PLUTARCH'S LIVES

VOLUME FIVE

A PATRICIAN ROMAN HOUSEHOLD

PLUTARCH'S LIVES

The Translation Called Dryden's

Corrected from the Greek and Revised by

A. H. CLOUGH

Sometime Fellow and Tutor of the Oriel College, Oxford, and Late Professor of the English Language and Literature at University College, London

With
Dr. William Smith's Historical Notes

IN FIVE VOLUMES

VOLUME FIVE

Illustrated

WILDSIDE PRESS

CONTENTS

Vol. V

	PAGE
DEMOSTHENES	1
CICERO	37
COMPARISON OF DEMOSTHENES WITH CICERO	95
DEMETRIUS	101
ANTONY	165
COMPARISON OF DEMETRIUS WITH ANTONY	255
DION	259
MARCUS BRUTUS	318
COMPARISON OF DION WITH BRUTUS	381
ARATUS	386
ARTAXERXES	441
GALBA	476
OTHO	509

ILLUSTRATIONS

VOL. V

A PATRICIAN ROMAN HOUSEHOLD,	*Frontispiece*
	FACING PAGE
DEMOSTHENES	34
MARCUS TULLIUS CICERO	92
"YES," SAID PYRRHUS, "ANOTHER SUCH VICTORY AND I SHALL BE UNDONE"	148
MARC ANTONY DELIVERS THE FUNERAL ORATION OVER THE DEAD BODY OF CÆSAR	178
JULIUS CÆSAR	240
THE BATTLE WITH THE LYCIANS	352
CYRUS THE GREAT	450

PLUTARCH'S LIVES

DEMOSTHENES[1]

TRANSLATED BY A WRITER UNNAMED.

WHOEVER it was, Sosius, that wrote the poem in honor of Alcibiades, upon his winning the chariot-race at the Olympian Games, whether it were Euripides, as is most commonly thought, or some other person, he tells us, that to a man's being happy it is in the first place requisite he should be born in "some famous city." But for him that would attain to true happiness, which for the most part is placed in the qualities and disposition of the mind, it is, in my opinion, of no other disadvantage to be of a mean, obscure country, than to be born of a small or plain-looking woman. For it were ridiculous to think that Iulis, a little part of Ceos, which itself is no great island, and Ægina, which an Athenian once said ought to be removed, like a small eye-sore from the port of Piræus, should breed good actors and poets,[2] and yet should never be able to produce a just, temperate, wise, and high-minded man. Other arts, whose end it is to acquire riches or

---

[1] The greatest of Athenian orators was born in the Attic demos of Pæania about 385 B. C. He employed his great influence for the good of his country. For fourteen years he continued the struggle against the aggressions of Philip of Macedonia and neither threats nor bribes could turn him from his purpose. He took poison and died in the temple of Poseidon on the island of Calauria, whence he had fled from Antipater's emissaries.—Dr. William Smith.

[2] Simonides, the lyric poet, was born at Iulis in Ceos; and Polus, the celebrated actor, who is mentioned in the account, further on, of Demosthenes's death, was a native of Ægina.

honor, are likely enough to wither and decay in poor and undistinguished towns; but virtue, like a strong and durable plant, may take root and thrive in any place where it can lay hold of an ingenuous nature, and a mind that is industrious. I, for my part, shall desire that for any deficiency of mine in right judgment or action, I myself may be, as in fairness, held accountable, and shall not attribute it to the obscurity of my birthplace.

But if any man undertake to write a history, that has to be collected from materials gathered by observation and the reading of works not easy to be got in all places, nor written always in his own language, but many of them foreign and dispersed in other hands, for him, undoubtedly, it is in the first place and above all things most necessary, to reside in some city of good note, addicted to liberal arts, and populous; where he may have plenty of all sorts of books, and upon inquiry may hear and inform himself of such particulars as, having escaped the pens of writers, are more faithfully preserved in the memories of men, lest his work be deficient in many things, even those which it can least dispense with.

But for me, I live in a little town, where I am willing to continue, lest it should grow less; and having had no leisure, while I was in Rome and other parts of Italy, to exercise myself in the Roman language, on account of public business and of those who came to be instructed by me in philosophy, it was very late, and in the decline of my age, before I applied myself to the reading of Latin authors. Upon which that which happened to me, may seem strange, though it be true; for it was not so much by the knowledge of words, that I came to the understanding of things, as by my experience of things I was enabled to follow the meaning of words. But to appreciate the graceful and ready pronunciation of the Roman tongue, to understand the various figures and connection of words, and such other ornaments, in which the beauty of speaking consists, is, I doubt not, an admirable and delightful accomplishment; but it requires a degree of practice and study which is not easy, and will better suit those who have more leisure, and time enough yet before them for the occupation.

And so in this fifth book of my Parallel Lives, in giving an account of Demosthenes and Cicero, my comparison of their natural dispositions and their characters will be formed upon their actions and their lives as statesmen, and I shall not pretend to criticize their orations one against the other, to show which of the two was the more charming or the more powerful speaker. For there, as Ion says,

> We are but like a fish upon dry land;

a proverb which Cæcilius [3] perhaps forgot, when he employed his always adventurous talents in so ambitious an attempt as a comparison of Demosthenes and Cicero: and, possibly, if it were a thing obvious and easy for every man *to know himself,* the precept had not passed for an oracle.

The divine power seems originally to have designed Demosthenes and Cicero upon the same plan, giving them many similarities in their natural characters, as their passion for distinction and their love of liberty in civil life, and their want of courage in dan-

---

[3] *Cæcilius,* who was so bold as to write *a comparison of Demosthenes and Cicero,* was a Greek rhetorician of Cale Acte, in Sicily, who lived in the time of Augustus, and whose books were much studied in the succeeding period. He and Dionysius of Halicarnassus are mentioned together. Suidas says his parents were slaves, his name, until he obtained the Roman citizenship, Archagathus, and that in religious opinions he was a Jew.

gers and war, and at the same time also to have added many accidental resemblances. I think there can hardly be found two other orators, who, from small and obscure beginnings, became so great and mighty; who both contested with kings and tyrants; both lost their daughters, were driven out of their country, and returned with honor; who, flying from thence again, were both seized upon by their enemies, and at last ended their lives with the liberty of their countrymen. So that if we were to suppose there had been a trial of skill between nature and fortune, as there is sometimes between artists, it would be hard to judge, whether that succeeded best in making them alike in their dispositions and manners, or this, in the coincidences of their lives. We will speak of the eldest first.

Demosthenes, the father of Demosthenes, was a citizen of good rank and quality, as Theopompus informs us, surnamed the Sword-maker, because he had a large workhouse, and kept servants skilful in that art at work. But of that which Æschines, the orator, said of his mother, that she was descended of one Gylon, who fled his country upon an accusation of treason, and of a barbarian woman, I can affirm nothing, whether he spoke true, or slandered and maligned her. This is certain, that Demosthenes, being as yet but seven years old, was left by his father in affluent circumstances, the whole value of his estate being little short of fifteen talents, and that he was wronged by his guardians, part of his fortune being embezzled by them, and the rest neglected; insomuch that even his teachers were defrauded of their salaries. This was the reason that he did not obtain the liberal education that he should have had; besides that on account of weakness and delicate health, his mother would not let him exert himself, and his teachers forbore to urge him. He was meagre and sickly from the first, and hence had his nickname of Batalus, given him, it is said, by the boys, in derision of his appearance; Batalus being, as some tell us, a certain enervated fluteplayer, in ridicule of whom Antiphanes wrote a play. Others speak of Batalus as a writer of wanton verses and drinking songs. And it would seem that some part of the body, not decent to be named, was at that time called *batalus* by the Athenians. But the name of Argas, which also they say was a nickname of Demosthenes, was given him for his behavior, as being savage and spiteful, *argas* being one of the poetical words for a snake; or for his disagreeable way of speaking, Argas being the name of a poet, who composed very harshly and disagreeably. So much, as Plato says, for such matters.

The first occasion of his eager inclination to oratory, they say, was this. Callistratus, the orator, being to plead in open court for Oropus, the expectation of the issue of that cause was very great, as well for the ability of the orator, who was then at the height of his reputation, as also for the fame of the action itself. Therefore, Demosthenes, having heard the tutors and schoolmasters agreeing among themselves to be present at this trial, with much importunity persuades his tutor to take him along with him to the hearing; who, having some acquaintance with the doorkeepers, procured a place where the boy might sit unseen, and hear what was said. Callistratus having got the day, and being much admired, the boy began to look upon his glory with a kind of emulation, observing how he was courted on all hands, and attended on his way by the multitude; but his wonder was more than all excited by the power of his eloquence, which seemed able to subdue and win over anything. From this time, therefore, bidding farewell to other sorts of learning and study, he now began to exercise himself, and to take pains in declaiming, as one that meant to be himself also an orator. He made use of Isæus as his guide to the art of speaking, though Isocrates at that time was giving lessons; whether, as some say, because he was an orphan, and was not able to pay Isocrates his appointed fee of ten minæ, or because he preferred Isæus's speaking, as being more business-like and effective in actual use. Hermippus says, that he met with certain memoirs without any author's name, in which it was written that Demosthenes was a scholar to Plato, and learnt much of his eloquence from him; and he also mentions Ctesibius, as reporting from Callias of Syracuse and some others, that Demosthenes secretly obtained a knowledge of the systems of Isocrates and Alcidamas, and mastered them thoroughly.

As soon, therefore, as he was grown up to man's estate, he began to go to law with his guardians, and to write orations against them; who, in the mean time, had recourse to various subterfuges and pleas for new trials, and Demosthenes, though he was thus, as Thucydides[4] says, taught his business in dangers, and by his own exertions was successful in his suit, was yet unable for all this to recover so much as a small fraction of his patrimony. He only attained some degree of confidence in speaking, and some competent experience in it. And having got a taste of the honor and power which are acquired by pleadings, he now

---

[4] "From the Persian war to the Peloponnesian, the Lacedæmonians and Athenians were continually engaged, one way or another, in military operations, and thus became," *says Thucydides,* "thoroughly well prepared and thoroughly expert in war, getting their training with real danger" (*I.,* 18); their lessons being taken at the peril of their lives if they failed, their military exercises performed not on parade, but in battle.

ventured to come forth, and to undertake public business. And, as it is said of Laomedon, the Orchomenian, that by advice of his physician, he used to run long distances to keep off some disease of his spleen, and by that means having, through labor and exercise, framed the habit of his body, he betook himself to the great garland games,[5] and became one of the best runners at the long race; so it happened to Demosthenes, who, first venturing upon oratory for the recovery of his own private property, by this acquired ability in speaking, and at length, in public business, as it were in the great games, came to have the preëminence of all competitors in the assembly. But when he first addressed himself to the people, he met with great discouragements, and was derided for his strange and uncouth style, which was cumbered with long sentences and tortured with formal arguments to a most harsh and disagreeable excess. Besides, he had, it seems, a weakness in his voice, a perplexed and indistinct utterance and a shortness of breath, which, by breaking and disjointing his sentences, much obscured the sense and meaning of what he spoke. So that in the end, being quite disheartened, he forsook the assembly; and as he was walking carelessly and sauntering about the Piræus, Eunomus, the Thriasian, then a very old man, seeing him, upbraided him, saying that his diction was very much like that of Pericles, and that he was wanting to himself through cowardice and meanness of spirit, neither bearing up with courage against popular outcry, nor fitting his body for action, but suffering it to languish through mere sloth and negligence.

Another time, when the assembly had refused to

---

[5] The Olympic, Pythian, Isthmian and Nemean Games, where the victors were crowned with garlands.

hear him, and he was going home with his head muffled up, taking it very heavily, they relate that Satyrus, the actor, followed him, and being his familiar acquaintance, entered into conversation with him. To whom, when Demosthenes bemoaned himself, that having been the most industrious of all the pleaders, and having almost spent the whole strength and vigor of his body in that employment, he could not yet find any acceptance with the people, that drunken sots, mariners, and illiterate fellows were heard, and had the hustings for their own, while he himself was despised, "You say true, Demosthenes," replied Satyrus, "but I will quickly remedy the cause of all this, if you will repeat to me some passage out of Euripides or Sophocles." Which when Demosthenes had pronounced, Satyrus presently taking it up after him, gave the same passage, in his rendering of it, such a new form, by accompanying it with the proper mien and gesture, that to Demosthenes it seemed quite another thing. By this being convinced how much grace and ornament language acquires from action, he began to esteem it a small matter, and as good as nothing for a man to exercise himself in declaiming, if he neglected enunciation and delivery. Hereupon he built himself a place to study in under ground, (which was still remaining in our time,) and hither he would come constantly every day to form his action, and to exercise his voice; and here he would continue, oftentimes without intermission, two or three months together, shaving one half of his head, that so for shame he might not go abroad, though he desired it ever so much.

Nor was this all, but he also made his conversation with people abroad, his common speech, and his business, subservient to his studies, taking from hence occasions and arguments as matter to work upon.

DEMOSTHENES

For as soon as he was parted from his company, down he would go at once into his study, and run over every thing in order that had passed, and the reasons that might be alleged for and against it. Any speeches, also, that he was present at, he would go over again with himself, and reduce into periods; and whatever others spoke to him, or he to them, he would correct, transform, and vary several ways. Hence it was, that he was looked upon as a person of no great natural genius, but one who owed all the power and ability he had in speaking to labor and industry. Of the truth of which it was thought to be no small sign, that he was very rarely heard to speak upon the occasion, but though he were by name frequently called upon by the people, as he sat in the assembly, yet he would not rise unless he had previously considered the subject, and came prepared for it. So that many of the popular pleaders used to make it a jest against him; and Pytheas once, scoffing at him, said that his arguments smelt of the lamp. To which Demosthenes gave the sharp answer, "It is true, indeed, Pytheas, that your lamp and mine are not conscious of the same things." To others, however, he would not much deny it, but would admit frankly enough, that he neither entirely wrote his speeches beforehand, nor yet spoke wholly extempore. And he would affirm, that it was the more truly popular act to use premeditation, such preparation being a kind of respect to the people; whereas, to slight and take no care how what is said is likely to be received by the audience, shows something of an oligarchical temper, and is the course of one that intends force rather than persuasion. Of his want of courage and assurance to speak off hand, they make it also another argument, that when he was at a loss, and discomposed, Demades would often rise up on the sudden to support him, but he was never observed to do the same for Demades.

Whence then, may some say, was it, that Æschines speaks of him as a person so much to be wondered at for his boldness in speaking? Or, how could it be, when Python, the Byzantine, "with so much confidence and such a torrent of words inveighed against"[6] the Athenians, that Demosthenes alone stood up to oppose him? Or, when Lamachus, the Myrinæan, had written a panegyric upon king Philip and Alexander, in which he uttered many things in reproach of the Thebans and Olynthians, and at the Olympic Games recited it publicly, how was it, that he, rising up, and recounting historically and demonstratively what benefits and advantages all Greece had received from the Thebans and Chalcidians, and on the contrary, what mischiefs the flatterers of the Macedonians had brought upon it, so turned the minds of all that were present that the sophist, in alarm at the outcry against him, secretly made his way out of the assembly? But Demosthenes, it should seem, regarded other points in the character of Pericles to be unsuited to him; but his reserve and his sustained manner, and his forbearing to speak on the sudden, or upon every occasion, as being the things to which principally he owed his greatness, these he followed, and endeavored to imitate, neither wholly neglecting the glory which present occasion offered, nor yet willing too often to expose his faculty to the mercy of chance. For, in fact, the orations which were spoken by him had much more of boldness and confidence in them than those that he wrote, if we may believe Eratosthenes, Demetrius the Phalerian, and the Comedians. Eratosthenes says

[6] These are his own words, quoted from the Oration on the Crown.

that often in his speaking he would be transported into a kind of ecstasy, and Demetrius, that he uttered the famous metrical adjuration to the people,

> By the earth, the springs, the rivers, and the streams,

as a man inspired, and beside himself. One of the comedians calls him a *rhopoperperethras*,[7] and another scoffs at him for his use of antithesis:—

> And what he took, took back; a phrase to please
> The very fancy of Demosthenes.

Unless, indeed, this also is meant by Antiphanes for a jest upon the speech on Halonesus, which Demosthenes advised the Athenians not to *take* at Philip's hands, but to *take back*.[8]

All, however, used to consider Demades, in the mere use of his natural gifts, an orator impossible to surpass, and that in what he spoke on the sudden, he excelled all the study and preparation of Demosthenes. And Ariston, the Chian, has recorded a judgment which Theophrastus passed upon the orators; for being asked what kind of orator he accounted Demosthenes, he answered, "Worthy of the city of Athens;" and then, what he thought of Demades, he answered, "Above it." And the same philosopher reports that Polyeuctus, the Sphettian, one of the Athenian politicians about that time, was wont to say,

---

[7] A loud declaimer about petty matters; from *rhopos*, small wares, and *perperos*, a loud talker.

[8] Halonesus had belonged to Athens, but had been seized by pirates, from whom Philip took it. He was willing to make a present of it to the Athenians, but Demosthenes warned them not on any account to *take* it, unless it were expressly understood that they *took* it *back*; Philip had no right to give what it was his duty to give back. The distinction thus put was apparently the subject of a great deal of pleasantry. Athenæus quotes five other passages from the comic writers, playing upon it in the same way.

that Demosthenes was the greatest orator, but Phocion the ablest, as he expressed the most sense in the fewest words. And, indeed, it is related, that Demosthenes himself, as often as Phocion stood up to plead against him, would say to his acquaintance, "Here comes the knife to my speech." Yet it does not appear whether he had this feeling for his powers of speaking, or for his life and character, and meant to say that one word or nod from a man who was really trusted, would go further than a thousand lengthy periods from others.

Demetrius, the Phalerian, tells us, that he was informed by Demosthenes himself, now grown old, that the ways he made use of to remedy his natural bodily infirmities and defects were such as these; his inarticulate and stammering pronunciation he overcame and rendered more distinct by speaking with pebbles in his mouth; his voice he disciplined by declaiming and reciting speeches or verses when he was out of breath, while running or going up steep places; and that in his house he had a large looking-glass, before which he would stand and go through his exercises. It is told that some one once came to request his assistance as a pleader, and related how he had been assaulted and beaten. "Certainly," said Demosthenes, "nothing of the kind can have happened to you." Upon which the other, raising his voice, exclaimed loudly, "What, Demosthenes, nothing has been done to me?" "Ah," replied Demosthenes, "now I hear the voice of one that has been injured and beaten." Of so great consequence towards the gaining of belief did he esteem the tone and action of the speaker. The action which he used himself was wonderfully pleasing to the common people; but by well-educated people, as, for example, by Demetrius, the Phalerian, it was looked upon as mean, humiliating, and unmanly. And

Hermippus says of Æsion, that, being asked his opinion concerning the ancient orators and those of his own time, he answered that it was admirable to see with what composure and in what high style they addressed themselves to the people; but that the orations of Demosthenes, when they are read, certainly appear to be superior in point of construction, and more effective.[9] His written speeches, beyond all question, are characterized by austere tone and by their severity. In his extempore retorts and rejoinders, he allowed himself the use of jest and mockery. When Demades said, "Demosthenes teach me! So might the sow teach Minerva!" he replied, "Was it this Minerva, that was lately found playing the harlot in Collytus?"[10] When a thief, who had the nickname of the Brazen, was attempting to upbraid him for sitting up late, and writing by candlelight, "I know very well," said he, "that you had rather have all lights out; and wonder not, O ye men of Athens, at the many robberies which are committed, since we have thieves of brass and walls of clay." But on these points, though we have much more to mention, we will add nothing at present. We will proceed to take an estimate of his character from his actions and his life as a statesman.

His first entering into public business was much

---

[9] Æsion was a fellow scholar with Demosthenes. The comparison in his remarks gives the superiority in manner to the old speakers, whom he remembered in his youth, but in construction, to Demosthenes, his contemporary.

[10] "Sus Minervam," the proverb. Collytus, together with Melite, formed the south-west, and, apparently, the more agreeable part of Athens. Plutarch, consoling a friend who was banished from his native city, tells him people cannot all live where they like best; it is not every Athenian can live in Collytus, nor does a man consider himself a miserable exile, who has to leave a house in Melite and take one in Diomea.

about the time of the Phocian war, as himself affirms, and may be collected from his Philippic orations. For of these, some were made after that action was over, and the earliest of them refer to its concluding events. It is certain that he engaged in the accusation of Midias when he was but two and thirty years old, having as yet no interest or reputation as a politician. And this it was, I consider, that induced him to withdraw the action, and accept a sum of money as a compromise. For of himself

He was no easy or good-natured man,[11]

but of a determined disposition, and resolute to see himself righted; however, finding it a hard matter and above his strength to deal with Midias, a man so well secured on all sides with money, eloquence, and friends, he yielded to the entreaties of those who interceded for him. But had he seen any hopes or possibility of prevailing, I cannot believe that three thousand drachmas could have taken off the edge of his revenge. The object which he chose for himself in the commonwealth was noble and just, the defence of the Grecians against Philip; and in this he behaved himself so worthily that he soon grew famous, and excited attention everywhere for his eloquence and courage in speaking. He was admired through all Greece. the king of Persia courted him, and by Philip himself he was more esteemed than all the other orators. His very enemies were forced to confess that they had to do with a man of mark; for such a character even Æschines and Hyperides give him, where they accuse and speak against him.

[11] *He was no easy or good-natured man* is from Iliad 20, 467,—said of Achilles. Tros, the son of Alastor, took hold of his knees and besought his mercy, little knowing that it was useless, since he was no easy or good-natured man.

So that I cannot imagine what ground Theopompus had to say, that Demosthenes was of a fickle, unsettled disposition, and could not long continue firm either to the same men or the same affairs; whereas the contrary is most apparent, for the same party and post in politics which he held from the beginning, to these he kept constant to the end; and was so far from leaving them while he lived, that he chose rather to forsake his life than his purpose. He was never heard to apologize for shifting sides like Demades, who would say, he often spoke against himself, but never against the city; nor as Melanopus, who, being generally against Callistratus, but being often bribed off with money, was wont to tell the people, "The man indeed is my enemy, but we must submit for the good of our country;" nor again as Nicodemus, the Messenian, who having first appeared on Cassander's side, and afterwards taken part with Demetrius, said the two things were not in themselves contrary, it being always most advisable to obey the conquerer. We have nothing of this kind to say against Demosthenes, as one who would turn aside or prevaricate, either in word or deed. There could not have been less variation in his public acts if they had all been played, so to say, from first to last, from the same score. Panætius, the philosopher, said, that most of his orations are so written, as if they were to prove this one conclusion, that what is honest and virtuous is for itself only to be chosen; as that of the Crown, that against Aristocrates, that for the Immunities,[12] and the Philippics; in all which he persuades his fellow-citizens to pursue not that which seems most pleasant, easy, or profitable; but declares

---

[12] *The oration for the Immunities* is that commonly called the oration against Leptines.

over and over again, that they ought in the first place to prefer that which is just and honorable, before their own safety and preservation. So that if he had kept his hands clean, if his courage for the wars had been answerable to the generosity of his principles, and the dignity of his orations, he might deservedly have his name placed, not in the number of such orators as Mœrocles, Polyeuctus, and Hyperides, but in the highest rank with Cimon, Thucydides, and Pericles.

Certainly amongst those who were contemporary with him, Phocion, though he appeared on the less commendable side in the commonwealth, and was counted as one of the Macedonian party, nevertheless, by his courage and his honesty, procured himself a name not inferior to those of Ephialtes, Aristides, and Cimon. But Demosthenes, being neither fit to be relied on for courage in arms, as Demetrius says, nor on all sides inaccessible to bribery (for how invincible soever he was against the gifts of Philip and the Macedonians, yet elsewhere he lay open to assault, and was overpowered by the gold which came down from Susa and Ecbatana), was therefore esteemed better able to recommend than to imitate the virtues of past times. And yet (excepting only Phocion), even in his life and manners, he far surpassed the other orators of his time. None of them addressed the people so boldly; he attacked the faults, and opposed himself to the unreasonable desires of the multitude, as may be seen in his orations. Theopompus writes, that the Athenians having by name selected Demosthenes, and called upon him to accuse a certain person, he refused to do it; upon which the assembly being all in an uproar, he rose up and said, "Your counsellor, whether you will or no, O ye men of Athens, you shall always have me; but a sycophant or false accuser, though you would have me, I shall never be." And his conduct in the case of Antiphon was perfectly aristocratical; whom, after he had been acquitted in the assembly, he took and brought before the court of Areopagus, and, setting at naught the displeasure of the people, convicted him there of having promised Philip to burn the arsenal; whereupon the man was condemned by that court, and suffered for it. He accused, also, Theoris, the priestess, amongst other misdemeanors, of having instructed and taught the slaves to deceive and cheat their masters, for which the sentence of death was passed upon her, and she was executed.

The oration which Apollodorus made use of, and by it carried the cause against Timotheus, the general, in an action of debt, it is said was written for him by Demosthenes; as also those against Phormion and Stephanus, in which latter case he was thought to have acted dishonorably, for the speech which Phormion used against Apollodorus was also of his making; he, as it were, having simply furnished two adversaries out of the same shop with weapons to wound one another. Of his orations addressed to the public assemblies, that against Androtion, and those against Timocrates and Aristocrates, were written for others, before he had come forward himself as a politician. They were composed, it seems, when he was but seven or eight and twenty years old. That against Aristogiton, and that for the Immunities, he spoke himself, at the request, as he says, of Ctesippus, the son of Chabrias, but, as some say, out of courtship to the young man's mother. Though, in fact, he did not marry her, for his wife was a woman of Samos, as Demetrius, the Magnesian, writes, in his book on Persons of the same Name. It is not certain whether his oration against Æschines, for Misconduct as Ambassador, was ever spoken; although Idomeneus says that Æschines wanted only thirty voices to condemn him. But this seems not to be correct, at least so far as may be conjectured from both their orations concerning the Crown; for in these, neither of them speaks clearly or directly of it, as a cause that ever came to trial. But let others decide this controversy.

It was evident, even in time of peace, what course Demosthenes would steer in the commonwealth; for whatever was done by the Macedonian, he criticized and found fault with, and upon all occasions was stirring up the people of Athens, and inflaming them against him. Therefore, in the court of Philip, no man was so much talked of, or of so great account as he; and when he came thither, one of the ten ambassadors who were sent into Macedonia, though all had audience given them, yet his speech was answered with most care and exactness. But in other respects, Philip entertained him not so honorably as the rest, neither did he show him the same kindness and civility with which he applied himself to the party of Æschines and Philocrates. So that, when the others commended Philip for his able speaking, his beautiful person, nay, and also for his good companionship in drinking, Demosthenes could not refrain from cavilling at these praises; the first, he said, was a quality which might well enough become a rhetorician, the second a woman, and the last was only the property of a sponge; no one of them was the proper commendation of a prince.

But when things came at last to war, Philip on the one side being not able to live in peace, and the Athenians, on the other side, being stirred up by Demosthenes, the first action he put them upon was the reducing of Eubœa, which, by the treachery of the tyrants, was brought under subjection to Philip. And on his proposition, the decree was voted, and they crossed over thither and chased the Macedonians out of the island. The next, was the relief of the Byzantines and Perinthians, whom the Macedonians at that time were attacking. He persuaded the people to lay aside their enmity against these cities, to forget the offences committed by them in the Confederate War, and to send them such succors as eventually saved and secured them. Not long after, he undertook an embassy through the States of Greece, which he solicited and so far incensed against Philip, that, a few only excepted, he brought them all into a general league. So that, besides the forces composed of the citizens themselves, there was an army consisting of fifteen thousand foot and two thousand horse, and the money to pay these strangers was levied and brought in with great cheerfulness. On which occasion it was, says Theophrastus, on the allies requesting that their contributions for the war might be ascertained and stated, Crobylus, the orator, made use of the saying, "War can't be fed at so much a day."[13] Now was all Greece up in arms, and in great expectation what would be the event. The Eubœans, the Achæans, the Corinthians, the Megarians, the Leucadians, and Corcyræans, their people and their cities, were all joined together in a league. But the hardest task was yet behind, left for Demosthenes, to draw the Thebans into this confederacy with the rest. Their country bordered next upon Attica, they had great forces for the war, and at that time they were accounted the best soldiers of all Greece, but it was no easy matter to make them

[13] *War can't be fed at so much a day* is a saying quoted in three other places by Plutarch,—once in the Life of Cleomenes, once in that of Crassus, and once in the miscellaneous works,—and in all these passages it is ascribed to king Archidamus, who commanded the Spartans in the first campaigns of the Peloponnesian war, and whose language, as reported by Thucydides, has something of this purport.

break with Philip, who, by many good offices, had so lately obliged them in the Phocian war; especially considering how the subjects of dispute and variance between the two cities were continually renewed and exasperated by petty quarrels, arising out of the proximity of their frontiers.

But after Philip, being now grown high and puffed up with his good success at Amphissa, on a sudden surprised Elatea and possessed himself of Phocis, and the Athenians were in a great consternation, none durst venture to rise up to speak, no one knew what to say, all were at a loss, and the whole assembly in silence and perplexity, in this extremity of affairs, Demosthenes was the only man who appeared, his counsel to them being alliance with the Thebans. And having in other ways encouraged the people, and, as his manner was, raised their spirits up with hopes, he, with some others, was sent ambassador to Thebes. To oppose him, as Marsyas says, Philip also sent thither his envoys, Amyntas and Clearchus, two Macedonians, besides Daochus, a Thessalian, and Thrasydæus. Now the Thebans, in their consultations, were well enough aware what suited best with their own interest, but every one had before his eyes the terrors of war, and their losses in the Phocian troubles were still recent; but such was the force and power of the orator, fanning up, as Theopompus says, their courage, and firing their emulation, that casting away every thought of prudence, fear, or obligation, in a sort of divine possession, they chose the path of honor, to which his words invited them. And this success, thus accomplished by an orator, was thought to be so glorious and of such consequence, that Philip immediately sent heralds to treat and petition for a peace: all Greece was aroused, and all up in arms to help. And the commanders-in-chief, not only of Attica, but of Bœotia, applied themselves to Demosthenes, and observed his directions. He managed all the assemblies of the Thebans, no less than those of the Athenians; he was beloved both by the one and by the other, and exercised the same supreme authority with both; and that not by unfair means, or without just cause, as Theopompus professes, but indeed it was no more than was due to his merit.

But there was, it should seem, some divinely-ordered fortune, commissioned, in the revolution of things, to put a period at this time to the liberty of Greece, which opposed and thwarted all their actions, and by many signs foretold what should happen. Such were the sad predictions uttered by the Pythian priestess, and this old oracle cited out of the Sibyl's verses,—

> The battle on Thermodon that shall be
> Safe at a distance I desire to see,
> Far, like an eagle, watching in the air.
> Conquered shall weep, and conqueror perish there.

This Thermodon, they say, is a little rivulet here in our country in Chæronea, running into the Cephisus. But we know of none that is so called at the present time; and can only conjecture that the streamlet which is now called Hæmon, and runs by the Temple of Hercules, where the Grecians were encamped, might perhaps in those days be called Thermodon, and after the fight, being filled with blood and dead bodies, upon this occasion, as we guess, might change its old name for that which it now bears. Yet Duris says that this Thermodon was no river, but that some of the soldiers, as they were pitching their tents and digging trenches about them, found a small stone statue, which, by the inscription, appeared to be the figure of Thermodon, carrying a wounded Amazon in his arms; and that there was another oracle current about it, as follows:—

> The battle on Thermodon that shall be,
> Fail not, black raven, to attend and see;
> The flesh of men shall there abound for thee.

In fine, it is not easy to determine what is the truth. But of Demosthenes it is said, that he had such great confidence in the Grecian forces, and was so excited by the sight of the courage and resolution of so many brave men ready to engage the enemy, that he would by no means endure they should give any heed to oracles, or hearken to prophecies, but gave out that he suspected even the prophetess herself, as if she had been tampered with to speak in favor of Philip. The Thebans he put in mind of Epaminondas, the Athenians, of Pericles, who always took their own measures and governed their actions by reason, looking upon things of this kind as mere pretexts for cowardice. Thus far, therefore, Demosthenes acquitted himself like a brave man. But in the fight he did nothing honorable, nor was his performance answerable to his speeches. For he fled, deserting his place disgracefully, and throwing away his arms, not ashamed, as Pytheas observed, to belie the inscription written on his shield, in letters of gold, "With good fortune."

In the meantime Philip, in the first moment of victory, was so transported with joy, that he grew extravagant, and going out, after he had drunk largely, to visit the dead bodies, he chanted the first words of the decree that had been passed on the motion of Demosthenes,

> The motion of Demosthenes, Demosthenes's son,[14]

dividing it metrically into feet, and marking the beats.

[14] Demosthenes Demosthenous, Paianieus, tad' eipen. "Demosthenes, the son of Demosthenes, of the Pæanian township, made this motion,"—the usual form of the commencement of the Votes of the Athenian Assembly.

But when he came to himself, and had well considered the danger he was lately under, he could not forbear from shuddering at the wonderful ability and power of an orator who had made him hazard his life and empire on the issue of a few brief hours. The fame of it also reached even to the court of Persia, and the king sent letters to his lieutenants, commanding them to supply Demosthenes with money, and to pay every attention to him, as the only man of all the Grecians who was able to give Philip occupation and find employment for his forces near home, in the troubles of Greece. This afterwards came to the knowledge of Alexander, by certain letters of Demosthenes which he found at Sardis, and by other papers of the Persian officers, stating the large sums which had been given him.

At this time, however, upon the ill success which now happened to the Grecians, those of the contrary faction in the commonwealth fell foul upon Demosthenes, and took the opportunity to frame several informations and indictments against him. But the people not only acquitted him of these accusations, but continued towards him their former respect, and still invited him, as a man that meant well, to take a part in public affairs. Insomuch that when the bones of those who had been slain at Chæronea were brought home to be solemnly interred, Demosthenes was the man they chose to make the funeral oration. They did not show, under the misfortunes which befell them, a base or ignoble mind, as Theopompus writes in his exaggerated style, but, on the contrary, by the honor and respect paid to their counsellor, they made it appear that they were noway dissatisfied with the counsels he had given them. The speech, therefore, was spoken by Demosthenes. But the subsequent decrees he would not allow to be passed in his own name, but made use of those of his friends, one after another, looking upon his own as unfortunate and inauspicious; till at length he took courage again after the death of Philip, who did not long outlive his victory at Chæronea. And this, it seems, was that which was foretold in the last verse of the oracle,

Conquered shall weep, and conqueror perish there.

Demosthenes had secret intelligence of the death of Philip, and laying hold of this opportunity to prepossess the people with courage and better hopes for the future, he came into the assembly with a cheerful countenance pretending to have had a dream that presaged some great good fortune for Athens; and, not long after, arrived the messengers who brought the news of Philip's death. No sooner had the people received it, but immediately they offered sacrifice to the gods, and decreed that Pausanias should be presented with a crown. Demosthenes appeared publicly in a rich dress, with a chaplet on his head, though it were but the seventh day since the death of his daughter, as is said by Æschines, who upbraids him upon this account, and rails at him as one void of natural affection towards his children. Whereas, indeed, he rather betrays himself to be of a poor, low spirit, and effeminate mind, if he really means to make wailings and lamentation the only signs of a gentle and affectionate nature, and to condemn those who bear such accidents with more temper and less passion. For my own part, I cannot say that the behavior of the Athenians on this occasion was wise or honorable, to crown themselves with garlands and to sacrifice to the Gods for the death of a Prince who, in the midst of his success and victories, when they were a conquered people, had used them with so much clemency and humanity. For besides provoking fortune, it was a base thing, and unworthy in itself, to make him a citizen of Athens, and pay him honors while he lived, and yet as soon as he fell by another's hand, to set no bounds to their jollity, to insult over him dead, and to sing triumphant songs of victory, as if by their own valor they had vanquished him. I must at the same time commend the behavior of Demosthenes, who, leaving tears and lamentations and domestic sorrows to the women, made it his business to attend to the interests of the commonwealth. And I think it the duty of him who would be accounted to have a soul truly valiant, and fit for government, that, standing always firm to the common good, and letting private griefs and troubles find their compensation in public blessings, he should maintain the dignity of his character and station, much more than actors who represent the persons of kings and tyrants, who, we see, when they either laugh or weep on the stage, follow, not their own private inclinations, but the course consistent with the subject and with their position. And if, moreover, when our neighbor is in misfortune, it is not our duty to forbear offering any consolation, but rather to say whatever may tend to cheer him, and to invite his attention to any agreeable objects, just as we tell people who are troubled with sore eyes, to withdraw their sight from bright and offensive colors to green, and those of a softer mixture, from whence can a man seek, in his own case, better arguments of consolation for afflictions in his family, than from the prosperity of his country, by making public and domestic chances count, so to say, together, and the better fortune of the state obscure and conceal the less happy circumstances of the individual. I have been induced to say so much, because I have known many readers melted by Æschines's language into a soft and unmanly tenderness.

But now to return to my narrative. The cities of Greece were inspirited once more by the efforts of Demosthenes to form a league together. The Thebans, whom he had provided with arms, set upon their garrison, and slew many of them; the Athenians made preparations to join their forces with them; Demosthenes ruled supreme in the popular assembly, and wrote letters to the Persian officers who commanded under the king of Asia, inciting them to make war upon the Macedonian, calling him child and simpleton.[15] But as soon as Alexander had settled matters in his own country, and came in person with his army into Bœotia, down fell the courage of the Athenians, and Demosthenes was hushed; the Thebans, deserted by them, fought by themselves, and lost their city. After which, the people of Athens, all in distress and great perplexity, resolved to send ambassadors to Alexander, and amongst others, made choice of Demosthenes for one; but his heart failing him for fear of the king's anger, he returned back from Cithæron, and left the embassy. In the mean time, Alexander sent to Athens, requiring ten of their orators to be delivered up to him, as Idomeneus and Duris have reported, but as the most and best historians say, he demanded these eight only,—Demosthenes, Polyeuctus, Ephialtes, Lycurgus, Mœrocles, Demon, Callisthenes, and Charidemus. It was upon this occasion that Demosthenes related to them the fable in which the sheep are said to deliver up their dogs to the wolves; himself and those who with him contended for the people's safety, being, in his comparison, the dogs that defended the flock, and Alexander "the Macedonian arch

[15] *Margites,* the name of the character held up to ridicule in an old poem ascribed to Homer,—the boy, who, though fully grown up, has never attained the sense or wits of a man.

wolf." He further told them, "As we see corn-masters sell their whole stock by a few grains of wheat which they carry about with them in a dish, as a sample of the rest, so you, by delivering up us, who are but a few, do at the same time unawares surrender up yourselves all together with us;" so we find it related in the history of Aristobulus, the Cassandrian. The Athenians were deliberating, and at a loss what to do, when Demades, having agreed with the persons whom Alexander had demanded, for five talents, undertook to go ambassador, and to intercede with the king for them; and whether it was that he relied on his friendship and kindness, or that he hoped to find him satiated, as a lion glutted with slaughter, he certainly went, and prevailed with him both to pardon the men, and to be reconciled to the city.

So he and his friends, when Alexander went away, were great men, and Demosthenes was quite put aside. Yet when Agis, the Spartan, made his insurrection, he also for a short time attempted a movement in his favor; but he soon shrunk back again, as the Athenians would not take any part in it, and, Agis being slain, the Lacedæmonians were vanquished. During this time it was that the indictment against Ctesiphon, concerning the Crown, was brought to trial. The action was commenced a little before the battle in Chæronea, when Chærondas was archon, but it was not proceeded with till about ten years after, Aristophon being then archon. Never was any public cause more celebrated than this, alike for the fame of the orators, and for the generous courage of the judges, who, though at that time the accusers of Demosthenes were in the height of power, and supported by all the favor of the Macedonians, yet would not give judgment against him, but acquitted him so honorably, that Æschines did not obtain the fifth part of their suffrages on his side, so that, immediately after, he left the city, and spent the rest of his life in teaching rhetoric about the island of Rhodes, and upon the continent of Ionia.

It was not long after that Harpalus fled from Alexander, and came to Athens out of Asia; knowing himself guilty of many misdeeds into which his love of luxury had led him, and fearing the king, who was now grown terrible even to his best friends. Yet this man had no sooner addressed himself to the people, and delivered up his goods, his ships, and himself to their disposal, but the other orators of the town had their eyes quickly fixed upon his money, and came in to his assistance, persuading the Athenians to receive and protect their suppliant. Demosthenes at first gave advice to chase him out of the country, and to beware lest they involved their city in a war upon an unnecessary and unjust occasion. But some few days after, as they were taking an account of the treasure, Harpalus, perceiving how much he was pleased with a cup of Persian manufacture, and how curiously he surveyed the sculpture and fashion of it, desired him to poise it in his hand, and consider the weight of the gold. Demosthenes, being amazed to feel how heavy it was, asked him what weight it *came to.* "To you," said Harpalus, smiling, "it shall *come with* twenty talents." And presently after, when night drew on, he sent him the cup with so many talents. Harpalus, it seems, was a person in singular skill to discern a man's covetousness by the air of his countenance, and the look and movements of his eyes. For Demosthenes could not resist the temptation, but admitting the present, like an armed garrison, into the citadel of his house, he surrendered himself up to the interest of Harpalus. The next day, he came into the assembly with his neck swathed about with wool and rollers, and when they called on him to rise up and speak, he made signs as if he had lost his voice. But the wits, turning the matter to ridicule, said that certainly the orator had been seized that night with no other than a silver quinsy. And soon after, the people, becoming aware of the bribery, grew angry, and would not suffer him to speak, or make any apology for himself, but ran him down with noise; and one man stood up, and cried out, "What, ye men of Athens, will you not hear the cup-bearer?"[16] So at length they banished Harpalus out of the city; and fearing lest they should be called to account for the treasure which the orators had purloined, they made a strict inquiry, going from house to house; only Callicles, the son of Arrhenidas, who was newly married, they would not suffer to be searched, out of respect, as Theopompus writes to the bride, who was within.

Demosthenes resisted the inquisition, and proposed a decree to refer the business to the court of Areopagus, and to punish those whom that court should find guilty. But being himself one of the first whom the court condemned, when he came to the bar, he was fined fifty talents, and committed to prison; where, out of shame of the crime for which he was condemned, and through the weakness of his body, growing incapable of supporting the confinement, he made his escape, by the carelessness of some and by the connivance of others of the citizens. We are told, at least, that he had not fled far from the city, when, finding that he was pursued by some of those who had

[16] *Will you not hear the cup-bearer?* is explained by the custom of drinking parties, that each guest as he took the cup in his hand should sing some verses. The cup in a man's hand was the signal for all to listen to him. Dacier cites this as the remark of M. Lefevre, Tannêguy Lefevre, his teacher and the father of Madame Dacier, known in the Latin of commentators as Tanaquillus Faber.

been his adversaries, he endeavored to hide himself. But when they called him by his name, and coming up nearer to him, desired he would accept from them some money which they had brought from home as a provision for his journey, and to that purpose only had followed him, when they entreated him to take courage, and to bear up against his misfortune, he burst out into much greater lamentation, saying, "But how is it possible to support myself under so heavy an affliction, since I leave a city in which I have such enemies, as in any other it is not easy to find friends." He did not show much fortitude in his banishment, spending his time for the most part in Ægina and Trœzen, and, with tears in his eyes, looking towards the country of Attica. And there remain upon record some sayings of his, little resembling those sentiments of generosity and bravery which he used to express when he had the management of the commonwealth. For, as he was departing out of the city, it is reported, he lifted up his hands towards the Acropolis, and said, "O Lady Minerva, how is it that thou takest delight in three such fierce untractable beasts, the owl, the snake, and the people?" The young men that came to visit and converse with him, he deterred from meddling with state affairs, telling them, that if at first two ways had been proposed to him, the one leading to the speaker's stand and the assembly, the other going direct to destruction, and he could have foreseen the many evils which attend those who deal in public business, such as fears, envies, calumnies, and contentions, he would certainly have taken that which led straight on to his death.

But now happened the death of Alexander, while Demosthenes was in this banishment which we have been speaking of. And the Grecians were once again up in arms, encouraged by the brave attempts of

Leosthenes, who was then drawing a circumvallation about Antipater, whom he held close besieged in Lamia. Pytheas, therefore, the orator, and Callimedon, called the Crab, fled from Athens, and taking sides with Antipater, went about with his friends and ambassadors to keep the Grecians from revolting and taking part with the Athenians. But, on the other side, Demosthenes, associating himself with the ambassadors that came from Athens, used his utmost endeavors and gave them his best assistance in persuading the cities to fall unanimously upon the Macedonians, and to drive them out of Greece. Phylarchus says that in Arcadia there happened a rencounter between Pytheas and Demosthenes, which came at last to downright railing, while the one pleaded for the Macedonians, and the other for the Grecians. Pytheas said, that as we always suppose there is some disease in the family to which they bring asses' milk, so wherever there comes an embassy from Athens, that city must needs be indisposed. And Demosthenes answered him, retorting the comparison: "Asses' milk is brought to restore health, and the Athenians come for the safety and recovery of the sick." With this conduct the people of Athens were so well pleased, that they decreed the recall of Demosthenes from banishment. The decree was brought in by Demon the Pæanian, cousin to Demosthenes. So they sent him a ship to Ægina, and he landed at the port of Piræus, where he was met and joyfully received by all the citizens, not so much as an Archon or a priest staying behind. And Demetrius, the Magnesian, says, that he lifted up his hands towards heaven, and blessed this day of his happy return, as far more honorable than that of Alcibiades; since he was recalled by his countrymen, not through any force or constraint put upon them, but by their own good-will and free inclinations. There remained only his pecuniary fine, which, according to law, could not be remitted by the people. But they found out a way to elude the law. It was a custom with them to allow a certain quantity of silver to those who were to furnish and adorn the altar for the sacrifice of Jupiter Soter. This office, for that turn, they bestowed on Demosthenes, and for the performance of it ordered him fifty talents, the very sum in which he was condemned.

Yet it was no long time that he enjoyed his country after his return, the attempts of the Greeks being soon all utterly defeated. For the battle at Cranon happened in Metagitnion, in Boëdromion the garrison entered into Munychia, and in the Pyanepsion following died Demosthenes after this manner.

Upon the report that Antipater and Craterus were coming to Athens, Demosthenes with his party took their opportunity to escape privily out of the city; but sentence of death was, upon the motion of Demades, passed upon them by the people. They dispersed themselves, flying some to one place, some to another; and Antipater sent about his soldiers into all quarters to apprehend them. Archias was their captain, and was thence called the exile-hunter. He was a Thurian born, and is reported to have been an actor of tragedies, and they say that Polus, of Ægina, the best actor of his time, was his scholar; but Hermippus reckons Archias among the disciples of Lacritus, the orator, and Demetrius says, he spent some time with Aneximenes. This Archias finding Hyperides the orator, Aristonicus of Marathon, and Himeræus, the brother of Demetrius the Phalerian, in Ægina, took them by force out of the temple of Æacus, whither they were fled for safety, and sent them to Antipater, then at Cleonæ, where they were all put to death; and Hyperides, they say, had his tongue cut out.

DEMOSTHENES

Demosthenes, he heard, had taken sanctuary at the temple of Neptune in Calauria, and, crossing over thither in some light vessels, as soon as he had landed himself, and the Thracian spear-men that came with him, he endeavored to persuade Demosthenes to accompany him to Antipater, as if he should meet with no hard usage from him. But Demosthenes, in his sleep the night before, had a strange dream. It seemed to him that he was acting a tragedy, and contended with Archias for the victory; and though he acquitted himself well, and gave good satisfaction to the spectators, yet for want of better furniture and provision for the stage, he lost the day. And so, while Archias was discoursing to him with many expressions of kindness, he sate still in the same posture, and looking up steadfastly upon him, "O Archias," said he, "I am as little affected by your promises now as I used formerly to be by your acting." Archias at this beginning to grow angry and to threaten him, "Now," said Demosthenes, "you speak like the genuine Macedonian oracle; before you were but acting a part. Therefore forbear only a little, while I write a word or two home to my family." Having thus spoken, he withdrew into the temple, and taking a scroll, as if he meant to write, he put the reed into his mouth, and biting it, as he was wont to do when he was thoughtful or writing, he held it there for some time. Then he bowed down his head and covered it. The soldiers that stood at the door, supposing all this to proceed from want of courage and fear of death, in derision called him effeminate, and faint-heated, and coward. And Archias, drawing near, desired him to rise up, and repeating the same kind of things he had spoken before, he once more promised him to make his peace with Antipater. But Demosthenes, perceiving that now the poison had pierced and seized his vitals, uncovered his head, and fixing his eyes upon Archias, "Now," said he, "as soon as you please you may commence the part of Creon in the tragedy, and cast out this body of mine unburied. But, O gracious Neptune, I for my part, while I am yet alive, arise up and depart out of this sacred place; though Antipater and the Macedonians have not left so much as thy temple unpolluted." After he had thus spoken and desired to be held up, because already he began to tremble and stagger, as he was going forward, and passing by the altar, he fell down, and with a groan gave up the ghost.

Ariston says that he took the poison out of a reed, as we have shown before. But Pappus, a certain historian whose history was recovered by Hermippus, says, that as he fell near the altar, there were found in his scroll this beginning only of a letter, and nothing more, "Demosthenes to Antipater." And that when his sudden death was much wondered at, the Thracians who guarded the doors reported that he took the poison into his hand out of a rag, and put it in his mouth, and that they imagined it had been gold which he swallowed; but the maid that served him, being examined by the followers of Archias, affirmed that he had worn it in a bracelet for a long time, as an amulet. And Eratosthenes also says that he kept the poison in a hollow ring, and that that ring was the bracelet which he wore about his arm. There are various other statements made by the many authors who have related the story, but there is no need to enter into their discrepancies; yet I must not omit what is said by Demochares, the relation of Demosthenes, who is of opinion, it was not by the help of poison that he met with so sudden and so easy a death, but that by the singular favor and providence of the gods he was thus rescued from the cruelty of the Macedonians.

DEMOSTHENES

He died on the sixteenth of Pyanepsion, the most sad and solemn day of the Thesmophoria, which the women observe by fasting in the temple of the goddess.

Soon after his death, the people of Athens bestowed on him such honors as he had deserved. They erected his statue of brass; they decreed that the eldest of his family should be maintained in the Prytaneum; and on the base of his statue was engraven the famous inscription,—

> Had you for Greece been strong, as wise you were,
> The Macedonian had not conquered her.

For it is simply ridiculous to say, as some have related, that Demosthenes made these verses himself in Calauria, as he was about to take the poison.

A little before he went to Athens, the following incident was said to have happened. A soldier, being summoned to appear before his superior officer, and answer to an accusation brought against him, put that little gold which he had into the hands of Demosthenes's statue. The fingers of this statue were folded one within another, and near it grew a small plane-tree, from which many leaves, either accidentally blown thither by the wind, or placed so on purpose by the man himself, falling together, and lying round about the gold, concealed it for a long time. In the end, the soldier returned, and found his treasure entire, and the fame of this incident was spread abroad. And many ingenious persons of the city competed with each other, on this occasion, to vindicate the integrity of Demosthenes, in several epigrams which they made on the subject.

As for Demades, he did not long enjoy the new honors he now came in for, divine vengeance for the death of Demosthenes pursuing him into Macedonia, where he was justly put to death by those whom he had basely flattered. They were weary of him before, but at this time the guilt he lay under was manifest and undeniable. For some of his letters were intercepted, in which he had encouraged Perdiccas[17] to fall upon Macedonia, and to save the Grecians, who, he said, hung only by an old rotten thread, meaning Antipater. Of this he was accused by Dinarchus, the Corinthian, and Cassander was so enraged, that he first slew his son in his bosom, and then gave orders to execute him; who might now at last, by his own extreme misfortunes, learn the lesson, that traitors, who make sale of their country, sell themselves first; a truth which Demosthenes had often foretold him, and he would never believe. Thus, Sosius, you have the life of Demosthenes, from such accounts as we have either read or heard concerning him.

[17] This, apparently, is one of Plutarch's slips of memory. It was not Perdiccas, but Antigonus; and so he tells the story himself in the life of Phocion.

I believe it has been more commonly said, as in the note above, that the mistaken statement is this, and that it was not Perdiccas, but Antigonus, to whom Demades had written. But Mr. Grote in his history takes this for the correct, and the passage in the life of Phocion for the incorrect account; during Demades's lifetime, Perdiccas, not Antigonus, had been formidable to Macedonia.

CICERO[1]

Translated by Thomas Fuller, D.D.

It is generally said that Helvia, the mother of Cicero, was both well born and lived a fair life; but of his father nothing is reported but in extremes. For whilst some would have him the son of a fuller, and educated in that trade, others carry back the origin of his family to Tollus Attius, an illustrious king of the Volscians, who waged war not without honor against the Romans. However, he who first of that house was surnamed Cicero seems to have been a person worthy to be remembered; since those who succeeded him not only did not reject, but were fond of that name, though vulgarly made a matter of reproach. For the Latins call a vetch *Cicer,* and a nick or dent at the tip of his nose, which resembled the opening in a vetch, gave him the surname of *Cicero.*

Cicero, whose story I am writing, is said to have replied with spirit to some of his friends, who recommended him to lay aside or change the name when he first stood for office and engaged in politics, that he

---

[1] Marcus Cicero was born on the 3rd of January, 106 B. C., and with his brother Quintus, early displayed aptitude for learning and received instruction from the best teachers at Rome. Cicero was not a great nor a strong statesman, but rather an eloquent and adroit politician. While his desire to maintain the republic unchanged was sincere and creditable, as a judge of character, in his idea of Pompey and as a judge of the times he failed. It is as an author that Cicero deserves the highest praise, for in his works the Latin language attains its highest perfection. His assassination occurred December 7, 43 B. C.— Dr. William Smith.

would make it his endeavor to render the name of Cicero more glorious than that of the Scauri and Catuli. And when he was quæstor in Sicily, and was making an offering of silver plate to the gods, and had inscribed his two names, Marcus and Tullius, instead of the third he jestingly told the artificer to engrave the figure of a vetch by them. Thus much is told us about his name.

Of his birth it is reported, that his mother was delivered without pain or labor, on the third of the new Calends,[2] the same day on which now the magistrates of Rome pray and sacrifice for the emperor. It is said, also, that a vision appeared to his nurse, and foretold the child she then suckled should afterwards become a great benefit to the Roman States. To such presages, which might in general be thought mere fancies and idle talk, he himself erelong gave the credit of true prophecies. For as soon as he was of an age to begin to have lessons, he became so distinguished for his talent, and got such a name and reputation amongst the boys, that their fathers would often visit the school, that they might see young Cicero, and might be able to say that they themselves had witnessed the quickness and readiness in learning for which he was renowned. And the more rude among

---

[2] The third of January. *The third of the new Calends, the day on which now the magistrates pray and sacrifice for the Emperor*, was, in imperial times, a well-known anniversary, known by the name of *Vota*. Capitolinus, in a passage of his life of Pertinax, quoted by Dacier, speaks of a thing happening *ante diem tertium Nonarum, Votis ipsis;* and in Facciolati a passage from Vopiscus is added, to the effect that the emperor Tacitus built a chapel for the worship of the good emperors, in which libations should be made *on his own birthday, on the feast of Parilia, on the Calends of January, and on the Vota.* The passage from Plato about the true, scholarlike, and philosophical temper is from the Republic.

them used to be angry with their children, to see them, as they walked together, receiving Cicero with respect into the middle place. And being, as Plato would have the scholar-like and philosophical temper, eager for every kind of learning, and indisposed to no description of knowledge or instruction, he showed, however, a more peculiar propensity to poetry; and there is a poem now extant, made by him when a boy, in tetrameter verse, called Pontius Glaucus. And afterwards, when he applied himself more curiously to these accomplishments, he had the name of being not only the best orator, but also the best poet of Rome. And the glory of his rhetoric still remains, notwithstanding the many new modes in speaking since his time; but his verses are forgotten and out of all repute, so many ingenious poets having followed him.

Leaving his juvenile studies, he became an auditor of Philo the Academic, whom the Romans, above all the other scholars of Clitomachus, admired for his eloquence and loved for his character. He also sought the company of the Mucii, who were eminent statesmen and leaders in the senate, and acquired from them a knowledge of the laws. For some short time he served in arms under Sylla, in the Marsian war. But perceiving the commonwealth running into factions, and from faction all things tending to an absolute monarchy, he betook himself to a retired and contemplative life, and conversing with the learned Greeks, devoted himself to study, till Sylla had obtained the government, and the commonwealth was in some kind of settlement.

At this time, Chrysogonus, Sylla's emancipated slave, having laid an information about an estate belonging to one who was said to have been put to death by proscription, he bought it himself for two thousand drachmas. And when Roscius, the son and heir of the dead, complained, and demonstrated the estate to be worth two hundred and fifty talents, Sylla took it angrily to have his actions questioned, and preferred a process against Roscius for the murder of his father, Chrysogonus managing the evidence. None of the advocates durst assist him, but fearing the cruelty of Sylla, avoided the cause. The young man, being thus deserted, came for refuge to Cicero. Cicero's friends encouraged him, saying he was not likely ever to have a fairer and more honorable introduction to public life; he therefore undertook the defence, carried the cause, and got much renown for it.

But fearing Sylla, he travelled into Greece, and gave it out that he did so for the benefit of his health. And indeed he was lean and meagre, and had such a weakness in his stomach, that he could take nothing but a spare and thin diet, and that not till late in the evening. His voice was loud and good, but so harsh and unmanaged that in vehemence and heat of speaking he always raised it to so high a tone, that there seemed to be reason to fear about his health.

When he came to Athens, he was a hearer of Antiochus of Ascalon, with whose fluency and elegance of diction he was much taken, although he did not approve of his innovations in doctrine. For Antiochus had now fallen off from the New Academy, as they call it, and forsaken the sect of Carneades, whether that he was moved by the argument of manifestness[3] and the senses, or, as some say, had been led by feelings of rivalry and opposition to the followers of Clitomachus and Philo to change his opinions, and in most

---

[3] According to a proposed correction, "by the manifestness of the senses." But the *enargeia*, or *manifestness* of things seen and felt, seems to be the recognized name of the argument against the sceptical views of the New Acadamy as to the possibility of certain knowledge. See Cicero's Academics, II. 6.

things to embrace the doctrine of the Stoics. But Cicero rather affected and adhered to the doctrines of the New Academy; and purposed with himself, if he should be disappointed of any employment in the commonwealth, to retire hither from pleading and political affairs, and to pass his life with quiet in the study of philosophy.

But after he had received the news of Sylla's death, and his body, strengthened again by exercise, was come to a vigorous habit, his voice managed and rendered sweet and full to the ear and pretty well brought into keeping with his general constitution, his friends at Rome earnestly soliciting him by letters, and Antiochus also urging him to return to public affairs, he again prepared for use his orator's instrument of rhetoric, and summoned into action his political faculties, diligently exercising himself in declamations, and attending the most celebrated rhetoricians of the time. He sailed from Athens for Asia and Rhodes. Amongst the Asian masters, he conversed with Xenocles of Adramyttium, Dionysius of Magnesia, and Menippus of Caria; at Rhodes, he studied oratory with Apollonius,[4] the son of Molon, and philosophy with Posidonius. Apollonius, we are told, not understanding Latin, requested Cicero to declaim in Greek. He complied willingly, thinking that his faults would thus be better pointed out to him. And after he finished, all his other hearers were astonished, and contended who should praise him most, but Apollonius, who had shown no signs of excitement whilst he was hearing him, so also now, when it was over, sate musing for some considerable time, without any remark. And when Cicero was discomposed at this, he said, "You have my praise and

[4] *Apollonius* was not *the son of Molon,* but Molon or Molo merely his own surname.

admiration, Cicero, and Greece my pity and commiseration, since those arts and that eloquence which are the only glories that remain to her, will now be transferred by you to Rome."

And now when Cicero, full of expectation, was again bent upon political affairs, a certain oracle blunted the edge of his inclination; for consulting the god of Delphi how he should attain most glory, the Pythoness answered, by making his own genius and not the opinion of the people the guide of his life; and therefore at first he passed his time in Rome cautiously, and was very backward in pretending to public offices, so that he was at that time in little esteem, and had got the names, so readily given by low and ignorant people in Rome, of Greek and Scholar.[5] But when his own desire of fame and the eagerness of his father and relations had made him take in earnest to pleading, he made no slow or gentle advance to the first place, but shone out in full lustre at once, and far surpassed all the advocates of the bar. At first, it is said, he, as well as Demosthenes, was defective in his delivery, and on that account paid much attention to the instructions, sometimes of Roscius the comedian, and sometimes of Æsop the tragedian. They tell of this Æsop, that whilst he was representing on the theatre Atreus deliberating the revenge of Thyestes, he was so transported beyond himself in the heat of action, that he struck with his sceptre one of the servants, who was running across the stage, so violently, that he laid him dead upon the place. And such afterwards

---

[5] *Greek* and *Scholar*, terms of reproach, are noticeable. *Greek* is in the original not *Hellen*, the proper national name, but *Graikos*, the Roman *Græcus*, a name never used of themselves by those whom we, after the Roman usage, call Greeks. *Scholar* is *scholasticos*, the learned fool or pedant of the late Greek witticisms.

was Cicero's delivery, that it did not a little contribute to render his eloquence persuasive. He used to ridicule loud speakers, saying that they shouted because they could not speak, like lame men who get on horseback because they cannot walk. And his readiness and address in sarcasm, and generally in witty sayings, was thought to suit a pleader very well, and to be highly attractive, but his using it to excess offended many, and gave him the repute of ill nature.

He was appointed quæstor in a great scarcity of corn, and had Sicily for his province, where, though at first he displeased many, by compelling them to send in their provisions to Rome, yet after they had had experience of his care, justice, and clemency, they honored him more than ever they did any of their governors before. It happened, also, that some young Romans of good and noble families, charged with neglect of discipline and misconduct in military service, were brought before the prætor in Sicily. Cicero undertook their defence, which he conducted admirably, and got them acquitted. So returning to Rome with a great opinion of himself for these things, a ludicrous incident befell him, as he tells us himself.[6] Meeting an eminent citizen in Campania, whom he accounted

[6] Cicero *tells us himself,* in his speech pro *Plancio.* Much had been said in praise of various good deeds done in the country by Laterensis, Plancius's opponent. "Very likely," says Cicero, "but at Rome so much is done, that one hardly knows what occurs in the provinces. I may be forgiven for speaking of my own quæstorship;" and he proceeds to mention the honors paid to him in Sicily. "I had done a good deal, and, I confess it frankly, I came away in the belief that all the talk at Rome was of nothing but my quæstorship. On my way home I visited Puteoli, where the best company is usually to be found, and here I was, I may say, struck to the earth when a friend accosted me with the inquiry, When I had left Rome, and what was the news? On my

his friend, he asked him what the Romans said and thought of his actions, as if the whole city had been filled with the glory of what he had done. His friend asked him in reply, "Where is it you have been, Cicero?" This for the time utterly mortified and cast him down, to perceive that the report of his actions had sunk into the city of Rome as into an immense ocean, without any visible effect or result in reputation. And afterwards considering with himself that the glory he contended for was an infinite thing, and that there was no fixed end nor measure in its pursuit, he abated much of his ambitious thoughts. Nevertheless, he was always excessively pleased with his own praise, and continued to the very last to be passionately fond of glory; which often interfered with the prosecution of his wisest resolutions.

On beginning to apply himself more resolutely to public business, he remarked it as an unreasonable and absurd thing that artificers, using vessels and instruments inanimate, should know the name, place, and use of every one of them, and yet the statesman, whose instruments for carrying out public measures are men, should be negligent and careless in the knowledge of persons. And so he not only acquainted himself with the names, but also knew the particular place where every one of the more eminent citizens dwelt, what lands he possessed, the friends he made use of, and those that were of his neighborhood, and when he travelled on any road in Italy, he could readily name and show the estates and seats of his friends and acquaint-

replying that I had just quitted my province, 'Oh, yes,' said he, 'Africa, I believe.' I began to be really offended, and said, a little scornfully, 'Sicily,' when one who stood by interposed, with the air of knowing every thing, 'Don't you know, he was quæstor at Syracuse?'"

ance. Having so small an estate, though a sufficient competency for his own expenses, it was much wondered at that he took neither fees nor gifts from his clients, and more especially, that he did not do so when he undertook the prosecution of Verres. This Verres, who had been prætor of Sicily, and stood charged by the Sicilians of many evil practices during his government there, Cicero succeeded in getting condemned, not by speaking, but in a manner by holding his tongue. For the prætors, favoring Verres, had deferred the trial by several adjournments to the last day, in which it was evident there could not be sufficient time for the advocates to be heard, and the cause brought to an issue. Cicero, therefore, came forward, and said there was no need of speeches; and after producing and examining witnesses, he required the judges to proceed to sentence. However, many witty sayings are on record, as having been used by Cicero on the occasion. When a man named Cæcilius, one of the freed slaves, who was said to be given to Jewish practices, would have put by the Sicilians, and undertaken the prosecution of Verres himself, Cicero asked, "What has a Jew to do with swine?" *verres* being the Roman word for a boar. And when Verres began to reproach Cicero with effeminate living, "you ought," replied he, "to use this language at home, to your sons;" Verres having a son who had fallen into disgraceful courses. Hortensius the orator, not daring directly to undertake the defence of Verres, was yet persuaded to appear for him at the laying on of the fine, and received an ivory sphinx for his reward; and when Cicero, in some passage of his speech, obliquely reflected on him, and Hortensius told him he was not skilful in solving riddles, "No," said Cicero, "and yet you have the Sphinx in your house!"

Verres was thus convicted; though Cicero, who set

the fine at seventy-five myriads,[7] lay under the suspicion of being corrupted by bribery to lessen the sum. But the Sicilians, in testimony of their gratitude, came and brought him all sorts of presents from the island, when he was ædile; of which he made no private profit himself, but used their generosity only to reduce the public price of provisions.

He had a very pleasant seat at Arpi,[8] he had also a farm near Naples, and another about Pompeii, but neither of any great value. The portion of his wife, Terentia, amounted to ten myriads, and he had a bequest valued at nine myriads of denarii; upon these he lived in a liberal but temperate style, with the learned Greeks and Romans that were his familiars. He rarely, if at any time, sat down to meat till sunset, and that not so much on account of business, as for his health and the weakness of his stomach. He was otherwise in the care of his body nice and delicate, appointing himself, for example, a set number of walks and rubbings. And after this manner managing the habit of his body, he brought it in time to be healthful, and capable of supporting many great fatigues and trials. His father's house he made over to his brother, living himself near the Palatine hill, that he might not give the trouble of long journeys to those that made suit to him. And, indeed, there were not fewer daily appearing at his door, to do their court to him, than there were that came to Crassus for his riches, or to Pompey for his power amongst the soldiers, these being at that

---

[7] Seventy-five ten thousands, i. e. 750,000 drachmas (about $150,000) Plutarch most likely counting the drachma as equivalent to the denarius. But the sum does not agree with the figures given in Cicero's own orations, and must be regarded as quite uncertain.

[8] Plutarch calls it Arpi, which is far from Rome, in Apulia, but it is, of course, Arpinum, Cicero's native place.

time the two men of the greatest repute and influence in Rome. Nay, even Pompey himself used to pay court to Cicero, and Cicero's public actions did much to establish Pompey's authority and reputation in the state.

Numerous distinguished competitors stood with him for the prætor's office; but he was chosen before them all, and managed the decision of causes with justice and integrity. It is related that Licinius Macer, a man himself of great power in the city, and supported also by the assistance of Crassus, was accused before him of extortion, and that, in confidence on his own interest and the diligence of his friends, whilst the judges were debating about the sentence, he went to his house, where hastily trimming his hair and putting on a clean gown, as already acquitted, he was setting off again to go to the Forum; but at his hall door meeting Crassus, who told him that he was condemned by all the votes, he went in again, threw himself upon his bed, and died immediately. This verdict was considered very creditable to Cicero, as showing his careful management of the courts of justice. On another occasion, Vatinius, a man of rude manners and often insolent in court to the magistrates, who had large swellings on his neck, came before his tribunal and made some request, and on Cicero's desiring further time to consider it, told him that he himself would have made no question about it, had he been prætor. Cicero, turning quickly upon him, answered, "But I, you see, have not the neck that you have."[9]

When there were but two or three days remaining in his office, Manilius was brought before him, and

[9] The strong, thick neck was both in Greek and Latin the sign of the pushing, unscrupulous man, who would take no refusal and stick at no doubt or difficulty. So in the life of Marius.

charged with peculation. Manilius had the good opinion and favor of the common people, and was thought to be prosecuted only for Pompey's sake, whose particular friend he was. And therefore, when he asked a space of time before his trial, Cicero allowed him but one day, and that the next only, the common people grew highly offended, because it had been the custom of the prætors to allow ten days at least to the accused; and the tribunes of the people having called him before the people, and accused him, he, desiring to be heard, said, that as he had always treated the accused with equity and humanity, as far as the law allowed, so he thought it hard to deny the same to Manilius, and that he had studiously appointed that day of which alone, as prætor, he was master, and that it was not the part of those that were desirous to help him, to cast the judgment of his cause upon another prætor. These things being said made a wonderful change in the people, and, commending him much for it, they desired that he himself would undertake the defence of Manilius; which he willingly consented to, and that principally for the sake of Pompey, who was absent. And, accordingly, taking his place before the people again, he delivered a bold invective upon the oligarchical party and on those who were jealous of Pompey.

Yet he was preferred to the consulship no less by the nobles than the common people, for the good of the city; and both parties jointly assisted his promotion, upon the following reasons. The change of government made by Sylla, which at first seemed a senseless one, by time and usage had now come to be considered by the people no unsatisfactory settlement. But there were some that endeavored to alter and subvert the whole present state of affairs, not from any good motives, but for their own private gain; and Pompey being at this time employed in the wars with the kings

of Pontus and Armenia, there was no sufficient force
at Rome to suppress any attempts at a revolution.
These people had for their head a man of bold, daring,
and restless character, Lucius Catiline, who was accused, besides other great offences, of deflouring his
virgin daughter, and killing his own brother; for
which latter crime, fearing to be prosecuted at law, he
persuaded Sylla to set him down, as though he were
yet alive, amongst those that were to be put to death
by proscription. This man the profligate citizens
choosing for their captain, gave faith to one another,
amongst other pledges, by sacrificing a man and eating of his flesh; and a great part of the young men of
the city were corrupted by him, he providing for every
one pleasures, drink, and women, and profusely supplying the expense of these debauches. Etruria, moreover, had all been excited to revolt, as well as a great
part of Gaul within the Alps. But Rome itself was
in the most dangerous inclination to change, on account of the unequal distribution of wealth and property, those of highest rank and greatest spirit having
impoverished themselves by shows, entertainments,
ambition of offices, and sumptuous buildings, and the
riches of the city having thus fallen into the hands of
mean and low-born persons. So that there wanted
but a slight impetus to set all in motion, it being in the
power of every daring man to overturn a sickly commonwealth.

Catiline, however, being desirous of procuring a
strong position to carry out his designs, stood for the
consulship, and had great hopes of success, thinking he
should be appointed, with Caius Antonius as his colleague, who was a man fit to lead neither in a good
cause nor in a bad one, but might be a valuable accession to another's power. These things the greatest
part of the good and honest citizens apprehending,

put Cicero upon standing for the consulship; whom the people readily receiving, Catiline was put by, so that he and Caius Antonius were chosen, although amongst the competitors he was the only man descended from a father of the equestrian, and not of the senatorial order.

Though the designs of Catiline were not yet publicly known, yet considerable preliminary troubles immediately followed upon Cicero's entrance upon the consulship. For, on the one side, those who were disqualified by the laws of Sylla from holding any public offices, being neither inconsiderable in power nor in number, came forward as candidates and caressed the people for them; speaking many things truly and justly against the tyranny of Sylla, only that they disturbed the government at an improper and unseasonable time; on the other hand, the tribunes of the people proposed laws to the same purpose, constituting a commission of ten persons, with unlimited powers, in whom as supreme governors should be vested the right of selling the public lands of all Italy and Syria and Pompey's new conquests, of judging and banishing whom they pleased, of planting colonies, of taking moneys out of the treasury, and of levying and paying what soldiers should be thought needful. And several of the nobility favored this law, but especially Caius Antonius, Cicero's colleague, in hopes of being one of the ten. But what gave the greatest fear to the nobles was, that he was thought privy to the conspiracy of Catiline, and not to dislike it, because of his great debts.

Cicero, endeavoring in the first place to provide a remedy against this danger, procured a decree assigning to him the province of Macedonia, he himself declining that of Gaul, which was offered to him. And this piece of favor so completely won over Antonius, that he was ready to second and respond to, like a hired player, whatever Cicero said for the good of the country. And now, having made his colleague thus tame and tractable, he could with greater courage attack the conspirators. And, therefore, in the senate, making an oration against the law of the ten commissioners, he so confounded those who proposed it, that they had nothing to reply. And when they again endeavored, and, having prepared things beforehand, had called the consuls before the assembly of the people, Cicero, fearing nothing, went first out, and commanded the senate to follow him, and not only succeeded in throwing out the law, but so entirely overpowered the tribunes by his oratory, that they abandoned all thought of their other projects.

For Cicero, it may be said, was the one man, above all others, who made the Romans feel how great a charm eloquence lends to what is good, and how invincible justice is, if it be well spoken; and that it is necessary for him who would dexterously govern a commonwealth, in action, always to prefer that which is honest before that which is popular, and in speaking, to free the right and useful measure from every thing that may occasion offence. An incident occurred in the theatre, during his consulship, which showed what his speaking could do. For whereas formerly the knights of Rome were mingled in the theatre with the common people, and took their places amongst them as it happened, Marcus Otho, when he was prætor, was the first who distinguished them from the other citizens, and appointed them a proper seat, which they still enjoy as their special place in the theatre. This the common people took as indignity done to them, and, therefore, when Otho appeared in the theatre, they hissed him; the knights, on the contrary, received him with loud clapping. The people repeated and increased their hissing; the knights continued their clapping. Upon this, turning upon one another, they broke out into insulting words, so that the theatre was in great disorder. Cicero, being informed of it, came himself to the theatre, and summoning the people into the temple of Bellona, he so effectually chid and chastised them for it, that, again returning into the theatre, they received Otho with loud applause, contending with the knights who should give him the greatest demonstrations of honor and respect.

The conspirators with Catiline, at first cowed and disheartened, began presently to take courage again. And assembling themselves together, they exhorted one another boldly to undertake the design before Pompey's return, who, as it was said, was now on his march with his forces for Rome. But the old soldiers of Sylla were Catiline's chief stimulus to action. They had been disbanded all about Italy, but the greatest number and the fiercest of them lay scattered among the cities of Etruria, entertaining themselves with dreams of new plunder and rapine amongst the hoarded riches of Italy. These, having for their leader Manlius, who had served with distinction in the wars under Sylla, joined themselves to Catiline, and came to Rome to assist him with their suffrages at the election. For he again pretended to the consulship, having resolved to kill Cicero in a tumult at the elections. Also, the divine powers seemed to give intimation of the coming troubles, by earthquakes, thunderbolts, and strange appearances. Nor was human evidence wanting, certain enough in itself, though not sufficient for the conviction of the noble and powerful Catiline. Therefore Cicero, deferring the day of election, summoned Catiline into the senate, and questioned him as to the charges made against him. Catiline, believing there were many in the senate desirous of change, and to give a specimen of himself to the conspirators present, returned an audacious answer, "What harm," said he, "when I see two bodies, the one lean and consumptive with a head, the other great and strong without one, if I put a head to that body which wants one!" This covert representation of the senate and the people excited yet greater apprehensions in Cicero. He put on armor, and was attended from his house by the noble citizens in a body; and a number of the young men went with him into the Plain. Here, designedly letting his tunic slip partly off from his shoulders, he showed his armor underneath, and discovered his danger to the spectators; who, being much moved at it, gathered round about him for his defence. At length, Catiline was by a general suffrage again put by, and Silanus and Murena chosen consuls.

Not long after this, Catiline's soldiers got together in a body in Etruria, and began to form themselves into companies, the day appointed for the design being near at hand. About midnight, some of the principal and most powerful citizens of Rome, Marcus Crassus, Marcus Marcellus, and Scipio Metellus went to Cicero's house, where, knocking at the gate, and calling up the porter, they commanded him to awake Cicero, and tell him they were there. The business was this: Crassus's porter after supper had delivered to him letters brought by an unknown person. Some of them were directed to others, but one to Crassus, without a name; this only Crassus read, which informed him that there was a great slaughter intended by Catiline, and advised him to leave the city. The others he did not open, but went with them immediately to Cicero, being affrighted at the danger, and to free himself of the suspicion he lay under for his familiarity with Catiline. Cicero, considering the matter, summoned the senate at break of day. The letters he brought with him, and delivered them to those to whom they were directed, commanding them to read them publicly; they all alike contained an account of the conspiracy. And when Quintus Arrius, a man of prætorian dignity, recounted to them, how soldiers were collecting in companies in Etruria, and Manlius stated to be in motion with a large force, hovering about those cities, in expectation of intelligence from Rome, the senate made a decree, to place all in the hands of the consuls, who should undertake the conduct of every thing, and do their best to save the state.[10] This was not a common thing, but only done by the senate in case of imminent danger.

After Cicero had received this power, he committed all affairs outside to Quintus Metellus, but the management of the city he kept in his own hands. Such a numerous attendance guarded him every day when he went abroad, that the greatest part of the market-place[11] was filled with his train when he entered it. Catiline, impatient of further delay, resolved himself to break forth and go to Manlius, but he commanded Marcius and Cethegus to take their swords, and go early in the morning to Cicero's gates, as if only intending to salute him, and then to fall upon him and slay him. This a noble lady, Fulvia, coming by night, discovered to Cicero, bidding him beware of Cethegus and Marcius. They came by break of day, and being denied entrance, made an outcry and disturbance at the gates, which excited all the more suspicion. But Cicero, going forth, summoned the senate into the

---

[10] "Dent operam consules ne quid respublica detrimenti capiat," the usual form for suspending other authority, and arming the consuls with discretionary power; much the same as placing the town in a state of siege.

[11] The Forum.

temple of Jupiter Stator, which stands at the end of the Sacred Street, going up to the Palatine. And when Catiline with others of his party also came, as intending to make his defence, none of the senators would sit by him, but all of them left the bench where he had placed himself. And when he began to speak, they interrupted him with outcries. At length Cicero, standing up, commanded him to leave the city, for since one governed the commonwealth with words, the other with arms, it was necessary there should be a wall betwixt them. Catiline, therefore, immediately left the town, with three hundred armed men; and assuming, as if he had been a magistrate, the rods, axes, and military ensigns, he went to Manlius, and having got together a body of near twenty thousand men, with these he marched to the several cities, endeavoring to persuade or force them to revolt. So it being now come to open war, Antonius was sent forth to fight him.

The remainder of those in the city whom he had corrupted, Cornelius Lentulus kept together and encouraged. He had the surname Sura, and was a man of a noble family, but a dissolute liver, who for his debauchery was formerly turned out of the senate, and was now holding the office of prætor for the second time, as the custom is with those who desire to regain the dignity of senator. It is said that he got the surname Sura upon this occasion; being quæstor in the time of Sylla, he had lavished away and consumed a great quantity of the public moneys, at which Sylla being provoked, called him to give an account in the senate; he appeared with great coolness and contempt, and said he had no account to give, but they might take this, holding up the calf of his leg, as boys do at ball, when they have missed. Upon which he was surnamed *Sura, sura* being the Roman word for the calf of the leg. Being at another time prosecuted at law, and having bribed some of the judges, he escaped only by two votes, and complained of the needless expense he had gone to in paying for a second, as one would have sufficed to acquit him. This man, such in his own nature, now inflamed by Catiline, false prophets and fortune-tellers had also corrupted with vain hopes, quoting to him fictitious verses and oracles, and proving from the Sibylline prophecies that there were three of the name Cornelius designed by fate to be monarchs of Rome; two of whom, Cinna and Sylla, had already fulfilled the decree, and that divine fortune was now advancing with the gift of monarchy for the remaining third Cornelius; and that therefore he ought by all means to accept it, and not lose opportunity by delay, as Catiline had done.

Lentulus, therefore, designed no mean or trivial matter, for he had resolved to kill the whole senate, and as many other citizens as he could, to fire the city, and spare nobody, except only Pompey's children, intending to seize and keep them as pledges of his reconciliation with Pompey. For there was then a common and strong report that Pompey was on his way homeward from his great expedition. The night appointed for the design was one of the Saturnalia; swords, flax, and sulphur they carried and hid in the house of Cethegus; and providing one hundred men, and dividing the city into as many parts, they had allotted to every one singly his proper place, so that in a moment many kindling the fire, the city might be in a flame all together. Others were appointed to stop up the aqueducts, and to kill those who should endeavor to carry water to put it out. Whilst these plans were preparing, it happened there were two ambassadors from the Allobroges staying in Rome; a nation at that time in a distressed condition, and very uneasy under the Roman government. These Lentulus and his party judging useful instruments to move and seduce Gaul to revolt, admitted into the conspiracy, and they gave them letters to their own magistrates, and letters to Catiline; in those they promised liberty, in these they exhorted Catiline to set all slaves free, and to bring them along with him to Rome. They sent also to accompany them to Catiline, one Titus, a native of Croton, who was to carry those letters to him.

These counsels of inconsidering men, who conversed together over wine and with women, Cicero watched with sober industry and forethought, and with most admirable sagacity, having several emissaries abroad, who observed and traced with him all that was done, and keeping also a secret correspondence with many who pretended to join in the conspiracy. He thus knew all the discourse which passed betwixt them and the strangers; and lying in wait for them by night, he took the Crotonian with his letters, the ambassadors of the Allobroges acting secretly in concert with him.

By break of day, he summoned the senate into the temple of Concord, where he read the letters and examined the informers. Junius Silanus further stated, that several persons had heard Cethegus say, that three consuls and four prætors were to be slain; Piso, also, a person of consular dignity, testified other matters of the like nature; and Caius Sulpicius, one of the prætors, being sent to Cethegus's house, found there a quantity of darts and of armor, and a still greater number of swords and daggers, all recently whetted. At length, the senate decreeing indemnity to the Crotonian upon his confession of the whole matter, Lentulus was convicted, abjured his office (for he was then prætor), and put off his robe edged with purple in the senate, changing it for another garment more agreeable to his present circumstances. He, thereupon, with the rest of his confederates present, was committed to the charge of the prætors in free custody.

It being evening, and the common people in crowds expecting without, Cicero went forth to them, and told them what was done, and then, attended by them, went to the house of a friend and near neighbor; for his own was taken up by the women, who were celebrating with secret rites the feast of the goddess whom the Romans call the Good, and the Greeks, the Women's goddess. For a sacrifice is annually performed to her in the consul's house, either by his wife or mother, in the presence of the vestal virgins. And having got into his friend's house privately, a few only being present, he began to deliberate how he should treat these men. The severest, and the only punishment fit for such heinous crimes, he was somewhat shy and fearful of inflicting, as well from the clemency of his nature, as also lest he should be thought to exercise his authority too insolently, and to treat too harshly men of the noblest birth and most powerful friendships in the city; and yet, if he should use them more mildly, he had a dreadful prospect of danger from them. For there was no likelihood, if they suffered less than death, they would be reconciled, but rather, adding new rage to their former wickedness, they would rush into every kind of audacity, while he himself, whose character for courage already did not stand very high with the multitude, would be thought guilty of the greatest cowardice and want of manliness.

Whilst Cicero was doubting what course to take, a portent happened to the women in their sacrificing. For on the altar, where the fire seemed wholly extinguished, a great and bright flame issued forth from the ashes of the burnt wood; at which others were affrighted, but the holy virgins called to Terentia, Cicero's wife, and bade her haste to her husband, and command him to execute what he had resolved for the good of his country, for the goddess had sent a great light to the increase of his safety and glory. Terentia, therefore, as she was otherwise in her own nature neither tender-hearted nor timorous, but a woman eager for distinction (who, as Cicero himself says,[12] would rather thrust herself into his public affairs, than communicate her domestic matters to him), told him these things, and excited him against the conspirators. So also did Quintus his brother, and Publius Nigidius, one of his philosophical friends, whom he often made use of in his greatest and most weighty affairs of state.

The next day, a debate arising in the senate about the punishment of the men, Silanus, being the first who was asked his opinion, said, it was fit they should be all sent to the prison, and there suffer the utmost penalty. To him all consented in order till it came to Caius Cæsar, who was afterwards dictator. He was then but a young man, and only at the outset of his career, but had already directed his hopes and policy to that course by which he afterwards changed the Roman state into a monarchy. Of this others foresaw nothing; but Cicero had seen reason for strong suspicion, though without obtaining any sufficient means of proof. And there were some indeed that said he was very near being discovered, and only just escaped him; others are of opinion that Cicero voluntarily overlooked and neglected the evidence against him, for fear of his friends and power; for it was very evident to everybody, that if Cæsar was to be accused with the conspirators, they were more likely to be saved with him, than he to be punished with them.

[12] *As Cicero himself says,*—not, it is said, in any of his extant writings.

When, therefore, it came to Cæsar's turn to give his opinion, he stood up and proposed that the conspirators should not be put to death, but their estates confiscated, and their persons confined in such cities in Italy as Cicero should approve, there to be kept in custody till Catiline was conquered. To this sentence, as it was the most moderate, and he that delivered it a most powerful speaker, Cicero himself gave no small weight, for he stood up, and, turning the scale on either side, spoke in favor partly of the former, partly of Cæsar's sentence. And all of Cicero's friends, judging Cæsar's sentence most expedient for Cicero, because he would incur the less blame if the conspirators were not put to death, chose rather the latter; so that Silanus, also, changing his mind, retracted his opinion, and said he had not declared for capital, but only the utmost punishment, which to a Roman senator is imprisonment. The first man who spoke against Cæsar's motion was Catulus Lutatius. Cato followed, and so vehemently urged in his speech the strong suspicion about Cæsar himself, and so filled the senate with anger and resolution, that a decree was passed for the execution of the conspirators. But Cæsar opposed the confiscation of their goods, not thinking it fair that those who had rejected the mildest part of his sentence should avail themselves of the severest. And when many insisted upon it, he appealed to the tribunes, but they would do nothing; till Cicero himself yielding, remitted that part of the sentence.

After this, Cicero went out with the senate to the conspirators; they were not all together in one place, but the several prætors had them, some one, some another, in custody. And first he took Lentulus from the Palatine, and brought him by the Sacred Street, through the middle of the market-place, a circle of the most eminent citizens encompassing and protecting him. The people, affrighted at what was doing, passed along in silence, especially the young men; as if, with fear and trembling, they were undergoing a rite of initiation into some ancient, sacred mysteries of aristocratic power. Thus passing from the market-place, and coming to the gaol, he delivered Lentulus to the officer, and commanded him to execute him; and after him Cethegus, and so all the rest in order, he brought and delivered up to execution. And when he saw many of the conspirators in the market-place, still standing together in companies, ignorant of what was done, and waiting for the night, supposing the men were still alive and in a possibility of being rescued, he called out in a loud voice, and said, "*They did live;*"[13] for so the Romans, to avoid inauspicious language, name those that are dead.

It was now evening, when he returned from the market-place to his own house, the citizens no longer attending him with silence, nor in order, but receiving him, as he passed, with acclamations and applauses, and saluting him as the saviour and founder of his country. A bright light shone through the streets from the lamps and torches set up at the doors, and the women showed lights from the tops of the houses, to honor Cicero, and to behold him returning home with a splendid train of the most principal citizens; amongst whom were many who had conducted great wars, celebrated triumphs, and added to the possessions of the Roman empire, both by sea and land. These, as they passed along with him, acknowledged to one another, that though the Roman people were indebted to several officers and commanders of that age for riches, spoils, and power, yet to Cicero alone they owed the safety and security of all these, for delivering them

---

[13] "Vixerunt."

from so great and imminent a danger. For though it might seem no wonderful thing to prevent the design, and punish the conspirators, yet to defeat the greatest of all conspiracies with so little disturbance, trouble, and commotion, was very extraordinary. For the greater part of those who had flocked in to Catiline, as soon as they heard the fate of Lentulus and Cethegus, left and forsook him, and he himself, with his remaining forces, joining battle with Antonius, was destroyed with his army.

And yet there were some who were very ready both to speak ill of Cicero, and to do him hurt for these actions; and they had for their leaders some of the magistrates of the ensuing year, as Cæsar, who was one of the prætors, and Metellus, and Bestia, the tribunes. These, entering upon their office some few days before Cicero's consulate expired, would not permit him to make any address to the people, but, throwing the benches before the Rostra, hindered his speaking, telling him he might, if he pleased, make the oath of withdrawal from office, and then come down again. Cicero, accordingly, accepting the conditions, came forward to make his withdrawal; and silence being made, he recited his oath, not in the usual, but in a new and peculiar form, namely, that he had saved his country, and preserved the empire; the truth of which oath all the people confirmed with theirs. Cæsar and the tribunes, all the more exasperated by this, endeavored to create him further trouble, and for this purpose proposed a law for calling Pompey home with his army, to put an end to Cicero's usurpation. But it was a very great advantage for Cicero and the whole commonwealth that Cato was at that time one of the tribunes. For he, being of equal power with the rest, and of greater reputation, could oppose their designs. He easily defeated their other projects, and, in an oration to the people, so highly extolled Cicero's consulate, that the greatest honors were decreed him, and he was publicly declared the Father of his Country, which title he seems to have obtained, the first man who did so, when Cato gave it him in this address to the people.

At this time, therefore, his authority was very great in the city; but he created himself much envy, and offended very many, not by any evil action, but because he was always lauding and magnifying himself. For neither senate, nor assembly of the people, nor court of judicature could meet, in which he was not heard to talk of Catiline and Lentulus. Indeed, he also filled his books and writings with his own praises, to such an excess as to render a style, in itself most pleasant and delightful, nauseous and irksome to his hearers; this ungrateful humor, like a disease, always cleaving to him. Nevertheless, though he was intemperately fond of his own glory, he was very free from envying others, and was, on the contrary, most liberally profuse in commending both the ancients and his contemporaries, as any one may see in his writings. And many such sayings of his are also remembered; as that he called Aristotle a river of flowing gold, and said of Plato's Dialogues, that if Jupiter were to speak, it would be in language like theirs. He used to call Theophrastus his special luxury. And being asked which of Demosthenes's orations he liked best, he answered, the longest. And yet some affected imitators of Demosthenes have complained of some words that occur in one of his letters,[14] to the effect that Demosthenes sometimes falls asleep in his speeches; for-

[14] The remark in disparagement of Demosthenes is not to be found in any one of *his letters* now remaining; but it is mentioned, says Coray, by Quintilian.

getting the many high encomiums he continually passes upon him, and the compliment he paid him when he named the most elaborate of all his orations, those he wrote against Antony, Philippics. And as for the eminent men of his own time, either in eloquence or philosophy, there was not one of them whom he did not, by writing or speaking favorably of him, render more illustrious. He obtained of Cæsar, when in power, the Roman citizenship for Cratippus, the Peripatetic, and got the court of Areopagus, by public decree, to request his stay at Athens, for the instruction of their youth, and the honor of their city. There are letters extant from Cicero to Herodes, and others to his son, in which he recommends the study of philosophy under Cratippus. There is one in which he blames Gorgias, the rhetorician, for enticing his son into luxury and drinking, and, therefore, forbids him his company. And this, and one other to Pelops, the Byzantine, are the only two of his Greek epistles which seem to be written in anger. In the first, he justly reflects on Gorgias, if he were what he was thought to be, a dissolute and profligate character; but in the other, he rather meanly expostulates and complains with Pelops, for neglecting to procure him a decree of certain honors from the Byzantines.

Another illustration of his love of praise is the way n which sometimes, to make his orations more striking, he neglected decorum and dignity. When Munatius, who had escaped conviction by his advocacy, immediately prosecuted his friend Sabinus, he said in the warmth of his resentment, "Do you suppose you were acquitted for your own merits, Munatius, and was it not that I so darkened the case, that court could not see your guilt?" When from the Rostra he had made an eulogy of Marcus Crassus, with much applause, and within a few days after again as publicly reproached him, Crassus called to him, and said, "Did not yourself two days ago, in this same place, commend me?" "Yes," said Cicero, "I exercised my eloquence in declaiming upon a bad subject." At another time, Crassus had said that no one of his family had ever lived beyond sixty years of age, and afterwards denied it, and asked, "What should put it into my head to say so?" "It was to gain the people's favor," answered Cicero; "you knew how glad they would be to hear it." When Crassus expressed admiration of the Stoic doctrine, that *the good man is always rich,* "Do you not mean," said Cicero, "their doctrine that *all things belong to the wise?*" Crassus being generally accused of covetousness. One of Crassus's sons, who was thought so exceedingly like a man of the name of Axius as to throw some suspicion on his mother's honor, made a successful speech in the senate. Cicero on being asked how he liked it, replied with the Greek words, *Axios Crassou.*[15]

When Crassus was about to go into Syria, he desired to leave Cicero rather his friend than his enemy, and, therefore, one day saluting him, told him he would come and sup with him, which the other as courteously received. Within a few days after, on some of Cicero's acquaintances interceding for Vatinius, as desirous of reconciliation and friendship, for he was then his enemy, "What," he replied, "does Vatinius also wish to come and sup with me?" Such was his way with Crassus. When Vatinius, who had swellings in

[15] Which may mean, either *worthy of Crassus,* or *Crassus's son Axius.* The jest on the Stoic doctrines is also rather obscure. Crassus appears to have praised the first dictum in its proper philosophical sense; that the only truly rich man is he who is virtuous; Cicero suggests, that a text which is more to Crassus's purpose is the other, that the wise man is the possessor of all things, that is may make himself as rich as he pleases.

his neck, was pleading a cause, he called him the *tumid* orator; and having been told by some one that Vatinius was dead, on hearing presently after that he was alive, "May the rascal perish," said he, "for his news not being true."

Upon Cæsar's bringing forward a law for the division of the lands in Campania amongst the soldiers, many in the senate opposed it; amongst the rest, Lucius Gellius, one of the oldest men in the house, said it should never pass whilst he lived. "Let us postpone it," said Cicero, "Gellius does not ask us to wait long." There was a man of the name of Octavius, suspected to be of African descent. He once said, when Cicero was pleading, that he could not hear him; "Yet there are holes," said Cicero, "in your ears."[16] When Metellus Nepos told him, that he had ruined more as a witness, than he had saved as an advocate, "I admit," said Cicero, "that I have more truth than eloquence." To a young man who was suspected of having given a poisoned cake to his father, and who talked largely of the invectives he meant to deliver against Cicero, "Better these," replied he, "than your cakes." Publius Sextius, having amongst other retained Cicero as his advocate in a certain cause, was yet desirous to say all for himself, and would not allow anybody to speak for him; when he was about to receive his acquittal from the judges, and the ballots were passing, Cicero called to him, "Make haste, Sextius, and use your time; tomorrow you will be nobody." He cited Publius Cotta to bear testimony in a certain cause, one who affected to be thought a lawyer, though ignorant and unlearned; to whom, when he had said, "I know nothing of the matter," he answered, "You think, perhaps, we

---

[16] The marks of the ears having been bored for ear-rings would be considered proof of his being of barbarian origin.

ask you about a point of law." To Metellus Nepos, who, in a dispute between them, repeated several times, "Who was your father, Cicero?" he replied, "Your mother has made the answer to such a question in your case more difficult;" Nepos's mother having been of ill repute. The son, also, was of a giddy, uncertain temper. At one time, he suddenly threw up his office of tribune, and sailed off into Syria to Pompey; and immediately after, with as little reason, came back again. He gave his tutor, Philagrus, a funeral with more than necessary attention, and then set up the stone figure of a crow over his tomb. "This," said Cicero, "is really appropriate; as he did not teach you to speak, but to fly about." When Marcus Appius, in the opening of some speech in a court of justice, said that his friend had desired him to employ industry, eloquence, and fidelity in that cause, Cicero answered, "And how have you had the heart not to accede to any one of his requests?"

To use this sharp raillery against opponents and antagonists in judicial pleading seems allowable rhetoric. But he excited much ill feeling by his readiness to attack any one for the sake of a jest. A few anecdotes of this kind may be added. Marcus Aquinius, who had two sons-in-law in exile, received from him the name of king Adrastus.[17] Lucius Cotta, an intemperate lover of wine, was censor when Cicero stood for the consulship. Cicero, being thirsty at the election, his friends stood round about him while he was drinking. "You have reason to be afraid," he

[17] Adrastus, king of Argos, married his daughters to the exiles, Tydeus and Polynices. The verse below, quoted from a tragedy, must refer to Laius and his son, born against the warning of the oracle, Œdipus. "Without Apollo's leave" would be a phrase like "invita Minerva" applied to any unsuccessful, or infelicitous, or injudicious proceeding.

said, "lest the censor should be angry with me for drinking water." Meeting one day Voconius with his three very ugly daughters, he quoted the verse,

> He reared a race without Apollo's leave.[18]

When Marcus Gellius, who was reputed the son of a slave, had read several letters in the senate with a very shrill, and loud voice, "Wonder not," said Cicero, "he comes of the criers." When Faustus Sylla, the son of Sylla the dictator, who had, during his dictatorship, by public bills proscribed and condemned so many citizens, had so far wasted his estate, and got into debt, that he was forced to publish his bills of sale, Cicero told him that he liked these bills much better than those of his father. By this habit he made himself odious with many people.

But Clodius's faction conspired against him upon the following occasion. Clodius was a member of a noble family, in the flower of his youth, and of a bold and resolute temper. He, being in love with Pompeia, Cæsar's wife, got privately into his house in the dress and attire of a music-girl; the women being at that time offering there the sacrifice which must not be seen by men, and there was no man present. Clodius, being a youth and beardless, hoped to get to Pompeia among the women without being taken notice of. But coming into a great house by night, he missed his way in the passages, and a servant belonging to Aurelia, Cæsar's mother, spying him wandering up and down, inquired his name. Thus being necessitated to speak, he told her he was seeking for one of Pompeia's maids, Abra by name; and she, perceiving it not to be

---

[18] *He reared a race against Apollo's will* is evidently a verse from a play on the subject of Œdipus; but nothing more is known of it.

a woman's voice, shrieked out, and called in the women; who, shutting the gates, and searching every place, at length found Clodius hidden in the chamber of the maid with whom he had come in. This matter being much talked about, Cæsar put away his wife, Pompeia, and Clodius was prosecuted for profaning the holy rites.

Cicero was at this time his friend, for he had been useful to him in the conspiracy of Catiline, as one of his forwardest assistants and protectors. But when Clodius rested his defence upon this point, that he was not then at Rome, but at a distance in the country, Cicero testified that he had come to his house that day, and conversed with him on several matters; which thing was indeed true, although Cicero was thought to testify it not so much for the truth's sake as to preserve his quiet with Terentia his wife. For she bore a grudge against Clodius on account of his sister Clodia's wishing, as it was alleged, to marry Cicero, and having employed for this purpose the intervention of Tullus, a very intimate friend of Cicero's; and his frequent visits to Clodia, who lived in their neighborhood, and the attentions he paid to her had excited Terentia's suspicions, and, being a woman of a violent temper, and having the ascendant over Cicero, she urged him on to taking a part against Clodius, and delivering his testimony. Many other good and honest citizens also gave evidence against him, for perjuries, disorders, bribing the people, and debauching women. Lucullus proved, by his women-servants, that he had debauched his youngest sister when she was Lucullus's wife; and there was a general belief that he had done the same with his two other sisters, Tertia, whom Marcius Rex, and Clodia, whom Metellus Celer had married; the latter of whom was called

Quadrantia,[19] because one of her lovers had deceived her with a purse of small copper money instead of silver, the smallest copper coin being called a *quadrant*. Upon this sister's account, in particular, Clodius's character was attacked. Notwithstanding all this, when the common people united against the accusers and witnesses and the whole party, the judges were affrighted, and a guard was placed about them for their defence; and most of them wrote their sentences on the tablets in such a way, that they could not well be read. It was decided, however, that there was a majority for his acquittal, and bribery was reported to have been employed; in reference to which Catulus remarked, when he next met the judges, "You were very right to ask for a guard, to prevent your money being taken from you." And when Clodius upbraided Cicero that the judges had not believed his testimony, "Yes," said he, "five and twenty of them trusted me, and condemned you, and the other thirty did not trust you, for they did not acquit you till they had got your money."

Cæsar, though cited, did not give his testimony against Clodius, and declared himself not convinced of his wife's adultery, but that he had put her away because it was fit that Cæsar's house should not be only free of the evil fact, but of the fame too.

Clodius, having escaped this danger, and having got himself chosen one of the tribunes, immediately attacked Cicero, heaping up all matters and inciting all persons against him. The common people he gained over with popular laws; to each of the consuls he decreed large provinces, to Piso, Macedonia, and to Gabinius, Syria; he made a strong party among the indigent citizens, to support him in his proceedings, and had always a body of armed slaves about him. Of

[19] *Quadrantia* in correct Latin is Quadrantaria.

the three men then in greatest power, Crassus was
Cicero's open enemy, Pompey indifferently made advances to both, and Cæsar was going with an army into
Gaul. To him, though not his friend (what had occurred in the time of the conspiracy having created
suspicions betweem them), Cicero applied, requesting
an appointment as one of his lieutenants in the province. Cæsar accepted him, and Clodius, perceiving
that Cicero would thus escape his tribunician authority, professed to be inclinable to a reconciliation, laid
the greatest fault upon Terentia, made always a favorable mention of him, and addressed him with kind
expressions, as one who felt no hatred or ill-will, but
who merely wished to urge his complaints in a moderate and friendly way. By these artifices, he so freed
Cicero of all his fears, that he resigned his appointment to Cæsar, and betook himself again to political
affairs. At which Cæsar being exasperated, joined
the party of Clodius against him, and wholly alienated
Pompey from him; he also himself declared in a public
assembly of the people, that he did not think Lentulus
and Cethegus, with their accomplices, were fairly and
legally put to death without being brought to trial.
And this, indeed, was the crime charged upon Cicero,
and this impeachment he was summoned to answer.
And so, as an accused man, and in danger for the
result, he changed his dress, and went round with his
hair untrimmed, in the attire of a suppliant, to beg
the people's grace. But Clodius met him in every
corner, having a band of abusive and daring fellows
about him, who derided Cicero for his change of dress
and his humiliation, and often, by throwing dirt and
stones at him, interrupted his supplication to the people.

However, first of all, almost the whole equestrian
order changed their dress with him, and no less than

twenty thousand young gentlemen followed him with their hair untrimmed, and supplicating with him to the people. And then the senate met, to pass a decree that the people should change their dress as in time of public sorrow. But the consuls opposing it, and Clodius with armed men besetting the senate-house, many of the senators ran out, crying out and tearing their clothes. But this sight moved neither shame nor pity; Cicero must either fly or determine it by the sword with Clodius. He entreated Pompey to aid him, who was on purpose gone out of the way, and was staying at his country-house in the Alban hills; and first he sent his son-in-law Piso to intercede with him, and afterwards set out to go himself. Of which Pompey being informed, would not stay to see him, being ashamed at the remembrance of the many conflicts in the commonwealth which Cicero had undergone in his behalf, and how much of his policy he had directed for his advantage. But being now Cæsar's son-in-law, at his instance he had set aside all former kindness, and, slipping out at another door, avoided the interview. Thus being forsaken by Pompey, and left alone to himself, he fled to the consuls. Gabinius was rough with him, as usual, but Piso spoke more courteously, desiring him to yield and give place for a while to the fury of Clodius, and to await a change of times, and to be now, as before, his country's savior from the peril of these troubles and commotions which Clodius was exciting.

Cicero, receiving this answer, consulted with his friends. Lucullus advised him to stay, as being sure to prevail at last; others to fly, because the people would soon desire him again, when they should have enough of the rage and madness of Clodius. This last Cicero approved. But first he took a statue of Minerva, which had been long set up and greatly honored in his house, and carrying it to the capitol, there dedicated it, with the inscription, "To Minerva, Patroness of Rome." And receiving an escort from his friends, about the middle of the night he left the city, and went by land through Lucania, intending to reach Sicily.

But as soon as it was publicly known that he was fled, Clodius proposed to the people a decree of exile, and by his own order interdicted him fire and water, prohibiting any within five hundred miles in Italy to receive him into their houses. Most people, out of respect for Cicero, paid no regard to this edict, offering him every attention, and escorting him on his way. But at Hipponium, a city of Lucania, now called Vibo, one Vibius, a Sicilian by birth, who, amongst many other instances of Cicero's friendship, had been made head of the state engineers when he was consul, would not receive him into his house, sending him word he would appoint a place in the country for his reception. Caius Vergilius, the prætor of Sicily, who had been on the most intimate terms with him, wrote to him to forbear coming into Sicily. At these things Cicero being disheartened, went to Brundusium, whence putting forth with a prosperous wind, a contrary gale blowing from the sea carried him back to Italy the next day. He put again to sea, and having reached Dyrrachium, on his coming to shore there, it is reported that an earthquake and a convulsion in the sea happened at the same time, signs which the diviners said intimated that his exile would not be long, for these were prognostics of change. Although many visited him with respect, and the cities of Greece contended which should honor him most, he yet continued disheartened and disconsolate, like an unfortunate lover, often casting his looks back upon Italy; and, indeed, he was become so poor-spirited, so humiliated and dejected by his misfortunes, as none could have expected in a man who had devoted so much of his life to study and learning. And yet he often desired his friends not to call him orator, but philosopher, because he had made philosophy his business, and had only used rhetoric as an instrument for attaining his objects in public life. But the desire of glory[20] has great power in washing the tinctures of philosophy out of the souls of men, and in imprinting the passions of the common people, by custom and conversation, in the minds of those that take a part in governing them, unless the politician be very careful so to engage in public affairs as to interest himself only in the affairs themselves, but not participate in the passions that are consequent to them.

Clodius, having thus driven away Cicero, fell to burning his farms and villas, and afterwards his city house, and built on the site of it a temple to Liberty. The rest of his property he exposed to sale by daily proclamation, but nobody came to buy. By these courses he became formidable to the noble citizens, and, being followed by the commonalty, whom he had filled with insolence and licentiousness, he began at last to try his strength against Pompey, some of whose arrangements in the countries he conquered, he attacked. The disgrace of this made Pompey begin to reproach himself for his cowardice in deserting Cicero,

[20] *Doxa*, the Greek word for "the desire of glory," should, perhaps, be translated "opinion." It is, in its original sense, "what people think," and is commonly used for people's *good* opinion, "glory," or "reputation." On the other hand, the philosophers employ it to express *opinion*, which may be false, as opposed to *knowledge*, which must be of the truth. If a philosopher, engaged in politics, does not confine his attention strictly to definite objects and acts, but lets himself be affected by the results, by people's good or bad *opinion* about them, his real convictions and *knowledge* will soon be overpowered.

and, changing his mind, he now wholly set himself with his friends to contrive his return. And when Clodius opposed it, the senate made a vote that no public measure should be ratified or passed by them till Cicero was recalled. But when Lentulus was consul, the commotions grew so high upon this matter, that the tribunes were wounded in the Forum, and Quintus, Cicero's brother, was left as dead, lying unobserved amongst the slain. The people began to change in their feelings; and Annius Milo, one of their tribunes, was the first who took confidence to summon Clodius to trial for acts of violence. Many of the common people and out of the neighboring cities formed a party with Pompey, and he went with them, and drove Clodius out of the Forum, and summoned the people to pass their vote. And, it is said, the people never passed any suffrage more unanimously than this. The senate, also, striving to outdo the people, sent letters of thanks to those cities which had received Cicero with respect in his exile, and decreed that his house and country-places, which Clodius had destroyed, should be rebuilt at the public charge.

Thus Cicero returned sixteen months after his exile, and the cities were so glad, and people so zealous to meet him, that what he boasted of afterwards, that Italy had brought him on her shoulders home to Rome, was rather less than the truth. And Crassus himself, who had been his enemy before his exile, went then voluntarily to meet him, and was reconciled, to please his son Publius, as he said, who was Cicero's affectionate admirer.

Cicero had not been long at Rome, when taking the opportunity of Clodius's absence, he went, with a great company, to the capitol, and there tore and defaced the tribunician tables, in which were recorded the acts done in the time of Clodius. And on Clodius calling him in question for this, he answered, that he, being of the patrician order, had obtained the office of tribune against law, and, therefore, nothing done by him was valid. Cato was displeased at this, and opposed Cicero, not that he commended Clodius, but rather disapproved of his whole administration; yet, he contended, it was an irregular and violent course for the senate to vote the illegality of so many decrees and acts, including those of Cato's own government in Cyprus and at Byzantium. This occasioned a breach between Cato and Cicero, which, though it came not to open enmity, yet made a more reserved friendship between them.

After this, Milo killed Clodius, and, being arraigned for the murder, he procured Cicero as his advocate. The senate, fearing lest the questioning of so eminent and high-spirited a citizen as Milo might disturb the peace of the city, committed the superintendence of this and of the other trials to Pompey, who should undertake to maintain the security alike of the city and of the courts of justice. Pompey, therefore, went in the night, and occupying the high grounds about it, surrounded the Forum with soldiers. Milo, fearing lest Cicero, being disturbed by such an unusual sight, should conduct his cause the less successfully, persuaded him to come in a litter into the Forum, and there repose himself till the judges were set, and the court filled. For Cicero, it seems, not only wanted courage in arms, but, in his speaking also, began with timidity, and in many cases scarcely left off trembling and shaking when he had got thoroughly into the current and the substance of his speech. Being to defend Licinius Murena against the prosecution of Cato, and being eager to outdo Hortensius, who had made his plea with great applause, he took so little rest that night, and was so disordered with thought and over-watching, that he spoke much worse than usual. And so now, on quitting his litter to commence the cause of Milo, at the sight of Pompey, posted, as it were, and encamped with his troops above, and seeing arms shining round about the Forum, he was so confounded, that he could hardly begin his speech, for the trembling of his body, and hesitance of his tongue; whereas Milo, meantime, was bold and intrepid in his demeanor, disdaining either to let his hair grow, or to put on the mourning habit. And this, indeed, seems to have been one principal cause of his condemnation. Cicero, however, was thought not so much to have shown timidity for himself, as anxiety about his friend.

He was made one of the priests, whom the Romans call Augurs, in the room of Crassus the younger, dead in Parthia. Then he was appointed, by lot, to the province of Cilicia, and set sail thither with twelve thousand foot and two thousand six hundred horse. He had orders to bring back Cappadocia to its allegiance to Ariobarzanes, its king; which settlement he effected very completely without recourse to arms. And perceiving the Cilicians, by the great loss the Romans had suffered in Parthia, and the commotions in Syria, to have become disposed to attempt a revolt, by a gentle course of government he soothed them back into fidelity. He would accept none of the presents that were offered him by the kings; he remitted the charge of public entertainments, but daily, at his own house, received the ingenious and accomplished persons of the province, not sumptuously, but liberally. His house had no porter, nor was he ever found in bed by any man, but early in the morning, standing or walking before his door, he received those who came to offer their salutations. He is said never once to have ordered any of those under his command to be beaten with rods, or to have their garments rent. He never gave contumelious language in his anger, nor inflicted punishment with reproach. He detected an embezzlement, to a large amount, in the public money, and thus relieved the cities from their burdens, at the same time that he allowed those who made restitution, to retain without further punishment their rights as citizens. He engaged too, in war, so far as to give a defeat to the banditti who infested Mount Amanus, for which he was saluted by his army Imperator. To Cæcilius,[21] the orator, who asked him to send him some panthers from Cicilia, to be exhibited on the theatre at Rome, he wrote, in commendation of his own actions, that there were no panthers in Cilicia, for they were all fled to Caria, in anger that in so general a peace they had become the sole objects of attack. On leaving his province, he touched at Rhodes, and tarried for some length of time at Athens, longing much to renew his old studies. He visited the eminent men of learning, and saw his former friends and companions; and after receiving in Greece the honors that were due to him, returned to the city, where every thing was now just as it were in a flame, breaking out into a civil war.

When the senate would have decreed him a triumph, he told them he had rather, so differences were accommodated, follow the triumphal chariot of Cæsar. In private, he gave advice to both, writing many letters to Cæsar, and personally entreating Pompey; doing his best to soothe and bring to reason both the one and the other. But when matters became incurable, and Cæsar was approaching Rome, and Pompey

---

[21] Probably Cælius. The Greek texts continually vary in these names, *Cæcilius* and *Cælius*. But whether Plutarch wrote it so or not, Cælius undoubtedly is the person, for we have Cicero's letter to him, in which he gives this answer (*Epist. ad Diversos II.*, 11).

durst not abide it, but, with many honest citizens, left the city, Cicero, as yet, did not join in the flight, and was reputed to adhere to Cæsar. And it is very evident he was in his thoughts much divided, and wavered painfully between both, for he writes in his epistles,[22] "To which side should I turn? Pompey has the fair and honorable plea for war; and Cæsar, on the other hand, has managed his affairs better, and is more able to secure himself and his friends. So that I know whom I should fly, not whom I should fly to." But when Trebatius, one of Cæsar's friends, by letter signified to him that Cæsar thought it was his most desirable course to join his party, and partake his hopes, but if he considered himself too old a man for this, then he should retire into Greece, and stay quietly there, out of the way of either party, Cicero, wondering that Cæsar had not written himself, gave an angry reply that he should not do any thing unbecoming his past life. Such is the account to be collected from his letters.

But as soon as Cæsar was marched into Spain, he immediately sailed away to join Pompey. And he was welcomed by all but Cato; who, taking him privately, chid him for coming to Pompey. As for himself, he said, it had been indecent to forsake that part in the commonwealth which he had chosen from the beginning; but Cicero might have been more useful to his country and friends, if, remaining neuter, he had attended and used his influence to moderate the result, instead of coming hither to make himself, without reason or necessity, an enemy to Cæsar, and a

---

[22] The passage describing what *he writes in his epistles* is a sort of summary of what we read in the seventh, eighth, and ninth books of the letters to Atticus; the last phrase is directly from VII., 7, "Ego vero quem fugiam habeo, quem sequar, non habeo."

partner in such great dangers. By this language, partly, Cicero's feelings were altered, and partly, also, because Pompey made no great use of him. Although, indeed, he was himself the cause of it, his not denying that he was sorry he had come, by his depreciating Pompey's resources, finding fault underhand with his counsels, and continually indulging in jests and sarcastic remarks on his fellow-soldiers. Though he went about in the camp with a gloomy and melancholy face himself, he was always trying to raise a laugh in others, whether they wished it or not. It may not be amiss to mention a few instances. To Domitius, on his preferring to a command one who was no soldier, and saying, in his defence, that he was a modest and prudent person, he replied, "Why did not you keep him for a tutor for your children?" On hearing Theophanes, the Lesbian, who was master of the engineers in the army, praised for the admirable way in which he had consoled the Rhodians for the loss of their fleet, "What a thing it is," he said, "to have a Greek in command!"[23] When Cæsar had been acting successfully, and in a manner blockading Pompey, Lentulus was saying it was reported that Cæsar's friends were out of heart; "Because," said Cicero, "they do not wish Cæsar well." To one Marcius, who had just come from Italy, and told them that there was a strong report at Rome that Pompey was blocked up, he said, "And you sailed hither to see it with your own eyes." To Nonius, encouraging them after a defeat

---

[23] *What a thing it is to have a Greek in command* is a scoff of course at the rhetorical gifts of the Greek, who could put a good color upon any disaster. The point of the answer at the end of the paragraph may perhaps be, "The first result of this expedient, this trick, or *stratagem*, as the Greek is, of circulating idle predictions, has been the loss of our camp."

to be of good hope, because there were seven eagles still left in Pompey's camp, "Good reason for encouragement," said Cicero, "if we were going to fight with jack-daws." Labienus insisted on some prophecies to the effect that Pompey would gain the victory; "Yes," said Cicero, "and the first step in the campaign has been losing our camp."

After the battle of Pharsalia was over, at which he was not present for want of health, and Pompey was fled, Cato, having considerable forces and a great fleet at Dyrrachium, would have had Cicero commander-in-chief, according to law, and the precedence of his consular dignity. And on his refusing the command, and wholly declining to take part in their plans for continuing the war, he was in the greatest danger of being killed, young Pompey and his friends calling him traitor, and drawing their swords upon him; only that Cato interposed, and hardly rescued and brought him out of the camp.

Afterwards, arriving at Brundusium, he tarried there sometime in expectation of Cæsar, who was delayed by his affairs in Asia and Egypt. And when it was told him that he was arrived at Tarentum, and was coming thence by land to Brundusium, he hastened towards him, not altogether without hope, and yet in some fear of making experiment of the temper of an enemy and conqueror in the presence of many witnesses. But there was no necessity for him either to speak or do any thing unworthy of himself; for Cæsar, as soon as he saw him coming a good way before the rest of the company, came down to meet him, saluted him, and, leading the way, conversed with him alone for some furlongs. And from that time forward he continued to treat him with honor and respect; so that, when Cicero wrote an oration in praise of Cato, Cæsar, in writing an answer to it, took occasion to commend Cicero's own life and eloquence, comparing him to Pericles and Theramenes. Cicero's oration was called Cato; Cæsar's, anti-Cato.

So also, it is related that when Quintus Ligarius was prosecuted for having been in arms against Cæsar, and Cicero had undertaken his defence, Cæsar said to his friends, "Why might we not as well once more hear a speech from Cicero? Ligarius, there is no question, is a wicked man and an enemy." But when Cicero began to speak, he wonderfully moved him, and proceeded in his speech with such varied pathos, and such a charm of language, that the color of Cæsar's countenance often changed, and it was evident that all the passions of his soul were in commotion. At length, the orator touching upon the Pharsalian battle,[24] he was so affected that his body trembled, and some of the papers he held dropped out of his hands. And thus he was overpowered, and acquitted Ligarius.

Henceforth, the commonwealth being changed into a monarchy, Cicero withdrew himself from public affairs, and employed his leisure in instructing those young men that would, in philosophy; and by the near intercourse he thus had with some of the noblest and highest in rank, he again began to possess great influence in the city. The work and object which he set himself was to compose and translate philosophical dialogues and to render logical and physical terms into the Roman idiom. For he it was, as it is said, who first or principally gave Latin names to *phantasia, syncatathesis, epokhe, catalepsis*,[25]

---

[24] The speech *pro Quinto Ligario ad Cæsarem* is extant; the passage about the battle of Pharsalia is in the third chapter.

[25] *Phantăsia*, sensation excited by some external object, "impulsione oblata extrinsecus," Cicero renders by *visum; syn-*

atomon, ameres, kenon, and other such technical terms, which, either by metaphors or other means of accommodation, he succeeded in making intelligible and expressible to the Romans. For his recreation, he exercised his dexterity in poetry, and when he was set to it, would make five hundred verses in a night. He spent the greatest part of his time at his country-house near Tusculum. He wrote to his friends that he led the life of Laertes,[26] either jestingly, as his custom was, or rather from a feeling of ambition for public employment, which made him impatient under the present state of affairs. He rarely went to the city, unless to pay his court to Cæsar. He was commonly the first amongst those who voted him honors, and sought out new terms of praise for himself and for his actions. As, for example, what he said of the statues of Pompey, which had been thrown down,

cătăthĕsis, the act of acceptance on our part, he calls *assensio* or *assensus; epŏkhē* is the suspension of assent, "suspensio assensionis"; *catalepsis,* or *comprehensio,* is the next step in perception after *assensio; ătŏmŏn* has been turned, but not by Cicero, into *insecabile;* he calls atoms *individua corpora,* or *individua,* using the same word also for *ămĕrĕs; kĕnon* is *inane* or *vacuum.* Most of these terms are introduced in the Academics, see I. 11, II. 6 and 18, and the curious illustration from Zeno in 47. Pointing with his left hand to his right, as it lay open and outspread. Here, said he, is sensation, *visum, phantasia;* letting the fingers begin to close, this, he proceeded, is assent, *syncatatehsis;* by closing his hand he exemplified comprehension or *catalepsis;* and, at last, seizing it with his left, such, he said, is knowledge. *Phantasia,* of course, is etymologically our *fancy,* and *epokhe,* in the sense of a point in time to pause at, our *epoch.*

[26] "Who," says the description in the first book of the Odyssey, "comes no more to the city, but lives away in pain and grief on his land, with one old woman to feed him, when he tires himself with tottering about his vineyard." So, also, when Ulysses goes to see him, in the last book. The passages in the Odyssey, describing the life of Laertes, are I. 190, XXIV. 226.

and were afterwards by Cæsar's orders set up again: that Cæsar, by this act of humanity, had indeed set up Pompey's statues, but he had fixed and established his own.

He had a design, it is said, of writing the history of his country, combining with it much of that of Greece, and incorporating in it all the stories and legends of the past that he had collected. But his purposes were interfered with by various public and various private unhappy occurrences and misfortunes; for most of which he was himself in fault. For first of all, he put away his wife Terentia, by whom he had been neglected in the time of the war, and sent away destitute of necessaries for his journey; neither did he find her kind when he returned into Italy, for she did not join him at Brundusium, where he staid a long time, nor would allow her young daughter, who undertook so long a journey, decent attendance, or the requisite expenses; besides, she left him a naked and empty house, and yet had involved him in many and great debts. These were alleged as the fairest reasons for the divorce. But Terentia, who denied them all, had the most unmistakable defence furnished her by her husband himself, who not long after married a young maiden for the love of her beauty, as Terentia upbraided him; or as Tiro, his emancipated slave, has written, for her riches, to discharge his debts. For the young woman was very rich, and Cicero had the custody of her estate, being left guardian in trust; and being indebted many myriads of money, he was persuaded by his friends and relations to marry her, notwithstanding his disparity of age, and to use her money to satisfy his creditors. Antony, who mentions this marriage in his answer to the Philippics, reproaches him for putting away a wife with whom he had lived to old age; adding some happy strokes of sarcasm on Cicero's domestic, inactive, unsoldier-like habits. Not long after this marriage, his daughter died in child-bed at Lentulus's house, to whom she had been married after the death of Piso, her former husband. The philosophers from all parts came to comfort Cicero; for his grief was so excessive, that he put away his new-married wife, because she seemed to be pleased at the death of Tullia. And thus stood Cicero's domestic affairs at this time.

He had no concern in the design that was now forming against Cæsar, although, in general, he was Brutus's most principal confidant, and one who was as aggrieved at the present, and as desirous of the former state of public affairs, as any other whatsoever. But they feared his temper, as wanting courage, and his old age, in which the most daring dispositions are apt to be timorous.

As soon, therefore, as the act was committed by Brutus and Cassius, and the friends of Cæsar were got together, so that there was fear the city would again be involved in a civil war, Antony, being consul, convened the senate, and made a short address recommending concord. And Cicero, following with various remarks such as the occasion called for, persuaded the senate to imitate the Athenians, and decree an amnesty [27] for what had been done in Cæsar's

[27] *Amnesteia*, the Greek original of *amnesty*, literally, an act of oblivion, a *not-remembering*, seems to have been a term first made for the occasion when Thrasybulus came back to Athens and the old democratic government was restored, after the expulsion of the thirty tyrants. Cicero expressly adduced the Athenian example, and suggested the Greek word. "Jeci fundamenta pacis, Atheniensiumque renovavi vetus exemplum; Græcum etiam verbum usurpavi, quo tum in sedandis discordiis erat usa civitas illa, etc." Philippic, I., 1, quoted in Mr. Long's note.

case, and to bestow provinces on Brutus and Cassius. But neither of these things took effect. For as soon as the common people, of themselves inclined to pity, saw the dead body of Cæsar borne through the market-place, and Antony showing his clothes filled with blood, and pierced through in every part with swords, enraged to a degree of frenzy, they made a search for the murderers, and with firebrands in their hands ran to their houses to burn them. They, however, being forewarned, avoided this danger; and expecting many more and greater to come, they left the city.

Antony on this was at once in exultation, and every one was in alarm with the prospect that he would make himself sole ruler, and Cicero in more alarm than any one. For Antony, seeing his influence reviving in the commonwealth, and knowing how closely he was connected with Brutus, was ill-pleased to have him in the city. Besides, there had been some former jealousy between them, occasioned by the difference of their manners. Cicero, fearing the event, was inclined to go as lieutenant with Dolabella into Syria. But Hirtius and Pansa, consuls elect as successors of Antony, good men and lovers of Cicero, entreated him not to leave them, undertaking to put down Antony if he would stay in Rome. And he, neither distrusting wholly, nor trusting them, let Dolabella go without him, promising Hirtius that he would go and spend his summer at Athens, and return again when he entered upon his office. So he set out upon his journey; but some delay occurring in his passage, new intelligence, as often happens, came suddenly from Rome, that Antony had made an astonishing change, and was doing all things and managing all public affairs at the will of the senate, and that there wanted nothing but his presence to bring things to a happy settlement. And therefore, blaming himself for his cowardice, he returned again to Rome, and was not deceived in his hopes at the beginning. For such multitudes flocked out to meet him, that the compliments and civilities which were paid him at the gates, and at his entrance into the city, took up almost one whole day's time.

On the morrow, Antony convened the senate, and summoned Cicero thither. He came not, but kept his bed, pretending to be ill with his journey; but the true reason seemed the fear of some design against him, upon a suspicion and intimation given him on his way to Rome. Antony, however, showed great offence at the affront, and sent soldiers, commanding them to bring him or burn his house; but many interceding and supplicating for him, he was contented to accept sureties. Ever after, when they met, they passed one another with silence, and continued on their guard, till Cæsar, the younger,[28] coming from Apollonia, entered on the first Cæsar's inheritance, and was engaged in a dispute with Antony about two thousand five hundred myriads of money, which Antony detained from the estate.

Upon this, Philippus, who married the mother, and Marcellus, who married the sister of young Cæsar, came with the young man to Cicero, and agreed with him that Cicero should give them the aid of his eloquence and political influence with the senate and people, and Cæsar give Cicero the defence of his riches and arms. For the young man had already a great party of the soldiers of Cæsar about him. And Cicero's readiness to join him was founded, it is said, on some yet stronger motives; for it seems, while Pompey and Cæsar were yet alive, Cicero, in his sleep, had fancied himself engaged in calling some of the

[28] Augustus.

sons of the senators into the capitol, Jupiter being about, according to the dream,[29] to declare one of them the chief ruler of Rome. The citizens, running up with curiosity, stood about the temple, and the youths, sitting in their purple-bordered robes, kept silence. On a sudden the doors opened, and the youths, arising one by one in order, passed round the god, who reviewed them all, and, to their sorrow, dismissed them; but when this one was passing by, the god stretched forth his right hand and said, "O ye Romans, this young man, when he shall be lord of Rome, shall put an end to all your civil wars." It is said that Cicero formed from his dream a distinct image of the youth, and retained it afterwards perfectly, but did not know who it was. The next day, going down into the Campus Martius, he met the boys returning from their gymnastic exercises, and the first was he, just as he had appeared to him in his dream. Being astonished at it, he asked him who were his parents. And it proved to be this young Cæsar, whose father was a man of no great eminence, Octavius, and his mother, Attia, Cæsar's sister's daughter; for which reason, Cæsar, who had no children, made him by will the heir of his house and property. From that time, it is said that Cicero studiously noticed the youth whenever he met him, and he as kindly received the civility; and by fortune he happened to be born when Cicero was consul.

These were the reasons spoken of; but it was principally Cicero's hatred of Antony, and a temper unable to resist honor, which fastened him to Cæsar, with

---

[29] *The dream* is described both by Suetonius and Dion Cassius, but is said by them to have been had by Catulus. Cicero, they say, dreamed he saw Jupiter letting down a youth (whom he afterwards, as in the other dream, recognized in Octavius) by golden chains from heaven, and putting into his hands a scourge.

the purpose of getting the support of Cæsar's power for his own public designs. For the young man went so far in his court to him, that he called him Father; at which Brutus was so highly displeased, that, in his epistles to Atticus he reflected on Cicero saying, it was manifest, by his courting Cæsar for fear of Antony, he did not intend liberty to his country, but an indulgent master to himself. Notwithstanding, Brutus took Cicero's son, then studying philosophy at Athens, gave him a command, and employed him in various ways, with a good result. Cicero's own power at this time was at the greatest height in the city, and he did whatsoever he pleased; he completely overpowered and drove out Antony, and sent the two consuls, Hirtius and Pansa, with an army, to reduce him; and, on the other hand, persuaded the senate to allow Cæsar the lictors and ensigns of a prætor, as though he were his country's defender. But after Antony was defeated in battle, and the two consuls slain, the armies united, and ranged themselves with Cæsar. And the senate, fearing the young man, and his extraordinary fortune, endeavored, by honors and gifts, to call off the soldiers from him, and to lessen his power; professing there was no further need of arms, now Antony was put to flight.

This giving Cæsar an affright, he privately sends some friends to entreat and persuade Cicero to procure the consular dignity for them both together; saying he should manage the affairs as he pleased, should have the supreme power, and govern the young man who was only desirous of name and glory. And Cæsar himself confessed, that in fear of ruin, and in danger of being deserted, he had seasonably made use of Cicero's ambition, persuading him to stand with him, and to accept the offer of his aid and interest for the consulship.

And now, more than at any other time, Cicero let himself be carried away and deceived, though an old man, by the persuasions of a boy. He joined him in soliciting votes, and procured the good-will of the senate, not without blame at the time on the part of his friends; and he, too, soon enough after, saw that he had ruined himself, and betrayed the liberty of his country. For the young man, once established, and possessed of the office of consul, bade Cicero farewell; and, reconciling himself to Antony and Lepidus, joined his power with theirs, and divided the government, like a piece of property, with them. Thus united, they made a schedule of above two hundred persons who were to be put to death. But the greatest contention in all their debates was on the question of Cicero's case. Antony would come to no conditions, unless he should be the first man to be killed. Lepidus held with Antony, and Cæsar opposed them both. They met secretly and by themselves, for three days together, near the town of Bononia. The spot was not far from the camp, with a river surrounding it. Cæsar, it is said, contended earnestly for Cicero the first two days; but on the third day he yielded, and gave him up. The terms of their mutual concessions were these: that Cæsar should desert Cicero, Lepidus his brother Paulus, and Antony, Lucius Cæsar, his uncle by his mother's side. Thus they let their anger and fury take from them the sense of humanity, and demonstrated that no beast is more savage than man, when possessed with power answerable to his rage.

Whilst these things were contriving, Cicero was with his brother at his country-house near Tusculum; whence, hearing of the proscriptions, they determined to pass to Astura, a villa of Cicero's near the sea, and to take shipping from thence for Macedonia to

Brutus, of whose strength in that province news had already been heard. They travelled together in their separate litters, overwhelmed with sorrow; and often stopping on the way till their litters came together, condoled with one another. But Quintus was the more disheartened, when he reflected on his want of means for his journey; for, as he said, he had brought nothing with him from home. And even Cicero himself had but a slender provision. It was judged, therefore, most expedient that Cicero should make what haste he could to fly, and Quintus return home to provide necessaries, and thus resolved, they mutually embraced, and parted with many tears.

Quintus, within a few days after, betrayed by his servants to those who came to search for him, was slain, together with his young son. But Cicero was carried to Astura, where, finding a vessel, he immediately went on board her, and sailed as far as Circæum with a prosperous gale; but when the pilots resolved immediately to set sail from thence, whether fearing the sea, or not wholly distrusting the faith of Cæsar, he went on shore, and passed by land a hundred furlongs, as if he was going for Rome. But losing resolution and changing his mind, he again returned to the sea, and there spent the night in fearful and perplexed thoughts. Sometimes he resolved to go into Cæsar's house privately, and there kill himself upon the altar of his household gods, to bring divine vengeance upon him; but the fear of torture put him off this course. And after passing through a variety of confused and uncertain counsels, at last he let his servants carry him by sea to Capitæ,[30] where he had a house, an

[30] This, as we find from other authority, means Caieta, the present Gaeta. Nothing is known of any such place as Capitæ. Formiæ, the present Mola di Gaeta, is close by; and here Cicero is known to have had a villa, the Formianum.

agreeable place to retire to in the heat of summer, when the Etesian winds are so pleasant.

There was at that place a chapel of Apollo, not far from the sea-side, from which a flight of crows rose with a great noise, and made towards Cicero's vessel as it rowed to land, and lighting on both sides of the yard, some croaked, others pecked the ends of the ropes. This was looked upon by all as an ill omen; and, therefore, Cicero went again ashore, and entering his house, lay down upon his bed to compose himself to rest. Many of the crows settled about the window, making a dismal cawing; but one of them alighted upon the bed where Cicero lay covered up, and with its bill by little and little pecked off the clothes from his face. His servants, seeing this, blamed themselves that they should stay to be spectators of their master's murder, and do nothing in his defence, whilst the brute creatures came to assist and take care of him in his undeserved affliction; and, therefore, partly by entreaty, partly by force, they took him up, and carried him in his litter towards the sea-side.

But in the mean time the assassins were come with a band of soldiers, Herennius, a centurion, and Popillius, a tribune, whom Cicero had formerly defended when prosecuted for the murder of his father. Finding the doors shut, they broke them open, and Cicero not appearing, and those within saying they knew not where he was, it is stated that a youth, who had been educated by Cicero in the liberal arts and sciences, an emancipated slave of his brother Quintus, Philologus by name, informed the tribune that the litter was on its way to the sea through the close and shady walks. The tribune, taking a few with him, ran to the place where he was to come out. And Cicero, perceiving Herennius running in the walks, commanded his servants to set down the litter; and strok-

MARCUS TILLIUS CICERO

ing his chin, as he used to do, with his left hand, he looked steadfastly upon his murderers, his person covered with dust, his beard and hair untrimmed, and his face worn with his troubles. So that the greatest part of those that stood by covered their faces while Herennius slew him. And thus was he murdered, stretching forth his neck out of the litter, being now in his sixty-fourth year. Herennius cut off his head, and, by Antony's command, his hands also, by which his Philippics were written; for so Cicero styled those orations he wrote against Antony, and so they are called to this day.

When these members of Cicero were brought to Rome, Antony was holding an assembly for the choice of public officers; and when he heard it, and saw them, he cried out, "Now let there be an end of our proscriptions." He commanded his head and hands to be fastened up over the Rostra, where the orators spoke; a sight which the Roman people shuddered to behold, and they believed they saw there not the face of Cicero, but the image of Antony's own soul. And yet amidst these actions he did justice in one thing, by delivering up Philologus to Pomponia, the wife of Quintus; who, having got his body into her power, besides other grievous punishments, made him cut off his own flesh by pieces, and roast and eat it; for so some writers have related. But Tiro, Cicero's emancipated slave, has not so much as mentioned the treachery of Philologus.

Some long time after, Cæsar, I have been told, visiting one of his daughter's sons, found him with a book of Cicero's in his hand. The boy for fear endeavored to hide it under his gown; which Cæsar perceiving, took it from him, and turning over a great part of the book standing, gave it him again, and said, "My child, this was a learned man, and a lover of his country."[31] And immediately after he had vanquished Antony, being then consul, he made Cicero's son his colleague in the office; and under that consulship, the senate took down all the statues of Antony, and abolished all the other honors that had been given him, and decreed that none of that family should thereafter bear the name of Marcus; and thus the final acts of the punishment of Antony were, by the divine powers, devolved upon the family of Cicero.

[31] It is not easy to find any proper equivalent for the word here translated by "learned." *Logios,* derived from *logos,* which is indifferently *speech* and *reason* (thinking and speaking being both powers of *articulating*), may be one who has thought much and well, one who has much to say, and one who can say it well.

COMPARISON OF DEMOSTHENES AND CICERO

THESE are the most memorable circumstances recorded in history of Demosthenes and Cicero which have come to our knowledge. But omitting an exact comparison of their respective faculties in speaking, yet thus much seems fit to be said; that Demosthenes, to make himself a master in rhetoric, applied all the faculties he had, natural or acquired, wholly that way; that he far surpassed in force and strength of eloquence all his contemporaries in political and judicial speaking, in grandeur and majesty all the panegyrical orators, and in accuracy and science all the logicians and rhetoricians of his day;[1] that Cicero was highly educated, and by his diligent study became a most accomplished general scholar in all these branches, having left behind him numerous philosophical treatises of his own on Academic principles; as, indeed, even in his written speeches, both political and judicial, we see him continually trying to show his learning by the way. And one may discover the different temper of each of them in their speeches. For Demosthenes's oratory was without all embellishment and jesting, wholly composed for real effect and seriousness; not smelling of the lamp, as Pytheas scoffingly said, but of the temperance, thoughtfulness, austerity, and grave earnestness of his temper.

---

[1] The political, the judicial, and the panegyrical departments were the three varieties of oratory. To the practitioners in these are added the *sophistæ*, the logic and rhetoric masters.

Whereas Cicero's love of mockery often ran him into scurrility; and in his love of laughing away serious arguments in judicial cases by jests and facetious remarks, with a view to the advantage of his clients, he paid too little regard to what was decent; saying, for example, in his defence of Cælius, that he had done no absurd thing in such plenty and affluence to indulge himself in pleasures, it being a kind of madness not to enjoy the things we possess, especially since the most eminent philosophers have asserted pleasure to be the chiefest good. So also we are told, that when Cicero, being consul, undertook the defence of Murena against Cato's prosecution, by way of bantering Cato, he made a long series of jokes upon the absurd *paradoxes,* as they are called, of the Stoic sect; so that a loud laughter passing from the crowd to the judges, Cato, with a quiet smile, said to those that sat next him, "My friends, what an amusing consul we have."

And, indeed, Cicero was by natural temper very much disposed to mirth and pleasantry, and always appeared with a smiling and serene countenance. But Demosthenes had constant care and thoughtfulness in his look, and a serious anxiety, which he seldom, if ever, laid aside; and, therefore, was accounted by his enemies, as he himself confessed, morose and ill-mannered.

Also, it is very evident, out of their several writings, that Demosthenes never touched upon his own praises but decently and without offence when there was need of it, and for some weightier end; but, upon other occasions modestly and sparingly. But Cicero's immeasurable boasting of himself in his orations argues him guilty of an uncontrollable appetite for distinction, his cry being evermore that arms should give place to the gown, and the soldier's laurel to the

DEMOSTHENES AND CICERO

tongue.[2] And at last we find him extolling not only his deeds and actions, but his orations also, as well those that were only spoken, as those that were published; as if he were engaged in a boyish trial of skill, who should speak best, with the rhetoricians, Isocrates and Anaximenes, not as one who could claim the task to guide and instruct the Roman nation, the

Soldiers full-armed, terrific to the foe.[3]

It is necessary, indeed, for a political leader to be an able speaker; but it is an ignoble thing for any man to admire and relish the glory of his own eloquence. And, in this matter, Demosthenes had a more than ordinary gravity and magnificence of mind, accounting his talent in speaking nothing more than a mere accomplishment and matter of practice, the success of which must depend greatly on the good-will and candor of his hearers, and regarding those who pride themselves on such accounts to be men of a low and petty disposition.

The power of persuading and governing the people did, indeed, equally belong to both, so that those who had armies and camps at command stood in need of their assistance; as Chares, Diopithes, and Leosthenes of Demosthenes's, Pompey and young Cæsar of Cicero's, as the latter himself admits in his Memoirs addressed to Agrippa and Mæcenas. But what are thought and commonly said most to demonstrate and try the tempers of men, namely, authority and

[2] Translating Cicero's famous verse upon himself—
Cedant arma togæ, concedat laurea linguæ.

[3] The verse *Soldier full-armed, terrific to the foe* is a fragment of one of Æschylus's elegies. Plutarch quotes it in three other places, in the minor works. It is No. 464 in Hermann's edition.

place, by moving every passion, and discovering every frailty, these are things which Demosthenes never received; nor was he ever in a position to give such proof of himself, having never obtained any eminent office, nor led any of those armies into the field against Philip which he raised by his eloquence. Cicero, on the other hand, was sent quæstor into Sicily, and proconsul into Cilicia and Cappadocia, at a time when avarice was at the height, and the commanders and governors who were employed abroad, as though they thought it a mean thing to steal, set themselves to seize by open force; so that it seemed no heinous matter to take bribes, but he that did it most moderately was in good esteem. And yet he, at this time, gave the most abundant proofs alike of his contempt of riches and of his humanity and good-nature. And at Rome, when he was created consul in name, but indeed received sovereign and dictatorial authority against Catiline and his conspirators, he attested the truth of Plato's prediction, that then the miseries of states would be at an end, when by a happy fortune supreme power, wisdom, and justice should be united in one.[4]

It is said, to the reproach of Demosthenes, that his eloquence was mercenary; that he privately made orations for Phormion and Apollodorus, though adversaries in the same cause; that he was charged with moneys received from the king of Persia, and condemned for bribes from Harpalus. And should we grant that all those (and they are not few) who have made these statements against him have spoken what is untrue, yet that Demosthenes was not the character to look without desire on the presents offered him out of respect and gratitude by royal persons, and that

[4] Or, as the dictum is in his Republic, "When the philosopher should be king."

one who lent money on maritime usury was likely to be thus indifferent, is what we cannot assert. But that Cicero refused, from the Sicilians when he was quæstor, from the king of Cappadocia when he was proconsul, and from his friends at Rome when he was in exile, many presents, though urged to receive them, has been said already.

Moreover, Demosthenes's banishment was infamous, upon conviction for bribery; Cicero's very honorable, for ridding his country of a set of villains. Therefore, when Demosthenes fled his country, no man regarded it; for Cicero's sake the senate changed their habit, and put on mourning, and would not be persuaded to make any act before Cicero's return was decreed. Cicero, however, passed his exile idly in Macedonia. But the very exile of Demosthenes made up a great part of the services he did for his country; for he went through the cities of Greece, and everywhere, as we have said, joined in the conflict on behalf of the Grecians, driving out the Macedonian ambassadors, and approving himself a much better citizen than Themistocles and Alcibiades did in the like fortune. And, after his return, he again devoted himself to the same public service, and continued firm to his opposition to Antipater and the Macedonians. Whereas Lælius reproached Cicero in the senate for sitting silent when Cæsar, a beardless youth, asked leave to come forward, contrary to the law, as a candidate for the consulship; and Brutus, in his epistles, charges him with nursing and rearing a greater and more heavy tyranny than that they had removed.

Finally, Cicero's death excites our pity; for an old man to be miserably carried up and down by his servants, flying and hiding himself from that death which was, in the course of nature, so near at hand; and yet at last to be murdered. Demosthenes, though he seemed at first a little to supplicate, yet, by his preparing and keeping the poison by him, demands our admiration; and still more admirable was his using it. When the temple of the god no longer afforded him a sanctuary, he took refuge, as it were, at a mightier altar, freeing himself from arms and soldiers, and laughing to scorn the cruelty of Antipater.

DEMETRIUS[1]

TRANSLATED BY JOHN NALSON, LL. D.

INGENIOUS men have long observed a resemblance between the arts and the bodily senses. And they were first led to do so, I think, by noticing the way in which, both in the arts and with our senses, we examine opposites. Judgment once obtained, the use to which we put it differs in the two cases. Our senses are not meant to pick out black rather than white, to prefer sweet to bitter, or soft and yielding to hard and resisting objects; all they have to do is to receive impressions as they occur, and report to the understanding the impressions as received. The arts, on the other hand, which reason institutes expressly to choose and obtain some suitable, and to refuse and get rid of some unsuitable object, have their proper concern in the consideration of the former; though, in a casual and contingent way, they must also, for the very rejection of them, pay attention to the latter. Medicine, to produce health, has to examine disease, and music, to create harmony, must investigate discord; and the supreme arts, of temperance, of justice, and of wis-

---

[1] Demetrius, surnamed Poliorcetes, king of Macedonia, was the son of Antigonus, King of Asia, and accompanied his father in his campaigns against Eumenes, 317, 316, B. C. Demetrius was one of the most remarkable characters of his age; in restless activity of mind, fertility of resource, and daring promptitude in the execution of his schemes he has perhaps never been surpassed. His besetting sin was his unbounded licentiousness. He died in imprisonment in 283 B. C., in the fifty-sixth year of his age.—Dr. William Smith.

dom, as they are acts of judgment and selection, exercised not on good and just and expedient only, but also on wicked, unjust, and inexpedient objects, do not give their commendations to the mere innocence whose boast is its inexperience of evil, and whose truer name is, by their award, simpleness and ignorance of what all men who live aright should know. The ancient Spartans, at their festivals, used to force their Helots to swallow large quantities of raw wine, and then to expose them at the public tables, to let the young men see what it is to be drunk. And, though I do not think it consistent with humanity or with civil justice to correct one man's morals by corrupting those of another, yet we may, I think, avail ourselves of the cases of those who have fallen into indiscretions, and have, in high stations, made themselves conspicuous for misconduct; and I shall not do ill to introduce a pair or two of such examples among these biographies, not, assuredly, to amuse and divert my readers, or give variety to my theme, but, as Ismenias, the Theban, used to show his scholars good and bad performers on the flute, and to tell them, "You should play like this man," and "You should not play like that," and as Antigenidas used to say, Young people would take great pleasure in hearing good playing, if first they were set to hear bad, so, and in the same manner, it seems to me likely enough that we shall be all the more zealous and more emulous to read, observe, and imitate the better lives, if we are not left in ignorance of the blameworthy and the bad.

For this reason, the following book contains the lives of Demetrius Poliorcetes,[2] and Antonius the

---

[2] Poliorcetes means the Besieger of Cities. *Triumvir* of the translation is, in Plutarch's Greek, *Autocrator*, the word corresponding to *Imperator*. It would, perhaps, be incorrect to give

DEMETRIUS 103

Triumvir; two persons who have abundantly justified the words of Plato,[3] that great natures produce great vices as well as virtues. Both alike were amorous and intemperate, war-like and munificent, sumptuous in their way of living, and overbearing in their manners. And the likeness of their fortunes carried out the resemblance in their characters. Not only were their lives each a series of great successes and great disasters, mighty acquisitions and tremendous losses of power, sudden overthrows, followed by unexpected recoveries, but they died, also, Demetrius in actual captivity to his enemies, and Antony on the verge of it.

Antigonus had by his wife, Stratonice, the daughter of Corrhæus, two sons; the one of whom, after the name of his uncle, he called Demetrius, the other had that of his grandfather Philip, and died young. This is the most general account, although some have related, that Demetrius was not the son of Antigonus, but of his brother; and that his own father dying young, and his mother being afterwards married to Antigonus, he was accounted to be his son.

this the significance attached to it by usage, when applied to Augustus and his successors. Yet, probably, to Plutarch the distinction between these and previous Military Autocrats did not seem so broad; and to say, "Antony the Emperor," would do little injustice to his meaning.

[3] For *the words of Plato, that great natures produce great vices as well as great virtues,* Coray refers to a passage in the Crito, "Would to heaven they were capable of accomplishing the greatest evils, as in this case, they might be capable of the greatest good!" But perhaps he alludes rather to the descriptions in the Republic, of the temptations and perils to which the best natures, the true philosophical, wisdom-loving minds are exposed—*from these come, when perverted and corrupted, those who do the greatest mischiefs to states alike, and individuals; as also those that do the greatest benefits, if haply they take this direction.*

Demetrius had not the height of his father Antigonus, though he was a tall man. But his countenance was one of such singular beauty and expression, that no painter or sculptor ever produced a good likeness of him. It combined grace and strength, dignity with boyish bloom, and, in the midst of youthful heat and passion, what was hardest of all to represent was a certain heroic look and air of kingly greatness. Nor did his character belie his looks, as no one was better able to render himself both loved and feared. For as he was the most easy and agreeable of companions, and the most luxurious and delicate of princes in his drinking and banquetting and daily pleasures, so in action there was never any one that showed a more vehement persistence, or a more passionate energy. Bacchus, skilled in the conduct of war, and after war in giving peace its pleasures and joys, seems to have been his pattern among the gods.

He was wonderfully fond of his father Antigonus; and the tenderness he had for his mother led him, for her sake, to redouble attentions, which it was evident were not so much owing to fear or duty as to the more powerful motives of inclination. It is reported, that, returning one day from hunting, he went immediately into the apartment of Antigonus, who was conversing with some ambassadors, and after stepping up and kissing his father, he sat down by him, just as he was, still holding in his hand the javelins which he had brought with him. Whereupon Antigonus, who had just dismissed the ambassadors with their answer, called out in a loud voice to them, as they were going, "Mention, also, that this is the way in which we two live together;" as if to imply to them that it was no slender mark of the power and security of his government that there was so perfect a good understanding between himself and his son. Such an unsociable, solitary thing is power, and so much of jealousy and distrust in it, that the first and greatest of the successors of Alexander could make it a thing to glory in that he was not so afraid of his son as to forbid his standing beside him with a weapon in his hand. And, in fact, among all the successors of Alexander, that of Antigonus was the only house which, for many descents, was exempted from crime of this kind; or, to state it exactly, Philip was the only one of this family who was guilty of a son's death. All the other families, we may fairly say, afforded frequent examples of fathers who brought their children, husbands their wives, children their mothers, to untimely ends; and that brothers should put brothers to death was assumed, like the postulates of mathematicians, as the common and recognized royal first principle of safety.

Let us here record an example in the early life of Demetrius, showing his natural humane and kindly disposition. It was an adventure which passed betwixt him and Mithridates, the son of Ariobarzanes, who was about the same age with Demetrius, and lived with him, in attendance on Antigonus; and although nothing was said or could be said to his reproach, he fell under suspicion, in consequence of a dream which Antigonus had. Antigonus thought himself in a fair and spacious field, where he sowed golden seed, and saw presently a golden crop come up; of which, however, looking presently again, he saw nothing remain but the stubble, without the ears. And as he stood by in anger and vexation, he heard some voices saying, Mithridates had cut the golden harvest and carried it off into Pontus. Antigonus, much discomposed with his dream, first bound his son by an oath not to speak, and then related it to him, adding, that he had resolved, in consequence, to lose no time in ridding himself of Mithridates, and making away with him. Demetrius was extremely distressed; and when the young man came, as usual, to pass his time with him, to keep his oath he forbore from saying a word, but, drawing him aside little by little from the company, as soon as they were by themselves, without opening his lips, with the point of his javelin he traced before him the words, "Fly, Mithridates." Mithridates took the hint, and fled by night into Cappadocia, where Antigonus's dream about him was quickly brought to its due fulfilment; for he got possession of a large and fertile territory; and from him descended the line of the kings of Pontus, which, in the eighth generation, was reduced by the Romans. This may serve for a specimen of the early goodness and love of justice that was part of Demetrius's natural character.

But as in the elements of the world, Empedocles [4] tells us, out of liking and dislike, there spring up contention and warfare, and all the more, the closer the contact, or the nearer the approach of the objects, even so the perpetual hostilities among the successors of Alexander were aggravated and inflamed, in particular cases, by juxtaposition of interests and of territories; as, for example, in the case of Antigonus and Ptolemy. News came to Antigonus that Ptolemy had crossed from Cyprus and invaded Syria, and was ravaging the country and reducing the cities. Remaining, therefore, himself in Phrygia, he sent Demetrius, now twenty-two years old, to make his first essay

[4] For the theory of *Empedocles as to the elements of the world*, compare Horace's phrase of the *rerum discordia concors*. Two verses, still remaining among the fragments of Empedocles, express this doctrine of attractions and repulsions.

"All things at one time in liking collect and combine into one thing.
All things again at another, divide and are severed in quarrel."

DEMETRIUS

as sole commander in an important charge. He, whose youthful heat outran his experience, advancing against an adversary trained in Alexander's school, and practised in many encounters, incurred a great defeat near the town of Gaza, in which eight thousand of his men were taken, and five thousand killed. His own tent, also, his money, and all his private effects and furniture, were captured. These, however, Ptolemy sent back, together with his friends, accompanying them with the humane and courteous message, that they were not fighting for any thing else but honor and dominion. Demetrius accepted the gift, praying only to the gods not to leave him long in Ptolemy's debt, but to let him have an early chance of doing the like to him. He took his disaster, also, with the temper not of a boy defeated in his attempt, but of an old and long-tried general, familiar with reverse of fortune; he busied himself in collecting his men, replenishing his magazines, watching the allegiance of the cities, and drilling his new recruits.

Antigonus received the news of the battle with the remark, that Ptolemy had beaten boys, and would now have to fight with men. But not to humble the spirit of his son, he acceded to his request, and left him to command on the next occasion.

Not long after, Cilles, Ptolemy's lieutenant, with a powerful army, took the field, and, looking upon Demetrius as already defeated by the previous battle, he had in his imagination driven him out of Syria before he saw him. But he quickly found himself deceived; for Demetrius came so unexpectedly upon him that he surprised both the general and his army, making him and seven thousand of the soldiers prisoners of war, and possessing himself of a large amount of treasure. But his joy in the victory was not so much for the prizes he should keep, as for those he could restore; and his thankfulness was less for the wealth and glory than for the means it gave him of requiting his enemy's former generosity. He did not, however, take it into his own hands, but wrote to his father. And on receiving leave to do as he liked, he sent back to Ptolemy Cilles and his friends, loaded with presents. This defeat drove Ptolemy out of Syria, and brought Antigonus from Celænæ, to enjoy the victory, and the sight of the son who had gained it.

Soon after, Demetrius was sent to bring the Nabathæan Arabs into obedience. And here he got into a district without water, and incurred considerable danger, but by his resolute and composed demeanor he overawed the barbarians, and returned after receiving from them a large amount of booty, and seven hundred camels. Not long after, Seleucus, whom Antigonus had formerly chased out of Babylon, but who had afterwards recovered his dominion by his own efforts and maintained himself in it, went with large forces on an expedition to reduce the tribes on the confines of India and the provinces near Mount Caucasus. And Demetrius, conjecturing that he had left Mesopotamia but slenderly guarded in his absence, suddenly passed the Euphrates with his army, and made his way into Babylonia unexpectedly; where he succeeded in capturing one of the two citadels, out of which he expelled the garrison of Seleucus, and placed in it seven thousand men of his own. And after allowing his soldiers to enrich themselves with all the spoil they could carry with them out of the country, he retired to the sea, leaving Seleucus more securely master of his dominions than before, as he seemed by this conduct to abandon every claim to a country which he treated like an enemy's. However, by a rapid advance, he rescued Halicarnassus from Ptolemy, who was besieging it. The glory which this act obtained them inspired both the father and son with a wonderful desire for freeing Greece, which Cassander and Ptolemy had everywhere reduced to slavery. No nobler or juster war was undertaken by any of the kings; the wealth they had gained while humbling, with Greek assistance, the barbarians being thus employed, for honor's sake and good repute, in helping the Greeks. When the resolution was taken to begin their attempt with Athens, one of his friends told Antigonus, if they captured Athens, they must keep it safe in their own hands, as by this gangway they might step out from their ships into Greece when they pleased. But Antigonus would not hear of it; he did not want a better or a steadier gangway than people's good-will; and from Athens, the beacon of the world, the news of their conduct would soon be handed on to all the world's inhabitants. So Demetrius, with a sum of five thousand talents, and a fleet of two hundred and fifty ships, set sail for Athens, where Demetrius the Phalerian was governing the city for Cassander, with a garrison lodged in the port of Munychia. By good fortune and skilful management he appeared before Piræus, on the twenty-sixth of Thargelion, before any thing had been heard of him. Indeed, when his ships were seen, they were taken for Ptolemy's, and preparations were commenced for receiving them; till at last, the generals discovering their mistake, hurried down, and all was alarm and confusion and attempts to push forward preparations to oppose the landing of this hostile force. For Demetrius, having found the entrances of the port undefended, stood in directly, and was by this time safely inside, before the eyes of everybody, and made signals from his ship, requesting a peaceable hearing. And on leave being given, he caused a herald with a loud voice to make proclamation that he was come thither by the command of his father, with no other design than what he prayed the gods to prosper with success, to give the Athenians their liberty, to expel the garrison, and to restore the ancient laws and constitution of the country.

The people, hearing this, at once threw down their shields, and, clapping their hands, with loud acclamations entreated Demetrius to land, calling him their deliverer and benefactor. And the Phalerian and his party, who saw that there was nothing for it but to receive the conqueror, whether he should perform his promises or not, sent, however, messengers to beg for his protection; to whom Demetrius gave a kind reception, and sent back with them Aristodemus of Miletus, one of his father's friends. The Phalerian, under the change of government, was more afraid of his fellow-citizens than of the enemy; but Demetrius took precautions for him, and, out of respect for his reputation and character, sent him with a safe conduct to Thebes, whither he desired to go. For himself, he declared he would not, in spite of all his curiosity, put his foot in the city, till he had completed its deliverance by driving out the garrison. So, blockading Munychia with a palisade and trench, he sailed off to attack Megara, where also there was one of Cassander's garrisons. But, hearing that Cratesipolis, the wife of Alexander son of Polysperchon, who was famous for her beauty was well disposed to see him, he left his troops near Megara, and set out with a few light-armed attendants for Patræ, where she was now staying. And, quitting these also, he pitched his tent apart from everybody, that the woman might pay her visit without being seen. This some of the enemy perceived, and suddenly attacked him; and, in his alarm, he was obliged to disguise himself in a shabby cloak, and run for it, narrowly escaping the shame of being made a prisoner, in reward for his foolish passion. And as it was, his tent and money were taken. Megara, however, surrendered, and would have been pillaged by the soldiers, but for the urgent intercession of the Athenians. The garrison was driven out, and the city restored to independence. While he was occupied in this, he remembered that Stilpo, the philosopher, famous for his choice of a life of tranquillity, was residing here. He, therefore, sent for him, and begged to know whether any thing belonging to him had been taken. "No," replied Stilpo, "I have not met with any one to take away knowledge." Pretty nearly all the servants in the city had been stolen away; and so, when Demetrius, renewing his courtesies to Stilpo, on taking leave of him said, "I leave your city, Stilpo, a city of freemen," "certainly," replied Stilpo, "there is not one serving man left among us all."

Returning from Megara, he sat down before the citadel of Munychia, which in a few days he took by assault, and caused the fortifications to be demolished; and thus having accomplished his design, upon the request and invitation of the Athenians he made his entrance into the upper city, where, causing the people to be summoned, he publicly announced to them that their ancient constitution was restored, and that they should receive from his father, Antigonus, a present of one hundred and fifty thousand measures of wheat, and such a supply of timber as would enable them to build a hundred galleys. In this manner did the Athenians recover their popular institutions, after the space of fifteen years from the time of the war of Lamia and the battle before Cranon, during which interval of time the government had been administered nominally as an oligarchy, but really by a single man, Demetrius the Phalerian being so powerful. But the excessive honors which the Athenians bestowed, for these noble and generous acts, upon Demetrius, created offence and disgust. The Athenians were the first who gave Antigonus and Demetrius the title of kings, which hitherto they had made it a point of piety to decline, as the one remaining royal honor still reserved for the lineal descendants of Philip and Alexander, in which none but they could venture to participate. Another name which they received from no people but the Athenians was that of the Tutelar Deities and Deliverers. And to enhance this flattery, by a common vote it was decreed to change the style of the city, and not to have the years named any longer from the annual archon; a priest of the two Tutelary Divinities, who was to be yearly chosen, was to have this honor, and all public acts and instruments were to bear their date by his name. They decreed, also, that the figures of Antigonus and Demetrius should be woven, with those of the gods, into the pattern of the great robe.[5] They consecrated the spot where Demetrius first alighted from his chariot, and built an altar there, with the name of the Altar of the Descent of Demetrius. They created two new tribes, calling them after the names of these princes, the Antigonid and the Demetriad; and to the Council, which consisted of five hundred persons, fifty being chosen out of every tribe, they added one hundred more to represent these new tribes. But the wildest proposal was one made by Stratocles, the great inventor of all these ingenious and exquisite compliments, enacting

[5] The *peplus,* the large, embroidered robe or shawl, the presentation of which to Minerva was the most striking part of the great Panathenaic festival. It was carried, like a sail or banner, set up on the mast in a sacred ship, and so taken in procession through the city, and finally was placed on the ancient statue of the goddess in the Acropolis.

that the members of any deputation that the ctiy should send to Demetrius or Antigonus should have the same title as those sent to Delphi or Olympia for the performance of the national sacrifices in behalf of the state, at the great Greek festivals.[6] This Stratocles was, in all respects, an audacious and abandoned character, and seemed to have made it his object to copy, by his buffoonery and impertinence, Cleon's old familiarity with the people. His mistress, Phylacion, one day bringing him a dish of brains and neckbones for his dinner, "Oh," said he, "I am to dine upon the things which we statesmen play at ball with." At another time, when the Athenians received their naval defeat near Amorgos, he hastened home before the news could reach the city, and, having a chaplet on his head, came riding through the Ceramicus, announcing that they had won a victory, and moved a vote for thanksgivings to the gods, and a distribution of meat among the people in their tribes. Presently after came those who brought home the wrecks from the battle; and when the people exclaimed at what he had done, he came boldly to face the outcry, and asked what harm there had been in giving them two days' pleasure.

Such was Stratocles. And, "adding flame to fire,"[7] as Aristophanes says, there was one who, to outdo Stratocles, proposed, that it should be decreed, that whensoever Demetrius should honor their city with his presence, they should treat him with the same show

---

[6] They should be called not *presbeutai*, deputies, envoys, or embassadors, but *theōroi*, religious delegates, a name given only to the representatives of a State at a religious ceremonial, sent to appear, not before men, but before a god.

[7] Aristophanes, Equites, 382.

of hospitable entertainment,[8] with which Ceres and Bacchus are received; and the citizen who exceeded the rest in the splendor and costliness of his reception should have a sum of money granted him from the public purse to make a sacred offering. Finally, they changed the name of the month of Munychion, and called it Demetrion; they gave the name of the Demetrian to the odd day between the end of the old and the beginning of the new month; and turned the feast of Bacchus, the Dionysia, into the Demetria, or feast of Demetrius. Most of these changes were marked by the divine displeasure. The sacred robe, in which, according to their decree, the figures of Demetrius and Antigonus had been woven with those of Jupiter and Minerva, was caught by a violent gust of wind, while the procession was conveying it through the Ceramicus, and was torn from the top to the bottom. A crop of hemlock, a plant which scarcely grew anywhere, even in the country thereabout, sprang up in abundance round the altars which they had erected to these new divinities. They had to omit the solemn procession at the feast of Bacchus, as upon the very day of its celebration there was such a severe and rigorous frost, coming quite out of its time, that not only the vines and fig-trees were killed, but almost all the wheat was destroyed in the blade. Accordingly, Philippides, an enemy to Stratocles, attacked him in a comedy, in the following verses:—

> He for whom frosts that nipped your vines were sent,
> And for whose sins the holy robe was rent,
> Who grants to men the gods' own honors, he,
> Not the poor stage, is now the people's enemy.

[8] *The show of hospitable entertainment with which Ceres and Bacchus are received,* when they were supposed to enter the city in procession in the times of their festivals.

Philippides[9] was a great favorite with king Lysimachus, from whom the Athenians received, for his sake, a variety of kindnesses. Lysimachus went so far as to think it a happy omen to meet or see Philippides at the outset of any enterprise or expedition. And, in general, he was well thought of for his own character, as a plain, uninterfering person, with none of the officious, self-important habits of a court. Once, when Lysimachus was solicitous to show him kindness, and asked what he had that he could make him a present of, "Any thing," replied Philippides, "but your state secrets." The stage-player, we thought, deserved a place in our narrative quite as well as the public speaker.

But that which exceeded all the former follies and flatteries was the proposal of Dromoclides of Sphettus; who, when there was a debate about sending to the Delphic Oracle to inquire the proper course for the consecration of certain bucklers, moved in the assembly that they should rather send to receive an oracle from Demetrius. I will transcribe the very words of the order, which was in these terms: "May it be happy and propitious. The people of Athens have decreed, that a fit person shall be chosen among the Athenian citizens, who shall be deputed to be sent to the Deliverer; and after he hath duly performed the sacrifices, shall inquire of the Deliverer, in what most religious and decent manner he will please to direct, at the earliest possible time, the consecration of the bucklers; and according to the answer the people shall

---

[9] *Philippides* was a comic writer of great distinction. He is one of the six whom the grammarians selected as the standards of the third, or, as it is called, the New, Attic Comedy. The list is as follows: Philemon, Menander, Diphilus, Philippides, Posidippus, Apollodorus.

act." With this befooling they completed the perversion of a mind which even before was not so strong or sound as it should have been.

During his present leisure in Athens, he took to wife Eurydice, a descendant of the ancient Miltiades, who had been married to Opheltas, the ruler of Cyrene, and after his death had come back to Athens. The Athenians took the marriage as a compliment and favor to the city. But Demetrius was very free in these matters, and was the husband of several wives at once; the highest place and honor among all being retained by Phila, who was Antipater's daughter, and had been the wife of Craterus, the one of all the successors of Alexander who left behind him the strongest feelings of attachment among the Macedonians. And for these reasons Antigonus had obliged him to marry her, notwithstanding the disparity of their years, Demetrius being quite a youth, and she much older; and when upon that account he made some difficulty in complying, Antigonus whispered in his ear the maxim from Euripides, broadly substituting a new word for the original, *serve*,—

> Natural or not,
> A man must *wed* where profit will be got.[10]

Any respect, however, which he showed either to Phila or to his other wives did not go so far as to prevent him from consorting with any number of mistresses, and bearing, in this respect, the worst character of all the princes of his time.

A summons now arrived from his father, ordering him to go and fight with Ptolemy in Cyprus, which he was obliged to obey, sorry as he was to abandon Greece. And in quitting this nobler and more glorious

---

[10] From the Phœnissæ, 898.

enterprise, he sent to Cleonides, Ptolemy's general, who was holding garrisons in Sicyon and Corinth, offering him money to let the cities be independent. But on his refusal, he set sail hastily, taking additional forces with him, and made for Cyprus; where, immediately upon his arrival, he fell upon Menelaus, the brother of Ptolemy, and gave him a defeat. But when Ptolemy himself came in person, with large forces both on land and sea, for some little time nothing took place beyond an interchange of menaces and lofty talk. Ptolemy bade Demetrius sail off before the whole armament came up, if he did not wish to be trampled under foot; and Demetrius offered to let him retire, on condition of his withdrawing his garrisons from Sicyon and Corinth. And not they alone, but all the other potentates and princes of the time, were in anxiety for the uncertain impending issue of the conflict; as it seemed evident, that the conquerer's prize would be, not Cyprus or Syria, but the absolute supremacy.

Ptolemy had brought a hundred and fifty galleys with him, and gave orders to Menelaus to sally, in the heat of the battle, out of the harbor of Salamis, and attack with sixty ships the rear of Demetrius. Demetrius, however, opposing to these sixty ten of his galleys, which were a sufficient number to block up the narrow entrance of the harbor, and drawing out his land forces along all the headlands running out into the sea, went into action with a hundred and eighty galleys, and, attacking with the utmost boldness and impetuosity, utterly routed Ptolemy, who fled with eight ships, the sole remnant of his fleet, seventy having been taken with all their men, and the rest destroyed in the battle; while the whole multitude of attendants, friends, and women, that had followed in the ships of burden, all the arms, treasure, and military engines fell, without exception, into the hands of

Demetrius, and were by him collected and brought into the camp. Among the prisoners was the celebrated Lamia, famed at one time for her skill on the flute, and afterwards renowned as a mistress. And although now upon the wane of her youthful beauty, and though Demetrius was much her junior, she exercised over him so great a charm, that all other women seemed to be amorous of Demetrius, but Demetrius amorous only of Lamia. After this signal victory, Demetrius came before Salamis; and Menelaus, unable to make any resistance, surrendered himself and all his fleet, twelve hundred horse, and twelve thousand foot, together with the place. But that which added more than all to the glory and splendor of the success was the humane and generous conduct of Demetrius to the vanquished. For, after he had given honorable funerals to the dead, he bestowed liberty upon the living; and that he might not forget the Athenians, he sent them, as a present, complete arms for twelve hundred men.

To carry this happy news, Aristodemus of Miletus, the most perfect flatterer belonging to the court, was despatched to Antigonus; and he, to enhance the welcome message, was resolved, it would appear, to make his most successful effort. When he crossed from Cyprus, he bade the galley which conveyed him come to anchor off the land; and, having ordered all the ship's crew to remain aboard, he took the boat, and was set ashore alone. Thus he proceeded to Antigonus, who, one may well imagine, was in suspense enough about the issue, and suffered all the anxieties natural to men engaged in so perilous a struggle. And when he heard that Aristodemus was coming alone, it put him into yet greater trouble; he could scarcely forbear from going out to meet him himself; he sent messenger on messenger, and friend after friend, to inquire what news. But Aristodemus, walking gravely and with a settled countenance, without making any answer, still proceeded quietly onward; until Antigonus, quite alarmed and no longer able to refrain, got up and met him at the gate, whither he came with a crowd of anxious followers now collected and running after him. As soon as he saw Antigonus within hearing, stretching out his hands, he accosted him with the loud exclamation, "Hail, king Antigonus! we have defeated Ptolemy by sea, and have taken Cyprus and sixteen thousand eight hundred prisoners." "Welcome, Aristodemus," replied Antigonus, "but, as you chose to torture us so long for your good news, you may wait awhile for the reward of it."

Upon this the people around gave Antigonus and Demetrius, for the first time, the title of kings. His friends at once set a diadem on the head of Antigonus; and he sent one presently to his son, with a letter addressed to him as King Demetrius. And when this news was told in Egypt, that they might not seem to be dejected with the late defeat, Ptolemy's followers also took occasion to bestow the style of king upon him; and the rest of the successors of Alexander were quick to follow the example. Lysimachus began to wear the diadem; and Seleucus, who had before received the name in all addresses from the barbarians, now also took it upon him in all business with the Greeks. Cassander still retained his usual superscription in his letters, but others, both in writing and speaking, gave him the royal title. Nor was this the mere accession of a name, or introduction of a new fashion. The men's own sentiments about themselves were disturbed, and their feelings elevated; a spirit of pomp and arrogance passed into their habits of life and conversation, as a tragic actor on the stage modifies, with a change of dress, his step, his voice, his motions in sitting down, his manner in addressing another. The punishments they inflicted were more violent after they had thus laid aside that modest style under which they formerly dissembled their power, and the influence of which had often made them gentler and less exacting to their subjects. A single flattering voice effected a revolution in the world.

Antigonus, extremely elevated with the success of his arms in Cyprus under the conduct of Demetrius, resolved to push on his good fortune, and to lead his forces in person against Ptolemy by land, whilst Demetrius should coast with a great fleet along the shore, to assist him by sea. The issue of the contest was intimated in a dream which Medius, a friend to Antigonus, had at this time in his sleep. He thought he saw Antigonus and his whole army running, as if it had been a race; that, in the first part of the course, he went off showing great strength and speed; gradually, however, his pace slackened; and at the end he saw him come lagging up, tired and almost breathless and quite spent. Antigonus himself met with many difficulties by land; and Demetrius, encountering a great storm at sea, was driven, with a loss of many of his ships, upon a dangerous coast without a harbor. So the expedition returned without effecting any thing. Antigonus, now nearly eighty years old, was no longer well able to go through the fatigues of a marching campaign, though rather on account of his great size and corpulence than from loss of strength; and for this reason he left things to his son, whose fortune and experience appeared sufficient for all undertakings, and whose luxury and expense and revelry gave him no concern. For though in peace he vented himself in his pleasures, and, when there was nothing to do, ran headlong into any excesses, in war he was as sober and abstemious as the most temperate character. The story is told, that once, after Lamia had gained open supremacy over him, the old man, when Demetrius coming home from abroad began to kiss him with unusual warmth, asked him if he took him for Lamia. At another time, Demetrius, after spending several days in a debauch, excused himself for his absence, by saying he had had a violent flux. "So I heard," replied Antigonus; "was it of Thasian wine, or Chian?" Once he was told his son was ill, and went to see him. At the door he met some young beauty. Going in, he sat down by the bed and took his pulse. "The fever," said Demetrius, "has just left me." "O yes," replied the father, "I met it going out at the door." Demetrius's great actions made Antigonus treat him thus easily. The Scythians in their drinking-bouts twang their bows to keep their courage awake amidst the dreams of indulgence; but he would resign his whole being, now, to pleasure, and now to action; and though he never let thoughts of the one intrude upon the pursuit of the other, yet, when the time came for preparing for war, he showed as much capacity as any man.

And indeed his ability displayed itself even more in preparing for, than in conducting a war. He thought he could never be too well supplied for every possible occasion, and took a pleasure, not to be satiated, in great improvements in ship-building and machines. He did not waste his natural genius and power of mechanical research on toys and idle fancies, turning, painting, and playing on the flute, like some kings, Aeropus, for example, king of Macedon, who spent his days in making small lamps and tables; or Attalus Philometor, whose amusement was to cultivate poisons, henbane and hellebore, and even hemlock, aconite, and dorycnium, which he used to sow himself in the royal gardens, and made it his business to gather the fruits and collect the juices in their season. The

Parthian kings took a pride in whetting and sharpening with their own hands the points of their arrows and javelins. But when Demetrius played the workman, it was like a king, and there was magnificence in his handicraft. The articles he produced bore marks upon the the face of them not of ingenuity only, but of a great mind and a lofty purpose. They were such as a king might not only design and pay for, but use his own hands to make; and while friends might be terrified with their greatness, enemies could be charmed with their beauty; a phrase which is not so pretty to the ear as it is true to the fact. The very people against whom they were to be employed could not forbear running to gaze with admiration upon his galleys of five and six ranges of oars, as they passed along their coasts; and the inhabitants of besieged cities came on their walls to see the spectacle of his famous *City-takers*. Even Lysimachus, of all kings of his time the greatest enemy of Demetrius, coming to raise the siege of Soli in Cilicia, sent first to desire permission to see his galleys and engines, and, having had his curiosity gratified by a view of them, expressed his admiration and quitted the place. The Rhodians, also, whom he long besieged, begged him, when they concluded a peace, to let them have some of his engines, which they might preserve as a memorial at once of his power and of their own brave resistance.

The quarrel between him and the Rhodians was on account of their being allies to Ptolemy, and in the siege the greatest of all the engines was planted against their walls. The base of it was exactly square, each side containing twenty-four cubits; it rose to a height of thirty-three cubits, growing narrower from the base to the top. Within were several apartments or chambers, which were to be filled with armed men, and in every story the front towards the enemy had windows for discharging missiles of all sorts, the whole being filled with soldiers for every description of fighting. And what was most wonderful was that, notwithstanding its size, when it was moved it never tottered or inclined to one side, but went forward on its base in perfect equilibrium, with a loud noise and great impetus, astounding the minds, and yet at the same time charming the eyes of all the beholders.

Whilst Demetrius was at this same siege, there were brought to him two iron cuirasses from Cyprus, weighing each of them no more than forty pounds, and Zoilus, who had forged them, to show the excellence of their temper, desired that one of them might be tried with a catapult missile, shot out of one of the engines at no greater distance than six and twenty paces; and, upon the experiment, it was found, that though the dart exactly hit the cuirass, yet it made no greater impression than such a slight scratch as might be made with the point of a style or graver. Demetrius took this for his own wearing, and gave the other to Alcimus the Epirot, the best soldier and strongest man of all his captains, the only one who used to wear armor to the weight of two talents, one talent being the weight which others thought sufficient. He fell during this siege in a battle near the theatre.

The Rhodians made a brave defence, insomuch that Demetrius saw he was making but little progress, and only persisted out of obstinacy and passion; and the rather because the Rhodians, having captured a ship in which some clothes and furniture, with letters from herself, were coming to him from Phila his wife, had sent on every thing to Ptolemy, and had not copied the honorable example of the Athenians, who, having surprised an express sent from king Philip, their enemy, opened all the letters he was charged with, excepting only those directed to queen Olympias, which they returned with the seal unbroken. Yet, although greatly provoked, Demetrius, into whose power it shortly after came to repay the affront, would not suffer himself to retaliate. Protogenes the Caunian had been making them a painting of the story of Ialysus,[11] which was all but completed, when it was taken by Demetrius in one of the suburbs. The Rhodians sent a herald begging him to be pleased to spare the work and not let it be destroyed; Demetrius's answer to which was that he would rather burn the pictures of his father than a piece of art which had cost so much labor. It is said to have taken Protogenes seven years to paint, and they tell us that Apelles, when he first saw it, was struck dumb with wonder, and called it, on recovering his speech, "a great labor and a wonderful success," adding, however, that it had not the graces which carried his own paintings as it were up to the heavens."[12] This picture, which

[11] This is the famous picture of Ialysus and his dog, spoken of by Cicero and Pliny, in which the foam on the dog's mouth was made by a happy throw of the sponge, while the painter in vexation was rubbing off his previous unsuccessful attempts.

"Lindus, Ialysus, and white Camirus" were already in Homer's day "the three departments of the inhabiters of Rhodes." Lindus, Ialysus and Camirus, grandchildren of the Sun, were the founders of the three towns. But the legends told of them, one of which was represented in the picture, have not come down to us.

The picture of *Ialysus* and his dog was still at Rhodes in Strabo's time, but was taken to Rome and placed, where Pliny saw it, and, no doubt, Plutarch also, in the Temple of Peace, built, after the end of the new civil wars, by Vespasian; and perished when the Temple was burnt in the reign of Commodus.

[12] The words, as reported by Ælian, were "a great labor and a great artist. But there is more execution than grace; add but that, and the work would reach the heavens." Apelles was the senior and had been the early patron of Protogenes.

came with the rest in the general mass to Rome, there perished by fire.

While the Rhodians were thus defending their city to the uttermost, Demetrius, who was not sorry for an excuse to retire, found one in the arrival of ambassadors from Athens, by whose mediation terms were made that the Rhodians should bind themselves to aid Antigonus and Demetrius against all enemies, Ptolemy excepted.

The Athenians entreated his help against Cassander, who was besieging the city. So he went thither with a fleet of three hundred and thirty ships, and many soldiers; and not only drove Cassander out of Attica, but pursued him as far as Thermopylæ, routed him, and became master of Heraclea, which came over to him voluntarily, and of a body of six thousand Macedonians, which also joined him. Returning hence, he gave their liberty to all the Greeks on this side Thermopylæ, and made alliance with the Bœotians, took Cenchreæ, and reducing the fortresses of Phyle and Panactum, in which were garrisons of Cassander, restored them to the Athenians. They, in requital, though they had before been so profuse in bestowing honors upon him, that one would have thought they had exhausted all the capacities of invention, showed they had still refinements of adulation to devise for him. They gave him, as his lodging, the back temple[13] in the Parthenon, and here he lived,

[13] The back temple, or *opisthodomos,* was the portion entered from the east end. There were here two chambers, a sort of vestibule, the *opisthodomos* proper, and an inner chamber immediately at the back of the statue in the great western hall or *hecatompedon.* In this, probably, Demetrius was lodged; and this, it is supposed, was the original maiden-chamber, or *Parthenon,* the goddess's private apartment. When this name was applied to the whole temple, the term *opisthodomos* would be extended to include the inner as well as the outer chamber.

under the immediate roof, as they meant it to imply, of his hostess, Minerva; no reputable or well-conducted guest to be quartered upon a maiden goddess. When his brother Philip was once put into a house where three young women were living, Antigonus, saying nothing to him, sent for his quartermaster, and told him, in the young man's presence, to find some less crowded lodgings for him.

Demetrius, however, who should, to say the least, have paid the goddess the respect due to an elder sister, for that was the purport of the city's compliment, filled the temple with such pollutions that the place seemed least profaned when his license confined itself to common women like Chrysis, Lamia, Demo, and Anticyra.

The fair name of the city forbids any further plain particulars; let us only record the severe virtue of the young Damocles, surnamed, and by that surname pointed out to Demetrius, the beautiful; who, to escape importunities, avoided every place of resort, and when at last followed into a private bathing room by Demetrius, seeing none at hand to help or deliver, seized the lid from the cauldron, and, plunging into the boiling water, sought a death untimely and unmerited, but worthy of the country and of the beauty that occasioned it. Not so Cleænetus, the son of Cleomedon, who, to obtain from Demetrius a letter of intercession to the people in behalf of his father, lately condemned in a fine of fifty talents, disgraced himself, and got the city into trouble. In deference to the letter, they remitted the fine, yet they made an edict prohibiting any citizen for the future to bring letters from Demetrius. But being informed that Demetrius resented this as a great indignity, they not only rescinded in alarm the former order, but put some of the proposers and advisers of it to death and banished others, and furthermore enacted and decreed, that whatsoever king Demetrius should in time to come ordain, should be accounted right towards the gods and just towards men; and when one of the better class of citizens said Stratocles must be mad to use such words, Demochares [14] of Leuconoe observed, he would be a fool not to be mad. For Stratocles was well rewarded for his flatteries; and the saying was remembered against Demochares, who was soon after sent into banishment. So fared the Athenians, after being relieved of the foreign garrison, and recovering what was called their liberty.

After this Demetrius marched with his forces into Peloponnesus, where he met with none to oppose him, his enemies flying before him, and allowing the cities to join him. He received into friendship all Acte,[15] as it was called, and all Arcadia except Mantinea. He bought the liberty of Argos, Corinth, and Sicyon, by paying a hundred talents to their garrisons to evacuate them. At Argos, during the feast of Juno, which happened at the time, he presided at the games, and, joining in the festivities with the multitude of the Greeks assembled there, he celebrated his marriage with Deidamia, daughter of Æacides, king of the Molossians, and sister of Pyrrhus. At Sicyon he told the people they had put the city just outside of the city, and, persuading them to remove to where they now live, gave their town not only a new site but a new name, Deme-

[14] Demochares of Leuconoe, a different man from Demochares of Soli, mentioned a little further on, is the sister's son of Demosthenes, and was himself eminent as a public speaker and political leader in Athens. Plutarch has given some account of him in his Lives of the Ten Orators, and has preserved a decree passed by the people to do him honor.

[15] The sea-coast of Argolis, opposite Ægina, in which lay the towns of Epidaurus and Trœzen.

trias, after himself. A general assembly met on the Isthmus, where he was proclaimed, by a great concourse of people, the Commander of Greece, like Philip and Alexander of old; whose superior he, in the present height of his prosperity and power, was willing enough to consider himself; and, certainly, in one respect he outdid Alexander, who never refused their title and their authority as such from his; whereof king of kings, though many kings received both their title and their authority as such from him; whereas Demetrius used to ridicule those who gave the name of king to any except himself and his father; and in his entertainments was well pleased when his followers, after drinking to him and his father as kings, went on to drink the healths of Seleucus,[16] with the title of Master of the Elephants; of Ptolemy, by the name of High Admiral; of Lysimachus, with the addition of Treasurer; and of Agathocles, with the style of Governor of the Island of Sicily. The other kings merely laughed when they were told of this vanity; Lysimachus alone expressed some indignation at being con-

[16] The description of the mockeries passed upon the other kings, *Seleucus, Master of the Elephants*, etc., appears to be taken from Phylarchus, the writer whom Plutarch follows in the life of Cleomenes. Athenæus (*VI.*, p. 261) quotes it as from the tenth book of Phylarchus's histories. *Lysimachus said he had never before seen a courtezan act a queen's part;* the women's parts on the Greek stage were performed by men. This again is quoted by Athenæus (*XIV.*, p. 614), from the sixth book of Phylarchus. Demetrius, sneering at the short and mean names of Lysimachus's courtiers and captains, said his court was like a comedy stage, there was not a single personage with three syllables to his name—contrasting Bithys and Paris, Lysimachus's friends, with his own Peucestes and Menelaus and Oxythemis, sounds worthy of the tragic stage. Lysimachus retorts, that he had never seen a harlot on the tragic stage, and Demetrius rejoins as in the text.

DEMETRIUS

sidered a eunuch; such being usually then selected for the office of treasurer. And, in general, there was a more bitter enmity between him and Lysimachus than with any of the others. Once, as a scoff at his passion for Lamia, Lysimachus said he had never before seen a courtezan act a queen's part; to which Demetrius rejoined that his mistress was quite as honest as Lysimachus's own Penelope.

But to proceed. Demetrius being about to return to Athens, signified by letter to the city that he desired immediate admission to the rites of initiation into the Mysteries, and wished to go through all the stages of the ceremony, from first to last, without delay. This was absolutely contrary to the rules, and a thing which had never been allowed before; for the lesser mysteries were celebrated in the month of Anthesterion, and the great solemnity in Boedromion, and none of the novices were finally admitted till they had completed a year after this latter. Yet all this notwithstanding, when in the public assembly these letters of Demetrius were produced and read, there was not one single person who had the courage to oppose them, except Pythodorus, the torch-bearer. But it signified nothing, for Stratocles at once proposed that the month of Munychion, then current, should by edict be reputed to be the month of Anthesterion; which being voted and done, and Demetrius thereby admitted to the lesser ceremonies, by another vote they turned the same month of Munychion into the other month of Boedromion; the celebration of the greater mysteries ensued, and Demetrius was fully admitted.[17]

---

[17] Literally, became an *Epoptes*, an initiate, adept, or communicant. The Lesser Mysteries, which were celebrated in Athens, and called (as Plutarch in the original calls them here) the Mysteries at Agra, or Agræ, a spot on the Ilissus, gave the rank

These proceedings gave the comedian, Philippides, a new occasion to exercise his wit upon Stratocles,

> ————whose flattering fear
> Into one month hath crowded all the year.

And on the vote that Demetrius should lodge in the Parthenon,

> Who turns the temple to a common inn,
> And makes the Virgin's house a house of sin.

Of all the disreputable and flagitious acts of which he was guilty in this visit, one that particularly hurt the feelings of the Athenians was that, having given command that they should forthwith raise for his service two hundred and fifty talents, and they to comply with his demands being forced to levy it upon the people with the utmost rigor and severity, when they presented him with the money, which they had with such difficulty raised, as if it were a trifling sum, he ordered it to be given to Lamia and the rest of his women to buy soap. The loss, which was bad enough, was less galling than the shame, and the words more intolerable than the act which they accompanied. Though, indeed, the story is variously reported; and some say it was the Thessalians, and not the Athenians, who were thus treated. Lamia, however, exacted contributions herself to pay for an entertainment she gave to the king, and her banquet was so renowned for its sumptuosity, that a description of it was drawn up by the Samian writer, Lynceus. Upon this occasion, one of the comic writers gave Lamia the

of *Mystes*, or Novice. The Great Mysteries followed in six months' time; and a complete year having elapsed after these, the Novices, at the next celebration of them, were conducted to Eleusis, and admitted to the inner sanctuary.

name of the real *Helepolis;* and Demochares of Soli called Demetrius *Mythus,* because the fable always has its Lamia, and so had he.[18]

And, in truth, his passion for this woman and the prosperity in which she lived were such as to draw upon him not only the envy and jealousy of all his wives, but the animosity even of his friends. For example, on Lysimachus's showing to some ambassadors from Demetrius the scars of the wounds which he had received upon his thighs and arms by the paws of the lion with which Alexander had shut him up, after hearing his account of the combat, they smiled and answered, that their king, also, was not without his scars, but could show upon his neck the marks of a Lamia, a no less dangerous beast. It was also matter of wonder that, though he had objected so much to Phila on account of her age, he was yet such a slave to Lamia, who was so long past her prime. One evening at supper, when she played the flute, Demetrius asked Demo, whom the men called Madness, what she thought of her. Demo answered she thought her an old woman. And when a quantity of sweetmeats were brought in, and the king said again, "See what presents I get from Lamia!" "My old mother," answered Demo, "will send you more, if you will make her your mistress." Another story is told of a criticism passed by Lamia on the famous judgment of Bocchoris. A young Egyptian had long made suit to Thonis, the

---

[18] *Helepolis,* the city-taker, is the name of the great engine. She alone was an engine sufficient to destroy a city. The Lamia is the hag of Greek fable (or *mythus*); she murders little children, and can take out her eyes and keep them by her in a pot. Plutarch in his essay on Inquisitiveness says, that we are too often like the Lamia in the fable,—we sit at home without our eyes, but as soon as we go abroad we take them out of the pot and put them on again, to spy our our neighbor's misdoings.

courtezan, offering a sum of gold for her favor. But before it came to pass, he dreamed one night that he had obtained it, and, satisfied with the shadow, felt no more desire for the substance. Thonis upon this brought an action for the sum. Bocchoris, the judge, on hearing the case, ordered the defendant to bring into court the full amount in a vessel, which he was to move to and fro in his hand, and the shadow of it was to be adjudged to Thonis. The fairness of this sentence Lamia contested, saying the young man's desire might have been satisfied with the dream, but Thonis's desire for the money could not be relieved by the shadow. Thus much for Lamia.

And now the story passes from the comic to the tragic stage in pursuit of the acts and fortunes of its subject. A general league of the kings, who were now gathering and combining their forces to attack Antigonus, recalled Demetrius from Greece. He was encouraged by finding his father full of a spirit and resolution for the combat that belied his years. Yet it would seem to be true, that if Antigonus could only have borne to make some trifling concessions, and if he had shown any moderation in his passion for empire, he might have maintained for himself till his death, and left to his son behind him, the first place among the kings. But he was of a violent and haughty spirit; and the insulting words as well as actions in which he allowed himself could not be borne by young and powerful princes, and provoked them into combining against him. Though now when he was told of the confederacy, he could not forbear from saying that this flock of birds would soon be scattered by one stone and a single shout. He took the field at the head of more than seventy thousand foot, and of ten thousand horse, and seventy-five elephants. His enemies had sixty-four thousand foot, five hundred more horse than he, elephants to the number of four hundred, and a hundred and twenty chariots. On their near approach to each other, an alteration began to be observable, not in the purposes, but in the presentiments of Antigonus. For whereas in all former campaigns he had ever shown himself lofty and confident, loud in voice and scornful in speech, often by some joke or mockery on the eve of battle expressing his contempt and displaying his composure, he was now remarked to be thoughtful, silent, and retired. He presented Demetrius to the army, and declared him his successor; and what every one thought stranger than all was that he now conferred alone in his tent with Demetrius; whereas in former time he had never entered into any secret consultations even with him; but had always followed his own advice, made his resolutions, and then giving out his commands. Once when Demetrius was a boy and asked him how soon the army would move, he is said to have answered him sharply, "Are you afraid lest you, of all the army, should not hear the trumpet?"

There were now, however, inauspicious signs, which affected his spirits. Demetrius, in a dream, had seen Alexander, completely armed, appear and demand of him what word they intended to give in the time of the battle; and Demetrius answering that he intended the word should be "Jupiter and Victory." "Then," said Alexander, "I will go to your adversaries and find my welcome with them." And on the morning of the combat, as the armies were drawing up, Antigonus, going out of the door of his tent, by some accident or other, stumbled and fell flat upon the ground, hurting himself a good deal. And on recovering his feet, lifting up his hands to heaven, he prayed the gods to grant him "either victory, or death without knowledge of defeat." When the armies engaged,

Demetrius, who commanded the greatest and best part of the cavalry, made a charge on Antiochus, the son of Seleucus, and, gloriously routing the enemy, followed the pursuit, in the pride and exultation of success, so eagerly, and so unwisely far, that it fatally lost him the day, for when, perceiving his error, he would have come in to the assistance of his own infantry, he was not able, the enemy with their elephants having cut off his retreat. And on the other hand, Seleucus, observing the main battle of Antigonus left naked of their horse, did not charge, but made a show of charging; and keeping them in alarm and wheeling about and still threatening an attack, he gave opportunity for those who wished it to separate and come over to him; which a large body of them did, the rest taking to flight. But the old king Antigonus still kept his post, and when a strong body of the enemies drew up to charge him, and one of those about him cried out to him, "Sir, they are coming upon you," he only replied, "What else should they do? but Demetrius will come to my rescue." And in this hope he persisted to the last, looking out on every side for his son's approach, until he was borne down by a whole multitude of darts, and fell. His other followers and friends fled, and Thorax of Larissa remained alone by the body.[19]

The battle having been thus decided, the kings who had gained the victory, carving up the whole vast empire that had belonged to Demetrius and Antigonus, like a carcass, into so many portions, added these new gains to their former possessions. As for Demetrius,

---

[19] This is the battle of Ipsus, referred to presently by Plutarch under that name, which in the account itself does not occur. He speaks, also, elsewhere of "the battle of Ipsus, at which all the kings of the world were gathered together." It determined the fortunes of Asia down to the time of the Roman conquests.

with five thousand foot and four thousand horse, he fled at his utmost speed to Ephesus, where it was the common opinion he would seize the treasures of the temple to relieve his wants; but he, on the contrary, fearing such an attempt on the part of his soldiers, hastened away, and sailed for Greece, his chief remaining hopes being placed in the fidelity of the Athenians, with whom he had left part of his navy and of his treasure and his wife Deidamia. And in their attachment he had not the least doubt but he should in this his extremity find a safe resource. Accordingly when, upon reaching the Cyclades, he was met by ambassadors from Athens, requesting him not to proceed to the city, as the people had passed a vote to admit no king whatever within their walls, and had conveyed Deidamia with honorable attendance to Megara, his anger and surprise overpowered him, and the constancy quite failed him which he had hitherto shown in a wonderful degree under his reverses, nothing humiliating or mean-spirited having as yet been seen in him under all his misfortunes. But to be thus disappointed in the Athenians, and to find the friendship he had trusted prove, upon trial, thus empty and unreal, was a great pang to him. And, in truth, an excessive display of outward honor would seem to be the most uncertain attestation of the real affection of a people for any king or potentate. Such shows lose their whole credit as tokens of affection (which has its virtue in the feelings and moral choice), when we reflect that they may equally proceed from fear. The same decrees are voted upon the latter motive as upon the former. And therefore judicious men do not look so much to statues, paintings, or divine honors that are paid them, as to their own actions and conduct, judging hence whether they shall trust these as a genuine, or discredit them as a forced homage. As in fact nothing is less unusual than for a people, even while offering compliments, to be disgusted with those who accept them greedily, or arrogantly, or without respect to the freewill of the givers.

Demetrius, shamefully used as he thought himself, was in no condition to revenge the affront. He returned a message of gentle expostulation, saying, however, that he expected to have his galleys sent to him, among which was that of thirteen banks of oars. And this being accorded him, he sailed to the Isthmus, and, finding his affairs in very ill condition, his garrisons expelled, and a general secession going on to the enemy, he left Pyrrhus to attend to Greece, and took his course to the Chersonesus, where he ravaged the territories of Lysimachus, and, by the booty which he took, maintained and kept together his troops, which were now once more beginning to recover and to show some considerable front. Nor did any of the other princes care to meddle with him on that side; for Lysimachus had quite as little claim to be loved, and was more to be feared for his power. But, not long after, Seleucus sent to treat with Demetrius for a marriage betwixt himself and Stratonice, daughter of Demetrius by Phila. Seleucus, indeed, had already, by Apama the Persian, a son named Antiochus, but he was possessed of territories that might well satisfy more than one successor, and he was the rather induced to this alliance with Demetrius, because Lysimachus had just married himself to one daughter of king Ptolemy, and his son Agathocles to another. Demetrius, who looked upon the offer as an unexpected piece of good fortune, presently embarked with his daughter, and with his whole fleet sailed for Syria. Having during his voyage to touch several times on the coast, among other places he landed in part of Cilicia, which, by the apportionment of the kings after the defeat of Antigonus, was allotted to Plistarchus, the brother of Cassander. Plistarchus, who took this descent of Demetrius upon his coasts as an infraction of his rights, and was not sorry to have something to complain of, hastened away to expostulate in person with Seleucus for entering separately into relations with Demetrius, the common enemy, without consulting the other kings.

Demetrius, receiving information of this seized the opportunity, and fell upon the city of Quinda, which he surprised, and took in it twelve hundred talents, still remaining of the treasure. With this prize, he hastened back to his galleys, embarked, and set sail. At Rhosus, where his wife Phila was now with him, he was met by Seleucus, and their communications with each other at once were put on a frank, unsuspecting, and kingly footing. First, Seleucus gave a banquet to Demetrius in his tent in the camp; then Demetrius received him in the ship of thirteen banks of oars. Meetings for amusements, conferences, and long visits for general intercourse succeeded, all without attendants or arms; until at length Seleucus took his leave, and in great state conducted Stratonice to Antioch. Demetrius meantime possessed himself of Cilicia, and sent Phila to her brother Cassander, to answer the complaints of Plistarchus. And here his wife Deidamia came by sea out of Greece to meet him, but not long after contracted an illness, of which she died. After her death, Demetrius, by the mediation of Seleucus, became reconciled to Ptolemy, and an agreement was made that he should marry his daughter Ptolemais. Thus far all was handsomely done on the part of Seleucus. But, shortly after, desiring to have the province of Cilicia from Demetrius for a sum of money, and being refused it, he then angrily demanded of him the cities of Tyre and Sidon, which seemed a mere piece of arbitrary dealing, and, indeed, an outrageous thing, that he, who was possessed of all the vast provinces between India and the Syrian sea, should think himself so poorly off as for the sake of two cities, which he coveted, to disturb the peace of his near connection, already a sufferer under a severe reverse of fortune. However, he did but justify the saying of Plato,[20] that the only certain way to be truly rich is not to have more property, but fewer desires. For whoever is always grasping at more avows that he is still in want, and must be poor in the midst of affluence.

But Demetrius, whose courage did not sink, resolutely sent him answer, that, though he were to lose ten thousand battles like that of Ipsus, he would pay no price for the good-will of such a son-in-law as Seleucus. He reinforced these cities with sufficient garrisons to enable them to make a defense against Seleucus; and, receiving information that Lachares, taking the opportunity of their civil dissensions, had set up himself as an usurper over the Athenians, he imagined that if he made a sudden attempt upon the city, he might now without difficulty get possession of it. He crossed the sea in safety, with a large fleet; but, passing along the coast of Attica, was met by a violent

[20] *The saying of Plato, that the way to be rich is not to have more property, but fewer desires,* is repeated in a variety of forms by both Greek and Roman moralists. Horace proposes (*Odes, III*, 16, 38) to enlarge his revenues by contracting his desires,—"Contracta melius parva cupidine Vectigalia porrigam." Cicero more than once recommends the affluence of frugality,—"Non intelligunt homines quam *magnum vectigal parsimonia.*" (*Paradox. VI.* 3.) Epicurus himself is recorded to have bidden his followers increase their incomes by curtailing their wishes, and add to their means by cutting down their wants. But I do not find where it occurs in Plato's extant writings.

storm, and lost the greater number of his ships, and a very considerable body of men on board of them As for him, he escaped, and began to make war in a petty manner with the Athenians, but finding himself unable to effect his design, he sent back orders for raising another fleet, and, with the troops which he had, marched into Peloponnesus, and laid siege to the city of Messena. In attacking which place, he was in danger of death; for a missile from an engine struck him in the face, and passed through the cheek into his mouth. He recovered, however, and, as soon as he was in a condition to take the field, won over divers cities which had revolted from him, and made an incursion into Attica, where he took Eleusis and Rhamnus, and wasted the country thereabout. And that he might straighten the Athenians by cutting off all manner of provision, a vessel laden with corn bound thither falling into his hands, he ordered the master and the super-cargo to be immediately hanged, thereby to strike a terror into others, that so they might not venture to supply the city with provisions. By which means they were reduced to such extremities, that a bushel of salt sold for forty drachmas, and a peck of wheat for three hundred. Ptolemy had sent to their relief a hundred and fifty galleys, which came so near as to be seen off Ægina; but this brief hope was soon extinguished by the arrival of three hundred ships, which came to reinforce Demetrius from Cyprus, Peloponnesus, and other places; upon which Ptolemy's fleet took to flight, and Lachares, the tyrant, ran away, leaving the city to its fate.

And now the Athenians, who before had made it capital for any person to propose a treaty or accommodation with Demetrius, immediately opened the nearest gates to send ambassadors to him, not so much out of hopes of obtaining any honorable conditions from his clemency as out of necessity, to avoid death by famine. For among many frightful instances of the distress they were reduced to, it is said that a father and son were sitting in a room together, having abandoned every hope, when a dead mouse fell from the ceiling; and for this prize they leaped up and came to blows. In this famine, it is also related, the philosopher Epicurus saved his own life, and the lives of his scholars, by a small quantity of beans, which he distributed to them daily by number.

In this condition was the city when Demetrius made his entrance and issued a proclamation that all the inhabitants should assemble in the theatre; which being done, he drew up his soldiers at the back of the stage, occupied the stage itself with his guards, and, presently coming in himself by the actor's passages, when the people's consternation had risen to its height, with his first words he put an end to it. Without any harshness of tone or bitterness of words, he reprehended them in a gentle and friendly way, and declared himself reconciled, adding a present of a hundred thousand bushels of wheat, and appointing as magistrates persons acceptable to the people. So Dromoclides the orator, seeing the people at a loss how to express their gratitude by any words or acclamations, and ready for any thing that would outdo the verbal encomiums of the public speakers, came forward, and moved a decree for delivering Piræus and Munychia into the hands of king Demetrius. This was passed accordingly, and Demetrius, of his own motion, added a third garrison, which he placed in the Museum, as a precaution against any new restiveness on the part of the people, which might give him the trouble of quitting his other enterprises.

He had not long been master of Athens before he had formed designs against Lacedæmon; of which

Archidamus, the king, being advertised, came out and met him, but he was overthrown in a battle near Mantinea; after which Demetrius entered Laconia, and, in a second battle near Sparta itself, defeated him again with the loss of two hundred Lacedæmonians slain, and five hundred taken prisoners. And now it was almost impossible for the city, which hitherto had never been captured, to escape his arms. But certainly there never was any king upon whom fortune made such short turns, nor any other life or story so filled with her swift and surprising changes, over and over again, from small things to great, from splendor back to humiliation, and from utter weakness once more to power and might. They say in his sadder vicissitudes he used sometimes to apostrophize fortune in the words of Æschylus—

> Thou liftest up, to cast us down again.[21]

And so at this moment, when all things seemed to conspire together to give him his heart's desire of dominion and power, news arrived that Lysimachus had taken all his cities in Asia, that Ptolemy had reduced all Cyprus with the exception of Salamis, and that in Salamis his mother and children were shut up and close besieged; and yet, like the woman in Archilochus,

> Water in one deceitful hand she shows,
> While burning fire within her other glows.

The same fortune that drew him off with these disastrous tidings from Sparta, in a moment after opened upon him a new and wonderful prospect, of the following kind. Cassander, king of Macedon, dying, and his eldest son, Philip, who succeeded him, not long sur-

[21] The fragment from Æschylus, *Thou lifest up, to cast us down again*, from an unknown play quoted also once elsewhere by Plutarch, is No. 312 in Hermann's edition.

viving his father, the two younger brothers fell at variance concerning the succession. And Antipater having murdered his mother Thessalonica, Alexander, the younger brother, called in to his assistance Pyrrhus out of Epirus, and Demetrius out of the Peloponnese. Pyrrhus arrived first, and, taking in recompense for his succor a large slice of Macedonia, had made Alexander begin to be aware that he had brought upon himself a dangerous neighbor. And, that he might not run a yet worse hazard from Demetrius, whose power and reputation were so great, the young man hurried away to meet him at Dium, whither he, who on receiving his letter had set out on his march, was now come. And, offering his greetings and grateful acknowledgments, he at the same time informed him that his affairs no longer required the presence of his ally, and thereupon he invited him to supper. There were not wanting some feelings of suspicion on either side already; and when Demetrius was now on his way to the banquet, some one came and told him that in the midst of the drinking he would be killed. Demetrius showed little concern, but, making only a little less haste, he sent to the principal officers of his army, commanding them to draw out the soldiers, and make them stand to their arms, and ordered his retinue (more numerous a good deal than that of Alexander) to attend him into the very room of the entertainment, and not to stir from thence till they saw him rise from the table. Thus Alexander's servants, finding themselves overpowered, had not courage to attempt any thing. And, indeed, Demetrius gave them no opportunity, for he made a very short visit, and, pretending to Alexander that he was not at present in health for drinking wine, left early. And the next day he occupied himself in preparations for departing, telling Alexander he had received intelligence that obliged

him to leave, and begging him to excuse so sudden a
parting; he would hope to see him further when his
affairs allowed him leisure. Alexander was only too
glad, not only that he was going, but that he was doing
so of his own motion, without any offence, and proposed to accompany him into Thessaly. But when
they came to Larissa, new invitations passed between
them, new professions of good-will, covering new conspiracies; by which Alexander put himself into the
power of Demetrius. For as he did not like to use
precautions on his own part, for fear Demetrius should
take the hint to use them on his, the very thing he
meant to do was first done to him. He accepted an
invitation, and came to Demetrius's quarters; and
when Demetrius, while they were still supping, rose
from the table and went forth, the young man rose
also, and followed him to the door, where Demetrius,
as he passed through, only said to the guards, "Kill
him that follows me," and went on; and Alexander
was at once despatched by them, together with such
of his friends as endeavored to come to his rescue, one
of whom, before he died, said, "You have been one day
too quick for us."

The night following was one, as may be supposed,
of disorder and confusion. And with the morning, the
Macedonians, still in alarm, and fearful of the forces
of Demetrius, on finding no violence offered, but only
a message sent from Demetrius desiring an interview
and opportunity for explanation of his actions, at last
began to feel pretty confident again, and prepared to
receive him favorably. And when he came, there was
no need of much being said; their hatred of Antipater
for his murder of his mother, and the absence of any
one better to govern them, soon decided them to proclaim Demetrius king of Macedon. And into Macedonia they at once started and took him. And the

Macedonians at home, who had not forgotten or forgiven the wicked deeds committed by Cassander on the family of Alexander, were far from sorry at the change. Any kind recollections that still might subsist, of the plain and simple rule of the first Antipater, went also to the benefit of Demetrius, whose wife was Phila, his daughter, and his son by her, a boy already old enough to be serving in the army with his father, was the natural successor to the government.

To add to this unexpected good fortune, news arrived that Ptolemy had dismissed his mother and children, bestowing upon them presents and honors; and also that his daughter Stratonice, whom he had married to Seleucus, was remarried to Antiochus, the son of Seleucus, and proclaimed queen of Upper Asia.

For Antiochus, it appears, had fallen passionately in love with Stratonice, the young queen, who had already made Seleucus the father of a son. He struggled very hard with the beginnings of this passion, and at last, resolving with himself that his desires were wholly unlawful, his malady past all cure, and his powers of reason too feeble to act, he determined on death, and thought to bring his life slowly to extinction by neglecting his person and refusing nourishment, under the pretence of being ill. Erasistratus, the physician who attended him, quickly perceived that love was his distemper, but the difficulty was to discover the object. He therefore waited continually in his chamber, and when any of the beauties of the court made their visits to the sick prince, he observed the emotions and alterations in the countenance of Antiochus, and watched for the changes which he knew to be indicative of the inward passions and inclinations of the soul. He took notice that the presence of other women produced no effect upon him; but when Stratonice came, as she often did, alone, or in company with Seleucus, to see

DEMETRIUS

him, he observed in him all Sappho's famous symptoms,[22]—his voice faltered, his face flushed up, his eyes glanced stealthily, a sudden sweat broke out on his skin, the beatings of his heart were irregular and violent, and, unable to support the excess of his passion, he would sink into a state of faintness, prostration, and pallor.

Erasistratus, reasoning upon these symptoms, and, upon the probability of things, considering that the king's son would hardly, if the object of his passion had been any other, have persisted to death rather than reveal it, felt, however, the difficulty of making a discovery of this nature to Seleucus. But, trusting to the tenderness of Seleucus for the young man, he put on all the assurance he could, and at last, on some opportunity, spoke out, and told him the malady was love, a love impossible to gratify or relieve. The king was extremely surprised, and asked, "Why impossible to relieve?" "The fact is," replied Erasistratus, "he is in love with my wife." "How!" said Seleucus, "and will our friend Erasistratus refuse to bestow his wife upon my son and only successor, when there is no other way to save his life?" "You," replied Erasistratus, "who are his father, would not do so, if he were in love with Stratonice." "Ah, my friend," answered Seleucus, "would to heaven any means, human or divine, could but convert his present passion to that; it would be well for me to part not only with Stratonice, but with my empire, to save Antiochus." This he said with the greatest passion, shedding tears as he spoke; upon

---

[22] Blessed as the gods the man who sits beside you, hears you speak, and sees you smile. For me, at the first sight of you, my speech fails, my tongue breaks, thin flame runs through me, my eyes are blinded, my ears tingle, a cold sweat overflows me, all my body trembles, my color goes, my very death seems coming upon me."

which Erasistratus, taking him by the hand, replied, "In that case, you have no need of Erasistratus; for you, who are the husband, the father, and the king, are the proper physician for your own family." Seleucus, accordingly, summoning a general assembly of his people, declared to them, that he had resolved to make Antiochus king, and Stratonice queen, of all the provinces of Upper Asia, uniting them in marriage; telling them, that he thought he had sufficient power over the prince's will, that he should find in him no repugnance to obey his commands; and for Stratonice, he hoped all his friends would endeavor to make her sensible, if she should manifest any reluctance to such a marriage, that she ought to esteem those things just and honorable which had been determined upon by the king as necessary to the general good. In this manner, we are told, was brought about the marriage of Antiochus and Stratonice.

To return to the affairs of Demetrius. Having obtained the crown of Macedon, he presently became master of Thessaly also. And, holding the greatest part of Peloponnesus, and, on this side the Isthmus, the cities of Megara and Athens, he now turned his arms against the Bœotians. They at first made overtures for an accommodation; but Cleonymus of Sparta having ventured with some troops to their assistance, and having made his way into Thebes, and Pisis, the Thespian, who was their first man in power and reputation, animating them to make a brave resistance, they broke off the treaty. No sooner, however, had Demetrius begun to approach the walls with his engines, but Cleonymus in affright secretly withdrew; and the Bœotians, finding themselves abandoned, made their submission. Demetrius placed a garrison in charge of their towns, and, having raised a large sum of money from them, he placed Hieronymus, the historian, in the office of governor and military commander over them, and was thought on the whole to have shown great clemency, more particularly to Pisis, to whom he did no hurt, but spoke with him courteously and kindly, and made him chief magistrate of Thespiæ. Not long after, Lysimachus was taken prisoner by Dromichætes, and Demetrius went off instantly in the hopes of possessing himself of Thrace, thus left without a king. Upon this, the Bœotians revolted again, and news also came that Lysimachus had regained his liberty. So Demetrius, turning back quickly and in anger, found on coming up that his son Antigonus had already defeated the Bœotians in battle, and therefore proceeded to lay siege again to Thebes.

But, understanding that Pyrrhus had made an incursion into Thessaly, and that he was advanced as far as Thermopylæ, leaving Antigonus to continue the siege, he marched with the rest of his army to oppose this enemy. Pyrrhus, however, made a quick retreat. So, leaving ten thousand foot and a thousand horse for the protection of Thessaly, he returned to the siege of Thebes, and there brought up his famous City-taker to the attack, which, however, was so laboriously and so slowly moved on account of its bulk and heaviness, that in two months it did not advance two furlongs. In the mean time the citizens made a stout defence, and Demetrius, out of heat and contentiousness very often, more than upon any necessity, sent his soldiers into danger; until at last Antigonus, observing how many men were losing their lives, said to him, "Why, my father, do we go on letting the men be wasted in this way, without any need of it?" But Demetrius, in a great passion, interrupted him: "And you, good sir, why do you afflict yourself for the matter? will dead men come to you for rations?" But that the soldiers might see he valued his own life at no dearer rate than theirs, he exposed himself freely, and was wounded with a javelin through his neck, which put him into great hazard of his life. But, notwithstanding, he continued the siege, and in conclusion took the town again. And after his entrance, when the citizens were in fear and trembling, and expected all the severities which an incensed conqueror could inflict, he only put to death thirteen, and banished some few others, pardoning all the rest. Thus the city of Thebes, which had not yet been ten years restored, in that short space was twice besieged and taken.

Shortly after, the festival of the Pythian Apollo was to be celebrated, and the Ætolians having blocked up all the passages to Delphi, Demetrius held the games and celebrated the feast at Athens, alleging it was great reason those honors should be paid in that place, Apollo being the paternal god of the Athenian people, and the reputed first founder of their race.[23]

From thence Demetrius returned to Macedon, and as he not only was of a restless temper himself, but saw also that the Macedonians were ever the best subjects when employed in military expeditions, but turbulent and desirous of change in the idleness of peace, he led them against the Ætolians, and, having wasted their country, he left Pantauchus with a great part of his army to complete the conquest, and with the rest he marched in person to find out Pyrrhus, who in like manner was advancing to encounter him. But so it fell out, that by taking different ways the two armies did not meet; but whilst Demetrius entered Epirus, and laid all waste before him, Pyrrhus fell upon Pantauchus, and, in a battle in which the two commanders

---

[23] Apollo was worshipped at Athens under the name of *Patroös*, Apollo paternal or ancestral; and Ion, the father of the Ionian name and nation, was the son of Apollo and Creüsa, begotten in the cave of Apollo and Pan, in the rocks of the Acropolis.

"YES," SAID PYRRHUS, "ANOTHER SUCH VICTORY AND I SHALL BE UNDONE"

met in person and wounded each other, he gained the victory, and took five thousand prisoners, besides great numbers slain on the field. The worst thing, however, for Demetrius was that Pyrrhus had excited less animosity as an enemy than admiration as a brave man. His taking so large a part with his own hand in the battle had gained him the greatest name and glory among the Macedonians. Many among them began to say that this was the only king in whom there was any likeness to be seen of the great Alexander's courage; the other kings, and particularly Demetrius, did nothing but personate him, like actors on a stage, in his pomp and outward majesty. And Demetrius truly was a perfect play and pageant, with his robes and diadems, his gold-edged purple and his hats with double streamers, his very shoes being of the richest purple felt, embroidered over in gold. One robe in particular, a most superb piece of work, was long in the loom in preparation for him, in which was to be wrought the representation of the universe and the celestial bodies. This, left unfinished when his reverses overtook him, not any one of the kings of Macedon, his successors, though divers of them haughty enough, ever presumed to use.

But it was not this theatric pomp alone which disgusted the Macedonians, but his profuse and luxurious way of living; and, above all, the difficulty of speaking with him or of obtaining access to his presence. For either he would not be seen at all, or, if he did give audience, he was violent and overbearing. Thus he made the envoys of the Athenians, to whom yet he was more attentive than to all the other Grecians, wait two whole years before they could obtain a hearing. And when the Lacedæmonians sent a single person on an embassy to him, he held himself insulted, and asked angrily whether it was the fact that the Lacedæmonians had sent but one ambassador. "Yes," was the happy reply he received, "one ambassador to one king."

Once when in some apparent fit of a more popular and acceptable temper he was riding abroad, a number of people came up and presented their written petitions. He courteously received all these, and put them up in the skirt of his cloak, while the poor people were overjoyed, and followed him close. But when he came upon the bridge of the river Axius, shaking out his cloak, he threw all into the river. This excited very bitter resentment among the Macedonians, who felt themselves to be not governed, but insulted. They called to mind what some of them had seen, and others had heard related of King Philip's unambitious and open, accessible manners. One day when an old woman had assailed him several times in the road and importuned him to hear her, after he had told her he had no time, "If so," cried she, "you have no time to be a king." And this reprimand so stung the king that after thinking of it a while he went back into the house, and, setting all other matters apart, for several days together he did nothing else but receive, beginning with the old woman, the complaints of all that would come. And to do justice, truly enough, might well be called a king's first business. "Mars," as says Timotheus, "is the tyrant;" but Law, in Pindar's words, the king of all.[24] Homer does not say that kings re-

---

[24] For *Law, in Pindar's words,* the *King of all,* see Boeckh, Fragmenta Incerta, 151, a famous and much debated passage quoted at greater length in Plato's Gorgias, p. 484, and in the Laws, pp. 690, 890. In Pindar's sense it is Enacted Law, making all things right by its own naturally appointed might. For Minos, the *familiar friend* of Jupiter, compare the life of Theseus, Vol. I. p. 13. The passage in Homer is in the Odyssey (*XIX.* 178), *the land of Crete in the mid dark sea is beautiful and fat, with*

DEMETRIUS 151

ceived at the hands of Jove besieging engines or ships of war, but sentences of justice, to keep and observe; nor is it the most warlike, unjust, and murderous, but the most righteous of kings, that has from him the name of Jupiter's "familiar friend" and scholar. Demetrius's delight was the title most unlike the choices of the king of gods. The divine names were those of the Defender and Keeper, his was that of the Besieger of Cities.[25] The place of virtue was given by him to that which, had he not been as ignorant as he was powerful, he would have known to be vice, and honor by his act was associated with crime. While he lay dangerously ill at Pella, Pyrrhus pretty nearly overran all Macedon, and advanced as far as the city of Edessa. On recovering his health, he quickly drove him out, and came to terms with him, being desirous not to employ his time in a string of petty local conflicts with a neighbor, when all his thoughts were fixed upon another design. This was no less than to endeavor the recovery of the whole empire which his father had possessed; and his preparations were suitable to his hopes, and the greatness of the enterprise. He had arranged for the levying of ninety-eight thousand foot, and nearly twelve thousand horse; and he had a fleet of five hundred galleys on the stocks, some

---

water flowing around it, full of people in great hosts, containing ninety cities . . . . one of which is Gnossus, where Minos reigned nine years, the familiar friend of great Zeus,—and there is a reference also in both places to the comments of Socrates in Plato's Minos, where, on the argument of Homer's phrase, Minos is pronounced the best of kings, and the story of the Minotaur and the labyrinth discarded as an Attic stage fable.

[25] Polieus and Poliuchus those of Zeus; Poliorcētes that of Demetrius. Jupiter's "familiar friend" is Minos. The passage about sentences of justice, which kings receive from Jupiter, is from Achilles's oath by his staff. Iliad, 1, 238.

building at Athens, others at Corinth and Chalcis, and in the neighborhood of Pella. And he himself was passing evermore from one to another of these places, to give his directions and his assistance to the plans, while all that saw were amazed, not so much at the number, as at the magnitude of the works. Hitherto, there had never been seen a galley with fifteen or sixteen ranges of oars. At a later time, Ptolemy Philopator built one of forty rows, which was two hundred and eighty cubits in length, and the height of her to the top of her stern forty-eight cubits; she had four hundred sailors and four thousand rowers, and afforded room besides for very near three thousand soldiers to fight on her decks. But this, after all, was for show, and not for service, scarcely differing from a fixed edifice ashore, and was not to be moved without extreme toil and peril; whereas these galleys of Demetrius were meant quite as much for fighting as for looking at, were not the less serviceable for their magnificence, and were as wonderful for their speed and general performance as for their size.

These mighty preparations against Asia, the like of which had not been made since Alexander first invaded it, united Seleucus, Ptolemy, and Lysimachus in a confederacy for their defence. They also despatched ambassadors to Pyrrhus, to persuade him to make a diversion by attacking Macedonia; he need not think there was any validity in a treaty which Demetrius had concluded, not as an engagement to be at peace with him, but as a means for enabling himself to make war first upon the enemy of his choice. So when Pyrrhus accepted their proposals, Demetrius, still in the midst of his preparations, was encompassed with war on all sides. Ptolemy, with a mighty navy, invaded Greece; Lysimachus entered Macedonia upon the side of Thrace, and Pyrrhus, from the Epirot border, both of them spoiling and wasting the country. Demetrius, leaving his son to look after Greece, marched to the relief of Macedon, and first of all to oppose Lysimachus. On his way, he received the news that Pyrrhus had taken the city Berœa; and the report quickly getting out among the soldiers, all discipline at once was lost, and the camp was filled with lamentations and tears, anger and execrations on Demetrius; they would stay no longer, they would march off, as they said, to take care of their country, friends, and families; but in reality the intention was to revolt to Lysimachus. Demetrius, therefore, thought it his business to keep them as far away as he could from Lysimachus, who was their own countryman, and for Alexander's sake kindly looked upon by many; they would be ready to fight with Pyrrhus, a new-comer and a foreigner, whom they could hardly prefer to himself. But he found himself under a great mistake in these conjectures. For when he advanced and pitched his camp near, the old admiration for Pyrrhus's gallantry in arms revived again; and as they had been used from time immemorial to suppose that the best king was he that was the bravest soldier, so now they were also told of his generous usage of his prisoners, and, in short, they were eager to have any one in the place of Demetrius, and well pleased that the man should be Pyrrhus. At first, some straggling parties only deserted, but in a little time the whole army broke out into an universal mutiny, insomuch that at last some of them went up, and told him openly that if he consulted his own safety he were best to make haste to be gone, for that the Macedonians were resolved no longer to hazard their lives for the satisfaction of his luxury and pleasure. And this was thought fair and moderate language, compared with the fierceness of the rest. So, withdrawing into his tent, and, like an actor rather than a real king, laying aside his stage-robes of royalty, he put on some common clothes and stole away. He was no sooner gone but the mutinous army were fighting and quarrelling for the plunder of his tent, but Pyrrhus, coming immediately, took possession of the camp without a blow, after which he, with Lysimachus, parted the realm of Macedon betwixt them, after Demetrius had securely held it just seven years.

As for Demetrius, being thus suddenly despoiled of every thing, he retired to Cassandrea. His wife Phila, in the passion of her grief, could not endure to see her hapless husband reduced to the condition of a private and banished man. She refused to entertain any further hope, and, resolving to quit a fortune which was never permanent except for calamity, took poison and died. Demetrius, determining still to hold on by the wreck, went off to Greece, and collected his friends and officers there. Menelaus, in the play of Sophocles,[26] to give an image of his vicissitudes of estate, says,—

> For me, my destiny, alas, is found
> Whirling upon the gods' swift wheel around,
> And changing still, and as the moon's fair frame
> Cannot continue for two nights the same,
> But out of shadow first a crescent shows,
> Thence into beauty and perfection grows,
> And when the form of plenitude it wears,
> Dwindles again, and wholly disappears.

This simile is yet truer of Demetrius and the phases of his fortunes, now on the increase, presently on the wane, now filling up and now falling away. And so, at this time of apparent entire obscuration and extinc-

---

[26] What was *the play of Sophocles*, to which the passage belongs, is unknown. This fragment (*No. 713 in Dindorf*) is only preserved to us by Plutarch, who quotes a part of it in two other places.

tion, his light again shone out, and accessions of strength, little by little, came in to fulfil once more the measure of his hope. At first he showed himself in the garb of a private man, and went about the cities without any of the badges of a king. One who saw him thus at Thebes applied to him, not inaptly, the lines of Euripides,

> Humbled to man, laid by the godhead's pride,
> He comes to Dirce and Ismenus' side.[27]

But erelong his expectations had reëntered the royal track, and he began once more to have about him the body and form of empire. The Thebans received back, as his gift, their ancient constitution. The Athenians had deserted him. They displaced Diphilus, who was that year the priest of the two Tutelar Deities, and restored the archons, as of old, to mark the year; and on hearing that Demetrius was not so weak as they had expected, they sent into Macedonia to beg the protection of Pyrrhus. Demetrius, in anger, marched to Athens, and laid close siege to the city. In this distress, they sent out to him Crates the philosopher, a person of authority and reputation, who succeeded so far, that what with his entreaties and the solid reasons which he offered, Demetrius was persuaded to raise the siege; and, collecting all his ships, he embarked a force of eleven thousand men with cavalry, and sailed away to Asia, to Caria and Lydia, to take those provinces from Lysimachus. Arriving at Miletus, he was met there by Eurydice, the sister of Phila, who brought along with her Ptolemais, one of her daughters by king Ptolemy, who had before been affianced to Demetrius, and with whom he now consum-

[27] The verses, *Humbled to man,* are from the beginning of the Bacchæ (4), spoken by Bacchus.

mated his marriage. Immediately after, he proceeded to carry out his project, and was so fortunate in the beginning, that many cities revolted to him; others, as particularly Sardis, he took by force; and some generals of Lysimachus, also, came over to him with troops and money. But when Agathocles, the son of Lysimachus, arrived with an army, he retreated into Phrygia, with an intention to pass into Armenia, believing that, if he could once plant his foot in Armenia, he might set Media in revolt, and gain a position in Upper Asia, where a fugitive commander might find a hundred ways of evasion and escape. Agathocles pressed hard upon him, and many skirmishes and conflicts occurred, in which Demetrius had still the advantage; but Agathocles straitened him much in his forage, and his men showed a great dislike to his purpose, which they suspected, of carrying them far away into Armenia and Media. Famine also pressed upon them, and some mistake occurred in their passage of the river Lycus, in consequence of which a large number were swept away and drowned. Still, however, they could pass their jests, and one of them fixed upon Demetrius's tent-door a paper with the first verse, slightly altered, of the Œdipus;—

>Child of the blind old man, Antigonus,
>Into what country are you bringing us?[28]

But at last, pestilence, as is usual, when armies are driven to such necessities as to subsist upon any food

---

[28] The two first lines of the Œdipus Coloneus.
>Child of the blind old man, Antigone,
>Into what country are you bringing me?

They called *Antigonus the blind old man*, since, as Plutarch himself records in the beginning of the life of Sertorius, he had lost one eye. There is a story in one of Plutarch's minor works which turns upon his being called a Cyclops.

they can get, began to assail them as well as famine. So that, having lost eight thousand of his men, with the rest he retreated and came to Tarsus, and because that city was within the dominions of Seleucus, he was anxious to prevent any plundering, and wished to give no sort of offence to Seleucus. But when he perceived it was impossible to restrain the soldiers in their extreme necessity, Agathocles also having blocked up all the avenues of Mount Taurus, he wrote a letter to Seleucus, bewailing first all his own sad fortunes, and proceedings with entreaties and supplications for some compassion on his part towards one nearly connected with him, who has fallen into such calamities as might extort tenderness and pity from his very enemies.

These letters so far moved Seleucus, that he gave orders to the governors of those provinces that they should furnish Demetrius with all things suitable to his royal rank, and with sufficient provisions for his troops. But Patrocles, a person whose judgment was greatly valued, and who was a friend highly trusted by Seleucus, pointed out to him, that the expense of maintaining such a body of soldiers was the least important consideration, but that it was contrary to all policy to let Demetrius stay in the country, since he, of all the kings of his time, was the most violent, and most addicted to daring enterprises; and he was now in a condition which might tempt persons of the greatest temper and moderation to unlawful and desperate attempts. Seleucus, excited by this advice, moved with a powerful army towards Cilicia; and Demetrius, astonished at this sudden alteration, betook himself for safety to the most inaccessible places of Mount Taurus; from whence he sent envoys to Seleucus, to request from him that he would permit him the liberty to settle with his army somewhere among the independent barbarian tribes, where he might be able to make himself a petty king, and end his life without further travel and hardship; or, if he refused him this, at any rate to give his troops food during the winter, and not expose him in this distressed and naked condition to the fury of his enemies.

But Seleucus, whose jealousy made him put an ill construction on all he said, sent him answer, that he would permit him to stay two months and no longer in Cataonia, provided he presently sent him the principal of his friends as hostages for his departure then; and in the mean time, he fortified all the passages into Syria. So that Demetrius, who saw himself thus, like a wild beast, in the way to be encompassed on all sides in the toils, was driven in desperation to his defence, overran the country, and in several engagements in which Seleucus attacked him, had the advantage of him. Particularly, when he was once assailed by the scythed chariots, he successfully avoided the charge and routed his assailants, and then, expelling the troops that were in guard of the passes, made himself master of the roads leading into Syria. And now, elated himself, and finding his soldiers also animated by these successes, he was resolved to push at all, and to have one deciding blow for the empire with Seleucus; who, indeed, was in considerable anxiety and distress, being averse to any assistance from Lysimachus, whom he both mistrusted and feared, and shrinking from a battle with Demetrius, whose desperation he knew, and whose fortune he had so often seen suddenly pass from the lowest to the highest.

But Demetrius, in the mean while, was taken with a violent sickness, from which he suffered extremely himself, and which ruined all his prospects. His men deserted to the enemy, or dispersed. At last, after forty days, he began to be so far recovered as to be able to rally his remaining forces, and marched as if he directly designed for Cilicia; but in the night, raising his camp without sound of trumpet, he took a countermarch, and, passing the mountain Amanus, he ravaged all the lower country as far as Cyrrhestica.

Upon this, Seleucus advancing towards him and encamping at no great distance, Demetrius set his troops in motion to surprise him by night. And almost to the last moment Seleucus knew nothing, and was lying asleep. Some deserter came with the tidings just so soon that he had time to leap, in great consternation, out of bed, and give the alarm to his men. And as he was putting on his boots to mount his horse, he bade the officers about him look well to it, for they had to meet a furious and terrible wild beast. But Demetrius, by the noise he heard in the camp, finding they had taken the alarm, drew off his troops in haste. With the morning's return he found Seleucus pressing hard upon him; so, sending one of his officers against the other wing, he defeated those that were opposed to himself. But Seleucus, lighting from his horse, pulling off his helmet, and taking a target, advanced to the foremost ranks of the mercenary soldiers, and, showing them who he was, bade them come over and join him, telling them that it was for their sakes only that he had so long forborne coming to extremities. And thereupon, without a blow more, they saluted Seleucus as their king, and passed over.

Demetrius, who felt that this was his last change of fortune, and that he had no more vicissitudes to expect, fled to the passes of Amanus, where, with a very few friends and followers, he threw himself into a dense forest, and there waited for the night, purposing, if possible, to make his escape towards Caunus, where he hoped to find his shipping ready to transport him. But upon inquiry, finding that they had not provisions even for that one day, he began to think of some other project. Whilst he was yet in doubt, his friend Sosigenes arrived, who had four hundred pieces of gold about him, and, with this relief, he again entertained hopes of being able to reach the coast, and, as soon as it began to be dark, set forward towards the passes. But, perceiving by the fires that the enemies had occupied them, he gave up all thought of that road, and retreated to his old station in the wood, but not with all his men; for some had deserted, nor were those that remained as willing as they had been. One of them, in fine, ventured to speak out, and say that Demetrius had better give himself up to Seleucus; which Demetrius, overhearing, drew out his sword, and would have passed it through his body, but that some of his friends interposed and prevented the attempt, persuading him to do as had been said. So at last he gave way, and sent to Seleucus, to surrender himself at discretion.

Seleucus, when he was told of it, said it was not Demetrius's good fortune that had found out this means for his safety, but his own, which had added to his other honors the opportunity of showing his clemency and generosity. And forthwith he gave order to his domestic officers to prepare a royal pavilion, and all things suitable to give him a splendid reception and entertainment. There was in the attendance of Seleucus one Apollonides, who formerly had been intimate with Demetrius. He was, therefore, as the fittest person, despatched from the king to meet Demetrius, that he might feel himself more at his ease, and might come with the confidence of being received as a friend and relative. No sooner was this message known, but the courtiers and officers, some few at first, and afterwards almost the whole of them, thinking Demetrius would presently become of great power with the king, hurried off, vying who should be foremost to pay him their respects. The effect of which was that compassion

DEMETRIUS   161

was converted into jealousy, and ill-natured, malicious people could the more easily insinuate to Seleucus that he was giving way to an unwise humanity, the very first sight of Demetrius having been the occasion of a dangerous excitement in the army. So, whilst Apollonides, in great delight, and after him many others, were relating to Demetrius the kind expressions of Seleucus, and he, after so many troubles and calamities, if indeed he had still any sense of his surrender of himself being a disgrace, had now, in confidence on the good hopes held out to him, entirely forgotten all such thoughts, Pausanias, with a guard of a thousand horse and foot, came and surrounded him; and, dispersing the rest that were with him, carried him, not to the presence of Seleucus, but to the Syrian Chersonese,[29] where he was committed to the safe custody of a strong guard. Sufficient attendance and liberal provision were here allowed him, space for riding and walking, a park with game for hunting, those of his friends and companions in exile who wished it had permission to see him, and messages of kindness, also, from time to time, were brought him from Seleucus, bidding him fear nothing, and intimating, that, so soon as Antiochus and Stratonice should arrive, he would receive his liberty.

Demetrius, however, finding himself in this condition, sent letters to those who were with his son, and to his captains and friends at Athens and Corinth, that

---

[29] The Syrian Chersonese is the river-peninsula formed by the Orontes and a neighboring lake, where Seleucus founded a town, and named it, in honor of Apame, his Persian wife, Apamea. Here were his stud-stables, and his great military depot for horses and elephants. It is far inland, up the river, and was long the capital of a division of Syria. The Macedonians called it Pella, after their Pella at home. Diodorus, in speaking of the captivity of Demetrius, says he was kept at Pella.

they should give no manner of credit to any letters written to them in his name, though they were sealed with his own signet, but that, looking upon him as if he were already dead, they should maintain the cities and whatever was left of his power, for Antigonus, as his successor. Antigonus received the news of his father's captivity with great sorrow; he put himself into mourning, and wrote letters to the rest of the kings, and to Seleucus himself, making entreaties, and offering not only to surrender whatever they had left, but himself to be a hostage for his father. Many cities, also, and princes joined in interceding for him; only Lysimachus sent and offered a large sum of money to Seleucus to take away his life. But he, who had always shown his aversion to Lysimachus before, thought him only the greater barbarian and monster for it. Nevertheless, he still protracted the time, reserving the favor, as he professed, for the intercession of Antiochus and Stratonice.

Demetrius, who had sustained the first stroke of his misfortune, in time grew so familiar with it, that, by continuance, it became easy. At first he persevered one way or other in taking exercise, in hunting, so far as he had means, and in riding. Little by little, however, after a while, he let himself grow indolent and indisposed for them, and took to dice and drinking, in which he passed most of his time, whether it were to escape the thoughts of his present condition, with which he was haunted when sober, and to drown reflection in drunkenness, or that he acknowledged to himself that this was the real happy life he had long desired and wished for, and had foolishly let himself be seduced away from it by a senseless and vain ambition, which had only brought trouble to himself and others; that highest good which he had thought to obtain by arms and fleets and soldiers, he had now discovered unexpectedly in idleness, leisure, and repose. As, indeed, what other end or period is there of all the wars and dangers which hapless princes run into, whose misery and folly it is, not merely that they make luxury and pleasure, instead of virtue and excellence, the object of their lives, but that they do not so much as know where this luxury and pleasure are to be found?

Having thus continued three years a prisoner in Chersonesus, for want of exercise, and by indulging himself in eating and drinking, he fell into a disease, of which he died at the age of fifty-four. Seleucus was ill-spoken of, and was himself greatly grieved, that he had yielded so far to his suspicions, and had let himself be so much outdone by the barbarian Dromichætes of Thrace, who had shown so much humanity and such a kingly temper in his treatment of his prisoner Lysimachus.

There was something dramatic and theatrical in the very funeral ceremonies with which Demetrius was honored. For his son Antigonus, understanding that his remains were coming over from Syria, went with all his fleet to the islands to meet them. They were there presented to him in a golden urn, which he placed in his largest admiral galley. All the cities where they touched in their passage sent chaplets to adorn the urn, and deputed certain of their citizens to follow in mourning, to assist at the funeral solemnity. When the fleet approached the harbor of Corinth, the urn, covered with purple, and a royal diadem upon it, was visible upon the poop, and a troop of young men attended in arms to receive it at landing. Xenophantus, the most famous musician of the day, played on the flute his most solemn measure, to which the rowers, as the ship came in, made loud response, their oars, like the funeral beating of the breast, keeping time with the cadences of the music. But Antigonus, in tears and mourning attire, excited among the spectators gathered on the shore the greatest sorrow and compassion. After crowns and other honors had been offered at Corinth, the remains were conveyed to Demetrias, a city to which Demetrius had given his name, peopled from the inhabitants of the small villages of Iolcus.

Demetrius left no other children by his wife Phila but Antigonus and Stratonice, but he had two other sons, both of his own name, one surnamed the Thin, by an Illyrian mother, and one who ruled in Cyrene, by Ptolemais. He had also, by Deidamia, a son, Alexander, who lived and died in Egypt; and there are some who say that he had a son by Eurydice, named Corrhabus. His family was continued in a succession of kings down to Perseus, the last, from whom the Romans took Macedonia.

And now, the Macedonian drama being ended, let us prepare to see the Roman.

ANTONY[1]

Translated by Charles Fraser, M. D.

The grandfather of Antony was the famous pleader, whom Marius put to death for having taken part with Sylla. His father was Antony, surnamed of Crete, not very famous or distinguished in public life, but a worthy, good man, and particularly remarkable for his liberality, as may appear from a single example. He was not very rich, and was for that reason checked in the exercise of his good-nature by his wife. A friend that stood in need of money came to borrow of him. Money he had none, but he bade a servant bring him water in a silver basin, with which, when it was brought, he whetted his face, as if he meant to shave, and, sending away the servant upon another errand, gave his friend the basin, desiring him to turn it to his purpose. And when there was, afterwards, a great inquiry for it in the house, and his wife was in a very ill humor, and was going to put the servants one by one to the search, he acknowledged what he had done, and begged her pardon.

[1] M. Antony, the Triumvir, was born about 83 B. C. He indulged in his early youth in every kind of dissipation and his affairs soon became deeply involved. After Cæsar's murder, March 15th, 44 B. C., Antony endeavored to succeed to his power, but found a new and unexpected rival in Cæsar's adopted son and great-nephew Octavianus, who finally overcame Antony at the memorable sea-fight off Actium, Sept. 2, 31 B. C. Antony and Cleopatra then fled to Alexandria, where the former put an end to his life the following year, 30 B. C. Cleopatra poisoned herself the same year.—Dr. William Smith.

His wife was Julia, of the family of the Cæsars, who, for her discretion and fair behavior, was not inferior to any of her time. Under her, Antony received his education, she being, after the death of his father, remarried to Cornelius Lentulus, who was put to death by Cicero for having been of Catiline's conspiracy. This, probably, was the first ground and occasion of that mortal grudge that Antony bore Cicero. He says, even, that the body of Lentulus was denied burial, till, by application made to Cicero's wife, it was granted to Julia. But this seems to be a manifest error, for none of those that suffered in the consulate of Cicero had the right of burial denied them. Antony grew up a very beautiful youth, but, by the worst of misfortunes, he fell into the acquaintance and friendship of Curio, a man abandoned to his pleasures; who, to make Antony's dependence upon him a matter of greater necessity, plunged him into a life of drinking and dissipation, and led him through a course of such extravagance, that he ran, at that early age, into debt to the amount of two hundred and fifty talents. For this sum, Curio became his surety; on hearing which, the elder Curio, his father, drove Antony out of his house. After this, for some short time, he took part with Clodius, the most insolent and outrageous demagogue of the time, in his course of violence and disorder; but, getting weary, before long, of his madness, and apprehensive of the powerful party forming against him, he left Italy, and travelled into Greece, where he spent his time in military exercises and in the study of eloquence. He took most to what was called the Asiatic taste in speaking, which was then at its height, and was, in many ways, suitable to his ostentatious, vaunting temper, full of empty flourishes and unsteady efforts for glory.

After some stay in Greece, he was invited by Gabinius, who had been consul, to make a campaign with him in Syria, which at first he refused, not being willing to serve in a private character, but, receiving a commission to command the horse, he went along with him. His first service was against Aristobulus, who had prevailed with the Jews to rebel. Here he was himself the first man to scale the largest of the works, and beat Aristobulus out of all of them; after which he routed, in a pitched battle, an army many times over the number of his, killed almost all of them, and took Aristobulus and his son prisoners. This war ended, Gabinius was solicited by Ptolemy to restore him to his kingdom of Egypt, and a promise made of ten thousand talents reward. Most of the officers were against this enterprise, and Gabinius himself did not much like it, though sorely tempted by the ten thousand talents. But Antony, desirous of brave actions, and willing to please Ptolemy, joined in persuading Gabinius to go. And whereas all were of opinion that the most dangerous thing before them was the march to Pelusium, in which they would have to pass over a deep sand, where no fresh water was to be hoped for, along the Ecregma and the Serbonian marsh (which the Egyptians call Typhon's breathing-hole, and which is, in probability, water left behind by, or making its way through from, the Red Sea, which is here divided from the Mediterranean by a narrow isthmus), Antony, being ordered thither with the horse, not only made himself master of the passes, but won Pelusium itself, a great city, took the garrison prisoners, and, by this means, rendered the march secure to the army, and the way to victory not difficult for the general to pursue. The enemy, also, reaped some benefit of his eagerness for honor. For when Ptolemy, after he had entered Pelusium, in his rage and spite against the Egyptians, designed to put them to the sword, Antony withstood him, and hindered the execution. In all the great and frequent skirmishes and battles, he gave continual proofs of his personal valor and military conduct; and once in particular, by wheeling about and attacking the rear of the enemy, he gave the victory to the assailants in the front, and received for this service signal marks of distinction. Nor was his humanity towards the deceased Archelaus less taken notice of. He had been formerly his guest and acquaintance, and, as he was now compelled, he fought him bravely while alive, but, on his death, sought out his body and buried it with royal honors. The consequence was that he left behind him a great name among the Alexandrians, and all who were serving in the Roman army looked upon him as a most gallant soldier.

He had also a very good and noble appearance; his beard was well grown, his forehead large, and his nose aquiline, giving him altogether a bold, masculine look, that reminded people of the faces of Hercules in paintings and sculptures. It was, moreover, an ancient tradition, that the Antonys were descended from Hercules, by a son of his called Anton; and this opinion he thought to give credit to, by the similarity of his person just mentioned, and also by the fashion of his dress. For, whenever he had to appear before large numbers, he wore his tunic girt low about the hips, a broadsword on his side, and over all a large, coarse mantle. What might seem to some very insupportable, his vaunting, his raillery, his drinking in public, sitting down by the men as they were taking their food, and eating, as he stood, off the common soldiers' tables, made him the delight and pleasure of the army. In love affairs, also, he was very agreeable; he gained many friends by the assistance he gave them in theirs, and took other people's raillery upon his own with good-humor. And his generous ways, his open and lavish hand in gifts and favors to his friends and fellow-soldiers, did a great deal for him in his first advance to power, and, after he had become great, long maintained his fortunes, when a thousand follies were hastening their overthrow. One instance of his liberality I must relate. He had ordered payment to one of his friends of twenty-five myriads of money, or *decies,* as the Romans call it, and his steward, wondering at the extravagance of the sum, laid all the silver in a heap, as he should pass by. Antony, seeing the heap, asked what it meant; his steward replied, "The money you have ordered to be given to your friend." So perceiving the man's malice, said he, "I thought the *decies* had been much more; 't is too little; let it be doubled." This, however, was at a later time.

When the Roman state finally broke up into two hostile factions, the aristocratical party joining Pompey, who was in the city, and the popular side seeking help from Cæsar, who was at the head of an army in Gaul, Curio, the friend of Antony, having changed his party and devoted himself to Cæsar, brought over Antony also to his service. And the influence which he gained with the people by his eloquence and by the money which was supplied by Cæsar enabled him to make Antony, first, tribune of the people, and then, augur. And Antony's accession to office was at once of the greatest advantage to Cæsar. In the first place, he resisted the consul Marcellus, who was putting under Pompey's orders the troops who were already collected, and was giving him power to raise new levies; he, on the other hand, making an order that they should be sent into Syria to reinforce Bibulus, who was making war with the Parthians, and that no one should give in his name to serve under Pompey. Next, when the senators would not suffer Cæsar's letters to be received or read in the senate, by virtue of his office he read them publicly, and succeeded so well, that many were brought to change their mind; Cæsar's demands, as they appeared in what he wrote, being just and reasonable. At length, two questions being put in the senate, the one, whether Pompey should dismiss his army, the other, if Cæsar his, some were for the former, for the latter all, except some few, when Antony stood up and put the question, if it would be agreeable to them that both Pompey and Cæsar should dismiss their armies. This proposal met with the greatest approval, they gave him loud acclamations, and called for it to be put to the vote. But when the consuls would not have it so, Cæsar's friends again made some new offers, very fair and equitable, but were strongly opposed by Cato, and Antony himself was commanded to leave the senate by the consul Lentulus. So, leaving them with execrations, and disguising himself in a servant's dress, hiring a carriage with Quintus Cassius, he went straight away to Cæsar, declaring at once, when they reached the camp, that affairs at Rome were conducted without any order or justice, that the privilege of speaking in the senate was denied the tribunes, and that he who spoke for common fair dealing was driven out and in danger of his life.

Upon this, Cæsar set his army in motion, and marched into Italy; and for this reason it is that Cicero writes in his Philippics,[2] that Antony was as much the cause of the civil war, as Helen was of the Trojan. But this is but a calumny. For Cæsar was not of so slight or weak a temper as to suffer himself to be carried away, by the indignation of the moment, into a

---

[2] The passage of *Cicero in his Philippics* is in the twenty-second chapter of the famous second Philippic;—"Ut Helena Trojanis, sic iste huic reipublicæ causa belli, causa pestis atque exitii fuit."

civil war with his country, upon the sight of Antony and Cassius seeking refuge in his camp, meanly dressed and in a hired carriage, without ever having thought of it or taken any such resolution long before. This was to him, who wanted a pretence of declaring war, a fair and plausible occasion; but the true motive that led him was the same that formerly led Alexander and Cyrus against all mankind, the unquenchable thirst of empire, and the distracted ambition of being the greatest man in the world, which was impracticable for him, unless Pompey were put down. So soon, then, as he had advanced and occupied Rome, and driven Pompey out of Italy, he purposed first to go against the legions that Pompey had in Spain, and then cross over and follow him with the fleet that should be prepared during his absence, in the mean time leaving the government of Rome to Lepidus, as prætor, and the command of the troops and of Italy to Antony, as tribune of the people. Antony was not long in getting the hearts of the soldiers, joining with them in their exercises, and for the most part living amongst them, and making them presents to the utmost of his abilities; but with all others he was unpopular enough. He was too lazy to pay attention to the complaints of persons who were injured; he listened impatiently to petitions; and he had an ill name for familiarity with other people's wives. In short, the government of Cæsar (which, so far as he was concerned himself, had the appearance of any thing rather than a tyranny), got a bad repute through his friends. And of these friends, Antony, as he had the largest trust, and committed the greatest errors, was thought the most deeply in fault.

Cæsar, however, at his return from Spain, overlooked the charges against him, and had no reason ever to complain, in the employments he gave him in the war, of any want of courage, energy, or military skill. He himself, going aboard at Brundusium, sailed over the Ionian Sea with a few troops, and sent back the vessels with orders to Antony and Gabinius to embark the army, and come over with all speed into Macedonia. Gabinius, having no mind to put to sea in the rough, dangerous weather of the winter season, was for marching the army round by the long land route; but Antony, being more afraid lest Cæsar might suffer from the number of his enemies, who pressed him hard, beat back Libo, who was watching with a fleet at the mouth of the haven of Brundusium, by attacking his galleys with a number of small boats, and, gaining thus an opportunity, put on board twenty thousand foot and eight hundred horse, and so set out to sea. And, being espied by the enemy and pursued, from this danger he was rescued by a strong south wind, which sprang up and raised so high a sea, that the enemy's galleys could make little way. But his own ships were driving before it upon a lee shore of cliffs and rocks running sheer to the water, where there was no hope of escape, when all of a sudden the wind turned about to southwest, and blew from land to the main sea, where Antony, now sailing in security, saw the coast all covered with the wreck of the enemy's fleet. For hither the galleys in pursuit had been carried by the gale, and not a few of them dashed to pieces. Many men and much property fell into Antony's hands; he took also the town of Lissus, and, by the seasonable arrival of so large a reinforcement, gave Cæsar great encouragement.

There was not one of the many engagements that now took place one after another in which he did not signalize himself; twice he stopped the army in its full flight, led them back to a charge, and gained the victory. So that not without reason his reputation, next to Cæsar's, was greatest in the army. And what opinion Cæsar himself had of him well appeared when for the final battle in Pharsalia, which was to determine every thing, he himself chose to lead the right wing, committing the charge of the left to Antony, as to the best officer of all that served under him. After the battle, Cæsar, being created dictator, went in pursuit of Pompey, and sent Antony to Rome, with the character of Master of the Horse, who is in office and power next to the dictator, when present, and in his absence is the first, and pretty nearly indeed the sole magistrate. For on the appointment of a dictator, with the one exception of the tribunes, all other magistrates cease to exercise any authority in Rome.

Dolabella, however, who was tribune, being a young man and eager for change, was now for bringing in a general measure for cancelling debts, and wanted Antony, who was his friend, and forward enough to promote any popular project, to take part with him in this step. Asinius and Trebellius were of the contrary opinion, and it so happened, at the same time, Antony was crossed by a terrible suspicion that Dolabella was too familiar with his wife; and in great trouble at this, he parted with her (she being his cousin, and daughter to Caius Antonius, the colleague of Cicero), and, taking part with Asinius, came to open hostilities with Dolabella, who had seized on the forum, intending to pass his law by force. Antony, backed by a vote of the senate that Dolabella should be put down by force of arms, went down and attacked him, killing some of his, and losing some of his own men; and by this action lost his favor with the commonalty, while with the better class and with all well conducted people his general course of life made him, as Cicero says, absolutely odious, utter disgust being excited by his drinking bouts at all hours, his wild expenses, his gross amours, the day spent in sleeping or walking off his debauches, and the night in banquets and at theatres, and in celebrating the nuptials of some comedian or buffoon. It is related that, drinking all night at the wedding of Hippias, the comedian, on the morning, having to harangue the people, he came forward, overcharged as he was, and vomited before them all, one of his friends holding his gown for him. Sergius, the player, was one of the friends who could do most with him; also Cytheris, a woman of the same trade, whom he made much of, and who, when he went his progress, accompanied him in a litter, and had her equipage, not in any thing inferior to his mother's; while every one, moreover, was scandalized at the sight of the golden cups that he took with him, fitter for the ornaments of a procession than the uses of a journey, at his having pavilions set up, and sumptuous morning repasts laid out by river sides and in groves, at his having chariots drawn by lions, and common women and singing girls quartered upon the houses of serious fathers and mothers of families. And it seemed very unreasonable that Cæsar, out of Italy, should lodge in the open field, and, with great fatigue and danger, pursue the remainder of a hazardous war, whilst others, by favor of his authority, should insult the citizens with their impudent luxury.

All this appears to have aggravated party quarrels in Rome, and to have encouraged the soldiers in acts of license and rapacity. And, accordingly, when Cæsar came home, he acquitted Dolabella, and, being created the third time consul, took, not Antony, but Lepidus, for his colleague. Pompey's house being offered for sale, Antony bought it, and, when the price was demanded of him, loudly complained. This, he tells us himself, and because he thought his former services had not been recompensed as they deserved, made him not follow Cæsar with the army into Libya. However, Cæsar, by dealing gently with his errors, seems to have succeeded in curing him of a good deal of his folly and extravagance. He gave up his former courses, and took a wife, Fulvia, the widow of Clodius the demagogue, a woman not born for spinning or housewifery, nor one that could be content with ruling a private husband, but prepared to govern a first magistrate, or give orders to a commander-in-chief. So that Cleopatra had great obligations to her for having taught Antony to be so good a servant, he coming to her hands tame and broken into entire obedience to the commands of a mistress. He used to play all sorts of sportive, boyish tricks, to keep Fulvia in good humor. As, for example, when Cæsar, after his victory in Spain, was on his return, Antony, among the rest, went out to meet him; and, a rumor being spread that Cæsar was killed and the enemy marching into Italy, he returned to Rome, and, disguising himself, came to her by night muffled up as a servant that brought letters from Antony. She, with great impatience, before she received the letter, asks if Antony were well, and instead of an answer he gives her the letter; and, as she was opening it, took her about the neck and kissed her. This little story of many of the same nature, I give as a specimen.

There was nobody of any rank in Rome that did not go some days' journeys to meet Cæsar on his return from Spain; but Antony was the best received of any, admitted to ride the whole journey with him in his carriage, while behind came Brutus Albinus, and Octavian, his niece's son, who afterwards bore his name and reigned so long over the Romans. Cæsar being created, the fifth time, consul, without delay chose Antony for his colleague, but, designing himself to give up his own consulate to Dolabella, he acquainted the senate with his resolution. But Antony opposed it with all his might, saying much that was bad against Dolabella, and receiving the like language in return, till Cæsar could bear with the indecency no longer, and deferred the matter to another time. Afterwards, when he came before the people to proclaim Dolabella, Antony cried out the auspices were unfavorable, so that at last Cæsar, much to Dolabella's vexation, yielded and gave it up. And it is credible that Cæsar was about as much disgusted with the one as the other. When some one was accusing them both to him, "It is not," said he, "these well fed, long haired men that I fear, but the pale and the hungry looking;" meaning Brutus and Cassius, by whose conspiracy he afterwards fell.

And the fairest pretext for that conspiracy was furnished, without his meaning it, by Antony himself. The Romans were celebrating their festival, called the Lupercalia, when Cæsar, in his triumphal habit, and seated above the Rostra in the market-place, was a spectator of the sports. The custom is, that many young noblemen and of the magistracy, anointed with oil and having straps of hide in their hands, run about and strike, in sport, at every one they meet. Antony was running with the rest; but, omitting the old ceremony, twining a garland of bay round a diadem, he ran up to the Rostra, and, being lifted up by his companions, would have put it upon the head of Cæsar, as if by that ceremony he were declared king. Cæsar seemingly refused, and drew aside to avoid it, and was applauded by the people with great shouts. Again Antony pressed it, and again he declined its acceptance. And so the dispute between them went on for some time, Antony's solicitations receiving but little encouragement from the shouts of a few friends, and Cæsar's refusal being accompanied with the general applause of the people; a curious thing enough, that they should submit with patience to the fact, and yet at the same time dread the name as the destruction of their liberty. Cæsar, very much discomposed at what had past, got up from his seat, and, laying bare his neck, said, he was ready to receive the stroke, if any one of them desired to give it. The crown was at last put on one of his statues, but was taken down by some of the tribunes, who were followed home by the people with shouts of applause. Cæsar, however, resented it, and deposed them.

These passages gave great encouragement to Brutus and Cassius, who, in making choice of trusty friends for such an enterprise, were thinking to engage Antony. The rest approved, except Trebonius, who told them that Antony and he had lodged and travelled together in the last journey they took to meet Cæsar, and that he had let fall several words, in a cautious way, on purpose to sound him; that Antony very well understood him, but did not encourage it; however, he had said nothing of it to Cæsar, but had kept the secret faithfully. The conspirators then proposed that Antony should die with him, which Brutus would not consent to, insisting that an action undertaken in defence of right and the laws must be maintained unsullied, and pure of injustice. It was settled that Antony, whose bodily strength and high office made him formidable, should, at Cæsar's entrance into the senate, when the deed was to be done, be amused outside by some of the party in a conversation about some pretended business.

So when all was proceeded with, according to their plan, and Cæsar had fallen in the senate-house, Antony, at the first moment, took a servant's dress, and hid himself. But, understanding that the conspirators had assembled in the Capitol, and had no further design upon any one, he persuaded them to come down, giving them his son as a hostage. That night Cassius supped at Antony's house, and Brutus with Lepidus. Antony then convened the senate, and spoke in favor of an act of oblivion, and the appointment of Brutus and Cassius to provinces. These measures the senate passed; and resolved that all Cæsar's acts should remain in force. Thus Antony went out of the senate with the highest possible reputation and esteem; for it was apparent that he had prevented a civil war, and had composed, in the wisest and most statesmanlike way, questions of the greatest difficulty and embarrassment. But these temperate counsels were soon swept away by the tide of popular applause, and the prospects, if Brutus were overthrown, of being without doubt the ruler-in-chief. As Cæsar's body was conveying to the tomb, Antony, according to the custom, was making his funeral oration in the market-place, and, perceiving the people to be infinitely affected with what he had said, he began to mingle with his praises language of commiseration, and horror at what had happened, and, as he was ending his speech, he took the under-clothes of the dead, and held them up, shewing them stains of blood and the holes of the many stabs, calling those that had done this act villains and bloody murderers. All which excited the people to such indignation, that they would not defer the funeral, but, making a pile of tables and forms in the very market-place, set fire to it; and every one, taking a brand, ran to the conspirators' houses, to attack them.

Upon this, Brutus and his whole party left the city, and Cæsar's friends joined themselves to Antony. Calpurnia, Cæsar's wife, lodged with him the best part of the property, to the value of four thousand talents; he got also into his hands all Cæsar's papers, wherein

MARC ANTONY DELIVERS THE FUNERAL ORATION OVER THE DEAD
BODY OF CAESAR

were contained journals of all he had done, and draughts of what he designed to do, which Antony made good use of; for by this means he appointed what magistrates he pleased, brought whom he would into the senate, recalled some from exile, freed others out of prison, and all this as ordered so by Cæsar. The Romans, in mockery, gave those who were thus benefited the name of Charonites,[3] since, if put to prove their patents, they must have recourse to the papers of the dead. In short, Antony's behavior in Rome was very absolute, he himself being consul, and his two brothers in great place; Caius, the one, being prætor, and Lucius, the other, tribune of the people.

While matters went thus in Rome, the young Cæsar, Cæsar's niece's son, and by testament left his heir, arrived at Rome from Apollonia, where he was when his uncle was killed. The first thing he did was to visit Antony, as his father's friend. He spoke to him concerning the money that was in his hands, and reminded him of the legacy Cæsar had made of seventy-five drachmas to every Roman citizen. Antony, at first, laughing at such discourse from so young a man, told him he wished he were in his health, and that he wanted good counsel and good friends, to tell him the burden of being executor to Cæsar would sit very uneasily upon his young shoulders. This was no answer to him; and, when he persisted in demanding the property, Antony went on treating him injuriously both in word and deed, opposed him when he stood for the tribune's office, and, when he was taking steps for the dedication

---

[3] Suetonius says *Orcini;* which was the common name given, even in the law-books, to slaves manumitted by their owner, after his death, by his will. *Charonitæ,* freedmen of Charon, may have been a Greek translation of the Latin *Orcini,* freedmen of Orcus, or the world below; or it was perhaps a more familiar word for the same thing.

of his father's golden chair, as had been enacted, he threatened to send him to prison if he did not give over soliciting the people. This made the young Cæsar apply himself to Cicero, and all those that hated Antony; by them he was recommended to the senate, while he himself courted the people, and drew together the soldiers from their settlements, till Antony got alarmed, and gave him a meeting in the Capitol, where, after some words, they came to an accommodation.

That night Antony had a very unlucky dream, fancying that his right hand was thunderstruck. And, some few days after, he was informed that Cæsar was plotting to take his life. Cæsar explained, but was not believed, so that the breach was now made as wide as ever; each of them hurried about all through Italy to engage, by great offers, the old soldiers that lay scattered in their settlements, and to be the first to secure the troops that still remained undischarged.

Cicero was at this time the man of greatest influence in Rome. He made use of all his art to exasperate people against Antony, and at length persuaded the senate to declare him a public enemy, to send Cæsar the rods and axes and other marks of honor usually given to prætors, and to issue orders to Hirtius and Pansa, who were the consuls, to drive Antony out of Italy. The armies engaged near Modena, and Cæsar himself was present and took part in the battle. Antony was defeated, but both the consuls were slain. Antony, in his flight, was overtaken by distresses of every kind, and the worst of all of them was famine. But it was his character in calamities to be better than at any other time. Antony, in misfortune, was most nearly a virtuous man. It is common enough for people, when they fall into great disasters, to discern what is right, and what they ought to do; but there are but few who in such extremities have the strength to obey their judgment, either in doing what it approves or avoiding what it condemns; and a good many are so weak as to give way to their habits all the more, and are incapable of using their minds. Antony, on this occasion, was a most wonderful example to his soldiers. He, who had just quitted so much luxury and sumptuous living, made no difficulty now of drinking foul water and feeding on wild fruits and roots. Nay, it is related they ate the very bark of trees, and, in passing over the Alps, lived upon creatures that no one before had ever been willing to touch.

The design was to join the army on the other side the Alps, commanded by Lepidus, who he imagined would stand his friend, he having done him many good offices with Cæsar. On coming up and encamping near at hand, finding he had no sort of encouragement offered him, he resolved to push his fortune and venture all. His hair was long and disordered, nor had he shaved his beard since his defeat; in this guise, and with a dark colored cloak flung over him, he came into the trenches of Lepidus, and began to address the army. Some were moved at his habit, others at his words, so that Lepidus, not liking it, ordered the trumpets to sound, that he might be heard no longer. This raised in the soldiers yet a greater pity, so that they resolved to confer secretly with him, and dressed Lælius and Clodius in women's clothes, and sent them to see him. They advised him without delay to attack Lepidus's trenches, assuring him that a strong party would receive him, and, if he wished it, would kill Lepidus. Antony, however, had no wish for this, but next morning marched his army to pass over the river that parted the two camps. He was himself the first man that stepped in, and, as he went through towards the other bank, he saw Lepidus's soldiers in great numbers reaching out their hands to help him, and beating down the works to make him way. Being entered into the camp, and finding himself absolute master, he nevertheless treated Lepidus with the greatest civility, and gave him the title of Father, when he spoke to him, and, though he had every thing at his own command, he left him the honor of being called the general. This fair usage brought over to him Munatius Plancus, who was not far off with a considerable force. Thus in great strength he repassed the Alps, leading with him into Italy seventeen legions and ten thousand horse, besides six legions which he left in garrison under the command of Varius, one of his familiar friends and boon companions, whom they used to call by the nickname of Cotylon.[4]

Cæsar, perceiving that Cicero's wishes were for liberty, had ceased to pay any further regard to him, and was now employing the mediation of his friends to come to a good understanding with Antony. They both met together with Lepidus in a small island, where the conference lasted three days. The empire was soon determined of, it being divided amongst them as if it had been their paternal inheritance. That which gave them all the trouble was to agree who should be put to death, each of them desiring to destroy his enemies and save his friends. But, in the end, animosity to those they hated carried the day against respect for relations and affection for friends; and Cæsar sacrificed Cicero to Antony, Antony gave up his uncle Lucius Cæsar, and Lepidus received permission to murder his brother Paulus, or, as others say, yielded his brother to them. I do not believe any thing ever took place more truly savage or barbarous than this composition, for, in this exchange of blood for blood, they were equally guilty of the lives they surrendered and

---

[4] From *Cotyle*, a cup.

of those they took; or, indeed, more guilty in the case
of their friends, for whose deaths they had not even
the justification of hatred. To complete the reconciliation, the soldiery, coming about them, demanded that
confirmation should be given to it by some alliance of
marriage; Cæsar should marry Clodia, the daughter
of Fulvia, wife to Antony. This also being agreed to,
three hundred persons were put to death by proscription. Antony gave orders to those that were to kill
Cicero, to cut off his head and right hand, with which
he had written his invectives against him; and, when
they were brought before him, he regarded them joyfully, actually bursting out more than once into laughter, and, when he had satiated himself with the sight
of them, ordered them to be hung up above the speaker's place in the forum, thinking thus to insult the
dead, while in fact he only exposed his own wanton
arrogance, and his unworthiness to hold the power that
fortune had given him. His uncle Lucius Cæsar, being closely pursued, took refuge with his sister, who,
when the murderers had broken into her house and
were pressing into her chamber, met them at the door,
and, spreading out her hands, cried out several times,
"You shall not kill Lucius Cæsar till you first despatch
me, who gave your general his birth;" and in this manner she succeeded in getting her brother out of the
way, and saving his life.

This triumvirate was very hateful to the Romans,
and Antony most of all bore the blame, because he
was older than Cæsar, and had greater authority than
Lepidus, and withal he was no sooner settled in his
affairs, but he returned to his luxurious and dissolute
way of living. Besides the ill reputation he gained
by his general behavior, it was some considerable disadvantage to him his living in the house of Pompey
the Great, who had been as much admired for his

temperance and his sober, citizen-like habits of life, as ever he was for having triumphed three times. They could not without anger see the doors of that house shut against magistrates, officers, and envoys, who were shamefully refused admittance, while it was filled inside with players, jugglers, and drunken flatterers, upon whom were spent the greatest part of the wealth which violence and cruelty procured. For they did not limit themselves to the forfeiture of the estates of such as were proscribed, defrauding the widows and families, nor were they contented with laying on every possible kind of tax and imposition; but, hearing that several sums of money were, as well by strangers as citizens of Rome, deposited in the hands of the vestal virgins, they went and took the money away by force. When it was manifest that nothing would ever be enough for Antony, Cæsar at last called for a division of property. The army was also divided between them, upon their march into Macedonia to make war with Brutus and Cassius, Lepidus being left with the command of the city.

However, after they had crossed the sea and engaged in operations of war, encamping in front of the enemy, Antony opposite Cassius, and Cæsar opposite Brutus, Cæsar did nothing worth relating, and all the success and victory were Antony's. In the first battle, Cæsar was completely routed by Brutus, his camp taken, he himself very narrowly escaping by flight. As he himself writes in his Memoirs, he retired before the battle, on account of a dream which one of his friends had. But Antony, on the other hand, defeated Cassius; though some have written that he was not actually present in the engagement, and only joined afterwards in the pursuit. Cassius was killed, at his own entreaty and order, by one of his most trusted freedmen, Pindarus, not being aware of Brutus's victory. After a few days' interval, they fought another battle, in which Brutus lost the day, and slew himself; and Cæsar being sick, Antony had almost all the honor of the victory. Standing over Brutus's dead body, he uttered a few words of reproach upon him for the death of his brother Caius, who had been executed by Brutus's order in Macedonia in revenge of Cicero; but, saying presently that Hortensius was most to blame for it, he gave order for his being slain upon his brother's tomb, and, throwing his own scarlet mantle, which was of great value, upon the body of Brutus, he gave charge to one of his own freedmen to take care of his funeral. This man, as Antony came to understand, did not leave the mantle with the corpse, but kept both it and a good part of the money that should have been spent in the funeral for himself; for which he had him put to death.

But Cæsar was conveyed to Rome, no one expecting that he would long survive. Antony, proposing to go to the eastern provinces to lay them under contribution, entered Greece with a large force. The promise had been made that every common soldier should receive for his pay five thousand drachmas; so it was likely there would be need of pretty severe taxing and levying to raise money. However, to the Greeks he showed at first reason and moderation enough; he gratified his love of amusement by hearing the learned men dispute, by seeing the games, and undergoing initiation; and in judicial matters he was equitable, taking pleasure in being styled a lover of Greece, but, above all, in being called a lover of Athens, to which city he made very considerable presents. The people of Megara wished to let him know that they also had something to show him, and invited him to come and see their senate-house. So he went and examined it, and on their asking him how he liked it, told them it was "not very large, but extremely *ruinous*."[5] At the same time, he had a survey made of the temple of the Pythian Apollo, as if he had designed to repair it, and indeed he had declared to the senate his intention so to do.

However, leaving Lucius Censorinus in Greece, he crossed over into Asia, and there laid his hands on the stores of accumulated wealth, while kings waited at his door, and queens were rivalling one another, who should make him the greatest presents or appear most charming in his eyes. Thus, whilst Cæsar in Rome was wearing out his strength amidst seditions and wars, Antony, with nothing to do amidst the enjoyments of peace, let his passions carry him easily back to the old course of life that was familiar to him. A set of harpers and pipers, Anaxenor and Xuthus, the dancing-man Metrodorus, and a whole Bacchic rout of the like Asiatic exhibitors, far outdoing in license and buffoonery the pests that had followed out of Italy, came in and possessed the court; the thing was past patience, wealth of all kinds being wasted on objects like these. The whole of Asia was like the city in Sophocles,[6] loaded, at one time,

———with incense in the air,
Jubilant songs, and outcries of despair.

When he made his entry into Ephesus, the women

[5] Antony's reply, *Not very large but extremely ruinous*, is meant for a jest in the manner which the Greeks called a surprise,—rather a favorite piece of pleasantry with them. Antony begins in the tone of compliments, *The building certainly could not be called large, but it was exceedingly—beautiful*, he seemed to be going to say, and for this he substitutes *rotten* or *ruinous*. *The Senate* in the next sentence must, I think, be the Senate, or Council, of Delphi.

[6] *The City in Sophocles* is Thebes in the time of the pestilence, described at the beginning of the Œdipus Tyrannus.

met him dressed up like Bacchantes, and the men and
boys like Satyrs and Fauns, and throughout the town
nothing was to be seen but spears wreathed about with
ivy, harps, flutes, and psaltries, while Antony in their
songs was Bacchus the Giver of Joy and the Gentle.
And so indeed he was to some, but to far more the
Devourer and the Savage;[7] for he would deprive persons of worth and quality of their fortunes to gratify
villains and flatterers, who would sometimes beg the
estates of men yet living, pretending they were dead,
and, obtaining a grant, take possession. He gave his
cook the house of a Magnesian citizen, as a reward for
a single highly successful supper, and, at last, when
he was proceeding to lay a second whole tribute on
Asia, Hybreas, speaking on behalf of the cities, took
courage, and told him broadly, but aptly enough for
Antony's taste, "If you can take two yearly tributes,
you can doubtless give us a couple of summers and a
double harvest time;" and put it to him in the plainest
and boldest way, that Asia had raised two hundred
thousand talents for his service: "If this has not been
paid to you, ask your collectors for it; if it has, and is
all gone, we are ruined men." These words touched
Antony to the quick, who was simply ignorant of most
things that were done in his name; not that he was so
indolent, as he was prone to trust frankly in all about
him. For there was much simplicity in his character;
he was slow to see his faults, but, when he did see
them, was extremely repentant, and ready to ask pardon of those he had injured; prodigal in his acts of

---

[7] "*Charidotes* and *Meilichius* in their songs, but too often, in reality, *Omestes* and *Agrionius*." These are epithets applied in various forms of worship to the Greek Dionysius or Bacchus. It was to Bacchus Omestes, the Devourer, that the Greeks, in the battle of Salamis, offered the Persian princes. See the story in the lives of Themistocles and Aristides.

reparation, and severe in his punishments, but his generosity was much more extravagant than his severity; his raillery was sharp and insulting, but the edge of it was taken off by his readiness to submit to any kind of repartee; for he was as well contented to be rallied, as he was pleased to rally others. And this freedom of speech was, indeed, the cause of many of his disasters. He never imagined that those who used so much liberty in their mirth would flatter or deceive him in business of consequence, not knowing how common it is with parasites to mix their flattery with boldness, as confectioners do their sweetmeats with something biting, to prevent the sense of satiety. Their freedoms and impertinences at table were designed expressly to give to their obsequiousness in council the air of being not complaisance, but conviction.

Such being his temper, the last and crowning mischief that could befall him came in the love of Cleopatra, to awaken and kindle to fury passions that as yet lay still and dormant in his nature, and to stifle and finally corrupt any elements that yet made resistance in him, of goodness and a sound judgement. He fell into the snare thus. When making preparation for the Parthian war, he sent to command her to make her personal appearance in Cilicia, to answer an accusation, that she had given great assistance, in the late wars, to Cassius. Dellius, who was sent on this message, had no sooner seen her face, and remarked her adroitness and subtlety in speech, but he felt convinced that Antony would not so much as think of giving any molestation to a woman like this; on the contrary, she would be the first in favor with him. So he set himself at once to pay his court to the Egyptian, and gave her his advice, "to go," in the Homeric style,

ANTONY

to Cilicia, "in her best attire,"[8] and bade her fear nothing from Antony, the gentlest and kindest of soldiers. She had some faith in the words of Dellius, but more in her own attractions, which, having formerly recommended her to Cæsar and the young Cnæus Pompey, she did not doubt might prove yet more successful with Antony. Their acquaintance was with her when a girl, young, and ignorant of the world, but she was to meet Antony in the time of life when women's beauty is most splendid, and their intellects are in full maturity.[9] She made great preparation for her journey, of money, gifts, and ornaments of value, such as so wealthy a kingdom might afford, but she brought with her her surest hopes in her own magic arts and charms.

She received several letters, both from Antony and from his friends, to summon her, but she took no account of these orders; and at last, as if in mockery of them, she came sailing up the river Cydnus, in a barge with gilded stern and outspread sails of purple, while oars of silver beat time to the music of flutes and fifes and harps. She herself lay all along, under a canopy of cloth of gold, dressed as Venus in a picture, and beautiful young boys, like painted Cupids, stood on each side to fan her. Her maids were dressed like Sea Nymphs and Graces, some steering at the rudder, some working at the ropes. The perfumes diffused themselves from the vessel to the shore, which was covered with multitudes, part following the galley up

---

[8] "To go to Ida in her best attire" is the verse, in which Plutarch merely substitutes Cilicia for Ida. See the Iliad, Book XIV. 162, where Juno is described as setting forth to beguile Jupiter from his watch on Mount Ida, while Neptune shall check the Trojans.

[9] She was now about twenty-eight years old.

the river on either bank, part running out of the city to see the sight. The market-place was quite emptied, and Antony at last was left alone sitting upon the tribunal; while the word went through all the multitude, that Venus was come to feast with Bacchus, for the common good of Asia. On her arrival, Antony sent to invite her to supper. She thought it fitter he should come to her; so, willing to show his good-humor and courtesy, he complied, and went. He found the preparations to receive him magnificent beyond expression, but nothing so admirable as the great number of lights; for on a sudden there was let down altogether so great a number of branches with lights in them so ingeniously disposed, some in squares, and some in circles, that the whole thing was a spectacle that has seldom been equalled for beauty.

The next day, Antony invited her to supper, and was very desirous to outdo her as well in magnificence as contrivance; but he found he was altogether beaten in both, and was so well convinced of it, that he was himself the first to jest and mock at his poverty of wit, and his rustic awkwardness. She, perceiving that his raillery was broad and gross, and savored more of the soldier than the courtier, rejoined in the same taste, and fell into it at once, without any sort of reluctance or reserve. For her actual beauty, it is said, was not in itself so remarkable that none could be compared with her, or that no one could see her without being struck by it, but the contact of her presence, if you lived with her, was irresistible; the attraction of her person, joining with the charm of her conversation, and the character that attended all she said or did, was something bewitching. It was a pleasure merely to hear the sound of her voice, with which, like an instrument of many strings, she could pass from one language to another; so that there were few of the barbarian nations that she answered by an interpreter; to most of them she spoke herself, as to the Æthiopians, Troglodytes, Hebrews, Arabians, Syrians, Medes, Parthians, and many others, whose language she had learnt; which was all the more surprising, because most of the kings her predecessors scarcely gave themselves the trouble to acquire the Egyptian tongue, and several of them quite abandoned the Macedonian.

Antony was so captivated by her, that, while Fulvia his wife maintained his quarrels in Rome against Cæsar by actual force of arms, and the Parthian troops, commanded by Labienus (the king's generals having made him commander-in-chief), were assembled in Mesopotamia, and ready to enter Syria, he could yet suffer himself to be carried away by her to Alexandria, there to keep holiday, like a boy, in play and diversion, squandering and fooling away in enjoyments that most costly, as Antiphon says, of all valuables, time. They had a sort of company, to which they gave a particular name, calling it that of the Inimitable Livers. The members entertained one another daily in turn, with an extravagance of expenditure beyond measure or belief. Philotas, a physician of Amphissa, who was at that time a student of medicine in Alexandria, used to tell my grandfather Lamprias, that, having some acquaintance with one of the royal cooks, he was invited by him, being a young man, to come and see the sumptuous preparations for supper. So he was taken into the kitchen, where he admired the prodigious variety of all things; but particularly, seeing eight wild boars roasting whole, says he, "Surely you have a great number of guests." The cook laughed at his simplicity, and told him there were not above twelve to sup, but that every dish was to be served up just roasted to a turn, and if any thing was but one minute ill-timed, it was spoiled; "And," said he, "maybe Antony will sup just now, maybe not this hour, maybe he will call for wine, or begin to talk, and will put it off. So that," he continued, "it is not one, but many suppers must be had in readiness, as it is impossible to guess at his hour." This was Philotas's story; who related besides, that he afterwards came to be one of the medical attendants of Antony's eldest son by Fulvia, and used to be invited pretty often, among other companions, to his table, when he was not supping with his father. One day another physician had talked loudly, and given great disturbance to the company, whose mouth Philotas stopped with this sophistical syllogism: "In some states of fever the patient should take cold water; every one who has a fever is in some state of fever; therefore in a fever cold water should always be taken." The man was quite struck dumb, and Antony's son, very much pleased, laughed aloud, and said, "Philotas, I make you a present of all you see there," pointing to a sideboard covered with plate. Philotas thanked him much, but was far enough from ever imagining that a boy of his age could dispose of things of that value. Soon after, however, the plate was all brought to him, and he was desired to set his mark upon it; and when he put it away from him, and was afraid to accept the present, "What ails the man?" said he that brought it; "do you know that he who gives you this is Antony's son, who is free to give it, if it were all gold? but if you will be advised by me, I would counsel you to accept of the value in money from us; for there may be amongst the rest some antique or famous piece of workmanship, which Antony would be sorry to part with." These anecdotes my grandfather told us Philotas used frequently to relate.

ANTONY 193

To return to Cleopatra; Plato admits four sorts of flattery,[10] but she had a thousand. Were Antony serious or disposed to mirth, she had at any moment some new delight or charm to meet his wishes; at every turn she was upon him, and let him escape her neither by day nor by night. She played at dice with him, drank with him, hunted with him; and when he exercised in arms, she was there to see. At night she would go rambling with him to disturb and torment people at their doors and windows, dressed like a servant-woman, for Antony also went in servant's disguise, and from these expeditions he often came home very scurvily answered, and sometimes even beaten severely, though most people guessed who it was. However, the Alexandrians in general liked it all well enough, and joined good humoredly and kindly in his frolic and play, saying they were much obliged to Antony for acting his tragic parts at Rome, and keeping his comedy for them. It would be trifling without end to be particular in his follies, but his fishing must not be forgotten. He went out one day to angle with Cleopatra, and, being so unfortunate as to catch nothing in the presence of his mistress, he gave secret orders to the fishermen to dive under water, and put fishes that had been already taken upon his hooks; and these he drew so fast that the Egyptian perceived

---

[10] See the Gorgias, chapter 19. The four Flatteries are the four Counterfeit Arts, which profess to do good to men's bodies and souls, and in reality only gratify their pleasures. The legislator's place is thus usurped by the sophist, the false reasoner, in deliberative assemblies; that of the judge by the rhetorician or pleader; the medical adviser is supplanted by the purveyor of luxuries; and the gymnastic teacher by the adorner of the person. The four genuine Arts are *nomothetike, dicanike, iatrike,* and *gumnastike;* the four corresponding Flatteries are *sophistike, rhetorike, opsopoiike,* and *kommotike.*

it. But, feigning great admiration, she told everybody how dexterous Antony was, and invited them next day to come and see him again. So, when a number of them had come on board the fishing boats, as soon as he had let down his hook, one of her servants was beforehand with his divers, and fixed upon his hook a salted fish from Pontus. Antony, feeling his line give, drew up the prey, and when, as may be imagined, great laughter ensued, "Leave," said Cleopatra, "the fishing-rod, general, to us poor sovereigns of Pharos and Canopus; your game is cities, provinces, and kingdoms."

Whilst he was thus diverting himself and engaged in this boys' play, two despatches arrived; one from Rome, that his brother Lucius and his wife Fulvia, after many quarrels among themselves, had joined in war against Cæsar, and, having lost all, had fled out of Italy; the other bringing little better news, that Labienus, at the head of the Parthians, was overrunning Asia, from Euphrates and Syria as far as Lydia and Ionia. So, scarcely at last rousing himself from sleep, and shaking off the fumes of wine, he set out to attack the Parthians, and went as far as Phœnicia; but, upon the receipt of lamentable letters from Fulvia, turned his course with two hundred ships to Italy. And, in his way, receiving such of his friends as fled from Italy, he was given to understand that Fulvia was the sole cause of the war, a woman of a restless spirit and very bold, and withal her hopes were that commotions in Italy would force Antony from Cleopatra. But it happened that Fulvia, as she was coming to meet her husband, fell sick by the way, and died at Sicyon, so that an accommodation was the more easily made. For when he reached Italy, and Cæsar showed no intention of laying any thing to his charge, and he on his part shifted the blame of every thing on

Fulvia, those that were friends to them would not suffer that the time should be spent in looking narrowly into the plea, but made a reconciliation first, and then a partition of the empire between them, taking as their boundary the Ionian Sea, the eastern provinces falling to Antony, to Cæsar the western, and Africa being left to Lepidus. And an agreement was made, that every one in their turn, as they thought fit, should make their friends consuls, when they did not choose to take the offices themselves.

These terms were well approved of, but yet it was thought some closer tie would be desirable; and for this, fortune offered occasion. Cæsar had an elder sister, not of the whole blood, for Attia was his mother's name, hers Ancharia. This sister, Octavia, he was extremely attached to, as, indeed, she was, it is said, quite a wonder of a woman. Her husband, Caius Marcellus, had died not long before, and Antony was now a widower by the death of Fulvia; for, though he did not disavow the passion he had for Cleopatra, yet he disowned any thing of marriage, reason, as yet, upon this point, still maintaining the debate against the charms of the Egyptian. Everybody concurred in promoting this new alliance, fully expecting that with the beauty, honor, and prudence of Octavia, when her company should, as it was certain it would, have engaged his affections, all would be kept in the safe and happy course of friendship. So, both parties being agreed, they went to Rome to celebrate the nuptials, the senate dispensing with the law by which a widow was not permitted to marry till ten months after the death of her husband.

Sextus Pompeius was in possession of Sicily, and with his ships, under the command of Menas, the pirate, and Menecrates, so infested the Italian coast, that no vessels durst venture into those seas. Sextus had behaved with much humanity towards Antony, having received his mother when she fled with Fulvia, and it was therefore judged fit that he also should be received into the peace. They met near the promontory of Misenum, by the mole of the port, Pompey having his fleet at anchor close by, and Antony and Cæsar their troops drawn up all along the shore. There it was concluded that Sextus should quietly enjoy the government of Sicily and Sardinia, he conditioning to scour the seas of all pirates, and to send so much corn every year to Rome.

This agreed on, they invited one another to supper, and by lot it fell to Pompey's turn to give the first entertainment, and Antony, asking where it was to be, "There," said he, pointing to the admiral-galley, a ship of six banks of oars, "that is the only house that Pompey is heir to of his father's."[11] And this he said, reflecting upon Antony, who was then in possession of his father's house. Having fixed the ship on her anchors, and formed a bridgeway from the promontory to conduct on board of her, he gave them a cordial welcome. And when they began to grow warm, and jests were passing freely on Antony and Cleopatra's loves, Menas, the pirate, whispered Pompey in the ear, "Shall I," said he, "cut the cables, and make you master not of Sicily only and Sardinia, but of the whole Roman empire?" Pompey, having considered a little while, returned him answer, "Menas, this might have been done without acquainting me; now we must rest content; I do not break my word." And so, having been entertained by the other two in their turns, he set sail for Sicily.

---

[11] "In Carinis," according to Dion Cassius, was the answer. "In the Carinæ," which might mean either the ships, or the quarter called the Carinæ, at Rome, in which stood his father's house.

After the treaty was completed, Antony despatched Ventidius into Asia, to check the advance of the Parthians, while he, as a compliment to Cæsar, accepted the office of priest to the deceased Cæsar. And in any state affair and matter of consequence, they both behaved themselves with much consideration and friendliness for each other. But it annoyed Antony, that in all their amusements, on any trial of skill or fortune, Cæsar should be constantly victorious. He had with him an Egyptian diviner, one of those who calculate nativities, who, either to make his court to Cleopatra, or that by the rules of his art he found it to be so, openly declared to him, that though the fortune that attended him was bright and glorious, yet it was overshadowed by Cæsar's; and advised him to keep himself as far distant as he could from that young man; "for your Genius," said he, "dreads his; when absent from him yours is proud and brave, but in his presence unmanly and dejected;" and incidents that occurred appeared to show that the Egyptian spoke truth. For whenever they cast lots for any playful purpose, or threw dice, Antony was still the loser; and repeatedly, when they fought game-cocks or quails, Cæsar's had the victory. This gave Antony a secret displeasure, and made him put the more confidence in the skill of his Egyptian. So, leaving the management of his home affairs to Cæsar, he left Italy, and took Octavia, who had lately borne him a daughter, along with him into Greece.

Here, whilst he wintered in Athens, he received the first news of Ventidius's successes over the Parthians, of his having defeated them in a battle, having slain Labienus and Pharnapates, the best general their king, Hyrodes, possessed. For the celebrating of which he made a public feast through Greece, and for the prizes which were contested at Athens he himself acted as steward, and, leaving at home the ensigns that are carried before the general, he made his public appearance in a gown and white shoes, with the steward's wands marching before; and he performed his duty in taking the combatants by the neck, to part them, when they had fought enough.

When the time came for him to set out for the war, he took a garland from the sacred olive, and, in obedience to some oracle, he filled a vessel with the water of the Clepsydra,[12] to carry along with him. In this interval, Pacorus, the Parthian king's son, who was marching into Syria with a large army, was met by Ventidius, who gave him battle in the country of Cyrrhestica, slew a large number of his men, and Pacorus among the first. This victory was one of the most renowned achievements of the Romans, and fully avenged their defeats under Crassus, the Parthians being obliged, after the loss of three battles successively, to keep themselves within the bounds of Media and Mesopotamia. Ventidius was not willing to push his good fortune further, for fear of raising some jealousy in Antony, but, turning his arms against those that had quitted the Roman interest, he reduced them to their former obedience. Among the rest, he besieged Antiochus, king of Commagene, in the city of Samosata, who made an offer of a thousand talents for his pardon, and a promise of submission to Antony's commands. But Ventidius told him that he must send to Antony, who was already on his march, and had sent word to Ventidius to make no terms with Antiochus, wishing that at any rate this one exploit might be ascribed to him, and that people might not

[12] The Clepsydra was a sacred spring, still to be found, inclosed in a chapel in the rock, on the north side of the Acropolis, near the cave of Apollo and Pan.

think that all his successes were won by his lieutenants. The siege, however, was long protracted; for when those within found their offers refused, they defended themselves stoutly, till, at last, Antony, finding he was doing nothing, in shame and regret for having refused the first offer, was glad to make an accommodation with Antiochus for three hundred talents. And, having given some orders for the affairs of Syria, he returned to Athens; and, paying Ventidius the honors he well deserved, dismissed him to receive his triumph. He is the only man that has ever yet triumphed for victories obtained over the Parthians; he was of obscure birth, but, by means of Antony's friendship, obtained an opportunity of showing his capacity, and doing great things; and his making such glorious use of it gave new credit to the current observation about Cæsar and Antony, that they were more fortunate in what they did by their lieutenants than in their own persons. For Sossius, also, had great success, and Canidius, whom he left in Armenia, defeated the people there, and also the kings of the Albanians and Iberians, and marched victorious as far as Caucasus, by which means the fame of Antony's arms had become great among the barbarous nations.

He, however, once more, upon some unfavorable stories, taking offence against Cæsar, set sail with three hundred ships for Italy, and, being refused admittance to the port of Brundusium, made for Tarentum. There his wife Octavia, who came from Greece with him, obtained leave to visit her brother, she being then great with child, having already borne her husband a second daughter; and as she was on her way, she met Cæsar, with his two friends Agrippa and Mæcenas, and, taking these two aside, with great entreaties and lamentations she told them, that of the most fortunate woman upon earth, she was in danger of becoming the most unhappy; for as yet every one's eyes were fixed upon her as the wife and sister of the two great commanders, but, if rash counsels should prevail, and war ensue, "I shall be miserable," said she, "without redress; for on what side soever victory falls, I shall be sure to be a loser." Cæsar was overcome by these entreaties, and advanced in a peaceable temper to Tarentum, where those that were present beheld a most stately spectacle; a vast army drawn up by the shore, and as great a fleet in the harbor, all without the occurrence of any act of hostility; nothing but the salutations of friends, and other expressions of joy and kindness, passing from one armament to the other. Antony first entertained Cæsar, this also being a concession on Cæsar's part to his sister; and when at length an agreement was made between them, that Cæsar should give Antony two of his legions to serve him in the Parthian war, and that Antony should in return leave with him a hundred armed galleys. Octavia further obtained of her husband, besides this, twenty light ships for her brother, and of her brother, a thousand foot for her husband. So, having parted good friends, Cæsar went immediately to make war with Pompey to conquer Sicily. And Antony, leaving in Cæsar's charge his wife and children, and his children by his former wife Fulvia, set sail for Asia.

But the mischief that thus long had lain still,[13] the passion for Cleopatra, which better thoughts had

---

[13] The soul of man has in it a driver and two horses, the one strong and willing, quick to obey, and eager for applause and for honorable praise; the other unruly and ill-conditioned, greedy and violent, whom only flogging and the goad can control. Do what the driver within us will, our better horse may be seduced at times from his duty, his evil yoke-fellow may obtain the mastery, and bear away all to destruction.

seemed to have lulled and charmed into oblivion, upon his approach to Syria, gathered strength again, and broke out into a flame. And, in fine, like Plato's restive and rebellious horse of the human soul,[14] flinging off all good and wholesome counsel, and breaking fairly loose, he sends Fonteius Capito to bring Cleopatra into Syria. To whom at her arrival he made no small or trifling present, Phœnicia, Cœle-Syria, Cyprus, great part of Cilicia, that side of Judæa which produces balm, that part of Arabia where the Nabathæans extend to the outer sea; profuse gifts, which much displeased the Romans. For, although he had invested several private persons in great governments and kingdoms, and bereaved many kings of theirs, as Antigonus of Judæa, whose head he caused to be struck off (the first example of that punishment being inflicted on a king), yet nothing stung the Romans like the shame of these honors paid to Cleopatra. Their dissatisfaction was augmented also by his acknowledging as his own the twin children he had by her, giving them the name of Alexandra and Cleopatra, and adding, as their surnames, the titles of Sun and Moon. But he, who knew how to put a good color on the most dishonest action, would say, that the greatness of the Roman empire consisted more in giving than in taking kingdoms, and that the way to carry noble blood through the world was by begetting in every place a new line and series of kings; his own ancestor had thus been born of Hercules; Hercules had not limited his hopes of progeny to a single womb, nor feared any law like Solon's, or any

---

[14] *The mischief that thus long had lain still* or *slept* has a metrical run in the Greek, and sounds like a tragic fragment. Plato's *restive and rebellious horse* is depicted in the Phædrus about the middle of the dialogue.

audit of procreation, but had freely let nature take her will in the foundation and first commencement of many families.[15]

After Phraates had killed his father Hyrodes, and taken possession of his kingdom, many of the Parthians left their country; among the rest, Monæses, a man of great distinction and authority, sought refuge with Antony, who, looking on his case as similar to that of Themistocles, and likening his own opulence and magnanimity to those of the former Persian kings, gave him three cities, Larissa, Arethusa, and Hierapolis, which was formerly called Bambyce. But when the king of Parthia soon recalled him, giving him his word and honor for his safety, Antony was not unwilling to give him leave to return, hoping thereby to surprise Phraates, who would believe that peace would continue; for he only made the demand of him, that he should send back the Roman ensigns which were taken when Crassus was slain, and the prisoners that remained yet alive. This done, he sent Cleopatra into Egypt, and marched through Arabia and Armenia; and, when his forces came together and were joined by those of his confederate kings (of whom there were very many, and the most consider-

---

[15] It may add interest to the details of Antony's Parthian campaign as related in the following pages to know that they are very likely taken from the narrative of an eye-witness. Strabo (XI. p. 523) tells us, that a history of the campaign was drawn up by Antony's friend and officer, Dellius, who served in it himself, and Plutarch, a little further on, speaks of Dellius as the historical writer, so that it is certain that he knew of his history. This is apparently the same Dellius who, as told before, was sent to summon Cleopatra to appear before Antony, and gave her the advice to go to Cilicia in her best attire. He deserted Antony before the battle of Actium, and he is generally identified with the *moriture Delli*, addressed in the third ode of the second book by Horace as a rich man living at his ease.

able, Artavasdes, king of Armenia, who came at the head of six thousand horse and seven thousand foot), he made a general muster. There appeared sixty thousand Roman foot, ten thousand horse, Spaniards and Gauls, who counted as Romans; and, of other nations, horse and foot, thirty thousand. And these great preparations, that put the Indians beyond Bactria into alarm, and made all Asia shake, were all, we are told, rendered useless to him because of Cleopatra. For, in order to pass the winter with her, the war was pushed on before its due time; and all he did was done without perfect consideration, as by a man who had no proper control over his faculties, who, under the effects of some drug or magic, was still looking back elsewhere, and whose object was much more to hasten his return than to conquer his enemies.

For, first of all, when he should have taken up his winter-quarters in Armenia, to refresh his men, who were tired with long marches, having come at least eight thousand furlongs, and then have taken the advantage in the beginning of the spring to invade Media, before the Parthians were out of winter-quarters, he had not patience to expect his time, but marched into the province of Atropatene, leaving Armenia on the left hand, and laid waste all that country. Secondly, his haste was so great, that he left behind the engines absolutely required for any siege, which followed the camp in three hundred wagons, and, among the rest, a ram eighty feet long; none of which was it possible, if lost or damaged, to repair or to make the like, as the provinces of the upper Asia produce no trees long or hard enough for such uses. Nevertheless, he left them all behind, as a mere impediment to his speed, in the charge of a detachment under the command of Statianus, the wagon-officer. He himself laid siege to Phraata, a principal city of the king of Media, wherein were that king's wife and children. And when actual need proved the greatness of his error in leaving the siege train behind him, he had nothing for it but to come up and raise a mound against the walls, with infinite labor and great loss of time. Meantime Phraates, coming down with a large army, and hearing that the wagons were left behind with the battering engines, sent a strong party of horse, by which Statianus was surprised, he himself and ten thousand of his men slain, the engines all broken in pieces, many taken prisoners, and, among the rest, king Polemon.

This great miscarriage in the opening of the campaign much discouraged Antony's army, and Artavasdes, king of Armenia, deciding that the Roman prospects were bad, withdrew with all his forces from the camp, although he had been the chief promoter of the war. The Parthians, encouraged by their success, came up to the Romans at the siege, and gave them many affronts; upon which Antony, fearing that the despondency and alarm of his soldiers would only grow worse if he let them lie idle, taking all the horse, ten legions, and three prætorian cohorts of heavy infantry, resolved to go out and forage, designing by this means to draw the enemy with more advantage to a battle. To effect this, he marched a day's journey from his camp, and, finding the Parthians hovering about, in readiness to attack him while he was in motion, he gave orders for the signal of battle to be hung out in the encampment, but, at the same time, pulled down the tents, as if he meant not to fight, but to lead his men home again; and so he proceeded to lead them past the enemy, who were drawn up in a half-moon, his orders being that the horse should charge as soon as the legions were come up near enough to second them. The Parthians, standing still

while the Romans marched by them, were in great
admiration of their army, and of the exact discipline
it observed, rank after rank passing on at equal distances in perfect order and silence, their pikes all
ready in their hands. But when the signal was given,
and the horse turned short upon the Parthians, and
with loud cries charged them, they bravely received
them, though they were at once too near for bowshot;
but the legions, coming up with loud shouts and rat-
tling of their arms, so frightened their horses and indeed the men themselves, that they kept their ground
no longer. Antony pressed them hard, in great hopes
that this victory should put an end to the war; the foot
had them in pursuit for fifty furlongs, and the horse
for thrice that distance, and yet the advantage sum-
med up, they had but thirty prisoners, and there were
but fourscore slain. So that they were all filled with
dejection and discouragement, to consider, that when
they were victorious, their advantage was so small, and
that when they were beaten, they lost so great a number of men as they had done when the carriages were
taken.

The next day, having put the baggage in order,
they marched back to the camp before Phraata, in
the way meeting with some scattering troops of the
enemy, and, as they marched further, with greater
parties, at length with the body of the enemy's army,
fresh and in good order, who defied them to battle,
and charged them on every side, and it was not without great difficulty that they reached the camp. There
Antony, finding that his men had in a panic deserted
the defence of the mound, upon a sally of the Medes,
resolved to proceed against them by decimation, as it
is called, which is done by dividing the soldiers into
tens, and, out of every ten, putting one to death, as it

happens by lot. The rest he gave orders should have, instead of wheat, their rations of corn in barley.

The war was now become grievous to both parties, and the prospect of its continuance yet more fearful to Antony, in respect that he was threatened with famine; for he could no longer forage without wounds and slaughter. And Phraates, on the other side, was full of apprehension that, if the Romans were to persist in carrying on the siege, the autumnal equinox being past and the air already closing in for cold, he should be deserted by his soldiers, who would suffer any thing rather than wintering in open field. To prevent which, he had recourse to the following deceit: he gave order to those of his men who had made most acquaintance among the Roman soldiers, not to pursue too close when they met them foraging, but to suffer them to carry off some provision; moreover, that they should praise their valor, and declare that it was not without reason that their king looked upon the Romans as the bravest men in the world. This done, upon further opportunity they rode nearer in, and, drawing up their horses by the men, began to revile Antony for his obstinacy; that whereas Phraates desired nothing more than peace, and an occasion to show how ready he was to save the lives of so many brave soldiers, he, on the contrary, gave no opening to any friendly offers, but sat awaiting the arrival of the two fiercest and worst enemies, winter and famine, from whom it would be hard for them to make their escape, even with all the good-will of the Parthians to help them. Antony, having these reports from many hands, began to indulge the hope; nevertheless, he would not send any message to the Parthian till he had put the question to these friendly talkers, whether what they said was said by order of their king. Receiving answer that it was, together with new encouragement to believe them, he sent some of his friends to demand once more the standards and prisoners, lest, if he should ask nothing, he might be supposed to be too thankful to have leave to retreat in quiet. The Parthian king made answer, that as for the standards and prisoners, he need not trouble himself; but if he thought fit to retreat, he might do it when he pleased, in peace and safety. Some few days, therefore, being spent in collecting the baggage, he set out upon his march. Upon which occasion, though there was no man of his time like him for addressing a multitude, or for carrying soldiers with him by the force of words, out of shame and sadness he could not find in his heart to speak himself, but employed Domitius Ænobarbus. And some of the soldiers resented it, as an undervaluing of them; but the greater number saw the true cause, and pitied it, and thought it rather a reason why they on their side should treat their general with more respect and obedience than ordinary.

Antony had resolved to return by the same way he came, which was through a level country clear of all trees; but a certain Mardian came to him (one that was very conversant with the manners of the Parthians, and whose fidelity to the Romans had been tried at the battle where the machines were lost), and advised him to keep the mountains close on his right hand, and not to expose his men, heavily armed, in a broad, open, riding country, to the attacks of a numerous army of light-horse and archers; that Phraates with fair promises had persuaded him from the siege on purpose that he might with more ease cut him off in his retreat; but, if so he pleased, he would conduct him by a nearer route, on which moreover he should find the necessaries for his army in greater abundance. Antony upon this began to consider what was best to be done; he was unwilling to seem to have any mistrust of the Parthians after their treaty; but holding it to be really best to march his army the shorter and more inhabited way, he demanded of the Mardian some assurance of his faith, who offered himself to be bound until the army came safe into Armenia. Two days he conducted the army bound, and, on the third, when Antony had given up all thought of the enemy, and was marching at his ease in no very good order, the Mardian, perceiving the bank of a river broken down, and the water let out and overflowing the road by which they were to pass, saw at once that this was the handiwork of the Parthians, done out of mischief, and to hinder their march; so he advised Antony to be upon his guard, for that the enemy was nigh at hand. And no sooner had he begun to put his men in order, disposing the slingers and dart-men in convenient intervals for sallying out, but the Parthians came pouring in on all sides, fully expecting to encompass them, and throw the whole army into disorder. They were at once attacked by the light troops, whom they galled a good deal with their arrows; but, being themselves as warmly entertained with the slings and darts, and many wounded, they made their retreat. Soon after, rallying up afresh, they were beat back by a battalion of Gallic horse, and appeared no more that day.

By their manner of attack Antony seeing what to do, not only placed the slings and darts as a rear guard, but also lined both flanks with them, and so marched in a square battle, giving order to the horse to charge and beat off the enemy, but not to follow them far as they retired. So that the Parthians, not doing more mischief for the four ensuing days than they received, began to abate in their zeal, and, complaining that the winter season was much advanced, pressed for returning home.

But, on the fifth day, Flavius Gallus, a brave and active officer, who had a considerable command in the army, came to Antony, desiring of him some light-infantry out of the rear, and some horse out of the front, with which he would undertake to do some considerable service. Which when he had obtained, he beat the enemy back, not withdrawing, as was usual, at the same time, and retreating upon the mass of the heavy infantry, but maintaining his own ground, and engaging boldly. The officers who commanded in the rear, perceiving how far he was getting from the body of the army, sent to warn him back, but he took no notice of them. It is said that Titius the quæstor snatched the standards and turned them round, upbraiding Gallus with thus leading so many brave men to destruction. But when he on the other side reviled him again, and commanded the men that were about him to stand firm, Titius made his retreat, and Gallus, charging the enemies in the front, was encompassed by a party that fell upon his rear, which at length perceiving, he sent a messenger to demand succor. But the commanders of the heavy infantry, Canidius amongst others, a particular favorite of Antony's seem here to have committed a great oversight. For, instead of facing about with the whole body, they sent small parties, and, when they were defeated, they still sent out small parties, so that by their bad management the rout would have spread through the whole army, if Antony himself had not marched from the van at the head of the third legion, and, passing this through among the fugitives, faced the enemies, and hindered them from any further pursuit.

In this engagement were killed three thousand, five thousand were carried back to the camp wounded, amongst the rest Gallus, shot through the body with four arrows, of which wounds he died. Antony went from tent to tent to visit and comfort the rest of them, and was not able to see his men without tears and a passion of grief. They, however, seized his hand with joyful faces, bidding him go and see to himself and not be concerned about them, calling him their emperor and their general, and saying that if he did well they were safe. For in short, never in all these times can history make mention of a general at the head of a more splendid army; whether you consider strength and youth, or patience and sufferance in labors and fatigues; but as for the obedience and affectionate respect they bore their general, and the unanimous feeling amongst small and great alike, officers and common soldiers, to prefer his good opinion of them to their very lives and being, in this part of military excellence it was not possible that they could have been surpassed by the very Romans of old. For this devotion, as I have said before, there were many reasons, as the nobility of his family, his eloquence, his frank and open manners, his liberal and magnificent habits, his familiarity in talking with everybody, and, at this time particularly, his kindness in assisting and pitying the sick, joining in all their pains, and furnishing them with all things necessary, so that the sick and wounded were even more eager to serve than those that were whole and strong.

Nevertheless, this last victory had so encouraged the enemy, that, instead of their former impatience were even more eager to serve than those that were the Romans, staying all night near the camp, in expectation of plundering their tents and baggage, which they concluded they must abandon; and in the morning new forces arrived in large masses, so that their number was grown to be not less, it is said, than forty thousand horse; and the king had sent the very guards that attended upon his own person, as to a sure and unquestioned victory. For he himself was never present in any fight. Antony, designing to harangue the soldiers, called for a mourning habit, that he might move them the more, but was dissuaded by his friends; so he came forward in the general's scarlet cloak, and addressed them, praising those that had gained the victory, and reproaching those that had fled, the former answering him with promises of success, and the latter excusing themselves, and telling him they were ready to undergo decimation, or any other punishment he should please to inflict upon them, only entreating that he would forget and not discompose himself with their faults. At which he lifted up his hands to heaven, and prayed the gods, that if to balance the great favors he had received of them any judgment lay in store, they would pour it upon his head alone, and grant his soldiers victory.

The next day they took better order for their march, and the Parthians, who thought they were marching rather to plunder than to fight, were much taken aback, when they came up and were received with a shower of missiles, to find the enemy not disheartened, but fresh and resolute. So that they themselves began to lose courage. But at the descent of a hill where the Romans were obliged to pass, they got together, and let fly their arrows upon them as they moved slowly down. But the full-armed infantry, facing round, received the light troops within; and those in the first rank knelt on one knee, holding their shields before them, the next rank holding theirs over the first, and so again others over these, much like the tiling of a house, or the rows of seats in a theatre, the whole affording sure defence against arrows, which glance upon them without doing any harm. The Parthians, seeing the Romans down upon their knees, could not imagine but that it must proceed from weariness; so that they laid down their bows, and, taking their spears, made a fierce onset, when the Romans, with a great cry, leapt upon their feet, striking hand to hand with their javelins, slew the foremost, and put the rest to flight. After this rate it was every day, and the trouble they gave made the marches short; in addition to which famine began to be felt in the camp, for they could get but little corn, and that which they got they were forced to fight for; and, besides this, they were in want of implements to grind it and make bread. For they left almost all behind, the baggage horses being dead or otherwise employed in carrying the sick and wounded. Provision was so scarce in the army that an Attic quart of wheat sold for fifty drachmas, and barley loaves for their weight in silver. And when they tried vegetables and roots, they found such as are commonly eaten very scarce, so that they were constrained to venture upon any they could get, and, among others, they chanced upon an herb that was mortal, first taking away all sense and understanding. He that had eaten of it remembered nothing in the world, and employed himself only in moving great stones from one place to another, which he did with as much earnestness and industry as if it had been a business of the greatest consequence. Through all the camp there was nothing to be seen but men grubbing upon the ground at stones, which they carried from place to place. But in the end they threw up bile and died, as wine, moreover, which was the one antidote, failed. When Antony saw them die so fast, and the Parthian still in pursuit, he was heard to exclaim several times over, "O, the Ten Thousand!" as if in admiration of the retreat of the Greeks with Xenophon, who, when they had a longer journey to make from Babylonia, and a more powerful enemy to deal with, nevertheless came home safe.

The Parthians, finding that they could not divide the Roman army, nor break the order of their battle, and that withal they had been so often worsted, once more began to treat the foragers with professions of humanity; they came up to them with their bows unbended, telling them that they were going home to their houses; that this was the end of their retaliation, and that only some Median troops would follow for two or three days, not with any design to annoy them, but for the defence of some of the villages further on. And, saying this, they saluted them and embraced them with a great show of friendship. This made the Romans full of confidence again, and Antony, on hearing of it, was more disposed to take the road through the level country, being told that no water was to be hoped for on that through the mountains. But while he was preparing thus to do, Mithridates came into the camp, a cousin to Monæses, of whom we related that he sought refuge with the Romans, and received in gift from Antony the three cities. Upon his arrival, he desired somebody might be brought to him that could speak Syriac or Parthian. One Alexander, of Antioch, a friend of Antony's, was brought to him, to whom the stranger, giving his name, and mentioning Monæses as the person who desired to do the kindness, put the question, did he see that high range of hills, pointing at some distance. He told him, yes. "It is there," said he, " the whole Parthian army lie in wait for your passage; for the great plains come immediately up to them, and they expect that, confiding in their promises, you will leave the way of the mountains, and take the level route. It is true that in passing over the mountains you will suffer the want of water, and the fatigue to which you have become familiar, but if you pass through the plains, Antony must expect the fortune of Crassus."

This said, he departed. Antony, in alarm, calling his friends in council, sent for the Mardian guide, who was of the same opinion. He told them that, with or without enemies, the want of any certain track in the plain, and the likelihood of their losing their way, were quite objection enough; the other route was rough and without water, but then it was but for a day. Antony, therefore, changing his mind, marched away upon this road that night, commanding that every one should carry water sufficient for his own use; but most of them being unprovided with vessels, they made shift with their helmets, and some with skins. As soon as they started, the news of it was carried to the Parthians, who followed them, contrary to their custom, through the night, and at sunrise attacked the rear, which was tired with marching and want of sleep, and not in condition to make any considerable defence. For they had got through two hundred and forty furlongs that night, and at the end of such a march to find the enemy at their heels, put them out of heart. Besides, having to fight for every step of the way increased their distress from thirst. Those that were in the van came up to a river, the water of which was extremely cool and clear, but brackish and medicinal, and, on being drunk, produced immediate pains in the bowels and a renewed thirst. Of this the Mardian had forewarned them, but they could not forbear, and, beating back those that opposed them, they drank of it. Antony ran from one place to another, begging they would have a little patience, that not far off there was a river of wholesome water, and that the rest of the way was so difficult for the horse, that the enemy could pursue them no further; and, saying this, he ordered to sound a retreat to call those back that were engaged, and commanded the tents should be set up, that the soldiers might at any rate refresh themselves in the shade.

But the tents were scarce well put up, and the Parthians beginning, according to their custom, to withdraw, when Mithridates came again to them, and informed Alexander, with whom he had before spoken, that he would do well to advise Antony to stay where he was no longer than needs he must, that, after having refreshed his troops, he should endeavor with all diligence to gain the next river, that the Parthians would not cross it, but so far they were resolved to follow them. Alexander made his report to Antony, who ordered a quantity of gold plate to be carried to Mithridates, who, taking as much as he could well hide under his clothes, went his way. And, upon this advice, Antony, while it was yet day, broke up his camp, and the whole army marched forward without receiving any molestation from the Parthians, though that night by their own doing was in effect the most wretched and terrible that they passed. For some of the men began to kill and plunder those whom they suspected to have any money, ransacked the baggage, and seized the money there. In the end, they laid hands on Antony's own equipage, and broke all his rich tables and cups, dividing the fragments amongst them. Antony, hearing such a noise and such a stirring to and fro all through the army, the belief prevailing that the enemy had routed and cut off a portion of the troops, called for one of his freedmen, then serving as one of his guards, Rhamnus by name, and made him take an oath that, whenever he should give him orders, he would run his sword through his body and cut off his head, that he might not fall alive into the hands of the Parthians, nor, when dead, be recognized as the general. While he was in this consternation, and all his friends about him in tears, the Mardian came up, and gave them all new life. He convinced them, by the coolness and humidity of the air, which they could feel in breathing it, that the river which he had spoken of was now not far off, and the calculation of the time that had been required to reach it came, he said, to the same result, for the night was almost spent. And, at the same time, others came with information that all the confusion in the camp proceeded only from their own violence and robbery among themselves. To compose this tumult, and bring them again into some order after their distraction, he commanded the signal to be given for a halt.

Day began to break, and quiet and regularity were just reappearing, when the Parthian arrows began to fly among the rear, and the light armed troops were ordered out to battle. And, being seconded by the heavy infantry, who covered one another as before described with their shields, they bravely received the enemy, who did not think convenient to advance any further, while the van of the army, marching forward leisurely in this manner came in sight of the river, and Antony, drawing up the cavalry on the banks to confront the enemy, first passed over the sick and wounded. And, by this time, even those who were engaged with the enemy had opportunity to drink at their ease; for the Parthians, on seeing the river, unbent their bows, and told the Romans they might pass over freely, and made them great compliments in praise of their valor. Having crossed without molestation, they rested themselves awhile, and presently went forward, not giving perfect credit to the fair words of their enemies. Six days after this last battle, they arrived at the river Araxes, which divides Media and Armenia, and seemed, both by its deepness and the violence of the current, to be very dangerous to pass. A report, also, had crept in amongst them, that the enemy was in ambush, ready to set upon them as soon as they should be occupied with their passage. But when they were got over on the other side, and found themselves in Armenia, just as if land was now sighted after a storm at sea, they kissed the ground for joy, shedding tears and embracing each other in their delight. But taking their journey through a land that abounded in all sorts of plenty, they ate, after their long want, with that excess of every thing they met with, that they suffered from dropsies and dysenteries.

Here Antony, making a review of his army, found that he had lost twenty thousand foot and four thousand horse, of which the better half perished, not by the enemy, but by diseases. Their march was of twenty-seven days from Phraata, during which they had beaten the Parthians in eighteen battles, though with little effect or lasting result, because of their being so unable to pursue. By which it is manifest that it was Artavasdes who lost Antony the benefit of the expedition. For had the sixteen thousand horsemen whom he led away out of Media, armed in the same style as the Parthians and accustomed to their manner of fight, been there to follow the pursuit when the Romans put them to flight, it is impossible they could have rallied so often after their defeats, and reappeared again as they did to renew their attacks. For this reason, the whole army was very earnest with Antony to march into Armenia to take revenge. But he, with more reflection, forbore to notice the desertion, and continued all his former courtesies, feeling that the army was wearied out, and in want of all manner of necessaries. Afterwards, however, entering Armenia, with invitations and fair promises he prevailed upon Artavasdes to meet him, when he seized him, bound him, and carried him to Alexandria, and there led him in a triumph; one of the things which most offended the Romans, who felt as if all the honors and solemn observances of their country were, for Cleopatra's sake, handed over to the Egyptians.

This, however, was at an after time. For the present, marching his army in great haste in the depth of winter through continual storms of snow, he lost eight thousand of his men, and came with much diminished numbers to a place called the White Village, between Sidon and Berytus, on the sea-coast, where he waited for the arrival of Cleopatra. And, being impatient of the delay she made, he bethought himself of shortening the time in wine and drunkenness, and yet could not endure the tediousness of a meal, but would start from the table and run to see if she were coming. Till at last she came into port, and brought with her clothes and money for the soldiers. Though some say that Antony only received the clothes from her, and distributed his own money in her name.

A quarrel presently happened between the king of Media and Phraates of Parthia, beginning, it is said, about the division of the booty that was taken from the Romans, and creating great apprehension in the Median lest he should lose his kingdom. He sent, therefore, ambassadors to Antony, with offers of entering into a confederate war against Phraates. And Antony, full of hopes at being thus asked, as a favor, to accept that one thing, horse and archers, the want of which had hindered his beating the Parthians before, began at once to prepare for a return to Armenia, there to join the Medes on the Araxes, and begin the war afresh. But Octavia, in Rome, being desirous to see Antony, asked Cæsar's leave to go to him; which he gave her, not so much, say most authors, to gratify his sister, as to obtain a fair pretence to begin the war upon her dishonorable reception. She no sooner arrived at Athens, but by letters from Antony she was informed of his new expedition, and his will that she should await him there. And, though she were much displeased, not being ignorant of the real reason of this usage, yet she wrote to him to know to what place he would be pleased she should send the things she had brought with her for his use; for she had brought clothes for his soldiers, baggage, cattle, money, and presents for his friends and officers, and two thousand chosen soldiers sumptuously armed, to form prætorian cohorts. This message was brought from Octavia to Antony by Niger, one of his friends, who added to it the praises she deserved so well. Cleopatra, feeling her rival already, as it were, at hand, was seized with fear, lest if to her noble life and her high alliance, she once could add the charm of daily habit and affectionate intercourse, she should become irresistible, and be his absolute mistress for ever. So she feigned to be dying for love of Antony, bringing her body down by slender diet; when he entered the room, she fixed her eyes upon him in a rapture, and when he left, seemed to languish and half faint away. She took great pains that he should see her in tears, and, as soon as he noticed it, hastily dried them up and turned away, as if it were her wish that he should know nothing of it. All this was acting while he prepared for Media; and Cleopatra's creatures were not slow to forward the design, upbraiding Antony with his unfeeling, hardhearted temper, thus letting a woman perish whose soul depended upon him and him alone. Octavia, it was true, was his wife, and had been married to him because it was found convenient for the affairs of her brother that it should be so, and she had the honor of the title; but Cleopatra, the sovereign queen of many nations, had been contented with the name of his mistress, nor did she shun or despise the character whilst she might see him, might live with him, and enjoy him; if she were bereaved of this, she would not survive the loss. In fine, they so melted and unmanned him, that, fully believing she would die if he forsook her, he put off the war and returned to Alexandria, deferring his Median expedition until next summer, though news came of the Parthians being all in confusion with intestine disputes. Nevertheless, he did some time after go into that country, and made an alliance with the king of Media, by marriage of a son of his by Cleopatra to the king's daughter, who was yet very young; and so returned, with his thoughts taken up about the civil war.

When Octavia returned from Athens, Cæsar, who considered she had been injuriously treated, commanded her to live in a separate house; but she refused to leave the house of her husband, and entreated him, unless he had already resolved, upon other motives, to make war with Antony, that he would on her account let it alone; it would be intolerable to have it said of the two greatest commanders in the world, that they had involved the Roman people in a civil war, the one out of passion for, the other out of resentment about, a woman. And her behavior proved her words to be sincere. She remained in Antony's house as if he were at home in it, and took the noblest and most generous care, not only of his children by her, but of those by Fulvia also. She received all the friends of Antony that came to Rome to seek office or upon any business, and did her utmost to prefer their requests to Cæsar; yet this her honorable deportment did but, without her meaning it, damage the reputation of Antony; the wrong he did to such a woman made him hated. Nor was the division he made among his sons at Alexandria less unpopular; it seemed a theatrical piece of insolence and contempt of his country. For, assembling the people in the exercise ground, and causing two golden thrones to be placed on a platform of silver, the one for him and the other for Cleopatra, and at their feet lower thrones for their children, he proclaimed Cleopatra queen of Egypt, Cyprus, Libya, and Cœle-Syria, and with her conjointly Cæsarion, the reputed son of the former Cæsar, who left Cleopatra with child, His own sons by Cleopatra were to have the style of kings of kings; to Alexander he gave Armenia and Media, with Parthia, so soon as it should be overcome; to Ptolemy, Phœnicia, Syria and Cilicia. Alexander was brought out before the people in the Median costume, the tiara and upright peak, and Ptolemy, in boots and mantle and Macedonian cap done about with the diadem; for this was the habit of the successors of Alexander, as the other was of the Medes and Armenians. And, as soon as they had saluted their parents, the one was received by a guard of Macedonians, the other by one of Armenians. Cleopatra was then, as at other times when she appeared in public, dressed in the habit of the goddess Isis, and gave audience to the people under the name of the New Isis.

Cæsar, relating these things in the senate, and often complaining to the people, excited men's minds against Antony. And Antony also sent messages of accusation against Cæsar. The principal of his charges were these: first, that he had not made any division with him of Sicily, which was lately taken from Pompey; secondly, that he had retained the ships he had lent him for the war; thirdly, that after deposing Lepidus, their colleague, he had taken for himself the army, governments, and revenues formerly appropriated to him; and, lastly, that he had parcelled out almost all Italy amongst his own soldiers, and left nothing for his. Cæsar's answer was as follows: that he had put Lepidus out of government because of his own misconduct; that what he had got in war he would divide with Antony, so soon as Antony gave him a share of Armenia; that Antony's soldiers had no claims in Italy, being in possession of Media and Parthia, the acquisitions which their brave actions under their general had added to the Roman empire.

Antony was in Armenia when this answer came to him, and immediately sent Canidius with sixteen legions towards the sea; but he, in the company of Cleopatra, went to Ephesus, whither ships were coming in from all quarters to form the navy, consisting, vessels of burden included, of eight hundred vessels, of which Cleopatra furnished two hundred, together with twenty thousand talents, and provision for the whole army during the war. Antony, on the advice of Domitius and some others, bade Cleopatra return into Egypt, there to expect the event of the war; but she, dreading some new reconciliation by Octavia's means, prevailed with Canidius, by a large sum of money, to speak in her favor with Antony, pointing out to him that it was not just that one that bore so great a part in the charge of the war should be robbed of her share of glory in the carrying it on; nor would it be politic to disoblige the Egyptians, who were so considerable a part of his naval forces; nor did he see how she was inferior in prudence to any one of the kings that were serving with him; she had long governed a great kingdom by herself alone, and long lived with him, and gained experience in public affairs. These arguments (so the fate that destined all to Cæsar would have it), prevailed; and when all their forces had met, they sailed together to Samos, and held high festivities. For, as it was ordered that all kings, princes, and governors, all nations and cities within the limits of Syria, the Mæotid Lake, Armenia, and Illyria, should bring or cause to be brought all munitions necessary for war, so was it also proclaimed that all stage-players should make their appearance at Samos; so that, while pretty nearly the whole world was filled with groans and lamentations, this one island for some days resounded with piping and harping, theatres filling, and choruses playing. Every city sent an ox as its contribution to the sacrifice, and the kings that accompanied Antony competed who should make the most magnificent feasts and the greatest presents; and men began to ask themselves, what would be done to celebrate the victory, when they went to such an expense of festivity at the opening of the war.

This over, he gave Priene to his players for a habitation,[16] and set sail for Athens, where fresh sports and play-acting employed him. Cleopatra, jealous of the honors Octavia had received at Athens (for Octavia was much beloved by the Athenians), courted the favor of the people with all sorts of attentions. The Athenians, in requital, having decreed her public honors, deputed several of the citizens to wait upon her at her house; amongst whom went Antony as one, he being an Athenian citizen, and he it was that made the speech. He sent orders to Rome to have Octavia removed out of his house. She left it, we are told, accompanied by all his children, except the eldest by Fulvia, who was then with his father, weeping and

---

[16] It seems to have been usual for the guild or company of performers in this part of Asia ("Ionia, as far as the Hellespont"), to have a city of their own, a sort of headquarters, whence they went out, and where once a year they held a festival of their own. Formerly, says Strabo, it had been Teos; intestine troubles drove them thence to Ephesus; king Attalus gave them Myonnesus; and afterwards Lebedus, in Roman times, a half abandoned town, "Gabiis desertior atque Fidenis vicus" was only too glad to receive them. See Strabo, XIV., 29.

grieving that she must be looked upon as one of the causes of the war. But the Romans pitied, not so much her, as Antony himself, and more particularly those who had seen Cleopatra, whom they could report to have no way the advantage of Octavia either in youth or in beauty.

The speed and extent of Antony's preparations alarmed Cæsar, who feared he might be forced to fight the decisive battle that summer. For he wanted many necessaries, and the people grudged very much to pay the taxes; freemen being called upon to pay a fourth part of their incomes, and freed slaves an eighth of their property, so that there were loud outcries against him, and disturbances throughout all Italy. And this is looked upon as one of the greatest of Antony's oversights, that he did not then press the war. For he allowed time at once for Cæsar to make his preparations, and for the commotions to pass over. For while people were having their money called for, they were mutinous and violent; but, having paid it, they held their peace. Titius and Plancus, men of consular dignity and friends to Antony, having been ill used by Cleopatra, whom they had most resisted in her design of being present in the war came over to Cæsar, and gave information of the contents of Antony's will, with which they were acquainted. It was deposited in the hands of the vestal virgins, who refused to deliver it up, and sent Cæsar word, if he pleased, he should come and seize it himself, which he did. And, reading it over to himself, he noted those places that were most for his purpose, and, having summoned the senate, read them publicly. Many were scandalized at the proceeding, thinking it out of reason and equity to call a man to account for what was not to be until after his death. Cæsar specially pressed what Antony said in his will about his burial; for he had ordered that even if he died in the city of Rome, his body, after being carried in state through the forum, should be sent to Cleopatra at Alexandria. Calvisius, a dependant of Cæsar's, urged other charges in connection with Cleopatra against Antony; that he had given her the library of Pergamus, containing two hundred thousand distinct volumes; that at a great banquet, in the presence of many guests, he had risen up and rubbed her feet, to fulfil some wager or promise; that he had suffered the Ephesians to salute her as their queen; that he had frequently at the public audience of kings and princes received amorous messages written in tablets made of onyx and crystal, and read them openly on the tribunal; that when Furnius, a man of great authority and eloquence among the Romans, was pleading, Cleopatra happening to pass by in her chair, Antony started up and left them in the middle of their cause, to follow at her side and attend her home.

Calvisius, however, was looked upon as the inventor of most of these stories. Antony's friends went up and down the city to gain him credit, and sent one of themselves, Geminius, to him, to beg him to take heed and not allow himself to be deprived by vote of his authority, and proclaimed a public enemy to the Roman state. But Geminius no sooner arrived in Greece but he was looked upon as one of Octavia's spies; at their suppers he was made a continual butt for mockery, and was put to sit in the least honorable places; all which he bore very well, seeking only an occasion of speaking with Antony. So, at supper, being told to say what business he came about, he answered he would keep the rest for a soberer hour, but one thing he had to say, whether full or fasting, that all would go well if Cleopatra would return to Egypt. And on Antony showing his anger at it, "You have done well, Geminius," said Cleopatra, "to

tell your secret without being put to the rack." So
Geminius, after a few days, took occasion to make his
escape and go to Rome. Many more of Antony's
friends were driven from him by the insolent usage
they had from Cleopatra's flatterers, amongst whom
were Marcus Silanus and Dellius the historian. And
Dellius says he was afraid of his life, and that Glaucus,
the physician, informed him of Cleopatra's design
against him. She was angry with him for having said
that Antony's friends were served with sour wine,
while at Rome Sarmentus, Cæsar's little page (his
delicia, as the Romans call it), drank Falernian.[17]

As soon as Cæsar had completed his preparations,
he had a decree made, declaring war on Cleopatra, and
depriving Antony of the authority which he had let a
woman exercise in his place. Cæsar added that he had
drunk potions that had bereaved him of his senses,
and that the generals they would have to fight with
would be Mardion the eunuch, Pothinus, Iras, Cleopatra's hair-dressing girl, and Charmion, who were
Antony's chief state-councillors.

These prodigies are said to have announced the
war. Pisaurum, where Antony had settled a colony,
on the Adriatic sea, was swallowed up by an earthquake; sweat ran from one of the marble statues of
Antony at Alba for many days together, and, though
frequently wiped off, did not stop. When he himself
was in the city of Patræ, the temple of Hercules was

[17] Suetonius tells us that it was one of the habitual amusements of Augustus to play and talk with children of this kind,
who were sought out for him chiefly in Syria and Mauritania.
They were specially selected for their smallness; but he had no
liking for dwarfs or deformed children, who were often kept by
other great people in Rome as their playthings, so called, *delicia*
or *deliciæ*, much in the same sense as the pet-bird of Catullus's
mistress, "Passer, deliciæ meæ puellæ."

struck by lightning, and, at Athens, the figure of Bacchus was torn by a violent wind out of the Battle of the Giants, and laid flat upon the theatre;[18] with both which deities Antony claimed connection, professing to be descended from Hercules, and from his imitating Bacchus in his way of living having received the name of Young Bacchus. The same whirlwind at Athens also brought down, from amongst many others which were not disturbed, the colossal statues of Eumenes and Attalus, which were inscribed with Antony's name. And in Cleopatra's admiral-galley, which was called the Antonias, a most inauspicious omen occurred. Some swallows had built in the stern of the galley, but other swallows came, beat the first away, and destroyed their nests.

When the armaments gathered for the war, Antony had no less than five hundred ships of war, including numerous galleys of eight and ten banks of oars, as richly ornamented as if they were meant for a triumph. He had a hundred thousand foot and twelve thousand horse. He had vassal kings attending, Bocchus of Libya, Tarcondemus of the Upper Cilicia, Archelaus of Cappadocia, Philadelphus of Paphlagonia, Mithridates of Commagene, and Sadalas of Thrace; all these were with him in person. Out of Pontus Polemon sent him considerable forces, as did also Malchus from Arabia, Herod the Jew, and Amyntas, king of Lycaonia and Galatia; also the Median king sent some troops to join him. Cæsar had two hundred and fifty galleys of war, eighty thousand foot, and horse about equal to the enemy. Antony's empire extended from Euphrates and Armenia to the Ionian sea and the Illyrians; Cæsar's from

[18] The Battle of the Giants with the Gods was a piece of sculpture in the south wall of the Acropolis, just above the Dionysiac theatre in the side of the rock underneath.

Illyria to the westward ocean, and from the ocean all along the Tuscan and Sicilian sea. Of Africa, Cæsar had all the coast opposite to Italy, Gaul, and Spain, as far as the Pillars of Hercules, and Antony the provinces from Cyrene to Æthiopia.

But so wholly was he now the mere appendage to the person of Cleopatra, that, although he was much superior to the enemy in land-forces, yet, out of complaisance to his mistress, he wished the victory to be gained by sea, and that, too, when he could not but see how, for want of sailors, his captains, all through unhappy Greece, were pressing every description of men, common travellers and ass-drivers, harvest laborers and boys, and for all this the vessels had not their complements, but remained, most of them, ill-manned and badly rowed. Cæsar, on the other side, had ships that were built not for size or show, but for service, not pompous galleys, but light, swift, and perfectly manned; and from his head-quarters at Tarentum and Brundusium he sent messages to Antony not to protract the war, but come out with his forces; he would give him secure roadsteads and ports for his fleet, and, for his land army to disembark and pitch their camp, he would leave him as much ground in Italy, inland from the sea, as a horse could traverse in a single course. Antony, on the other side, with the like bold language, challenged him to a single combat, though he were much the older; and, that being refused, proposed to meet him in the Pharsalian fields, where Cæsar and Pompey had fought before. But whilst Antony lay with his fleet near Actium, where now stands Nicopolis, Cæsar seized his opportunity, and crossed the Ionian sea, securing himself at a place in Epirus called the Ladle.[19] And when those about

---

[19] Toryne is the name which has this meaning.

Antony were much disturbed, their land-forces being a good way off, "Indeed," said Cleopatra, in mockery, "we may well be frightened if Cæsar has got hold of the Ladle!"

On the morrow, Antony, seeing the enemy sailing up, and fearing lest his ships might be taken for want of the soldiers to go on board of them, armed all the rowers, and made a show upon the decks of being in readiness to fight; the oars were mounted as if waiting to be put in motion, and the vessels themselves drawn up to face the enemy on either side of the channel of Actium, as though they were properly manned, and ready for an engagement. And Cæsar, deceived by this stratagem, retired. He was also thought to have shown considerable skill in cutting off the water from the enemy by some lines of trenches and forts, water not being plentiful anywhere else, nor very good. And again, his conduct to Domitius was generous, much against the will of Cleopatra. For when he had made his escape in a little boat to Cæsar, having then a fever upon him, although Antony could not but resent it highly, yet he sent after him his whole equipage, with his friends and servants; and Domitius, as if he would give a testimony to the world how repentant he had become on his desertion and treachery being thus manifest, died soon after. Among the kings, also, Amyntas and Deiotarus went over to Cæsar. And the fleet was so unfortunate in every thing that was undertaken, and so unready on every occasion, that Antony was driven again to put his confidence in the land-forces. Canidius, too, who commanded the legions, when he saw how things stood, changed his opinion, and now was of advice that Cleopatra should be sent back, and that, retiring into Thrace or Macedonia, the quarrel should be decided in a land fight. For Dicomes, also, the king of the Getæ, promised to come and join him with a great army, and it would not be any kind of disparagement to him to yield the sea to Cæsar, who, in the Sicilian wars, had had such long practice in ship-fighting; on the contrary, it would be simply ridiculous for Antony, who was by land the most experienced commander living, to make no use of his well-disciplined and numerous infantry, scattering and wasting his forces by parcelling them out in the ships. But for all this, Cleopatra prevailed that a sea-fight should determine all, having already an eye to flight, and ordering all her affairs, not so as to assist in gaining a victory, but to escape with the greatest safety from the first commencement of a defeat.

There were two long walls, extending from the camp to the station of the ships, between which Antony used to pass to and fro without suspecting any danger. But Cæsar, upon the suggestion of a servant that it would not be difficult to surprise him, laid an ambush, which, rising up somewhat too hastily, seized the man that came just before him, he himself escaping narrowly by flight.

When it was resolved to stand to a fight at sea, they set fire to all the Egyptian ships except sixty; and of these the best and largest, from ten banks down to three, he manned with twenty thousand full-armed men, and two thousand archers. Here it is related that a foot captain, one that had fought often under Antony, and had his body all mangled with wounds, exclaimed, "O, my general, what have our wounds and swords done to displease you, that you should give your confidence to rotten timbers? Let Egyptians and Phœnicians contend at sea, give us the land, where we know well how to die upon the spot or gain the victory." To which he answered nothing, but, by his look and motion of his hand seeming to bid him be

of good courage, passed forwards, having already, it
would seem, no very sure hopes, since when the masters
proposed leaving the sails behind them, he commanded
they should be put aboard, "For we must not," said
he, "let one enemy escape."

That day and the three following the sea was so
rough they could not engage. But on the fifth there
was a calm, and they fought; Antony commanding
with Publicola the right, and Cœlius the left squadron,
Marcus Octavius and Marcus Insteius the centre.
Cæsar gave the charge of the left to Agrippa, commanding in person on the right. As for the land-
forces, Canidius was general for Antony, Taurus for
Cæsar; both armies remaining drawn up in order
along the shore. Antony in a small boat went from
one ship to another, encouraging his soldiers, and bidding them stand firm, and fight as steadily on their
large ships as if they were on land. The masters he
ordered that they should receive the enemy lying still
as if they were at anchor, and maintain the entrance
of the port, which was a narrow and difficult passage.
Of Cæsar they relate, that, leaving his tent and going
round, while it was yet dark, to visit the ships, he met
a man driving an ass, and asked him his name. He
answered him that his own name was "Fortunate, and
my ass," says he, "is called Conquerer."[20] And afterwards, when he disposed the beaks of the ships in that
place in token of his victory, the statue of this man
and his ass in bronze were placed amongst them.
After examining the rest of his fleet, he went in a
boat to the right wing, and looked with much admiration at the enemy lying perfectly still in the straits,
in all appearance as if they had been at anchor. For
some considerable length of time he actually thought

---

[20] Eutychus the name of the man, and Nicon that of the ass.

they were so, and kept his own ships at rest, at a distance of about eight furlongs from them. But about noon a breeze sprang up from the sea, and Antony's men, weary of expecting the enemy so long, and trusting to their large tall vessels, as if they had been invincible, began to advance the left squadron. Cæsar was overjoyed to see them move, and ordered his own right squadron to retire, that he might entice them out to sea as far as he could, his design being to sail round and round, and so with his light and well-manned galleys to attack these huge vessels, which their size and their want of men made slow to move and difficult to manage.

When they engaged, there was no charging or striking of one ship by another, because Antony's, by reason of their great bulk, were incapable of the rapidity required to make the stroke effectual, and, on the other side, Cæsar's durst not charge head to head on Antony's, which were all armed with solid masses and spikes of brass; nor did they like even to run in on their sides, which were so strongly built with great squared pieces of timber, fastened together with iron bolts, that their vessels' beaks would easily have been shattered upon them. So that the engagement resembled a land fight, or, to speak yet more properly, the attack and defense of a fortified place; for there were always three or four vessels of Cæsar's about one of Antony's, pressing them with spears, javelins, poles, and several inventions of fire, which they flung among them, Antony's men using catapults also, to pour down missiles from wooden towers. Agrippa drawing out the squadron under his command to outflank the enemy, Publicola was obliged to observe his motions, and gradually to break off from the middle squadron, where some confusion and alarm ensued, while Arruntius[21] engaged them. But the fortune of the day was still undecided, and the battle equal, when on a sudden Cleopatra's sixty ships were seen hoisting sail and making out to sea in full flight, right through the ships that were engaged. For they were placed behind the great ships, which, in breaking through, they put into disorder. The enemy was astonished to see them sailing off with a fair wind towards Peloponnesus. Here it was that Antony showed to all the world that he was no longer actuated by the thoughts and motives of a commander or a man, or indeed by his own judgment at all, and what was once said as a jest, that the soul of a lover lives in some one else's body, he proved to be a serious truth. For, as if he had been born part of her, and must move with her wheresoever she went, as soon as he saw her ship sailing away, he abandoned all that were fighting and spending their lives for him, and put himself aboard a galley of five ranks of oars, taking with him only Alexander of Syria and Scellias, to follow her that had so well begun his ruin and would hereafter accomplish it.

She, perceiving him to follow, gave the signal to come aboard. So, as soon as he came up with them, he was taken into the ship. But without seeing her or letting himself be seen by her, he went forward by himself, and sat alone, without a word, in the ship's prow, covering his face with his two hands. In the meanwhile, some of Cæsar's light Liburnian ships, that were in pursuit, came in sight. But on Antony's commanding to face about, they all gave back except Eurycles the Laconian, who pressed on, shaking a lance from the deck, as if he meant to hurl it at him. Antony, standing at the prow, demanded of him,

[21] Arruntius commanded in Cæsar's centre.

"Who is this that pursues Antony?" "I am," said he, "Eurycles, the son of Lachares, armed with Cæsar's fortune to revenge my father's death." Lachares had been condemned for a robbery, and beheaded by Antony's orders. However, Eurycles did not attack Antony, but ran with full force upon the other admiral-galley (for there were two of them), and with the blow turned her round, and took both her and another ship, in which was a quantity of rich plate and furniture. So soon as Eurycles was gone, Antony returned to his posture, and sate silent, and thus he remained for three days, either in anger with Cleopatra, or wishing not to upbraid her, at the end of which they touched at Tænarus. Here the women of their company succeeded first in bringing them to speak, and afterwards to eat and sleep together. And, by this time, several of the ships of burden and some of his friends began to come in to him from the rout, bringing news of his fleet's being quite destroyed, but that the land-forces, they thought, still stood firm. So that he sent messengers to Canidius to march the army with all speed through Macedonia into Asia. And, designing himself to go from Tænarus into Africa, he gave one of the merchant ships, laden with a large sum of money, and vessels of silver and gold of great value, belonging to the royal collections, to his friends, desiring them to share it amongst them, and provide for their own safety. They refusing his kindness with tears in their eyes, he comforted them with all the goodness and humanity imaginable, entreating them to leave him, and wrote letters in their behalf to Theophilus, his steward, at Corinth, that he would provide for their security, and keep them concealed till such time as they could make their peace with Cæsar. This Theophilus was the father of Hipparchus, who had such interest with Antony, who was the first of all his freedmen that went over to Cæsar, and who settled afterwards at Corinth. In this posture were affairs with Antony.

But at Actium, his fleet, after a long resistance to Cæsar, and suffering the most damage from a heavy sea that set in right ahead, scarcely, at four in the afternoon, gave up the contest, with the loss of not more than five thousand men killed, but of three hundred ships taken, as Cæsar himself has recorded. Only few had known of Antony's flight; and those who were told of it could not at first give any belief to so incredible a thing, as that a general who had nineteen entire legions and twelve thousand horse upon the seashore, could abandon all and fly away; and he, above all, who had so often experienced both good and evil fortune, and had in a thousand wars and battles been inured to changes. His soldiers, however, would not give up their desires and expectations, still fancying he would appear from some part or other, and showed such a generous fidelity to his service, that, when they were thoroughly assured that he was fled in earnest, they kept themselves in a body seven days, making no account of the messages that Cæsar sent to them. But at last, seeing that Canidius himself, who commanded them, was fled from the camp by night, and that all their officers had quite abandoned them, they gave way, and made their submission to the conqueror. After this, Cæsar set sail for Athens, where he made a settlement with Greece, and distributed what remained of the provision of corn that Antony had made for his army among the cities, which were in a miserable condition, despoiled of their money, their slaves, their horses, and beasts of service. My great-grandfather Nicarchus used to relate, that the whole body of the people of our city were put in requisition to carry each one a certain measure of corn upon their shoulders to the sea-side near Anticyra, men standing by to quicken them with the lash. They had made one journey of the kind, but when they had just measured out the corn and were putting it on their backs for a second, news came of Antony's defeat, and so saved Chæronea, for all Antony's purveyors and soldiers fled upon the news, and left them to divide the corn among themselves.

When Antony came into Africa, he sent on Cleopatra from Parætonium into Egypt, and staid himself in the most entire solitude that he could desire, roaming and wandering about with only two friends, one a Greek, Aristocrates, a rhetorician, and the other a Roman, Lucilius, of whom we have elsewhere spoken, how, at Philippi, to give Brutus time to escape, he suffered himself to be taken by the pursuers, pretending he was Brutus. Antony gave him his life, and on this account he remained true and faithful to him to the last.

But when also the officer who commanded for him in Africa, to whose care he had committed all his forces there, took them over to Cæsar, he resolved to kill himself, but was hindered by his friends. And coming to Alexandria, he found Cleopatra busied in a most bold and wonderful enterprise. Over the small space of land which divides the Red Sea from the sea near Egypt, which may be considered also the boundary between Asia and Africa, and in the narrowest place is not much above three hundred furlongs across, over this neck of land Cleopatra had formed a project of dragging her fleet, and setting it afloat in the Arabian Gulf, thus with her soldiers and her treasure to secure herself a home on the other side, where she might live in peace, far away from war and slavery. But the first galleys which were carried over being burnt by the Arabians of Petra, and Antony not

ANTONY

knowing but that the army before Actium still held together, she desisted from her enterprise, and gave orders for the fortifying all the approaches to Egypt. But Antony, leaving the city and the conversation of his friends, built him a dwelling-place in the water, near Pharos, upon a little mole which he cast up in the sea, and there, secluding himself from the company of mankind, said he desired nothing but to live the life of Timon; as, indeed, his case was the same, and the ingratitude and injuries which he suffered from those he had esteemed his friends, made him hate and mistrust all mankind.

This Timon was a citizen of Athens, and lived much about the Peloponnesian war, as may be seen by the comedies of Aristophanes[22] and Plato, in which he is ridiculed as the hater and enemy of mankind. He avoided and repelled the approaches of every one, but embraced with kisses and the greatest show of affection Alcibiades, then in his hot youth. And when Apemantus was astonished, and demanded the reason,

---

[22] Two passages are extant in *the comedies of Aristophanes* in which Timon is mentioned,—the 1549th line of the Birds, in which Prometheus calls himself a Timon, a sort of god-misanthrope among the dieties, and lines 805-820 of the Lysistrata, where his solitary, man-hating life is briefly depicted. *Plato,* the comic poet, was another contemporary. So also was Phrynichus, a fragment of whom, describing Timon's habits, is preserved by a grammarian. But it seems to have been in the next century by Antiphanes, one of the two great leaders of the second or Middle Attic Comedy (quoted by Plutarch, Vol. V. p. 10, as ridiculing Demosthenes), that Timon was elevated to be the ideal of the misanthrope, and made the vehicle for general invective on mankind. Antiphanes wrote a play called Timon. This passage in Plutarch is the most historical account that we have of Timon, though it is from Lucian's dialogue in the century following Plutarch that the modern representations have been chiefly derived. Some have thought that Lucian probably copied Antiphanes, but this is quite conjectural.

he replied that he knew this young man would one day do infinite mischief to the Athenians. He never admitted any one into his company, except at times this Apemantus, who was of the same sort of temper, and was an imitator of his way of life. At the celebration of the festival of flagons,[23] these two kept the feast together, and Apemantus saying to him, "What a pleasant party, Timon!" "It would be," he answered, "if you were away." One day he got up in a full assembly on the speaker's place, and when there was a dead silence and great wonder at so unusual a sight, he said, "Ye men of Athens, I have a little plot of ground, and in it grows a fig-tree, on which many citizens have been pleased to hang themselves; and now, having resolved to build in that place, I wished to announce it publicly that any of you who may be desirous may go and hang yourselves before I cut it down." He died and was buried at Halæ, near the sea, where it so happened that, after his burial, a land-slip took place on the point of the shore, and the sea, flowing in, surrounded his tomb, and made it inaccessible to the foot of man. It bore this inscription:—

> Here am I laid, my life of misery done.
> Ask not my name, I curse you every one.

And this epitaph was made by himself while yet alive; that which is more generally known is by Callimachus:—

> Timon, the misanthrope, am I below.
> Go, and revile me, traveller, only go.

Thus much of Timon, of whom much more might

---

[23] "The Flagons," or *Choës*, was the second day of the Anthesterian feast of Bacchus, and was observed by the Athenians as a special day of conviviality, when they met in parties, and drank together.

ANTONY

be said. Canidius now came, bringing word in person of the loss of the army before Actium. Then he received news that Herod of Judea was gone over to Cæsar with some legions and cohorts, and that the other kings and princes were in like manner deserting him, and that, out of Egypt, nothing stood by him. All this, however, seemed not to disturb him, but, as if he were glad to put away all hope, that with it he might be rid of all care, and leaving his habitation by the sea, which he called the Timoneum, he was received by Cleopatra in the palace, and set the whole city into a course of feasting, drinking, and presents. The son of Cæsar and Cleopatra was registered among the youths, and Antyllus, his own son by Fulvia, received the gown without the purple border, given to those that are come of age; in honor of which the citizens of Alexandria did nothing but feast and revel for many days. They themselves broke up the Order of the Inimitable Livers, and constituted another in its place, not inferior in splendor, luxury, and sumptuosity, calling it that of the Diers together.[24] For all those that said they would die with Antony and Cleopatra gave in their names, for the present passing their time in all manner of pleasures and a regular succession of banquets. But Cleopatra was busied in making a collection of all varieties of poisonous drugs, and, in order to see which of them were the least painful in the operation, she had them tried upon prisoners condemned to die. But, finding that the quick poisons always worked with sharp pains, and that the less painful were slow, she next tried venomous animals,

---

[24] It was a name well known on the stage. There were two, if not three, comedies, called the *Synapothneskontes,* and one of them had been translated into Latin by Plautus, as the *Commorientes.*

and watched with her own eyes whilst they were applied, one creature to the body of another. This was her daily practice, and she pretty well satisfied herself that nothing was comparable to the bite of the asp, which, without convulsion or groaning, brought on a heavy drowsiness and lethargy, with a gentle sweat on the face, the senses being stupefied by degrees; the patient, in appearance, being sensible of no pain, but rather troubled to be disturbed or awakened, like those that are in a profound natural sleep.

At the same time, they sent ambassadors to Cæsar into Asia, Cleopatra asking for the kingdom of Egypt for her children, and Antony, that he might have leave to live as a private man in Egypt, or, if that were thought too much, that he might retire to Athens. In lack of friends, so many having deserted, and others not being trusted, Euphronius, his son's tutor, was sent on this embassy. For Alexas of Laodicea, who, by the recommendation of Timagenes, became acquainted with Antony at Rome, and had been more powerful with him than any Greek, and was, of all the instruments which Cleopatra made use of to persuade Antony, the most violent, and the chief subverter of any good thoughts that, from time to time, might rise in his mind in Octavia's favor, had been sent before to dissuade Herod from desertion; but, betraying his master, stayed with him, and, confiding in Herod's interest, had the boldness to come into Cæsar's presence. Herod, however, was not able to help him, for he was immediately put in chains, and sent into his own country, where, by Cæsar's order, he was put to death. This reward of his treason Alexas received while Antony was yet alive.

Cæsar would not listen to any proposals for Antony, but he made answer to Cleopatra, that there was no reasonable favor which she might not expect, if

JULIUS CAESAR

she put Antony to death, or expelled him from Egypt. He sent back with the ambassadors his own freedman Thyrsus, a man of understanding, and not at all ill-qualified for conveying the messages of a youthful general to a woman so proud of her charms and possessed with the opinion of the power of her beauty. But by the long audiences he received from her, and the special honors which she paid him, Antony's jealousy began to be awakened; he had him seized, whipped, sent back; writing Cæsar word that the man's busy, impertinent ways had provoked him; in his circumstances he could not be expected to be very patient: "But if it offend you," he added, "you have got my freedman, Hipparchus, with you; hang him up and scourge him to make us even." But Cleopatra, after this, to clear herself, and to allay his jealousies, paid him all the attentions imaginable. When her own birthday came, she kept it as was suitable to their fallen fortunes; but his was observed with the utmost prodigality of splendor and magnificence, so that many of the guests sate down in want, and went home wealthy men. Meantime, continual letters came to Cæsar from Agrippa, telling him his presence was extremely required at Rome.

And so the war was deferred for a season. But, the winter being over, he began his march; he himself by Syria, and his captains through Africa. Pelusium being taken, there went a report as if it had been delivered up to Cæsar by Seleucus not without the consent of Cleopatra; but she, to justify herself, gave up into Antony's hands the wife and children of Seleucus to be put to death. She had caused to be built, joining to the temple of Isis, several tombs and monuments of wonderful height, and very remarkable for the workmanship; thither she removed her treasure, her gold, silver, emeralds, pearls, ebony, ivory, cinnamon, and, after all, a great quantity of torchwood and tow. Upon which Cæsar began to fear lest she should, in a desperate fit, set all these riches on fire; and, therefore, while he was marching towards the city with his army, he omitted no occasion of giving her new assurances of his good intentions. He took up his position in the Hippodrome, where Antony made a fierce sally upon him, routed the horse, and beat them back into their trenches, and so returned with great satisfaction to the palace, where, meeting Cleopatra, armed as he was, he kissed her, and commended to her favor one of his men, who had most signalized himself in the fight, to whom she made a present of a breastplate and helmet of gold; which he having received, went that very night and deserted to Cæsar.

After this, Antony sent a new challenge to Cæsar, to fight him hand to hand; who made him answer that he might find several other ways to end his life; and he, considering with himself that he could not die more honorably than in battle, resolved to make an effort both by land and sea. At supper, it is said, he bade his servants help him freely, and pour him out wine plentifully, since to-morrow, perhaps, they should not do the same, but be servants to a new master, whilst he should lie on the ground, a dead corpse, and nothing. His friends that were about him wept to hear him talk so; which he perceiving, told them he would not lead them to a battle in which he expected rather an honorable death than either safety or victory. That night, it is related, about the middle of it, when the whole city was in a deep silence and general sadness, expecting the event of the next day, on a sudden was heard the sound of all sorts of instruments, and voices singing in tune, and the cry of a crowd of people shouting and dancing, like a troop of bacchanals on its way. This tumultuous procession seemed to take its course right through the middle of the city to the gate nearest the enemy; here it became loudest, and suddenly passed out. People who reflected considered this to signify that Bacchus, the god whom Antony had always made it his study to copy and imitate, had now forsaken him.

As soon as it was light, he marched his infantry out of the city, and posted them upon a rising ground, from whence he saw his fleet make up to the enemy. There he stood in expectation of the event; but, as soon as the fleets came near to one another, his men saluted Cæsar's with their oars; and, on their responding, the whole body of the ships, forming into a single fleet, rowed up direct to the city. Antony had no sooner seen this, but the horse deserted him, and went over to Cæsar; and his foot being defeated, he retired into the city, crying out that Cleopatra had betrayed him to the enemies he had made for her sake. She, being afraid lest in his fury and despair he might do her a mischief, fled to her monument, and letting down the falling doors, which were strong with bars and bolts, she sent messengers who should tell Antony she was dead. He, believing it, cried out, "Now, Antony, why delay longer? Fate has snatched away the only pretext for which you could say you desired yet to live." Going into his chamber, and there loosening and opening his coat of armor, "I am not," said he, "troubled, Cleopatra, to be at present bereaved of you, for I shall soon be with you; but it distresses me that so great a general should be found of a tardier courage than a woman." He had a faithful servant, whose name was Eros; he had engaged him formerly to kill him when he should think it necessary, and now he put him to his promise. Eros drew his sword, as designing to kill him, but, suddenly turning round, he slew himself. And as he fell dead at his feet, "It is well done, Eros," said Antony; "you show your master how to do what you had not the heart to do yourself;" and so he ran himself into the belly, and laid himself upon the couch. The wound, however, was not immediately mortal; and the flow of blood ceasing when he lay down, presently he came to himself, and entreated those that were about him to put him out of his pain; but they all fled out of the chamber, and left him crying out and struggling, until Diomede, Cleopatra's secretary, came to him, having orders from her to bring him into the monument.

When he understood she was alive, he eagerly gave order to the servants to take him up, and in their arms was carried to the door of the building. Cleopatra would not open the door, but, looking from a sort of window, she let down ropes and cords, to which Antony was fastened; and she and her two women, the only persons she had allowed to enter the monument, drew him up. Those that were present say that nothing was ever more sad than this spectacle, to see Antony, covered all over with blood and just expiring, thus drawn up, still holding up his hands to her, and lifting up his body with the little force he had left. As, indeed, it was no easy task for the women; and Cleopatra, with all her force, clinging to the rope, and straining with her head to the ground, with difficulty pulled him up, while those below encouraged her with their cries, and joined in all her effort and anxiety. When she had got him up, she laid him on the bed, tearing all her clothes, which she spread upon him; and, beating her breasts with her hands, lacerating herself, and disfiguring her own face with the blood from his wounds, she called him her lord, her husband, her emperor, and seemed to have pretty nearly forgotten all her own evils, she was so intent upon his misfortunes. Antony, stopping her lamentations as well as he could, called for wine to drink, either that he was thirsty, or that he imagined that it might put him the sooner out of pain. When he had drunk, he advised her to bring her own affairs, so far as might be honorably done, to a safe conclusion, and that, among all the friends of Cæsar, she should rely on Proculeius; that she should not pity him in this last turn of fate, but rather rejoice for him in remembrance of his past happiness, who had been of all men the most illustrious and powerful, and, in the end, had fallen not ignobly, a Roman by a Roman overcome.

Just as he breathed his last, Proculeius arrived from Cæsar; for when Antony gave himself his wound, and was carried in to Cleopatra, one of his guards, Dercetæus, took up Antony's sword and hid it; and when he saw his opportunity, stole away to Cæsar, and brought him the first news of Antony's death, and withal showed him the bloody sword. Cæsar, upon this, retired into the inner part of his tent, and, giving some tears to the death of one that had been nearly allied to him in marriage, his colleague in empire, and companion in so many wars and dangers, he came out to his friends, and, bringing with him many letters, he read to them with how much reason and moderation he had always addressed himself to Antony, and in return what overbearing and arrogant answers he received. Then he sent Proculeius to use his utmost endeavors to get Cleopatra alive into his power; for he was afraid of losing a great treasure, and, besides, she would be no small addition to the glory of his triumph. She, however, was careful not to put herself in Proculeius's power; but from within her monument, he standing on the outside of a door, on the level of the ground, which was strongly barred, but so that they might well enough hear one another's voice, she held a conference with him; she demanding that her kingdom might be given to her children, and he bidding her be of good courage, and trust Cæsar for every thing.

Having taken particular notice of the place, he returned to Cæsar, and Gallus was sent to parley with her the second time; who, being come to the door, on purpose prolonged the conference, while Proculeius fixed his scaling-ladders in the window through which the women had pulled up Antony. And so entering, with two men to follow him, he went straight down to the door where Cleopatra was discoursing with Gallus. One of the two women who were shut up in the monument with her cried out, "Miserable Cleopatra, you are taken prisoner!" Upon which she turned quick, and, looking at Proculeius, drew out her dagger, which she had with her to stab herself. But Proculeius ran up quickly, and, seizing her with both his hands, "For shame," said he, "Cleopatra; you wrong yourself and Cæsar much, who would rob him of so fair an occasion of showing his clemency, and would make the world believe the most gentle of commanders to be a faithless and implacable enemy." And so, taking the dagger out of her hand, he also shook her dress to see if there were any poison hid in it. After this, Cæsar sent Epaphroditus, one of his freedmen, with orders to treat her with all the gentleness and civility possible, but to take the strictest precautions to keep her alive.

In the meanwhile, Cæsar made his entry into Alexandria, with Areius the philosopher at his side, holding him by the hand and talking with him; desiring that all his fellow-citizens should see what honor was paid to him, and should look up to him accordingly from the very first moment. Then, entering the exercise-ground, he mounted a platform erected for the purpose, and from thence commanded the citizens (who, in great fear and consternation, fell prostrate at his feet) to stand up, and told them, that he freely acquitted the people of all blame, first, for the sake of Alexander, who built their city; then, for the city's sake itself, which was so large and beautiful; and, thirdly, to gratify his friend Areius.

Such great honor did Areius receive from Cæsar; and by his intercession many lives were saved, amongst the rest that of Philostratus, a man, of all the professors of logic that ever were, the most ready in extempore speaking, but quite destitute of any right to call himself one of the philosophers of the Academy. Cæsar, out of disgust at his character, refused all attention to his entreaties. So, growing a long, white beard, and dressing himself in black, he followed behind Areius, shouting out the verse,

> The wise, if they are wise, will save the wise.

Which Cæsar hearing, gave him his pardon, to prevent rather any odium that might attach to Areius, than any harm that Philostratus might suffer.

Of Antony's children, Antyllus, his son by Fulvia, being betrayed by his tutor, Theodorus, was put to death; and while the soldiers were cutting off his head, his tutor contrived to steal a precious jewel which he wore about his neck, and put it into his pocket, and afterwards denied the fact, but was convicted and crucified. Cleopatra's children, with their attendants, had a guard set on them, and were treated very honorably. Cæsarion, who was reputed to be the son of Cæsar the Dictator, was sent by his mother, with a great sum of money, through Æthiopia, to pass into India; but his tutor, a man named Rhodon, about as honest as Theodorus, persuaded him to turn back, for that Cæsar had designed to make him king. Cæsar consulting what was best to be done with him, Areius, we are told, said,

> Too many *Cæsars* are not well.[25]

So, afterwards, when Cleopatra was dead, he was killed.

Many kings and great commanders made petition to Cæsar for the body of Antony, to give him his funeral rites; but he would not take away his corpse from Cleopatra, by whose hands he was buried with royal splendor and magnificence, it being granted to her to employ what she pleased on his funeral. In this extremity of grief and sorrow, and having inflamed and ulcerated her breasts with beating them, she fell into a high fever, and was very glad of the occasion, hoping, under this pretext, to abstain from food, and so to die in quiet without interference. She had her own physician, Olympus, to whom she told the truth, and asked his advice and help to put an end to herself, as Olympus himself has told us, in a narrative which he wrote of these events. But Cæsar, suspecting her purpose, took to menacing language about her children, and excited her fears for them, before which engines her purpose shook and gave way, so that she suffered those about her to give her what meat or medicine they pleased.

Some few days after, Cæsar himself came to make her a visit and comfort her. She lay then upon her

---

[25] A parody on Homer's famous words,

> *Too many leaders are not well;* the way
> Is to have one commander to obey,
> One king, of Zeus appointed for the sway

ouk agathon polukaisarie being a slight variation upon *ouk agathon polukoiranie*. *Kaisar* is the Greek form of Cæsar; and *Koiran*, or *Koiranos*, is a captain or chief.

pallet-bed in undress, and, on his entering in, sprang up from off her bed, having nothing on but the one garment next her body, and flung herself at his feet, her hair and face looking wild and disfigured, her voice quivering, and her eyes sunk in her head. The marks of the blows she had given herself were visible about her bosom, and altogether her whole person seemed no less afflicted than her soul. But, for all this, her old charm, and the boldness of her youthful beauty had not wholly left her, and, in spite of her present condition, still sparkled from within, and let itself appear in all the movements of her countenance. Cæsar, desiring her to repose herself, sat down by her; and, on this opportunity, she said something to justify her actions, attributing what she had done to the necessity she was under, and to her fear of Antony; and when Cæsar, on each point, made his objections, and she found herself confuted, she broke off at once into language of entreaty and deprecation, as if she desired nothing more than to prolong her life. And at last, having by her a list of her treasure, she gave it into his hands; and when Seleucus, one of her stewards, who was by, pointed out that various articles were omitted, and charged her with secreting them, she flew up and caught him by the hair, and struck him several blows on the face. Cæsar smiling and withholding her, "Is it not very hard, Cæsar," said she, "when you do me the honor to visit me in this condition I am in, that I should be accused by one of my own servants of laying by some women's toys, not meant to adorn, be sure, my unhappy self, but that I might have some little present by me to make your Octavia and your Livia, that by their intercession I might hope to find you in some measure disposed to mercy?" Cæsar was pleased to hear her talk thus, being now assured that she was desirous to live. And, therefore, letting her know that the things she had laid by she might dispose of as she pleased, and his usage of her should be honorable above her expectation, he went away, well satisfied that he had overreached her, but, in fact, was himself deceived.

There was a young man of distinction among Cæsar's companions, named Cornelius Dolabella. He was not without a certain tenderness for Cleopatra, and sent her word privately, as she had besought him to do, that Cæsar was about to return through Syria, and that she and her children were to be sent on within three days. When she understood this, she made her request to Cæsar that he would be pleased to permit her to make oblations to the departed Antony; which being granted, she ordered herself to be carried to the place where he was buried, and there, accompanied by her women, she embraced his tomb with tears in her eyes, and spoke in this manner: "O, dearest Antony," said she, "it is not long since that with these hands I buried you; then they were free, now I am a captive, and pay these last duties to you with a guard upon me, for fear that my just griefs and sorrows should impair my servile body, and make it less fit to appear in their triumph over you. No further offerings or libations expect from me; these are the last honors that Cleopatra can pay your memory, for she is to be hurried away far from you. Nothing could part us whilst we lived, but death seems to threaten to divide us. You, a Roman born, have found a grave in Egypt; I, an Egyptian, am to seek that favor, and none but that, in your country. But if the gods below, with whom you now are, either can or will do any thing (since those above have betrayed us), suffer not your living wife to be abandoned; let me not be led in triumph to your shame, but hide me and bury me here with you, since, amongst all my bitter misfortunes, nothing has afflicted me like this brief time that I have lived away from you."

Having made these lamentations, crowning the tomb with garlands and kissing it, she gave orders to prepare her a bath, and, coming out of the bath, she lay down and made a sumptuous meal. And a country fellow brought her a little basket, which the guards intercepting and asking what it was, the fellow put the leaves which lay uppermost aside, and showed them it was full of figs; and on their admiring the largeness and beauty of the figs, he laughed, and invited them to take some, which they refused, and, suspecting nothing, bade him carry them in. After her repast, Cleopatra sent to Cæsar a letter which she had written and sealed; and, putting everybody out of the monument but her two women, she shut the doors. Cæsar, opening her letter, and finding pathetic prayers and entreaties that she might be buried in the same tomb with Antony, soon guessed what was doing. At first he was going himself in all haste, but, changing his mind, he sent others to see. The thing had been quickly done. The messengers came at full speed, and found the guards apprehensive of nothing; but on opening the doors, they saw her stone-dead, lying upon a bed of gold, set out in all her royal ornaments. Iras, one of her women, lay dying at her feet, and Charmion, just ready to fall, scarcely able to hold up her head, was adjusting her mistress's diadem. And when one that came in said angrily, "Was this well done of your lady, Charmion?" "Extremely well," she answered, "and as became the descendant of so many kings"; and as she said this, she fell down dead by the bedside.

Some relate that an asp was brought in amongst those figs and covered with the leaves, and that Cleo-

patra had arranged that it might settle on her before
she knew, but, when she took away some of the figs
and saw it, she said, "So here it is," and held out her
bare arm to be bitten. Others say that it was kept in
a vase, and that she vexed and pricked it with a golden
spindle till it seized her arm. But what really took
place is known to no one. Since it was also said that
she carried poison in a hollow bodkin, about which she
wound her hair; yet there was not so much as a spot
found, or any symptom of poison upon her body, nor
was the asp seen within the monument; only something
like the trail of it was said to have been noticed on the
sand by the sea, on the part towards which the building faced and where the windows were. Some relate
that two faint puncture-marks were found on Cleopatra's arms, and to this account Cæsar seems to have
given credit; for in his triumph there was carried a
figure of Cleopatra, with an asp clinging to her. Such
are the various accounts. But Cæsar, though much
disappointed by her death, yet could not but admire
the greatness of her spirit, and gave order that her
body should be buried by Antony with royal splendor
and magnificence. Her women, also, received honorable burial by his directions. Cleopatra had lived nine
and thirty years, during twenty-two of which she had
reigned as queen, and for fourteen had been Antony's
partner in his empire. Antony, according to some authorities, was fifty-three, according to others, fifty-six
years old. His statues were all thrown down, but
those of Cleopatra were left untouched; for Archibius,
one of her friends, gave Cæsar two thousand talents
to save them from the fate of Antony's.

Antony left by his three wives seven children, of
whom only Antyllus, the eldest, was put to death by
Cæsar; Octavia took the rest, and brought them up

with her own. Cleopatra, his daughter by Cleopatra, was given in marriage to Juba, the most accomplished of kings; and Antony, his son by Fulvia, attained such high favor, that whereas Agrippa was considered to hold the first place with Cæsar, and the sons of Livia the second, the third, without dispute, was possessed by Antony. Octavia, also, having had by her first husband, Marcellus, two daughters, and one son named Marcellus, this son Cæsar adopted, and gave him his daughter in marriage; as did Octavia one of the daughters to Agrippa. But Marcellus dying almost immediately after his marriage, she, perceiving that her brother was at a loss to find elsewhere any sure friend to be his son-in-law, was the first to recommend that Agrippa should put away her daughter and marry Julia. To this Cæsar first, and then Agrippa himself, gave assent; so Agrippa married Julia, and Octavia, receiving her daughter, married her to the young Antony. Of the two daughters whom Octavia had borne to Antony, the one was married to Domitius Ahenobarbus;[26] and the other, Antonia, famous for her beauty and discretion, was married to Drusus, the son of Livia, and step-son to Cæsar. Of these parents were born Germanicus and Claudius. Claudius reigned later; and of the children of Germanicus, Caius, after a reign of distinction, was killed with his wife and child; Agrippina, after bearing a son, Lucius Domitius, to Ahenobarbus, was married to Claudius Cæsar, who adopted Domitius, giving him the name of Nero Germanicus. He was emperor in our time, and put his mother to death, and with his madness and folly came not far from ruining the Roman empire, being Antony's descendant in the fifth generation.

[26] Ahenobarbus, in this line, is the son of Domitius who deserted before Actium, and is the father of Ahenobarbus mentioned

below. The stem, showing the three emperors of Antony's race, is as follows:—

Mark Antony = Octavia, sister of the Emperor Augustus.

Antonia = L. Domitius Ahenobarbus   Antonia = Druses, brother of the Emperor Tiberius.

Agrippina (I.) = Germanicus   The Emperor Claudius.
daughter of
Agrippa and
Julia daughter
of Augustus.

Cn. Domitius Ahenobarbus = Agrippina (II)   The Emperor [Caligula,

Lucius Domitius, the Emperor Nero.

COMPARISON OF DEMETRIUS AND ANTONY

As both are great examples of the vicissitudes of fortune, let us first consider in what way they attained their power and glory. Demetrius heired a kingdom already won for him by Antigonus, the most powerful of the Successors,[1] who, before Demetrius grew to be a man, traversed with his armies and subdued the greater part of Asia. Antony's father was well enough in other respects, but was no warrior, and could bequeathe no great legacy of reputation to his son, who had the boldness, nevertheless, to take upon him the government, to which birth gave him no claim, which had been held by Cæsar, and became the inheritor of his great labors. And such power did he attain, with only himself to thank for it, that, in a division of the whole empire into two portions, he took and received the nobler one; and, absent himself, by his mere subalterns and lieutenants often defeated the Parthians, and drove the barbarous nations of the Caucasus back to the Caspian Sea. Those very things that procured him ill-repute bear witness to his greatness. Antigonus considered Antipater's daughter Phila, in spite of the disparity of her years, an advantageous match for Demetrius. Antony was thought disgraced by his marriage with Cleopatra, a queen superior in power and glory to all, except Arsaces, who were kings in her time. Antony was so great as to be thought by others worthy of higher things than his own desires.

As regards the right and justice of their aims at em-

[1] The Successors of Alexander, the *diadochi*, usually known in the Greek historians by this title.

pire, Demetrius need not be blamed for seeking to rule a people that had always had a king to rule them. Antony, who enslaved the Roman people, just liberated from the rule of Cæsar, followed a cruel and tyrannical object. His greatest and most illustrious work, his successful war with Brutus and Cassius, was done to crush the liberties of his country and of his fellow-citizens. Demetrius, till he was driven to extremity, went on, without intermission, maintaining liberty in Greece, and expelling the foreign garrisons from the cities; not like Antony, whose boast was to have slain in Macedonia those who had set up liberty in Rome. As for the profusion and magnificence of his gifts, one point for which Antony is lauded, Demetrius so far outdid them, that what he gave to his enemies was far more than Antony ever gave to his friends. Antony was renowned for giving Brutus honorable burial; Demetrius did so to all the enemy's dead, and sent the prisoners back to Ptolemy with money and presents.

Both were insolent in prosperity, and abandoned themselves to luxuries and enjoyments. Yet it cannot be said that Demetrius, in his revellings and dissipations, ever let slip the time for action; pleasures with him attended only the superabundance of his ease, and his Lamia, like that of the fable, belonged only to his playful, half-waking, half-sleeping hours. When war demanded his attention, his spear was not wreathed with ivy, nor his helmet redolent of unguents; he did not come out to battle from the women's chamber, but,

---

[2] The quotation from Euripides, *the minister of the unpriestly* or unhallowed *Mars,* is an uncertain fragment, No. cxii. in Matthiæ. A second *Taphosiris* (tomb of Osiris) is distinguished by Strabo from the more important inland town of the same name, and described as a rocky place on the coast, and a favorite resort for pleasure parties from Alexandria.

hushing the bacchanal shouts and putting an end to the orgies, he became at once, as Euripides² calls it, "the minister of the unpriestly Mars;" and, in short, he never once incurred disaster through indolence or self-indulgence. Whereas Antony, like Hercules in the picture where Omphale is seen removing his club and stripping him of his lion's skin, was over and over again disarmed by Cleopatra, and beguiled away, while great actions and enterprises of the first necessity fell, as it were, from his hands, to go with her to the sea-shore of Canopus and Taphosiris, and play about. And in the end, like another Paris, he left the battle to fly to her arms; or rather, to say the truth, Paris fled when he was already beaten; Antony fled first, and, to follow Cleopatra, abandoned his victory.

There was no law to prevent Demetrius from marrying several wives; from the time of Philip and Alexander, it had become usual with Macedonian kings, and he did no more than was done by Lysimachus and Ptolemy. And those he married he treated honorably. But Antony, first of all, in marrying two wives at once, did a thing which no Roman had ever allowed himself; and then he drove away his lawful Roman wife to please the foreign and unlawful woman. And so Demetrius incurred no harm at all; Antony procured his ruin by his marriage. On the other hand, no licentious acts of Antony's can be charged with that impiety which marks those of Demetrius. Historical writers tell us that the very dogs are excluded from the whole Acropolis, because of their gross, uncleanly habits. The very Parthenon itself saw Demetrius consorting with harlots and debauching free women of Athens. The vice of cruelty, also, remote as it seems from the indulgence of voluptuous desires, must be attributed to him, who, in the pursuit of his pleasures, allowed, or to say more truly, compelled the death of the most beautiful and most chaste of the Athenians, who found no way but this to escape his violence. In one word, Antony himself suffered by his excesses, and other people by those of Demetrius.

In his conduct to his parents, Demetrius was irreproachable. Antony gave up his mother's brother, in order that he might have leave to kill Cicero, this itself being so cruel and shocking an act, that Antony would hardly be forgiven if Cicero's death had been the price of this uncle's safety. In respect of breaches of oaths and treaties, the seizure of Artabazes, and the assassination of Alexander, Antony may urge the plea which no one denies to be true, that Artabazes first abandoned and betrayed him in Media; Demetrius is alleged by many to have invented false pretexts for his act, and not to have retaliated for injuries, but to have accused one whom he injured himself.

The achievements of Demetrius are all his own work. Antony's noblest and greatest victories were won in his absence by his lieutenants. For their final disasters they have both only to thank themselves; not, however, in an equal degree. Demetrius was deserted, the Macedonians revolted from him; Antony deserted others, and ran away while men were fighting for him at the risk of their lives. The fault to be found with the one is that he had thus entirely alienated the affections of his soldiers; the other's condemnation is that he abandoned so much love and faith as he still possessed. We cannot admire the death of either, but that of Demetrius excites our greater contempt. He let himself become a prisoner, and was thankful to gain a three years' accession of life in captivity. He was tamed like a wild beast by his belly, and by wine; Antony took himself out of the world in a cowardly, pitiful, and ignoble manner, but still in time to prevent the enemy having his person in their power.

DION[1]

TRANSLATED BY ROBERT UVEDALE, LL. D.

IF it be true, Sosius Senecio, that, as Simonides tells us,

"Of the Corinthians Troy does not complain"[2]

for having taken part with the Achæans in the siege, because the Trojans also had Corinthians (Glaucus, who sprang from Corinth), fighting bravely on their side, so also it may be fairly said that neither Romans nor Greeks can quarrel with the Academy, each nation being equally represented in the following pair of lives, which will give an account of Brutus and of Dion,—Dion, who was Plato's own hearer, and Brutus, who was brought up in his philosophy. They came from one and the selfsame school, where they had been trained alike, to run the race of honor; nor need we wonder that in the performance of actions

---

[1] Dion, a Syracusan, was born about 408 B. C. He became an ardent disciple of Plato, when that philosopher visited Syracuse in the reign of the elder Dionysius, and he dreamed of making Syracuse a free city and of giving liberty to the Greek cities in Sicily. He carried to excess the austerity of the philosopher. But when he found himself master of Syracuse, about 355 B. C., he was unwilling to give the citizens the liberty which they expected, and his despotic conduct soon caused discontent. A conspiracy was formed against him and he was assassinated 353 B. C.—Dr. William Smith.

[2] Aristotle, in his Rhetoric, takes the verse of Simonides in quite a different sense. The Corinthians, he says, thought Simonides meant it to their disparagement, as if those could have little worth whom their enemies did not think it worth while to complain

often most nearly allied and akin, they both bore evidence to the truth of what their guide and teacher had said, that, without the concurrence of power and success with justice and prudence, public actions do not attain their proper, great, and noble character. For as Hippomachus the wrestling-master affirmed, he could distinguish his scholars at a distance, though they were but carrying meat from the shambles, so it is very probable that the principles of those who have had the same good education should appear with a resemblance in all their actions, creating in them a certain harmony and proportion, at once agreeable and becoming.

We may also draw a close parallel of the lives of the two men from their fortunes, wherein chance, even more than their own designs, made them nearly alike. For they were both cut off by an untimely death, not being able to accomplish those ends which through many risks and difficulties they aimed at. But, above all, this is most wonderful; that by preternatural interposition both of them had notice given of their approaching death by an unpropitious form, which visibly appeared to them. Although there are people who utterly deny any such thing, and say that no man

of. Thirteen letters professing to be Plato's have come down to us, almost all relating to these more eventful passages of his life, and addressed to Dion, Dion's friends, and Dionysius himself. It is of course highly probable that letters of this description would be fabricated,—it is more probable, perhaps, that any extant compositions of the kind should be fictitious, than that they should be genuine. These which we have are not what we should expect Plato's letters to be, and yet, on the other hand, are not what we should expect to have been written for him. Plutarch quotes the fourth and seventh; and some critics have considered these to be, not Plato's own, but early compositions by some immediate disciples, written in his name, as a defence of his conduct. Mr. Grote appears to treat the whole collection as genuine.

in his right senses ever yet saw any supernatural phantom or apparition, but that children only, and silly women, or men disordered by sickness, in some aberration of the mind or distemperature of the body, have had empty and extravagant imaginations, whilst the real evil genius, superstition, was in themselves. Yet if Dion and Brutus, men of solid understanding, and philosophers, not to be easily deluded by fancy or discomposed by any sudden apprehension, were thus affected by visions, that they forthwith declared to their friends what they had seen, I know not how we can avoid admitting again the utterly exploded opinion of the oldest times, that evil and beguiling spirits, out of an envy to good men, and a desire of impeding their good deeds, make efforts to excite in them feelings of terror and distraction, to make them shake and totter in their virtue, lest by a steady and unbiased perseverance they should obtain a happier condition than these beings after death. But I shall leave these things for another opportunity, and, in this twelfth book of the lives of great men compared one with another, begin with his who was the elder.

Dionysius the First, having possessed himself of the government, at once took to wife the daughter of Hermocrates, the Syracusan. She, in an outbreak which the citizens made before the new power was well settled, was abused in such a barbarous and outrageous manner, that for shame she put an end to her own life. But Dionysius, when he was reëstablished and confirmed in his supremacy, married two wives together, one named Doris, of Locri, the other, Aristomache, a native of Sicily, and daughter of Hipparinus, a man of the first quality in Syracuse, and colleague with Dionysius when he was first chosen general with unlimited powers for the war. It is said he married them both in one day, and no one ever knew which of the two he first made his wife; and ever after he divided his kindness equally between them, both accompanying him together at his table, and in his bed by turns. Indeed, the Syracusans were urgent that their own countrywoman might be preferred before the stranger; but Doris, to compensate for her foreign extraction, had the good fortune to be the mother of the son and heir of the family, whilst Aristomache continued a long time without issue, though Dionysius was very desirous to have children by her, and, indeed, caused Doris's mother to be put to death, laying to her charge that she had given drugs to Aristomache, to prevent her being with child.

Dion, Aristomache's brother, at first found an honorable reception for his sister's sake; but his own worth and parts soon procured him a nearer place in his brother-in-law's affection, who, among other favors, gave special command to his treasurers to furnish Dion with whatever money he demanded, only telling him on the same day what they had delivered out. Now, though Dion was before reputed a person of lofty character, of a noble mind, and daring courage, yet these excellent qualifications all received a great development from the happy chance which conducted Plato into Sicily; not assuredly by any human device or calculation, but some supernatural power, designing that this remote cause should hereafter occasion the recovery of the Sicilians' lost liberty and the subversion of the tyrannical government, brought the philosopher out of Italy to Syracuse, and made acquaintance between him and Dion. Dion was, indeed, at this time extremely young in years, but of all the scholars that attended Plato he was the quickest and aptest to learn, and the most prompt and eager to practise, the lessons of virtue, as Plato himself reports of him, and his own actions sufficiently testify.

For though he had been bred up under a tyrant in habits of submission, accustomed to a life, on the one hand of servility and intimidation, and yet on the other of vulgar display and luxury, the mistaken happiness of people that knew no better thing than pleasure and self-indulgence, yet, at the first taste of reason and a philosophy that demands obedience to virtue, his soul was set in a flame, and in the simple innocence of youth, concluding, from his own disposition, that the same reasons would work the same effects upon Dionysius, he made it his business, and at length obtained the favor of him, at a leisure hour, to hear Plato.

At this their meeting, the subject-matter of their discourse in general was human virtue, but, more particularly, they disputed concerning fortitude, which Plato proved tyrants, of all men, had the least pretence to; and thence proceeding to treat of justice, asserted the happy estate of the just, and the miserable condition of the unjust; arguments which Dionysius would not hear out, but, feeling himself, as it were, convicted by his words, and much displeased to see the rest of the auditors full of admiration for the speaker and captivated with his doctrine, at last, exceedingly exasperated, he asked the philosopher in a rage, what business he had in Sicily. To which Plato answered, "I came to seek a virtuous man." "It seems then," replied Dionysius, "you have lost your labor." Dion, supposing that this was all, and that nothing further could come of his anger, at Plato's request, conveyed him aboard a galley, which was conveying Pollis, the Spartan, into Greece. But Dionysius privately dealt with Pollis, by all means to kill Plato in the voyage; if not, to be sure to sell him for a slave; he would, of course, take no harm of it, being the same just man as before; he would enjoy that happiness, though he lost his liberty. Pollis, therefore, it is stated, carried Plato to Ægina, and there sold him; the Æginetans, then at war with Athens, having made a decree that whatever Athenian was taken on their coasts should forthwith be exposed to sale. Notwithstanding, Dion was not in less favor and credit with Dionysius than formerly, but was intrusted with the most considerable employments, and sent on important embassies to Carthage, in the management of which he gained very great reputation. Besides, the usurper bore with the liberty he took to speak his mind freely, he being the only man who upon any occasion durst boldly say what he thought, as, for example, in the rebuke he gave him about Gelon. Dionysius was ridiculing Gelon's government, and, alluding to his name, said, he had been the laughing-stock of Sicily.[3] While others seemed to admire and applaud the quibble, Dion very warmly replied, "Nevertheless, it is certain that you are sole governor here, because you were trusted for Gelon's sake; but for your sake no man will ever hereafter be trusted again." For, indeed, Gelon had made a monarchy appear the best, whereas Dionysius had convinced men that it was the worst, of governments.

Dionysius had three children by Doris, and by Aristomache four, two of which were daughters, Sophrosyne and Arete. Sophrosyne was married to his son Dionysius; Arete, to his brother Thearides, after whose death, Dion received his niece Arete to wife. Now when Dionysius was sick and like to die, Dion endeavored to speak with him in behalf of the children he had by Aristomache, but was still prevented by the physicians, who wanted to ingratiate themselves with the next successor, who also, as Timæus reports, gave

---

[3] *Gelona*, he said, had been the *gelota* of Sicily; *Gelona* being equivalent to Gelon, and *gelota* meaning laughter, or ridicule.

him a sleeping potion which he asked for, which produced an insensibility only followed by his death.

Nevertheless, at the first council which the young Dionysius held with his friends, Dion discoursed so well of the present state of affairs, that he made all the rest appear in their politics but children, and in their votes rather slaves than counsellors, who timorously and disingenuously advised what would please the young man, rather than what would advance his interest. But that which startled them most was the proposal he made to avert the imminent danger they feared of a war with the Carthaginians, undertaking, if Dionysius wanted peace, to sail immediately over into Africa, and conclude it there upon honorable terms; but, if he rather preferred war, then he would fit out and maintain at his own cost and charges fifty galleys ready for the service.

Dionysius wondered much at his greatness of mind, and received his offer with satisfaction. But the other courtiers thinking his generosity reflected upon them, and jealous of being lessened by his greatness, from hence took all occasions by private slanders to render him obnoxious to the young man's displeasure; as if he designed by his power at sea to surprise the government, and by the help of those naval forces confer the supreme authority upon his sister Aristomache's children. But, indeed, the most apparent and the strongest grounds for dislike and hostility existed already in the difference of his habits, and his reserved and separate way of living. For they, who, from the beginning, by flatteries and all unworthy artifices, courted the favor and familiarity of the prince, youthful and voluptuously bred, ministered to his pleasures, and sought how to find him daily some new amours and occupy him in vain amusements, with wine or with women, and in other dissipations; by which means, the tyranny, like iron softened in the fire, seemed, indeed, to the subject to be more moderate and gentle, and to abate somewhat of its extreme severity; the edge of it being blunted, not by the clemency, but rather the sloth and degeneracy of the sovereign, whose dissoluteness, gaining ground daily, and growing upon him, soon weakened and broke those "adamantine chains," with which his father, Dionysius, said he had left the monarchy fastened and secured. It is reported of him, that, having begun a drunken debauch, he continued it ninety days without intermission;[4] in all which time no person on business was allowed to appear, nor was any serious conversation heard at court, but drinking, singing, dancing, and buffoonery reigned there without control.

It is likely then they had little kindness for Dion, who never indulged himself in any youthful pleasure or diversion. And so his very virtues were the matter of their calumnies, and were represented under one or other plausible name as vices; they called his gravity pride, his plaindealing self-will, the good advice he gave was all construed into reprimand, and he was censured for neglecting and scorning those in whose misdemeanors he declined to participate. And to say the truth, there was in his natural character something stately, austere, reserved, and unsociable in conversation, which made his company unpleasant and disagreeable not only to the young tyrant, whose ears had been corrupted by flatteries; many also of Dion's own intimate friends, though they loved the integrity and generosity of his temper, yet blamed his manner, and thought he treated those with whom he had to do,

---

[4] *Ninety* seems an impossible number; Amiot, in his translation, has *three* ("trois jours"), which seems, on the other hand, too little.

less courteously and affably than became a man engaged in civil business. Of which Plato also afterwards wrote to him; and, as it were, prophetically advised him carefully to avoid an arbitrary temper, whose proper helpmate was a solitary life. And, indeed, at this very time, though circumstances made him so important, and, in the danger of the tottering government, he was recognized as the only or the ablest support of it, yet he well understood that he owed not his high position to any good-will or kindness, but to the mere necessities of the usurper.

And, supposing the cause of this to be ignorance and want of education, he endeavored to induce the young man into a course of liberal studies, and to give him some knowledge of moral truths and reasonings, hoping he might thus lose his fear of virtuous living, and learn to take pleasure in laudable actions. Dionysius, in his own nature, was not one of the worst kind of tyrants, but his father, fearing that if he should come to understand himself better, and converse with wise and reasonable men, he might enter into some design against him, and dispossess him of his power, kept him closely shut up at home; where, for want of other company, and ignorant how to spend his time better, he busied himself in making little chariots, candlesticks, stools, tables, and other things of wood. For the elder Dionysius was so diffident and suspicious, and so continually on his guard against all men, that he would not so much as let his hair be trimmed with any barber's or hair-cutter's instruments, but made one of his artificers singe him with a live coal. Neither were his brother or his son allowed to come into his apartment in the dress they wore, but they, as all others, were stript to their skins by some of the guard, and, after being seen naked, put on other clothes before they were admitted into the presence. When his brother Leptines was once describing the situation of a place, and took a javelin from one of the guard to draw the plan of it, he was extremely angry with him, and had the soldier who gave him the weapon put to death. He declared, the more judicious his friends were, the more he suspected them; because he knew, that were it in their choice, they would rather be tyrants themselves than the subjects of a tyrant. He slew Marsyas, one of his captains whom he had preferred to a considerable command, for dreaming that he killed him; without some previous waking thought and purpose of the kind, he could not, he supposed, have had that fancy in his sleep. So timorous was he, and so miserable a slave to his fears, yet very angry with Plato, because he would not allow him to be the valiantest man alive.

Dion, as we said before, seeing the son thus deformed and spoilt in character for want of teaching, exhorted him to study, and to use all his entreaties to persuade Plato, the first of philosophers, to visit him in Sicily, and, when he came, to submit himself to his direction and advice; by whose instructions he might conform his nature to the truths of virtue, and, living after the likeness of the Divine and glorious Model of Being, out of obedience to whose control the general confusion is changed into the beautiful order of the universe, so he in like manner might be the cause of great happiness to himself and to all his subjects, who, obliged by his justice and moderation, would then willingly pay him obedience as their father, which now grudgingly, and upon necessity, they are forced to yield him as their master. Their usurping tyrant he would then no longer be, but their lawful king. For fear and force, a great navy and standing army of ten thousand hired barbarians are not, as his father had said, the adamantine chains which secure the regal power, but the love, zeal, and affection inspired by clemency and justice; which, though they seem more pliant than the stiff and hard bonds of severity, are nevertheless the strongest and most durable ties to sustain a lasting government. Moreover, it is mean and dishonorable that a ruler, while careful to be splendid in his dress, and luxurious and magnificent in his habitation, should, in reason and power of speech, make no better show than the commonest of his subjects, nor have the princely palace of his mind adorned according to his royal dignity.

Dion frequently entertaining the king upon this subject, and, as occasion offered, repeating some of the philosopher's sayings, Dionysius grew impatiently desirous to have Plato's company, and to hear him discourse. Forthwith, therefore, he sent letter upon letter to him to Athens, to which Dion added his entreaties; also several philosophers of the Pythagorean sect from Italy sent their recommendations, urging him to come and obtain a hold upon this pliant, youthful soul, which his solid and weighty reasonings might steady, as it were, upon the seas of absolute power and authority. Plato, as he tells us himself, out of shame more than any other feeling, lest it should seem that he was all mere theory, and that of his own good-will he would never venture into action, hoping withal, that if he could work a cure upon one man, the head and guide of the rest, he might remedy the distempers of the whole island of Sicily, yielded to their requests.

But Dion's enemies, fearing an alteration in Dionysius, persuaded him to recall from banishment Philistus, a man of learned education, and at the same time of great experience in the ways of tyrants, and who might serve as a counterpoise to Plato and his philosophy. For Philistus from the beginning had been a great instrument in establishing the tyranny, and for a long time had held the office of captain of the citadel. There was a report, that he had been intimate with the mother of Dionysius the first, and not without his privity. And when Leptines, having two daughters by a married woman whom he had debauched, gave one of them in marriage to Philistus, without acquainting Dionysius, he, in great anger, put Leptines's mistress in prison, and banished Philistus from Sicily. Whereupon, he fled to some of his friends on the Adriatic coast, in which retirement and leisure it is probable he wrote the greatest part of his history; for he returned not into his country during the reign of that Dionysius.

But after his death, as is just related, Dion's enemies occasioned him to be recalled home, as fitter for their purpose, and a firm friend to the arbitrary government. And this, indeed, immediately upon his return he set himself to maintain; and at the same time various calumnies and accusations against Dion were by others brought to the king; as that he held correspondence with Theodotes and Heraclides, to subvert the government; as, doubtless, it is likely enough, that Dion had entertained hopes, by the coming of Plato, to mitigate the rigid and despotic severity of the tyranny, and to give Dionysius the character of a fair and lawful governor; and had determined, if he should continue averse to that, and were not to be reclaimed, to depose him, and restore the commonwealth to the Syracusans; not that he approved a democratic government, but thought it altogether preferable to a tyranny, when a sound and good aristocracy[5] could not be procured.

[5] The word *aristocracy* is used in its Platonic sense, which in the modern use it has lost, namely, a government by the best (the most wise and virtuous) citizens.

This was the state of affairs when Plato came into Sicily, who, at his first arrival, was received with wonderful demonstration of kindness and respect. For one of the royal chariots, richly ornamented, was in attendance to receive him when he came on shore; Dionysius himself sacrificed to the gods in thankful acknowledgment for the great happiness which had befallen his government. The citizens, also, began to entertain marvellous hopes of a speedy reformation, when they observed the modesty which now ruled in the banquets, and the general decorum which prevailed in all the court, their tyrant himself also behaving with gentleness and humanity in all their matters of business that came before him. There was a general passion for reasoning and philosophy, insomuch that the very palace, it is reported, was filled with dust by the concourse of the students in mathematics who were working their problems there.[6] Some few days after, it was the time of one of the Syracusan sacrifices, and when the priest, as he was wont, prayed for the long and safe continuance of the tyranny, Dionysius, it is said, as he stood by, cried out, "Leave off praying for evil upon us." This sensibly vexed Philistus and his party, who conjectured, that if Plato, upon such brief acquaintance, had so far transformed and altered the young man's mind, longer converse and greater intimacy would give him such influence and authority, that it would be impossible to withstand him.

Therefore, no longer privately and apart, but jointly and in public, all of them, they began to slander Dion, noising it about that he had charmed and bewitched Dionysius by Plato's sophistry, to the end that when he was persuaded voluntarily to part with

[6] The floors being spread with sand, in which the geometrical figures, according to the common Greek habit, would be drawn.

his power, and lay down his authority, Dion might take it up, and settle it upon his sister Aristomache's children. Others professed to be indignant that the Athenians, who formerly had come to Sicily with a great fleet and a numerous land-army, and perished miserably without being able to take the city of Syracuse, should now, by means of one sophister, overturn the sovereignty of Dionysius; inveigling him to cashier his guard of ten thousand lances, dismiss a navy of four hundred galleys, disband an army of ten thousand horse and many times over that number of foot, and go seek in the schools an unknown and imaginary bliss, and learn by the mathematics how to be happy; while, in the mean time, the substantial enjoyments of absolute power, riches, and pleasure would be handed over to Dion and his sister's children.

By these means, Dion began to incur at first suspicion, and by degrees more apparent displeasure and hostility. A letter, also, was intercepted and brought to the young prince, which Dion had written to the Carthaginian agents, advising them, that, when they treated with Dionysius concerning the peace, they should not come to their audience without communicating with him; they would not fail to obtain by this means all that they wanted. When Dionysius had shown this to Philistus, and consulted with him, as Timæus, relates, about it, he overreached Dion by a feigned reconciliation, professing, after some fair and reasonable expression of his feelings, that he was at friends with him, and thus, leading him alone to the sea-side, under the castle wall, he showed him the letter, and taxed him with conspiring with the Carthaginians against him. And when Dion essayed to speak in his own defence, Dionysius suffered him not; but immediately forced him aboard a boat, which lay there for that purpose, and commanded the sailors to set him ashore on the coast of Italy.

When this was publicly known, and was thought very hard usage, there was much lamentation in the tyrant's own household on account of the women,[7] but the citizens of Syracuse encouraged themselves, expecting that for his sake some disturbance would ensue; which, together with the mistrust others would now feel, might occasion a general change and revolution in the state. Dionysius, seeing this, took alarm, and endeavored to pacify the women and others of Dion's kindred and friends; assuring them that he had not banished, but only sent him out of the way for a time, for fear of his own passion, which might be provoked some day by Dion's self-will into some act which he should be sorry for. He gave also two ships to his relations, with liberty to send into Peloponnesus for him whatever of his property or servants they thought fit.

Dion was very rich, and had his house furnished with little less than royal splendor and magnificence. These valuables his friends packed up and conveyed to him, besides many rich presents which were sent him by the women and his adherents. So that, so far as wealth and riches went, he made a noble appearance among the Greeks, and they might judge, by the affluence of the exile, what was the power of the tyrant.

Dionysius immediately removed Plato into the castle,[8] designing, under color of an honorable and kind reception, to set a guard upon him, lest he should fol-

---

[7] Dion's wife, Arete, and sister, Aristomache.

[8] The castle, citadel, or *acropolis*, is the island of Ortygia (now the modern town), which Dionysius had strongly fortified, which was held by the barbarian garrison, and in which the tyrannic family lived and kept their court.

low Dion, and declare to the world in his behalf, how injuriously he had been dealt with. And, moreover, time and conversation (as wild beasts by use grow tame and tractable) had brought Dionysius to endure Plato's company and discourse, so that he began to love the philosopher, but with such an affection as had something of the tyrant in it, requiring of Plato that he should, in return of his kindness, love him only, and attend to him above all other men; being ready to permit to his care the chief management of affairs, and even the government, too, upon condition that he would not prefer Dion's friendship before his. This extravagant affection was a great trouble for Plato, for it was accompanied with petulant and jealous humors, like the fond passions of those that are desperately in love; frequently he was angry and fell out with him, and presently begged and entreated to be friends again. He was beyond measure desirous to be Plato's scholar, and to proceed in the study of philosophy, and yet he was ashamed of it with those who spoke against it and professed to think it would ruin him.

But a war about this time breaking out, he sent Plato away, promising him in the summer to recall Dion, though in this he broke his word at once; nevertheless, he remitted to him his revenues, desiring Plato to excuse him as to the time appointed, because of the war, but, as soon as he had settled a peace, he would immediately send for Dion, requiring him in the interim to be quiet, and not raise any disturbance, nor speak ill of him among the Grecians. This Plato endeavored to effect, by keeping Dion with him in the Academy, and busying him in philosophical studies.

Dion sojourned in the Upper Town of Athens, with Callippus, one of his acquaintance; but for his pleasure he bought a seat in the country, which afterwards, when he went into Sicily, he gave to Speusippus,[9] who had been his most frequent companion while he was at Athens, Plato so arranging it, with the hope that Dion's austere temper might be softened by agreeable company, with an occasional mixture of seasonable mirth. For Speusippus was of the character to afford him this; we find him spoken of in Timon's Silli,[10] as "good at a jest." And Plato himself, as it happened, being called upon to furnish a chorus of boys, Dion took upon him the ordering and management of it, and defrayed the whole expense, Plato giving him this opportunity to oblige the Athenians, which was likely to procure his friend more kindness than himself credit. Dion went also to see several other cities, visiting the noblest and most statesmanlike persons in Greece, and joining in their recreations and entertainments in their times of festival. In all which, no sort of vulgar ignorance, or tyrannic assumption, or luxuriousness was remarked in him; but, on the contrary, a great deal of temperance, generosity, and courage, and a well-becoming taste for reasoning and philosophic discourses. By which means he gained the love and admiration of all men, and in many cities had public honors decreed him; the Lacedæmonians making him a citizen of Sparta, without regard to the displeasure of Dionysius, though at that time he was aiding them in their wars against the Thebans.

It is related that once, upon invitation, he went to pay a visit to Ptœodorus the Megarian, a man, it would seem, of wealth and importance; and when, on account of the concourse of people about his doors, and the press of business, it was very troublesome and

[9] Plato's nephew and successor in the School of the Academy.

[10] Satiric poems, so called, in which a good deal of ridicule was thrown on the philosophers.

difficult to get access to him, turning about to his friends who seemed concerned and angry at it, "What reason," said he, "have we to blame Ptœodorus, when we ourselves used to do no better when we were at Syracuse?"

After some little time, Dionysius, envying Dion, and jealous of the favor and interest he had among the Grecians, put a stop upon his incomes, and no longer sent him his revenues, making his own commissioners trustees of the estate. But, endeavoring to obviate the ill-will and discredit which, upon Plato's account, might accrue to him among the philosophers, he collected in his court many reputed learned men; and, ambitiously desiring to surpass them in their debates, he was forced to make use, often incorrectly, of arguments he had picked up from Plato. And now he wished for his company again, repenting he had not made better use of it when he had it, and had given no greater heed to his admirable lessons. Like a tyrant, therefore, inconsiderate in his desires, headstrong and violent in whatever he took a will to, on a sudden he was eagerly set on the design of recalling him, and left no stone unturned, but addressed himself to Archytas the Pythagorean (his acquaintance and friendly relations with whom owed their origin to Plato), and persuaded him to stand as surety for his engagements, and to request Plato to revisit Sicily.

Archytas therefore sent Archedemus, and Dionysius some galleys, with divers friends, to entreat his return; moreover, he wrote to him himself expressly and in plain terms, that Dion must never look for any favor or kindness, if Plato would not be prevailed with to come into Sicily; but if Plato did come, Dion should be assured of whatever he desired. Dion also received letters full of solicitations from his sister and his wife, urging him to beg Plato to gratify Dionysius in this request, and not give him an excuse for further ill-doing. So that, as Plato says of himself, the third time he set sail for the Strait of Scylla,[11]

"Venturing again Charybdis's dangerous gulf."

This arrival brought great joy to Dionysius, and no less hopes to the Sicilians, who were earnest in their prayers and good wishes that Plato might get the better of Philistus, and philosophy triumph over tyranny. Neither was he unbefriended by the women, who studied to oblige him; and he had with Dionysius that peculiar credit which no man else ever obtained, namely, liberty to come into his presence without being examined or searched. When he would have given him a considerable sum of money, and, on several repeated occasions, made fresh offers, which Plato as often declined, Aristippus the Cyrenæan, then present, said that Dionysius was very safe in his munificence, he gave little to those who were ready to take all they could get, and a great deal to Plato, who would accept of nothing.

After the first compliments of kindness were over, when Plato began to discourse of Dion, he was at first diverted by excuses for delay, followed soon after by complaints and disgusts, though not as yet observable to others, Dionysius endeavoring to conceal them, and, by other civilities and honorable usage, to draw him off from his affection to Dion. And for some time Plato himself was careful not to let any thing of this dishonesty and breach of promise appear, but bore with it, and dissembled his annoyance. While matters stood thus between them, and, as they thought, they

---

[11] It is *Sicily* in the manuscripts, and in the old text, but there can be no doubt about altering it to *Scylla*, which is more apposite in itself, and is found with the verse following from the Odyssey (xii., 428), in Plato's own letters (Ep. 7).

were unobserved and undiscovered, Helicon the Cyzicenian, one of Plato's follower's foretold an eclipse of the sun, which happened according to his prediction; for which he was much admired by the tyrant, and rewarded with a talent of silver; whereupon Aristippus, jesting with some others of the philosophers, told them, he also could predict something extraordinary; and on their entreating him to declare it, "I foretell," said he, "that before long there will be a quarrel between Dionysius and Plato."

At length Dionysius made sale of Dion's estate, and converted the money to his own use, and removed Plato from an apartment he had in the gardens of the palace to lodgings among the guards he kept in pay, who from the first had hated Plato, and sought opportunity to make away with him, supposing he advised Dionysius to lay down the government and disband his soldiers.

When Archytas understood the danger he was in, he immediately sent a galley with messengers to demand him of Dionysius; alleging that he stood engaged for his safety, upon the confidence of which Plato had come to Sicily. Dionysius, to palliate his secret hatred, before Plato came away, treated him with great entertainments and all seeming demonstrations of kindness, but could not forbear breaking out one day into the expression, "No doubt, Plato, when you are at home among the philosophers, your companions, you will complain of me, and reckon up a great many of my faults." To which Plato answered with a smile, "The Academy will never, I trust, be at such a loss for subjects to discuss as to seek one in you." Thus, they say, Plato was dismissed; but his own writings do not altogether agree with this account.

Dion was angry at all this, and not long after declared open enmity to Dionysius, on hearing what had been done with his wife; on which matter Plato, also, had had some confidential correspondence with Dionysius. Thus it was. After Dion's banishment, Dionysius, when he sent Plato back, had desired him to ask Dion privately, if he would be averse to his wife's marrying another man. For there went a report, whether true, or raised by Dion's enemies, that his marriage was not pleasing to him, and that he lived with his wife on uneasy terms. When Plato therefore came to Athens, and had mentioned the subject to Dion, he wrote a letter to Dionysius, speaking of other matters openly, but on this in language expressly designed to be understood by him alone, to the effect that he had talked with Dion about the business, and that it was evident he would highly resent the affront, if it should be put into execution. At that time, therefore, while there were yet great hopes of an accommodation, he took no new steps with his sister, suffering her to live with Dion's child. But when things were come to that pass, that no reconciliation could be expected, and Plato, after his second visit, was again sent away in displeasure, he then forced Arete, against her will, to marry Timocrates, one of his favorites; in this action coming short even of his father's justice and lenity; for he, when Polyxenus, the husband of his sister, Theste, became his enemy, and fled in alarm out of Sicily, sent for his sister, and taxed her, that being privy to her husband's flight, she had not declared it to him. But the lady, confident and fearless, made him this reply: "Do you believe me, brother, so bad a wife, or so timorous a woman, that, having known my husband's flight, I would not have borne him company, and shared his fortunes? I knew nothing of it; since otherwise it had been my better lot to be called the wife of the exile Polyxenus, than the sister of the tyrant Dionysius." It is said, he admired her free and ready answer, as did the Syracusans, also, her courage and virtue, insomuch that she retained her dignity and princely retinue after the dissolution of the tyranny, and, when she died, the citizens, by public decree, attended the solemnity of her funeral. And the story, though a digression from the present purpose, was well worth the telling.

From this time, Dion set his mind upon warlike measures; with which Plato, out of respect for past hospitalities, and because of his age,[12] would have nothing to do. But Speusippus and the rest of his friends assisted and encouraged him, bidding him deliver Sicily, which with lift-up hands implored his help, and with open arms was ready to receive him. For when Plato was staying at Syracuse, Speusippus, being oftener than he in company with the citizens, had more thoroughly made out how they were inclined; and though at first they had been on their guard, suspecting his bold language, as though he had been set on by the tyrant to trepan them, yet at length they trusted him. There was but one mind and one wish or prayer among them all, that Dion would undertake the design, and come, though without either navy, men, horse, or arms; that he would simply put himself aboard any ship, and lend the Sicilians his person and name against Dionysius. This information from Speusippus encouraged Dion, who, concealing his real purpose, employed his friends privately to raise what men they could; and many statesmen and philosophers were assisting to him, as, for instance, Eudemus the Cyprian, on whose death Aristotle wrote his Dialogue of the Soul, and Timonides the Leucadian. They also engaged on his side Miltas the Thessalian, who was a prophet, and had studied in the Academy. But

---

[12] He was now seventy years old.

of all that were banished by Dionysius, who were not fewer than a thousand, five and twenty only joined in the enterprise; the rest were afraid, and abandoned it. The rendezvous was in the island Zacynthus, where a a small force of not quite eight hundred men came together, all of them, however, persons already distinguished in plenty of previous hard service, their bodies well trained and practised, and their experience and courage amply sufficient to animate and embolden to action the numbers whom Dion expected to join him in Sicily.

Yet these men, when they first understood the expedition was against Dionysius, were troubled and disheartened, blaming Dion, that, hurried on like a madman by mere passion and despair, he rashly threw both himself and them into certain ruin. Nor were they less angry with their commanders and mustermasters, that they had not in the beginning let them know the design. But when Dion in his address to them had set forth the unsafe and weak condition of arbitrary government, and declared that he carried them rather for commanders than soldiers, the citizens of Syracuse and the rest of the Sicilians having been long ready for a revolt, and when, after him, Alcimenes, an Achæan of the highest birth and reputation, who accompanied the expedition, harangued them to the same effect, they were contented.

It was now the middle of summer, and the Etesian winds blowing steadily on the seas, the moon was at the full, when Dion prepared a magnificent sacrifice to Apollo, and with great solemnity marched his soldiers to the temple in all their arms and accoutrements. And after the sacrifice, he feasted them all in the racecourse[13] of the Zacynthians, where he had made pro-

---

[13] The enclosed *Stadium* or Greek circus.

vision for their entertainment. And when here they beheld with wonder the quantity and the richness of the gold and silver plate, and the tables laid to entertain them, all far exceeding the fortunes of a private man, they concluded with themselves, that a man now past the prime of life, who was master of so much treasure, would not engage himself in so hazardous an enterprise without good reason of hope, and certain and sufficient assurances of aid from friends over there. Just after the libations were made,[14] and the accompanying prayers offered, the moon was eclipsed; which was no wonder to Dion, who understood the revolutions of eclipses, and the way in which the moon is overshadowed and the earth interposed between her and the sun. But because it was necessary that the soldiers, who were surprised and troubled at it, should be satisfied and encouraged, Miltas the diviner, standing up in the midst of the assembly, bade them be of good cheer, and expect all happy success, for that the divine powers foreshowed that something at present glorious and resplendent should be eclipsed and obscured; nothing at this time being more splendid than the sovereignty of Dionysius, their arrival in Sicily should dim this glory, and extinguish this brightness. Thus Miltas, in public, descanted upon the incident. But concerning a swarm of bees which settled on the poop of Dion's ship, he privately told him and his friends, that he feared the great actions they were like to perform, though for a time they should thrive and flourish, would be of short continuance, and soon suffer a decay. It is reported, also, that many prodigies happened to Dionysius at that time. An eagle, snatching a javelin from one of the guard, carried it

[14] Just when the dinner itself was over, and the dessert and drinking of wine about to follow.

aloft, and from thence let it fall into the sea. The water of the sea that washed the castle walls was for a whole day sweet and potable, as many that tasted it experienced. Pigs were farrowed perfect in all their other parts, but without ears. This the diviners declared to portend revolt and rebellion, for that the subjects would no longer give ear to the commands of their superiors. They expounded the sweetness of the water to signify to the Syracusans a change from hard and grievous times into easier and more happy circumstances. The eagle being the bird of Jupiter, and the spear an emblem of power and command, this prodigy was to denote that the chief of the gods designed the end and dissolution of the present government. These things Theopompus relates in his history.

Two ships of burden carried all Dion's men; a third vessel, of no great size, and two galleys of thirty oars attended them. In addition to his soldiers' own arms, he carried two thousand shields, a very great number of darts and lances, and abundant stores of all manner of provisions, that there might be no want of any thing in their voyage; their purpose being to keep out at sea during the whole voyage, and use the winds, since all the land was hostile to them, and Philistus, they had been told, was in Iapygia with a fleet, looking out for them. Twelve days they sailed with a fresh and gentle breeze; on the thirteenth, they made Pachynus, the Sicilian cape. There Protus, the chief pilot, advised them to land at once and without delay, for if they were forced again from the shore, and did not take advantage of the headland, they might ride out at sea many nights and days, waiting for a southerly wind in the summer season. But Dion, fearing a descent too near his enemies, and desirous to begin at a greater distance, and further on in the country, sailed on past Pachynus. They had not gone far, before stress of weather, the wind blowing hard at north, drove the fleet from the coast; and it being now about the time that Arcturus rises, a violent storm of wind and rain came on, with thunder and lightning, the mariners were at their wits' end, and ignorant what course they ran, until on a sudden they found they were driving with the sea on Cercina, the island on the coast of Africa, just where it is most craggy and dangerous to run upon. Upon the cliffs there they escaped narrowly of being forced and staved to pieces; but, laboring hard at their oars, with much difficulty they kept clear until the storm ceased. Then, lighting by chance upon a vessel, they understood they were upon the Heads, as it is called, of the Great Syrtis; and when they were now again disheartened by a sudden calm, and beating to and fro without making any way, a soft air began to blow from the land, when they expected any thing rather than wind from the south and scarce believed the happy change of their fortune. The gale gradually increasing, and beginning to blow fresh, they clapped on all their sails, and, praying to the gods, put out again into the open sea, steering right from Africa for Sicily. And, running steady before the wind, the fifth day they arrived at Minoa, a little town of Sicily, in the dominion of the Carthaginians, of which Synalus, an acquaintance and friend of Dion's, happened at that time to be governor; who, not knowing it was Dion and his fleet, endeavored to hinder his men from landing; but they rushed on shore with their swords in their hands, not slaying any of their opponents (for this Dion had forbidden, because of his friendship with the Carthaginians), but forced them to retreat, and, following close, pressed in a body with them into the place, and took it. As soon as the two commanders met, they mutually saluted each other;

Dion delivered up the place again to Synalus, without the least damage done to any one therein, and Synalus quartered and entertained the soldiers, and supplied Dion with what he wanted.

They were most of all encouraged by the happy accident of Dionysius's absence at this nick of time; for it appeared that he was lately gone with eighty sail of ships to Italy. Therefore, when Dion was desirous that the soldiers should refresh themselves there, after their tedious and troublesome voyage, they would not be prevailed with, but, earnest to make the best use of that opportunity, they urged Dion to lead them straight on to Syracuse. Leaving therefore their baggage, and the arms they did not use, Dion desired Synalus to convey them to him as he had occasion, and marched directly to Syracuse.

The first that came in to him upon his march were two hundred horse of the Agrigentines who were settled near Ecnomum, and, after them, the Geloans. But the news soon flying to Syracuse, Timocrates, who had married Dion's wife, the sister of Dionysius, and was the principal man among his friends now remaining in the city, immediately despatched a courier to Dionysius with letters announcing Dion's arrival; while he himself took all possible care to prevent any stir or tumult in the city, where all were in great excitement, but as yet continued quiet, fearing to give too much credit to what was reported. A very strange accident happened to the messenger who was sent with the letters; for being arrived in Italy, as he travelled through the land of Rhegium, hastening to Dionysius at Caulonia, he met one of his acquaintance, who was carrying home part of a sacrifice. He accepted a piece of the flesh, which his friend offered him, and proceeded on his journey with all speed; having travelled a good part of the night, and being through weariness forced to take a little rest, he laid himself down in the next convenient place he came to, which was in a wood near the road. A wolf, scenting the flesh, came and seized it as it lay fastened to the letter-bag, and with the flesh carried away the bag also, in which were the letters to Dionysius. The man, awaking and missing his bag, sought for it up and down a great while, and, not finding it, resolved not to go to the king without his letters, but to conceal himself, and keep out of the way.

Dionysius, therefore, came to hear of the war in Sicily from other hands, and that a good while after. In the mean time, as Dion proceeded in his march, the Camarineans joined his forces, and the country people in the territory of Syracuse rose and joined him in a large body. The Leontines and Campanians,[15] who, with Timocrates, guarded the Epipolæ, receiving a false alarm which was spread in purpose by Dion, as if he intended to attack their cities first, left Timocrates, and hastened off to carry succor to their own homes. News of which being brought to Dion, where he lay near Macræ,[16] he raised his camp by night, and came to the river Anapus, which is distant from the city about ten furlongs; there he made a halt, and sacrificed by the river, offering vows to the rising sun. The soothsayers declared that the gods promised him victory; and they that were present, seeing him assisting at the sacrifice with a garland on his head, one and all crowned themselves with gar-

[1] The Campanians were mercenaries of the native Italian population, whom the elder Dionysius had settled on Sicilian lands and in Sicilian-Greek cities. Perhaps by the Leontines and Campanians he means the Campanians settled in Leontini.

[16] Macræ is an unknown name; the real name is probably Acræ, which is a place mentioned by Thucydides.

lands. There were about five thousand that had joined his forces in their march; who, though but ill-provided, with such weapons as came next to hand, made up by zeal and courage for the want of better arms; and when once they were told to advance, as if Dion were already conqueror, they ran forward with shouts and acclamations, encouraging each other with the hopes of liberty.

The most considerable men and better sort of the citizens of Syracuse, clad all in white, met him at the gates. The populace set upon all that were of Dionysius's party, and principally searched for those they called setters or informers,[17] a number of wicked and hateful wretches, who made it their business to go up and down the city, thrusting themselves into all companies, that they might inform Dionysius what men said, and how they stood affected. These were the first that suffered, being beaten to death by the crowd. Timocrates, not being able to force his way to the garrison that kept the castle,[18] took horse, and fled out of the city, filling all the places where he came with fear and confusion, magnifying the amount of Dion's forces, that he might not be supposed to have deserted his charge without good reason for it. By this time Dion was come up, and appeared in the sight of the people; he marched first in a rich suit of arms, and by him on one hand his brother, Megacles, on the other, Callippus the Athenian, crowned with gar-

---

[17] These, by the name given to them, which is feminine here, and masculine in one of Plutarch's minor works (*De Curiositate*, 16), seem to have been of both sexes.

[18] He was posted in the fort at the other extremity of the town, Euryalus, high at the end of the broad rising ground, sloping up from the junction with the island, up and over which the town had spread. This fort is what Dion is presently said to take, the "Epipolæ."

lands. Of the foreign soldiers, a hundred followed as his guard, and their several officers led the rest in good order; the Syracusans looking on and welcoming them, as if they believed the whole to be a sacred and religious procession, to celebrate the solemn entrance, after an absence of forty-eight years, of liberty and popular government.

Dion entered by the Menitid gate,[19] and, having by sound of trumpet quieted the noise of the people, he caused proclamation to be made, that Dion and Megacles, who were come to overthrow the tyrannical government, did declare the Syracusans and all other Sicilians to be free from the tyrant. But, being desirous to harangue the people himself, he went up through the Achradina. The citizens on each side the way brought victims for sacrifice, set out their tables and goblets, and as he passed by each door threw flowers and ornaments upon him, with vows and acclamations, honoring him as a god. There was under the castle and the Pentapyla[20] a lofty and conspicuous sundial, which Dionysius had set up. Getting up upon the top of that, he made an oration to the people, calling upon them to maintain and defend their liberty; who, with great expressions of joy and acknowledgment, created Dion and Megacles generals, with plenary powers, joining in commission with them, at their desire and entreaty, twenty colleagues, of whom half were of those that had returned with them out of banishment. It seemed also to the diviners a most happy omen, that Dion, when he made

[19] Menitid in the manuscripts, but more probably the *Temenitid* gates, near the statue of Apollo, called Temenites, who had here his *temenos*, or sacred lot of ground.

[20] The Five Gates, the entrance to the citadel or acropolis in Ortygia.

his address to the people, had under his feet the stately monument which Dionysius had been at such pains to erect; but because it was a sundial on which he stood when he was made general, they expressed some fears that the great actions he had performed might be subject to change, and admit some rapid turn and declination of fortune.

After this, Dion, taking the Epipolæ, released the citizens who were imprisoned there, and then raised a wall to invest the castle. Seven days after Dionysius arrived by sea, and got into the citadel, and about the same time came carriages bringing the arms and ammunition which Dion had left with Synalus. These he distributed among the citizens; and the rest that wanted furnished themselves as well as they could, and put themselves in the condition of zealous and serviceable men-at-arms.

Dionysius sent agents, at first privately, to Dion, to try what terms they could make with him. But he declaring that any overtures they had to make must be made in public to the Syracusans as a free people, envoys now went and came between the tyrant and the people, with fair proposals, and assurances that they should have abatements of their tributes and taxes, and freedom from the burdens of military expeditions, all which should be made according to their own approbation and consent with him. The Syracusans laughed at these offers, and Dion returned answer to the envoys that Dionysius must not think to treat with them upon any other terms but resigning the government; which if he would actually do, he would not forget how nearly he was related to him, or be wanting to assist him in procuring oblivion for the past, and whatever else was reasonable and just. Dionysius seemed to consent to this, and sent his agents again, desiring some of the Syracusans to come into the citadel and discuss with him in person the terms to which on each side they might be willing, after fair debate, to consent. There were therefore some deputed, such as Dion approved of; and the general rumor from the castle was, that Dionysius would voluntarily resign his authority, and rather do it himself as his own good deed, than let it be the act of Dion. But this profession was a mere trick to amuse the Syracusans. For he put the deputies that were sent to him in custody, and by break of day, having first, to encourage his men, made them drink plentifully of raw wine, he sent the garrison of mercenaries out to make a sudden sally against Dion's works. The attack was quite unexpected, and the barbarians set to work boldly with loud cries to pull down the cross-wall, and assailed the Syracusans so furiously that they were not able to maintain their post. Only a party of Dion's hired soldiers, on first taking the alarm, advanced to the rescue; neither did they at first know what to do, or how to employ the aid they brought, not being able to hear the commands of their officers, amidst the noise and confusion of the Syracusans, who fled from the enemy and ran in among them, breaking through their ranks, until Dion, seeing none of his orders could be heard, resolved to let them see by example what they ought to do, and charged into the thickest of the enemy. The fight about him was fierce and bloody, he being as well known by the enemy as by his own party, and all running with loud cries to the quarter where he fought. Though his time of life was on longer that of the bodily strength and agility for such a combat, still his determination and courage were sufficient to maintain him against all that attacked him; but, while bravely driving them back, he was wounded in the hand with a lance, his body armor also had been much battered, and was scarcely any longer serviceable to protect him, either against missiles or blows hand to hand. Many spears and javelins had passed into it through the shield, and, on these being broken back, he fell to the ground, but was immediately rescued, and carried off by his soldiers. The command-in-chief he left to Timonides, and, mounting a horse, rode about the city, rallying the Syracusans that fled; and, ordering up a detachment of the foreign soldiers out of Achradina, where they were posted on guard, he brought them as a fresh reserve, eager for battle, upon the tired and failing enemy, who were already well inclined to give up their design. For having hopes at their first sally to retake the whole city, when beyond their expectation they found themselves engaged with bold and practised fighters, they fell back towards the castle. As soon as they gave ground, the Greek soldiers pressed the harder upon them, till they turned and fled within the walls. There were lost in this action seventy-four of Dion's men, and a very great number of the enemy. This being a signal victory, and principally obtained by the valor of the foreign soldiers, the Syracusans rewarded them in honor of it with a hundred minæ, and the soldiers on their part presented Dion with a crown of gold.

Soon after, there came heralds from Dionysius, bringing Dion letters from the women of his family, and one addressed outside, "To his father, from Hipparinus;" this was the name of Dion's son, though Timæus says, he was, from his mother Arete's name, called Aretæus; but I think credit is rather to be given to Timonides's report, who was his father's fellow-soldier and confidant. The rest of the letters were read publicly, containing many solicitations and humble requests of the women; that professing to be from his son, the heralds would not have them open publicly, but Dion, putting force upon them, broke the seal. It was from Dionysius, written in the terms of it to Dion, but in effect to the Syracusans, and so worded that, under a plausible justification of himself and entreaty to him, means were taken for rendering him suspected by the people. It reminded him of the good service he had formerly done the usurping government, it added threats to his dearest relations, his sister, son, and wife, if he did not comply with the contents, also passionate demands mingled with lamentations, and, most to the purpose of all, urgent recommendations to him not to destroy the government, and put the power into the hands of men who always hated him, and would never forget their old piques and quarrels; let him take the sovereignty himself, and so secure the safety of his family and his friends.

When this letter was read, the Syracusans were not, as they should have been, transported with admiration at the unmovable constancy and magnanimity of Dion, who withstood all his dearest interests to be true to virtue and justice, but, on the contrary, they saw in this their reason for fearing and suspecting that he lay under an invincible necessity to be favorable to Dionysius; and they began therefore to look out for other leaders, and the rather, because to their great joy they received the news that Heraclides was on his way. This Heraclides was one of those whom Dionysius had banished, a very good soldier, and well known for the commands he had formerly had under the tyrant; yet a man of no constant purpose, of a fickle temper, and least of all to be relied upon when he had to act with a colleague in any honorable command. He had had a difference formerly with Dion in Peloponnesus, and had resolved, upon his own means, with what ships and soldiers he had, to

make an attack upon Dionysius. When he arrived at
Syracuse, with seven galleys and three small vessels,
he found Dionysius already close besieged, and the
Syracusans high and proud of their victories. Forthwith, therefore, he endeavored by all ways to make
himself popular; and, indeed, he had in him naturally
something that was very insinuating and taking with
a populace that loves to be courted. He gained his
end, also, the easier, and drew the people over to his
side, because of the dislike they had taken to Dion's
grave and stately manner, which they thought overbearing and assuming; their successes having made
them so careless and confident, that they expected
popular arts and flatteries from their leaders, before
they had in reality secured a popular government.

Getting therefore together in an irregular assembly, they chose Heraclides their admiral; but when
Dion came forward, and told them, that conferring
this trust upon Heraclides was in effect to withdraw
that which they had granted him, for he was no longer
their generalissimo if another had the command of
the navy, they repealed their order, and, though much
against their wills, cancelled the new appointment.
When this business was over, Dion invited Heraclides
to his house, and pointed out to him, in gentle terms,
that he had not acted wisely or well to quarrel with
him upon a punctilio of honor, at a time when the least
false step might be the ruin of all; and then, calling a
fresh assembly of the people, he there named Heraclides admiral, and prevailed with the citizens to allow
him a life-guard, as he himself had.

Heraclides openly professed the highest respect
for Dion, and made him great acknowledgments for
this favor, attending him with all deference, as ready
to receive his commands; but underhand he kept up
his dealings with the populace and the unrulier citi-

zens, unsettling their minds and disturbing them with his complaints, and putting Dion into the utmost perplexity and disquiet. For if he advised to give Dionysius leave to quit the castle, he would be exposed to the imputation of sparing and protecting him; if, to avoid giving offence or suspicion, he simply continued the siege, they would say he protracted the war, to keep his office of general the longer, and overawe the citizens.

There was one Sosis, notorious in the city for his bad conduct and his impudence, yet a favorite with the people, for the very reason that they liked to see it made a part of popular privileges to carry free speech to this excess of license. This man, out of a design against Dion, stood up one day in an assembly, and, having sufficiently railed at the citizens as a set of fools, that could not see how they had made an exchange of a dissolute and drunken for a sober and watchful despotism, and thus having publicly declared himself Dion's enemy, took his leave. The next day, he was seen running through the streets, as if he fled from some that pursued him, almost naked, wounded in the head, and bloody all over. In this condition, getting people about him in the market-place, he told them that he had been assaulted by Dion's men; and, to confirm what he said, showed them the wounds he had received in his head. And a good many took his part, exclaiming loudly against Dion for his cruel and tyrannical conduct, stopping the mouths of the people by bloodshed and peril of life. Just as an assembly was gathering in this unsettled and tumultuous state of mind, Dion came before them, and made it appear how this Sosis was brother to one of Dionysius's guard, and that he was set on by him to embroil the city in tumult and confusion; Dionysius having now no way left for his security but to make his advantage of their dissensions and distractions. The surgeons, also, having searched the wound, found it was rather razed, than cut with a downright blow; for the wounds made with a sword are, from their mere weight, most commonly deepest in the middle, but this was very slight, and all along of an equal depth; and it was not one continued wound, as if cut at once, but several incisions, in all probability made at several times, as he was able to endure the pain. There were credible persons, also, who brought a razor, and showed it in the assembly, stating that they met Sosis running in the street, all bloody, who told them that he was flying from Dion's soldiers, who had just attacked and wounded him; they ran at once to look after them and met no one, but spied this razor lying under a hollow stone near the place from which they observed he came.

Sosis was now likely to come by the worst of it. But when, to back all this, his own servants came in, and gave evidence that he had left his house alone before break of day, with the razor in his hand, Dion's accusers withdrew themselves, and the people by a general vote condemned Sosis to die, being once again well satisfied with Dion and his proceedings.

Yet they were still as jealous as before of his soldiers, and the rather, because the war was now carried on principally by sea; Philistus being come from Iapygia with a great fleet to Dionysius's assistance. They supposed, therefore, that there would be no longer need of the soldiers, who were all landsmen and armed accordingly: these were rather, indeed, they thought, in a condition to be protected by themselves, who were seamen, and had their power in their shipping. Their good opinion of themselves was also much enhanced by an advantage they got in an engagement by sea, in which they took Philistus pris-

oner, and used him in a barbarous and cruel manner.
Ephorus relates that when he saw his ship was taken
he slew himself. But Timonides, who was with Dion
from the very first, and was present at all the events
as they occurred, writing to Speusippus the philosopher, relates the story thus: that Philistus's galley
running aground, he was taken prisoner alive, and
first disarmed, then stripped of his corslet, and exposed naked, being now an old man, to every kind of
contumely; after which they cut off his head, and gave
his body to the boys of the town, bidding them drag
it through the Achradina, and then throw it into the
Quarries. Timæus, to increase the mockery, adds
further, that the boys tied him by his lame leg, and so
drew him through the streets, while the Syracusans
stood by laughing and jesting at the sight of that
very man thus tied and dragged about by the leg, who
had told Dionysius, that, so far from flying on horseback from Syracuse, he ought to wait till he should
be dragged out by the heels. Philistus, however, has
stated, that this was said to Dionysius by another, and
not by himself.

Timæus avails himself of this advantage, which
Philistus truly enough affords against himself in his
zealous and constant adherence to the tyranny, to
vent his own spleen and malice against him. They,
indeed, who were injured by him at the time are perhaps excusable, if they carried their resentment to
the length of indignities to his dead body; but they
who write history afterwards, and were noway
wronged by him in his lifetime, and have received assistance from his writings, in honor should not with
opprobrious and scurrilous language upbraid him for
those misfortunes, which may well enough befall even
the best of men. On the other side, Ephorus is as
much out of the way in his encomiums. For, however

ingenious he is in supplying unjust acts and wicked conduct with fair and worthy motives, and in selecting decorous and honorable terms, yet when he does his best, he does not himself stand clear of the charge of being the greatest lover of tyrants, and the fondest admirer of luxury and power and rich estates and alliances of marriage with absolute princes. He that neither praises Philistus for his conduct, nor insults over his misfortunes, seems to me to take the fittest course.

After Philistus's death, Dionysius sent to Dion, offering to surrender the castle, all the arms, provisions, and garrison-soldiers, with full pay for them for five months, demanding in return that he might have safe conduct to go unmolested into Italy, and there to continue, and also to enjoy the revenues of Gyarta, a large and fruitful territory belonging to Syracuse, reaching from the sea-side to the middle of the country. Dion rejected these proposals, and referred him to the Syracusans. They, hoping in a short time to take Dionysius alive, dismissed his ambassadors summarily. But he, leaving his eldest son, Apollocrates, to defend the castle, and putting on board his ships the persons and the property that he set most value upon, took the opportunity of a fair wind, and made his escape, undiscovered by the admiral Heraclides and his fleet.

The citizens loudly exclaimed against Heraclides for this neglect; but he got one of their public speakers, Hippo by name, to go among them, and make proposals to the assembly for a redivision of lands, alleging that the first beginning of liberty was equality, and that poverty and slavery were inseparable companions. In support of this, Heraclides spoke, and used the faction in favor of it to overpower Dion.

who opposed it; and, in fine, he persuaded the people to ratify it by their vote, and further to decree, that the foreign soldiers should receive no pay, and that they would elect new commanders, and so be rid of Dion's oppression. The people, attempting, as it were, after their long sickness of despotism, all at once to stand on their legs, and to do the part, for which they were yet unfit, of freemen, stumbled in all their actions; and yet hated Dion, who, like a good physician, endeavored to keep the city to a strict and temperate regimen.

When they met in the assembly to choose their commanders, about the middle of summer, unusual and terrible thunders, with other inauspicious appearances, for fifteen days together, dispersed the people, deterring them, on grounds of religious fear, from creating new generals. But, at last, the popular leaders, having found a fair and clear day, and having got their party together, were proceeding to an election, when a draught-ox, who was used to the crowd and noise of the streets, but for some reason or other grew unruly to his driver, breaking from his yoke, ran furiously into the theatre where they were assembled, and set the people flying and running in all directions before him in the greatest disorder and confusion; and from thence went on, leaping and rushing about, over all that part of the city which the enemies afterwards made themselves masters of. However, the Syracusans, not regarding all this, elected five and twenty captains, and, among the rest, Heraclides; and underhand tampered with Dion's men, promising, if they would desert him, and enlist themselves in their service, to make them citizens of Syracuse, with all the privileges of natives. But they would not hear the proposals, but, to show their fidelity and courage, with their swords in their hands, placing Dion for his security in the midst of their battalion, conveyed him out of the city, not offering violence to any one, but upbraiding those they met with their baseness and ingratitude. The citizens, seeing they were but few, and did not offer any violence, despised them; and, supposing that with their large numbers they might with ease overpower and cut them off before they got out of the city, fell upon them in the rear.

Here Dion was in a great strait, being necessitated either to fight against his own countrymen, or tamely suffer himself and his faithful soldiers to be cut in pieces. He used many entreaties to the Syracusans, stretching out his hands towards the castle, that was full of their enemies, and showing them the soldiers, who in great numbers appeared on the walls and watched what was doing. But when no persuasions could divert the impulse of the multitude, and the whole mass, like the sea in a storm, seemed to be driven before the breath of the demagogues, he commanded his men, not to charge them, but to advance with shouts and clashing of their arms, which being done, not a man of them stood his ground; all fled at once through the streets, though none pursued them. For Dion immediately commanded his men to face about, and led them towards the city of the Leontines.

The very women laughed at the new captains for this retreat; so to redeem their credit, they bid the citizens arm themselves again, and followed after Dion, and came up with him as he was passing a river. Some of the light-horse rode up and began to skirmish. But when they saw Dion no more tame and calm, and no signs in his face of any fatherly tenderness towards his countrymen, but with an angry countenance, as resolved not to suffer their indignities any longer, bidding his men face round and form in their ranks for the onset, they presently turned their backs more basely than before, and fled to the city, with the loss of some few of their men.

The Leontines received Dion very honorably, gave money to his men, and made them free of their city; sending envoys to the Syracusans, to require them to do the soldiers justice, who, in return, sent back other agents to accuse Dion. But when a general meeting of the confederates met in the town of the Leontines, and the matter was heard and debated, the Syracusans were held to be in fault. They, however, refused to stand to the award of their allies, following their own conceit, and making it their pride to listen to no one, and not to have any commanders but those who would fear and obey the people.

About this time, Dionysius sent in a fleet, under the command of Nypsius the Neapolitan, with provisions and pay for the garrison. The Syracusans fought him, had the better, and took four of his ships; but they made very ill use of their good success, and, for want of good discipline, fell in their joy to drinking and feasting in an extravagant manner, with so little regard to their main interest, that, when they thought themselves sure of taking the castle, they actually lost their city. Nypsius, seeing the citizens in this general disorder, spending day and night in their drunken singing and revelling, and their commanders well pleased with the frolic, or at least not daring to try and give any orders to men in their drink, took advantage of this opportunity, made a sally, and stormed their works; and, having made his way through these, let his barbarians loose upon the city, giving up it and all that were in it to their pleasure.

The Syracusans quickly saw their folly and misfortune, but could not, in the distraction they were in, so soon redress it. The city was in actual process of being sacked, the enemy putting the men to the sword, demolishing the fortifications, and dragging the women and children with lamentable shrieks and cries prisoners into the castle. The commanders, giving all for lost, were not able to put the citizens in any tolerable posture of defence, finding them confusedly mixed up and scattered among the enemy. While they were in this condition, and the Achradina in danger to be taken, every one was sensible who he was in whom all their remaining hopes rested, but no man for shame durst name Dion, whom they had so ungratefully and foolishly dealt with. Necessity at last forcing them, some of the auxiliary troops and horsemen cried out, "Send for Dion and his Peloponnesians from the Leontines." No sooner was the venture made and the name heard among the people, but they gave a shout for joy, and, with tears in their eyes, wished him there, that they might once again see that leader at the head of them, whose courage and bravery in the worst of dangers they well remembered, calling to mind not only with what an undaunted spirit he always behaved himself, but also with what courage and confidence he inspired them when he led them against the enemy. They immediately, therefore, despatched Archonides and Telesides of the confederate troops, and of the horsemen Hellanicus and four others. These, traversing the road between at their horses' full speed, reached the town of the Leontines in the evening. The first thing they did was to leap from their horses and fall at Dion's feet, relating with tears the sad condition the Syracusans were in. Many of the Leontines and Peloponnesians began to throng about them, guessing by their speed and the manner of their address that something extraordinary had occurred.

Dion at once led the way to the assembly, and, the people being gathered together in a very little time, Archonides and Hellanicus and the others came in among them, and in short declared the misery and distress of the Syracusans, begging the foreign soldiers to forget the injuries they had received, and assist the afflicted, who had suffered more for the wrong they had done, than they themselves who received it would (had it been in their power) have inflicted upon them. When they had made an end, there was a profound silence in the theatre; Dion then stood up, and began to speak, but tears stopped his words; his soldiers were troubled at his grief, but bade him take good courage and proceed. When he had recovered himself a little, therefore, "Men of Peloponnesus," he said, "and of the confederacy, I asked for your presence here, that you might consider your own interests. For myself, I have no interests to consult while Syracuse is perishing, and, though I may not save it from destruction, I will nevertheless hasten thither, and be buried in the ruins of my country. Yet if you can find in your hearts to assist us, the most inconsiderate and unfortunate of men, you may to your eternal honor again retrieve this unhappy city. But if the Syracusans can obtain no more pity nor relief from you, may the gods reward you for what you have formerly valiantly done for them, and for your kindness to Dion, of whom speak hereafter as one who deserted you not when you were injured and abused, nor afterwards forsook his fellow-citizens in their afflictions and misfortunes."

Before he had yet ended his speech, the soldiers leapt up, and with a great shout testified their readiness for the service, crying out, to march immediately to the relief of the city. The Syracusan messengers hugged and embraced them, praying the gods to send down blessings upon Dion and the Peloponnesians. When the noise was pretty well over, Dion gave orders that all should go to their quarters to prepare for their march, and, having refreshed themselves, come ready armed to their rendezvous in the place where they now were, resolving that very night to attempt the rescue.

Now at Syracuse, Dionysius's soldiers, as long as day continued, ransacked the city, and did all the mischief they could; but when night came on, they retired into the castle, having lost some few of their number. At which the factious ringleaders taking heart, and hoping the enemy would rest content with what they had done and make no further attempt upon them, persuaded the people again to reject Dion, and, if he came with the foreign soldiers, not to admit him; advising them not to yield, as inferior to them in point of honor and courage, but to save their city and defend their liberties and properties themselves. The populace, therefore, and their leaders sent messengers to Dion to forbid him to advance, while the noble citizens and the horse sent others to him to desire him to hasten his march; for which reason he slacked his pace, yet did not remit his advance. And in the course of the night, the faction that was against him set a guard upon the gates of the city to hinder him from coming in. But Nypsius made another sally out of the castle with a far greater number of men, and those far more bold and eager than before, who quite ruined what of the rampart was left standing, and fell in, pell-mell, to sack and ravage the city. The slaughter was now very great, not only of the men, but of the women also and children; for they regarded not so much the plunder, as to destroy and kill all they met. For Dionysius, despairing to regain the kingdom, and mortally hating the Syracusans, resolved to bury his lost sovereignty in the ruin and desolation of Syracuse. The soldiers, therefore, to anticipate Dion's succors, resolved upon the most complete and ready way of destruction, to lay the city in ashes, firing all at hand with torches and lamps, and at distance with flaming arrows, shot from their bows. The citizens fled every way before them; they who, to avoid the fire, forsook their houses were taken in the streets and put to the sword; they who betook themselves for refuge into the houses were forced out again by the flames, many buildings being now in a blaze, and many falling in ruins upon them as they fled past.

This fresh misfortune by general consent opened the gates for Dion. He had given up his rapid advance, when he received advice that the enemies were retreated into the castle; but, in the morning, some horse brought him the news of another assault, and, soon after, some of those who before opposed his coming fled now to him, to entreat him he would hasten his relief. The pressure increasing, Heraclides sent his brother, and after him his uncle, Theodotes, to beg him to help them: for that now they were not able to resist any longer; he himself was wounded, and the greatest part of the city either in ruins or in flames. When Dion met this sad news, he was about sixty furlongs distant from the city. When he had acquainted the soldiers with the exigency, and exhorted them to behave themselves like men, the army no longer marched but ran forwards, and by the way were met by messengers upon messengers entreating them to make haste. By the wonderful eagerness of the soldiers and their extraordinary speed, Dion quickly came to the city and entered what is called the Hecatompedon, sending his light-armed men at once to charge the enemy, that, seeing them, the Syracusans might take courage. In the mean time, he drew up in good order his full-armed men and all the citizens that came in and joined him; forming his battalions deep, and distributing his officers in many separate commands, that he might be able to attack from many quarters at once, and so be more alarming to the enemy.

So, having made his arrangements and offered vows to the gods, when he was seen in the streets advancing at the head of his men to engage the enemy, a confused noise of shouts, congratulations, vows, and prayers was raised by the Syracusans, who now called Dion their deliverer and tutelar deity, and his soldiers their friends, brethren, and fellow-citizens. And, indeed, at that moment, none seemed to regard themselves, or value their safeties, but to be concerned more for Dion's life than for all their own together, as he marched at the head of them to meet the danger, through blood and fire and over heaps of dead bodies that lay in his way.

And indeed the posture of the enemy was in appearance terrible; for they were flushed and ferocious with victory, and had posted themselves very advantageously along the demolished works, which made the access to them very hazardous and difficult. Yet that which disturbed Dion's soldiers most was the apprehension they were in of the fire, which made their march very troublesome and difficult; for the houses being in flames on all sides, they were met everywhere with the blaze, and, treading upon burning ruins and every minute in danger of being overwhelmed with falling houses, through clouds of ashes and smoke they labored hard to keep their order and maintain their ranks. When they came near to the enemy, the approach was so narrow and uneven that but few of them could engage at a time; but at length, with loud cheers and much zeal on the part of the Syracusans, encouraging them and joining with them, they beat off Nypsius's men, and put them to flight. Most of them escaped into the castle, which was near at hand; all that could not get in were pursued and picked up here and there by the soldiers, and put to the sword. The present exigency, however, did not suffer the citizens to take immediate benefit of their victory in such mutual congratulations and embraces as became so great a success; for now all were busily employed to save what houses were left standing, laboring hard all night, and scarcely so could master the fire.

The next day, not one of the popular haranguers durst stay in the city, but all of them, knowing their own guilt, by their flight confessed it, and secured their lives. Only Heraclides and Theodotes went voluntarily and surrendered themselves to Dion, acknowledging that they had wronged him, and begging he would be kinder to them than they had been just to him; adding, how much it would become him who was master of so many excellent accomplishments, to moderate his anger and be generously compassionate to ungrateful men, who were here before him, making their confession, that, in all the matter of their former enmity and rivalry against him, they were now absolutely overcome by his virtue. Though they thus humbly addressed him, his friends advised him not to pardon these turbulent and ill conditioned men, but to yield them to the desires of his soldiers, and utterly root out of the commonwealth the ambitious affectation of popularity, a disease as pestilent and pernicious as the passion for tyranny itself. Dion endeavored to satisfy them, telling them that other generals exercised and trained themselves for the most part in the practices of war and arms; but that he had long studied in the Academy how to conquer anger, and not let emulation and envy conquer him; that to do this it is not sufficient that a man be obliging and kind to his friends, and those that have deserved well of him, but rather, gentle and ready to forgive in the case of those who do wrong; that he wished to let the world see that he valued not himself so much upon excelling Heraclides in ability and conduct, as he did in outdoing him in justice and clemency; herein to have the advantage is to excel indeed; whereas the honor of success in war is never entire; fortune will be sure to dispute it, though no man should pretend to have a claim. What if Heraclides be perfidious, malicious, and base, must Dion therefore sully or injure his virtue by passionate concern for it? For, though the laws determine it juster to revenge an injury than to do an injury, yet it is evident that both, in the nature of things, originally proceed from the same deficiency and weakness. The malicious humor of men, though perverse and refractory, is not so savage and invincible but it may be wrought upon by kindness, and altered by repeated obligations. Dion, making use of these arguments, pardoned and dismissed Heraclides and Theodotes.

And now, resolving to repair the blockade about the castle, he commanded all the Syracusans to cut each man a stake and bring it to the works; and then, dismissing them to refresh themselves, and take their rest, he employed his own men all night, and by morning had finished his line of palisade; so that both the enemy and the citizens wondered, when day returned, to see the work so far advanced in so short a time. Burying therefore the dead, and redeeming the prisoners, who were near two thousand, he called a public assembly, where Heraclides made a motion that Dion should be declared general with full powers at land and sea. The better citizens approved well of it, and called on the people to vote it so. But the mob of sailors and handicraftsmen would not yield that Heraclides should lose his command of the navy; believing him, if otherwise an ill man, at any rate to be more citizenlike than Dion, and readier to comply with the people. Dion therefore submitted to them in this, and consented Heraclides should continue admiral. But when they began to press the project of the redistribution of lands and houses, he not only opposed it, but repealed all the votes they had formerly made upon that account, which sensibly vexed them. Heraclides, therefore, took a new advantage of him, and, being at Messene, harangued the soldiers and ships' crews that sailed with him, accusing Dion that he had a design to make himself absolute. And yet at the same time he held private correspondence for a treaty with Dionysius by means of Pharax the Spartan. Which when the noble citizens of Syracuse had intimation of, there arose a sedition in the army, and the city was in great distress and want of provisions; and Dion now knew not what course to take, being also blamed by all his friends for having thus fortified against himself such a perverse and jealous and utterly corrupted man as Heraclides was.

Pharax at this time lay encamped at Neapolis, in the territory of Agrigentum. Dion, therefore, led out the Syracusans, but with an intent not to engage him till he saw a fit opportunity. But Heraclides and his seamen exclaimed against him, that he delayed fighting on purpose that he might the longer continue his command; so that, much against his will, he was forced to an engagement and was beaten, his loss, however, being inconsiderable, and that occasioned chiefly by the dissension that was in the army. He rallied his men, and, having put them in good order and encouraged them to redeem their credit, resolved upon a second battle. But, in the evening, he received advice that Heraclides with his fleet was on his way to Syracuse, with the purpose to possess himself of the city and keep him and his army out. Instantly, therefore, taking with him some of the strongest and most active of his men, he rode off in the dark, and about nine the next morning was at the gates, having ridden seven hundred furlongs that night. Heraclides, though he strove to make all the speed he could, yet, coming too late, tacked and stood out again to sea; and, being unresolved what course to steer, accidentally he met Gæsylus the Spartan, who told him he was come from Lacedæmon to head the Sicilians, as Gylippus had formerly done. Heraclides was only too glad to get hold of him, and fastening him as it might be a sort of amulet to himself, he showed him to the confederates, and sent a herald to Syracuse to summon them to accept the Spartan general. Dion returned answer that they had generals enough, and, if they wanted a Spartan to command them, he could supply that office, being himself a citizen of Sparta. When Gæsylus saw this, he gave up all pretensions, and sailed in to Dion, and reconciled Heraclides to him, making Heraclides swear the most solemn oaths to perform what he engaged, Gæsylus himself also undertaking to maintain Dion's right, and inflict chastisement on Heraclides if he broke his faith.

The Syracusans then laid up their navy, which was at present a great charge and of little use to them, but an occasion of differences and dissensions among the generals, and pressed on the siege, finishing the wall of blockade with which they invested the castle. The besieged, seeing no hopes of succors and their provisions failing, began to mutiny; so that the son of Dionysius, in despair of holding out longer for his father, capitulated, and articled with Dion to deliver up the castle with all the garrison soldiers and ammunition; and so, taking his mother and sisters and manning five galleys, he set out to go to his father, Dion seeing him safely out, and scarce a man in all the city not being there to behold the sight, as indeed they called even on those that were not present, out of pity that they could not be there, to see this happy day and the sun shining on a free Syracuse. And as this expulsion of Dionysius is even now always cited as one of the greatest and most remarkable examples of fortune's vicissitudes, how extraordinary may we imagine their joy to have been, and how entire their satisfaction who had totally subverted the most potent tyranny that ever was by very slight and inconsiderable means!

When Apollocrates was gone, and Dion coming to take possession of the castle, the women could not stay while he made his entry, but ran to meet him at the gate. Aristomache led Dion's son, and Arete followed after weeping, fearful and dubious how to salute or address her husband, after living with another man. Dion first embraced his sister, then his son; when Aristomache bringing Arete to him, "O Dion," said she, "your banishment made us all equally miserable; your return and victory has cancelled all sorrows, excepting this poor sufferer's, whom I, unhappy, saw compelled to be another's, while you were yet alive. Fortune has now given you the sole disposal of us; how will you determine concerning her hard fate? In what relation must she salute you as her uncle, or as her husband?" This speech of Aristomache's brought tears from Dion, who with great affection embraced his wife, gave her his son, and desired her to retire to his own house, where he continued to reside when he had delivered up the castle to the Syracusans.

For though all things had now succeeded to his

wish, yet he desired not to enjoy any present advantage of his good fortune, except to gratify his friends, reward his allies, and bestow upon his companions of former time in Athens and the soldiers that had served him some special mark of kindness and honor, striving herein to outdo his very means in his generosity. As for himself, he was content with a very frugal and moderate competency, and was indeed the wonder of all men, that when not only Sicily and Carthage, but all Greece looked to him as in the height of prosperity, and no man living greater than he, no general more renowned for valor and success, yet in his garb, his attendance, his table, he seemed as if he rather commoned with Plato in the Academy than lived among hired captains and paid soldiers, whose solace of their toils and dangers it is to eat and drink their fill, and enjoy themselves plentifully every day. Plato indeed wrote to him that the eyes of all the world were now upon him; but it is evident that he himself had fixed his eye upon one place in one city, the Academy, and considered that the spectators and judges there regarded not great actions, courage, or fortune, but watched to see how temperately and wisely he could use his prosperity, how evenly he could behave himself in the high condition he now was in. Neither did he remit any thing of his wonted stateliness in conversation or serious carriage to the people; he made it rather a point to maintain it, notwithstanding that a little condescension and obliging civility were very necessary for his present affairs; and Plato, as we said before, rebuked him, and wrote to tell him that self-will keeps house with solitude. But certainly his natural temperament was one that could not bend to complaisance; and, besides, he wished to work the Syracusans back the other way, out of their present excess of license and caprice.

Heraclides began again to set up against him, and, being invited by Dion to make one of the Council, refused to come, saying he would give his opinion as a private citizen in the public assembly. Next he complained of Dion because he had not demolished the citadel, and because he had hindered the people from throwing down Dionysius's tomb and doing despite to the dead; moreover he accused him for sending to Corinth for counsellors and assistants in the government, thereby neglecting and slighting his fellow-citizens. And indeed he had sent messages for some Corinthians to come to him, hoping by their means and presence the better to settle that constitution he intended; for he designed to suppress the unlimited democratic government, which indeed is not a government, but, as Plato calls it, a market-place of governments,[21] and to introduce and establish a mixed polity, on the Spartan and Cretan model, between a commonwealth and a monarchy, wherein an aristocratic body should preside, and determine all matters of greatest consequence; for he saw also that the Corinthians were chiefly governed by something like an oligarchy, and the people but little concerned in public business.

Now knowing that Heraclides would be his most considerable adversary, and that in all ways he was a turbulent, fickle, and factious man, he gave way to some whom formerly he hindered when they designed to kill him, who, breaking in, murdered Heraclides in

[21] See the Republic, National Library Edition Vol. II., Book VII.—In the absolutely democratic state of things there is no fixed form of government at all; every man is his own government; so that the philosophic inquirer in search of the best form of polity should certainly, says Plato in his irony, be directed hither to this mart and magazine of governments, where he may find every variety of rule of life and conduct. A public rule of life and conduct is what Plato means by government.

his own house. His death was much resented by the citizens. Nevertheless, when Dion made him a splendid funeral, followed the dead body with all his soldiers, and then addressed them, they understood that it would have been impossible to have kept the city quiet, as long as Dion and Heraclides were competitors in the government.

Dion had a friend called Callippus, an Athenian, who, Plato says, first made acquaintance and afterwards obtained familiarity with him, not from any connection with his philosophic studies, but on occasion afforded by the celebration of the mysteries, and in the way of ordinary society. This man went with him in all his military service, and was in great honor and esteem; being the first of his friends who marched by his side into Syracuse, wearing a garland upon his head, having behaved himself very well in all the battles, and made himself remarkable for his gallantry. He, finding that Dion's principal and most considerable friends were cut off in the war, Heraclides now dead, and the people without a leader, and that the soldiers had a great kindness for him, like a perfidious and wicked villain, in hopes to get the chief command of Sicily as his reward for the ruin of his friend and benefactor, and, as some say, being also bribed by the enemy with twenty talents to destroy Dion, inveigled and engaged several of the soldiers in a conspiracy against him, taking this cunning and wicked occasion for his plot. He daily informed Dion of what he heard or what he feigned the soldiers said against him; whereby he gained that credit and confidence, that he was allowed by Dion to consort privately with whom he would, and talk freely against him in any company, that he might discover who were his secret and factious maligners. By this means, Callippus in a short time got together a cabal of all the seditious malecontents in the city; and if any one who would not be drawn in advised Dion that he was tampered with, he was not troubled or concerned at it, believing Callippus did it in compliance with his directions.

While this conspiracy was afoot, a strange and dreadful apparition was seen by Dion. As he sat one evening in a gallery in his house alone and thoughtful, hearing a sudden noise he turned about, and saw at the end of the colonnade, by clear daylight, a tall woman, in her countenance and garb like one of the tragical Furies, with a broom in her hand, sweeping the floor. Being amazed and extremely affrighted, he sent for some of his friends, and told them what he had seen, entreating them to stay with him and keep him company all night; for he was excessively discomposed and alarmed, fearing that if he were left alone the spectre would again appear to him. He saw it no more. But a few days after, his only son, being almost grown up to man's estate, upon some displeasure and pet he had taken upon a childish and frivolous occasion, threw himself headlong from the top of the house and broke his neck.

While Dion was under this affliction, Callippus drove on his conspiracy, and spread a rumor among the Syracusans, that Dion, being now childless, was resolved to send for Dionysius's grandson, Apollocrates, who was his wife's nephew and sister's grandson, and make him his heir and successor.[22] By this time, Dion

---

[22] He was the son of Sophrosyne, who was sister to Arete, Dion's wife; Sophrosyne (Temperance) and Arete (perhaps Virtue) being the two daughters of the elder Dionysius by Aristomache, Dion's sister.

Doris of Locri=Dionysius I.=Aristomache, Dion's sister.

Dionysius II.=Sophrosyne   Arete=Dion.

and his wife and sister began to suspect what was
doing, and from all hands information came to them of
the plot. Dion, being troubled, it is probable, for Heraclides's murder, which was like to be a blot and stain
upon his life and actions, in continual weariness and
vexation, declared he had rather die a thousand times,
and open his breast himself to the assassin, than live
not only in fear of his enemies but suspicious of his
friends. But Callippus, seing the women very in-
quisitive to search to the bottom of the business, took
alarm, and came to them, utterly denying it with tears
in his eyes, and offering to give them whatever assurances of his fidelity they desired. They required that
he should take the Great Oath, which was after this
manner. The juror went into the sanctuary of Ceres
and Proserpine, where, after the performance of some
ceremonies, he was clad in the purple vestment of the
goddess, and, holding a lighted torch in his hand, took
his oath. Callippus did as they required, and forswore
the fact. And indeed he so little valued the goddesses,
that he stayed but till the very festival of Proserpine,
whom he had sworn, and on that very day committed
his intended murder; as truly he might well enough
disregard the day, since he must at any other time as
impiously offend her, when he who had acted as her
initiating priest should shed the blood of her wor-
shipper.[23]

There were a great many in the conspiracy; and as
Dion was at home with several of his friends in a room
with tables for entertainment in it, some of the conspirators beset the house around, others secured the
doors and windows. The actual intended murderers

---

[23] This seems to refer to the origin of the acquaintance between Callippus and Dion.—Callippus had acted as *mystagogus*
when Dion was initiated as a *mystes* in the Eleusinian ceremony.

were some Zacynthians, who went inside in their under-dresses without swords. Those outside shut the doors upon them and kept them fast. The murderers fell on Dion, endeavoring to stifle and crush him; then, finding they were doing nothing, they called for a sword, but none durst open the door. There were a great many within with Dion, but every one was for securing himself, supposing that by letting him lose his life he should save his own, and therefore no man ventured to assist him. When they had waited a good while, at length Lycon the Syracusan reached a short sword in at the window to one of the Zacynthians, and thus, like a victim at a sacrifice, this long time in their power, and trembling[24] for the blow, they killed him. His sister, and wife big with child, they hurried to prison, who, poor lady, in her unfortunate condition, was there brought to bed of a son, which, by the consent of the keepers, they intended to bring up, the rather because Callippus began already to be embroiled in troubles.

After the murder of Dion, he was in great glory, and had the sole government of Syracuse in his hands; and to that effect wrote to Athens, a place which, next the immortal gods, being guilty of such an abominable crime, he ought to have regarded with shame and fear. But true it is, what is said of that city, that the good men she breeds are the most excellent, and the bad the most notorious; as their country also produces the most delicious honey and the most deadly hemlock. Callippus, however, did not long continue to scandalize fortune and upbraid the gods with his prosperity, as though they connived at and bore with the wretched man, while he purchased riches and power by heinous impieties, but he quickly received the punishment he

---

[24] This word is uncertain.

deserved. For, going to take Catana, he lost Syracuse; whereupon they report he said, he had lost a city and got a bauble.²⁵ Then, attempting Messena, he had most of his men cut off, and, among the rest, Dion's murderers. When no city in Sicily would admit him, but all hated and abhorred him, he went into Italy and took Rhegium; and there, being in distress and not able to maintain his soldiers, he was killed by Leptines and Polysperchon, and, as fortune would have it, with the same sword by which Dion was murdered, which was known by the size, being but short, as the Spartan swords, and the workmanship of it very curious and artificial. Thus Callippus received the reward of his villanies.

When Aristomache and Arete were released out of prison, Hicetes, one of Dion's friends, took them to his house, and seemed to intend to entertain them well and like a faithful friend. Afterwards, being persuaded by Dion's enemies, he provided a ship and pretended to send them into Peloponnesus, but commanded the sailors, when they came out to sea, to kill them and throw them overboard. Others say that they and the little boy were thrown alive into the sea. This man also escaped not the due recompense of his wickedness, for he was taken by Timoleon and put to death, and the Syracusans, to revenge Dion, slew his two daughters; of all which I have given a more particular account in the life of Timoleon.

²⁵ Literally, a cheese-scraper;—there seems to be some probability, independent of this passage, for supposing that the name *Catana* or *Patana* had this meaning.

MARCUS BRUTUS[1]

TRANSLATED BY R. DUKE, FELLOW OF TRINITY COLLEGE (THE TRANSLATOR OF THE LIFE OF THESUS).

MARCUS BRUTUS was descended from that Junius Brutus to whom the ancient Romans erected a statue of brass in the capitol among the images of their kings with a drawn sword in his hand, in remembrance of his courage and resolution in expelling the Tarquins and destroying the monarchy. But that ancient Brutus was of a severe and inflexible nature, like steel of too hard a temper, and having never had his character softened by study and thought, he let himself be so far transported with his rage and hatred against tyrants, that, for conspiring with them, he proceeded to the execution even of his own sons. But this Brutus, whose life we now write, having to the goodness of his disposition added the improvements of learning and the study of philosophy, and having stirred up his natural parts, of themselves grave and gentle, by applying himself to business and public affairs, seems

[1] Marcus Brutus joined Pompey (although he was the murderer of Brutus' father) on the breaking out of the civil war 49 B. C., but after the battle of Pharsalia 48 B. C., he was not only pardoned by Cæsar but received from him the greatest marks of favor and confidence. Notwithstanding all the obligations he was under to Cæsar, he was persuaded by Cassius to murder his benefactor under the delusive idea of again establishing the republic. An ardent student, he appears to have been deficient in judgment and original power. Being defeated at Philippi, he put an end to his own life 42 B. C.—Dr. William Smith.

to have been of a temper exactly framed for virtue; insomuch that they who were most his enemies upon account of his conspiracy against Cæsar, if in that whole affair there was any honorable or generous part, referred it wholly to Brutus, and laid whatever was barbarous and cruel to the charge of Cassius, Brutus's connection and familiar friend, but not his equal in honesty and pureness of purpose. His mother, Servilia, was of the family of Servilius Ahala, who, when Spurius Mælius worked the people into a rebellion and designed to make himself king, taking a dagger under his arm, went forth into the market-place, and, upon pretence of having some private business with him, came up close to him, and, as he bent his head to hear what he had to say, struck him with his dagger and slew him. And thus much, as concerns his descent by the mother's side, is confessed by all; but as for his father's family, they who for Cæsar's murder bore any hatred or ill-will to Brutus say that he came not from that Brutus who expelled the Tarquins, there being none of his race left after the execution of his two sons; but that his ancestor was a plebian, son of one Brutus, a steward, and only rose in the latest times to office or dignity in the commonwealth. But Posidonius the philosopher writes that it is true indeed what the history relates, that two of the sons of Brutus who were of men's estate were put to death, but that a third, yet an infant, was left alive, from whom the family was propagated down to Marcus Brutus; and further, that there were several famous persons of this house in his time whose looks very much resembled the statute of Junius Brutus. But of this subject enough.

Cato the philosopher was brother to Servilia, the mother of Brutus, and he it was whom of all the Romans his nephew most admired and studied to imitate, and he afterwards married his daughter Porcia. Of all the sects of the Greek philosophers, though there was none of which he had not been a hearer and in which he had not made some proficiency, yet he chiefly esteemed the Platonists; and, not much approving of the modern and middle Academy, as it is called, he applied himself to the study of the ancient. He was all his lifetime a great admirer of Antiochus of the city of Ascalon, and took his brother Aristus into his own house for his friend and companion, a man for his learning inferior indeed to many of the philosophers, but for the evenness of his temper and steadiness of his conduct equal to the best. As for Empylus, of whom he himself and his friends often make mention in their epistles, as one that lived with Brutus, he was a rhetorician, and has left behind him a short but well-written history of the death of Cæsar, entitled Brutus.

In Latin, he had by exercise attained a sufficient skill to be able to make public addresses and to plead a cause; but in Greek, he must be noted for affecting the sententious and short Laconic way of speaking in sundry passages of his epistles; as when, in the beginning of the war, he wrote thus to the Pergamenians: "I hear you have given Dolabella money; if willingly, you must own you have injured me; if unwillingly, show it by giving willingly to me." And another time to the Samians: "Your counsels are remiss and your performances slow: what think ye will be the end?" And of the Patareans thus: "The Xanthians, suspecting my kindness, have made their country the grave of their despair; the Patareans, trusting themselves to me, enjoy in all points their former liberty; it is in your power to choose the judgment of the

Patareans or the fortune of the Xanthians." And
this is the style for which some of his letters are to be
noted.[2]

When he was but a very young man, he accompanied his uncle Cato, to Cyprus, when he was sent
there against Ptolemy. But when Ptolemy killed
himself, Cato, being by some necessary business detained in the isle of Rhodes, had already sent one of
his friends, named Canidius, to take into his care and
keeping the treasure of the king; but presently, not
feeling sure of his honesty, he wrote to Brutus to sail
immediately for Cyprus out of Pamphylia, where he
then was staying to refresh himself, being but just
recovered of a fit of sickness. He obeyed his orders,
orders, but with a great deal of unwillingness, as well
out of respect to Canidius, who was thrown out of this
employment by Cato with so much disgrace, as also
because he esteemed such a commission mean, and unsuitable to him, who was in the prime of his youth, and
given to books and study. Nevertheless, applying
himself to the business, he behaved himself so well in
it that he was highly commended by Cato, and, having
turned all the goods of Ptolemy into ready money, he
sailed with the greatest part of it in his own ship to
Rome.

But upon the general separation into two factions,
when, Pompey and Cæsar taking up arms against one
another, the whole empire was turned into confusion,
it was commonly believed that he would take Cæsar's
side; for his father in past time had been put to death
by Pompey. But he, thinking it his duty to prefer
the interest of the public to his own private feelings,
and judging Pompey's to be the better cause, took

[2] Noted, I believe ne means, for their false style—as not to be
imitated.

part with him; though formerly he used not so much as to salute or take any notice of Pompey, if he happened to meet him, esteeming it a pollution to have the least conversation with the murderer of his father. But now, looking upon his as the general of his country, he placed himself under his command, and set sail for Cilicia in quality of lieutenant to Sestius, who had the government of that province. But finding no opportunity there of doing any great service, and hearing that Pompey and Cæsar were now near one another and preparing for the battle upon which all depended, he came of his own accord to Macedonia to partake in the danger. At his coming it is said that Pompey was so surprised and so pleased, that, rising from his chair in the sight of all who were about him, he saluted and embraced him, as one of the chiefest of his party. All the time that he was in the camp, excepting that which he spent in Pompey's company, he employed in reading and in study, which he did not neglect even the day before the great battle. It was the middle of summer, and the heat was very great, the camp having been pitched near some marshy ground, and the people that carried Brutus's tent were a long while before they came. Yet though upon these accounts he was extremely harassed and out of order, having scarcely by the middle of the day anointed himself and eaten a sparing meal, whilst most others were either laid to sleep or taken up with the thoughts and apprehensions of what would be the issue of the fight, he spent his time until the evening in writing an epitome of Polybius.

It is said that Cæsar had so great a regard for him that he ordered his commanders by no means to kill Brutus in the battle, but to spare him, if possible, and bring him safe to him, if he would willingly surrender himself; but if he made any resistance, to suffer him to escape rather than do him any violence. And this he is believed to have done out of a tenderness to Servilia, the mother of Brutus; for Cæsar had, it seems, in his youth been very intimate with her, and she passionately in love with him; and, considering that Brutus was born about that time in which their loves were at the highest, Cæsar had a belief that he was his own child. The story is told, that when the great question of the conspiracy of Catiline, which had like to have been the destruction of the commonwealth, was debated in the senate, Cato and Cæsar were both standing up, contending together on the decision to be come to; at which time a little note was delivered to Cæsar from without, which he took and read silently to himself. Upon this Cato, cried out aloud, and accused Cæsar of holding correspondence with and receiving letters from the enemies of the commonwealth; and when many other senators exclaimed against it, Cæsar delivered the note as he had received it to Cato, who reading it found it to be a love-letter from his own sister Servilia, and threw it back again to Cæsar with the words, "Keep it, you drunkard," and returned to the subject of the debate. So public and notorious was Servilia's love to Cæsar.

After the great overthrow at Pharsalia, Pompey himself having made his escape to the sea, and Cæsar's army storming the camp, Brutus stole privately out by one of the gates leading to marshy ground full of water and covered with reeds, and, travelling through the night, got safe to Larissa. From Larissa he wrote to Cæsar, who expressed a great deal of joy to hear that he was safe, and, bidding him come, not only forgave him freely, but honored and esteemed him among his chiefest friends. Now when nobody could give any certain account which way Pompey had fled, Cæsar took a little journey alone with Brutus, and tried what was his opinion herein, and after some discussion which passed between them, believing that Brutus's conjecture was the right one, laying aside all other thoughts, he set out directly to pursue him towards Egypt. But Pompey, having reached Egypt, as Brutus guessed his design was to do, there met his fate.

Brutus in the mean time gained Cæsar's forgiveness for his friend Cassius; and pleading also in defence of the king of the Lybians,[3] though he was overwhelmed with the greatness of the crimes alleged against him, yet by his entreaties and deprecations to Cæsar in his behalf, he preserved to him a great part of his kingdom. It is reported that Cæsar, when he first heard Brutus speak in public, said to his friends, "I know not what this young man intends, but, whatever he intends, he intends vehemently."[4] For his natural firmness of mind, not easily yielding, or complying in favor of every one that entreated his kindness, once set into action upon motives of right reason and deliberate moral choice, whatever direction it thus took, it was pretty sure to take effectively, and to work in such a way as not to fail in its object. No flattery could ever prevail with him to listen to unjust petitions; and he held that to be overcome by the importunities of shameless and fawning entreaties, though some compliment it with the name of modesty and bashfulness, was the worst disgrace a great man could suffer. And he used to say, that he always felt

---

[3] Deiotarus, king of the Galatians of Asia Minor, is the person meant. The error is supposed to be Plutarch's.

[4] *Quidquid vult, valde vult;* the words are recorded by Cicero in the Letters to Atticus, xiv., 1,—where Brutus's speech in favor of Deiotarus is also mentioned.

as if they who could deny nothing could not have behaved well in the flower of their youth.

Cæsar, being about to make his expedition into Africa against Cato and Scipio, committed to Brutus the government of Cisalpine Gaul, to the great happiness and advantage of that province. For while people in other provinces were in distress with the violence and avarice of their governors, and suffered as much oppression as if they had been slaves and captives of war, Brutus, by his easy government, actually made them amends for their calamities under former rulers, directing moreover all their gratitude for his good deeds to Cæsar himself; insomuch that it was a most welcome and pleasant spectacle to Cæsar, when in his return he passed through Italy, to see the cities that were under Brutus's command and Brutus himself increasing his honor and joining agreeably in his progress.

Now several prætorships being vacant, it was all men's opinion, that that of the chiefest dignity, which is called the prætorship of the city, would be conferred either upon Brutus or Cassius; and some say that, there having been some little difference upon former accounts between them, this competition set them much more at variance, though they were connected in their families, Cassius having married Junia, the sister of Brutus. Others say that the contention was raised between them by Cæsar's doing, who had privately given each of them such hopes of his favor as led them on, and provoked them at last into this open competition and trial of their interest. Brutus had only the reputation of his honor and virtue to oppose to the many and gallant actions performed by Cassius against the Parthians. But Cæsar, having heard each side, and deliberating about the matter among his friends, said, "Cassius has the stronger plea, but we must let Brutus be first prætor." So another prætorship was given to Cassius; the gaining of which could not so much oblige him, as he was incensed for the loss of the other. And in all other things Brutus was partaker of Cæsar's power as much as he desired; for he might, if he had pleased, have been the chief of all his friends, and had authority and command beyond them all, but Cassius and the company he met with him drew him off from Cæsar. Indeed, he was not yet wholly reconciled to Cassius, since that competition which was between them; but yet he gave ear to Cassius's friends, who were perpetually advising him not to be so blind as to suffer himself to be softened and won upon by Cæsar, but to shun the kindness and favors of a tyrant, which they intimated that Cæsar showed him, not to express any honor to his merit or virtue, but to unbend his strength, and undermine his vigor of purpose.

Neither was Cæsar wholly without suspicion of him, nor wanted informers that accused Brutus to him; but he feared, indeed, the high spirit and the great character and the friends that he had, but thought himself secure in his moral disposition. When it was told him that Antony and Dolabella designed some disturbance, "It is not," said he, "the fat and the long-haired men that I fear, but the pale and the lean," meaning Brutus and Cassius. And when some maligned Brutus to him, and advised him to beware of him, taking hold of his flesh with his hand, "What," he said, "do you think that Brutus will not wait out the time of this little body?" as if he thought none so fit to succeed him in his power as Brutus. And indeed it seems to be without doubt that Brutus might have been the first man in the commonwealth, if he had had patience but a little time to be second to Cæsar, and would have suffered his power to decline after it was come to its highest pitch, and the fame of his great actions to die away by degrees. But Cassius, a man of a fierce disposition, and one that out of private malice, rather than love of the public, hated Cæsar, not the tyrant, continually fired and stirred him up. Brutus felt the rule an oppression, but Cassius hated the ruler; and, among other reasons on which he grounded his quarrel against Cæsar, the loss of his lions which he had procured when he was edile elect was one: for Cæsar, finding these in Megara, when that city was taken by Calenus, seized them to himself. These beasts, they say, were a great calamity to the Megarians; for, when their city was just taken, they broke open the lions' dens, and pulled off their chains and let them loose, that they might run upon the enemy that was entering the city; but the lions turned upon them themselves, and tore to pieces a great many unarmed persons running about, so that it was a miserable spectacle even to their enemies to behold.

And this, some say, was the chief provocation that stirred up Cassius to conspire against Cæsar; but they are much in the wrong. For Cassius had from his youth a natural hatred and rancor against the whole race of tyrants, which he showed when he was but a boy, and went to the same school with Faustus, the son of Sylla; for, on his boasting himself amongst the boys, and extolling the sovereign power of his father, Cassius rose up and struck him two or three boxes on the ear; which when the guardians and relations of Faustus designed to inquire into and to prosecute, Pompey forbade them, and, sending for both the boys together, examined the matter himself. And Cassius then is reported to have said thus, "Come, then, Faustus, dare to speak here those words that provoked me, that I may strike you again as I did before." Such was the disposition of Cassius.

But Brutus was roused up and pushed on to the undertaking by many persuasions of his familiar friends, and letters and invitations from unknown citizens. For under the statue of his ancestor Brutus, that overthrew the kingly government, they wrote the words, "O that we had a Brutus now!" and, "O that Brutus were alive!" And Brutus's own tribunal, on which he sate as prætor, was filled each morning with writings such as these: "You are asleep, Brutus," and, "You are not a true Brutus." Now the flatterers of Cæsar were the occasion of all this, who, among other invidious honors which they strove to fasten upon Cæsar, crowned his statues by night with diadems, wishing to incite the people to salute him king instead of dictator. But quite the contrary came to pass, as I have more particularly related in the life of Cæsar.

When Cassius went about soliciting friends to engage in this design against Cæsar, all whom he tried readily consented, if Brutus would be head of it; for their opinion was that the enterprise wanted not hands or resolution, but the reputation and authority of a man such as he was, to give as it were the first religious sanction, and by his presence, if by nothing else, to justify the undertaking; that without him they should go about this action with less heart, and should lie under greater suspicions when they had done it, for, if their cause had been just and honorable, people would be sure that Brutus would not have refused it. Cassius, having considered these things with himself, went to Brutus, and made him the first visit after their falling out; and after the compliments of reconciliation had passed, and former kindnesses were renewed between them, he asked him if he designed to be present in the senate on the Calends of March, for it was discoursed, he said, that Cæsar's friends intended then to move that he might be made king. When Brutus answered, that he would not be there, "But what," says Cassius, "if they should send for us?" "It will be my business then," replied Brutus, "not to hold my peace, but to stand up boldly, and die for the liberty of my country." To which Cassius with some emotion answered, "But what Roman will suffer you to die? What, do you not know yourself, Brutus? Or do you think that those writings that you find upon your prætor's seat were put there by weavers and shopkeepers, and not by the first and most powerful men of Rome? From other prætors, indeed, they expect largesses and shows and gladiators, but from you they claim, as an hereditary debt, the extirpation of tyranny; they are all ready to suffer any thing on your account, if you will but show yourself such as they think you are and expect you should be." Which said, he fell upon Brutus, and embraced him; and after this, they parted each to try their several friends.

Among the friends of Pompey there was one Caius Ligarius, whom Cæsar had pardoned, though accused for having been in arms against him. This man, not feeling so thankful for having been forgiven as he felt oppressed by that power which made him need a pardon, hated Cæsar, and was one of Brutus's most intimate friends. Him Brutus visited, and, finding him sick, "O Ligarius," says he, "what a time have you found out to be sick in!" At which words Ligarius, raising himself and leaning on his elbow, took Brutus by the hand, and said, "But, O Brutus, if you are on any design worthy of yourself, I am well."

From this time, they tried the inclinations of all their acquaintance that they durst trust, and communicated the secret to them, and took into the design not only their familiar friends, but as many as they believed bold and brave and despisers of death.

For which reason they concealed the plot from Cicero, though he was very much trusted and as well beloved by them all, lest, to his own disposition, which was naturally timorous, adding now the wariness and caution of old age, by his weighing, as he would do, every particular, that he might not make one step without the greatest security, he should blunt the edge of their forwardness and resolution in a business which required all the despatch imaginable. As indeed there were also two others that were companions of Brutus, Statilius the Epicurean, and Favonius the admirer of Cato, whom he left out for this reason: as he was conversing one day with them, trying them at a distance, and proposing some such question to be disputed of as among philosophers, to see what opinion they were of, Favonius declared his judgment to be that a civil war was worse than the most illegal monarchy; and Statilius held that, to bring himself into troubles and danger upon the account of evil or foolish men, did not become a man that had any wisdom or discretion. But Labeo, who was present, contradicted them both; and Brutus, as if it had been an intricate dispute, and difficult to be decided, held his peace for that time, but afterwards discovered the whole design to Labeo, who readily undertook it. The next thing that was thought convenient, was to gain the other Brutus, surnamed Albinus, a man of himself of no great bravery or courage, but considerable for the number of gladiators that he was maintaining for a public show, and the great confidence that Cæsar put in him. When Cassius and Labeo spoke with him concerning the matter, he gave them no answer; but, seeking an interview with Brutus himself alone, and finding that he was their captain, he readily consented to partake in the action. And among the others, also, the most and best were gained by the name of Brutus. And, though they neither gave nor took any oath of secrecy, nor used any other sacred rite to assure their fidelity to each other, yet all kept their design so close, were so wary, and held it so silently among themselves, that, though by prophecies and apparitions and signs in the sacrifices the gods gave warning of it, yet could it not be believed.

Now Brutus, feeling that the noblest spirits of Rome for virtue, birth, or courage were depending upon him, and surveying with himself all the circumstances of the dangers they were to encounter, strove indeed as much as possible, when abroad, to keep his uneasiness of mind to himself, and to compose his thoughts; but at home, and especially at night, he was not the same man, but sometimes against his will his working care would make him start out of his sleep, and other times he was taken up with further reflection and consideration of his difficulties, so that his wife that lay with him could not choose but take notice that he was full of unusual trouble, and had in agitation some dangerous and perplexing question. Porcia, as was said before, was the daughter of Cato, and Brutus, her cousin-german, had married her very young, though not a maid, but after the death of her former husband, by whom she had one son, that was named Bibulus; and there is a little book, called Memoirs of Brutus, written by him, yet extant. This Porcia, being addicted to philosophy, a great lover of her husband, and full of an understanding courage, resolved not to inquire into Brutus's secrets before she had made this trial of herself. She turned all her attendants out of her chamber, and, taking a little knife, such as they use to cut nails with, she gave herself a deep gash in the thigh; upon which followed a great flow of blood, and, soon after, violent pains and a shivering fever, occasioned by the wound. Now when Brutus was extremely anxious and afflicted for her, she, in the height of all her pain, spoke thus to him: "I, Brutus, being the daughter of Cato, was given to you in marriage, not like a concubine, to partake only in the common intercourse of bed and board, but to bear a part in all your good and all your evil fortunes; and for your part, as regards your care for me, I find no reason to complain; but from me, what evidence of my love, what satisfaction can you receive, if I may not share with you in bearing your hidden griefs, nor be admitted to any of your counsels that require secrecy and trust? I know very well that women seem to be of too weak a nature to be trusted with secrets; but certainly, Brutus, a virtuous birth and education, and the company of the good and honorable, are of some force to the forming our manners; and I can boast that I am the daughter of Cato and the wife of Brutus, in which two titles though before I put less confidence, yet now I have tried myself, and find that I can bid defiance to pain." Which words having spoken, she showed him her wound, and related to him the trial that she had made of her constancy; at which he being astonished, lifted up his hands to heaven, and begged the assistance of the gods in his enterprise, that he might show himself a husband worthy of such a wife as Porcia. So then he comforted his wife.

But a meeting of the senate being appointed, at which it was believed that Cæsar would be present, they agreed to make use of that opportunity: for then they might appear all together without suspicion; and, besides, they hoped that all the noblest and leading men of the commonwealth, being then assembled, as soon as the great deed was done, would immediately stand forward, and assert the common liberty. The very place, too, where the senate was to meet, seemed to be by divine appointment favorable to their purpose. It was a portico, one of those joining the theatre, with a large recess,[5] in which there stood a statue of Pompey, erected to him by the commonwealth, when he adorned that part of the city with the porticos and the theatre. To this place it was that the senate was summoned for the middle of March (the Ides of March is the Roman name for the day); as if some more than human power were leading the man thither, there to meet his punishment for the death of Pompey.

As soon as it was day, Brutus, taking with him a dagger, which none but his wife knew of, went out. The rest met together at Cassius's house, and brought forth his son, that was that day to put on the manly gown, as it is called, into the forum; and from thence, going all to Pompey's porch, stayed there, expecting Cæsar to come without delay to the senate. Here it was chiefly that any one who had known what they had purposed, would have admired the unconcerned temper and the steady resolution of these men in their most dangerous undertaking; for many of them, being prætors, and called upon by their office to judge and determine causes, did not only hear calmly all that made application to them and pleaded against each other before them, as if they were free from all other thoughts, but decided causes with as much accuracy and judgment as they had heard them with attention

---

[5] An *exedra*. These were chambers or saloons attached to colonnades and porticos, as, for example, to those which surrounded the great buildings for public amusements, called the thermæ, from the baths, which formed but one part of them. They might be said to correspond to modern reading-rooms, and were used by the lecturers in rhetoric and philosophy. For Pompey's famous theatre, see his Life, in Vol. IV., p. 101, and a note at the end of the volume.

and patience. And when one person refused to stand to the award of Brutus, and with great clamor and many attestations appealed to Cæsar, Brutus, looking round about him upon those that were present, said, "Cæsar does not hinder me, nor will he hinder me, from doing according to the laws."

Yet there were many unusual incidents that disturbed them and by mere chance were thrown in their way. The first and chiefest was the long stay of Cæsar, though the day was far spent, and his being detained at home by his wife, and forbidden by the soothsayers to go forth, upon some defect that appeared in his sacrifice. Another was this: There came a man up to Casca, one of the company, and, taking him by the hand, "You concealed," said he, "the secret from us, but Brutus has told me all." At which words when Casca was surprised, the other said laughing, "How come you to be so rich of a sudden, that you should stand to be chosen edile?" So near was Casca to let out the secret, upon the mere ambiguity of the other's expression. Then Popilius Lænas, a senator, having saluted Brutus and Cassius more earnestly than usual, whispered them softly in the ear and said, "My wishes are with you, that you may accomplish what you design, and I advise you to make no delay, for the thing is now no secret." This said, he departed, and left them in great suspicion that the design had taken wind. In the mean while, there came one in all haste from Brutus's house, and brought him news that his wife was dying. For Porcia, being extremely disturbed with expectation of the event, and not able to bear the greatness of her anxiety, could scarce keep herself within doors; and at every little noise or voice she heard, starting up suddenly, like those possessed with the bacchic frenzy, she asked every one that came in from the forum what Brutus was doing, and sent

one messenger after another to inquire. At last, after
long expectation, the strength of her body could hold
out no longer; her mind was overcome with her doubts
and fears, and she lost the control of herself, and began to faint away. She had not time to betake herself
to her chamber, but, sitting as she was amongst her
women, a sudden swoon and a great stupor seized her,
and her color changed, and her speech was quite lost.
At this sight, her women made a loud cry, and many
of the neighbors running to Brutus's door to know
what was the matter, the report was soon spread
abroad that Porcia was dead; though with her wom-
en's help she recovered in a little while, and came
to herself again. When Brutus received this news,
he was extremely troubled, nor without reason, yet
was not so carried away by his private grief as to quit
his public purpose.

For now news was brought that Cæsar was coming,
carried in a litter. For, being discouraged by the ill
omens that attended his sacrifice, he had determined
to undertake no affairs of any great importance that
day, but to defer them till another time, excusing himself that he was sick. As soon as he came out of his
litter, Popilius Lænas, he who but a little before had
wished Brutus good success in his undertaking, coming up to him, conversed a great while with him, Cæsar standing still all the while, and seeming to be very
attentive. The conspirators (to give them this name),
not being able to hear what he said, but guessing by
what themselves were conscious of that this conference
was the discovery of their treason, were again disheartened, and, looking upon one another, agreed from
each other's countenances that they should not stay to
be taken, but should all kill themselves. And now
when Cassius and some others were laying hands upon
their daggers under their robes, and were drawing

them out, Brutus, viewing narrowly the looks and gesture of Lænas, and finding that he was earnestly petitioning and not accusing, said nothing, because there were many strangers to the conspiracy mingled amongst them, but by a cheerful countenance encouraged Cassius. And after a little while, Lænas, having kissed Cæsar's hand, went away, showing plainly that all his discourse was about some particular business relating to himself.

Now when the senate was gone in before to the chamber where they were to sit, the rest of the company placed themselves close about Cæsar's chair, as if they had some suit to make to him, and Cassius, turning his face to Pompey's statue, is said to have invoked it, as if it had been sensible of his prayers. Trebonius, in the meanwhile, engaged Antony's attention at the door, and kept him in talk outside. When Cæsar entered, the whole senate rose up to him. As soon as he was set down, the men all crowded round about him, and set Tillius Cimber, one of their own number, to intercede in behalf of his brother, that was banished; they all joined their prayers with his, and took Cæsar by the hand, and kissed his head and his breast. But he putting aside at first their supplications, and afterwards, when he saw they would not desist, violently rising up, Tillius with both hands caught hold of his robe and pulled it off from his shoulders, and Casca, that stood behind him, drawing his dagger, gave him the first, but a slight wound, about the shoulder. Cæsar snatching hold of the handle of the dagger, and crying out aloud in Latin, "Villain Casca, what do you?" he, calling in Greek, to his brother, bade him come and help. And by this time, finding himself struck by a great many hands, and looking round about him to see if he could force his way out, when he saw Brutus with his dagger drawn against him, he let go Casca's hand, that he had hold of, and, covering his head with his robe, gave up his body to their blows. And they so eagerly pressed towards the body, and so many daggers were hacking together, that they cut one another; Brutus, particularly, received a wound in his hand, and all of them were besmeared with the blood.

Cæsar, being thus slain, Brutus, stepping forth into the midst, intended to have made a speech, and called back and encouraged the senators to stay; but they all affrighted ran away in great disorder, and there was a great confusion and press at the door, though none pursued or followed. For they had come to an express resolution to kill nobody besides Cæsar, but to call and invite all the rest to liberty. It was indeed the opinion of all the others, when they consulted about the execution of their design, that it was necessary to cut off Antony with Cæsar, looking upon him as an insolent man, an affecter of monarchy, and one that, by his familiar intercourse, had gained a powerful interest with the soldiers. And this they urged the rather, because at that time to the natural loftiness and ambition of his temper there was added the dignity of being consul and colleague to Cæsar. But Brutus opposed this counsel, insisting first upon the injustice of it, and afterwards giving them hopes that a change might be worked in Antony. For he did not despair but that so highly gifted and honorable a man, and such a lover of glory as Antony, stirred up with emulation of their great attempt, might, if Cæsar were once removed, lay hold of the occasion to be joint restorer with them of the liberty of his country. Thus did Brutus save Antony's life. But he, in the general consternation, put himself into a plebeian habit, and fled. But Brutus and his party marched up to the capitol, in their way showing their hands all bloody, and their naked swords, and proclaiming liberty to the people. At first all places were filled with cries and shouts; and the wild running to and fro, occasioned by the sudden surprise and passion that every one was in, increased the tumult in the city. But no other bloodshed following, and no plundering of the goods in the streets, the senators and many of the people took courage and went up to the men in the capitol; and, a multitude being gathered together, Brutus made an oration to them, very popular, and proper for the state that affairs were then in. Therefore, when they applauded his speech, and cried out to him to come down, they all took confidence and descended into the forum; the rest promiscuously mingled with one another, but many of the most eminent persons, attending Brutus, conducted him in the midst of them with great honor from the capitol, and placed him in the rostra. At the sight of Brutus, the crowd, though consisting of a confused mixture and all disposed to make a tumult, were struck with reverence, and expected what he would say with order and with silence, and, when he began to speak, heard him with quiet and attention. But that all were not pleased with this action they plainly showed when, Cinna beginning to speak and accuse Cæsar, they broke out into a sudden rage, and railed at him in such language, that the whole party thought fit again to withdraw to the capitol. And there Brutus, expecting to be besieged, dismissed the most eminent of those that had accompanied them thither, not thinking it just that they who were not partakers of the fact should share in the danger.

But the next day, the senate being assembled in the temple of the Earth,[6] and Antony and Plancus and

---

[6] The temple of Tellus, in the Carinæ.

Cicero having made orations recommending concord in general and an act of oblivion, it was decreed, that the men should not only be put out of all fear or danger, but that the consuls should see what honors and dignities were proper to be conferred upon them. After which done, the senate broke up; and, Antony having sent his son as an hostage to the capitol, Brutus and his company came down, and mutual salutes and invitations passed amongst them, the whole of them being gathered together. Antony invited and entertained Cassius, Lepidus did the same to Brutus, and the rest were invited and entertained by others, as each of them had acquaintance or friends. And as soon as it was day, the senate met again and voted thanks to Antony for having stifled the beginning of a civil war; afterwards Brutus and his associates that were present received encomiums, and had provinces assigned and distributed among them. Crete was alloted to Brutus, Africa to Cassius, Asia to Trebonius, Bithynia to Cimber, and to the other Brutus Gaul about the Po.

After these things, they began to consider of Cæsar's will, and the ordering of his funeral. Antony desired that the will might be read, and that the body should not have a private or dishonorable interment, lest that should further exasperate the people. This Cassius violently opposed, but Brutus yielded to it, and gave leave; in which he seems to have a second time committed a fault. For as before in sparing the life of Antony he could not be without some blame from his party, as thereby setting up against the conspiracy a dangerous and difficult enemy, so now, in suffering him to have the ordering of the funeral, he fell into a total and irrecoverable error. For first, it appearing by the will that Cæsar had bequeathed to the Roman people seventy-five drachmas a man, and given to the public his gardens beyond Tiber (where now the temple of Fortune stands), the whole city was fired with a wonderful affection for him, and a passionate sense of the loss of him. And when the body was brought forth into the forum, Antony, as the custom was, making a funeral oration in the praise of Cæsar, and finding the multitude moved with his speech, passing into the pathetic tone, unfolded the bloody garment of Cæsar, showed them in how many places it was pierced, and the number of his wounds. Now there was nothing to be seen but confusion; some cried out to kill the murderers, others (as was formerly done when Clodius led the people) tore away the benches and tables out of the shops round about, and, heaping them all together, built a great funeral pile, and, having put the body of Cæsar upon it, set it on fire, the spot where this was done being moreover surrounded with a great many temples and other consecrated places, so that they seemed to burn the body in a kind of sacred solemnity. As soon as the fire flamed out, the multitude, flocking in some from one part and some from another, snatched the brands that were half burnt out of the pile, and ran about the city to fire the houses of the murderers of Cæsar. But they, having beforehand well fortified themselves, repelled this danger.

There was, however, a kind of poet, one Cinna, not at all concerned in the guilt of the conspiracy, but on the contrary one of Cæsar's friends. This man dreamed that he was invited to supper by Cæsar, and that he declined to go, but that Cæsar entreated and pressed him to it very earnestly; and at last, taking him by the hand, led him into a very deep and dark place, whither he was forced against his will to follow in great consternation and amazement. After this vision, he had a fever the most part of the night; nevertheless in the morning, hearing that the body of Cæsar was to be carried forth to be interred, he was ashamed not to be present at the solemnity, and came abroad and joined the people, when they were already infuriated by the speech of Antony. And perceiving him, and taking him not for that Cinna who indeed he was, but for him that a little before in a speech to the people had reproached and inveighed against Cæsar, they fell upon him and tore him to pieces.

This action chiefly, and the alteration that Antony had wrought, so alarmed Brutus and his party, that for their safety they retired from the city. The first stay they made was at Antium, with a design to return again as soon as the fury of the people had spent itself and was abated, which they expected would soon and easily come to pass in an unsettled multitude, apt to be carried away with any sudden and impetuous passion, especially since they had the senate favorable to them; which, though it took no notice of those that had torn Cinna to pieces, yet made a strict search and apprehended in order to punishment those that had assaulted the houses of the friends of Brutus and Cassius. By this time, also, the people began to be dissatisfied with Antony, who they perceived was setting up a kind of monarchy for himself; they longed for the return of Brutus, whose presence they expected and hoped for at the games and spectacles which he, as prætor, was to exhibit to the public. But he, having intelligence that many of the old soldiers that had borne arms under Cæsar, by whom they had had lands and cities given them, lay in wait for him, and by small parties at a time had stolen into the city, would not venture to come himself; however, in his absence there were most magnificent and costly shows exhibited to the people; for, having bought up a great number of all sorts of wild beasts, he gave order that not any of them should be returned or saved, but that all should be spent freely at the public spectacles. He himself made a journey to Naples to procure a considerable number of players, and hearing of one Canutius, that was very much praised for his acting upon the stage, he wrote to his friends to use all their entreaties to bring him to Rome (for, being a Grecian, he could not be compelled); he wrote also to Cicero, begging him by no means to omit being present at the shows.

This was the posture of affairs when another sudden alteration was made upon the young Cæsar's coming to Rome. He was son to the niece of Cæsar, who adopted him, and left him his heir by his will. At the time when Cæsar was killed, he was following his studies at Apollonia, where he was expecting also to meet Cæsar on his way to the expedition which he had determined on against the Parthians; but, hearing of his death, he immediately came to Rome, and, to ingratiate himself with the people, taking upon himself the name of Cæsar, and punctually distributing among the citizens the money that was left them by the will, he soon got the better of Antony; and by money and largesses, which he liberally dispersed amongst the soldiers, he gathered together and brought over to his party a great number of those that had served under Cæsar. Cicero himself, out of the hatred which he bore to Antony, sided with young Cæsar; which Brutus took so ill that he treated with him very sharply in his letters,[7] telling him, that he perceived Cicero could well enough endure a tyrant, but was afraid that he

---

[7] Letters of Brutus to Cicero and to Atticus, in which the phrases quoted by Plutarch occur, have come down to us in a series from Cicero to Brutus (*Epist. ad Brutum, I.* 16, 17). But this whole collection also is regarded with suspicion.

who hated him should be the man; that in writing and speaking so well of Cæsar, he showed that his aim was to have an easy slavery." "But our forefathers," said Brutus, "could not brook even gentle masters." Further he added, that for his own part he had not as yet fully resolved whether he should make war or peace; but that as to one point he was fixed and settled, which was, never to be a slave; that he wondered Cicero should fear the dangers of a civil war, and not be much more afraid of a dishonorable and infamous peace; that the very reward that was to be given him for subverting Antony's tyranny was the privilege of establishing Cæsar as tyrant in his place. This is the tone of Brutus's first letters to Cicero.

The city being now divided into two factions, some betaking themselves to Cæsar, and others to Antony, the soldiers selling themselves, as it were, by public outcry, and going over to him that would give them most, Brutus began to despair of any good event of such proceedings, and, resolving to leave Italy, passed by land through Lucania and came to Elea[8] by the sea-side. From hence it was thought convenient that Porcia should return to Rome. She was overcome with grief to part from Brutus, but strove as much as was possible to conceal it; but, in spite of all her constancy, a picture which she found there accidentally betrayed it. It was a Greek subject, Hector parting from Andromache when he went to engage the Greeks, giving his young son Astyanax into her arms, and she fixing her eyes upon it. When she looked at this piece, the resemblance it bore to her own condition made her burst into tears, and several times a day she went to see the picture, and wept before it. Upon this occasion, when Acilius, one of Brutus's friends, repeated

[8] Velia, called Elea in Greek, a little south of Pæstum.

out of Homer the verses, where Andromache speaks to Hector:—

> But Hector, you
> To me are father and are mother too,
> My brother, and my loving husband true,

Brutus, smiling, replied, "But I must not answer Porcia, as Hector did Andromache,

> 'Mind you your loom, and to your maids give law.'

For though the natural weakness of her body hinders her from doing what only the strength of men can perform, yet she has a mind as valiant and as active for the good of her country as the best of us." This narrative is in the memoirs of Brutus written by Bibulus, Porcia's son.

Brutus took ship from hence, and sailed to Athens where he was received by the people with great demonstrations of kindness, expressed in their acclamations and the honors that were decreed him. He lived there with a private friend, and was a constant auditor of Theomnestus the Academic and Cratippus the Peripatetic, with whom he so engaged in philosophical pursuits, that he seemed to have laid aside all thoughts of public business, and to be wholly at leisure for study. But all this while, being unsuspected, he was secretly making preparation for war; in order to which he sent Herostratus into Macedonia to secure the commanders there to his side, and he himself won over and kept at his disposal all the young Romans that were then students at Athens. Of this number was Cicero's son, whom he everywhere highly extols, and says that whether sleeping or waking he could not choose but admire a young man of so great a spirit and such a hater of tyranny.

At length he began to act openly, and to appear in public business, and, being informed that there were several Roman ships full of treasure that in their course from Asia were to come that way, and that they were commanded by one of his friends, he went to meet him about Carystus. Finding him there, and having persuaded him to deliver up the ships, he made a more than usually splendid entertainment, for it happened also to be his birthday. Now when they came to drink, and were filling their cups with hopes for victory to Brutus and liberty to Rome, Brutus, to animate them the more, called for a larger bowl, and holding it in his hands, on a sudden upon no occasion or forethought pronounced aloud this verse:—

But fate my death and Leto's son have wrought.[9]

And some writers add that in the last battle which he fought at Philippi the word that he gave to his soldiers was Apollo, and from thence conclude that this sudden unaccountable exclamation of his was a presage of the overthrow that he suffered there.

Antistius, the commander of these ships, at his parting gave him fifty thousand myriads of the money that he was conveying to Italy; and all the soldiers yet remaining of Pompey's army, who after their general's defeat wandered about Thessaly, readily and joyfully flocked together to join him. Besides this, he took from Cinna five hundred horse that he was carrying to Dolabella into Asia. After that, he sailed to Demetrias, and there seized a great quantity of arms, that had been provided by the command of the deceased Cæsar for the Parthian war, and were now to be sent to Antony. Then Macedonia was put into his hands and delivered up by Hortensius the prætor, and all the kings and potentates round about came and of-

[9] Leto is the Greek name of the mother of Apollo, for which Latona is the Latin form. The verse is from the sixteenth Iliad (849) part of the dying words of Patroclus.

fered their services. So when news was brought that Caius, the brother of Antony, having passed over from Italy, was marching on directly to join the forces that Vatinius commanded in Dyrrhachium and Apollonia, Brutus resolved to anticipate him, and to seize them first, and in all haste moved forwards with those that he had about him. His march was very difficult, through rugged places and in a great snow, but so swift that he left those that were to bring his provisions for the morning meal a great way behind. And now, being very near to Dyrrachium, with fatigue and cold he fell into the distemper called Bulimia. This is a disease that seizes both men and cattle after much labor, and especially in a great snow; whether it is caused by the natural heat, when the body is seized with cold, being forced all inwards, and consuming at once all the nourishment laid in, or whether the sharp and subtile vapor which comes from the snow as it dissolves, cuts the body, as it were, and destroys the heat which issues through the pores; for the sweatings seem to arise from the heat meeting with the cold, and being quenched by it on the surface of the body. But this I have in another place discussed more at large.[10]

Brutus, growing very faint, and there being none in the whole army that had any thing for him to eat, his servants were forced to have recourse to the enemy, and going as far as to the gates of the city, begged bread of the sentinels that were upon duty. As soon as they heard of the condition of Brutus, they came themselves, and brought both meat and drink along with them; in return for which, Brutus, when he took

[10] Plutarch discusses the nature of this ravenous or famishing *oxhunger* (as the Greek word is), in the Symposiac Questions (*VI.* 8).

the city, showed the greatest kindness, not to them only, but to all the inhabitants, for their sakes. Caius Antonius, in the mean time, coming to Apollonia, summoned all the soldiers that were near that city to join him there; but finding that they nevertheless went all to Brutus, and suspecting that even those of Apollonia were inclined to the same party, he quitted that city, and came to Buthrotum, having first lost three cohorts of his men, that in their march thither were cut to pieces by Brutus. After this, attempting to make himself master of some strong places about Byllis which the enemy had first seized, he was overcome in a set battle by young Cicero, to whom Brutus gave the command, and whose conduct he made use of often and with much success. Caius himself was surprised in a marshy place, at a distance from his supports; and Brutus, having him in his power, would not suffer his soldiers to attack, but manœuvring about the enemy with his horse, gave command that none of them should be killed, for that in a little time they would all be of his side; which accordingly came to pass, for they surrendered both themselves and their general. So that Brutus had by this time a very great and considerable army. He showed all marks of honor and esteem to Caius for a long time, and left him the use of the ensigns of his office, though, as some report, he had several letters from Rome, and particularly from Cicero, advising him to put him to death. But at last, perceiving that he began to corrupt his officers, and was trying to raise a mutiny amongst his soldiers, he put him aboard a ship and kept him close prisoner. In the mean time the soldiers that had been corrupted by Caius retired to Apollonia, and sent word to Brutus, desiring him to come to them thither. He answered that this was not the custom of the Romans, but that it became those who had offended to come themselves to their general and beg forgiveness of their offences; which they did, and accordingly received their pardon.

As he was preparing to pass into Asia, tidings reached him of the alteration that had happened at Rome; where the young Cæsar, assisted by the senate, in opposition to Antony, and having driven his competitor out of Italy, had begun himself to be very formidable, suing for the consulship contrary to law, and maintaining large bodies of troops of which the commonwealth had no manner of need. And then, perceiving that the senate, dissatisfied with his proceedings, began to cast their eyes abroad upon Brutus, and decreed and confirmed the government of several provinces to him, he had taken the alarm. Therefore despatching messengers to Antony, he desired that there might be a reconciliation, and a friendship between them. Then, drawing all his forces about the city, he made himself be chosen consul, though he was but a boy, being scarce twenty years old, as he himself writes in his memoirs. At his first entry upon the consulship he immediately ordered a judicial process to be issued out against Brutus and his accomplices for having murdered a principal man of the city, holding the highest magistracies of Rome, without being heard or condemned; and appointed Lucius Cornificius to accuse Brutus, and Marcus Agrippa to accuse Cassius. None appearing to the accusation, the judges were forced to pass sentence and condemn them both. It is reported, that when the crier from the tribunal, as the custom was, with a loud voice cited Brutus to appear, the people groaned audibly, and the noble citizens hung down their heads for grief. Publius Silicius was seen to burst out into tears, which was the cause that not long after he was put down in the list of those that were proscribed. After this, the three men, Cæsar, Antony, and Lepidus, being perfectly reconciled, shared the provinces among themselves, and made up the catalogue of proscription, wherein were set those that were designed for slaughter, amounting to two hundred men, in which number Cicero was slain.

This news being brought to Brutus in Macedonia, he was under a compulsion, and sent orders to Hortensius that he should kill Caius Antonius in revenge of the death of Cicero his friend, and Brutus[11] his kinsman, who was also proscribed and slain. Upon this account it was that Antony, having afterwards taken Hortensius in the battle of Philippi, slew him upon his brother's tomb. But Brutus expresses himself as more ashamed for the cause of Cicero's death than grieved for the misfortune of it, and says he cannot help accusing his friends at Rome, that they were slaves more through their own doing than that of those who now were their tyrants; they could be present and see and yet suffer those things which even to hear related ought to them to have been insufferable.

Having made his army, that was already very considerable, pass into Asia, he ordered a fleet to be prepared in Bithynia and about Cyzicus. But going himself through the country by land, he made it his business to settle and confirm all the cities, and gave audience to the princes of the parts through which he passed. And he sent orders into Syria to Cassius to come to him, and leave his intended journey into Egypt; letting him understand, that it was not to gain an empire for themselves, but to free their country, that they went thus wandering about and had got an army together whose business it was to destroy the

[11] Decimus Brutus Albinus, who had been put to death by Antony's orders in Cisalpine Gaul.

tyrants; that therefore, if they remembered and resolved to persevere in their first purpose, they ought not to be too far from Italy, but make what haste they could thither, and endeavor to relieve their fellow-citizens from oppression.

Cassius obeyed his summons, and returned, and Brutus went to meet him; and at Smyrna they met, which was the first time they had seen one another since they parted at the Piræus in Athens, one for Syria, and the other for Macedonia. They were both extremely joyful and had great confidence of their success at the sight of the forces that each of them had got together, since they who had fled from Italy, like the most despicable exiles, without money, without arms, without a ship or a soldier or a city to rely on, in a little time after had met together so well furnished with shipping and money, and an army both of horse and foot, that they were in a condition to contend for the empire of Rome.

Cassius was desirous to show no less respect and honor to Brutus than Brutus did to him; but Brutus was still beforehand with him, coming for the most part to him, both because he was the elder man, and of a weaker constitution than himself. Men generally reckoned Cassius a very expert soldier, but of a harsh and angry nature, and one that desired to command rather by fear than love; though, on the other side, among his familiar acquaintance he would easily give way to jesting, and play the buffoon. But Brutus, for his virtue, was esteemed by the people, beloved by his friends, admired by the best men, and hated not by his enemies themselves. For he was a man of a singularly gentle nature, of a great spirit, insensible of the passions of anger or pleasure or covetousness; steady and inflexible to maintain his purpose for what he thought right and honest. And that which gained him the greatest affection and reputation was the entire faith in his intentions. For it had not ever been supposed that Pompey the Great himself, if he had overcome Cæsar, would have submitted his power to the laws, instead of taking the management of the state upon himself, soothing the people with the specious name of consul or dictator, or some other milder title than king. And they were well persuaded that Cassius, being a man governed by anger and passion and carried often, for his interest's sake, beyond the bounds of justice, endured all these hardships of war and travel and danger most assuredly to obtain dominion to himself, and not liberty to the people. And as for the former disturbers of the peace of Rome, whether a Cinna, a Marius, or a Carbo, it is manifest that they, having set their country as a stake for him that should win, did almost own in express terms that they fought for empire. But even the enemies of Brutus did not, they tell us, lay this accusation to his charge; nay, many heard Antony himself say that Brutus was the only man that conspired against Cæsar out of a sense of the glory and the apparent justice of the action, but that all the rest rose up against the man himself, from private envy and malice of their own. And it is plain by what he writes himself, that Brutus did not so much rely upon his forces, as upon his own virtue. For thus he speaks in a letter to Atticus, shortly before he was to engage with the enemy: that his affairs were in the best state of fortune that he could wish; for that either he should overcome, and restore liberty to the people of Rome, or die, and be himself out of the reach of slavery; that other things being certain and beyond all hazard, one thing was yet in doubt, whether they should live or die free men. He adds further, that Mark Antony had received a just punishment for his folly, who, when he might

have been numbered with Brutus and Cassius and
Cato, would join himself to Octavius;[12] that though
they should not now be both overcome, they soon
would fight between themselves. And in this he seems
to have been no ill prophet.

Now when they were at Smyrna, Brutus desired of
Cassius that he might have part of the great treasure
that he had heaped up, because all his own was expended in furnishing out such a fleet of ships as was
sufficient to keep the whole interior sea[13] in their
power. But Cassius's friends dissuaded him from
this; "for," said they, "it is not just that the money
which you with so much parsimony keep and with so
much envy have got, should be given to him to be disposed of in making himself popular, and gaining the
favor of the soldiers." Notwithstanding this, Cassius gave him a third part of all that he had; and then
they parted each to their several commands. Cassius,
having taken Rhodes, behaved himself there with no
clemency; though at his first entry, when some had
called him lord and king, he answered, that he was
neither king nor lord, but the destroyer and punisher
of a king and lord. Brutus, on the other part, sent
to the Lycians to demand from them a supply of
money and men; but Naucrates, their popular leader,
persuaded the cities to resist, and they occupied several little mountains and hills, with a design to hinder
Brutus's passage. Brutus at first sent out a party of
horse, which, surprising them as they were eating,

[12] Octavius is the name which Brutus studiously gives to the
young Cæsar, afterwards called Augustus, who was indeed by
birth and blood properly so named, and only as an adopted son
had ceased to be Octavius, and had become Cæsar Octavianus.

[13] The *interior* sea is the Mediterranean, for which, as a whole,
the Greeks and Romans had no distinguishing name.

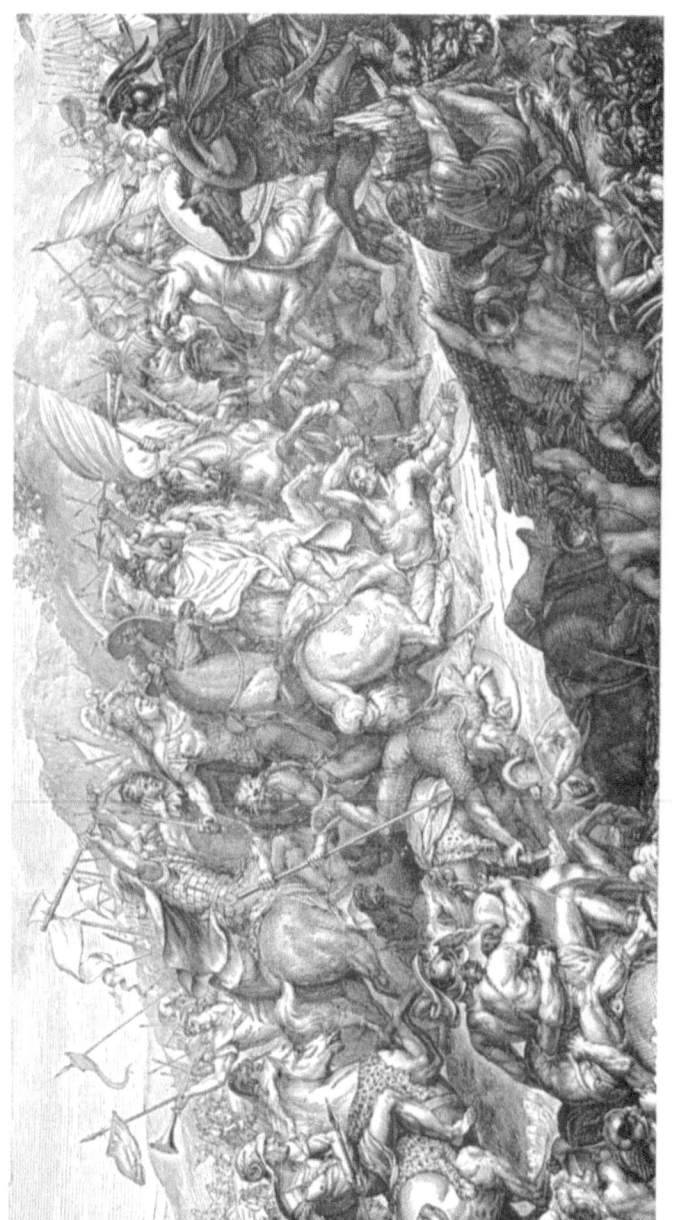

THE BATTLE WITH THE LYCIANS

killed six hundred of them; and afterwards, having taken all their small towns and villages round about, he set all his prisoners free without ransom, hoping to win the whole nation by good-will. But they continued obstinate, taking in anger what they had suffered, and despising his goodness and humanity; until, having forced the most warlike of them into the city of Xanthus, he besieged them there. They endeavored to make their escape by swimming and diving through the river that flows by the town, but were taken by nets let down for that purpose in the channel, which had little bells at the top, which gave present notice of any that were taken in them. After that, they made a sally in the night, and seizing several of the battering engines, set them on fire; but being perceived by the Romans, were beaten back to their walls, and, there being a strong wind, it carried the flames to the battlements of the city with such fierceness, that several of the adjoining houses took fire. Brutus, fearing lest the whole city should be destroyed, commanded his own soldiers to assist, and quench the fire.

But the Lycians were on a sudden possessed with a strange and incredible desperation; such a frenzy as cannot be better expressed than by calling it a violent appetite to die, for both women and children, the bondmen and the free, those of all ages and of all conditions strove to force away the soldiers that came in to their assistance, from the walls; and themselves gathering together reeds and wood, and whatever combustible matter they found, spread the fire over the whole city, feeding it with whatever fuel they could, and by all possible means exciting its fury, so that the flame, having dispersed itself and encircled the whole city, blazed out in so terrible a manner, that Brutus, being extremely afflicted at their calamity, got on horseback and rode round the walls, earnestly desirous to preserve the city, and, stretching forth his hands to the Xanthians, begged of them that they would spare themselves and save their town. Yet none regarded his entreaties, but by all manner of ways strove to destroy themselves; not only men and women, but even boys and little children, with a hideous outcry, leaped, some into the fire, others from the walls, others fell upon their parents' swords, baring their throats and desiring to be struck. After the destruction of the city, there was found a woman who had hanged herself with her young child hanging from her neck, and the torch in her hand, with which she had fired her own house. It was so tragical a sight, that Brutus could not endure to see it, but wept at the very relation of it, and proclaimed a reward to any soldier that could save a Xanthian. And it is said that an hundred and fifty only were found, to have their lives saved against their wills. Thus the Xanthians, after a long space of years, the fated period of their destruction having, as it were, run its course, repeated by their desperate deed the former calamity of their forefathers, who after the very same manner in the Persian war had fired their city and destroyed themselves.

Brutus, after this, finding the Patareans resolved to make resistance and hold out their city against him, was very unwilling to besiege it, and was in great perplexity lest the same frenzy might seize them too. But having in his power some of their women, who were his prisoners, he dismissed them all without any ransom; who, returning and giving an account to their husbands and fathers, who were of the greatest rank, what an excellent man Brutus was, how temperate and how just, persuaded them to yield themselves and put their city into his hands. From this time all the cities round about came into his power, submitting

themselves to him, and found him good and merciful
even beyond their hopes. For though Cassius at the
same time had compelled the Rhodians to bring in all
the silver and gold that each of them privately was
possessed of, by which he raised a sum of eight thousand
talents, and besides this had condemned the public
to pay the sum of five hundred talents more, Brutus,
not having taken above a hundred and fifty talents
from the Lycians, and having done them no other
manner of injury, parted from thence with his army
to go into Ionia.

Through the whole course of this expedition, Brutus
did many memorable acts of justice in dispensing
rewards and punishments to such as had deserved
either; but one in particular I will relate, because he
himself, and all the noblest Romans, were gratified
with it above all the rest. When Pompey the Great,
being overthrown from his great power by Cæsar, had
fled to Egypt, and landed near Pelusium, the protectors
of the young king consulted among themselves
what was fit to be done on that occasion, nor could
they all agree in the same opinion, some being for receiving
him, others for driving him from Egypt. But
Theodotus, a Chian by birth, and then attending upon
the king as a paid teacher of rhetoric, and for want of
better men admitted into the council, undertook to
prove to them, that both parties were in the wrong,
those that counselled to receive Pompey, and those
that advised to send him away; that in their present
case one thing only was truly expedient, to seize him
and to kill him; and ended his argument with the proverb,
that "dead men don't bite." The council agreed
to his opinion, and Pompey the Great (an example
of incredible and unforeseen events) was slain, as the
sophister himself had the impudence to boast, through
the rhetoric and cleverness of Theodotus. Not long

after, when Cæsar came to Egypt, some of the murderers received their just reward and suffered the evil death they deserved. But Theodotus, though he had borrowed on from fortune a little further time for a poor despicable and wandering life, yet did not lie hid from Brutus as he passed through Asia; but being seized by him and executed, had his death made more memorable than was his life.

About this time, Brutus sent to Cassius to come to him at the city of Sardis, and, when he was on his journey, went forth with his friends to meet him; and the whole army in array saluted each of them with the name of Imperator. Now (as it usually happens in business of great concern and where many friends and many commanders are engaged), several jealousies of each other and matters of private accusation having passed between Brutus and Cassius, they resolved, before they entered upon any other business, immediately to withdraw into some apartment; where, the door being shut and they two alone, they began first to expostulate, then to dispute hotly, and accuse each other; and finally were so transported into passion as to fall to hard words, and at last burst out into tears. Their friends who stood without were amazed, hearing them loud and angry, and feared lest some mischief might follow, but yet durst not interrupt them, being commanded not to enter the room. However, Marcus Favonius, who had been an ardent admirer of Cato, and, not so much by his learning or wisdom as by his wild, vehement manner, maintained the character of a philosopher, was rushing in upon them, but was hindered by the attendants. But it was a hard matter to stop Favonius, wherever his wildness hurried him; for he was fierce in all his behavior, and ready to do any thing to get his will. And though he was a senator, yet, thinking that one of the least of his excellences, he valued himself more upon a sort of cynical liberty of speaking what he pleased, which sometimes, indeed, did away with the rudeness and unseasonableness of his addresses with those that would interpret it in jest. This Favonius, breaking by force through those that kept the doors, entered into the chamber, and with a set voice declaimed the verses that Homer makes Nestor use,—

Be ruled, for I am older than ye both.[14]

At this Cassius laughed; but Brutus thrust him out, calling him impudent dog and counterfeit Cynic;[15] but yet for the present they let it put an end to their dispute, and parted. Cassius made a supper that night, and Brutus invited the guests; and when they were set down, Favonius, having bathed, came in among them. Brutus called out aloud and told him he was not invited, and bade him go to the upper couch; but he violently thrust himself in, and lay down on the middle one;[16] and the entertainment passed in sportive talk, not wanting either wit or philosophy.

The next day after, upon the accusation of the

[14] Nestor's address to Agamemnon and Achilles in the midst of their quarrel, in the first book of the Iliad (I., 259). Favonius might very aptly quote the whole passage from Homer:
Ah me, truly great grief to the land of Achaia is coming,
Truly would Priam be glad and all the children of Priam,
And every Trojan else be greatly rejoiced in his spirit,
Should he be told the news of you contending together,
Who are in counsel best of the Danaans, and in the battle.
Be persuaded; you are, both of you, younger than I am.
I have consorted ere this with men much greater than you are—etc.

[15] "Impudent dog is of course pointed at the derivation of the term *Cynic*. They had called Antisthenes *Cyna*, or dog, and *Cynic* was the epithet of those that copied his manner.

[16] Of the three couches or sofas (for their breadth more re-

Sardians, Brutus publicly disgraced and condemned Lucius Pella, one that had been censor of Rome, and employed in offices of trust by himself, for having embezzled the public money. This action did not a little vex Cassius; for but a few days before, two of his own friends being accused of the same crime, he only admonished them in private, but in public absolved them, and continued them in his service; and upon this occasion he accused Brutus of too much rigor and severity of justice in a time which required them to use more policy and favor. But Brutus bade him remember the Ides of March, the day when they killed Cæsar, who himself neither plundered nor pillaged mankind, but was only the support and strength of those that did; and bade him consider, that if there was any color for justice to be neglected, it had been better to suffer the injustice of Cæsar's friends than to give impunity to their own; "for then," said he, "we could have been accused of cowardice only; whereas now we are liable to the accusation of injustice, after all our pain and dangers which we endure."[17] By which we may perceive what was Brutus's purpose, and the rule of his actions.

About the time that they were going to pass out of Asia into Europe, it is said that a wonderful sign was seen by Brutus. He was naturally given to much watching, and by practice and moderation in his diet

---

sembling beds) which formed the furniture of the Roman dining-room, the *triclinium*, the middle was the couch of honor, and the lower that of the master of the house. Brutus would be on the one, Cassius on the other.

[17] The last words are uncertain; the common reading seems in part to be derived from Amyot, whose translation has had for Plutarch's translators an authority almost like that of the Vulgate.

had reduced his allowance of sleep to a very small amount of time. He never slept in the daytime, and in the night then only when all his business was finished, and when, every one else being gone to rest, he had nobody to discourse with him. But at this time, the war being begun, having the whole state of it to consider and being solicitous of the event, after his first sleep, which he let himself take after his supper, he spent all the rest of the night in settling his most urgent affairs; which if he could despatch early and so make a saving of any leisure, he employed himself in reading until the third watch, at which time the centurions and tribunes were used to come to him for orders. Thus one night before he passed out of Asia, he was very late all alone in his tent, with a dim light burning by him, all the rest of the camp being hushed and silent; and reasoning about something with himself and very thoughtful, he fancied some one came in, and, looking up towards the door, he saw a terrible and strange appearance of an unnatural and frightful body standing by him without speaking. Brutus boldly asked it, "What are you, of men or gods, and upon what business come to me?" The figure answered, "I am your evil genius, Brutus; you shall see me at Philippi." To which Brutus, not at all disturbed, replied, "Then I shall see you."

As soon as the apparition vanished, he called his servants to him, who all told him they had neither heard any voice nor seen any vision. So then he continued watching till the morning, when he went to Cassius, and told him of what he had seen. He, who followed the principles of Epicurus's philosophy, and often used to dispute with Brutus concerning matters of this nature, spoke to him thus upon this occasion: "It is the opinion of our sect, Brutus, that not all that we feel or see is real and true; but that the sense is a most slippery and deceitful thing, and the mind yet more quick and subtle to put the sense in motion and affect it with every kind of change upon no real occasion of fact; just as an impression is made upon wax; and the soul of man, which has in itself both what imprints and what is imprinted on, may most easily, by its own operations, produce and assume every variety of shape and figure. This is evident from the sudden changes of our dreams; in which the imaginative principle,[18] once started by any trifling matter, goes through a whole series of most diverse emotions and appearances. It is its nature to be ever in motion, and its motion is fantasy or conception. But besides all this, in your case, the body, being tired and distressed with continual toil, naturally works upon the mind, and keeps it in an excited and unusual condition. But that there should be any such thing as supernatural beings,[19] or, if there were, that they should have human shape or voice or power that can reach to us, there is no reason for believing; though I confess I could wish that there were such beings, that we might not rely upon our arms only, and our horses and our navy, all which are so numerous and powerful, but might be confident of the assistance of gods also, in this our most sacred and honorable attempt." With such discourses as these Cassius soothed the mind of Brutus. But just as the troops were going on board, two eagles

[18] The Greek term for the *imaginative principle* is the *phantasticon* (*phantasia* and memory are, says Aristotle, what brutes have); it is imagination in its lowest sense of the faculty of reproducing images. It is always, says Cassius, in motion, and its motion consists in seeing, hearing, and perceiving things of its own making.

[19] *Supernatural beings* is, in the Greek, daimones, daimons, or, etymologically—dæmons, unseen, preterhuman agencies; *gods* is the proper word (*theos*, the Latin *deus*) usually so rendered.

flew and lighted on the first two ensigns, and crossed over the water with them, and never ceased following the soldiers and being fed by them till they came to Philippi, and there, but one day before the fight, they both flew away.

Brutus had already reduced most of the places and people of these parts; but they now marched on as far as to the coast opposite Thasos, and, if there were any city or man of power that yet stood out, brought them all to subjection. At this point Norbanus was encamped, in a place called the Straits, near Symbolum. Him they surrounded in such sort that they forced him to dislodge and quit the place; and Norbanus narrowly escaped losing his whole army, Cæsar by reason of sickness being too far behind; only Antony came to his relief with such wonderful swiftness that Brutus and those with him did not believe when they heard he was come. Cæsar came up ten days after, and encamped over against Brutus, and Antony over against Cassius.

The space between the two armies is called by the Romans the Campi Philippi. Never had two such large Roman armies come together to engage each other. That of Brutus was somewhat less in number than that of Cæsar, but in the splendidness of the men's arms and richness of their equipage it wonderfully exceeded; for most of their arms were of gold and silver, which Brutus had lavishly bestowed among them. For though in other things he had accustomed his commanders to use all frugality and self-control, yet he thought that the riches which soldiers carried about them in their hands and on their bodies would add something of spirit to those that were desirous of glory, and would make those that were covetous and lovers of gain fight the more valiantly to preserve the arms which were their estate.

Cæsar made a view and lustration[20] of his army within his trenches, and distributed only a little corn and but five drachmas to each soldier for the sacrifice they were to make. But Brutus, either pitying this poverty, or disdaining this meanness of spirit in Cæsar, first, as the custom was, made a general muster and lustration of the army in the open field, and then distributed a great number of beasts for sacrifice to every regiment, and fifty drachmas to every soldier; so that in the love of his soldiers and their readiness to fight for him Brutus had much the advantage. But at the time of lustration it is reported that an unlucky omen happened to Cassius; for his lictor, presenting him with a garland that he was to wear at sacrifice, gave it him the wrong way up. Further, it is said that some time before, at a certain solemn procession, a golden image of Victory, which was carried before Cassius, fell down by a slip of him that carried it. Besides this there appeared many birds of prey daily about the camp, and swarms of bees were seen in a place within the trenches, which place the soothsayers ordered to be shut out from the camp, to remove the superstition which insensibly began to infect even Cassius himself and shake him in his Epicurean philosophy, and had wholly seized and subdued the soldiers; from whence it was that Cassius was reluctant to put all to the hazard of a present battle, but advised rather to draw out the war until further time, considering that they were stronger in money and provisions, but in num-

---

[20] The lustration was a general cleaning, to which, as to many other disagreeable things, it was made a point to assign a sacred character. So in the Iliad (I., 312), while the ship is sailing, carrying back his daughter to Chryses and conveying the propitiation to Apollo, "Agamemnon bids the people clean themselves of their pollutions; they clean themselves, and cast their pollutions in the sea."

bers of men and arms inferior. But Brutus, on the contrary, was still, as formerly, desirous to come with all speed to the decision of a battle; that so he might either restore his country to her liberty, or else deliver from their misery all those numbers of people whom they harassed with the expenses and the service and exactions of the war. And finding also his light-horse in several skirmishes still to have had the better, he was the more encouraged and resolved; and some of the soldiers having deserted and gone to the enemy, and others beginning to accuse and suspect one another, many of Cassius's friends in the council changed their opinions to that of Brutus. But there was one of Brutus's party, named Atellius, who opposed his resolution, advising rather that they should tarry over the winter. And when Brutus asked him in how much better a condition he hoped to be a year after, his answer was, "If I gain nothing else, yet I shall live so much the longer." Cassius was much displeased at this answer; and among the rest, Atellius was had in much disesteem for it. And so it was presently resolved to give battle the next day.

Brutus that night at supper showed himself very cheerful and full of hope, and reasoned on subjects of philosophy with his friends, and afterwards went to his rest. But Messala says that Cassius supped privately with a few of his nearest acquaintance, and appeared thoughtful and silent, contrary to his temper and custom; that after supper he took him earnestly by the hand, and speaking to him, as his manner was when he wished to show affection, in Greek, said, "Bear witness for me, Messala, that I am brought into the same necessity as Pompey the Great was before me, of hazarding the liberty of my country upon one battle; yet ought we to be of courage, relying on our good fortune, which it were unfair to mistrust, though we take evil counsels." These, Messala says, were the last words that Cassius spoke before he bade him farewell; and that he was invited to sup with him the next night, being his birthday.[21]

As soon as it was morning, the signal of battle, the scarlet coat, was set out in Brutus's and Cassius's camps, and they themselves met in the middle space between their two armies. There Cassius spoke thus to Brutus: "Be it as we hope, O Brutus, that this day we may overcome, and all the rest of our time may live a happy life together; but since the greatest of human concerns are the most uncertain, and since it may be difficult for us ever to see one another again, if the battle should go against us, tell me, what is your resolution concerning flight and death?" Brutus answered, "When I was young, Cassius, and unskillful in affairs, I was led, I know not how, into uttering a bold sentence in philosophy, and blamed Cato for killing himself, as thinking it an irreligious act, and not a valiant one among men, to try to evade the divine course of things, and not fearlessly to receive and undergo the evil that shall happen, but run away from it. But now in my own fortunes I am of another mind; for if Providence shall not dispose what we now undertake according to our wishes, I resolve to put no further hopes or warlike preparations to the proof, but will die contented with my fortune. For I already have given up my life to my country on the Ides of March; and have lived since then a second life for her sake, with liberty and honor."[22] Cassius at these words

---

[21] The text is a little ambiguous, but it appears, by another authority, that the birthday was that of Cassius, so that Messala was the invited guest, not *vice versa*.

[22] He means, I believe, that he considers himself to have given away his life once for all on the Ides of March; since then he

smiled, and, embracing Brutus, said, "With these resolutions let us go on upon the enemy; for either we ourselves shall conquer, or have no cause to fear those that do." After this they discoursed among their friends about the ordering of the battle; and Brutus desired of Cassius that he might command the right wing, though it was thought that this was more fit for Cassius, in regard both of his age and his experience. Yet even in this Cassius complied with Brutus, and placed Messala with the valiantest of all his legions in the same wing, so Brutus immediately drew out his horse, excellently well equipped, and was not long in bringing up his foot after them.

Antony's soldiers were casting trenches from the marsh by which they were encamped, across the plain, to cut off Cassius's communciations with the sea. Cæsar was to be at hand with his troops to support them, but he was not able to be present himself, by reason of his sickness; and his soldiers, not much expecting that the enemy would come to a set battle, but only make some excursions with their darts and light arms to disturb the men at work in the trenches, and not taking notice of the troops drawn up against them ready to give battle, were amazed when they heard the confused and great outcry that came from the trenches. In the meanwhile Brutus had sent his tickets, in which was the word of battle, to the officers; and himself riding about to all the troops, encouraged the soldiers; but there were but of them that understood the word before they engaged; the most of them, not staying to have it delivered to them, with one impulse and

did not regard himself to have, properly, any life of his own at all; he had, however, for his country's sake lived a subsequent, second, and as it were extra life, and this, too, honorably. "The divine course of things" just above is in the Greek *the daimon*, the word rendered by "Providence" is *God,* or a *god.*

cry ran upon the enemy. This disorder caused an unevenness in the line, and the legions got severed and divided one from another; that of Messala first, and afterwards the other adjoining, went beyond the left wing of Cæsar; and having just touched the extremity, without slaughtering any great number, passing round that wing, fell directly into Cæsar's camp. Cæsar himself, as his own memoirs tell us, had but just before been conveyed away, Marcus Artorius, one of his friends, having had a dream bidding Cæsar be carried out of the camp. And it was believed that he was slain; for the soldiers had pierced his litter, which was left empty, in many places with their darts and pikes. There was a great slaughter in the camp that was taken, and two thousand Lacedæmonians that were newly come to the assistance of Cæsar were all cut off together.

The rest of the army, that had not gone round but had engaged the front, easily overthrew them, finding them in great disorder, and slew upon the place three legions; and being carried on with the stream of victory, pursuing those that fled, fell into the camp with them, Brutus himself being there. But they that were conquered took the advantage in their extremity of what the conquerors did not consider. For they fell upon that part of the main body which had been left exposed and separated, where the right wing had broke off from them and hurried away in the pursuit; yet they could not break into the midst of their battle, but were received with strong resistance and obstinacy. Yet they put to flight the left wing, where Cassius commanded, being in great disorder, and ignorant of what had passed on the other wing; and, pursuing them to their camp, they pillaged and destroyed it, neither of their generals being present; for Antony, they say, to avoid the fury of the first onset, had retired into the marsh that was hard by; and Cæsar was nowhere to be found after his being conveyed out of the tents; though some of the soldiers showed Brutus their swords bloody, and declared that they had killed him, describing his person and his age. By this time also the centre of Brutus's battle had driven back their opponents with great slaughter; and Brutus was everywhere plainly conqueror, as on the other side Cassius was conquered. And this one mistake was the ruin of their affairs, that Brutus did not come to the relief of Cassius, thinking that he, as well as himself, was conqueror; and that Cassius did not expect the relief of Brutus, thinking that he too was overcome. For as a proof that the victory was on Brutus's side, Messala urges his taking three eagles and many ensigns of the enemy without losing any of his own. But now, returning from the pursuit after having plundered Cæsar's camp, Brutus wondered that he could not see Cassius's tent standing high, as it was wont, and appearing above the rest, nor other things appearing as they had been; for they had been immediately pulled down and pillaged by the enemy upon their first falling into the camp. But some that had a quicker and longer sight than the rest acquainted Brutus that they saw a great deal of shining armor and silver targets moving to and fro in Cassius's camp, and that they thought, by their number and the fashion of their armor, they could not be those that they left to guard the camp; but yet that there did not appear so great a number of dead bodies thereabouts as it was probable there would have been after the actual defeat of so many legions. This first made Brutus suspect Cassius's misfortune, and, leaving a guard in the enemy's camp, he called back those that were in the pursuit, and rallied them together to lead them to the relief of Cassius, whose fortune had been as follows.

First, he had been angry at the onset that Brutus's soldiers made, without the word of battle or command to charge. Then, after they had overcome, he was as much displeased to see them rush on to the plunder and spoil, and neglect to surround and encompass the rest of the enemy. Besides this, letting himself act by delay and expectation, rather than command boldly and with a clear purpose, he got hemmed in by the right wing of the enemy, and, his horse making with all haste their escape and flying towards the sea, the foot also began to give way, which he perceiving labored as much as ever he could to hinder their flight and bring them back; and, snatching an ensign out of the hand of one that fled, he stuck it at his feet, though he could hardly keep even his own personal guard together. So that at last he was forced to fly with a few about him to a little hill that overlooked the plain. But he himself, being weak-sighted, discovered nothing, only the destruction of his camp, and that with difficulty. But they that were with him saw a great body of horse moving towards him, the same whom Brutus had sent. Cassius believed these were enemies, and in pursuit of him; however, he sent away Titinius, one of those that were with him, to learn what they were. As soon as Brutus's horse saw him coming, and knew him to be a friend and a faithful servant of Cassius, those of them that were his more familiar acquaintance, shouting out for joy and alighting from their horses, shook hands and embraced him, and the rest rode round about him singing and shouting, through their excess of gladness at the sight of him. But this was the occasion of the greatest mischief that could be. For Cassius really thought that Titinius had been taken by the enemy, and cried out,

"Through too much fondness of life, I have lived to endure the sight of my friend taken by the enemy before my face." After which words he retired into an empty tent, taking along with him only Pindarus, one of his freedmen, whom he had reserved for such an occasion ever since the disasters in the expedition against the Parthians, when Crassus was slain. From the Parthians he came away in safety; but now, pulling up his mantle over his head, he made his neck bare, and held it forth to Pindarus, commanding him to strike. The head was certainly found lying severed from the body. But no man ever saw Pindarus after, from which some suspected that he had killed his master without his command. Soon after they perceived who the horsemen were, and saw Titinius, crowned with garlands, making what haste he could towards Cassius. But as soon as he understood by the cries and lamentations of his afflicted friends the unfortunate error and death of his general, he drew his sword, and having very much accused and upbraided his own long stay, that had caused it, he slew himself.

Brutus, as soon as he was assured of the defeat of Cassius, made haste to him; but heard nothing of his death till he came near his camp. Then having lamented over his body, calling him "the last of the Romans," it being impossible that the city should ever produce another man of so great a spirit, he sent away the body to be buried at Thasos, lest celebrating his funeral within the camp might breed some disorder. He then gathered the soldiers together and comforted them; and, seeing them destitute of all things necessary, he promised to every man two thousand drachmas in recompense of what he had lost. They at these words took courage, and were astonished at the magnificence of the gift; and waited upon him at his parting with shouts and praises, magnifying him for the only general of all the four who was not overcome in the battle. And indeed the action itself testified that it was not without reason he believed he should conquer; for with a few legions he overthrew all that resisted him; and if all his soldiers had fought, and the most of them had not passed beyond the enemy in pursuit of the plunder, it is very likely that he had utterly defeated every part of them.

There fell of his side eight thousand men, reckoning the servants of the army, whom Brutus calls Briges; and on the other side, Messala says his opinion is that there were slain above twice that number. For which reason they were more out of heart than Brutus, until a servant of Cassius, named Demetrius, came in the evening to Antony, and brought to him the garment which he had taken from the dead body, and his sword; at the sight of which they were so encouraged, that, as soon as it was morning, they drew out their whole force into the field, and stood in battle array. But Brutus found both his camps wavering and in disorder; for his own, being filled with prisoners, required a guard more strict than ordinary over them; and that of Cassius was uneasy at the change of general, besides some envy and rancor, which those that were conquered bore to that part of the army which had been conquerors. Wherefore he thought it convenient to put his army in array, but to abstain from fighting. All the slaves that were taken prisoners, of whom there was a great number that were mixed up, not without suspicion, among the soldiers, he commanded to be slain; but of the freemen and citizens, some he dismissed, saying that among the enemy they were rather prisoners than with him, for with them they were captives and slaves, but with him freemen and citizens of Rome. But he was forced to hide and help them to escape privately, perceiving that his friends and officers were bent upon revenge against them. Among the captives there was one Volumnius, a player, and Sacculio, a buffoon; of these Brutus took no manner of notice, but his friends brought them before him, and accused them that even then in that condition they did not refrain from their jests and scurrilous language. Brutus, having his mind taken up with other affairs, said nothing to their accusation; but the judgment of Messala Corvinus was, that they should be whipped publicly upon a stage, and so sent naked to the captains of the enemy, to show them what sort of fellow drinkers and companions they took with them on their campaigns. At this some that were present laughed; and Publius Casca, he that gave the first wound to Cæsar, said, "We do ill to jest and make merry at the funeral of Cassius. But you, O Brutus," he added, "will show what esteem you have for the memory of that general, according as you punish or preserve alive those who will scoff and speak shamefully of him." To this Brutus, in great discomposure, replied, "Why then, Casca, do you ask me about it, and not do yourselves what you think fitting?" This answer of Brutus was taken for his consent to the death of these wretched men; so they were carried away and slain.

After this he gave the soldiers the reward that he had promised them; and having slightly reproved them for having fallen upon the enemy in disorder without the word of battle or command, he promised them, that if they behaved themselves bravely in the next engagement, he would give them up two cities to spoil and plunder, Thessalonica and Lacedæmon. This is the one indefensible thing of all that is found fault with in the life of Brutus; though true it may be that Antony and Cæsar were much more cruel in the rewards that they gave their soldiers after victory; for they drove out, one might almost say, all the old inhabitants of Italy, to put their soldiers in possession of other men's lands and cities. But indeed their only design and end in undertaking the war was to obtain dominion and empire, whereas Brutus, for the reputation of his virtue, could not be permitted either to overcome or save himself but with justice and honor, especially after the death of Cassius, who was generally accused of having been his adviser to some things that he had done with less clemency. But now, as in a ship, when the rudder is broken by a storm, the mariners fit and nail on some other piece of wood instead of it, striving against the danger not well, but as well as in that necessity they can, so Brutus, being at the head of so great an army, in a time of such uncertainty, having no commander equal to his need, was forced to make use of those that he had, and to do and to say many things according to their advice; which was, in effect, whatever might conduce to the bringing of Cassius's soldiers into better order. For they were very headstrong and intractable, bold and insolent in the camp for want of their general, but in the field cowardly and fearful, remembering that they had been beaten.

Neither were the affairs of Cæsar and Antony in any better posture; for they were straitened for provision, and, the camp being in a low ground, they expected to pass a very hard winter. For being driven close upon the marshes, and a great quantity of rain, as is usual in autumn, having fallen after the battle, their tents were all filled with mire and water, which through the coldness of the weather immediately froze. And while they were in this condition, there was news brought to them of their loss at sea. For Brutus's fleet fell upon their ships, which were bringing a great supply of soldiers out of Italy, and so entirely defeated them, that but very few of the men escaped being slain, and they too were forced by famine to feed upon the sails and tackle of the ship. As soon as they heard this, they made what haste they could to come to the decision of a battle, before Brutus should have notice of his good success. For it had so happened that the fight both by sea and land was on the same day, but by some misfortune, rather than the fault of his commanders, Brutus knew not of his victory twenty days after. For had he been informed of this, he would not have been brought to a second battle, since he had sufficient provisions for his army for a long time, and was very advantageously posted, his camp being well sheltered from the cold weather, and almost inaccessible to the enemy, and his being absolute master of the sea, and having at land overcome on that side wherein he himself was engaged, would have made him full of hope and confidence. But it seems, the state of Rome not enduring any longer to be governed by many, but necessarily requiring a monarchy, the divine power, that it might remove out of the way the only man that was able to resist him that could control the empire, cut off his good fortune from coming to the ears of Brutus; though it came but a very little too late, for the very evening before the fight, Clodius, a deserter from the enemy, came and announced that Cæsar had received advice of the loss of his fleet, and for that reason was in such haste to come to a battle. But his story met with no credit, nor was he so much as seen by Brutus, being simply set down as one that had had no good information, or invented lies to bring himself into favor.

The same night, they say, the vision appeared again to Brutus, in the same shape that it did before, but vanished without speaking. But Publius Volumnius, a philosopher, and one that had from the beginning borne arms with Brutus, makes no mention of this apparition, but says that the first eagle was covered with a swarm of bees, and that there was one of the captains whose arm of itself sweated oil of roses, and, though they often dried and wiped it, yet it would not cease; and that immediately before the battle, two eagles falling upon each other fought in the space between the two armies, that the whole field kept incredible silence and all were intent upon the spectacle, until at last that which was on Brutus's side yielded and fled. But the story of the Ethiopian is very famous, who meeting the standard-bearer at the opening the gate of the camp, was cut to pieces by the soldiers, that took it for an ill omen.

Brutus, having brought his army into the field and set them in array against the enemy, paused a long while before he would fight; for, as he was reviewing the troops, suspicions were excited, and informations laid against some of them. Besides, he saw his horse not very eager to begin the action, and waiting to see what the foot would do. Then suddenly Camulatus, a very good soldier, and one whom for his valor he highly esteemed, riding hard by Brutus himself, went over to the enemy, the sight of which grieved Brutus exceedingly. So that partly out of anger, and partly out of fear of some greater treason and desertion, he immediately drew on his forces upon the enemy, the sun now declining, about three of the clock in the afternoon. Brutus on his side had the better, and pressed hard on the left wing, which gave way and retreated; and the horse too fell in together with the foot, when they saw the enemy in disorder. But the other wing, when the officers extended the line to avoid its being encompassed, the numbers being inferior, got drawn out too thin in the centre, and was so weak here that they could not withstand the charge, but at the first onset fled. After defeating these, the enemy at once took Brutus in the rear, who all the while performed all that was possible for an expert general and valiant soldier, doing every thing in the peril, by counsel and by hand, that might recover the victory. But that which had been his superiority in the former fight was to his prejudice in this second. For in the first fight, that part of the enemy which was beaten was killed on the spot; but of Cassius's soldiers that fled few had been slain, and those that escaped, daunted with their defeat, infected the other and larger part of the army with their want of spirit and their disorder. Here Marcus, the son of Cato, was slain, fighting and behaving himself with great bravery in the midst of the youth of the highest rank and greatest valor. He would neither fly nor give the least ground, but, still fighting and declaring who he was and naming his father's name, he fell upon a heap of dead bodies of the enemy. And of the rest, the bravest were slain in defending Brutus.

There was in the field one Lucilius, an excellent man and a friend of Brutus, who, seeing some barbarian horse taking no notice of any other in the pursuit, but galloping at full speed after Brutus, resolved to stop them, though with the hazard of his life; and, letting himself fall a little behind, he told them that he was Brutus. They believed him the rather, because he prayed to be carried to Antony, as if he feared Cæsar, but durst trust him. They, overjoyed with their prey, and thinking themselves wonderfully fortunate, carried him along with them in the night, having first sent messengers to Antony of their coming. He was much pleased, and came to meet them; and all the rest that heard that Brutus was taken and brought alive, flocked together to see him, some pitying his fortune, others accusing him of a meanness unbecoming his former glory, that out of too much love of life he would be a prey to barbarians. When they came near together, Antony stood still, considering with himself in what manner he should receive Brutus. But Lucilius, being brought up to him, with great confidence said: "Be assured, Antony, that no enemy either has taken or ever shall take Marcus Brutus alive (forbid it, heaven, that fortune should ever so much prevail above virtue), but he shall be found, alive or dead, as becomes himself. As for me, I am come hither by a cheat that I put upon your soldiers, and am ready, upon this occasion, to suffer any severities you will inflict." All were amazed to hear Lucilius speak these words. But Antony, turning himself to those that brought him, said: "I perceive, my fellow-soldiers, that you are concerned and take it ill that you have been thus deceived, and think yourselves abused and injured by it; but know that you have met with a booty better than you sought. For you were in search of an enemy, but you have brought me here a friend. For indeed I am uncertain how I should have used Brutus, if you had brought him alive; but of this I am sure, that it is better to have such men as Lucilius our friends than our enemies." Having said this, he embraced Lucilius, and for the present commended him to the care of one of his friends, and ever after found him a steady and a faithful friend.

Brutus had now passed a little brook, running among trees and under steep rocks, and, it being night, would go no further, but sat down in a hollow place with a great rock projecting before it, with a few of his officers and friends about him. At first, looking up to heaven, that was then full of stars, he

MARCUS BRUTUS

repeated two verses, one of which, Volumnius writes, was this:—

<blockquote>Punish, great Jove, the author of these ills.[23]</blockquote>

The other he says he has forgot. Soon after, naming severally all his friends that had been slain before his face in the battle, he groaned heavily, especially at the mentioning of Flavius and Labeo, the latter his lieutenant, and the other chief officer of his engineers. In the mean time, one of his companions, that was very thirsty and saw Brutus in the same condition, took his helmet and ran to the brook for water, when, a noise being heard from the other side of the river, Volumnius, taking Dardanus, Brutus's armor-bearer, with him, went out to see what it was. They returned in a short space, and enquired about the water. Brutus, smiling with much meaning, said to Volumnius, "It is all drunk; but you shall have some more fetched." But he that had brought the first water, being sent again, was in great danger of being taken by the enemy, and, having received a wound, with much difficulty escaped.

Now Brutus guessing that not many of his men were slain in the fight, Statyllius undertook to dash through the enemy (for there was no other way), and to see what was become of their camp; and promised, if he found all things there safe, to hold up a torch for a signal, and then return. The torch was held up, for Statyllius got safe to the camp; but when

---

[23] *Punish, great Jove,* Euripides, Medea, 332. It has been thought that by *the verse* which *Volumnius says he forgot* we may understand two which Dion Cassius gives. "Alas, poor Virtue, you were, it seems, a mere word, I practised you as a reality, but you were the slave of fortune." This, however, was a very well-known commonplace on the subject, and Dion's statement must be considered quite doubtful.

after a long time he did not return, Brutus said, "If Statyllius be alive, he will come back." But it happened that in his return he fell into the enemy's hands, and was slain.

The night now being far spent, Brutus, as he was sitting, leaned his head towards his servant Clitus and spoke to him; he answered him not, but fell a weeping. After that, he drew aside his armor-bearer, Dardanus, and had some discourse with him in private. At last, speaking to Volumnius in Greek, he reminded him of their common studies and former discipline, and begged that he would take hold of his sword with him, and help him to thrust it through him. Volumnius put away his request, and several others did the like; and some one saying, that there was no staying there, but they needs must fly, Brutus, rising up, said, "Yes, indeed, we must fly, but not with our feet, but with our hands." Then giving each of them his right hand, with a countenance full of pleasure, he said, that he found an infinite satisfaction in this, that none of his friends had been false to him; that as for fortune, he was angry with that only for his country's sake; as for himself, he thought himself much more happy than they who had overcome, not only as he had been a little time ago, but even now in his present condition; since he was leaving behind him such a reputation of his virtue as none of the conquerors with all their arms and riches should ever be able to acquire, no more than they could hinder posterity from believing and saying, that, being unjust and wicked men, they had destroyed the just and the good, and usurped a power to which they had no right. After this, having exhorted and entreated all about him to provide for their own safety, he withdrew from them with two or three only of his peculiar friends;

Strato was one of these, with whom he had contracted an acquaintance when they studied rhetoric together. Him he placed next to himself, and, taking hold of the hilt of his sword and directing it with both his hands, he fell upon it, and killed himself. But others say, that not he himself, but Strato, at the earnest entreaty of Brutus, turning aside his head, held the sword, upon which he violently throwing himself, it pierced his breast, and he immediately died. This same Strato, Messala, a friend of Brutus, being after reconciled to Cæsar, brought to him once at his leisure, and with tears in his eyes said, "This, O Cæsar, is the man that did the last friendly office to my beloved Brutus." Upon which Cæsar received him kindly; and had good use of him in his labors and his battles at Actium, being one of the Greeks that proved their bravery in his service. It is reported of Messala himself, that, when Cæsar once gave him this commendation, that though he was his fiercest enemy at Philippi in the cause of Brutus, yet he had shown himself his most entire friend in the fight at Actium, he answered, "You have always found me, Cæsar, on the best and justest side."

Brutus's dead body was found by Antony, who commanded the richest purple mantle that he had to be thrown over it, and afterwards the mantle being stolen, he found the thief, and had him put to death. He sent the ashes of Brutus to his mother Servilia. As for Porcia his wife, Nicolaus the philosopher and Valerius Maximus write, that, being desirous to die, but being hindered by her friends, who continually watched her, she snatched some burning charcoal out of the fire, and, shutting it close in her mouth, stifled herself, and died. Though there is a letter current from Brutus to his friends, in which he laments the death of Porcia, and accuses them for neglecting her so that she desired to die rather than languish with her disease. So that it seems Nicolaus was mistaken in the time; for this epistle (if it indeed is authentic, and truly Brutus's) gives us to understand the malady and love of Porcia, and the way in which her death occurred.

COMPARISON OF DION AND BRUTUS

THERE are noble points in abundance in the characters of these two men, and one to be first mentioned is their attaining such a height of greatness upon such inconsiderable means; and on this score Dion has by far the advantage. For he had no partner to contest his glory, as Brutus had in Cassius, who was not, indeed, his equal in proved virtue and honor, yet contributed quite as much to the service of the war by his boldness, skill, and activity; and some there be who impute to him the rise and beginning of the whole enterprise, saying that it was he who roused Brutus, till then indisposed to stir, into action against Cæsar. Whereas Dion seems of himself to have provided not only arms, ships, and soldiers, but likewise friends and partners for the enterprise. Neither did he, as Brutus, collect money and forces from the war itself, but, on the contrary, laid out of his own substance, and employed the very means of his private sustenance in exile for the liberty of his country. Besides this, Brutus and Cassius, when they fled from Rome, could not live safe or quiet, being condemned to death and pursued, and were thus of necessity forced to take arms and hazard their lives in their own defence, to save themselves, rather than their country. On the other hand, Dion enjoyed more ease, was more safe, and his life more pleasant in his banishment, than was the tyrant's who had banished him, when he flew to action, and ran the risk of all to save Sicily.

Take notice, too, that it was not the same thing for the Sicilians to be freed from Dionysius, and for the

Romans to be freed from Cæsar. The former owned himself a tyrant, and vexed Sicily with a thousand oppressions; whereas Cæsar's supremacy, certainly, in the process for attaining it, had inflicted no little trouble on its opponents, but, once established and victorious, it had indeed the name and appearance, but fact that was cruel or tyrannical there was none. On the contrary, in the malady of the times and the need of a monarchical government, he might be thought to have been sent, as the gentlest physician, by no other than a divine intervention. And thus the common people instantly regretted Cæsar, and grew enraged and implacable against those that killed him. Whereas Dion's chief offence in the eyes of his fellow-citizens was his having let Dionysius escape, and not having demolished the former tyrant's tomb.

In the actual conduct of war, Dion was a commander without fault, improving to the utmost those counsels which he himself gave, and, where others led him into disaster, correcting and turning every thing to the best. But Brutus seems to have shown little wisdom in engaging in the final battle, which was to decide every thing, and, when he failed, not to have done his business in seeking a remedy; he gave all up, and abandoned his hopes, not venturing against fortune even as far as Pompey did, when he had still means enough to rely on in his troops, and was clearly master of all the seas with his ships.

The greatest thing charged on Brutus is, that he, being saved by Cæsar's kindness, having saved all the friends whom he chose to ask for, he moreover, accounted a friend, and preferred above many, did yet lay violent hands upon his preserver. Nothing like this could be objected against Dion; quite the contrary, whilst he was of Dionysius's family and his friend, he did good service, and was useful to him; but driven from his country, wronged in his wife, and his estate lost, he openly entered upon a war just and lawful. Does not, however, the matter turn the other way? For the chief glory of both was their hatred of tyranny, and abhorrence of wickedness. This was unmixed and sincere in Brutus; for he had no private quarrel with Cæsar, but went into the risk singly for the liberty of his country. The other, had he not been privately injured, had not fought. This is plain from Plato's epistles, where it is shown that he was turned out, and did not forsake the court to wage war upon Dionysius. Moreover, the public good made Brutus Pompey's friend (instead of his enemy as he had been) and Cæsar's enemy; since he proposed for his hatred and his friendship no other end and standard but justice. Dion was very serviceable to Dionysius whilst in favor; when no longer trusted, he grew angry and fell to arms. And, for this reason, not even were his own friends all of them satisfied with his undertaking, or quite assured that, having overcome Dionysius, he might not settle the government on himself, deceiving his fellow-citizens by some less obnoxious name than tyranny. But the very enemies of Brutus would say that he had no other end or aim, from first to last, save only to restore to the Roman people their ancient government.

And apart from what has just been said, the adventure against Dionysius was nothing equal with that against Cæsar. For none that was familiarly conversant with Dionysius but scorned him for his life of idle amusement with wine, women, and dice; whereas it required an heroic soul and a truly intrepid and unquailing spirit so much as to entertain the thought of crushing Cæsar, so formidable for his ability, his power, and his fortune, whose very name disturbed the slumbers of the Parthian and Indian kings. Dion was no sooner seen in Sicily but thousands ran in to him and joined him against Dionysius; whereas the renown of Cæsar, even when dead, gave strength to his friends; and his very name so heightened the person that took it, that from a simple boy he presently became the chief of the Romans; and he could use it for a spell against the enmity and power of Antony. If any object that it cost Dion great trouble and difficulties to overcome the tyrant, whereas Brutus slew Cæsar naked and unprovided, yet this itself was the result of the most consummate policy and conduct, to bring it about that a man so guarded around, and so fortified at all points, should be taken naked and unprovided. For it was not on the sudden, nor alone, nor with a few, that he fell upon and killed Cæsar; but after long concerting the plot, and placing confidence in a great many men, not one of whom deceived him. For he either at once discerned the best men, or by confiding in them made them good. But Dion, either making a wrong judgment, trusted himself with ill men, or else by his employing them made ill men of good; either of the two would be a reflection on a wise man. Plato also is severe upon him, for choosing such for friends as betrayed him.

Besides, when Dion was killed, none appeared to revenge his death. Whereas Brutus, even amongst his enemies, had Antony that buried him splendidly; and Cæsar also took care his honors should be preserved. There stood at Milan in Gaul, within the Alps, a brazen statue, which Cæsar in after-times noticed (being a real likeness,[1] and a fine work of art), and passing by it, presently stopped short, and in the hearing of many commanded the magistrates to come

[1] *A real likeness,* i. e., an *iconic* statue; compare the first note on the Life of Lysander, Vol. III., —.

before him. He told them their town had broken their league, harboring an enemy. The magistrates at first simply denied the thing, and, not knowing what he meant, looked one upon another, when Cæsar, turning towards the statue and gathering his brows, said, "Pray, is not that our enemy who stands there?" They were all in confusion, and had nothing to answer; but he, smiling, much commended the Gauls, as who had been firm to their friends, though in adversity, and ordered that the statue should remain standing as he found it.

ARATUS[1]

Translated by John Bateman, M.D.

The philosopher Chrysippus, O Polycrates, quotes an ancient proverb, not as really it should be, apprehending, I suppose, that it sounded too harshly, but so as he thought it would run best, in these words,

> Who praise their fathers but the generous sons?

But Dionysodorus the Trœzenian proves him to be wrong, and restores the true reading, which is thus,—

> Who praise their fathers but degenerate sons?

telling us that the proverb is meant to stop the mouth of those who, having no merit of their own, take refuge in the virtues of their ancestors, and make their advantage of praising them. But, as Pindar hath it,

> He that by nature doth inherit
> From ancestors a noble spirit,[2]

as you do, who make your life the copy of the fairest originals of your family,—such, I say, may take great

---

[1] Aratus, the celebrated general of the Achæans, sons of Clinias, was born at Sicyon 271 B. C. He excelled more in negotiation than in war, and in his war with the Ætolians and Spartans he was often defeated. Indeed, it must be admitted that he showed positive cowardice in battle strangely contrasted with the boldness of his plans and policy. Dissensions arose between Philip and Aratus and the latter was eventually poisoned by the King's order 213 B. C.—Dr. William Smith.

[2] The quotation from Pindar is from the eighth Pythian ode, line 44.

ARATUS

satisfaction in being reminded, both by hearing others speak and speaking themselves, of the best of their progenitors. For they assume not the glory of praises earned by others out of any want of worth of their own, but, affiliating their own deeds to those of their ancestors, give them honor as the authors both of their descent and manners. Therefore I have sent to you the life which I have written of your fellow-citizen and forefather Aratus, to whom you are no discredit in point either of reputation or of authority, not as though you had not been most diligently careful to inform yourself from the beginning concerning his actions, but that your sons, Polycrates and Pythocles, may both by hearing and reading become familiar with those family examples which it behooves them to follow and imitate. It is a piece of self-love, and not of the love of virtue, to imagine one has already attained to what is best.[3]

The city of Sicyon, from the time that it first fell off from the pure and Doric aristocracy (its harmony being destroyed, and a mere series of seditions and personal contests of popular leaders ensuing), continued to be distempered and unsettled, changing from one tyrant to another, until, Cleon being slain, Timoclides and Clinias, men of the most repute and power amongst the citizens, were chosen to the magistracy. And the commonwealth now seeming to be in a pretty settled condition, Timoclides died, and Abantidas, the son of Paseas, to possess himself of the tyranny, killed Clinias, and, of his kindred and friends, slew some and banished others. He sought also to kill his son Aratus, whom he left behind him, being but seven years old. This boy in the general disorder getting out of the

---

[3] These last words are very doubtful; most likely they are not what Plutarch wrote.

house with those that fled, and wandering about the city helpless and in great fear, by chance got undiscovered into the house of a woman who was Abantidas's sister, but married to Prophantus, the brother of Clinias, her name being Soso. She, being of a generous temper, and believing the boy had by some supernatural guidance fled to her for shelter, hid him in the house, and at night sent him away to Argos.

Aratus, being thus delivered and secured from this danger, conceived from the first and ever after nourished a vehement and burning hatred against tyrants, which strengthened with his years. Being therefore bred up amongst his father's acquaintance and friends at Argos with a liberal education, and perceiving his body to promise good health and stature, he addicted himself to the exercises of the palæstra, to that degree that he competed in the five games,[4] and gained some crowns; and indeed in his statues one may observe a certain kind of athletic cast, and the sagacity and majesty of his countenance does not dissemble his full diet and the use of the hoe.[5] Whence it came to pass that he less studied eloquence than perhaps became a statesman, and yet he was more accomplished in speaking than many believe, judging by the commentaries which he left behind him, written carelessly and by the way, as fast as he could do it, and in such words as first came to his mind.

In the course of time, Dinias and Aristoteles the logician killed Abantidas, who used to be present in the market-place at their discussions, and to make one in

---

[4] The *pentathlum*, or five exercises of leaping, running, wrestling, the discus, and the dart. The palæstra is the wrestling or exercising ground.

[5] The hoe exercise was used by those who trained for the games.

them; till they, taking the occasion, insensibly accustomed him to the practice, and so had opportunity to contrive and execute a plot against him. After him Paseas, the father of Abantidas, taking upon him the government, was assassinated by Nicocles, who himself set up for tyrant. Of him it is related that he was strikingly like Periander the son of Cypselus, just as it is said that Orontes the Persian bore a great resemblance to Alcmæon the son of Amphiaraus, and that Lacedæmonian youth, whom Myrsilus relates to have been trodden to pieces by the crowd of those that came to see him upon that report, to Hector.

This Nicocles governed four months, in which, after he had done all kinds of mischief to the city, he very nearly let it fall into the hands of the Ætolians. By this time Aratus, being grown a youth, was in much esteem, both for his noble birth and his spirit and disposition, which, while neither insignificant nor wanting in energy, were solid, and tempered with a steadiness of judgment beyond his years. For which reason the exiles had their eyes most upon him, nor did Nicocles less observe his motions, but secretly spied and watched him, not out of apprehension of any such considerable or utterly audacious attempt, but suspecting he held correspondence with the kings, who were his father's friends and acquaintance. And, indeed, Aratus first attempted this way; but finding that Antigonus, who had promised fair, neglected him and delayed the time, and that his hopes from Egypt and Ptolemy were long to wait for, he determined to cut off the tyrant by himself.

And first he broke his mind to Aristomachus and Ecdelus, the one an exile of Sicyon, the other, Ecdelus, an Arcadian of Megalopolis, a philosopher, and a man of action, having been the familiar friend of Arcesilaus the Academic at Athens. These readily consenting, he communicated with the other exiles, whereof some few, being ashamed to seem to despair of success, engaged in the design; but most of them endeavored to divert him from his purpose, as one that for want of experience was too rash and daring.

Whilst he was consulting to seize upon some post in Sicyonia, from whence he might make war upon the tyrant, there came to Argos a certain Sicyonian, newly escaped out of prison, brother to Xenocles, one of the exiles, who being by him presented to Aratus informed him, that that part of the wall over which he escaped was, inside, almost level with the ground, adjoining a rocky and elevated place, and that from the outside it might be scaled with ladders. Aratus, hearing this, despatches away Xenocles with two of his own servants, Seuthas and Technon, to view the wall, resolving, if possible, secretly and with one risk to hazard all on a single trial, rather than carry on a contest as a private man against a tyrant by long war and open force. Xenocles, therefore, with his companions, returning, having taken the height of the wall, and declaring the place not to be impossible or indeed difficult to get over, but that it was not easy to approach it undiscovered, by reason of some small but uncommonly savage and noisy dogs belonging to a gardener hard by, he immediately undertook the business.

Now the preparation of arms gave no jealousy, because robberies and petty forays were at that time common everywhere between one set of people and another; and for the ladders, Euphranor, the machine-maker, made them openly, his trade rendering him unsuspected, though one of the exiles. As for men, each of his friends in Argos furnished him with ten apiece out of those few they had, and he armed thirty of his own servants, and hired some few soldiers of Xenophilus, the chief of the robber captains, to whom it was given out that they were to march into the territory of Sicyon to seize the king's stud; most of them were sent before, in small parties, to the tower of Polygnotus, with orders to wait there; Caphisias also was despatched beforehand lightly armed, with four others, who were, as soon as it was dark, to come to the gardener's house, pretending to be travellers, and, procuring their lodging there, to shut up him and his dogs; for there was no other way of getting past. And for the ladders, they had been made to take in pieces, and were put into chests, and sent before hidden upon waggons. In the mean time, some of the spies of Nicocles appearing in Argos, and being said to go privately about watching Aratus, he came early in the morning into the market-place, showing himself openly and conversing with his friends; then he anointed himself in the exercise ground, and, taking with him thence some of the young men that used to drink and spend their time with him, he went home; and presently after several of his servants were seen about the market-place, one carrying garlands, another buying flambeaus, and a third speaking to the women that used to sing and play at banquets, all which things the spies observing were deceived, and said laughing to one another, "Certainly nothing can be more timorous than a tyrant, if Nicocles, being master of so great a city and so numerous a force, stands in fear of a youth that spends what he has to subsist upon in his banishment in pleasures and day-debauches;" and, being thus imposed upon, they returned home.

But Aratus, departing immediately after his morning meal, and coming to his soldiers at Polygnotus's tower, led them to Nemea; where he disclosed, to most of them for the first time, his true design, making them large promises and fair speeches, and marched towards the city, giving for the word Apollo victorious, propor-

tioning his march to the motion of the moon, so as to
have the benefit of her light upon the way, and to be
in the garden, which was close to the wall, just as she
was setting. Here Caphisias came to him, who had not
secured the dogs, which had run away before he could
catch them, but had only made sure of the gardener.
Upon which most of the company being out of heart
and desiring to retreat, Aratus encouraged them to go
on, promising to retire in case the dogs were too troublesome;
and at the same time sending forward those
that carried the ladders, conducted by Ecdelus and
Mnasitheus, he followed them himself leisurely, the
dogs already barking very loud and following the steps
of Ecdelus and his companions. However, they got
to the wall, and reared the ladders with safety. But
as the foremost men were mounting them, the captain
of the watch that was to be relieved by the morning
guard passed on his way with the bell, and there were
many lights, and a noise of people coming up. Hearing
which, they clapt themselves close to the ladders,
and so were unobserved; but as the other watch also
was coming up to meet this, they were in extreme danger
of being discovered. But when this also went by
without observing them, immediately Mnasitheus and
Ecdelus got upon the wall, and, possessing themselves
of the approaches inside and out, sent away Technon
to Aratus, desiring him to make all the haste he could.

Now there was no great distance from the garden
to the wall and to the tower, in which latter a large
hound was kept. The hound did not hear their steps
of himself, whether that he were naturally drowsy, or
overwearied the day before, but, the gardener's curs
awaking him, he first began to growl and grumble in
response, and then as they passed by to bark out aloud.
And the barking was now so great, that the sentinel
opposite shouted out to the dog's keeper to know why

the dog kept such a barking, and whether any thing
was the matter; who answered, that it was nothing,
but only that his dog had been set barking by the
lights of the watch and the noise of the bell. This
reply much encouraged Aratus's soldiers, who thought
the dog's keeper was privy to their design, and wished
to conceal what was passing, and that many others in
the city were of the conspiracy. But when they came
to scale the wall, the attempt then appeared both to
require time and to be full of danger, for the ladders
shook and tottered extremely unless they mounted
them leisurely and one by one, and time pressed, for
the cocks began to crow, and the country people that
used to bring things to the market would be coming
to the town directly. Therefore Aratus made haste
to get up himself, forty only of the company being
already upon the wall, and, staying but for a few more
of those that were below, he made straight to the tyrant's house and the general's office, where the mercenary soldiers passed the night, and, coming suddenly
upon them, and taking them prisoners without killing
any one of them, he immediately sent to all his friends
in their houses to desire them to come to him, which
they did from all quarters. By this time the day began
to break, and the theatre was filled with a multitude
that were held in suspense by uncertain reports and
knew nothing distinctly of what had happened, until a
public crier came forward and proclaimed that Aratus,
the son of Clinias, invited the citizens to recover their
liberty.

Then at last assured that what they so long looked
for was come to pass, they pressed in throngs to the
tyrant's gates to set them on fire. And such a flame
was kindled, the whole house catching fire, that it was
seen as far as Corinth; so that the Corinthians, wondering what the matter could be, were upon the point

of coming to their assistance. Nicocles fled away secretly out of the city by means of certain underground passages, and the soldiers, helping the Sicyonians to quench the fire, plundered the house. This Aratus hindered not, but divided also the rest of the riches of the tyrants amongst the citizens. In this exploit, not one of those engaged in it was slain, nor any of the contrary party, fortune so ordering the action as to be clear and free from civil bloodshed. He restored eighty exiles who had been expelled by Nicocles, and no less than five hundred who had been driven out by former tyrants and had endured a long banishment, pretty nearly, but this time, of fifty years' duration. These returning, most of them very poor, were impatient to enter upon their former possessions, and, proceeding to their several farms and houses, gave great perplexity to Aratus, who considered that the city without was envied for its liberty and aimed at by Antigonus, and within was full of disorder and sedition. Wherefore, as things stood, he thought it best to associate it to the Achæan community, and so, although Dorians, they of their own will took upon them the name and citizenship of the Achæans, who at that time had neither great repute nor much power. For the most of them lived in small towns, and their territory was neither large nor fruitful, and the neighboring sea was almost wholly without a harbor, breaking direct upon a rocky shore. But yet these above others made it appear that the Grecian courage was invincible, whensoever it could only have order and concord within itself and a prudent general to direct it. For though they had scarcely been counted as any part of the ancient Grecian power, and at this time did not equal the strength of one ordinary city, yet by prudence and unanimity, and because they knew how not to envy and malign, but to obey and follow him amongst them that was most eminent for virtue, they not only preserved their own liberty in the midst of so many great cities, military powers, and monarchies, but went on steadily saving and delivering from slavery great numbers of the Greeks.

As for Aratus, he was in his behavior a true statesman, high-minded, and more intent upon the public than his private concerns, a bitter hater of tyrants, making the common good the rule and law of his friendships and enmities. So that indeed he seems not to have been so faithful a friend, as he was a reasonable and gentle enemy, ready, according to the needs of the state, to suit himself on occasion to either side; concord between nations, brotherhood between cities, the council and the assembly unanimous in their votes, being the objects above all other blessings to which he was passionately devoted; backward, indeed, and diffident in the use of arms and open force, but in effecting a purpose underhand, and outwitting cities and potentates without observation, most politic and dexterous. Therefore, though he succeeded beyond hope in many enterprises which he undertook, yet he seems to have left quite as many unattempted, though feasible enough, for want of assurance. For it should seem, that, as the sight of certain beasts is strong in the night but dim by day, the tenderness of the humors of their eyes not bearing the contact of the light, so there is also one kind of human skill and sagacity which is easily daunted and disturbed in actions done in the open day and before the world, and recovers all its self-possession in secret and covert enterprises; which inequality is occasioned in noble minds for want of philosophy, a mere wild and uncultivated fruit of a virtue without true knowledge coming up; as might be made out by examples.

Aratus, therefore, having associated himself and

his city to the Achæans, served in the cavalry, and made himself much beloved by his commanding officers for his exact obedience; for though he had made so large an addition to the common strength as that of his own credit and the power of his country, yet he was as ready as the most ordinary person to be commanded by the Achæan general of the time being, whether he were a man of Dymæ, or of Tritæa, or any yet meaner town than these. Having also a present of five and twenty talents sent him from the king, he took them, but gave them all to his fellow-citizens, who wanted money, amongst other purposes, for the redemption of those who had been taken prisoners.

But the exiles being by no means to be satisfied, disturbing continually those that were in possession of their estates, Sicyon was in great danger of falling into perfect desolation; so that, having no hope left but in the kindness of Ptolemy, he resolved to sail to him, and to beg so much money of him as might reconcile all parties. So he set sail from Mothone beyond Malea, designing to make the direct passage. But the pilot not being able to keep the vessel up against a strong wind and high waves that came in from the open sea, he was driven from his course, and with much ado got to shore in Andros,[6] an enemy's land, possessed by Antigonus, who had a garrison there. To avoid which he immediately landed, and, leaving the ship, went up into the country a good way from the sea, having along with him only one friend, called Ti-

---

[6] *Adria* is the reading of the manuscripts, which cannot be right. *Andria,* or the territory of Andros, is one conjecture, and *Hydrea* is another. Both islands are far out of the course from Mothone to Egypt, Andros the furthest, but Aratus would hardly be thought to have gone from Hydrea to Eubœa, which is near enough to Andros to make the supposition in this case not unnatural.

manthes; and throwing themselves into some ground
thickly covered with wood, they had but an ill night's
rest of it. Not long after, the commander of the
troops came, and, enquiring for Aratus, was deceived
by his servants, who had been instructed to say that he
had fled at once over into the island of Euboea. However, he declared the ship, the property on board of
her, and the servants, to be lawful prize, and detained
them accordingly. As for Aratus, after some few
days, in his extremity by good fortune a Roman ship
happened to put in just at the spot in which he made
his abode, sometimes peeping out to seek his opportunity, sometimes keeping close. She was bound for
Syria; but going aboard, he agreed with the master to
land him in Caria. In which voyage he met with no
less danger on the sea than before. From Caria being
after much time arrived in Egypt, he immediately
went to the king, who had a great kindness for him,
and had received from him many presents of drawings
and paintings out of Greece. Aratus had a very good
judgment in them, and always took care to collect and
send him the most curious and finished works, especially those of Pamphilus and Melanthus.

For the Sicyonian pieces were still in the height of
their reputation, as being the only ones whose colors
were lasting; so that Apelles himself, even after he had
become well known and admired, went thither, and
gave a talent to be admitted into the society of the
painters there, not so much to partake of their skill,
which he wanted not, but of their credit. And accordingly Aratus, when he freed the city, immediately took
down the representations of the rest of the tyrants, but
demurred a long time about that of Aristratus, who
flourished in the time of Philip. For this Aristratus
was painted by Melanthus and his scholars, standing
by a chariot, in which a figure of Victory was carried,

Apelles himself having had a hand in it, as Polemon the geographer reports. It was an extraordinary piece, and therefore Aratus was fain to spare it for the workmanship, and yet, instigated by the hatred he bore the tyrants, commanded it to be taken down. But Nealces the painter, one of Aratus's friends, entreated him, it is said, with tears in his eyes, to spare it, and, finding he did not prevail with him, told him at last he should carry on his war with the tyrants, but with the tyrants alone: "Let therefore the chariot and the Victory stand, and I will take means for the removal of Aristratus;" to which Aratus consenting, Nealces blotted out Aristratus, and in his place painted a palm-tree, not daring to add any thing else of his own invention. The feet of the defaced figure of Aristratus are said to have escaped notice, and to be hid under the chariot. By these means Aratus got favor with the king, who, after he was more fully acquainted with him, loved him so much the more, and gave him for the relief of his city one hundred and fifty talents; forty of which he immediately carried away with him, when he sailed to Peloponnesus, but the rest the king divided into instalments, and sent them to him afterwards at different times.

Assuredly it was a great thing to procure for his fellow-citizens a sum of money, a small portion of which had been sufficient, when presented by a king to other captains and popular leaders, to induce them to turn dishonest, and betray and give away their native countries to him. But it was a much greater, that by means of this money he effected a reconciliation and good understanding between the rich and poor, and created quiet and security for the whole people. His moderation, also, amidst so great power was very admirable. For being declared sole arbitrator and plenipotentiary for settling the questions of property in the case of the exiles, he would not accept the commission alone, but, associating with himself fifteen of the citizens, with great pains and trouble he succeeded in adjusting matters, and established peace and good-will in the city, for which good service, not only all the citizens in general bestowed extraordinary honors upon him, but the exiles, apart by themselves, erecting his statue in brass, inscribed on it these elegiac verses:—

> Your counsels, deeds, and skill for Greece in war
> Known beyond Hercules's pillars are;
> But we this image, O Aratus, gave
> Of you who saved us, to the gods who save,
> By you from exile to our homes restored,
> That virtue and that justice to record,
> To which the blessing Sicyon owes this day
> Of Wealth that's shared alike, and laws that all obey.

By his success in effecting these things, Aratus secured himself from the envy of his fellow-citizens, on account of the benefits they felt he had done them; but king Antigonus being troubled in his mind about him, and designing either wholly to bring him over to his party, or else to make him suspected by Ptolemy, besides other marks of his favor shown to him, who had little mind to receive them, added this too, that, sacrificing to the gods in Corinth, he sent portions to Aratus at Sicyon, and at the feast, where were many guests, he said openly, "I thought this Sicyonian youth had been only a lover of liberty and of his fellow citizens, but now I look upon him as a good judge of the manners and actions of kings. For formerly he despised us, and, placing his hopes further off, admired the Egyptian riches, hearing so much of their elephants, fleets, and palaces. But after seeing all these at a nearer distance, perceiving them to be but mere stage show and pageantry, he is now come over to us. And for my part I willingly receive him, and, resolving to make great use of him myself, command you to look upon him as a friend." These words were soon taken hold of by those that envied and maligned him, who strove which of them should, in their letters to Ptolemy, attack him with the worst calumnies, so that Ptolemy sent to expostulate the matter with him; so much envy and ill-will did there always attend the so much contended for, and so ardently and passionately aspired to, friendships of princes and great men.

But Aratus, being now for the first time chosen general of the Achæans, ravaged the country of Locris and Calydon, just over against Achæa, and then went to assist the Bœotians with ten thousand soldiers, but came not up to them until after the battle near Chæronea had been fought, in which they were beaten by the Ætolians, with the loss of Abœocritus the Bœotarch, and a thousand men besides. A year after, being again elected general,[7] he resolved to attempt the capture of the Acro-Corinthus, not so much for the advantage of the Sicyonians or Achæans, as considering that by expelling the Macedonian garrison he should free all Greece alike from a tyranny which oppressed every part of her. Chares the Athenian, having the good fortune to get the better, in a certain battle, of the king's generals, wrote to the people of Athens that this victory was "sister to that at Marathon." And so may this action be very safely termed sister to those of Pelopidas the Theban and Thrasybulus the Athenian, in which they slew the tyrants; except, perhaps, it exceed them upon this account, that it was not against natural Grecians, but against

---

[7] Not one year after, but eight, as we find from Polybius. Plutarch's phrase is a little ambiguous; it is possible that the word eight has slipped out.

a foreign and stranger domination. The Isthmus, rising like a bank between the seas, collects into a single spot and compresses together the whole continent of Greece; and Acro-Corinthus, being a high mountain springing up out of the very middle of what here is Greece, wheresoever it is held with a garrison, stands in the way and cuts off all Peloponnesus from intercourse of every kind, free passage of men and arms, and all traffic by sea and land, and makes him lord of all, that is master of it. Wherefore the younger Philip did not jest, but said very true, when he called the city of Corinth "the fetters of Greece." So that this post was always much contended for, especially by the kings and tyrants; and so vehemently was it longed for by Antigonus, that his passion for it came little short of that of frantic love; he was continually occupied with devising how to take it by surprise from those that were then masters of it, since he despaired to do it by open force.

Therefore Alexander, who held the place, being dead, poisoned by him, as is reported, and his wife Nicæa succeeding in the government and the possession of Acro-Corinthus, he immediately made use of his son, Demetrius, and, giving her pleasing hopes of a royal marriage and of a happy life with a youth, whom a woman now growing old might well find agreeable, with this lure of his son he succeeded in taking her; but the place itself she did not deliver up, but continued to hold it with a very strong garrison, of which he seeming to take no notice, celebrated the wedding in Corinth, entertaining them with shows and banquets every day, as one that had nothing else in his mind but to give himself up for awhile to indulgence in pleasure and mirth. But when the moment came, and Amœbeus began to sing in the theatre, he waited himself upon Nicæa to the play, she being carried in a royally-decorated chair, extremely pleased with her new honor, not dreaming of what was intended. As soon, therefore, as they were come to the turning which led up to the citadel, he desired her to go on before him to the theatre, but for himself, bidding farewell to the music, farewell to the wedding, he went on faster than one would have thought his age would have admitted to the Acro-Corinthus, and, finding the gate shut, knocked with his staff, commanding them to open, which they within, being amazed, did. And having thus made himself master of the place, he could not contain himself for joy; but, though an old man, and one that had seen so many turns of fortune, he must needs revel it in the open streets and the midst of the market-place, crowned with garlands and attended with flute-women, inviting everybody he met to partake in his festivity. So much more does joy without discretion transport and agitate the mind than either fear or sorrow. Antigonus, therefore, having in this manner possessed himself of Acro-Corinthus, put a garrison into it of those he trusted most, making Persæus the philosopher governor.

Now Aratus, even in the lifetime of Alexander, had made an attempt, but, a confederacy being made between Alexander and the Achæans, he desisted. But now he started afresh, with a new plan of effecting the thing, which was this: there were in Corinth four brothers, Syrians born, one of whom, called Diocles, served as a soldier in the garrison, but the three others, having stolen some gold of the king's, came to Sicyon, to one Ægias, a banker, whom Aratus made use of in his business. To him they immediately sold part of their gold, and the rest one of them, called Erginus, coming often thither, exchanged by parcels. Becoming, by this means, familiarly acquainted with

Ægias, and being by him led into discourses concerning the fortress, he told him that in going up to his brother he had observed, in the face of the rock, a side-cleft, leading to that part of the wall of the castle which was lower than the rest. At which Ægias joking with him and saying, "So, you wise man, for the sake of a little gold you have broken into the king's treasure; when you might, if you chose, get money in abundance for a single hour's work, burglary, you know, and treason being punished with the same death," Erginus laughed and told him then, he would break the thing to Diocles (for he did not altogether trust his other brothers), and, returning within a few days, he bargained to conduct Aratus to that part of the wall where it was no more than fifteen feet high, and to do what else should be necessary, together with his brother Diocles.

Aratus, therefore, agreed to give them sixty talents if he succeeded, but if he failed in his enterprise, and yet he and they came off safe, then he would give each of them a house and a talent. Now the threescore talents being to be deposited in the hands of Ægias for Erginus and his partners, and Aratus neither having so much by him, nor willing, by borrowing it from others, to give any one a suspicion of his design, he pawned his plate and his wife's golden ornaments to Ægias for the money. For so high was his temper, and so strong his passion for noble actions, that, even as he had heard that Phocion and Epaminondas were the best and justest of the Greeks, because they refused the greatest presents and would not surrender their duty for money, so he now chose to be at the expense of this enterprise privately, and to advance all the cost out of his own property, taking the whole hazard on himself for the sake of the rest that did not so much as know what was doing. And who indeed can withhold, even now, his admiration for and his sympathy with the generous mind of one, who paid so largely to purchase so great a risk, and lent out his richest possessions to have an opportunity to expose his own life, by entering among his enemies in the dead of the night, without desiring any other security for them than the hope of a noble success.

Now the enterprise, though dangerous enough in itself, was made much more so by an error happening through mistake in the very beginning. For Technon, one of Aratus's servants, was sent away to Diocles, that they might together view the wall. Now he had never seen Diocles, but made no question of knowing him by the marks Erginus had given him of him; namely, that he had curly hair, a swarthy complexion, and no beard. Being come, therefore, to the appointed place, he stayed waiting for Erginus and Diocles outside the town, in front of the place called Ornis. In the mean time, Dionysius, elder brother to Erginus and Diocles, who knew nothing at all of the matter, but much resembled Diocles, happened to pass by. Technon, upon this likeness, all being in accordance with what he had been told, asked him if he knew Erginus; and on his replying that he was his brother, taking it for granted that he was speaking with Diocles, not so much as asking his name or staying for any other token, he gave him his hand, and began to discourse with him and ask him questions about matters agreed upon with Erginus. Dionysius, cunningly taking the advantage of his mistake, seemed to understand him very well, and returning towards the city, led him on, still talking, without any suspicion. And being now near the gate, he was just about to seize on him, when by chance again Erginus met them, and, apprehending the cheat and the danger, beckoned to Technon to make his escape, and immediately both of them, betaking themselves to their heels, ran away as fast as they could to Aratus, who for all this despaired not, but immediately sent away Erginus to Dionysius to bribe him to hold his tongue. And he not only effected that, but also brought him along with him to Aratus. But, when they had him, they no longer left him at liberty, but binding him, they kept him close shut up in a room, whilst they prepared for executing their design.

All things being now ready, he commanded the rest of his forces to pass the night by their arms, and taking with him four hundred chosen men, few of whom knew what they were going about, he led them to the gates by the temple of Juno. It was the midst of summer, and the moon was at full, and the night so clear without any clouds, that there was danger lest the arms glistening in the moonlight should discover them. But as the foremost of them came near the city, a mist came off from the sea, and darkened the city itself and the outskirts about it. Then the rest of them, sitting down, put off their shoes, because men both make less noise and also climb surer, if they go up ladders barefooted, but Erginus, taking with him seven young men dressed like travellers, got unobserved to the gate, and killed the sentry with the other guards. And at the same time the ladders were clapped to the walls, and Aratus, having in great haste got up a hundred men, commanded the rest to follow as they could, and immediately drawing up his ladders after him, he marched through the city with his hundred men towards the castle, being already overjoyed that he was undiscovered, and not doubting of the success. But while still they were some way off, a watch of four men came with a light, who did not see them, because they were still in the shade of the moon, but were seen plainly enough themselves as they came on directly towards them. So withdrawing a little way amongst some walls and plots for houses, they lay in wait for them; and three of them they killed. But the fourth, being wounded in the head with a sword, fled, crying out that the enemy was in the city. And immediately the trumpets sounded, and all the city was in an uproar at what had happened, and the streets were full of people running up and down, and many lights were seen shining both below in the town, and above in the castle, and a confused noise was to be heard in all parts.

In the mean time, Aratus was hard at work struggling to get up the rocks, at first slowly and with much difficulty, straying continually from the path, which lay deep, and was overshadowed with the crags, leading to the wall with many windings and turnings; but the moon immediately and as if by miracle, it is said, dispersing the clouds, shone out and gave light to the most difficult part of the way, until he got to that part of the wall he desired, and there she overshadowed and hid him, the clouds coming together again. Those soldiers whom Aratus had left outside the gate, near Juno's temple, to the number of three hundred, entering the town, now full of tumult and lights, and not knowing the way by which the former had gone, and finding no track of them, slunk aside, and crowded together in one body under a flank of the cliff that cast a strong shadow, and there stood and waited in great distress and perplexity. For, by this time, those that had gone with Aratus were attacked with missiles from the citadel, and were busy fighting, and a sound of cries of battle came down from above, and a loud noise, echoed back and back from the mountain sides, and therefore confused and uncertain whence it proceeded, was heard on all sides.

They being thus in doubt which way to turn themselves, Archelaus, the commander of Antigonus's troops, having a great number of soldiers with him, made up towards the castle with great shouts and noise of trumpets to fall upon Aratus's people, and passed by the three hundred, who, as if they had risen out of an ambush, immediately charged him, killing the first they encountered, and so affrighted the rest, together with Archelaus, that they put them to flight and pursued them until they had quite broke and dispersed them about the city. No sooner were these defeated, but Erginus came to them from those that were fighting above, to acquaint them that Aratus was engaged with the enemy, who defended themselves very stoutly, and there was a fierce conflict at the very wall, and need of speedy help. They therefore desired him to lead them on without delay, and, marching up, they by their shouts made their friends understand who they were, and encouraged them; and the full moon, shining on their arms, made them, in the long line by which they advanced, appear more in number to the enemy than they were; and the echo of the night multiplied their shouts. In short, falling on with the rest, they made the enemy give way, and were masters of the castle and garrison, day now beginning to be bright, and the rising sun shining out upon their success. By this time, also, the rest of his army came up to Aratus from Sicyon, the Corinthians joyfully receiving them at the gates and helping them to secure the king's party.

And now, having put all things into a safe posture, he came down from the castle to the theatre, an infinite number of people crowding thither to see him and to hear what he would say to the Corinthians. Therefore drawing up the Achæans on each side of the stage-passages, he came forward himself upon the stage, with his corslet still on, and his face showing the effects of all his hard work and want of sleep, so that his natural exultation and joyfulness of mind were overborne by the weariness of his body. The people, as soon as he came forth, breaking out into great applauses and congratulations, he took his spear in his right hand, and, resting his body upon it with his knee a little bent, stood a good while in that posture, silently receiving their shouts and acclamations, while they extolled his valor and wondered at his fortune; which being over, standing up, he began an oration in the name of the Achæans, suitable to the late action, persuading the Corinthians to associate themselves to the Achæans, and withal delivered up to them the keys of their gates, which had never been in their power since the time of King Philip. Of the captains of Antigonus, he dismissed Archelaus, whom he had taken prisoner, and Theophrastus, who refused to quit his post, he put to death. As for Persæus, when he saw the castle was lost, he had got away to Cenchreæ, where, some time after, discoursing with one that said to him that the wise man only is a true general, "Indeed," he replied, "none of Zeno's maxims once pleased me better than this, but I have been converted to another opinion by the young man of Sicyon." This is told by many of Persæus. Aratus, immediately after, made himself master of the temple of Juno and haven of Lechæum, seized upon five and twenty of the king's ships, together with five hundred horses and four hundred Syrians; these he sold. The Achæans kept guard in the Acro-Corinthus with a body of four hundred soldiers, and fifty dogs with as many keepers.

The Romans, extolling Philopœmen, called him the last of the Grecians, as if no great man had ever since his time been bred amongst them. But I should call this capture of the Acro-Corinthus the last of the Grecian exploits, being comparable to the best of them, both for the daringness of it, and the success, as was presently seen by the consequences. For the Megarians, revolting from Antigonus, joined Aratus, and the Trœzenians and Epidaurians enrolled themselves in the Achæan community, and issuing forth for the first time, he entered Attica, and passing over into Salamis, he plundered the island, turning the Achæan force every way, as if it were just let loose out of prison and set at liberty. All freemen whom he took he sent back to the Athenians without ransom, as a sort of first invitation to them to come over to the league. He made Ptolemy become a confederate of the Achæans, with the privilege of command both by sea and land. And so great was his power with them, that since he could not by law be chosen their general every year, yet every other year he was, and by his counsels and actions was in effect always so. For they perceived that neither riches nor reputation, nor the friendship of kings, nor the private interest of his own country, nor any thing else was so dear to him as the increase of the Achæan power and greatness. For he believed that the cities, weak individually, could be preserved by nothing else but a mutual assistance under the closest bond of the common interest; and, as the members of the body live and breathe by the union of all in a single natural growth, and on the dissolution of this, when once they separate, pine away and putrify, in the same manner are cities ruined by being dissevered, as well as preserved when, as the members of one great body they enjoy the benefit of that providence and counsel that govern the whole.

Now being distressed to see that, whereas the chief neighboring cities enjoyed their own laws and lib-

erties, the Argives were in bondage, he took counsel
for destroying their tyrant Aristomachus, being very
desirous both to pay his debt of gratitude to the city
where he had been bred up, by restoring it its liberty,
and to add so considerable a town to the Achæans.
Nor were there some wanting who had the courage to
undertake the thing, of whom Æschylus and Charimenes the soothsayer were the chief. But they wanted
swords; for the tyrant had prohibited the keeping of
any under a great penalty. Therefore Aratus, having
provided some small daggers at Corinth and hidden
them in the packsaddles of some packhorses that carried ordinary ware, sent them to Argos. But Charimenes letting another person into the design,
Æschylus and his partners were angry at it, and
henceforth would have no more to do with him, and
took their measures by themselves, and Charimenes,
on finding this, went, out of anger, and informed
against them, just as they were on their way to attack
the tyrant; however, the most of them made a shift
to escape out of the market-place, and fled to Corinth.
Not long after, Aristomachus was slain by some
slaves, and Aristippus, a worse tyrant than he, seized
the government. Upon this, Aratus, mustering all
the Achæans present that were of age, hurried away
to the aid of the city, believing that he should find the
people ready to join with him. But the greater number being by this time habituated to slavery and content to submit, and no one coming to join him, he was
obliged to retire, having moreover exposed the Achæans to the charge of committing acts of hostility in
the midst of peace; upon which account they were sued
before the Mantineans, and, Aratus, not making his
appearance, Aristippus gained the cause and had
damages allowed him to the value of thirty minæ.
And now hating and fearing Aratus, he sought means

ARATUS

to kill him, having the assistance herein of king Antigonus; so that Aratus was perpetually dogged and watched by those that waited for an opportunity to do this service. But there is no such safeguard of a ruler as the sincere and steady good-will of his subjects, for, where both the common people and the principal citizens have their fears not of but for their governor, he sees with many eyes and hears with many ears whatsoever is doing. Therefore I cannot but here stop short a little in the course of my narrative, to describe the manner of life which the so much envied arbitrary power and the so much celebrated and admired pomp and pride of absolute government obliged Aristippus to lead.

For though Antigonus was his friend and ally, and though he maintained numerous soldiers to act as his body-guard, and had not left one enemy of his alive in the city, yet he was forced to make his guards encamp in the colonnade about his house; and for his servants, he turned them all out immediately after supper, and then, shutting the doors upon them, he crept up into a small upper chamber, together with his mistress, through a trap-door, upon which he placed his bed, and there slept after such a fashion, as one in his condition can be supposed to sleep, that is, interruptedly and in fear. The ladder was taken away by the woman's mother, and locked up in another room; in the morning she brought it again, and putting it to, called up this brave and wonderful tyrant, who came crawling out like some creeping thing out of its hole. Whereas, Aratus, not by force of arms, but lawfully and by his virtue, lived in possession of a firmly settled command, wearing the ordinary coat and cloak, being the common and declared enemy of all tyrants, and has left behind him a noble race of descendants surviving among the Grecians to this day; while those occupiers of citadels and maintainers of body-guards, who made all this use of arms and gates and bolts to protect their lives, in some few cases perhaps escaped, like the hare from the hunters; but in no instance have we either house or family, or so much as a tomb to which any respect is shown, remaining to preserve the memory of any one of them.

Against this Aristippus, therefore, Aratus made many open and many secret attempts, whilst he endeavored to take Argos, though without success; once, particularly, clapping scaling ladders in the night to the wall, he desperately got up upon it with a few of his soldiers, and killed the guards that opposed him. But the day appearing, the tyrant set upon him with all hands, whilst the Argives, as if it had not been their liberty that was contended for, but some Nemean game going on for which it was their privilege to assign the prize, like fair and impartial judges, sat looking on in great quietness. Aratus, fighting bravely, was run through the thigh with a lance, yet he maintained his ground against the enemy till night, and, had he been able to go on and hold out that night also, he had gained his point; for the tyrant thought of nothing but flying, and had already shipped most of his goods. But Aratus, having no intelligence of this, and wanting water, being disabled himself by his wound, retreated with his soldiers.

Despairing henceforth to do any good this way, he fell openly with his army into Argolis, and plundered it, and, in a fierce battle with Aristippus near the river Chares, he was accused of having withdrawn out of the fight, and thereby abandoned the victory. For whereas one part of his army had unmistakably got the better, and was pursuing the enemy at a good distance from him, he yet retreated in confusion into his camp, not so much because he was overpressed by those with whom he was engaged, as out of mistrust of success and through a panic fear. But when the other wing, returning from the pursuit, showed themselves extremely vexed, that though they had put the enemy to flight and killed many more of his men than they had lost, yet those that were in a manner conquered should erect a trophy as conquerors, being much ashamed he resolved to fight them again about the trophy, and the next day but one drew up his army to give them battle. But, perceiving that they were reinforced with fresh troops, and came on with better courage than before, he durst not hazard a fight, but retired, and sent to request a truce to bury his dead. However, by his dexterity in dealing personally with men and managing political affairs, and by his general favor, he excused and obliterated this fault, and brought in Cleonæ to the Achæan association, and celebrated the Nemean games at Cleonæ, as the proper and more ancient place for them. The games were also celebrated by the Argives at the same time, which gave the first occasion to the violation of the privilege of safe conduct and immunity, always granted to those that came to compete for the prizes, the Achæans at that time selling as enemies all those they caught going through their country after joining in the games at Argos. So vehement and implacable a hater was he of the tyrants.

Not long after, having notice that Aristippus had a design upon Cleonæ, but was afraid of him, because he then was staying in Corinth, he assembled an army by public proclamation, and, commanding them to take along with them provisions for several days, he marched to Cenchreæ, hoping by this stratagem to entice Aristippus to fall upon Cleonæ, when he supposed him far enough off. And so it happened, for he immediately brought his forces against it from Argos. But Aratus, returning from Cenchreæ to Corinth in the dusk of the evening, and setting posts of his troops in all the roads, led on the Achæans, who followed him in such good order and with so much speed and alacrity, that they were undiscovered by Aristippus, not only whilst upon their march, but even when they got, still in the night, into Cleonæ, and drew up in order of battle. As soon as it was morning, the gates being opened and the trumpets sounding, he fell upon the enemy with great cries and fury, routed them at once, and kept close in pursuit, following the course which he most imagined Aristippus would choose, there being many turns that might be taken. And so the chase lasted as far as Mycenæ, where the tyrant was slain by a certain Cretan called Tragiscus, as Dinias reports. Of the common soldiers, there fell above fifteen hundred. Yet though Aratus had obtained so great a victory, and that too without the loss of a man, he could not make himself master of Argos nor set it at liberty, because Agias and the younger Aristomachus got into the town with some of the king's forces, and seized upon the government. However, by this exploit he spoiled the scoffs and jests of those that flattered the tyrants, and in their raillery would say that the Achæan general was usually troubled with a looseness when he was to fight a battle, that the sound of a trumpet struck him with a drowsiness and a giddiness, and that, when he had drawn up his army and given the word, he used to ask his lieutenants and officers whether there was any further need of his presence now the die was cast, and then went aloof, to await the result at a distance. For indeed these stories were so generally listened to, that, when the philosophers disputed whether to have one's heart

beat and to change color upon any apparent danger
be an argument of fear, or rather of some distemperature and chilliness of bodily constitution, Aratus was
always quoted as a good general, who was always thus
affected in time of battle.

Having thus despatched Aristippus, he advised
with himself how to overthrow Lydiades, the Megalopolitan, who held usurped power over his country.
This person was naturally of a generous temper, and
not insensible of true honor, and had been led into this
wickedness, not by the ordinary motives of other
tyrants, licentiousness and rapacity, but being young,
and stimulated with the desire of glory, he had let his
mind be unwarily prepossessed with the vain and false
applauses given to tyranny, as some happy and glorious thing. But he no sooner seized the government,
than he grew weary of the pomp and burden of it.
And at once emulating the tranquillity and fearing
the policy of Aratus, he took the best of resolutions,
first, to free himself from hatred and fear, from soldiers and guards, and, secondly, to be the public benefactor of his country. And sending for Aratus, he
resigned the government, and incorporated his city
into the Achæan community. The Achæans, applaud-
ing this generous action, chose him their general; upon
which, desiring to outdo Aratus in glory, amongst
many other uncalled-for things, he declared war
against the Lacedæmonians; which Aratus opposing
was thought to do it out of envy; and Lydiades was
the second time chosen general, though Aratus acted
openly against him, and labored to have the office
conferred upon another. For Aratus himself had the
command every other year, as has been said. Lydiades,
however, succeeded so well in his pretensions, that he
was thrice chosen general, governing alternately, as
did Aratus; but at last, declaring himself his professed

enemy, and accusing him frequently to the Achæans, he was rejected, and fell into contempt, people now seeing that it was a contest between a counterfeit and a true, unadulterated virtue, and, as Æsop tells us that the cuckoo once, asking the little birds why they flew away from her, was answered, because they feared she would one day prove a hawk, so Lydiades's former tyranny still cast a doubt upon the reality of his change.

But Aratus gained new honor in the Ætolian war. For the Archæans resolving to fall upon the Ætolians on the Megarian confines, and Agis also, the Lacedæmonian king, who came to their assistance with an army, encouraging them to fight, Aratus opposed this determination. And patiently enduring many reproaches, many scoffs and jeerings at his soft and cowardly temper, he would not, for any appearance of disgrace, abandon what he judged to be the true common advantage, and suffered the enemy to pass over Geranea into Peloponnesus without a battle. But when, after they had passed by, news came that they had suddenly captured Pellene, he was no longer the same man, nor would he hear of any delay, or wait to draw together his whole force, but marched towards the enemy with such as he had about him to fall upon them, as they were indeed now much less formidable through the intemperances and disorders committed in their success. For as soon as they entered the city, the common soldiers dispersed and went hither and thither into the houses, quarrelling and fighting with one another about the plunder; and the officers and commanders were running about after the wives and daughters of the Pellenians, on whose heads they put their own helmets, to mark each man his prize, and prevent another from seizing it. And in this posture were they when news came that Aratus was ready to fall upon them. And in the midst of the consternation likely to ensue in the confusion they were in, before all of them heard of the danger, the outmost of them, engaging at the gates and in the suburbs with the Achæans, were already beaten and put to flight, and, as they came headlong back, filled with their panic those who were collecting and advancing to their assistance.

In this confusion, one of the captives, daughter of Epigethes, a citizen of repute, being extremely handsome and tall, happened to be sitting in the temple of Diana, placed there by the commander of the band of chosen men, who had taken her and put his crested helmet upon her. She, hearing the noise, and running out to see what was the matter, stood in the temple gates, looking down from above upon those that fought, having the helmet upon her head; in which posture she seemed to the citizens to be something more than human, and struck fear and dread into the enemy, who believed it to be a divine apparition; so that they lost all courage to defend themselves. But the Pellenians tell us that the image of Diana stands usually untouched, and when the priestess happens at any time to remove it to some other place, nobody dares look upon it, but all turn their faces from it; for not only is the sight of it terrible and hurtful to mankind, but it makes even the trees, by which it happens to be carried, become barren and cast their fruit. This image, therefore, they say, the priestess produced at that time, and, holding it directly in the faces of the Ætolians, made them lose their reason and judgment. But Aratus mentions no such thing in his commentaries, but says, that, having put to flight the Ætolians, and falling in pell-mell with them into the city, he drove them out by main force, and killed seven hundred of them. And the action was extolled as one of the most famous exploits, and Timanthes the painter made a picture of the battle, giving by his composition a most lively representation of it.

But many great nations and potentates combining against the Achæans, Aratus immediately treated for friendly arrangements with the Ætolians, and, making use of the assistance of Pantaleon, the most powerful man amongst them, he not only made a peace, but an alliance between them and the Achæans. But being desirous to free the Athenians, he got into disgrace and ill-repute among the Achæans, because, notwithstanding the truce and suspension of arms made between them and the Macedonians, he had attempted to take the Piræus. He denies this fact in his commentaries, and lays the blame on Erginus, by whose assistance he took Acro-Corinthus, alleging that he upon his own private account attacked the Piræus, and, his ladders happening to break, being hotly pursued, he called out upon Aratus as if present, by which means deceiving the enemy, he got safely off. This excuse, however, sounds very improbable; for it is not in any way likely that Erginus, a private man and a Syrian stranger, should conceive in his mind so great an attempt without Aratus at his back, to tell him how and when to make it, and to supply him with the means. Nor was it twice or thrice, but very often, that, like an obstinate lover, he repeated his attempts on the Piræus, and was so far from being discouraged by his disappointments, that his missing his hopes but narrowly was an incentive to him to proceed the more boldly in a new trial. One time amongst the rest, in making his escape through the Thriasian plain, he put his leg out of joint, and was forced to submit to many operations with the knife before he was cured, so that for a long time he was carried in a litter to the wars.

And when Antigonus [8] was dead, and Demetrius succeeded him in the kingdom, he was more bent than ever upon Athens, and in general quite despised the Macedonians. And so, being overthrown in battle near Phylacia by Bithys, Demetrius's general, and there being a very strong report that he was either taken or slain, Diogenes, the governor of the Piræus, sent letters to Corinth, commanding the Achæans to quit that city, seeing Aratus was dead. When these letters came to Corinth, Aratus happened to be there in person, so that Diogenes's messengers, being sufficiently mocked and derided, were forced to return to their master. King Demetrius himself also sent a ship, wherein Aratus was to be brought to him in chains. And the Athenians, exceeding all possible fickleness of flattery to the Macedonians, crowned themselves with garlands upon the first news of his death. And so in anger he went at once and invaded Attica, and penetrated as far as the Academy, but then suffering himself to be pacified, he did no further act of hostility. And the Athenians afterwards, coming to a due sense of his virtue, when upon the death of Demetrius they attempted to recover their liberty, called him in to their assistance; and although at that time another person was general of the Achæans, and he himself had long kept his bed with a sickness, yet, rather than fail the city in a time of need, he was carried thither in a litter, and helped to persuade Diogenes the governor to deliver up the Piræus, Munychia, Salamis, and Sunium to the Athenians in consideration of a hundred and fifty talents, of which Aratus himself contributed twenty to the city. Upon

---

[8] Antigonus Gonatas, the son of Demetrius Poliorcetes, and friend of Zeno, the founder of the stoic philosophy, was succeeded by Demetrius, his son.

this, the Æginetans and the Hermionians immediately joined the Achæans, and the greatest part of Arcadia entered their confederacy; and the Macedonians being occupied with various wars upon their own confines and with their neighbors, the Achæan power, the Ætolians also being in alliance with them, rose to great height.

But Aratus, still bent on effecting his old project, and impatient that tyranny should maintain itself in so near a city as Argos, sent to Aristomachus to persuade him to restore liberty to that city, and to associate it to the Achæans, and that, following Lydiades's example, he should rather choose to be the general of a great nation, with esteem and honor, than the tyrant of one city, with continual hatred and danger. Aristomachus slighted not the message, but desired Aratus to send him fifty talents, with which he might pay off the soldiers. In the meantime, whilst the money was providing, Lydiades, being then general, and extremely ambitious that this advantage might seem to be of his procuring for the Achæans, accused Aratus to Aristomachus, as one that bore an irreconcilable hatred to the tyrants, and, persuading him to commit the affair to his management, he presented him to the Achæans. But there the Achæan council gave a manifest proof of the great credit Aratus had with them and the good-will they bore him. For when he, in anger, spoke against Aristomachus's being admitted into the association, they rejected the proposal, but when he was afterwards pacified and came himself and spoke in its favor, they voted every thing cheerfully and readily, and decreed that the Argives and Phliasians should be incorporated into their commonwealth, and the next year they chose Aristomachus general. He, being in good credit with the Achæans, was very desirous to invade Laconia, and for that purpose sent for Aratus from Athens. Aratus wrote to him to dissuade him as far as he could from that expedition, being very unwilling the Achæans should be engaged in a quarrel with Cleomenes, who was a daring man, and making extraordinary advances to power. But Aristomachus resolving to go on, he obeyed and served in person, on which occasion he hindered Aristomachus from fighting a battle, when Cleomenes came upon them at Pallantium; and for this act was accused by Lydiades, and, coming to an open conflict with him in a contest for the office of general, he carried it by the show of hands, and was chosen general the twelfth time.

This year, being routed by Cleomenes near the Lycæum, he fled, and, wandering out of the way in the night, was believed to be slain; and once more it was confidently reported so throughout all Greece. He, however, having escaped this danger and rallied his forces, was not content to march off in safety, but, making a happy use of the present conjuncture, when nobody dreamed any such thing, he fell suddenly upon the Mantineans, allies of Cleomenes, and, taking the city, put a garrison into it, and made the stranger inhabitants free of the city; procuring, by this means, those advantages for the beaten Achæans, which, being conquerors, they would not easily have obtained. The Lacedæmonians again invading the Megalopolitan territories, he marched to the assistance of the city, but refused to give Cleomenes, who did all he could to provoke him to it, any opportunity of engaging him in a battle, nor could be prevailed upon by the Megalopolitans, who urged him to it extremely. For besides that by nature he was ill suited for set battles, he was then much inferior in numbers, and was to deal with a daring leader, still in the heat of youth, while he himself, now past the prime of courage and come to a chastised ambition, felt it his business to maintain by prudence the glory, which he had obtained, and the other was only aspiring to by forwardness and daring.

So that though the light-armed soldiers had sallied out and driven the Lacedæmonians as far as their camp, and had come even to their tents, yet would not Aratus lead his men forward, but, posting himself in a hollow water-course in the way thither, stopped and prevented the citizens from crossing this. Lydiades, extremely vexed at what was going on, and loading Aratus with reproaches, entreated the horse that together with him they would second them that had the enemy in chase, and not let a certain victory slip out of their hands, nor forsake him that was going to venture his life for his country. And being reinforced with many brave men that turned after him, he charged the enemy's right wing, and routing it, followed the pursuit without measure or discretion, letting his eagerness and hopes of glory tempt him on into broken ground, full of planted fruit-trees and cut up with broad ditches, where, being engaged by Cleomenes, he fell, fighting gallantly the noblest of battles, at the gate of his country. The rest, flying back to their main body and troubling the ranks of the full-armed infantry, put the whole army to the rout. Aratus was extremely blamed, being suspected to have betrayed Lydiades, and was constrained by the Achæans, who withdrew in great anger, to accompany them to Ægium, where they called a council, and decreed that he should no longer be furnished with money, nor have any more soldiers hired for him, but that, if he would make war, he should pay them himself.

This affront he resented so far as to resolve to give up the seal and lay down the office of general; but upon second thoughts he found it best to have patience, and presently marched with the Achæans to

Orchomenus and fought a battle with Megistonus, the step-father of Cleomenes, where he got the victory, killing three hundred men and taking Megistonus prisoner. But whereas he used to be chosen general every other year, when his turn came and he was called to take upon him that charge, he declined it, and Timoxenus was chosen in his stead. The true cause of which was not the pique he was alleged to have taken at the people, but the ill circumstances of the Achæan affairs. For Cleomenes did not now invade them gently and tenderly as hitherto, as one controlled by the civil authorities, but having killed the Ephors, divided the lands, and made many of the stranger residents free of the city, he was responsible to no one in his government; and therefore fell in good earnest upon the Achæans, and put forward his claim to the supreme military command. Wherefore Aratus is much blamed, that in a stormy and tempestuous time, like a cowardly pilot, he should forsake the helm, when it was even perhaps his duty to have insisted, whether they would or no, on saving them; or if he thought the Achæan affairs desperate, to have yielded all up to Cleomenes, and not to have let Peloponnesus fall once again into barbarism with Macedonian garrisons, and Acro-Corinthus be occupied with Illyric and Gaulish soldiers, and, under the specious name of Confederates, to have made those masters of the cities whom he had held it his business by arms and by policy to baffle and defeat, and, in the memoirs he left behind him, loaded with reproaches and insults. And say that Cleomenes was arbitrary and tyrannical, yet was he descended from the Heraclidæ, and Sparta was his country, the obscurest citizen of which deserved to be preferred to the generalship before the best of the Macedonians by those that had any regard to the honor of Grecian birth. Besides, Cleomenes sued for that command over the Achæans as one that would return the honor of that title with real kindnesses to the cities; whereas Antigonus,[9] being declared absolute general by sea and land, would not accept the office unless Acro-Corinthus were by special agreement put into his hands, following the example of Æsop's hunter; for he would not get up and ride the Achæans, who desired him so to do, and offered their backs to him by embassies and popular decrees, till, by a garrison and hostages, they had allowed him to bit and bridle them. Aratus exhausts all his powers of speech to show the necessity that was upon him. But Polybius writes, that long before this, and before there was any necessity, apprehending the daring temper of Cleomenes, he communicated secretly with Antigonus, and that he had beforehand prevailed with the Megalopolitans to press the Achæans to crave aid from Antigonus. For they were the most harassed by the war, Cleomenes continually plundering and ransacking their country. And so writes also Phylarchus, who, unless seconded by the testimony of Polybius, would not be altogether credited; for he is seized with enthusiasm when he so much as speaks a word of Cleomenes, and as if he were pleading, not writing a history, goes on throughout defending the one and accusing the other.

The Achæans, therefore, lost Mantinea, which was recovered by Cleomenes, and being beaten in a great fight near Hecatombæum, so general was the consternation, that they immediately sent to Cleomenes to desire him to come to Argos and take the command upon him. But Aratus, as soon as he understood that he was coming, and was got as far as Lerna with his

[9] This Antigonus is Antigonus Doson (or going to give), a cousin to Demetrius now dead, whom he succeeded as the guardian of Philip, Demetrius's son, of whom we presently hear.

ARATUS

troops, fearing the result, sent ambassadors to him, to request him to come accompanied with three hundred only, as to friends and confederates, and, if he mistrusted any thing, he should receive hostages. Upon which Cleomenes, saying this was mere mockery and affront, went away, sending a letter to the Achæans full of reproaches and accusation against Aratus. And Aratus also wrote letters against Cleomenes; and bitter revilings and railleries were current on both hands, not sparing even their marriages and wives. Hereupon Cleomenes sent a herald to declare war against the Achæans, and in the mean time missed very narrowly of taking Sicyon by treachery. Turning off at a little distance, he attacked and took Pellene, which the Achæan general abandoned, and not long after took also Pheneus and Penteleum. Then immediately the Argives voluntarily joined with him, and the Phliasians received a garrison, and in short nothing among all their new acquisitions held firm to the Achæans. Aratus was encompassed on every side with clamor and confusion; he saw the whole of Peloponnesus shaking around him, and the cities everywhere set in revolt by men desirous of innovations.

For indeed no place remained quiet or satisfied with the present condition; even amongst the Sicyonians and Corinthians themselves, many were well known to have had private conferences with Cleomenes, who long since, out of desire to make themselves masters of their several cities, had been discontented with the present order of things. Aratus, having absolute power given him to bring these to condign punishment, executed as many of them as he could find at Sicyon, but going about to find them out and punish them at Corinth also, he irritated the people, already unsound in feeling and weary of the Achæan government. So collecting tumultuously in the temple of Apollo, they sent for Aratus, having determined to take or kill him before they broke out into open revolt. He came accordingly, leading his horse in his hand, as if he suspected nothing. Then several leaping up and accusing and reproaching him, with mild words and a settled countenance he bade them sit down, and not stand crying out upon him in a disorderly manner, desiring, also, that those that were about the door might be let in, and saying so, he stepped out quietly, as if he would give his horse to somebody. Clearing himself thus of the crowd, and speaking without discomposure to the Corinthians that he met, commanding them to go to Apollo's temple, and being now, before they were aware, got near to the citadel, he leaped upon his horse, and commanding Cleopater, the governor of the garrison, to have a special care of his charge, he galloped to Sicyon, followed by thirty of his soldiers, the rest leaving him and shifting for themselves. And not long after it being known that he was fled, the Corinthians pursued him, but not overtaking him, they immediately sent for Cleomenes and delivered up the city to him, who, however, thought nothing they could give was so great a gain, as was the loss of their having let Aratus get away. Nevertheless, being strengthened by the accession of the people of the Acte, as it is called, who put their towns into his hands, he proceeded to carry a palisade and lines of circumvallation around the Acro-Corinthus.

But Aratus being arrived at Sicyon, the body of the Achæans there flocked to him, and, in an assembly there held, he was chosen general with absolute power, and he took about him a guard of his own citizens, it being now three and thirty years since he first took a part in public affairs among the Achæans, having in that time been the chief man in credit and power of all Greece; but he was now deserted on all hands, helpless and overpowered, drifting about amidst the waves and danger on the shattered hulk of his native city. For the Ætolians, whom he applied to, declined to assist him in his distress, and the Athenians, who were well affected to him, were diverted from lending him any succor by the authority of Euclides and Micion. Now whereas he had a house and property in Corinth, Cleomenes meddled not with it, nor suffered anybody else to do so, but calling for his friends and agents, he bade them hold themselves responsible to Aratus for every thing, as to him they would have to render their account; and privately he sent to him Tripylus, and afterwards Megistonus, his own step-father, to offer him, besides several other things, a yearly pension of twelve talents, which was twice as much as Ptolemy allowed him, for he gave him six; and all that he demanded was to be declared commander of the Achæans, and together with them to have the keeping of the citadel of Corinth. To which Aratus returning answer that affairs were not so properly in his power as he was in the power of them, Cleomenes, believing this a mere evasion, immediately entered the country of Sicyon, destroying all with fire and sword, and besieged the city three months, whilst Aratus held firm, and was in dispute with himself whether he should call in Antigonus upon condition of delivering up the citadel of Corinth to him; for he would not lend him assistance upon any other terms.

In the mean time the Achæans assembled at Ægium, and called for Aratus; but it was very hazardous for him to pass thither, while Cleomenes was encamped before Sicyon; besides, the citizens endeavored to stop him by their entreaties, protesting that they would not suffer him to expose himself to so evident danger, the enemy being so near; the women, also, and children hung about him, weeping and embracing him as their common father and defender. But he, having comforted and encouraged them as well as he could, got on horseback, and being accompanied with ten of his friends and his son, then a youth, got away to the sea-side, and finding vessels there waiting off the shore, went on board of them and sailed to Ægium to the assembly; in which it was decreed that Antigonus should be called in to their aid, and should have the Acro-Corinthus delivered to him. Aratus also sent his son to him with the other hostages. The Corinthians, extremely angry at this proceeding, now plundered his property, and gave his house as a present to Cleomenes.

Antigonus being now near at hand with his army, consisting of twenty thousand Macedonian foot and one thousand three hundred horse, Aratus, with the Members of Council,[10] went to meet him by sea, and got, unobserved by the enemy, to Pegæ, having no great confidence either in Antigonus or the Macedonians. For he was very sensible that his own greatness had been made out of the losses he had caused them, and that the first great principle of his public conduct had been hostility to the former Antigonus. But perceiving the necessity that was now upon him, and the pressure of the time, that lord and master of those we call rulers, to be inexorable, he resolved to put all to the venture. So soon, therefore, as Antigonus was told that Aratus was coming up to him, he saluted the rest of the company after the ordinary

---

[10] The *demiurgi,* ten in number, one for each Achæan town, formed a sort of Executive Council under the Chief Magistrate or General. Next under them came a Great Council of a hundred and twenty members; and as the base of all, the general Assembly.

manner, but him he received at the very first approach with especial honor, and finding him afterwards to be both good and wise, admitted him to his nearer familiarity. For Aratus was not only useful to him in the management of great affairs, but singularly agreeable also as the private companion of a king in his recreations. And therefore, though Antigonus was young, yet as soon as he observed the temper of the man to be proper for a prince's friendship, he made more use of him than of any other, not only of the Achæans, but also of the Macedonians that were about him. So that the thing fell out to him just as the god had foreshown in a sacrifice. For it is related that, as Aratus was not long before offering sacrifice, there was found in the liver two gall-bags inclosed in the same caul of fat; whereupon the soothsayer told him that there should very soon be the strictest friendship imaginable between him and his greatest and most mortal enemies; which prediction he at that time slighted, having in general no great faith in soothsayings and prognostications, but depending most upon rational deliberation. At an after time, however, when, things succeeding well in the war Antigonus made a great feast at Corinth, to which he invited a great number of guests, and placed Aratus next above himself, and presently calling for a coverlet, asked him if he did not find it cold, and on Aratus's answering "Yes, extremely cold," bade him come nearer, so that when the servants brought the coverlet, they threw it over them both, then Aratus remembering the sacrifice, fell a laughing, and told the king the sign which had happened to him, and the interpretation of it. But this fell out a good while after.

So Aratus and the king, plighting their faith to each other at Pegæ, immediately marched towards the enemy, with whom they had frequent engagements near the city, Cleomenes maintaining a strong position, and the Corinthians making a very brisk defence. In the mean time, Aristoteles the Argive, Aratus's friend, sent privately to him to let him know, that he would cause Argos to revolt, if he would come thither in person with some soldiers. Aratus acquainted Antigonus, and, taking fifteen hundred men with him, sailed in boats along the shore as quickly as he could from the Isthmus to Epidaurus. But the Argives had not patience till he could arrive, but, making a sudden insurrection, fell upon Cleomenes's soldiers, and drove them into the citadel. Cleomenes having news of this, and fearing lest, if the enemy should possess themselves of Argos, they might cut off his retreat home, leaves the Acro-Corinthus and marches away by night to help his men. He got thither first, and beat off the enemy, but Aratus appearing not long after, and the king approaching with his forces, he retreated to Mantinea, upon which all the cities again came over to the Achæans, and Antigonus took possession of the Acro-Corinthus. Aratus, being chosen general by the Argives, persuaded them to make a present to Antigonus of the property of the tyrants and the traitors. As for Aristomachus, after having put him to the rack in the town of Cenchreæ, they drowned him in the sea; for which, more than any thing else, Aratus was reproached, that he could suffer a man to be so lawlessly put to death, who was no bad man, had been one of his long acquaintance, and at his persuasion had abdicated his power, and annexed the city to the Achæans.

And already the blame of the other things that were done began to be laid to his account; as that they so lightly gave up Corinth to Antigonus, as if it had been an inconsiderable village; that they had suffered him, after first sacking Orchomenus, then to put into it a Macedonian garrison; that they made a decree that no letters nor embassy should be sent to any other king without the consent of Antigonus, that they were forced to furnish pay and provision for the Macedonian soldiers, and celebrated sacrifices, processions, and games in honor of Antigonus, Aratus's citizens setting the example and receiving Antigonus, who was lodged and entertained at Aratus's house. All these things they treated as his fault, not knowing that having once put the reins into Antigonus's hands, and let himself be borne by the impetus of regal power, he was no longer master of any thing but one single voice, the liberty of which it was not so very safe for him to use. For it was very plain that Aratus was much troubled at several things, as appeared by the business about the statues. For Antigonus replaced the statues of the tyrants of Argos that had been thrown down, and on the contrary threw down the statues of all those that had taken the Acro-Corinthus, except that of Aratus, nor could Aratus, by all his entreaties, dissuade him. Also, the usage of the Mantineans by the Achæans seemed not in accordance with the Grecian feelings and manners. For being masters of their city by the help of Antigonus, they put to death the chief and most noted men amongst them; and of the rest, some they sold, others they sent, bound in fetters, into Macedonia, and made slaves of their wives and children; and of the money thus raised, a third part they divided among themselves, and the other two thirds were distributed among the Macedonians. And this might seem to have been justified by the law of retaliation; for although it be a barbarous thing for men of the same nation and blood thus to deal with one another in their fury, yet necessity makes it, as Simonides says, sweet and something excusable,[11] being the proper thing, in the mind's painful and inflamed condition, to give alleviation and relief. But for what was afterwards done to that city, Aratus cannot be defended on any ground either of reason or necessity. For the Argives having had the city bestowed on them by Antigonus, and resolving to people it, he being then chosen as the new founder, and being general at that time, decreed that it should no longer be called Mantinea, but Antigonea, which name it still bears. So that he may be said to have been the cause that the old memory of the "beautiful Mantinea"[12] has been wholly extinguished, and the city to this day has the name of the destroyer and slayer of its citizens.

After this, Cleomenes, being overthrown in a great battle near Sellasia, forsook Sparta and fled into Egypt, and Antigonus, having shown all manner of kindness and fair-dealing to Aratus, retired into Macedonia. There, falling sick, he sent Philip, the heir of the kingdom, into Peloponnesus, being yet scarce a youth, commanding him to follow above all the counsel of Aratus, to communicate with the cities through him, and through him to make acquaintance with the Achæans; and Aratus, receiving him accordingly, so managed him as to send him back to Macedon both well affected to himself and full of desire and ambition to take an honorable part in the affairs of Greece.

When Antigonus was dead, the Ætolians, despising the sloth and negligence of the Achæans, who, hav-

[11] The fragment of Simonides is only known by this mention of it. It is probably confined to the words *sweet and something excusable.*

[12] Iliad 2, 607, where in that catalogue of the Arcadians present in the war, are mentioned "they that held Tegea, and the beautiful Mantinea."

ing learnt to be defended by other men's valor and to shelter themselves under the Macedonian arms, lived in ease and without any discipline, now attempted to interfere in Peloponnesus. And plundering the land of Patræ and Dyme in their way, they invaded Messene and ravaged it; at which Aratus being indignant, and finding that Timoxenus, then general, was hesitating and letting the time go by, being now on the point of laying down his office, in which he himself was chosen to succeed him, he anticipated the proper term by five days, that he might bring relief to the Messenians. And mustering the Achæans, who were both in their persons unexercised in arms and in their minds relaxed and averse to war, he met with a defeat at Caphyæ. Having thus begun the war, as it seemed, with too much heat and passion, he then ran into the other extreme, cooling again and desponding so much, that he let pass and overlooked many fair opportunities of advantage given by the Ætolians, and allowed them to run riot, as it were, throughout all Peloponnesus, with all manner of insolence and licentiousness. Wherefore, holding forth their hands once more to the Macedonians, they invited and drew in Philip to intermeddle in the affairs of Greece, chiefly hoping, because of his affection and trust that he felt for Aratus, they should find him easy-tempered, and ready to be managed as they pleased.

But the king, being now persuaded by Apelles, Megaleas, and other courtiers, that endeavored to ruin the credit Aratus had with him, took the side of the contrary faction, and joined them in canvassing to have Eperatus chosen general by the Achæans. But he being altogether scorned by the Achæans, and, for the want of Aratus to help, all things going wrong, Philip saw he had quite mistaken his part, and, turning about and reconciling himself to Aratus, he was wholly his; and his affairs now going on favorably both for his power and reputation, he depended upon him altogether as the author of all his gains in both respects; Aratus hereby giving a proof to the world that he was as good a nursing father of a kingdom as he had been of a democracy, for the actions of the king had in them the touch and color of his judgment and character. The moderation which the young man showed to the Lacedæmonians, who had incurred his displeasure, and his affability to the Cretans, by which in a few days he brought over the whole island to his obedience, and his expedition against the Ætolians, so wonderfully successful, brought Philip reputation for hearkening to good advice, and to Aratus for giving it; for which things the king's followers envying him more than ever, and finding they could not prevail against him by their secret practices, began openly to abuse and affront him at the banquets and over their wine, with every kind of petulance and impudence; so that once they threw stones at him as he was going back from supper to his tent. At which Philip being much offended, immediately fined them twenty talents; and finding afterwards that they still went on disturbing matters and doing mischief in his affairs, he put them to death.

But with his run of good success, prosperity began to puff him up, and various extravagant desires began to spring and show themselves in his mind; and his natural bad inclinations, breaking through the artificial restraints he had put upon them, in a little time laid open and discovered his true and proper character. And in the first place, he privately injured the younger Aratus in his wife, which was not known of a good while, because he was lodged and entertained at their house; then he began to be more rough and untractable in the domestic politics of Greece, and showed plainly that he was wishing to shake himself loose of Aratus. This the Messenian affairs first gave occasion to suspect. For they falling into sedition, and Aratus being just too late with his succors, Philip, who got into the city one day before him, at once blew up the flame of contention amongst them, asking privately, on the one hand, the Messenian generals, if they had not laws whereby to suppress the insolence of the common people, and on the other, the leaders of the people, whether they had not hands to help themselves against their oppressors. Upon which gathering courage, the officers attempted to lay hands on the heads of the people, and they on the other side, coming upon the officers with the multitude, killed them, and very near two hundred persons with them.

Philip having committed this wickedness, and doing his best to set the Messenians by the ears together more than before, Aratus arrived there, and both showed plainly that he took it ill himself, and also he suffered his son bitterly to reproach and revile him. It should seem that the young man had an attachment for Philip, and so at this time one of his expressions to him was, that he no longer appeared to him the handsomest, but the most deformed of all men, after so foul an action. To all which Philip gave him no answer, though he seemed so angry as to make it expected he would, and though several times he cried out aloud, while the young man was speaking. But as for the elder Aratus, seeming to take all that he said in good part, and as if he were by nature a politic character and had a good command of himself, he gave him his hand and led him out of the theatre, and carried him with him to the Ithomatas,[13] to sacrifice there to Jupiter, and take a view of the place, for it is a post as fortifiable as the Acro-Corinthus, and, with a garrison in it, quite as strong and as impregnable to the attacks of all around it. Philip therefore went up hither, and having offered sacrifice, receiving the entrails of the ox with both his hands from the priest, he showed them to Aratus and Demetrius the Pharian, presenting them sometimes to the one and sometimes to the other, asking them what they judged, by the tokens in the sacrifice, was to be done with the fort; was he to keep it for himself, or restore it to the Messenians. Demetrius laughed and answered, "If you have in you the soul of a soothsayer, you will restore it, but if of a prince, you will hold the ox by both the horns," meaning to refer to Peloponnesus, which would be wholly in his power and at his disposal if he added the Ithomatas to the Acro-Corinthus. Aratus said not a word for a good while; but Philip entreating him to declare his opinion, he said: "Many and great hills are there in Crete, and many rocks in Bœotia and Phocis, and many remarkable strong-holds both near the sea and in the midland in Acarnania, and yet all these people obey your orders, though you have not possessed yourself of any one of those places. Robbers nest themselves in rocks and precipices; but the strongest fort a king can have is confidence and affection. These have opened to you the Cretan sea; these make you master of Peloponnesus, and by the help of these, young as you are, are

[13] The Ithomatas (the name of the god himself) is used to mean the mount Ithome as sacred to and occupied by the temple of the Ithometan Jupiter, Zeus Ithomatas. Mount Ithome is said to be rather higher than the Acro-Corinthus, and even more remarkable in appearance.

ARATUS

you become captain of the one, and lord of the other." While he was still speaking, Philip returned the entrails to the priest, and drawing Aratus to him by the hand, "Come, then," said he, "let us follow the same course;" as if he felt himself forced by him, and obliged to give up the town.

From this time Aratus began to withdraw from court, and retired by degrees from Philip's company; when he was preparing to march into Epirus, and desired him that he would accompany him thither, he excused himself and stayed at home, apprehending that he should get nothing but discredit by having any thing to do with his actions. But when, afterwards, having shamefully lost his fleet against the Romans and miscarried in all his designs, he returned into Peloponnesus, where he tried once more to beguile the Messenians by his artifices, and failing in this, began openly to attack them and to ravage their country, then Aratus fell out with him downright, and utterly renounced his friendship; for he had begun then to be fully aware of the injuries done to his son in his wife, which vexed him greatly, though he concealed them from his son, as he could but know he had been abused, without having any means to revenge himself. For, indeed, Philip seems to have been an instance of the greatest and strangest alteration of character; after being a mild king and modest and chaste youth, he became a lascivious man and most cruel tyrant; though in reality this was not a change of his nature, but a bold unmasking, when safe opportunity came, of the evil inclinations which his fear had for a long time made him dissemble.

For that the respect he at the beginning bore to Aratus had a great alloy of fear and awe appears evidently from what he did to him at last. For being desirous to put him to death, not thinking himself, whilst he was alive, to be properly free as a man, much less at liberty to do his pleasure as a king or tyrant, he durst not attempt to do it by open force, but commanded Taurion, one of his captains and familiars, to make him away secretly by poison, if possible, in his absence. Taurion, therefore, made himself intimate with Aratus, and gave him a dose, not of your strong and violent poisons, but such as cause gentle, feverish heats at first, and a dull cough, and so by degrees bring on certain death. Aratus perceived what was done to him, but, knowing that it was in vain to make any words of it, bore it patiently and with silence, as if it had been some common and usual distemper. Only once, a friend of his being with him in his chamber, he spat some blood, which his friend observing and wondering at, "These, O Cephalon," said he, "are the wages of a king's love."

Thus died he in Ægium, in his seventeenth generalship. The Achæans were very desirous that he should be buried there with a funeral and monument suitable to his life, but the Sicyonians treated it as a calamity to them if he were interred anywhere but in their city, and prevailed with the Achæans to grant them the disposal of the body.

But there being an ancient law that no person should be buried within the walls of their city, and besides the law also a strong religious feeling about it, they sent to Delphi to ask counsel of the Pythoness, who returned this answer:—

> Sicyon, whom oft he rescued, "Where," you say,
> "Shall we the relics of Aratus lay?"
> The soil that would not lightly o'er him rest,
> Or to be under him would feel opprest,
> Were in the sight of earth and seas and skies unblest.

This oracle being brought, all the Achæans were well pleased at it, but especially the Sicyonians, who,

ARATUS

changing their mourning into public joy, immediately fetched the body from Ægium, and in a kind of solemn procession brought it into the city, being crowned with garlands, and arrayed in white garments, with singing and dancing, and, choosing a conspicuous place, they buried him there, as the founder and savior of their city. The place is to this day called Aratium, and there they yearly make two solemn sacrifices to him, the one on the day he delivered the city from tyranny, being the fifth of the month Dæsius, which the Athenians call Anthesterion, and this sacrifice they call Soteria;[14] the other in the month of his birth, which is still remembered. Now the first of these was performed by the priest of Jupiter Soter, the second by the priest of Aratus, wearing a band around his head, not pure white, but mingled with purple. Hymns were sung to the harp by the singers of the feasts of Bacchus; the procession was led up by the president of the public exercises, with the boys and young men; these were followed by the councillors wearing garlands, and other citizens such as pleased. Of these observances, some small traces, it is still made a point of religion not to omit, on the appointed day; but the greatest part of the ceremonies have through time and other intervening accidents been disused.

And such, as history tells us, was the life and manners of the elder Aratus. And for the younger, his

---

[14] *Soteria,* the feast of deliverance or safety, in which the priest of Zeus *Soter,* the savior or deliverer, performed the rite. The *singers,* or *professional people, of the feasts of Bacchus,* is the proper term used elsewhere for ordinary actors, including the performers in the choruses; the president of the gymnastic exercises, the *gymnasiarchus,* was in the times of political insignificance an important magistrate in the decaying Greek towns; compare the story at the beginning of the Life of Lucullus.

son, Philip, abominably wicked by nature and a savage abuser of his power, gave him such poisonous medicines, as though they did not kill him indeed, yet made him lose his senses, and run into wild and absurd attempts and desire to do actions and satisfy appetites that were ridiculous and shameful. So that his death, which happened to him while he was yet young and in the flower of his age, cannot be so much esteemed a misfortune as a deliverance and end of his misery. However, Philip paid dearly, all through the rest of his life, for these impious violations of friendship and hospitality. For, being overcome by the Romans, he was forced to put himself wholly into their hands, and, being deprived of his other dominions and surrendering all his ships except five, he had also to pay a fine of a thousand talents, and to give his son for hostage, and only out of mere pity he was suffered to keep Macedonia and its dependences; where continually putting to death the noblest of his subjects and the nearest relations he had, he filled the whole kingdom with horror and hatred of him. And whereas amidst so many misfortunes he had but one good chance, which was the having a son of great virtue and merit, him, through jealousy and envy at the honor the Romans had for him, he caused to be murdered, and left his kingdom to Perseus, who, as some say, was not his own child, but supposititious, born of a sempstress called Gnathænion. This was he whom Paulus Æmilius led in triumph, and in whom ended the succession of Antigonus's line and kingdom. But the posterity of Aratus continued still in our days at Sicyon and Pellene.

ARTAXERXES[1]

TRANSLATED BY MR. OAKLY.

THE first Artaxerxes, among all the kings of Persia the most remarkable for a gentle and noble spirit, was surnamed the Long-handed,[2] his right hand being longer than his left, and was the son of Xerxes. The second, whose story I am now writing, who had the surname of the Mindful,[2] was the grandson of the former, by his daughter Parysatis, who brought Darius four sons, the eldest Artaxerxes, the next Cyrus, and two younger than these, Ostanes and Oxathres. Cyrus took his name of the ancient Cyrus, as he, they say, had his from the sun, which, in the Persian language, is called Cyrus. Artaxerxes was at first called Arsicas; Dinon says Oarses; but it is utterly improbable that Ctesias (however otherwise he may have filled his books with a perfect farrago of incredible and senseless fables) should be ignorant of the name of the king with whom he lived as his physician, attending upon himself, his wife, his mother, and his children.

Cyrus, from his earliest youth, showed something of a headstrong and vehement character; Artaxerxes,

---

[1] Artaxerxes Mnemon, succeeded his father, Darius II., and reigned 405-359 B. C. He was succeeded by his son Ochus who had caused the destruction of two of his brothers, in order to secure the succession and who ruled under the name of Artaxerxes III. Plutarch is one of the chief authorities on this period of history.—Dr. William Smith.

[2] Artaxerxes Longimanus and Artaxerxes Mnemon.

on the other side, was gentler in every thing, and of a nature more yielding and soft in its action. He married a beautiful and virtuous wife, at the desire of his parents, but kept her as expressly against their wishes. For king Darius, having put her brother to death, was purposing likewise to destroy her. But Arsicas, throwing himself at his mother's feet, by many tears, at last, with much ado, persuaded her that they should neither put her to death nor divorce her from him. However, Cyrus was his mother's favorite, and the son whom she most desired to settle in the throne. And therefore, his father Darius now lying ill, he, being sent for from the sea to the court, set out thence with full hopes that by her means he was to be declared the successor to the kingdom. For Parysatis had the specious plea in his behalf, which Xerxes on the advice of Demaratus had of old made use of, that she had borne him Arsicas when he was a subject, but Cyrus when a king. Notwithstanding, she prevailed not with Darius, but the eldest son Arsicas was proclaimed king, his name being changed into Artaxerxes; and Cyrus remained satrap of Lydia, and commander in the maritime provinces.

It was not long after the decease of Darius that the king, his successor, went to Pasargadæ, to have the ceremony of his inauguration consummated by the Persian priests. There is a temple dedicated to a warlike goddess, whom one might liken to Minerva; into which when the royal person to be initiated has passed, he must strip himself of his own robe, and put on that which Cyrus the first wore before he was king; then, having devoured a frail of figs, he must eat turpentine, and drink a cup of sour milk. To which if they superadd any other rites, it is unknown to any but those that are present at them. Now Artaxerxes being about to address himself to this solemnity, Tisaphernes came to him, bringing a certain priest, who, having trained up Cyrus in his youth in the established discipline of Persia, and having taught him the Magian philosophy, was likely to be as much disappointed as any man that his pupil did not succeed to the throne. And for that reason his veracity was the less questioned when he charged Cyrus as though he had been about to lie in wait for the king in the temple, and to assault and assassinate him as he was putting off his garment. Some affirm that he was apprehended upon this impeachment, others that he had entered the temple and was pointed out there, as he lay lurking, by the priest. But as he was on the point of being put to death, his mother clasped him in her arms, and, entwining him with the tresses of her hair, joined his neck close to her own, and by her bitter lamentation and intercession to Artaxerxes for him, succeeded in saving his life; and sent him away again to the sea and to his former province. This, however, could no longer content him; nor did he so well remember his delivery as his arrest, his resentment for which made him more eagerly desirous of the kingdom than before.

Some say that he revolted from his brother, because he had not a revenue allowed him sufficient for his daily meals; but this is on the face of it absurd. For had he had nothing else, yet he had a mother ready to supply him with whatever he could desire out of her own means. But the great number of soldiers who were hired from all quarters and maintained, as Xenophon informs us, for his service, by his friends and connections, is in itself a sufficient proof of his riches. He did not assemble them together in a body, desiring as yet to conceal his enterprise; but he had agents everywhere, enlisting foreign soldiers upon various pretences; and, in the mean time, Parysatis, who was with the king, did her best to put aside all suspicions, and Cyrus himself always wrote in a humble and dutiful manner to him, sometimes soliciting favor, sometimes making counter-charges against Tisaphernes, as if his jealousy and contest had been wholly with him. Moreover, there was a certain natural dilatoriness in the king, which was taken by many for clemency. And, indeed, in the beginning of his reign, he did seem really to emulate the gentleness of the first Artaxerxes, being very accessible in his person, and liberal to a fault in the distribution of honors and favors. Even in his punishments, no contumely or vindictive pleasure could be seen; and those who offered him presents were as much pleased with his manner of accepting, as were those who received gifts from him with his graciousness and amiability in giving them. Nor truly was there any thing, however inconsiderable, given him, which he did not deign kindly to accept of; insomuch that when one Omises had presented him with a very large pomegranate, "By Mithras," said he, "this man, were he intrusted with it, would turn a small city into a great one."

Once when some were offering him one thing, some another, as he was on a progress, a certain poor laborer, having got nothing at hand to bring him, ran to the river side, and, taking up water in his hands, offered it to him; with which Artaxerxes was so well pleased that he sent him a goblet of gold and a thousand darics. To Euclidas, the Lacedæmonian, who had made a number of bold and arrogant speeches to him, he sent word by one of his officers, "You have leave to say what you please to me, and I, you should remember, may both say and do what I please to you." Teribazus once, when they were hunting, came up and pointed out to the king that his royal robe was torn; the king asked him what he wished him to do; and when Teribazus replied "May it please you to put on another and give me that," the king did so, saying withal, "I give it you, Teribazus, but I charge you not to wear it." He, little regarding the injunction, being not a bad, but a light-headed, thoughtless man, immediately the king took it off, put it on, and bedecked himself further with royal golden necklaces and women's ornaments, to the great scandal of everybody, the thing being quite unlawful. But the king laughed and told him, "You have my leave to wear the trinkets as a woman, and the robe of state as a fool." And whereas none usually sat down to eat with the king besides his mother and his wedded wife, the former being placed above, and the other below him, Artaxerxes invited also to his table his two younger brothers, Ostanes and Oxathres. But what was the most popular thing of all among the Persians was the sight of his wife Statira's chariot, which always appeared with its curtains down, allowing her countrywomen to salute and approach her, which made the queen a great favorite with the people.

Yet busy, factious men, that delighted in change, professed it to be their opinion that the times needed Cyrus, a man of a great spirit, an excellent warrior, and a lover of his friends, and that the largeness of their empire absolutely required a bold and enterprising prince. Cyrus, then, not only relying upon those of his own province near the sea, but upon many of those in the upper countries near the king, commenced the war against him. He wrote to the Lacedæmonians, bidding them come to his assistance and supply him with men, assuring them that to those who came to him on foot he would give horses, and to the horsemen chariots; that upon those who had farms he

would bestow villages, and those who were lords of
villages he would make so of cities; and that those
who would be his soldiers should receive their pay, not
by count, but by weight. And among many other high
praises of himself, he said he had the stronger soul;
was more a philosopher and a better Magian; and
could drink and bear more wine than his brother, who,
as he averred, was such a coward and so little like a
man, that he could neither sit his horse in hunting nor
his throne in time of danger. The Lacedæmonians, his
letter being read, sent a staff to Clearchus, commanding him to obey Cyrus in all things. So Cyrus marched
towards the king, having under his conduct a numerous host of barbarians, and but little less than thirteen
thousand stipendiary Grecians; alleging first one
cause, then another, for his expedition. Yet the true
reason lay not long concealed, but Tisaphernes went
to the king in person to declare it. Thereupon, the
court was all in an uproar and tumult, the queen-
mother bearing almost the whole blame of the enterprise, and her retainers being suspected and accused.
Above all, Statira angered her by bewailing the war
and passionately demanding where were now the
pledges and the intercessions which saved the life
of him that conspired against his brother; "to the end,"
she said, "that he might plunge us all into war and
trouble." For which words Parysatis hating Statira,
and being naturally inplacable and savage in her anger
and revenge, consulted how she might destroy her.
But since Dinon tells us that her purpose took effect
in the time of the war, and Ctesias says it was after it,
I shall keep the story for the place to which the latter
assigns it, as it is very unlikely that he, who was actually present, should not know the time when it happened, and there was no motive to induce him designedly to misplace its date in his narrative of it, though

it is not infrequent with him in his history to make excursions from truth into mere fiction and romance.

As Cyrus was upon the march, rumors and reports were brought him, as though the king still deliberated, and were not minded to fight and presently to join battle with him; but to wait in the heart of his kingdom until his forces should have come in thither from all parts of his dominions. He had cut a trench through the plain ten fathoms in breadth, and as many in depth, the length of it being no less than four hundred furlongs. Yet he allowed Cyrus to pass across it, and to advance almost to the city of Babylon. Then Teribazus, as the report goes, was the first that had the boldness to tell the king that he ought not to avoid the conflict, nor to abandon Media, Babylon, and even Susa, and hide himself in Persis, when all the while he had an army many times over more numerous than his enemies, and an infinite company of governors and captains that were better soldiers and politicians than Cyrus. So at last he resolved to fight, as soon as it was possible for him. Making, therefore, his first appearance, all on a sudden, at the head of nine hundred thousand well-marshalled men, he so startled and surprised the enemy, who with the confidence of contempt were marching on their way in no order, and with their arms not ready for use, that Cyrus, in the midst of much noise and tumult, was scarce able to form them for battle. Moreover, the very manner in which he led on his men, silently and slowly, made the Grecians stand amazed at his good discipline; who had expected irregular shouting and leaping, much confusion and separation between one body of men and another, in so vast a multitude of troops. He also placed the choicest of his armed chariots in the front of his own phalanx over against the Grecian troops, that a violent charge with these might cut open their ranks before they closed with them.

But as this battle is described by many historians, and Xenophon in particular as good as shows it us by eyesight, not as a past event, but as a present action, and by his vivid account makes his hearers feel all the passions and join in all the dangers of it, it would be folly in me to give any larger account of it than barely to mention any things omitted by him which yet deserve to be recorded. The place, then, in which the two armies were drawn out is called Cunaxa, being about five hundred furlongs distant from Babylon. And here Clearchus beseeching Cyrus before the fight to retire behind the combatants,[3] and not expose himself to hazard, they say he replied, "What is this, Clearchus? Would you have me, who aspire to empire, show myself unworthy of it?" But if Cyrus committed a great fault in entering headlong into the midst of danger, and not paying any regard to his own safety, Clearchus was as much to blame, if not more, in refusing to lead the Greeks against the main body of the enemy, where the king stood, and in keeping his right wing close to the river, for fear of being surrounded. For if he wanted, above all other things, to be safe, and considered it his first object to sleep in a whole skin, it had been his best way not to have stirred from home. But, after marching in arms ten thousand furlongs from the sea-coast, simply on his own choosing, for the purpose of placing Cyrus on the throne, to look about and select a position which would

---

[3] The manuscripts read, the *Macedonians*—which Amyot seems to have turned into Greeks (derrière la bataille des Grecs) —to make the meaning right; as there were of course no Macedonians. A later correction has been Lacedæmonians; but *makedonon*, Macedonians, is more justly taken as a corruption of *makhomenon*, combatants.

enable him, not to preserve him under whose pay and conduct he was, but himself to engage with more ease and security, seemed much like one that through fear of present dangers had abandoned the purpose of his actions, and been false to the design of his expedition. For it is evident from the very event of the battle that none of those who were in array around the king's person could have stood the shock of the Grecian charge; and had they been beaten out of the field, and Artaxerxes either fled or fallen, Cyrus would have gained by the victory, not only safety, but a crown. And, therefore, Clearchus, by his caution, must be considered more to blame for the result in the destruction of the life and fortune of Cyrus, than he by his heat and rashness. For had the king made it his business to discover a place, where having posted the Grecians, he might encounter them with the least hazard, he would never have found out any other but that which was remote from himself and those near him; of his defeat in which he was insensible, and, though Clearchus had the victory, yet Cyrus could not know of it, and could take no advantage of it before his fall. Cyrus knew well enough what was expedient to be done, and commanded Clearchus with his men to take their place in the centre. Clearchus replied that he would take care to have all arranged as was best, and then spoiled all.

For the Grecians, where they were, defeated the barbarians till they were weary, and chased them successfully a very great way. But Cyrus being mounted upon a noble but a headstrong and hard-mouthed horse, bearing the name, as Ctesias tells us, of Pasacas, Artagerses, the leader of the Cadusians, galloped up to him, crying aloud, "O most unjust and senseless of men, who are the disgrace of the honored name of Cyrus, are you come here leading the wicked Greeks on a wicked journey, to plunder the good things of the Persians, and this with the intent of slaying your lord and brother, the master of ten thousand times ten thousand servants that are better men than you? as you shall see this instant; for you shall lose your head here, before you look upon the face of the king." Which when he had said, he cast his javelin at him. But the coat of mail stoutly repelled it, and Cyrus was not wounded; yet the stroke falling heavy upon him, he reeled under it. Then Artagerses turning his horse, Cyrus threw his weapon, and sent the head of it through his neck near the shoulder bone. So that it is almost universally agreed to by all the authors that Artagerses was slain by him.

But as to the death of Cyrus, since Xenophon, as being himself no eye-witness of it, has stated it simply and in few words, it may not be amiss perhaps to run over on the one hand what Dinon, and on the other, what Ctesias has said of it.

Dinon then affirms, that, after the death of Artagerses, Cyrus, furiously attacking the guard of Artaxerxes, wounded the king's horse, and so dismounted him, and when Teribazus had quickly lifted him up upon another, and said to him, "O king, remember this day, which is not one to be forgotten," Cyrus, again spurring up his horse, struck down Artaxerxes. But at the third assault the king being enraged, and saying to those near him that death was more eligible, made up to Cyrus, who furiously and blindly rushed in the face of the weapons opposed to him. So the king struck him with a javelin, as likewise did those that were about him. And thus Cyrus falls, as some say, by the hand of the king; as others, by the dart of a Carian, to whom Artaxerxes, for a reward of his achievement, gave the privilege of carrying ever after a golden cock upon his spear before the first ranks of

CYRUS THE GREAT

the army in all expeditions. For the Persians call the men of Caria cocks, because of the crests with which they adorn their helmets.

But the account of Ctesias, to put it shortly, omitting many details, is as follows: Cyrus, after the death of Artagerses, rode up against the king, as he did against him, neither exchanging a word with the other. But Ariæus, Cyrus's friend, was beforehand with him, and darted first at the king, yet wounded him not. Then the king cast his lance at his brother, but missed him, though he both hit and slew Satiphernes, a noble man and a faithful friend to Cyrus. Then Cyrus directed his lance against the king, and pierced his breast with it quite through his armor, two inches deep, so that he fell from his horse with the stroke. At which those that attended him being put to flight and disorder, he, rising with a few, among whom was Ctesias, and making his way to a little hill not far off, rested himself. But Cyrus, who was in the thick of the enemy, was carried off a great way by the wildness of his horse, the darkness which was now coming on making it hard for them to know him, and for his followers to find him. However, being made elate with victory, and full of confidence and force, he passed through them, crying out, and that more than once, in the Persian language, "Clear the way, villains, clear the the way;" which they indeed did, throwing themselves down at his feet. But his tiara dropped off his head, and a young Persian, by name Mithridates, running by, struck a dart into one of his temples near his eye, not knowing who he was; out of which wound much blood gushed, so that Cyrus, swooning and senseless, fell off his horse. The horse escaped, and ran about the field; but the companion of Mithridates took the trappings, which fell off, soaked with blood. And as Cyrus slowly began to come to himself, some eunuchs

who were there tried to put him on another horse, and
so convey him safe away. And when he was not able
to ride, and desired to walk on his feet, they led and
supported him, being indeed dizzy in the head and
reeling, but convinced of his being victorious, hearing,
as he went, the fugitives saluting Cyrus as king, and
praying for grace and mercy. In the mean time, some
wretched, poverty-stricken Caunians, who in some
pitiful employment as camp-followers had accompanied the king's army, by chance joined these attendants of Cyrus, supposing them to be of their own
party. But when, after a while, they made out that
their coats over their breastplates were red, whereas
all the king's people wore white ones, they knew that
they were enemies. One of them, therefore, not
dreaming that it was Cyrus, ventured to strike him
behind with a dart. The vein under the knee was cut
open, and Cyrus fell, and at the same time struck his
wounded temple against a stone, and so died. Thus
runs Ctesias's account, tardily, with the slowness of
a blunt weapon, effecting the victim's death.

When he was now dead, Artasyras, the king's eye,[4]
passed by on horseback, and, having observed the
eunuchs lamenting, he asked the most trusty of them,
"Who is this, Pariscas, whom you sit here deploring?"
He replied, "Do you not see, O Artasyras, that it is my
master, Cyrus?" Then Artasyras wondering, bade the
eunuch be of good cheer, and keep the dead body safe.
And going in all haste to Artaxerxes, who had now

---

[4] The *King's eyes* and the *King's ears* were the official titles
of particular officers of the Persian government, and are mentioned by Aristotle and Xenophon. Aristophanes also brings upon
the stage, in his Acharnians, a grotesque personage with the name
of the *King's eye*, whom certain ambassadors have brought down
to Athens out of Persia, and who utters some barbarous Greek
words.

given up all hope of his affairs, and was in great suffering also with his thirst and his wound, he with much joy assured him that he had seen Cyrus dead. Upon this, at first, he set out to go in person to the place, and commanded Artasyras to conduct him where he lay. But when there was a great noise made about the Greeks, who were said to be in full pursuit, conquering and carrying all before them, he thought it best to send a number of persons to see; and accordingly thirty men went with torches in their hands. Meantime, as he seemed to be almost at the point of dying from thirst, his eunuch Satibarzanes ran about seeking drink for him; for the place had no water in it, and he was at a good distance from his camp. After a long search he at last luckily met with one of those poor Caunian camp-followers, who had in a wretched skin about four pints of foul and stinking water, which he took and gave to the king; and when he had drunk all off, he asked him if he did not dislike the water; but he declared by all the gods, that he never so much relished either wine, or water out of the lightest or purest stream. "And therefore," said he, "if I fail myself to discover and reward him who gave it to you, I beg of heaven to make him rich and prosperous."

Just after this, came back the thirty messengers, with joy and triumph in their looks, bringing him the tidings of his unexpected fortune. And now he was also encouraged by the number of soldiers that again began to flock in and gather about him; so that he presently descended into the plain with many lights and flambeaus round about him. And when he had come near the dead body, and, according to a certain law of the Persians, the right hand and head had been lopped off from the trunk, he gave orders that the latter should be brought to him, and, grasping the hair of it, which was long and bushy, he showed it to those who were still uncertain and disposed to fly. They were amazed at it, and did him homage; so that there were presently seventy thousand of them got about him, and entered the camp again with him. He had led out to the fight, as Ctesias affirms, four hundred thousand men. But Dinon and Xenophon aver that there were many more than forty myriads actually engaged. As to the number of the slain, as the catalogue of them was given up to Artaxerxes, Ctesias says, they were nine thousand, but that they appeared to him no fewer than twenty thousand. Thus far there is something to be said on both sides. But it is a flagrant untruth on the part of Ctesias to say that he was sent along with Phalinus the Zacynthian and some others to the Grecians. For Xenophon knew well enough that Ctesias was resident at court; for he makes mention of him, and had evidently met with his writings. And, therefore, had he come, and been deputed the interpreter of such momentous words, Xenophon surely would not have struck his name out of the embassy to mention only Phalinus. But Ctesias, as is evident, being excessively vain-glorious, and no less a favorer of the Lacedæmonians and Clearchus, never fails to assume to himself some province in his narrative, taking opportunity, in these situations, to introduce abundant high praise of Clearchus and Sparta.

When the battle was over, Artaxerxes sent goodly and magnificent gifts to the son of Artagerses, whom Cyrus slew. He conferred likewise high honors upon Ctesias and others, and, having found out the Caunian who gave him the bottle of water, he made him, of a poor, obscure man, a rich and an honorable person. As for the punishments he inflicted upon delinquents, there was a kind of harmony betwixt them and the crimes. He gave order that one Arbaces, a

Mede, that had fled in the fight to Cyrus, and again at his fall had come back, should, as a mark that he was considered a dastardly and effeminate, not a dangerous or treasonable man, have a common harlot set upon his back, and carry her about for a whole day in the market-place. Another, besides that he had deserted to them, having falsely vaunted that he had killed two of the rebels, he decreed that three needles should be struck through his tongue. And both supposing that with his own hand he had cut off Cyrus, and being willing that all men should think and say so, he sent rich presents to Mithridates, who first wounded him, and charged those by whom he conveyed the gifts to him to tell him, that "the king has honored you with these his favors, because you found and brought him the horse-trappings of Cyrus." The Carian, also, from whose wound in the ham Cyrus died, suing for his reward, he commanded those that brought it to him to say that "the king presents you with this as a second remuneration for the good news told him; for first Artasyras, and, next to him, you assured him of the decease of Cyrus." Mithridates retired without complaint, though not without resentment. But the unfortunate Carian was fool enough to give way to a natural infirmity. For being ravished with the sight of the princely gifts that were before him, and being tempted thereupon to challenge and aspire to things above him, he deigned not to accept the king's present as a reward for good news, but indignantly crying out and appealing to witnesses, he protested that he, and none but he, had killed Cyrus, and that he was unjustly deprived of the glory. These words, when they came to his ear, much offended the king, so that forthwith he sentenced him to be beheaded. But the queen mother, being in the king's presence, said, "Let not the king so lightly discharge this pernicious Carian; let him receive from me the fitting punishment of what he dares to say." So when the king had consigned him over to Parysatis, she charged the executioners to take up the man, and stretch him upon the rack for ten days, then, tearing out his eyes, to drop molten brass into his ears till he expired.

Mithridates, also, within a short time after, miserably perished by the like folly; for being invited to a feast where were the eunuchs both of the king and of the queen mother, he came arrayed in the dress and the golden ornaments which he had received from the king. After they began to drink, the eunuch that was the greatest in power with Parysatis thus speaks to him: "A magnificent dress, indeed, O Mithridates, is this which the king has given you; the chains and bracelets are glorious, and your scymetar of invaluable worth; how happy has he made you, the object of every eye!" To whom he, being a little overcome with the wine replied, "What are these things, Sparamizes? Sure I am, I showed myself to the king in that day of trial to be one deserving greater and costlier gifts than these." At which Sparamizes smiling, said, "I do not grudge them to you Mithridates; but since the Grecians tell us that wine and truth go together, let me hear now, my friend, what glorious or mighty matter was it to find some trappings that had slipped off a horse, and to bring them to the king?" And this he spoke, not as ignorant of the truth, but desiring to unbosom him to the company, irritating the vanity of the man, whom drink had now made eager to talk and incapable of controlling himself. So he forebore nothing, but said out, "Talk you what you please of horse-trappings, and such trifles; I tell you plainly, that this hand was the death of Cyrus. For I threw not my dart as Artagerses did, in vain and to no purpose, but only just missing his eye, and hitting him right on the temple, and piercing him through, I brought him to the ground; and of that wound he died." The rest of the company, who saw the end and the hapless fate of Mithridates as if it were already completed, bowed their heads to the ground; and he who entertained them said, "Mithridates, my friend, let us eat and drink now, revering the fortune of our prince, and let us waive discourse which is too weighty for us."

Presently after, Sparamizes told Parysatis what he said, and she told the king, who was greatly enraged at it, as having the lie given him, and being in danger to forfeit the most glorious and most pleasant circumstance of his victory. For it was his desire that every one, whether Greek or barbarian, should believe that in the mutual assaults and conflicts between him and his brother, he, giving and receiving a blow, was himself indeed wounded, but that the other lost his life. And, therefore, he decreed that Mithridates should be put to death in boats; which execution is after the following manner: Taking two boats framed exactly to fit and answer each other, they lay down in one of them the malefactor that suffers, upon his back; then, covering it with the other, and so setting them together that the head, hands, and feet of him are left outside, and the rest of his body lies shut up within, they offer him food, and if he refuse to eat it, they force him to do it by pricking his eyes; then, after he has eaten, they drench him with a mixture of milk and honey, pouring it not only into his mouth, but all over his face. They then keep his face continually turned towards the sun; and it becomes completely covered up and hidden by the multitude of flies that settle on it. And as within the boats he does what those that eat and drink must needs do, creeping things and vermin spring out of the corruption and rottenness of the excrement, and these entering into the bowels of him, his body is consumed. When the man is manifestly dead, the uppermost boat being taken off, they find his flesh devoured, and swarms of such noisome creatures preying upon and, as it were, growing to his inwards. In this way Mithridates, after suffering for seventeen days, at last expired.

Masabates, the king's eunuch, who had cut off the hand and head of Cyrus, remained still as a mark for Parysatis's vengeance. Whereas, therefore, he was so circumspect, that he gave her no advantage against him, she framed this kind of snare for him. She was a very ingenious woman in other ways, and was an excellent player at dice, and, before the war, had often played with the king. After the war, too, when she had been reconciled to him, she joined readily in all amusements with him, played at dice with him, was his confidant in his love matters, and in every way did her best to leave him as little as possible in the company of Statira, both because she hated her more than any other person, and because she wished to have no one so powerful as herself. And so once when Artaxerxes was at leisure, and inclined to divert himself, she challenged him to play at dice with her for a thousand Darics, and purposely let him win them, and paid him down in gold. Yet, pretending to be concerned for her loss, and that she would gladly have her revenge for it, she pressed him to begin a new game for a eunuch; to which he consented. But first they agreed that each of them might except five of their most trusty eunuchs, and that out of the rest of them the loser should yield up any the winner should make choice of. Upon these conditions they played. Thus being bent upon her design, and thoroughly in earnest with her game, and the dice also running luckily for her, when she had got the game, she demanded Masabates, who was not in the number of the five excepted. And before the king could suspect the matter, having delivered him up to the tormentors, she enjoined them to flay him alive, to set his body upon three stakes, and to stretch his skin upon stakes separately from it.

These things being done, and the king taking them ill, and being incensed against her, she with raillery and laughter told him, "You are a comfortable and happy man indeed, if you are so much disturbed for the sake of an old rascally eunuch, when I, though I have thrown away a thousand Darics, hold my peace and acquiesce in my fortune." So the king, vexed with himself for having been thus deluded, hushed up all. But Statira both in other matters openly opposed her, and was angry with her for thus, against all law and humanity, sacrificing to the memory of Cyrus the king's faithful friends and eunuchs.

Now after that Tisaphernes had circumvented and by a false oath had betrayed Clearchus and the other commanders, and, taking them, had sent them bound in chains to the king, Ctesias says that he was asked by Clearchus to supply him with a comb; and that when he had it, and had combed his head with it, he was much pleased with this good office, and gave him a ring, which might be a token of the obligation to his relatives and friends in Sparta; and that the engraving upon this signet was a set of Caryatides dancing.[5] He tells us that the soldiers, his fellow captives, used to purloin a part of the allowance of food sent to

---

[5] Carya, or Caryæ, was a spot in Laconia sacred to Artemis and the nymphs, where there was an image of Artemis Caryatid. Here continues Pausanias, the Lacedæmonian maidens hold yearly dances, and perform a particular dance of the country. Pausanias, III., 10.

Clearchus, giving him but little of it; which thing Ctesias says he rectified, causing a better allowance to be conveyed to him, and that a separate share should be distributed to the soldiers by themselves; adding that he ministered to and supplied him thus by the interest and at the instance of Parysatis. And there being a portion of ham sent daily with his other food to Clearchus, she, he says, advised and instructed him, that he ought to bury a small knife in the meat, and thus send it to his friend, and not leave his fate to be determined by the king's cruelty; which he, however, he says, was afraid to do. However, Artaxerxes consented to the entreaties of his mother, and promised her with an oath that he would spare Clearchus; but afterwards, at the instigation of Statira, he put every one of them to death except Menon. And thenceforward he says, Parysatis watched her advantage against Statira, and made up poison for her; not a very probable story, or a very likely motive to account for her conduct, if indeed he means that out of respect to Clearchus she dared to attempt the life of the lawful queen, that was mother of those who were heirs of the empire. But it is evident enough, that this part of his history is a sort of funeral exhibition in honor of Clearchus. For he would have us believe, that, when the generals were executed, the rest of them were torn in pieces by dogs and birds; but as for the remains of Clearchus, that a violent gust of wind, bearing before it a vast heap of earth, raised a mound to cover his body, upon which, after a short time, some dates having fallen there, a beautiful grove of trees grew up and overshadowed the place, so that the king himself declared his sorrow, concluding that in Clearchus he put to death a man beloved of the gods.

Parysatis, therefore, having from the first entertained a secret hatred and jealousy against Statira, seeing that the power she herself had with Artaxerxes was founded upon feelings of honor and respect for her, but that Statira's influence was firmly and strongly based upon love and confidence, was resolved to contrive her ruin, playing at hazard, as she thought, for the greatest stake in the world. Among her attendant women there was one that was trusty and in the highest esteem with her, whose name was Gigis; who, as Dinon avers, assisted in making up the poison. Ctesias allows her only to have been conscious of it, and that against her will; charging Belitaras with actually giving the drug, whereas Dinon says it was Melantas. The two women had begun again to visit each other and to eat together; but though they had thus far relaxed their former habits of jealousy and variance, still, out of fear and as a matter of caution, they always ate of the same dishes and of the same parts of them. Now there is a small Persian bird, in the inside of which no excrement is found, only a mass of fat, so that they suppose the little creature lives upon air and dew. It is called *rhyntaces*. Ctesias affirms, that Parysatis, cutting a bird of this kind into two pieces with a knife, one side of which had been smeared with the drug, the other side being clear of it, ate the untouched and wholesome part herself, and gave Statira that which was thus infected; but Dinon will not have it to be Parysatis, but Melantas, that cut up the bird and presented the envenomed part of it to Statira, who, dying with dreadful agonies and convulsions, was herself sensible of what had happened to her, and aroused in the king's mind suspicion of his mother, whose savage and implacable temper he knew. And therefore proceeding instantly to an inquest, he seized upon his mother's domestic servants that attended at her table, and put them upon the rack. Parysatis kept Gigis at home with her a long time, and, though the king commanded her, she would not produce her. But she, at last, herself desiring that she might be dismissed to her own home by night, Artaxerxes had intimation of it, and, lying in wait for her, hurried her away, and adjudged her to death. Now poisoners in Persia suffer thus by law. There is a broad stone, on which they place the head of the culprit, and then with another stone beat and press it, until the face and head itself are all pounded to pieces; which was the punishment Gigis lost her life by. But to his mother, Artaxerxes neither said nor did any other hurt, save that he banished and confined her, not much against her will, to Babylon, protesting that while she lived he would not come near that city. Such was the condition of the king's affairs in his own house.

But when all his attempts to capture the Greeks that had come up with Cyrus, though he desired to do so no less than he had desired to overcome Cyrus and maintain his throne, proved unsuccessful, and they though they had lost both Cyrus and their own generals, nevertheless escaped, as it were, out of his very palace, making it plain to all men that the Persian king and his empire were mighty indeed in gold and luxury and women, but otherwise were mere show and vain display, upon this, all Greece took courage, and despised the barbarians; and especially the Lacedæmonians thought it strange if they should not now deliver their countrymen that dwelt in Asia from their subjection to the Persians, nor put an end to the contumelious usage of them. And first having an army under the conduct of Thimbron, then under Dercyllidas, but doing nothing memorable, they at last committed the war to the management of their king Agesilaus, who, when he had arrived with his men in Asia, as soon as he had landed them, fell actively to work, and got himself great renown. He defeated Tisaphernes in a pitched battle, and set many cities in revolt. Upon this, Artaxerxes, perceiving what was his wisest way of waging the war, sent Timocrates the Rhodian into Greece, with large sums of gold, commanding him by a free distribution of it to corrupt the leading men in the cities, and to excite a Greek war against Sparta. So Timocrates following his instructions, the most considerable cities conspiring together, and Peloponnesus being in disorder, the ephors remanded Agesilaus from Asia. At which time, they say, as he was upon his return, he told his friends that Artaxerxes had driven him out of Asia with thirty thousand archers; the Persian coin having an archer stamped upon it.

Artaxerxes scoured the seas, too, of the Lacedæmonians, Conon the Athenian and Pharnabazus being his admirals. For Conon, after the battle of Ægospotami, resided in Cyprus; not that he consulted his own mere security, but looking for a vicissitude of affairs with no less hope than men wait for a change of wind at sea. And perceiving that his skill wanted power, and that the king's power wanted a wise man to guide it, he sent him an account by letter of his projects, and charged the bearer to hand it to the king, if possible, by the mediation of Zeno the Cretan or Polycritus the Mendæan (the former being a dancing-master, the latter a physician), or, in the absence of them both, by Ctesias; who is said to have taken Conon's letter, and foisted into the contents of it a request, that the king would also be pleased to send over Ctesias to him, who was likely to be of use on the sea-coast. Ctesias, however, declares that the king, of his own accord, deputed him to this service. Artaxerxes, however, defeating the Lacedæmonians in a sea-fight at Cnidos, under the conduct of Pharnabazus and Conon, after he had stripped them of their sovereignty by sea, at the same time, brought, so to say, the whole of Greece over to him, so that upon his own terms he dictated the celebrated peace among them, styled the peace of Antalcidas. This Antalcidas was a Spartan, the son of one Leon, who, acting for the king's interest, induced the Lacedæmonians to covenant to let all the Greek cities in Asia and the islands adjacent to it become subject and tributary to him, peace being upon these conditions established among the Greeks, if indeed the honorable name of peace can fairly be given to what was in fact the disgrace and betrayal of Greece, a treaty more inglorious than had ever been the result of any war to those defeated in it.

And therefore Artaxerxes, though always abominating other Spartans, and looking upon them, as Dinon says, to be the most impudent men living, gave wonderful honor to Antalcidas when he came to him into Persia; so much so that one day, taking a garland of flowers and dipping it in the most precious ointment, he sent it to him after supper, a favor which all were amazed at. Indeed he was a person fit to be thus delicately treated, and to have such a crown, who had among the Persians thus made fools of Leonidas and Callicratidas. Agesilaus, it seems, on some one having said, "O the deplorable fate of Greece, now that the Spartans turn Medes!" replied, "Nay, rather it is the Medes who become Spartans." But the subtilty of the repartee did not wipe off the infamy of the action. The Lacedæmonians soon after lost their sovereignty in Greece by their defeat at Leuctra; but they had already lost their honor by this treaty. So long then as Sparta continued to be the first state in Greece, Artaxerxes continued to Antalcidas the honor of being called his friend and his guest; but when, routed and humbled at the battle of Leuctra, being under great distress for money, they had despatched Agesilaus into Egypt, and Antalcidas went up to Artaxerxes, beseeching him to supply their necessities, he so despised, slighted, and rejected him, that finding himself, on his return, mocked and insulted by his enemies, and fearing also the ephors, he starved himself to death. Ismenias, also, the Theban, and Pelopidas, who had already gained the victory at Leuctra, arrived at the Persian court; where the latter did nothing unworthy of himself. But Ismenias, being commanded to do obeisance to the king, dropped his ring before him upon the ground, and so, stooping to take it up, made a show of doing him homage. He was so gratified with some secret intelligence which Timagoras the Athenian sent in to him by the hand of his secretary, Beluris, that he bestowed upon him ten thousand darics, and because he was ordered, on account of some sickness, to drink cow's milk, there were fourscore milch kine driven after him; also, he sent him a bed, furniture, and servants for it, the Grecians not having skill enough to make it, as also chairmen to carry him, being infirm in body, to the sea-side. Not to mention the feast made for him at court, which was so princely and splendid that Ostanes, the king's brother, said to him, "O, Timagoras, do not forget the sumptuous table you have sat at here; it was not put before you for nothing;" which was indeed rather a reflection upon his treason than to remind him of the king's bounty. And indeed the Athenians condemned Timagoras to death for taking bribes.

But Artaxerxes gratified the Grecians in one thing in lieu of the many wherewith he plagued them, and that was by taking off Tisaphernes, their most hated and malicious enemy, whom he put to death; Parysatis adding her influence to the charges made against him. For the king did not persist long in his wrath with his mother, but was reconciled to her, and sent for her, being assured that she had wisdom and courage fit for royal power, and there being now no cause discernible but that they might converse together without suspicion or offence. And from thence forward humoring the king in all things according to his heart's desire, and finding fault with nothing that he did, she obtained great power with him, and was gratified in all her requests. She perceived he was desperately in love with Atossa, one of his own two daughters, and that he concealed and checked his passion chiefly for fear of herself, though, if we may believe some writers, he had privately given way to it with the young girl already. As soon as Parysatis suspected it, she displayed a greater fondness for the young girl than before, and extolled both her virtue and beauty to him, as being truly imperial and majestic. In fine, she persuaded him to marry her and declare her to be his lawful wife, overriding all the principles and the laws by which the Greeks hold themselves bound, and regarding himself as divinely appointed for a law to the Persians, and the supreme arbitrator of good and evil. Some historians further affirm, in which number is Heraclides of Cuma, that Artaxerxes married not only this one, but a second daughter also, Amestris, of whom we shall speak by and by. But he so loved Atossa when she became his consort, that when leprosy had run through her whole body, he was not in the least offended at it; but putting up his prayers to Juno for her, to this one alone of all the deities he made obeisance, by laying his hands upon the earth; and his satraps and favorites made such offerings to the goddess by his direction, that all along for sixteen furlongs, betwixt the court and her temple, the road was filled up with gold and silver, purple and horses, devoted to her.

He waged war out of his own kingdom with the Egyptians, under the conduct of Pharnabazus and Iphicrates, but was unsuccessful by reason of their dissensions. In his expedition against the Cadusians, he went himself in person with three hundred thousand footmen and ten thousand horse. And making an incursion into their country, which was so mountainous as scarcely to be passable, and withal very misty, producing no sort of harvest of corn or the like, but with pears, apples, and other tree-fruits feeding a warlike and valiant breed of men, he unawares fell into great distresses and dangers. For there was nothing to be got, fit for his men to eat, of the growth of that place, nor could any thing be imported from any other. All they could do was to kill their beasts of burden, and thus an ass's head could scarcely be bought for sixty drachmas. In short, the king's own table failed; and there were but few horses left; the rest they had spent for food. Then Teribazus, a man often in great favor with his prince for his valor, and as often out of it for his buffoonery, and particularly at that time in humble estate and neglected, was the deliverer of the king and his army. There being two kings amongst the Cadusians, and each of them encamping separately, Teribazus, after he made his application to Artaxerxes and imparted his design to him, went to one of the princes, and sent away his son privately to the other. So each of them deceived his man, assuring him that the other prince had deputed an ambassador to Artaxerxes, suing for friendship and alliance for himself alone; and, therefore, if he were wise, he told him, he must apply himself to his master before he had decreed any thing, and he, he said, would lend him his assistance in all things. Both

of them gave credit to these words, and because they
supposed they were each intrigued against by the
other, they both sent their envoys, one along with
Teribazus, and the other with his son. All this taking
some time to transact, fresh surmises and suspicions
of Teribazus were expressed to the king, who began
to be out of heart, sorry that he had confided in him,
and ready to give ear to his rivals who impeached
him. But at last he came, and so did his son, bringing
the Cadusian agents along with them, and so there
was a cessation of arms and a peace signed with both
the princes. And Teribazus, in great honor and distinction, set out homewards in the company of the
king; who, indeed, upon this journey made it appear
plainly that cowardice and effeminacy are the effects,
not of delicate and sumptuous living, as many suppose, but of a base and vicious nature, actuated by
false and bad opinions. For notwithstanding his
golden ornaments, his robe of state, and the rest of
that costly attire, worth no less than twelve thousand
talents, with which the royal person was constantly
clad, his labors and toils were not a whit inferior to
those of the meanest persons in his army. With his
quiver by his side and his shield on his arm, he led
them on foot, quitting his horse, through craggy and
steep ways, insomuch that the sight of his cheerfulness and unwearied strength gave wings to the soldiers, and so lightened the journey, that they made
daily marches of above two hundred furlongs.

After they had arrived at one of his own mansions,
which had beautiful ornamented parks in the midst of
a region naked and without trees, the weather being
very cold, he gave full commission to his soldiers to
provide themselves with wood by cutting down any,
without exception, even the pine and cypress. And
when they hesitated and were for sparing them, being

large and goodly trees, he, taking up an axe himself, felled the greatest and most beautiful of them. After which his men used their hatchets, and piling up many fires, passed away the night at their ease. Nevertheless, he returned not without the loss of many and valiant subjects, and of almost all his horses. And supposing that his misfortunes and the ill success of his expedition made him despised in the eyes of his people, he looked jealously on his nobles, many of whom he slew in anger, and yet more out of fear. As, indeed, fear is the bloodiest passion in princes; confidence, on the other hand, being merciful, gentle, and unsuspicious. So we see among wild beasts, the intractable and least tamable are the most timorous and most easily startled; the nobler creatures, whose courage makes them trustful, are ready to respond to the advances of men.

Artaxerxes, now being an old man, perceived that his sons were in controversy about his kingdom, and that they made parties among his favorites and peers. Those that were equitable among them thought it fit, that as he had received it, so he should bequeathe it, by right of age, to Darius. The younger brother, Ochus, who was hot and violent, had indeed a considerable number of the courtiers that espoused his interest, but his chief hope was that by Atossa's means he should win his father. For he flattered her with the thoughts of being his wife and partner in the kingdom after the death of Artaxerxes. And truly it was rumored that already Ochus maintained a too intimate correspondence with her. This, however, was quite unknown to the king; who, being willing to put down in good time his son Ochus's hopes, lest, by his attempting the same things his uncle Cyrus did, wars and contentions might again afflict his kingdom, proclaimed Darius, then twenty-five[6] years old, his successor, and gave him leave to wear the upright hat, as they call it. It was a rule and usage of Persia, that the heir apparent to the crown should beg a boon, and that he that declared him so should give whatever he asked, provided it were within the sphere of his power. Darius therefore requested Aspasia, in former time the most prized of the concubines of Cyrus, and now belonging to the king. She was by birth a Phocæan, of Ionia, born of free parents, and well educated. Once when Cyrus was at supper, she was led in to him with other women, who, when they were sat down by him, and he began to sport and dally and talk jestingly with them, gave way freely to his advances. But she stood by in silence, refusing to come when Cyrus called her, and when his chamberlains were going to force her towards him, said, "Whosoever lays hands on me shall rue it;" so that she seemed to the company a sullen and rude-mannered person. However, Cyrus was well pleased, and laughed, saying to the man that brought the women, "Do you not see of a certainty that this woman alone of all that came with you is truly noble and pure in character?" After which time he began to regard her, and loved her above all of her sex, and called her the Wise. But Cyrus being slain in the fight, she was taken among the spoils of his camp.

Darius, in demanding her, no doubt much offended his father, for the barbarian people keep a very jealous and watchful eye over their carnal pleasures, so

[6] The manuscripts read "fifty,"*pentecostom*, corrected on conjecture to *pemptom kai eikoston*. Fifty seems inconsistent with the language of Plutarch a little further on, where he speaks of him as a young man. But the length of the reign of Artaxerxes, if it really lasted, as Plutarch says, for sixty-two years, is quite out of keeping with this youthfulness of the son and declared successor; and scarcely compatible at all with the story of his passion for Aspasia.

that it is death for a man not only to come near and touch any concubine of his prince, but likewise on a journey to ride forward and pass by the carriages in which they are conveyed. And though, to gratify his passion, he had against all law married his daughter Atossa, and had besides her no less than three hundred and sixty concubines selected for their beauty, yet being importuned for that one by Darius, he urged that she was a free-woman, and allowed him to take her, if she had an inclination to go with him, but by no means to force her away against it. Aspasia, therefore, being sent for, and, contrary to the king's expectation, making choice of Darius, he gave him her indeed, being constrained by law, but when he had done so, a little after he took her from him. For he consecrated her priestess to Diana of Ecbatana, whom they name Anaitis, that she might spend the remainder of her days in strict chastity, thinking thus to punish his son, not rigorously, but with moderation, by a revenge chequered with jest and earnest. But he took it heinously, either that he was passionately fond of Aspasia, or because he looked upon himself as affronted and scorned by his father. Teribazus, perceiving him thus minded, did his best to exasperate him yet further, seeing in his injuries a representation of his own, of which the following is the account: Artaxerxes, having many daughters, promised to give Apama to Pharnabazus to wife, Rhodogone to Orontes, and Amestris to Teribazus; whom alone of the three he disappointed, by marrying Amestris himself. However, to make him amends, he betrothed his youngest daughter Atossa to him. But after he had, being enamored of her too, as has been said, married her, Teribazus entertained an irreconcilable enmity against him. As indeed he was seldom at any other time steady in his temper, but uneven and inconsiderate; so that whether he were in the number of the choicest favorites of his prince, or whether he were offensive and odius to him, he demeaned himself in neither condition with moderation; but if he was advanced he was intolerably insolent, and in his degradation not submissive and peaceable in his deportment, but fierce and haughty.

And therefore Teribazus was to the young prince flame added upon flame, ever urging him, and saying, that in vain those wear their hats upright who consult not the real success of their affairs, and that he was ill befriended of reason if he imagined, whilst he had a brother, who, through the women's apartments, was seeking a way to the supremacy, and a father of so rash and fickle a humor, that he should by succession infallibly step up into the throne. For he that out of fondness to an Ionian girl has eluded a law sacred and inviolable among the Persians is not likely to be faithful in the performance of the most important promises. He added, too, that it was not all one for Ochus not to attain to, and for him to be put by his crown; since Ochus as a subject might live happily, and nobody could hinder him; but he, being proclaimed king, must either take up his sceptre or lay down his life. These words presently inflamed Darius; what Sophocles says being indeed generally true:—

Quick travels the persuasion to what's wrong.[7]

For the path is smooth, and upon an easy descent, that leads us to our own will; and the most part of us desire what is evil through our strangeness to and ignorance of good. And in this case, no doubt, the greatness of the empire and the jealousy Darius had of Ochus furnished Teribazus with material for his persuasions. Nor was Venus wholly unconcerned, in the matter, in regard, namely, of his loss of Aspasia.

[7] An uncertain fragment, No. 57; 714 in Dindorf.

Darius, therefore, resigned himself up to the dictates of Teribazus; and many now conspiring with them, a eunuch gave information to the king of their plot and the way how it was to be managed, having discovered the certainty of it, that they had resolved to break into his bed-chamber by night, and there to kill him as he lay. After Artaxerxes had been thus advised, he did not think fit, by disregarding the discovery, to despise so great a danger, nor to believe it when there was little or no proof of it. Thus then he did: he charged the eunuch constantly to attend and accompany the conspirators wherever they were; in the mean while, he broke down the party-wall of the chamber behind his bed, and placed a door in it to open and shut, which covered up with tapestry; so the hour approaching, and the eunuch having told him the precise time in which the traitors designed to assassinate him, he waited for them in his bed, and rose not up till he had seen the faces of his assailants and recognized every man of them. But as soon as he saw them with their swords drawn and coming up to him, throwing up the hanging, he made his retreat into the inner chamber, and, bolting to the door, raised a cry. Thus when the murderers had been seen by him, and had attempted him in vain, they with speed went back through the same doors they came in by, enjoining Teribazus and his friends to fly, as their plot had been certainly detected. They, therefore, made their escape different ways; but Teribazus was seized by the king's guards, and after slaying many, while they were laying hold on him, at length being struck through with a dart at a distance, fell. As for Darius, who was brought to trial with his children, the king appointed the royal judges to sit over him, and because he was not himself present, but accused Darius by proxy, he commanded his scribes to write down the opinion of every one of the judges, and show it to him. And after they had given their sentences, all as one man, and condemned Darius to death, the officers seized on him and hurried him to a chamber not far off. To which place the executioner when summoned, came with a razor in his hand, with which men of his employment cut off the heads of offenders. But when he saw that Darius was the person thus to be punished, he was appalled and started back, offering to go out, as one that had neither power nor courage enough to behead a king; yet at the threats and commands of the judges, who stood at the prison door, he returned, and grasping the hair of his head and bringing his face to the ground with one hand, he cut through his neck with the razor he had in the other. Some affirm that sentence was passed in the presence of Artaxerxes; that Darius, after he had been convicted by clear evidence, falling prostrate before him, did humbly beg his pardon; that instead of giving it, he, rising up in rage and drawing his scymetar, smote him till he had killed him; that then, going forth into the court, he worshipped the sun, and said, "Depart in peace, ye Persians, and declare to your fellow-subjects how the mighty Oromasdes hath dealt out vengeance to the contrivers of unjust and unlawful things."

Such, then, was the issue of this conspiracy. And now Ochus was high in his hopes, being confident in the influence of Atossa; but yet was afraid of Ariaspes, the only male surviving besides himself, of the legitimate offspring of his father, and of Arsames, one of his natural sons. For indeed Ariaspes was already claimed as their prince by the wishes of the Persians, not because he was the elder brother, but because he excelled Ochus in gentleness, plaindealing, and good-nature; and on the other hand Arsames appeared, by his wisdom, fitted for the throne, and that he was dear to his father, Ochus well knew. So he laid snares for them both, and being no less treacherous than bloody, he made use of the cruelty of his nature against Arsames, and of his craft and wiliness against Ariaspes. For he suborned the king's eunuchs and favorites to convey to him menacing and harsh expressions from his father, as though he had decreed to put him to a cruel and ignominious death. When they daily communicated these things as secrets, and told him at one time that the king would do so to him ere long, and at another, that the blow was actually close impending, they so alarmed the young man, struck such a terror into him, and cast such a confusion and anxiety upon his thoughts, that, having prepared some poisonous drugs, he drank them, that he might be delivered from his life. The king, on hearing what kind of death he died, heartily lamented him, and was not without a suspicion of the cause of it. But being disabled by his age to search into and prove it, he was, after the loss of his son, more affectionate than before to Arsames, did manifestly place his greatest confidence in him, and made him privy to his counsels. Whereupon Ochus had no longer patience to defer the execution of his purpose, but having procured Arpates, Teribazus's son, for the undertaking, he killed Arsames by his hand. Artaxerxes at that time had but a little hold on life, by reason of his extreme age, and so, when he heard of the fate of Arsames, he could not sustain it at all, but sinking at once under the weight of his grief and distress, expired, after a life of ninety-four years, and a reign of sixty-two. And then he seemed a moderate and gracious governor, more especially as compared to his son Ochus, who outdid all his predecessors in bloodthirstiness and cruelty.

GALBA[1]

TRANSLATED BY ANDREW TAYLOR, FELLOW OF KING'S COLLEGE, CAMBRIDGE.

IPHICRATES the Athenian used to say that it is best to have a mercenary soldier fond of money and of pleasures, for thus he will fight the more boldly, to procure the means to gratify his desires. But most have been of opinion, that the body of an army, as well as the natural one, when in its healthy condition, should make no efforts apart, but in compliance with its head. Wherefore they tell us that Paulus Æmilius, on taking command of the forces in Macedonia, and finding them talkative and impertinently busy, as though they were all commanders, issued out his orders that they should have only ready hands and keen swords, and leave the rest to him. And Plato, who can discern no use of a good ruler or general, if his men are not on their part obedient and conformable (the virtue of obeying, as of ruling, being in his opinion one that does not exist without first a noble nature, and then a philosophic education, where the eager and active powers are allayed with the gentler and hu-

---

[1] Sulpicius Galba, Roman Emperor from June, 68 A. D., January, 69 A. D., was born Dec. 24th, 3 B. C. Claudius entrusted him in 45 with the administration of Africa, where he governed with wisdom and integrity. He lived in retirement several years, fearing Nero, who gave him the government of Hispania Tarraconensis for 8 years, 61-68. As Emperor, during his short reign his severity and avarice made him unpopular and he was assassinated 69 A. D.—Dr. William Smith.

maner sentiments), may claim in confirmation of his doctrines sundry mournful instances elsewhere, and, in particular, the events that followed among the Romans upon the death of Nero, in which plain proofs were given that nothing is more terrible than a military force moving about in an empire upon uninstructed and unreasoning impulses. Demades, after the death of Alexander, compared the Macedonian army to the Cyclops after his eye was out, seeing their many disorderly and unsteady motions. But the calamities of the Roman government might be likened to the motions of the giants that assailed heaven, convulsed as it was, and distracted, and from every side recoiling, as it were, upon itself, not so much by the ambition of those who were proclaimed emperors, as by the covetousness and license of the soldiery, who drove commander after commander out, like nails one upon another.

Dionysius, in raillery, said of the Pheræan[2] who enjoyed the government of Thessaly only ten months, that he had been a tragedy-king, but the Cæsars' house in Rome, the Palatium, received in a shorter space of time no less than four emperors, passing, as it were, across the stage, and one making room for another to enter.

This was the only satisfaction of the distressed, that they needed not require any other justice on their oppressors, seeing them thus murder each other, and first of all, and that most justly, the one that ensnared them first, and taught them to expect such happy results from a change of emperors, sullying a good work by the pay he gave for its being done,

---

[2] The name has fallen out of the text. Alexander, according to some, but more probably Lycophron, was the tyrant of Pheræ in Thessaly who is referred to.

and turning revolt against Nero into nothing better than treason.

For, as already related,[3] Nymphidius Sabinus, captain of the guards, together with Tigellinus,[4] after Nero's circumstances were now desperate, and it was perceived that he designed to fly into Egypt, persuaded the troops to declare Galba emperor, as if Nero had been already gone, promising to all the court and Prætorian soldiers, as they are called, seven thousand five hundred drachmas[5] apiece, and to those in service abroad twelve hundred and fifty drachmas each; so vast a sum for a largess as it was impossible any one could raise, but he must be infinitely more exacting and oppressive than ever Nero was. This quickly brought Nero to his grave, and soon after Galba too; they murdered the first in expectation of the promised gift, and not long after the other because they did not obtain it from him; and then, seeking about to find some one who would purchase at such a rate, they consumed themselves in a succession of treacheries and rebellions before they obtained their demands. But to give a particular relation of all that passed would require a history in full form; I have only to notice what is properly to my purpose, namely, what the Cæsars did and suffered.

Sulpicius Galba is owned by all to have been the richest private person that ever came to the imperial seat. And besides the additional honor of being of the family of the Servii, he valued himself more especially for his relationship to Catulus, the most eminent citizen

---

[3] This seems to refer to a lost biography of Nero.

[4] Nymphidius and Tigellinus were the two prefects of the prætorian guards, whose camp was in the city, and who were the household troops of the emperor.

[5] About $1500.

of his time both for virtue and renown, however he may have voluntarily yielded to others as regards power and authority. Galba was also akin to Livia, the wife of Augustus, by whose interest he was preferred to the consulship by the emperor.[6] It is said of him that he commanded the troops well in Germany, and, being made proconsul in Libya, gained a reputation that few ever had. But his quiet manner of living and his sparingness in expenses and his disregard of appearance gave him, when he became emperor, an ill-name for meanness, being, in fact, his worn-out credit for regularity and moderation. He was entrusted by Nero with the government of Spain, before Nero had yet learned to be apprehensive of men of great repute. To the opinion, moreover, entertained of his mild natural temper, his old age added a belief that he would never act incautiously.

There while Nero's iniquitous agents[7] savagely and cruelly harassed the provinces under Nero's authority, he could afford no succor, but merely offer this only ease and consolation, that he seemed plainly to sympathize, as a fellow-sufferer, with those who were condemned upon suits and sold. And when lampoons were made upon Nero and circulated and sung everywhere about, he neither prohibited them, nor showed any indignation on behalf of the emperor's agents, and for this was the more beloved; as also that he was now well acquainted with them, having been in chief power there eight years at the time when Junius

---

[6] Literally, "he came out as consul from the Palatium;" i. e., as the nominee of the emperor; the Palatium being the name for the Cæsars' residence, which was gradually coming to occupy the whole Palatine Hill or Palatium.

[7] The imperial proctors, or procurators, who collected the special imperial revenues for the *fiscus* or privy purse.

Vindex,[8] general of the forces in Gaul, began his insurrection against Nero. And it is reported that letters came to Galba before it fully broke out into an open rebellion, which he neither seemed to give credit to, nor on the other hand to take means to let Nero know; as other officers did, sending to him the letters which came to them, and so spoiled the design, as much as in them lay, who yet afterwards shared in the conspiracy, and confessed they had been treacherous to themselves as well as him. At last Vindex, plainly declaring war, wrote to Galba, encouraging him to take the government upon him, and give a head to this strong body, the Gaulish provinces, which could already count a hundred thousand men in arms, and were able to arm a yet greater number if occasion were. Galba laid the matter before his friends, some of whom thought it fit to wait, and see what movement there might be and what inclinations displayed at Rome for the revolution. But Titus Vinius, captain of his prætorian guard,[9] spoke thus: "Galba, what means this inquiry? To question whether we shall continue faithful to Nero is, in itself, to cease to be faithful.[10] Nero is our enemy, and we must by no means decline the help of Vindex: or else we must at once denounce him, and march to attack him, because he wishes you to be the governor of the Romans,

---

[8] His name was not Junius, but Julius, which came no doubt from the house of the Cæsars; he was of Gaulish blood, and his father or grandfather may have received the citizenship from Cæsar himself.

[9] Every Roman commander-in-chief (for which prætor was originally the title, borne, for example, in old time, by the consuls) had his body-guard, or prætorian cohort. This had been the model for the imperial prætorians in the city.

[10] "Nam qui deliberant desciverunt."—*Tacitus.*

rather than Nero their tyrant." Thereupon Galba, by an edict, appointed a day when he would receive manumissions,[11] and general rumor and talk beforehand about his purpose brought together a great crowd of men so ready for a change, that he scarcely appeared, stepping up to the tribunal, but they with one consent saluted him emperor. That title he refused at present to take upon him; but after he had a while inveighed against Nero, and bemoaned the loss of the more conspicuous of those that had been destroyed by him, he offered himself and service to his country, not by the titles of Cæsar or emperor, but as the lieutenant of the Roman senate and people.

Now that Vindex did wisely in inviting Galba to the empire, Nero himself bore testimony; who, though he seemed to despise Vindex and altogether to slight the Gauls and their concerns, yet when he heard of Galba (as by chance he had just bathed and sat down to his morning meal), at this news he overturned the table. But the senate having voted Galba an enemy, presently, to make his jest, and likewise to personate a confidence among his friends, "This is a very happy opportunity," he said, "for me, who sadly want such a booty as that of the Gauls, which must all fall in as lawful prize; and Galba's estate I can use or sell at once, he being now an open enemy." And accordingly he had Galba's property exposed to sale, which when Galba heard of, he sequestered all that was Nero's in Spain, and found far readier bidders.

Many now began to revolt from Nero, and pretty nearly all adhered to Galba; only Clodius Macer in Africa, and Virginius Rufus, commander of the German forces in Gaul, followed counsel of their own;

[11] No act for the manumission of a slave was valid by the Roman law, unless a declaration was made to the magistrate.

yet these two were not of one and the same advice, for Clodius, being sensible of the rapines and murders to which he had been led by cruelty and covetousness, was in perplexity, and felt it was not safe for him either to retain or quit his command. But Virginius, who had the command of the strongest legions, by whom he was many repeated times saluted emperor and pressed to take the title upon him, declared that he neither would assume that honor himself, nor see it given to any other than whom the senate should elect.

These things at first did not a little disturb Galba, but when presently Virginius and Vindex were in a manner forced by their armies, having got the reins, as it were, out of their hands, to a great encounter and battle, in which Vindex, having seen twenty thousand of the Gauls destroyed, died by his own hand, and when the report straight spread abroad, that all desired Virginius, after this great victory, to take the empire upon him, or else they would return to Nero again, Galba, in great alarm at this, wrote to Virginius, exhorting him to join with him for the preservation of the empire and the liberty of the Romans, and so retiring with his friends into Clunia, a town in Spain, he passed away his time, rather repenting his former rashness, and wishing for his wonted ease and privacy, than setting about what was fit to be done.

It was now summer, when on a sudden, a little before dusk, comes a freedman, Icelus by name, having arrived in seven days from Rome; and being informed where Galba was reposing himself in private, he went straight on, and pushing by the servants of the chamber, opened the door and entered the room, and told him, that Nero being yet alive but not appearing, first the army, and then the people and senate, declared Galba emperor; not long after, it was reported that

Nero was dead; "but I," said he, "not giving credit to common fame, went myself to the body and saw him lying dead, and only then set out to bring you word." This news at once made Galba great again, and a crowd of people came hastening to the door, all very confident of the truth of his tidings, though the speed of the man was almost incredible. Two days after came Titus Vinius with sundry others from the camp, who gave an account in detail of the orders of the senate, and for this service was considerably advanced. On the freedman, Galba conferred the honor of the gold ring,[12] and Icelus, as he had been before, now taking the name of Marcianus, held the first place of the freedmen.

But at Rome, Nymphidius Sabinus, not gently and little by little, but at once, and without exception, engrossed all power to himself; Galba, being an old man (seventy-three years of age), would scarcely, he thought, live long enough to be carried in a litter to Rome; and the troops in the city were from old time attached to him, and now bound by the vastness of the promised gift, for which they regarded him as their benefactor, and Galba as their debtor. Thus presuming on his interest, he straightway commanded Tigellinus, who was in joint commission with himself, to lay down his sword;[13] and giving entertainments, he invited the former consuls and command-

[12] The gold ring had been the mark of the Roman citizen of the equestrian or cavalry class; these were the rings which Hannibal collected at Cannæ. But the gold ring was given also by the personal favor of the emperor, and was a sort of beginning of a royal power of conferring nobility. Any freeborn citizen thus distinguished took equestrian rank, and a freedman that of a freeborn citizen or *ingenuus*.

[13] His sword of office as prefect, together with himself, of the prætorian guard.

ers, making use of Galba's name for the invitation; but at the same time prepared many in the camp to propose that a request should be sent to Galba that he should appoint Nymphidius sole prefect for life without a colleague. And the modes which the senate took to show him honor and increase his power, styling him their benefactor, and attending daily at his gates, and giving him the compliment of heading with his own name and confirming all their acts, carried him on to a yet greater degree of arrogance, so that in a short time he became an object, not only of dislike, but of terror, to those that sought his favor. When the consuls themselves had despatched their couriers with the decrees of the senate to the emperor, together with the sealed diplomas,[14] which the authorities in all the towns where horses or carriages are changed, look at and on that certificate hasten the couriers forward with all their means, he was highly displeased that his seal had not been used, and none of his soldiers employed on the errand. Nay, he even deliberated what course to take with the consuls themselves, but upon their submission and apology he was at last pacified. To gratify the people, he did not interfere with their beating to death any that fell into their hands of Nero's party. Amongst others, Spiclus,[15] the gladiator, was killed in the forum by being thrown under Nero's statues, which they dragged about the place over his body. Aponius, one of those who had been concerned in accusations, they

---

[14] This is the beginning of the system, still followed on the continent of Europe, of a state-post for conveyance. The *diplomata*, or *double*-papers, were issued for this special purpose, sealed under the republic by the consuls, now by the emperors. Persons who wished for the use of the state's horses and carriages got them; couriers with despatches, of course, had them.

[15] Spicillus.

knocked to the ground, and drove carts loaded with stones over him. And many others they tore in pieces, some of them no way guilty, insomuch that Mauriscus,[16] a person of great account and character, told the senate that he feared, in a short time, they might wish for Nero again.

Nymphidius, now advancing towards the consummation of his hopes, did not refuse to let it be said that he was the son of Caius Cæsar,[17] Tiberius's successor; who, it is told, was well acquainted with his mother in his early youth, a woman indeed handsome enough, the offspring of Callistus, one of Cæsar's freedmen, and a certain sempstress. But it is plain that Caius's familiarity with his mother was of too late date to give him any pretensions, and it was suspected he might, if he pleased, claim a father in Martianus, the gladiator, whom his mother, Nymphidia, took a passion for, being a famous man in his way, whom also he much more resembled. However, though he certainly owned Nymphidia for his mother, he ascribed meantime the downfall of Nero to himself alone, and thought he was not sufficiently rewarded with the honors and riches he enjoyed, (nay, though to all was added the company of Sporus, whom he immediately sent for while Nero's body was yet burning on the pile, and treated as his consort, with the name of Poppæa,) but he must also aspire to the empire. And at Rome he had friends who took measures for him

---

[16] *Mauriscus, both really and in reputation one of the best of the city,* is probably Julius Mauricus, mentioned with honor both by Tacitus and Pliny. *Tacit. Hist. IV.* 40; *Agricola,* 45; *Plin. Ep. IV.* 22.) He was exiled under Domitian. He appears (*Plin. Ep. I.* 5) to have been the brother of Arulenus Rusticus, Plutarch's auditor at Rome, for whom see the Life of Plutarch, Vol I.

[17] The emperor Caligula, always called Caius; though Caius Cæsar is not always Caligula.

secretly, as well as some women and some members
of the senate also, who worked underhand to assist
him. And into Spain he despatched one of his friends,
named Gellianus, to view the posture of affairs.

But all things succeeded well with Galba after
Nero's death; only Virginius Rufus, still standing
doubtful, gave him some anxiety, lest he should listen
to the suggestions of some who encouraged him to
take the government upon him, having, at present,
besides the command of a large and warlike army, the
new honors of the defeat of Vindex and the subjuga-
tion of one considerable part of the Roman empire,
namely, the entire Gaul, which had seemed shaking
about upon the verge of open revolt. Nor had any
man indeed a greater name and reputation than Virginius, who had taken a part of so much consequence
in the deliverance of the empire at once from a cruel
tyranny and a Gallic war. But he, standing to his
first resolves, reserved to the senate the power of elect-
ing an emperor. Yet when it was now manifest that
Nero was dead, the soldiers pressed him hard to it,
and one of the tribunes, entering his tent with his
drawn sword, bade him either take the government or
that. But after Fabius Valens, having the command
of one legion, had first sworn fealty to Galba, and
letters from Rome came with tidings of the resolves
of the senate, at last with much ado he persuaded the
army to declare Galba emperor. And when Flaccus
Hordeonius came by Galba's commission as his successor, he handed over to him his forces, and went
himself to meet Galba on his way, and having met
him, turned back to attend him; in all which no apparent displeasure nor yet honor was shown him. Galba's
feelings of respect for him prevented the former; the
latter was checked by the envy of his friends, and particularly of Titus Vinius, who, acting in the desire of

hindering Virginius's promotion, unwittingly aided his happy genius in rescuing him from those hazards and hardships which other commanders were involved in, and securing him the safe enjoyment of a quiet life and peaceable old age.

Near Narbo, a city in Gaul, the deputation of the senate met Galba, and, after they had delivered their compliments, begged him to make what haste he could to appear to the people, that impatiently expected him. He discoursed with them courteously and unassumingly, and in his entertainment, though Nymphidius had sent him royal furniture and attendance of Nero's, he put all aside, and made use of nothing but his own, for which he was well spoken of, as one who had a great mind, and was superior to little vanities. But in a short time, Vinius, by declaring to him that these noble, unpompous, citizen-like ways were a mere affectation of popularity, and a petty bashfulness at assuming his proper greatness, induced him to make use of Nero's supplies, and in his entertainments not to be afraid of a regal sumptuosity. And in more than one way the old man let it gradually appear that he had put himself under Vinius's disposal.

Vinius was a person of an excessive covetousness, and not quite free from blame in respect to women. For being a young man, newly entered into the service under Calvisius Sabinus, upon his first campaign, he brought his commander's wife, a licentious woman, in a soldier's dress, by night into the camp, and was found with her in the very general's quarters, the *principia,* as the Romans call them. For which insolence Caius Cæsar cast him into prison, from whence he was fortunately delivered by Caius's death. Afterwards, being invited by Claudius Cæsar to supper, he privily conveyed away a silver cup, which Cæsar hearing of, invited him again the next day, and gave order to his servants to set before him no silver plate, but only earthen ware. And this offence, through the comic mildness of Cæsar's reprimand, was treated rather as a subject of jest than as a crime. But the acts to which now, when Galba was in his hands and his power was so extensive, his covetous temper led him were the causes, in part, and in part the provocation, of tragical and fatal mischiefs.

Nymphidius became very uneasy upon the return out of Spain of Gellianus, whom he had sent to pry into Galba's actions, understanding that Cornelius Laco was appointed commander of the court guards, and that Vinius was the great favorite, and that Gellianus had not been able so much as to come nigh, much less have any opportunity to offer any words in private, so narrowly had he been watched and observed. Nymphidius, therefore, called together the officers of the troops, and declared to them that Galba of himself was a good, well-meaning old man, but did not act by his own counsel, and was ill-guided by Vinius and Laco; and lest, before they were aware, they should engross the authority Tigellinus had with the troops, he proposed to them to send deputies from the camp, acquainting him that if he pleased to remove only these two from his counsel and presence, he would be much more welcome to all at his arrival. Wherein when he saw he did not prevail (it seeming absurd and unmannerly to give rules to an old commander what friends to retain or displace, as if he had been a youth newly taking the reins of authority into his hands), adopting another course, he wrote himself to Galba letters in alarming terms, one while as if the city were unsettled, and had not yet recovered its tranquillity; then that Clodius Macer withheld the corn-ships from Africa; that the legions in Germany began to be mutinous, and that he heard the like of those in Syria and Judæa. But Galba not minding him much nor giving credit to his stories, he resolved to make his attempt beforehand, though Clodius Celsus, a native of Antioch, a person of sense, and friendly and faithful to Nymphidius, told him he was wrong, saying he did not believe one single street in Rome would ever give him the title of Cæsar. Nevertheless many also derided Galba, amongst the rest Mithridates of Pontus, saying, that as soon as this wrinkled, bald-headed man should be seen publicly at Rome, they would think it an utter disgrace ever to have had such a Cæsar.

At last it was resolved, about midnight, to bring Nymphidius into the camp, and declare him emperor. But Antonius Honoratus, who was first among the tribunes, summoning together in the evening those under his command, charged himself and them severely with their many and unreasonable turns and alterations, made without any purpose or regard to merit, simply as if some evil genius hurried them from one treason to another. "What though Nero's miscarriages," said he, "gave some color to your former acts, can you say you have any plea for betraying Galba in the death of a mother, the blood of a wife, or the degradation of the imperial power upon the stage and amongst players? Neither did we desert Nero for all this, until Nymphidius had persuaded us that he had first left us and fled into Egypt. Shall we, therefore, send Galba after, to appease Nero's shade, and, for the sake of making the son of Nymphidia emperor, take off one of Livia's family, as we have already the son of Agrippina? Rather, doing justice on him, let us revenge Nero's death, and show ourselves true and faithful by preserving Galba."

The tribune having ended his harangue, the soldiers assented, and encouraged all they met with to persist in their fidelity to the emperor, and, indeed, brought over the greatest part. But presently hearing a great shout, Nymphidius, imagining, as some say, that the soldiers called for him, or hastening to be in time to check any opposition and gain the doubtful, came on with many lights, carrying in his hand a speech in writing, made by Cingonius Varro, which he had got by heart, to deliver to the soldiers. But seeing the gates of the camp shut up, and large numbers standing armed about the walls, he began to be afraid. Yet drawing nearer, he demanded what they meant, and by whose orders they were then in arms; but hearing a general acclamation, all with one consent crying out that Galba was their emperor, advancing towards them, he joined in the cry, and likewise commanded those that followed him to do the same. The guard notwithstanding permitted him to enter the camp only with a few, where he was presently struck with a dart, which Septimius, being before him, received on his shield; others, however, assaulted him with their naked swords, and on his flying, pursued him into a soldier's cabin, where they slew him. And dragging his body thence, they placed a railing about it, and exposed it next day to public view. When Galba heard of the end which Nymphidius had thus come to, he commanded that all his confederates who had not at once killed themselves should immediately be despatched; amongst whom were Cingonius, who made his oration, and Mithridates, formerly mentioned. It was, however, regarded as arbitrary and illegal, and though it might be just, yet by no means popular, to take off men of their rank and quality without a hearing. For every one expected another scheme of government, being deceived, as is usual, by the first plausible pretences; and the death of Petronius Turpilianus, who was of consular dignity, and had remained faithful to Nero, was yet more keenly resented. Indeed, the taking off of Macer in Africa by Trebonius, and Fonteius by Valens in Germany, had a fair pretence, they being dreaded as armed commanders, having their soldiers at their bidding; but why refuse Turpilianus, an old man and unarmed, permission to try to clear himself, if any part of the moderation and equity at first promised were really to come to a performance? Such were the comments to which these actions exposed him. When he came within five and twenty furlongs or thereabouts of the city, he happened to light on a disorderly rabble of the seamen,[13] who beset him as he passed. These were they whom Nero made soldiers, forming them into a legion. They so rudely crowded to have their commission confirmed, that they did not let Galba either be seen or heard by those that had come out to meet their new emperor; but tumultuously pressed on with loud shouts to have colors to their legion, and quarters assigned them. Galba put them off until another time, which they interpreting as a denial, grew more insolent and mutinous, following and crying out, some of them with their drawn swords in their hands. Upon seeing which, Galba commanded the horse to ride over them, when they were soon routed, not a man standing his ground, and many of them were slain, both there and in the pursuit; an ill omen, that Galba should make his first entry through so much blood and among dead bodies. And now he was looked upon with terror and alarm by any who had entertained contempt of him at the sight of his age and apparent infirmities.

---

[13] The classiarii, levied from the rowers in the fleet, and employed in the regular service on shore.

But when he desired presently to let it appear what a change would be made from Nero's profuseness and sumptuosity in giving presents, he much missed his aim, and fell so short of magnificence, that he scarcely came within the limits of decency. When Canus, who was a famous musician, played at supper for him, he expressed his approbation, and bade the bag be brought to him; and taking a few gold pieces, put them in with this remark, that it was out of his own purse, and not on the public account. He ordered the largesses which Nero had made to actors and wrestlers and such like to be strictly required again, allowing only the tenth part to be retained; though it turned to very small account, most of those persons expending their daily income as fast as they received it, being rude, improvident livers; upon which he had further inquiry made as to those who had bought or received from them, and called upon these people to refund. The trouble was infinite, the exactions being prosecuted far, touching a great number of persons, bringing disrepute on Galba, and general hatred on Vinius, who made the emperor appear base-minded and mean to the world, whilst he himself was spending profusely, taking whatever he could get, and selling to any buyer. Hesiod tells us to drink without stinting of

The end and the beginning of the cask.[19]

And Vinius, seeing his patron old and decaying, made the most of what he considered to be at once the first of his fortune and the last of it.

Thus the aged man suffered in two ways: first, through the evil deeds which Vinius did himself, and, next, by his preventing or bringing into disgrace those just acts which he himself designed. Such was

[19] The line from Hesiod in 366 in the Works and Days.

the punishing Nero's adherents. When he destroyed the bad, amongst whom were Helius, Polycletus, Petinus, and Patrobius, the people mightily applauded the act, crying out, as they were dragged through the forum, that it was a goodly sight, grateful to the gods themselves, adding, however, that the gods and men alike demanded justice on Tigellinus, the very tutor and prompter of all the tyranny. This good man, however, had taken his measures beforehand, in the shape of a present and a promise to Vinius. Turpilianus could not be allowed to escape with life, though his one and only crime had been that he had not betrayed or shown hatred to such a ruler as Nero. But he who had made Nero what he became, and afterwards deserted and betrayed him whom he had so corrupted, was allowed to survive as an instance that Vinius could do any thing, and an advertisement that those that had money to give him need despair of nothing. The people, however, were so possessed with the desire of seeing Tigellinus dragged to execution, that they never ceased to require it at the theatre and in the race-course, till they were checked by an edict from the emperor himself, announcing that Tigellinus could not live long, being wasted with a consumption, and requesting them not to seek to make his government appear cruel and tyrannical. So the dissatisfied populace were laughed at, and Tigellinus made a splendid feast, and sacrificed in thanksgiving for his deliverance: and after supper, Vinius, rising from the emperor's table, went to revel with Tigellinus, taking his daughter, a widow, with him; to whom Tigellinus presented his compliments, with a gift of twenty-five myriads of money, and bade the superintendent of his concubines take off a rich necklace from her own neck and tie it about hers, the value of it being estimated at fifteen myriads.

After this, even reasonable acts were censured; as, for example, the treatment of the Gauls who had been in the conspiracy with Vindex. For people looked upon their abatement of tribute and admission to citizenship as a piece, not of clemency on the part of Galba, but of money-making on that of Vinius. And thus the mass of the people began to look with dislike upon the government. The soldiers were kept on a while in expectation of the promised donative, supposing that if they did not receive the full, yet they should have at least as much as Nero gave them. But when Galba, on hearing they began to complain, declared greatly, and like a general, that he was used to enlist and not to buy his soldiers, when they heard of this, they conceived an implacable hatred against him; for he did not seem to defraud them merely himself in their present expectations, but to give an ill precedent, and instruct his successors to do the like. This heart-burning, however, was as yet at Rome a thing undeclared, and a certain respect for Galba's personal presence somewhat retarded their motions, and took off their edge, and their having no obvious occasion for beginning a revolution curbed and kept under, more or less, their resentments. But those forces that had been formerly under Virginius, and now were under Flaccus in Germany, valuing themselves much upon the battle they had fought with Vindex, and finding now no advantage of it, grew very refractory and intractable towards their officers: and Flaccus they wholly disregarded, being incapacitated in body by unintermitted gout, and, besides, a man of little experience in affairs. So at one of their festivals, when it was customary for the officers of the army to wish all health and happiness to the emperor, the common soldiers began to murmur loudly, and on their officers persisting in the ceremony, responded with the words, "If he deserves it."

When some similar insolence was committed by the legions under Vitellius,[20] frequent letters with the information came to Galba from his agents; and taking alarm at this, and fearing that he might be despised not only for his old age, but also for want of issue, he determined to adopt some young man of distinction, and declare him his successor. There was at this time in the city Marcus Otho, a person of fair extraction, but from his childhood one of the few most debauched, voluptuous, and luxurious livers in Rome. And as Homer gives Paris in several places the title of "fair Helen's love," making a woman's name the glory and addition to his, as if he had nothing else to distinguish him, so Otho was renowned in Rome for nothing more than his marriage with Poppæa, whom Nero had a passion for when she was Crispinus's wife. But being as yet respectful to his own wife, and standing in awe of his mother, he engaged Otho underhand to solicit her. For Nero lived familiarly with Otho, whose prodigality won his favor, and he was well pleased when he took the freedom to jest upon him as mean and penurious. Thus when Nero one day perfumed himself with some rich essence and favored Otho with a sprinkle of it, he, entertaining Nero next day, ordered gold and silver pipes to disperse the like on a sudden freely, like water, throughout the room. As to Poppæa, he was

---

[20] The uniform reading is *Tigellinus*, who cannot have been mentioned in this place. He commanded no troops of any kind now; he was no longer prætorian prefect and Plutarch is clearly speaking of armies at a distance. *The legions under Vitellius* may very well be meant. Flaccus commanded those in the Upper or Southern Germany (the Rhine from Basle to Mayence), Vitellius in the Lower, at Cologne.

beforehand with Nero, and first seducing her himself, then, with the hope of Nero's favor, he prevailed with her to part with her husband, and brought her to his own house as his wife, and was not content afterwards to have a share in her, but grudged to have Nero for a claimant, Poppæa herself, they say, being rather pleased than otherwise with this jealousy; she sometimes excluded Nero, even when Otho was not present, either to prevent his getting tired with her, or, as some say, not liking the prospect of an imperial marriage, though willing enough to have the emperor as her lover. So that Otho ran the risk of his life, and strange it was he escaped, when Nero, for this very marriage, killed his wife and sister. But he was beholden to Seneca's friendship, by whose persuasions and entreaty Nero was prevailed with to despatch him as prætor into Lusitania, on the shores of the Ocean; where he behaved himself very agreeably and indulgently to those he had to govern, well knowing this command was but to color and disguise his banishment.

When Galba revolted from Nero, Otho was the first governor of any of the provinces that came over to him, bringing all the gold and silver he possessed in the shape of cups and tables, to be coined into money, and also what servants he had fitly qualified to wait upon a prince. In all other points, too, he was faithful to him, and gave him sufficient proof that he was inferior to none in managing public business. And he so far ingratiated himself, that he rode in the same carriage with him during the whole journey, several days together. And in this journey and familiar companionship, he won over Vinius also, both by his conversation and presents, but especially by conceding to him the first place, securing the second, by his interest, for himself. And he had the advantage of

GALBA

him in avoiding all odium and jealousy, assisting all petitioners, without asking for any reward, and appearing courteous and of easy access towards all, especially to the military men, for many of whom he obtained commands, some immediately from the emperor, others by Vinius's means, and by the assistance of the two favorite freedmen, Icelus and Asiaticus,[21] these being the men in chief power in the court. As often as he entertained Galba, he gave the cohort on duty, in addition to their pay, a piece of gold for every man there, upon pretence of respect to the emperor, while really he undermined him, and stole away his popularity with the soldiers.

So Galba consulting about a successor, Vinius introduced Otho, yet not even this gratis, but upon promise that he would marry his daughter, if Galba should make him his adopted son and successor to the empire. But Galba, in all his actions, showed clearly that he preferred the public good before his own private interest, not aiming so much to pleasure himself as to advantage the Romans by his selection. Indeed, he does not seem to have been so much as inclined to make choice of Otho, had it been but to inherit his own private fortune, knowing his extravagant and luxurious character, and that he was already plunged in debt five thousand myriads deep. So he listened to Vinius, and made no reply, but mildly suspended his determination. Only he appointed himself consul, and Vinius his colleague, and it was the general expectation that he would declare his successor at the beginning of the new year. And the soldiers desired nothing more than that Otho should be the person.

---

[21] Asiaticus was the freedman and favorite, not of Galba, but of Vitellius. His time came later. Plutarch has brought him in here by a mistake.

But the forces in Germany broke out into their mutiny whilst he was yet deliberating, and anticipated his design. All the soldiers in general felt much resentment against Galba for not having given them their expected largess, but these troops made a pretence of a more particular concern, that Virginius Rufus was cast off dishonorably, and that the Gauls who had fought with them were well rewarded, while those who had refused to take part with Vindex were punished; and Galba's thanks seemed all to be for him, to whose memory he had done honor after his death with public solemnities as though he had been made emperor by his means only. Whilst these discourses passed openly throughout the army, on the first day of the first month of the year, the Calends, as they call it, of January, Flaccus summoning them to take the usual anniversary oath of fealty to the emperor, they overturned and pulled down Galba's statues, and having sworn in the name of the senate and people of Rome, departed. But the officers now feared anarchy and confusion, as much as rebellion; and one of them came forward and said: "What will become of us, my fellow-soldiers, if we neither set up another general, nor retain the present one? This will not be so much to desert from Galba as to decline all subjection and command. It is useless to try and maintain Flaccus Hordeonius, who is but a mere shadow and image of Galba. But Vitellius, commander of the other Germany, is but one day's march distant, whose father was censor and thrice consul, and in a manner co-emperor with Claudius Cæsar; and he himself has the best proof to show of his bounty and largeness of mind, in the poverty with which some reproach him. Him let us make choice of, that all may see we know how to choose an emperor better than either Spaniards or Lusitanians." Which motion whilst some assented to, and others gainsaid, a certain standard-bearer slipped out and carried the news to Vitellius,[22] who was entertaining much company by night. This, taking air, soon passed through the troops, and Fabius Valens, who commanded one legion, riding up next day with a large body of horse, saluted Vitellius emperor. He had hitherto seemed to decline it, professing a dread he had to undertake the weight of the government; but on this day, being fortified, they say, by wine and a plentiful noon-day repast, he began to yield, and submitted to take on him the title of Germanicus they gave him, but desired to be excused as to that of Cæsar. And immediately the army under Flaccus also, putting away their fine and popular oaths in the name of the senate, swore obedience to Vitellius as emperor, to observe whatever he commanded.

Thus Vitellius was publicly proclaimed emperor in Germany; which news coming to Galba's ear, he no longer deferred his adoption; yet knowing that some of his friends were using their interest for Dolabella, and the greatest number of them for Otho, neither of whom he approved of, on a sudden, without any one's privity, he sent for Piso, the son of Crassus and Scribonia, whom Nero slew, a young man in general of excellent dispositions for virtue, but his most eminent qualities those of steadiness and austere gravity. And so he set out to go to the camp to declare him Cæsar and successor to the empire. But at his very

[22] Vitellius, "commander of the other," that is, the Lower "Germany," or Lower Rhine, was at Cologne, with his troops quartered near. The army of the Upper Rhine, or at least this part of it, was in winter-quarters, one day's journey distant. The standard-bearer reached Vitellius, says Tacitus, the same night. Fabius Valens belonged to the Lower Province, and was in quarters near Cologne.

first going forth, many signs appeared in the heavens, and when he began to make a speech to the soldiers, partly extempore, and partly reading it, the frequent claps of thunder and flashes of lightning and the violent storm of rain that burst on both the camp and the city were plain discoveries that the divine powers did not look with favor or satisfaction on this act of adoption, that would come to no good result. The soldiers, also, showed symptoms of hidden discontent, and wore sullen looks, no distribution of money being even now made to them. However, those that were present and observed Piso's countenance and voice could not but feel admiration to see him so little overcome by so great a favor, of the magnitude of which at the same time he seemed not at all insensible. Otho's aspect, on the other hand, did not fail to let many marks appear of his bitterness and anger at his disappointment; since to have been the first man thought of for it, and to have come to the very point of being chosen, and now to be put by, was in his feelings a sign of the displeasure and ill-will of Galba towards him. This filled him with fears and apprehensions, and sent him home with a mind full of various passions, whilst he dreaded Piso, hated Galba, and was full of wrath and indignation against Vinius. And the Chaldeans and soothsayers about him would not permit him to lay aside his hopes or quit his design, chiefly Ptolemæus, insisting much on a prediction he had made, that Nero should not murder Otho, but he himself should die first, and Otho succeed as emperor; for the first proving true, he thought he could not distrust the rest. But none perhaps stimulated him more than those that professed privately to pity his hard fate and compassionate him for being thus ungratefully dealt with by Galba; especially Nymphidius's and Tigellinus's creatures, who, being now cast off and reduced

GALBA 501

to low estate, were eager to put themselves upon him, exclaiming at the indignity he had suffered, and provoking him to revenge himself.

Amongst these were Veturius and Barbius, the one an *optio,* the other a *tesserarius* (these are men who have the duties of messengers and scouts[23]), with whom Onomastus, one of Otho's freedmen, went to the camp, to tamper with the army, and brought over some with money, others with fair promises, which was no hard matter, they being already corrupted, and only wanting a fair pretence. It had been otherwise more than the work of four days (which elapsed between the adoption and murder) so completely to infect them as to cause a general revolt. On the sixth day ensuing,[24] the eighteenth, as the Romans call it, before the Calends of February, the murder was done. On that day, in the morning, Galba sacrificed in the Palatium, in the presence of his friends, when Umbricius, the priest, taking up the entrails, and speaking not ambiguously, but in plain words, said that there were signs of great troubles ensuing, and dangerous snares laid for the life of the emperor. Thus Otho had even been discovered by the finger of the god; being there just behind Galba, hearing all that was said, and seeing what was pointed out to them by Umbricius. His countenance changed to every color in his fear, and he was betraying no small discomposure, when Onomastus, his freedman, came

---

[23] The *optio* was a sort of second or *sub*-centurion; the *tesserarius* distributed the *tesseræ* or billets of the watchword. These two men both belonged to the corps of *speculatores,* and it almost seems that this is the word which Plutarch means to explain in what follows, as if the words "of the *speculatores*" had dropped out of the text after *tesserarius.*

[24] The fifteenth of January.

up and acquainted him that the master-builders had come, and were waiting for him at home. Now that was the signal for Otho to meet the soldiers. Pretending then that he had purchased an old house, and was going to show the defects to those that had sold it to him, he departed; and passing through what is called Tiberius's house,[25] he went on into the forum, near the spot where a golden pillar stands, at which all the several roads through Italy terminate.

Here, it is related, no more than twenty-three received and saluted him emperor; so that, although he was not in mind as in body enervated with soft living and effeminacy,[26] being in his nature bold and fearless enough in danger, nevertheless, he was afraid to go on. But the soldiers that were present would not suffer him to recede, but came with their drawn swords about his chair, commanding the bearers to take him up, whom he hastened on, saying several times over to himself, "I am a lost man." Several persons overheard the words, who stood by wondering, rather than alarmed, because of the small number that attempted such an enterprise. But as they marched on through the forum, about as many more met him, and here and there three or four at a time joined in. Thus returning towards the camp, with their bare swords in their hands, they saluted him as Cæsar, whereupon Martialis, the tribune in charge of the watch, who was, they say, noways privy to it, but

[25] The *domus Tiberiana* was a more retired portion of the imperial buildings on the Palatine. Galba was sacrificing in the temple of the Palatine Apollo. Otho left him and went out by a side-entrance from the buildings, got into the street below and went to the Golden Milestone, in the forum, just by the Temple of Saturn.

[26] "Non erat Othoni mollis, neque corpori similis animus." Tacitus Hist. II., 22.

GALBA

was simply surprised at the unexpectedness of the thing, and afraid to refuse, permitted him entrance. And after this, no man made any resistance; for they that knew nothing of the design, being purposely encompassed by the conspirators, as they were straggling here and there, first submitted for fear, and afterwards were persuaded into compliance. Tidings came immediately to Galba in the Palatium, whilst the priest was still present and the sacrifices at hand, so that persons who were most entirely incredulous about such things, and most positive in their neglect of them, were astonished, and began to marvel at the divine event. A multitude of all sorts of people now began to run together out of the forum; Vinius and Laco and some of Galba's freedmen drew their swords and placed themselves beside him; Piso went forth and addressed himself to the guards on duty in the court; and Marius Celsus, a brave man, was despatched to the Illyrian legion, stationed in what is called the Vipsanian chamber,[27] to secure them.

Galba now consulting whether he should go out, Vinius dissuaded him, but Celsus[28] and Laco encouraged him by all means to do so, and sharply reprimanded Vinius. But on a sudden a rumor came hot that Otho was slain in the camp; and presently ap-

---

[27] The Vipsanian Portico was away in the new region, on the edge of the Campus Martius, taking its name from Vipsanius Agrippa, who built here the Pantheon, on one side of the great road out of the city (now the Corso), and laid out on the other the Campus Agrippæ, one of the ornaments of which was this Portico, mentioned by Horace as a place of fashionable resort:—
——— Ut bene notum
Porticus Agrippæ et via te conspexerit Appi,
Ire tamen restat Numa quo devenit et Ancus.

[28] Celsus should, I think, be Icelus, who occurs in this connection in Tacitus. Celsus had already left the Palatine to go to the Porch of Agrippa and bring up the Illyrian troops.

peared one Julius Atticus, a man of some distinction
in the guards, running up with his drawn sword, crying out that he had slain Cæsar's enemy; and pressing
through the crowd that stood in his way, he presented
himself before Galba with his bloody weapon, who,
looking on him, demanded, "Who gave you your
orders?"[29] And on his answering that it had been his
duty and the obligation of the oath he had taken, the
people applauded, giving loud acclamations, and
Galba got into his chair and was carried out to sacrifice to Jupiter, and so to show himself publicly. But
coming into the forum, there met him there, like a
turn of wind, the opposite story, that Otho had made
himself master of the camp. And as usual in a crowd
of such a size, some called to him to return back, others
to move forward; some encouraging him to be bold
and fear nothing, others bade him be cautious and distrust. And thus whilst his chair was tossed to and
fro, as it were on the waves, often tottering, there appeared first horse, and straightway heavy-armed foot,
coming through Paulus's court,[30] and all with one
accord crying out, "Down with this private man."
Upon this, the crowd of people set off running, not to
fly and disperse, but to possess themselves of the
colonnades and elevated places of the forum, as it
might be to get places to see a spectacle. And as soon
as Atillius Vergilio knocked down one of Galba's
statues, this was taken as the declaration of war, and
they[31] sent a discharge of darts upon Galba's litter,

[29] "Commilito, quis jussit?" Fellow soldier, who bade it?" are the words in Tacitus.

[30] The Basilica Pauli, on the other side of the forum, the side nearer the camp.

[31] Not the people, as the grammar might seem to imply, but the soldiers. Atillius Vergilio was one of the men of the cohort on duty attending Galba.

and, missing their aim, came up and attacked him nearer hand with their naked swords. No man resisted or offered to stand up in his defence, save one only, a centurion, Sempronius Densus,[32] the single man among so many thousands that the sun beheld that day act worthily of the Roman empire, who, though he had never received any favor from Galba, yet out of bravery and allegiance endeavored to defend the litter. First, lifting up his switch of vine, with which the centurions correct the soldiers when disorderly, he called aloud to the aggressors, charging them not to touch their emperor. And when they came upon him hand to hand, he drew his sword, and made a defence for a long time, until at last he was cut under the knees and brought to the ground.

Galba's chair was upset at the spot called the Lacus Curtius,[33] where they ran up and struck at him as he lay in his corslet. He, however, offered his throat, bidding them "Strike, if it be for the Romans' good."[34] He received several wounds on his legs and arms, and at last was struck in the throat, as most say, by one Camurius, a soldier of the fifteenth legion. Some name Terentius, others Lecanius; and there are

[32] Indrisus, or Indister, is the name in the manuscripts; Densus is introduced in its place on the authority of Tacitus, in whose narrative, however, it is Piso, not Galba, who is defended by him. This is clear from the context; it is curious, however, that there should be a difference of reading; and, indeed, most of the manuscripts make it Galba whom he attends; and so it is in Dion Cassius also.

[33] The Lacus Curtius, so called, was just in the middle of the open space of the forum.

[34] "Ferirent si ita e republica videretur," are the words in Tacitus, who says, however, that there were many different stories of what he said; those who killed him could not be expected to care what it was; "non interfuit occidentium quid diceret."

others that say it was Fabius Fabulus, who, it is reported, cut off the head and carried it away in the skirt of his coat, the baldness making it a difficult thing to take hold of. But those that were with him would not allow him to keep it covered up, but bade him let every one see the brave deed he had done; so that after a while he stuck upon the lance the head of the aged man that had been their grave and temperate ruler, their supreme priest and consul, and, tossing it up in the air, ran like a bacchanal, twirling and flourishing with it, while the blood ran down the spear. But when they brought the head to Otho, "Fellow-soldiers," he cried out, "this is nothing, unless you show me Piso's too," which was presented him not long after. The young man, retreating upon a wound received, was pursued by one Murcus, and slain at the temple of Vesta. Titus Vinius was also despatched, avowing himself to have been privy to the conspiracy against Galba by calling out that they were killing him contrary to Otho's pleasure. However, they cut off his head, and Laco's too, and brought them to Otho, requesting a boon.

And as Archilochus says—

> When six or seven lie breathless on the ground,
> 'Twas I, 'twas I, say thousands, gave the wound.

Thus many that had no share in the murder wetted their hands and swords in blood, and came and showed them to Otho, presenting memorials suing for a gratuity. Not less than one hundred and twenty were identified afterwards from their written petitions; all of whom Vitellius sought out and put to death. There came also into the camp Marius Celsus, and was accused by many voices of encouraging the soldiers to assist Galba, and was demanded to death by the multitude. Otho had no desire for this, yet, fearing an absolute denial, he professed that he did not wish to take him off so soon, having many matters yet to learn from him; and so committed him safe to the custody of those he most confided in.

Forthwith a senate was convened, and as if they were not the same men, or had other gods to swear by, they took that oath in Otho's name which he himself had taken in Galba's and had broken; and withal conferred on him the titles of Cæsar and Augustus; whilst the dead carcasses of the slain lay yet in their consular robes in the market-place. As for their heads, when they could make no other use of them, Vinius's they sold to his daughter for two thousand five hundred drachmas; Piso's was begged by his wife Verania; Galba's they gave to Patrobius's servants;[35] who when they had it, after all sorts of abuse and indignities, tumbled it into the place where those that suffer death by the emperor's orders are usually cast, called Sessorium. Galba's body was conveyed away by Priscus Helvidius by Otho's permission, and buried in the night by Argius, his freedman.

Thus you have the history of Galba, a person inferior to few Romans, either for birth or riches, rather exceeding all of his time in both, having lived in great honor and reputation in the reigns of five emperors, insomuch that he overthrew Nero rather by his fame and repute in the world than by actual force and power. Of all the others that joined in Nero's deposition, some were by general consent regarded as unworthy, others had only themselves to vote them deserving of the empire. To him the title was offered, and by him it was accepted; and simply lending his

---

[35] Patrobius has already been mentioned as one of Nero's freedmen who were put to death by Galba's orders soon after his entering the city.

name to Vindex's attempt, he gave to what had been called rebellion before, the name of a civil war, by the presence of one that was accounted fit to govern. And, therefore, as he considered that he had not so much sought the position as the position had sought him, he proposed to command those whom Nymphidius and Tigellinus had wheedled into obedience, no otherwise than Scipio formerly and Fabricius and Camillus had commanded the Romans of their times. But being now overcome with age, he was indeed among the troops and legions an upright ruler upon the antique model; but for the rest, giving himself up to Vinius, Laco, and his freedmen, who made their gain of all things, no otherwise than Nero had done to his insatiate favorites, he left none behind him to wish him still in power, though many to compassionate his death.

OTHO[1]

TRANSLATED BY SAMUEL GARTH, M. D.
(THE AUTHOR OF THE DISPENSARY, THE "WELL-NATURED GARTH," GRATEFULLY REMEMBERED BY POPE; A SHORT ACCOUNT OF WHOM IS GIVEN IN JOHNSON'S LIVES OF THE POETS).

THE new emperor went early in the morning to the capitol, and sacrificed; and, having commanded Marius Celsus to be brought, he saluted him, and with obliging language desired him rather to forget his accusation than remember his acquittal; to which Celsus answered neither meanly nor ungratefully, that his very crime ought to recommend his integrity, since his guilt had been his fidelity to Galba, from whom he had never received any personal obligations. Upon which they were both of them admired by those that were present, and applauded by the soldiers.

In the senate, Otho said much in a gentle and popular strain. He was to have been consul for part of that year himself, but he gave the office to Virginius Rufus, and displaced none that had been named for the consulship by either Nero or Galba. Those

---

[1] Otho was born about 32 A. D. Having succeeded in his conspiracy which resulted in the death of the emperor Galba, Otho was proclaimed emperor. Meantime Vitellius had been proclaimed emperor by the German troops at Cologne. Otho was defeated and put an end to his own life in the thirty-seventh year of his age, having been emperor from January 15th to April 16th, 69 A. D.—Dr. William Smith.

that were remarkable for their age and dignity he promoted to the priesthoods; and restored the remains of their fortunes, that had not yet been sold, to all those senators that were banished by Nero and recalled by Galba. So that the nobility and chief of the people, who were at first apprehensive that no human creature, but some supernatural penal, or vindictive power had seized the empire, began now to flatter themselves with hopes of a government that smiled upon them thus early.

Besides, nothing gratified or gained the whole Roman people more than his justice in relation to Tigellinus. It was not seen how he was in fact already suffering punishment, not only by the very terror of retribution which he saw the whole city requiring as a just debt, but with several incurable diseases also; not to mention those unhallowed frightful excesses among impure and prostituted women, to which, at the very close of life, his lewd nature clung, and in them gasped out, as it were, its last; these, in the opinion of all reasonable men, being themselves the extremest punishment, and equal to many deaths. But it was felt like a grievance by people in general that he continued yet to see the light of day, who had been the occasion of the loss of it to so many persons, and such persons, as had died by his means. Wherefore Otho ordered him to be sent for, just as he was contriving his escape by means of some vessels that lay ready for him on the coast near where he lived, in the neighborhood of Sinuessa. At first he endeavored to corrupt the messenger, by a large sum of money, to favor his design; but when he found this was to no purpose, he made him as considerable a present, as if he had really connived at it, only entreating him to stay till he had shaved; and so took that opportunity, and with his razor despatched himself.

And while giving the people this most righteous satisfaction of their desires, for himself he seemed to have no sort of regard for any private injuries of his own. And at first, to please the populace, he did not refuse to be called Nero in the theatre, and did not interfere when some persons displayed Nero's statues to public view. And Cluvius Rufus says,[2] imperial letters, such as are sent with couriers, went into Spain with the name of Nero affixed adoptively to that of Otho; but as soon as he perceived this gave offence to the chief and most distinguished citizens, it was omitted.

After he had begun to model the government in this manner, the paid soldiers began to murmur, and endeavored to make him suspect and chastise the nobility, either really out of a concern for his safety, or wishing, upon this pretence, to stir up trouble and warfare. Thus, whilst Crispinus, whom he had ordered to bring him the seventeenth cohort from Ostia, began to collect what he wanted after it was dark, and was putting the arms upon the waggons,[3] some of the most turbulent cried out that Crispinus was disaf-

[2] Cluvius Rufus, at this time, was governor of Spain. *Adoptively*, which seems to be the best of two readings, would mean that he should add the name of Nero to his own in the same way as that of Cæsar was subsequently, without any proper claim to it, taken by the emperors who had no connection with the Cæsar family.

[3] It would appear that Plutarch understood the arms to have been collected and the men to have broken out into this tumult at Ostia. The real fact was that, having ordered a body of men up from Ostia, Otho directed Crispinus to procure arms to equip them from the magazine in the prætorian camp. On seeing him removing these arms by night, the prætorians took the alarm, declared he was taking them to the senators who meant to arm their slaves with them and attack Otho, and so set off at once to protect him.

fected, that the senate was practising something against the emperor, and that those arms were to be employed against Cæsar, and not for him. When this report was once set afoot, it got the belief and excited the passions of many; they broke out into violence; some seized the waggons, and others slew Crispinus and two centurions that opposed them; and the whole number of them, arraying themselves in their arms, and encouraging one another to stand by Cæsar, marched to Rome. And hearing there that eighty of the senators were at supper with Otho, they flew to the palace, and declared it was a fair opportunity to take off Cæsar's enemies at one stroke. A general alarm ensued of an immediate coming sack of the city. All were in confusion about the palace, and Otho himself in no small consternation, being not only concerned for the senators (some of whom had brought their wives to supper thither), but also feeling himself to be an object of alarm and suspicion to them, whose eyes he saw fixed on him in silence and terror. Therefore he gave orders to the prefects to address the soldiers and do their best to pacify them, while he bade the guests rise, and leave by another door. They had only just made their way out, when the soldiers rushed into the room, and called out, "Where are Cæsar's enemies?" Then Otho, standing up on his couch, made use both of arguments and entreaties, and by actual tears at last, with great difficulty, persuaded them to desist. The next day he went to the camp, and distributed a bounty of twelve hundred and fifty drachmas a man amongst them; then commended them for the regard and zeal they had for his safety, but told them, that there were some who were intriguing among them, who not only accused his own clemency, but had also misrepresented their loyalty; and, therefore, he desired their assistance in doing justice upon them. To which when they all consented, he was satisfied with the execution of two only, whose deaths he knew would be regretted by no one man in the whole army.

Such conduct, so little expected from him, was regarded by some with gratitude and confidence; others looked upon his behavior as a course to which necessity drove him, to gain the people to the support of the war. For now there were certain tidings that Vitellius had assumed the sovereign title and authority, and frequent expresses brought accounts of new accessions to him; others, however, came, announcing that the Pannonian, Dalmatian, and Mœsian legions, with their officers, adhered to Otho. Erelong also came favorable letters from Mucianus and Vespasian, generals of two formidable armies, the one in Syria, the other in Judæa, to assure him of their firmness to his interest: in confidence whereof he was so exalted that he wrote to Vitellius not to attempt any thing beyond his post; and offered him large sums of money and a city, where he might live his time out in pleasure and ease. These overtures at first were responded to by Vitellius with equivocating civilities; which soon, however, turned into an interchange of angry words; and letters passed between the two, conveying bitter and shameful terms of reproach, which were not false indeed, for that matter, only it was senseless and ridiculous for each to assail the other with accusations to which both alike must plead guilty. For it were hard to determine which of the two had been most profuse, most effeminate, which was most a novice in military affairs, and most involved in debt through previous want of means.

As to the prodigies and apparitions that happened about this time, there were many reported which none could answer for, or which were told in different ways,

but one which everybody actually saw with their eyes
was the statue in the capitol, of Victory carried in a
chariot, with the reins dropped out of her hands, as if
she were grown too weak to hold them any longer;
and a second, that Caius Cæsar's[4] statue in the island
of Tiber, without any earthquake or wind to account
for it, turned round from west to east; and this they
say, happened about the time when Vespasian and
his party first openly began to put themselves forward. Another incident, which the people in general
thought an evil sign, was the inundation of the Tiber;
for though it happened at a time when rivers are usually at their fullest, yet such height of water and so
tremendous a flood had never been known before, nor
such a destruction of property, great part of the city
being under water, and especially the corn market,
so that it occasioned a great dearth for several days.

But when news was now brought that Cæcina and
Valens, commanding for Vitellius, had possessed
themselves of the Alps, Otho sent Dolabella (a patrician, who was suspected by the soldiery of some ill
design), for whatever reason, whether it were fear of
him or of any one else, to the town of Aquinum, to
give encouragement there; and proceeding then to
choose which of the magistrates should go with him to
the war, he named amongst the rest Lucius, Vitellius's
brother, without distinguishing him by any new marks
either of his favor or displeasure. He also took the
greatest precautions for Vitellius's wife and mother,
that they might be safe, and free from all apprehension for themselves. He made Flavius Sabinus, Vespasian's brother, governor of Rome, either in honor to
the memory of Nero, who had advanced him formerly

---

[4] Caius Cæsar is here the great Cæsar, Julius Cæsar as we call
him; "divus Julius" in Tacitus.

to that command, which Galba had taken away, or else to show his confidence in Vespasian by his favor to his brother.

After he came to Brixillum, a town of Italy near the Po, he stayed behind himself, and ordered the army to march under the conduct of Marius Celsus, Suetonius Paulinus, Gallus, and Spurina, all men of experience and reputation, but unable to carry their own plans and purposes into effect, by reason of the ungovernable temper of the army, which would take orders from none but the emperor whom they themselves had made their master. Nor was the enemy under much better discipline, the soldiers there also being haughty and disobedient upon the same account, but they were more experienced and used to hard work; whereas Otho's men were soft from their long easy living and lack of service, having spent most of their time in theatres and at state-shows and on the stage; while moreover they tried to cover their deficiencies by arrogance and vain display, pretending to decline their duty not because they were unable to do the thing commanded but because they thought themselves above it. So that Spurina had like to have been cut in pieces for attempting to force them to their work; they assailed him with insolent language, accusing him of a design to betray and ruin Cæsar's interest; nay, some of them that were in drink forced his tent in the night, and demanded money for the expenses of their journey, which they must at once take, they said, to the emperor, to complain of him.

However, the contemptuous treatment they met with at Placentia did for the present good service to Spurina, and to the cause of Otho. For Vitellius's men marched up to the walls, and upbraided Otho's upon the ramparts, calling them players, dancers, idle spectators of Pythian and Olympic games, but novices in the art of war, who never so much as looked on at a battle; mean souls, that triumphed in the beheading of Galba, an old man unarmed, but had no desire to look real enemies in the face. Which reproaches so inflamed them, that they kneeled at Spurina's feet, entreated him to give his orders, and assured him no danger or toil should be too great or too difficult for them. Whereupon when Vitellius's forces made a vigorous attack on the town, and brought up numerous engines against the walls, the besieged bravely repulsed them, and, repelling the enemy with great slaughter, secured the safety of a noble city, one of the most flourishing places in Italy.

Besides, it was observed that Otho's officers were much more inoffensive, both towards the public and to private men, than those of Vitellius; among whom was Cæcina, who used neither the language nor the apparel of a citizen, an overbearing, foreign-seeming man, of gigantic stature, and always dressed in trews and sleeves, after the manner of the Gauls, whilst he conversed with Roman officials and magistrates. His wife, too, travelled along with him, riding in splendid attire on horseback, with a chosen body of cavalry to escort her. And Fabius Valens, the other general, was so rapacious, that neither what he plundered from enemies nor what he stole or got as gifts and bribes from his friends and allies could satisfy his wishes. And it was said that it was in order to have time to raise money that he had marched so slowly that he was not present at the former attack. But some lay the blame on Cæcina, saying, that out of a desire to gain the victory by himself before Fabius joined him, he committed sundry other errors of lesser consequence, and by engaging unseasonably and when he could not do so thoroughly, he very nearly brought all to ruin.

When he found himself beat off at Placentia, he

set off to attack Cremona, another large and rich city. In the mean time, Annius Gallus marched to join Spurina at Placentia; but having intelligence that the siege was raised, and that Cremona was in danger, he turned to its relief, and encamped just by the enemy, where he was daily reinforced by other officers. Cæcina placed a strong ambush of heavy infantry in some rough and woody country, and gave orders to his horse to advance, and if the enemy should charge them, then to make a slow retreat, and draw them into the snare. But his stratagem was discovered by some deserters to Celsus, who attacked with a good body of horse, but followed the pursuit cautiously, and succeeded in surrounding and routing the troops in the ambuscade; and if the infantry which he ordered up from the camp had come soon enough to sustain the horse, Cæcina's whole army, in all appearance, had been totally routed. But Paulinus, moving too slowly, was accused of acting with a degree of needless caution not to have been expected from one of his reputation. So that the soldiers incensed Otho against him, accused him of treachery, and boasted loudly that the victory had been in their power, and that if it was not complete, it was owing to the mismanagement of their generals; all which Otho did not so much believe as he was willing to appear not to disbelieve. He therefore sent his brother Titianus, with Proculus, the prefect of the guards, to the army, where the latter was general in reality, and the former in appearance. Celsus and Paulinus had the title of friends and counsellors, but not the least authority or power. At the same time, there was nothing but quarrel and disturbance amongst the enemy, especially where Valens commanded; for the soldiers here, being informed of what had happened at the ambuscade, were enraged because they had not been permitted to be present to strike a blow in defence of the lives of so many men that had died in that action. Valens, with much difficulty, quieted their fury, after they had now begun to throw missiles at him, and quitting his camp, joined Cæcina.

About this time, Otho came to Bedriacum, a little town near Cremona, to the camp, and called a council of war; where Proculus and Titianus declared for giving battle, while the soldiers were flushed with their late success, saying they ought not to lose their time and opportunity and present height of strength, and wait for Vitellius to arrive out of Gaul. But Paulinus told them that the enemy's whole force was present, and that there was no body of reserve behind; but that Otho, if he would not be too precipitate, and choose the enemy's time, instead of his own, for the battle, might expect reinforcements out of Mœsia and Pannonia, not inferior in numbers to the troops that were already present. He thought it probable, too, that the soldiers, who were then in heart before they were joined, would not be less so when the forces were all come up. Besides, the deferring battle could not be inconvenient to them that were sufficiently provided with all necessaries; but the others, being in an enemy's country, must needs be exceedingly straitened in a little time. Marius Celsus was of Paulinus's opinion; Annius Gallus, being absent and under the surgeon's hands through a fall from his horse, was consulted by letter, and advised Otho to stay for those legions that were marching from Mœsia. But after all he did not follow the advice; and the opinion of those that declared for a battle prevailed.

There are several reasons given for this determination, but the most apparent is this: that the prætorian soldiers, as they are called, who serve as guards, not relishing the military discipline which they now had begun a little more to experience, and longing for their amusements and unwarlike life among the shows of Rome, would not be commanded, but were eager for a battle, imagining that upon the first onset they should carry all before them. Otho also himself seems not to have shown the proper fortitude in bearing up against the uncertainty, and, out of effeminacy and want of use, had not patience for the calculations of danger, and was so uneasy at the apprehension of it, that he shut his eyes, and like one going to leap from a precipice, left every thing to fortune. This is the account Secundus the rhetorician, who was his secretary, gave of the matter But others would tell you that there are many movements in both armies for acting in concert; and if it were possible for them to agree, then they should proceed to choose one of their most experienced officers that were present; if not, they should convene the senate, and invest it with the power of election. And it is not improbable that, neither of the emperors then bearing the title having really any reputation, such purposes were really entertained among the genuine, serviceable, and sober-minded part of the soldiers. For what could be more odious and unreasonable than that the evils which the Roman citizens had formerly thought it so lamentable to inflict upon each other for the sake of a Sylla or a Marius, a Cæsar or a Pompey, should now be undergone anew, for the object of letting the empire pay the expenses of the gluttony and intemperance of Vitellius, or the looseness and effeminacy of Otho? It is thought that Celsus, upon such reflections, protracted the time in order to a possible accommodation; and that Otho pushed on things to an extremity to prevent it.

He himself returned to Brixillum, which was another false step, both because he withdrew from the combatants all the motives of respect and desire to gain his favor, which his presence would have supplied, and because he weakened the army by detaching some of his best and most faithful troops for his horse and foot guards.

About the same time also happened a skirmish on the Po. As Cæcina was laying a bridge over it, Otho's men attacked him, and tried to prevent it. And when they did not succeed, on their putting into their boats torchwood with a quantity of sulphur and pitch, the wind on the river suddenly caught their material that they had prepared against the enemy, and blew it into a light. First came smoke, and then a clear flame, and the men, getting into great confusion and jumping overboard, upset the boats, and put themselves ludicrously at the mercy of their enemies. Also the Germans attacked Otho's gladiators upon a small island in the river, routed them, and killed a good many.

All which made the soldiers at Bedriacum full of anger, and eagerness to be led to battle. So Proculus led them out of Bedriacum to a place fifty furlongs off, where he pitched his camp so ignorantly and with such a ridiculous want of foresight, that the soldiers suffered extremely for want of water, thought it was the spring time, and the plains all around were full of running streams and rivers that never dried up. The next day he proposed to attack the enemy, first making a march of not less than a hundred furlongs; but to this Paulinus objected, saying they ought to wait, and not immediately after a journey engage men who would have been standing in their arms and arranging themselves for battle at their leisure, whilst they were making a long march with all their beasts of burden and their camp followers to encumber them. As the generals were arguing about this matter, a Numidian courier came from Otho with orders to lose no time, but give battle. Accordingly they consented, and moved. As soon as Cæcina had notice, he was much surprised, and quitted his post on the river to hasten to the camp. In the mean time, the men had armed themselves mostly, and were receiving the word from Valens; so while the legions took up their position, they sent out the best of their horse in advance.

Otho's foremost troops, upon some groundless rumor, took up the notion that the commanders on the other side would come over; and accordingly, upon their first approach, they saluted them with the friendly title of fellow-soldiers. But the others returned the compliment with anger and disdainful words; which not only disheartened those that had given the salutation, but excited suspicions of their fidelity amongst the others on their side, who had not. This caused a confusion at the very first onset. And nothing else that followed was done upon any plan; the baggage-carriers, mingling up with the fighting men, created great disorder and division, as well as the nature of the ground; the ditches and pits in which were so many, that they were forced to break their ranks to avoid and go round them, and so to fight without order and in small parties. There were but two legions, one of Vitellius's, called The Ravenous,[5] and another of Otho's, called The Assistant, that got out into the open outspread level and engaged in proper form, fighting, one main body against the other, for some length of time. Otho's men were

[5] All the legions seem to have had these high-sounding additions to the numbers that denoted them. There are a great many on record. The Twenty-first the Ravenous, and The First the Assistant, UNA ET VICESIMA RAPAX and PRIMA ADJUTRIX, were the style of the two here mentioned.

strong and bold, but had never been in battle before; Vitellius's had seen many wars, but were old and past their strength. So Otho's legion charged boldly, drove back their opponents, and took the eagle, killing pretty nearly every man in the first rank, till the others, full of rage and shame, returned the charge, slew Orfidius, the commander of the legion, and took several standards. Varus Alfenus, with his Batavians, who are the natives of an island of the Rhine, and are esteemed the best of the German horse, fell upon the gladiators, who had a reputation both for valor and skill in fighting. Some few of these did their duty, but the greatest part of them made towards the river, and, falling in with some cohorts stationed there, were cut off. But none behaved so ill as the prætorians, who, without ever so much as meeting the enemy, ran away, broke through their own body that stood, and put them into disorder. Notwithstanding this, many of Otho's men routed those that were opposed to them, broke right into them, and forced their way to the camp through the very middle of their conquerors

As for their commanders, neither Proculus nor Paulinus ventured to reënter with the troops; they turned aside, and avoided the soldiers, who had already charged the miscarriage upon their officers. Annius Gallus received into the town and rallied the scattered parties, and encouraged them with an assurance that the battle was a drawn one and the victory had in many parts been theirs. Marius Celsus, collecting the officers, urged the public interest; Otho himself, if he were a brave man, would not, after such an expense of Roman blood, attempt any thing further; especially since even Cato and Scipio, though the liberty of Rome was then at stake, had been accused of being too prodigal of so many brave men's lives as were lost in Africa, rather than submit to Cæsar after the battle of Pharsalia had gone against them. For though all persons are equally subject to the caprice of fortune, yet all good men have one advantage she cannot deny, which is this, to act reasonably under misfortunes.

This language was well accepted amongst the officers, who sounded the private soldiers, and found them desirous of peace; and Titianus also gave directions that envoys should be sent in order to a treaty. And accordingly it was agreed that the conference should be between Celsus and Gallus on one part, and Valens with Cæcina on the other. As the two first were upon their journey, they met some centurions, who told them the troops were already in motion, marching for Bedriacum, but that they themselves were deputed by their generals to carry proposals for an accommodation. Celsus and Gallus expressed their approval, and requested them to turn back and carry them to Cæcina. However, Celsus, upon his approach, was in danger from the vanguard, who happened to be some of the horse that had suffered at the ambush. For as soon as they saw him, they hallooed, and were coming down upon him; but the centurions came forward to protect him, and the other officers crying out and bidding them desist, Cæcina came up to inform himself of the tumult, which he quieted, and, giving a friendly greeting to Celsus, took him in his company and proceeded towards Bedriacum. Titianus, meantime, had repented of having sent the messengers; and placed those of the soldiers who were more confident upon the walls once again, bidding the others also go and support them. But when Cæcina rode up on his horse and held out his hand, no one did or said to the contrary; those on the walls greeted his men with salutations, others opened the gates and went out, and mingled freely with those they met; and instead of acts of hostility, there was nothing but mutual shaking of hands and congratulations, every one taking the oaths and submitting to Vitellius.

This is the account which the most of those that were present at the battle give of it, yet own that the disorder they were in, and the absence of any unity of action would not give them leave to be certain as to particulars. And when I myself travelled afterwards over the field of battle, Mestrius Florus,[6] a man of consular degree, one of those who had been, not willingly, but by command, in attendance on Otho at the time, pointed out to me an ancient temple, and told me, that as he went that way after the battle, he observed a heap of bodies piled up there to such a height, that those on the top of it touched the pinnacles of the roof. How it came to be so, he could neither discover himself nor learn from any other person; as indeed, he said, in civil wars it generally happens that greater numbers are killed when an army is routed, quarter not being given, because captives are of no advantage to the conquerors; but why the carcases should be heaped up after that manner is not easy to determine.

Otho, at first, as it frequently happens, received some uncertain rumors of the issue of the battle. But when some of the wounded that returned from the field informed him rightly of it, it is not, indeed, so much to be wondered at that his friends should bid him not give all up as lost or let his courage sink; but the feeling shown by the soldiers is something that exceeds all belief. There was not one of them would either go over to the conqueror or show any disposi-

---

[6] Mestrius Florus is also mentioned as a *consular* by Suetonius (*Vespasian*, 22). Vespasian made a witty retort to him.

tion to make terms for himself, as if their leader's cause was desperate; on the contrary, they crowded his gates, called out to him with the title of emperor, and as soon as he appeared, cried out and entreated him, catching hold of his hand, and throwing themselves upon the ground, and with all the moving language of tears and persuasion, besought him to stand by them, not abandon them to their enemies, but employ in his service their lives and persons, which would not cease to be his so long as they had breath; so urgent was their zealous and universal importunity. And one obscure and private soldier, after he had drawn his sword, addressed himself to Otho: "By this, Cæsar, judge our fidelity; there is not a man amongst us but would strike thus to serve you;" and so stabbed himself. Notwithstanding this, Otho stood serene and unshaken, and, with a face full of constancy and composure, turned himself about and looked at them, replying thus: "This day, my fellow-soldiers, which gives me such proofs of your affection, is preferable even to that on which you saluted me emperor; deny me not, therefore, the yet higher satisfaction of laying down my life for the preservation of so many brave men; in this, at least, let me be worthy of the empire, that is, to die for it. I am of opinion the enemy has neither gained an entire nor a decisive victory; I have advice that the Mœsian army is not many days' journey distant, on its march to the Adriatic; Asia, Syria, and Egypt, and the legions that are serving against the Jews, declare for us; the senate is also with us, and the wives and children of our opponents are in our power; but alas, it is not in defence of Italy against Hannibal or Pyrrhus or the Cimbri that we fight; Romans combat here against Romans, and, whether we conquer or are defeated, our country suffers and we commit a crime: victory, to whichever it fall, is gained at her expense. Believe it many times over, I can die with more honor than I can reign. For I cannot see at all, how I should do any such great good to my country by gaining the victory, as I shall by dying to establish peace and unanimity and to save Italy from such another unhappy day."

As soon as he had done, he was resolute against all manner of argument or persuasion, and taking leave of his friends and the senators that were present, he bade them depart, and wrote to those that were absent, and sent letters to the towns, that they might have every honor and facility in their journey. Then he sent for Cocceius, his brother's son,[7] who was yet a boy, and bade him be in no apprehension of Vitellius, whose mother and wife and family he had treated with the same tenderness as his own; and also told him that this had been his reason for delaying to adopt him, which he had meant to do, as his son; he had desired that he might share his power, if he conquered, but not be involved in his ruin, if he failed. "Take notice," he added, "my boy, of these my last words, that you neither too negligently forget, nor too zealously remember, that Cæsar was your uncle." By and by he heard a tumult amongst the soldiers at the door, who were treating the senators with menaces for preparing to withdraw; upon which, out of regard to their safety, he showed himself once more in public, but not with a gentle aspect and in a persuading manner as before; on the contrary, with a countenance that discovered indignation and authority, he commanded such as were disorderly to leave the place, and was not disobeyed.

[7] More correctly, Cocceianus, Salvius Cocceianus, the son of Titianus.

It was now evening, and feeling thirsty, he drank
some water, and then took two daggers that belonged
to him, and when he had carefully examined their
edges, he laid one of them down, and put the other in
his robe, under his arm, then called his servants, and
distributed some money amongst them, but not inconsiderately, nor like one too lavish of what was not his
own; for to some he gave more, to others less, all
strictly in moderation, and distinguishing every one's
particular merit. When this was done, he dismissed
them, and passed the rest of the night in so sound a
sleep, that the officers of his bed-chamber heard him
snore. In the morning, he called for one of his freedmen, who had assisted him in arranging about the
senators, and bade him bring him an account if they
were safe. Being informed they were all well and
wanted nothing, "Go then," said he, "and show yourself to the soldiers, lest they should cut you to pieces
for being accessory to my death." As soon as he was
gone, he held his sword upright under him with both
his hands, and falling upon it, expired with no more
than one single groan, to express his sense of the
pang, or to inform those that waited without. When
his servants therefore raised their exclamations of
grief, the whole camp and city were at once filled
with lamentation; the soldiers immediately broke in
at the doors with a loud cry, in passionate distress,
and accusing themselves that they had been so negligent in looking after that life which was laid down to
preserve theirs. Nor would a man of them quit the
body to secure his own safety with the approaching
enemy; but having raised a funeral pile, and attired
the body, they bore it thither, arrayed in their arms,
those among them greatly exulting, who succeeded
in getting first under the bier and becoming its bearers. Of the others, some threw themselves down be-

fore the body and kissed his wound, others grasped his hand, and others that were at a distance knelt down to do him obeisance. There were some who, after putting their torches to the pile, slew themselves, though they had not, so far as appeared, either any particular obligations to the dead, or reason to apprehend ill usage from the victor. Simply it would seem, no king, legal or illegal, had ever been possessed with so extreme and vehement a passion to command others, as was that of these men to obey Otho. Nor did their love of him cease with his death; it survived and changed erelong into a mortal hatred to his successor, as will be shown in its proper place.

They placed the remains of Otho in the earth, and raised over them a monument which neither by its size nor the pomp of its inscription might excite hostility.[8] I myself have seen it, at Brixillum; a plain structure, and the epitaph only this: To the memory of Marcus Otho. He died in his thirty-eighth year, after a short reign of about three months, his death being as much applauded as his life was censured; for if he lived not better than Nero, he died more nobly. The soldiers were displeased with Pollio, one of their two prefects,[9] who bade them immediately swear allegiance to Vitellius; and when they understood that some of the senators were still upon the spot, they made no opposition to the departure of the rest, but

[8] "Modicum et mansurum" Tacitus calls it. The inscription has been corrected on conjecture from Memory to Manes (*diamosi* instead of *delosei*), so that it is supposed to have stood DIIS MANIBUS MARCI OTHONIS.

[9] The two prefects were Plotius Firmus and Licinius Proculus. Probably Pollio is a mistake or corruption, and Plotius or Proculus should be the name. The words at the end of the preceding paragraph seem to refer to a continuation of the series, a life of Vitellius.

only disturbed the tranquillity of Virginius Rufus with an offer of the government, and moving in one body to his house in arms, they first entreated him, and then demanded of him to accept of the empire, or at least to be their mediator. But he, that refused to command them when conquerors, thought it ridiculous to pretend to it now they were beat, and was unwilling to go as their envoy to the Germans, whom in past time he had compelled to do various things that they had not liked; and for these reasons he slipped away through a private door. As soon as the soldiers perceived this, they owned Vitellius, and so got their pardon, and served under Cæcina.

The lives of Galba and Otho recall us to that of Plutarch himself. There can be little question that they are his genuine work; any difference in tone may be easily accounted for by difference in subject, and we feel perhaps the effects of his having been studying Tacitus. The visit to Bedriacum may accordingly be added to the brief sum of Plutarch's recorded Italian experiences.

Among the notable people with whom he came into connection should have been mentioned, perhaps, Dio Chrysostom, the eloquent speaker to whom in the catalogue of his writings he is said to have dedicated one of his minor works, and king Philopappus, so well known by the monument to him remaining on the Museum Hill at Athens; who appears as resident in Athens at the time of one of the scenes in the Symposiac Questions.

There were, apparently, lives of both the Scipios; and the elder perhaps not the younger (as stated in *Vol. I.*), was compared with Epaminondas.

The most complete summary of all the notices of Plutarch's life and circumstances to be found both in his own works and elsewhere is in the preface by Westermann to the edition of the Greek text by Bekker, published by Bernhard Tauchnitz. This I had not seen until after the Preface in Vol. I. had been printed.
—A. H. Clough.

INDEX

INDEX

OF HISTORICAL AND GEOGRAPHICAL PROPER NAMES

ABANTES, of Eubœa, Theseus, i. 5.
ABANTIDAS, tyrant of Sicyon, Aratus, v. 387, 388.
ABAS, a river in Asia, Pompey, iv. 107.
ABDERA, in Thrace, Alexander, iv. 253.
ABILLIUS, a son of Romulus, Romulus, i. 58.
ABŒOCRITUS, the Bœotarch, defeated by the Ætolians, Aratus, v. 400.
ABOLUS, a river in Sicily, Timoleon, ii. 161.
ABRA, a maid, Cicero, v. 68.
ABRIORIX or AMBIORIX, the Gaul, Cæsar, iv. 315.
ABROTONON, mother of Themistocles, Themistocles, i. 244.
ABULETES, a Persian, Alexander, iv. 274.
ABYDOS, in Troas, Alcibiades, ii. 40, 43, 53; Cæsar, iv. 364.
ACADEMIA, Theseus, i. 36.
ACADEMY, the garden at Athens, Solon, i. 178; Sylla, iii. 169; Cimon, iii. 233.
ACADEMY, school of philosophy, Philopœmen, ii. 395; Lucullus, iii. 299; Comparison of Lucullus and Cimon, iii. 302; Phocion, iv. 371, 382; Cicero, v. 40; Dion, v. 259, 274, 278, 280, 306, 311; Brutus, v. 320, 344; Aratus v. 389, 419.
ACAMANTIS, Attic tribe, Pericles, i. 340.
ACANTHIANS, Lysander, iii. 113, 134.
ACARNANIA, Pericles, i. 365, 367; Pyrrhus, iii. 8; Agesilaus, iv. 32; Aratus, v. 161.
ACARNANIANS, Numa, i. 161; Alexander, iv. 165, 204; Cleomenes, iv. 552.
ACASTUS, son of Pelias, Sylla, iii. 204.
ACCA LARENTIA, wife of Faustulus, Romulus, i. 45.
ACERRÆ, in Cisalpine Gaul, Marcellus, ii. 267.
ACESTODORUS, a writer, Themistocles, i. 261.
ACHÆAN HARBOR, Lucullus, iii. 258.
ACHÆANS of Phthiotis, Pericles, i. 365; Pelopidas, ii. 255, 259; Flamininus, ii. 436.
ACHÆA and ACHÆANS, Pericles, i. 367; Cato the Elder, ii. 359; Philopœmen, ii. 396, and following; Flamininus, ii. 428, 441, 445, 446; Comparison of Philopœmen and Flamininus, ii. 454, and following; Agesilaus, iv. 32; Agis, iv. 510, 511; Cleomenes, iv. 523, and following; Demosthenes, v. 19; Aratus, v. 394, and following.
ACHAÏCUS, surname of Mummius, Marius, iii. 52.
ACHARNÆ, in Attica, Themistocles, i. 273; Pericles, i. 384.
ACHELOUS, river in Acarnania, Pericles, i. 367.

533

INDEX

ACHILLAS, an Egyptian, Pompey, iv. 165-170; Cæsar, iv. 342, 343.
ACHILLES, Theseus, i. 37; Camillus, i. 299; Alcibiades, ii. 33; Aristides, ii. 319; Philopœmen, ii. 395, 405; Pyrrhus, iii. 1, 9, 16; Comparison of Lysander and Sylla, iii. 211; Agesilaus, iv. 8; Pompey, iv. 97; Alexander, iv. 197, 198; Cleomenes, iv. 558.
ACHILLES, a Macedonian, Pyrrhus, iii. 3.
ACHRADINA, or ACRADINA, in Syracuse, Timoleon, ii. 142, 143, 146; Marcellus, ii. 284; Dion, v. 288, 291, 296, 301.
ACILÆ or ACRILLÆ, in Sicily, Marcellus, ii. 283.
CAIUS ACILIUS, an historian, Romulus, i. 70; Cato the Elder, ii. 380.
MANIUS ACILIUS (Glabrio), Cato the Elder, ii. 363, 366, 367; Philopœmen, ii. 416, 421 (under the name of MANIUS); Flamininus, ii. 443, 444; Sylla, iii. 170.
ACILIUS, friend of Brutus, Brutus, v. 343.
ACILIUS, a soldier of Cæsar, Cæsar, iv. 304.
ACONTIUM, a mountain in Bœotia, Sylla, iii. 178, 181.
ACRÆ or MACRÆ, in Sicily, Dion, v. 286.
ACRO-CORINTHUS, castle or citadel of Corinth, Cleomenes, iv. 537, 542; Aratus, v. 401, and following.
ACRON, king of the Ceninenses, Romulus, i. 60, 61; Comparison of Romulus and Theseus, i. 82; Marcellus, ii. 270.
ACROTATUS, son of Cleomenes, king of Sparta, Agis, iv. 499.
ACROTATUS, son of Areus, grandson of the first Acrotatus, Pyrrhus, iii. 39, 42; Agis, iv. 499.
ACRURIUM, a mountain in Phocis, Phocion, iv. 406.

ACTÆON, a Platæan hero, Aristides, ii. 324.
ACTÆON, two of that name, Sertorius, iii. 405.
ACTE, coast of Argolis, Demetrius, v. 127; Aratus, v. 426.
ACTIUM, Pompey, iv. 89; Antony, v. 228, 229, 235, 237, 239; Brutus, v. 379.
ACUPHIS, of Nysa, Alexander, iv. 262.
ADA, queen of Caria, Alexander, iv. 209.
ADÆUS, or IDÆUS, secretary to Agesilaus, Agesilaus, iv. 19.
ADIABENIANS, in Asia, Lucullus, iii. 276, 280.
ADIGE, the river, Marius, iii. 79, 80.
ADIMANTUS, archon at Athens, Themistocles, i. 250.
ADIMANTUS, an Athenian general, Alcibiades, ii. 54.
ADMETUS, beloved of Apollo, Numa, i. 139.
ADMETUS, king of the Molossians, Themistocles, i. 273.
ADONIS, Alcibiades, ii. 25; Nicias, iii. 327.
ADRAMYTTIUM, in Mysia, Cicero, v. 41.
ADRANITANS, Timoleon, ii. 134.
ADRANUM, a town in Sicily, Timoleon, ii. 134.
ADRANUS, a Sicilian deity, Timoleon, ii. 133.
ADRASTEA MOUNT, near Cyzicum, Lucullus, iii. 255.
ADRASTUS, king of the Argives, Theseus, i. 32.
ADRASTUS, a nickname, Cicero, v. 67.
ADRIA, a city of the Tyrrhenians, Camillus, i. 301.
ADRIA, a corrupt reading, Aratus, v. 396, n.
ADRIANUS, legate of Lucullus, Lucullus, iii. 264.
ADRIATIC SEA, Camillus, i. 301, 332;

INDEX 585

Æmilius Paulus, ii. 179; Antony, v. 226; Dion, v. 270; Otho, v. 525.
ADRUMETUM, a town in Africa, Cato the Younger, iv. 481.
ÆACIDÆ, Themistocles, i. 248; Pyrrhus, iii. 38.
ÆACIDES, son of Arybas, king of the Molossians, father of Pyrrhus, Pyrrhus, iii. 1-3; Demetrius, v. 127.
ÆACUS, Theseus, i. 274; Alexander, iv. 179; Demosthenes, v. 32.
ÆANTIS, Attic tribe, Aristides, ii. 335.
ÆDEPSUS, town of Eubœa, Sylla, iii. 189.
ÆDUI or EDUI, a Gallic tribe, Cæsar, iv. 317.
ÆGÆ, a town in Æolia, Themistocles, i. 274.
ÆGÆ, in Macedonia, Pyrrhus, iii. 38; Alexander, iv. 238.
ÆGEIS, Attic tribe, Alcibiades, ii. 29; Nicias, iii. 326.
ÆGESTEANS, people of Segesta in Sicily, Nicias, iii. 308, 325, 328.
ÆGEUS, father of Theseus, Theseus, i. 4, and following; Comparison of Theseus and Romulus, i. 82, 83; Cimon, iii. 224.
ÆGIALIA, island on the coast of Laconia, Cleomenes, iv. 554, 555.
ÆGIAS, banker at Sicyon, Aratus, v. 402, 403.
ÆGICORES, Attic tribe, Solon, i. 201.
ÆGINA, Themistocles, i. 263, 265, 267; Pericles, i. 348, 386; Aristides, ii. 319; Lysander, iii. 122; Demosthenes, v. 1, 30, 31, 32; Demetrius, v. 139; Dion, v. 264.
ÆGINETANS, Themistocles, i. 248; Pericles, i. 379; Lysander, iii. 129; Nicias, iii. 316; Comparison, iii. 403; Dion, v. 264; Aratus, v. 420.
ÆGIUM, town of Achæa, Cato the Elder, ii. 364; Cleomenes, iv. 537, 548; Aratus, v. 422, 427, 428, 438, 439.
ÆGLE, daughter of Panopeus, Theseus, i. 19-31.
ÆGOSPOTAMI, town in Thrace, Alcibiades, ii. 54; Lysander, iii. 122, 123, 126; Artaxerxes, v. 463.
ÆLIA, wife of Sylla, iii. 161.
ÆLII, Æmilius Paulus, ii. 174.
SEXTUS ÆLIUS, Flamininus, ii. 424.
ÆLIUS TUBERO, Æmilius Paulus, ii. 174, 201, 203.
ÆMILIA, wife of Scipio Africanus, Æmilius Paulus, ii. 170.
ÆMILIA, stepdaughter of Sylla and wife of Pompey, Sylla, iii. 200; Pompey, iv. 68, 69.
ÆMILII, Numa, i. 146; Æmilius Paulus, ii. 170.
ÆMILIUS, son of Pythagoras, Numa, i. 146; Æmilius Paulus, ii. 170.
QUINTUS ÆMILIUS, Pyrrhus, iii. 29.
LUCIUS ÆMILIUS PAULUS. See PAULUS.
MARCUS ÆMILIUS (Lucius Æmilius Mamercinus), Camillus, i. 336.
MARCUS ÆMILIUS LEPIDUS, Æmilius Paulus, ii. 215.
ÆMILIUS, the crier, Æmilius Paulus, ii. 214.
ÆMILIUS, quæstor (censor?), Numa, i. 147.
ÆMYLIA, daughter of Æneas, Romulus, i. 42.
ÆNARIA, island on the coast of Campania, Marius, iii. 97, 101.
ÆNEAS, Romulus, i. 42, 43; Comparison of Romulus and Theseus, i. 85; Camillus, i. 308; Coriolanus, ii. 95; Flamininus, ii. 440.
ÆNUS, a city of Thrace, Cato the Younger, iv. 424.
ÆOLIA in Asia Minor, Themistocles, i. 275.
ÆOLUS, islands of, Camillus, i. 295.
ÆPEA, town of Cyprus, Solon, i. 205.

ÆQUIANS, Camillus, i. 286, 323, 326; Coriolanus, ii. 111.
AEROPUS, friend of Pyrrhus, Pyrrhus, iii. 10.
AEROPUS, king of Macedon, Demetrius, v. 121.
ÆSCHINES, the orator, Solon, i. 186; Demosthenes, v. 4, 14, 17, 24, 27.
ÆSCHINES, of Lampra, Aristides, ii. 326.
ÆSCHINES, scholar of Socrates, Pericles, i. 372, 383; Aristides, ii. 343.
ÆSCHYLUS, an Argive, Aratus, v. 410.
ÆSCHYLUS, kinsman of Timoleon, Timoleon, ii. 123.
ÆSCHYLUS, the tragic poet, Theseus, i. 1, 32; Romulus, i. 51; Themistocles, i. 262; Aristides, ii. 312; Cimon, iii. 225; Pompey, iv. 58; Alexander, iv. 188; the Comparison of Demosthenes and Cicero, v. 97; Demetrius, v. 142.
ÆSCULAPIUS, Numa, i. 139; Pompey, iv. 89.
ÆSION, fellow scholar of Demosthenes, Demosthenes, v. 13.
ESON, a river of Macedon, Æm. Paulus, ii. 188.
ÆSOP, or ÆSOPUS, a tragedian, Cicero, v. 42.
ÆSOP, the fabulist, Solon, i. 182, 207; Pelopidas, ii. 259; Crassus, iii. 395; Aratus, v. 416, 424.
ÆSUVIAN MEADOW, Poplicola, i. 222.
ÆTOLIA and ÆTOLIANS, Cato the Elder, ii. 366; Philopœmen, ii. 403, 413; Flamininus, ii. 428, and after; Pyrrhus, iii. 9; Nicias, iii. 315; Alexander, iv. 249; Agis, iv. 510; Cleomenes, iv. 532, 540, 558; Demetrius, v. 148; Aratus, v. 389, and in several places after.
ÆTHRA, mother of Theseus, Theseus, i. 4, 5, 37.
AFIDIUS (or FUFIDIUS?), follower of Sylla, Sylla, iii. 198.

AFRANIUS, lieutenant of Pompey, Sertorius, iii. 429; Pompey, iv. 105, 108, 112, 119, 150, 151; Cæsar, iv. 329, 334, 346.
AFRICA. See LIBYA; and for AFRICANUS see SCIPIO.
AGAMEMNON, Pericles, i. 377; Pelopidas, ii. 243; Lysander, iii. 130; Nicias, iii. 314; Sertorius, iii. 405; Agesilaus, iv. 8, 10, 14.
AGARISTE, mother of Pericles, Pericles, i. 340.
AGATHARCHUS, a painter, Pericles, i. 357; Alcibiades, ii. 23.
AGATHOCLEA, Cleomenes, iv. 557.
AGATHOCLES, son of Lysimachus, Demetrius, v. 136, 156, 157.
AGATHOCLES of Syracuse, Pyrrhus, iii. 11, 19; Demetrius, v. 128.
AGAVE, Crassus, iii. 395.
AGESIAS of Acharnæ, Aristides, ii. 326.
AGESILAUS, king of Sparta, Life, iv. 3; Comparison, iv. 171; Lycurgus, i. 105, 130; Timoleon, ii. 164, 165; Pelopidas, ii. 236; Flamininus, ii. 437; Lysander, iii. 139, 143, 145, 151; Cimon, iii. 242; Phocion, iv. 370; Agis, iv. 498, 499, 510; Artaxerxes, v. 463, 465.
AGESILAUS, a Spartan, uncle of Agis IV., Agis, iv. 499, 502, 505, 509, 512, 515, 516.
AGESIPOLIS I., son of Pausanias, king of Sparta, Pelopidas, ii. 225; Agesilaus, iv. 30, 35; Agis, iv. 499.
AGESIPOLIS II., son of Cleombrotus, king of Sparta, Agis, iv. 499.
AGESISTRATA, mother of Agis, Agis, iv. 499, 515-518.
AGIADÆ, Lysander, iii. 143, 151; Agis, iv. 498.
AGIAS, at Argos, Aratus, v. 414.
AGIATIS, daughter of Gylippus, Cleomenes, iv. 520, 544.
AGIS II., son of Archidamus II.,

INDEX

king of Sparta, Lycurgus, i. 103, 115, 116; Alcibiades, ii. 34-36, 50, 57; Lysander, iii. 122, 128, 139; Agesilaus, iv. 3-6.

AGIS III., son of Archidamus III., king of Sparta, Agesilaus, iv. 22; Agis, iv. 499; Demosthenes, v. 27.

AGIS IV., son of Eudamidas, king of Sparta, Life, iv. 495; Comparison, iv. 619; Agesilaus, iv. 57; Cleomenes, iv. 520-524, 525; Aratus, v. 416.

AGNONIDES or HAGNONIDES, a sycophant, Phocion, iv. 401, 406-408, 411.

AGNUS (more correctly HAGNUS), Attic township, Theseus, i. 12.

AGRAULE, in Attica, Themistocles, i. 271.

AGRAULOS, daughter of Cecrops, Alcibiades, ii. 21.

AGRIGENTUM, in Sicily, Timoleon, ii. 163; Pyrrhus, iii. 31; Dion, v. 285, 308.

MARCUS AGRIPPA, Augustus Cæsar's friend, Comparison of Cicero and Demosthenes, v. 97; Antony, v. 199, 231, 232, 241, 253; Brutus, v. 348.

MENENIUS AGRIPPA, Coriolanus, ii. 65.

AGRIPPINA, Nero's mother, Antony, v. 253; Galba, v. 489.

AGYLÆUS, an ephor, Cleomenes, iv. 528.

SERVILIUS AHALA, Brutus, v. 319.

AHENOBARBUS, a surname, Æm. Paulus, ii. 198. See DOMITIUS.

AJAX, Theseus, i. 31; Solon, i. 185; Alcibiades, ii. 1; Pompey, iv. 159.

AIDONEUS, king of the Molossians, Theseus, i. 34, 38.

AIUS LOCUTIUS, Camillus, i. 320.

ALBA, a town of Latium, Romulus, i. 42, 48, 49, 51, 69, 75; Comparison of Romulus and Theseus, i. 82; Pompey, iv. 132, 170; Cæsar, iv. 353; Antony, v. 226.

ALBANS, Camillus, i. 302; Alban Lake, Camillus, i. 287-289; Alban farm, Sylla, iii. 199; Alban hills, Cicero, v. 72; Alban mount, Marcellus, ii. 289.

ALBANIANS, a people of Asia, Lucullus, iii. 277; Pompey, iv. 106, 108, 111, 120; Antony, v. 199.

DECIMUS BRUTUS ALBINUS. See under BRUTUS.

LUCIUS ALBINUS or ALBINIUS, Camillus, i. 309.

POSTUMIUS ALBINUS, an historian, Cato the Elder, ii. 364.

ALBINUS, a Roman general, Marius, iii. 61.

ALBINUS, Sylla's lieutenant, Sylla, iii. 161.

ALCÆUS, an epigram-writer, Flamininus, ii. 433, 434.

ALCÆUS, of Sardis, Pompey, iv. 110.

ALCANDER, a Spartan, Lycurgus, i. 101.

ALCETAS, a Macedonian general, brother of Perdiccas, Eumenes, iii. 446, 451; Alexander, iv. 258.

ALCETAS, son of Tharrhypas, Pyrrhus, iii. 1.

ALCIBIADES, Life, ii. 1; Comparison, ii. 112; Lycurgus, i. 111; Numa, i. 146; Pericles, i. 368, 390; Pelopidas, ii. 224; Aristides, ii. 318, 345; Flamininus, ii. 437; Lysander, iii. 116, 118, 123, 124, 135, 139; Comparison of Lysander and Sylla, iii. 211; Nicias, iii. 318, and after; Comparison of Nicias and Crassus, iii. 399, 400; Agesilaus, iv. 5, 6; Demosthenes, v. 1, 31; Comparison of Demosthenes and Cicero, v. 99; Antony, v. 237.

ALCIDAMAS, an orator, Demosthenes, v. 6.

ALCIMENES, an Achæan, Dion, v. 281.

ALCIMUS, promontory in Attica, Themistocles, i. 284.

ALCIMUS, an Epirot, Demetrius, v. 123.
ALCMÆON, in command of the Athenians, Solon, i. 186, 208.
ALCMÆON, of Agraule, Themistocles, i. 271; Aristides, ii. 344.
ALCMÆON, son of Amphiaraus, Alcibiades, ii. 1; Aratus, v. 389.
ALCMAN, a Lacedæmonian poet, Lycurgus, i. 119, 127; Sylla, iii.. 204.
ALCMENA, mother of Hercules, Theseus, i. 7; Romulus, i. 79; Lysander, iii. 148.
ALCYONEUS, son of Antigonus, Pyrrhus, iii. 51.
ALEA, in Bœotia, Lysander, iii. 148.
ALESIA, town in Gaul, Cæsar, iv. 318, 319.
ALEXANDER of Antioch, follower of Antony, Antony, v. 213, 215, 233.
ALEXANDER, son of Antony and Cleopatra, Antony, v. 201, 221.
ALEXANDER, son of Cassander, Pyrrhus, iii. 8; Demetrius, v. 141-144; Comparison of Demetrius and Antony, v. 258.
ALEXANDER, an Aristotelian philosopher, a teacher of Crassus, Crassus, iii. 354.
ALEXANDER, grandson of Craterus, Aratus, v. 401, 402.
ALEXANDER, son of Demetrius Poliorcetes, Demetrius, v. 164.
ALEXANDER, a freedman, Pompey, iv. 62.
ALEXANDER I., king of Macedon, Aristides, ii. 329, 330; Cimon, iii. 234.
ALEXANDER II., king of Macedon, Pelopidas, ii. 249.
ALEXANDER THE GREAT, Life, iv. 178; Theseus, i. 5; Camillus, i. 305; Æm. Paulus, ii. 182, 197, 201; Pelopidas, ii. 258; Aristides, ii. 325; Flamininus, ii. 431, 451; Pyrrhus, iii. 10, 13, 26; Comparison of Nicias and Crassus, iii. 403; Eumenes, iii. 441, 443, 447, 448, 457, 463, 464; Agesilaus, iv. 22; Pompey, iv. 59, 106, 121; Comparison of Pompey and Agesilaus, iv. 173; Cæsar, iv. 299; Phocion, iv. 378, 385-388, 390, 392, 400, 401; Demosthenes, v. 10, 23, 26, 27, 30; Demetrius, v. 133, 143, 149; Antony, v. 171, 221, 247; Comparison, v. 257; Galba, v. 477; also Philopœmen, ii. 398.
ALEXANDER the Myndian, a writer, Marius, iii. 72.
ALEXANDER, son of Perseus, Æm. Paulus, ii. 213.
ALEXANDER, of Pheræ, Pelopidas, ii. 248-261.
ALEXANDER, son of Polysperchon, Phocion, iv. 405; Demetrius, v. 110.
ALEXANDER, son of Pyrrhus, Pyrrhus, iii. 11.
ALEXANDER, son of Roxana, Pyrrhus, iii. 4.
ALEXANDER, general of the Thracians, Æm. Paulus, ii. 190.
ALEXANDRIA and ALEXANDRIANS, Lucullus, iii. 246; Pompey, iv. 127; Alexander, iv. 214; Cæsar, iv. 341, 343; Cato the Younger, iv. 452; Cleomenes, iv. 556, 558, 564; Antony, v. 168, 191, 193, 218, 220, 221, 225, 236, 239.
ALEXANDRIDES or ANAXANDRIDES, Lysander, iii. 134.
ALEXANDROPOLIS, Alexander, iv. 189.
ALEXAS, of Laodicea, friend of Antony, Antony, v. 240.
ALEXICRATES, an Epirot, Pyrrhus's cupbearer, Pyrrhus, iii. 6.
ALEXIPPUS, a physician, Alexander, iv. 238.
ALFENUS VARUS, general of Vitellius, Otho, v. 522.
ALLIA, river of Italy, Camillus, i. 305, 313.

INDEX

ALLOBROGES, Gallic tribe, Cicero, v. 56, 57.
ALOPECE, township in Attica, Themistocles, i. 283; Pericles, i. 353; Aristides, ii. 308.
ALOPECUS, a hill in Bœotia, Lysander, iii. 150.
ALSÆA (more probably Alea or Asea), in Arcadia, Cleomenes, iv. 527.
ALYCUS, son of Sciron, Theseus, i. 36.
AMANTIUS (Matius?), Cæsar's friend, Cæsar, iv. 344.
AMANUS, mountain in Cilicia, Pompey, iv. 112; Cicero, v. 78; Demetrius, v. 159.
AMARSYAS, Theseus, i. 16.
AMATHUSIANS, of Cyprus, Theseus, i. 19, 20.
AMAZONS, Theseus, i. 27-31; Comparison of Theseus and Romulus, i. 82; Pericles, i. 382; Lucullus, iii. 273; Pompey, iv. 107; Alexander, iv. 243; Demosthenes, v. 21.
AMAZONIUM, at Athens, Theseus, i. 29; at Chalcis, Theseus, i. 30.
AMBIORIX, or ABRIORIX, king of the Gauls, Cæsar, iv. 315.
AMBRACIA, in Acarnania, Pericles, i. 365; Pyrrhus, iii. 8, 11.
AMBRONES, a Celtic tribe, Marius, iii. 60, 65-67.
QUINTUS FABIUS AMBUSTUS, ambassador, Numa, i. 152; Camillus, i. 289, 303.
AMERIA, town in Umbria, Marius, iii. 72.
AMESTRIS, Artaxerxes, v. 466, 471.
AMINIAS of Decelea, Themistocles, i. 262; Comparison of Aristides and Cato, ii. 389.
AMINIAS, a Phocian, Pyrrhus, iii. 44.
AMISUS, town in Pontus, Lucullus, iii. 260, 261, 267, 287, 288; Pompey, iv. 110, 116.

AMMON, Lysander, iii. 137, 144; Cimon, iii. 241; Nicias, iii. 326; Alexander, iv. 180, 216, 217, 250.
AMMON, son of Jupiter and Pasiphae, Agis, iv. 505.
AMMONIUS, a philosopher, Plutarch's teacher, Themistocles, i. 284.
AMNÆUS, Cato the Younger, iv. 434.
AMŒBEAS, a harp-player, Aratus, v. 401.
AMOMPHARETUS, a Spartan, Solon, i. 186; Aristides, ii. 331.
AMORGOS, island in the Ægean Sea, Demetrius, v. 113.
AMPHARES, a Spartan, Agis, iv. 515-518.
AMPHIARAUS, Aristides, ii. 312, 334; Aratus, v. 389.
AMPHICRATES, an orator, Lucullus, iii. 272.
AMPHICTYONS, Solon, i. 186; Themistocles, i. 269; Sylla, iii. 169, 170; Cimon, iii. 224.
AMPHILOCHIA, in western Greece, Pyrrhus, iii. 8.
AMPHIPOLIS, town in Thrace, Lycurgus, i. 123; Æm. Paulus, ii. 197; Cimon, iii. 224; Nicias, iii. 319; Pompey, iv. 161.
AMPHISSA, a town of Locris, Demosthenes, v. 20; Antony, v. 191.
AMPHITHEUS, a Theban, Lysander, iii. 146.
AMPHITROPE, in Attica, Aristides, ii. 344.
AMPHITRYON, Lysander, iii. 148.
AMULIUS, king of Alba, Romulus, i. 44, 46-47, 69; Comparison of Theseus and Romulus, i. 82.
AMYCLA, a Spartan woman, Alcibiades, ii. 1; Compare Lycurgus, i. 110.
AMYCLAS, father of Daphne, Agis, iv. 505.
AMYNTAS, a Macedonian, Alexander, iv. 205.

AMYNTAS, envoy of Philip, Demosthenes, v. 20.
AMYNTAS, king of Lycaonia and Galatia, Antony, v. 227, 229.
ANACES, a title of Castor and Pollux, Theseus, i. 37; Numa, i. 154.
ANACHARSIS, the Scythian philosopher, Solon, i. 181.
ANACREON, the poet, Pericles, i. 339, 376.
LUCIUS ANALIUS, a senator, Comparison of Crassus and Nicias, iii. 399.
ANAPHLYSTUS, an Attic township, Cimon, iii. 239.
ANAPUS, a river of Sicily, Timoleon, ii. 146; Dion, v. 286.
ANAXAGORAS, of Clazomenæ, philosopher, Themistocles, i. 246; Pericles, i. 342-344, 347, 364, 382, 383; Lysander, iii. 126; Nicias, iii. 341.
ANAXANDRIDES (in the text ALEXANDRIDES), of Delphi, Lysander, iii. 134.
ANAXARCHUS of Abdera, a philosopher, Alexander, iv. 188, 218, 253, 254.
ANAXENOR, a harper, Antony, v. 186.
ANAXIDAMUS of Chæronea, Sylla, iii. 178, 182.
ANAXILAS, a Spartan, Solon, i. 186.
ANAXILAUS, of Byzantium, Alcibiades, ii. 46.
ANAXIMENES, an orator, Poplicola, i. 224; Demosthenes, v. 32; Comparison of Demosthenes and Cicero, v. 97.
ANAXO, a woman of Trœzen, Theseus, i. 31; Comparison of Theseus and Romulus, i. 85.
ANCHARIA, mother of Octavia, Antony, v. 195.
ANCHARIUS, a senator, Marius, iii. 106.
ANCUS MARCIUS, Numa, i. 147, 166;

Coriolanus, ii. 59 (given under MARCIUS).
ANDOCIDES, an Athenian orator, Themistocles, i. 284; Alcibiades, ii. 29, 30; Nicias, iii. 326.
ANDRO of Halicarnassus, a writer, Theseus, i. 27.
ANDROCLEON, an Epirot, Pyrrhus, iii. 2.
ANDROCLES, an Athenian demagogue, Alcibiades, ii. 26.
ANDROCLIDES, a Theban, Pelopidas, ii. 225, 226; Lysander, iii. 146 (? the same).
ANDROCLIDES, an Epirot, Pyrrhus, iii. 2.
ANDROCLIDES, an author, Lysander, iii. 121.
ANDROCOTTUS, an Indian king, Alexander, iv. 266.
ANDROCRATES, a Platæan hero, Aristides, ii. 324, 325.
ANDROCYDES, a Cyzicenian painter, Pelopidas, ii. 247.
ANDROGEUS, son of Minos, Theseus, i. 13, 14; Comparison of Theseus and Romulus, i. 83.
ANDROMACHE, Pelopidas, ii. 252; Alexander, iv. 251; Brutus, v. 343, 344.
ANDROMACHUS, of Carrhæ, Crassus, iii. 390.
ANDROMACHUS, of Tauromenium, Timoleon, ii. 131.
ANDRONICUS, of Rhodes, Sylla, iii. 189.
ANDROS, island in the Ægean, Themistocles, i. 269; Pericles, i. 354; Alcibiades, ii. 51; Pelopidas, ii. 221; and (?) Aratus, v. 396.
ANDROTION, Demosthenes, v. 17.
ANDROTION, a writer, Solon, i. 192.
ANGELUS, an Epirot, Pyrrhus, iii. 2.
LUCIUS ANICIUS, a Roman officer, Æm. Paulus, ii. 183.
ANIENUS, Cæsar, iv. 351.
ANIO, a river, Poplicola, i. 236; Camillus, i. 333; Coriolanus, ii. 65.

INDEX 541

ANIUS, a river in Epirus, Cæsar, iv. 331. (Aous or Æas).
CAIUS ANNIUS, sent by Sylla into Spain, Sertorius, iii. 413.
ANNIUS, who killed the orator Antonius, Marius, iii. 108.
TITUS ANNIUS, Ti. Gracchus, iv. 584.
ANNIUS GALLUS, one of Otho's generals, Otho, v. 515, 517, 518, 523.
ANTÆUS, Theseus, i. 10; Sertorius, iii. 416.
ANTAGORAS of Chios, Aristides, ii. 340.
ANTALCIDAS, the Spartan, Lycurgus, i. 105; Pelopidas, ii. 236, 253; Agesilaus, iv. 33, 38, 45; Artaxerxes, v. 464, 465.
ANTEMNA, or ANTEMNÆ, Romulus, i. 62; Sylla, iii. 196.
ANTENOR, Numa, i. 146.
ANTEROS, Alcibiades, ii. 8.
ANTHEDON, in Bœotia, Sylla, iii. 190.
ANTHEMION, Alcibiades, ii. 8; Coriolanus, ii. 76.
ANTHEMOCRITUS, a herald, Pericles, i. 381.
ANTHO, daughter of Amulius, Romulus, i. 44.
VALERIUS ANTIAS. See VALERIUS.
ANTIATES, Coriolanus, ii. 69, 74, 83, 84, 109.
ANTICLIDES, a writer, Alexander, iv. 243.
ANTICRATES, a Laconian, Agesilaus, iv. 50.
ANTICYRA, Demetrius, v. 126.
ANTICYRA, a town in Phocis, Antony, v. 236.
ANTIGENES, chief officer of the Argyraspids, Eumenes, iii. 456, 462; Alexander, iv. 276.
ANTIGENES, a writer, Alexander, iv. 243.
ANTIGENIDAS, a flute-player, Demetrius, v. 102.
ANTIGONE, daughter of Philip and Berenice, Pyrrhus, iii. 5, 7, 11.
ANTIGONE, of Pydna, Alexander, iv. 247.
ANTIGONEA, the new name of Mantinea, Aratus, v. 432.
ANTIGONIS, or Antigonid, Attic tribe, Demetrius, v. 112.
ANTIGONUS, father of Demetrius Poliorcetes, Romulus, i. 62; Æm. Paulus, ii. 176, 209; Pelopidas, ii. 220, 221; Pyrrhus, iii. 4, 10; Sertorius, iii. 406; Eumenes, iii. 444, 450, and following; Comparison of Eumenes and Sertorius, iii. 468; Alexander, iv. 284; Phocion, iv. 400, 401; Demetrius, v. 103, and following; Comparison of Antony and Demetrius, v. 255; Aratus, v. 440.
ANTIGONUS GONATAS, king of Macedon, son of Demetrius Poliorcetes, Æm. Paulus, ii. 176; Pyrrhus, iii. 37, 38, 44, and following; Demetrius, v. 147, 162, 164; Aratus, v. 389, 394, and following to 419.
ANTIGONUS DOSON, king of Macedon, Coriolanus, ii. 72; Æm. Paulus, ii. 176; Cleomenes, iv. 537, 538, 542, and following; Aratus, v. 424, 427-433; Philopœmen, ii. 400-404.
ANTIGONUS, king of the Jews, Antony, v. 201.
ANTIGONUS, a writer, Romulus, i. 63.
ANTILIBANUS, Alexander, iv. 212.
ANTILOCHUS, a poet, Lysander, iii. 134.
ANTIMACHUS, poet of Colophon, Timoleon, ii. 164; Lysander, iii. 134.
ANTIMACHUS, poet of Teos, Romulus, i. 54.
ANTIOCH on Daphne, the Syrian capital, Lucullus, iii. 270; Pompey, iv. 112; Cato the Younger,

iv. 426; Demetrius, v. 137; Galba, v. 489.
ANTIOCH of Mygdonia (Nisibis), Lucullus, iii. 287.
ANTIOCHUS, an Athenian tribe, Aristides, ii. 308, 315.
ANTIOCHUS of Ascalon, an Academic philosopher, Lucullus, iii. 281, 299; Cicero, v. 41; Brutus, v. 320.
ANTIOCHUS, an Athenian pilot, Alcibiades, ii. 53; Lysander, iii. 117; Comparison of Lysander and Sylla, iii. 211.
ANTIOCHUS, of Commagene, Antony, v. 198, 199.
ANTIOCHUS I., Soter, son of Seleucus, Demetrius, v. 133, 136, 137, 144, 161, 162.
ANTIOCHUS III., the Great, Æm. Paulus, ii. 172, 176; Cato the Elder, ii. 363, 364, 366; Comparison of Aristides and Cato, ii. 389, 393; Philopœmen, ii. 414, 416; Flamininus, ii. 434, 435, 438, 442, 444, 446, 449; Sylla, iii. 170; Lucullus, iii. 257, 285; Crassus, iii. 386.
ANTIOPE, an Amazon, Theseus, i. 27; Comparison of Theseus and Romulus, i. 85.
ANTIORUS, son of Lycurgus, i. 132.
ANTIPATER, governor of Macedonia, Camillus, i. 306; Comparison of Alcibiades and Coriolanus, ii. 114; Comparison of Aristides and Cato, ii. 390; Eumenes, iii. 444-447, 451, 455; Agesilaus, iv. 22; Alexander, iv. 193, 206, 236, 243, 244, 249, 258, 261, 274, 278, 281, 284; Phocion, iv. 366, 387, 393, 396-404; Agis, iv. 496, 498; Demosthenes, v. 31-34, 36; Comparison of Demosthenes and Cicero, v. 99, 100; Demetrius, v. 116, 144; Comparison of Antony and Demetrius, v. 255.
ANTIPATER, son of Cassander, Pyrrhus, iii. 8; Demetrius, v. 142, 144.
ANTIPATER of Tarsus, a Stoic, Marius, iii. 111; Ti. Gracchus, iv. 575.
ANTIPATER of Tyre, a Stoic philosopher, Cato the Younger, iv. 417.
ANTIPHANES, a comic poet, Demosthenes, v. 5, 11.
ANTIPHATES, an Athenian, Themistocles, i. 266.
ANTIPHILUS, an Athenian general, Phocion, iv. 394, 395.
ANTIPHON, an orator, Alcibiades, ii. 6; Nicias, iii. 314; Antony, v. 191 [perhaps another].
ANTIPHON, a criminal, Demosthenes, v. 17.
ANTISTHENES, a philosopher, Lycurgus, i. 131; Pericles, i. 338; Alcibiades, ii. 1.
ANTISTIA, wife of Appius Claudius, Ti. Gracchus, iv. 569.
ANTISTIA, wife of Pompey, iv. 63, 68, 69.
ANTISTIUS (Appuleius?), in command of ships, Brutus, v. 345.
ANTISTIUS, father-in-law of Pompey, iv. 62, 69.
ANTIUM, a town of Latium, Fabius, i. 397; Coriolanus, ii. 83, 86-88, 91, 109; Brutus, v. 341.
ANTON, son of Hercules, Antony, v. 168.
ANTONIA, daughter of Mark Antony and Octavia, Antony, v. 253.
MARCUS ANTONIUS, the orator, Marius, iii. 107, 108; Pompey, iv. 90; Antony, v. 165.
ANTONIUS CRETICUS, father of the triumvir, Antony, v. 165.
CAIUS ANTONIUS, son of the orator, Cicero, v. 49, 50, 55, 62; Antony, v. 173.
CAIUS ANTONIUS, brother of the triumvir, Antony, v. 179, 185; Brutus, v. 347, 349.

INDEX 543

LUCIUS ANTONIUS, brother of the triumvir, Antony, v. 179, 194.
ANTONIUS, Iulus, son of Mark Antony and Fulvia, Antony, v. 253.
ANTONIUS HONORATUS, tribune, Galba, v. 489.
PUBLIUS ANTONIUS, Cæsar, iv. 289.
ANTONIUS, Lucius Antonius Saturninus in Domitian's time, Æm. Paulus, ii. 199.
ANTONIUS, murderer of Sertorius, Sertorius, iii. 439.
ANTONY, Marcus Antonius the triumvir, Life, v. 165; Comparison, v. 255; Numa, i. 163; Æm. Paulus, ii. 214; Pompey, iv. 141, 142, 154; Cæsar, iv. 323, and after; Cato the Younger, iv. 494; Cicero, v. 85, and after; Demetrius, v. 102, 103; Brutus, v. 326, 337, and after; Comparison, v. 384.
QUINTUS ANTYLLIUS, C. Gracchus iv. 609; Comparison, iv. 623.
ANTYLLUS, the son of Mark Antony and Fulvia, Antony, v. 192, 239, 247, 252.
ANYTUS, son of Anthemion, Alcibiades, ii. 8, 9; Coriolanus, ii. 76.
AOLLIUS or ABILLIUS, son of Romulus, Romulus, i. 58.
AOUS or ÆAS or ANIUS, river in Epirus, Cæsar, iv. 296.
APAMA, wife of Seleucus, Demetrius, v. 136.
APAMA, daughter of Artaxerxes, Artaxerxes, v. 471.
APAMA, daughter of Artabazus, wife of Ptolemy, sister of Barsine, Eumenes, iii. 442.
APELLES, a Macedonian, Aratus, v. 433.
APELLES, the painter, Alexander, iv. 182; Demetrius, v. 124; Aratus, v. 397.
APELLICON of Teos, Sylla, iii. 189.
APEMANTUS, an Athenian, Antony, v. 287.

APERANTIANS, a people of Thessaly, Flamininus, ii. 443.
APHETÆ, a port in Thessaly, Themistocles, i. 252.
APHIDNÆ, in Attica, Theseus, i. 34-36; Comparison, i. 86.
APHIDNUS, Theseus, i. 34, 36.
APHYTÆ, a town in Thrace, Lysander, iii. 137.
APOLLOCRATES, son of Dionysius the Younger, Dion, v. 297, 310, 314.
APOLLODORUS, an Athenian, Demosthenes, v. 17; Comparison, v. 98.
APOLLODORUS, governor of Babylon, Alexander, iv. 280.
APOLLODORUS the Phalerian, Cato the Younger, iv. 465.
APOLLODORUS, a Sicilian, Cæsar, iv. 342.
APOLLODORUS, a writer, Lycurgus, i. 88.
APOLLONIA, in Epirus, Sylla, iii. 190; Cæsar, iv. 330; Cicero, v. 87; Antony, v. 179; Brutus, v. 342, 347.
APOLLONIA, in Mysia, Lucullus, iii. 257.
APOLLONIA, in Sicily, Timoleon, ii. 150.
APOLLONIDES, Demetrius, v. 160.
APOLLONIDES, Stoic philosopher, Cato the Younger, iv. 487, 488, 490.
APOLLONIUS, son of Molon, an orator, Cæsar, iv. 288; Cicero, v. 41.
APOLLONIUS, tyrant of Zenodotia, Crassus, iii. 372.
APOLLOPHANES of Cyzicus, Agesilaus, iv. 17.
APOLLOTHEMIS, a writer, Lycurgus, i. 132.
APONIUS, an informer, Galba, v. 484.
APOTHETÆ, a chasm under Taygetus, Lycurgus, i. 110.
The APPIAN WAY, Cæsar, iv. 291.
The APPII, Æm. Paulus, ii. 214.
APPIUS CLAUDIUS, Cæcus, Pyrrhus, iii. 25, 27.

544 INDEX

APPIUS CLAUDIUS, consul B. C. 212, Comparison of Fabius and Pericles, i. 432; Marcellus, ii. 276, 278.

APPIUS, Claudius, consul B. C. 177, Poplicola, i. 221.

APPIUS CLAUDIUS, consul B. C. 143, Æm. Paulus, ii. 214; Ti. Gracchus, iv. 568, 576, 581.

APPIUS CLAUDIUS, consul B. C. 54, Lucullus, iii. 267, 269, 271, 272, 283; Pompey, iv. 139; Cæsar, iv. 311.

APPIUS CLAUDIUS, Sylla, iii. 195.

MARCUS APPIUS, Cicero, v. 67.

APPIUS CLAUSUS, a Sabine, Poplicola, i. 235; the same as APPIUS CLAUDIUS, Coriolanus, ii. 83.

APSEPHION (in the text, APHEPSION). Archon at Athens, Cimon, iii. 225.

APSUS, river in Illyria, Flamininus, ii. 425.

APTERA, in Crete, Pyrrhus, iii. 45.

LUCIUS APULEIUS, Camillus, i. 298.

APULIA, in Italy, Marcellus, ii. 293.

AQUILLII, Poplicola, i. 217-220.

MANIUS AQUILLIUS, Marius, iii. 68.

AQUILLIUS, tribune of the people, Cato the Younger, iv. 461.

MARCUS AQUINIUS, Cicero, v. 67.

AQUINUM, in Latium, Otho, v. 514.

AQUINUS, lieutenant of Metellus, Sertorius, iii. 421.

ARABIA and ARABIANS, Theseus, i. 4; Lucullus, iii. 270, 277, and after; Crassus, iii. 377, and after; Pompey, iv. 111, and after; Alexander, iv. 212; Antony, v. 201, 202, 227, 236.

ARACHOSIA, Eumenes, iii. 466.

ARACUS, a Spartan, Lysander, iii. 120.

ARAR, a river of Gaul, Cæsar, iv. 307, 317.

ARATERION, near Gargettus, in Attica, Theseus, i. 38.

ARATUS of Sicyon, Life, v. 386; Philopœmen, ii. 395, 403, 404; Agis, iv. 510, 511; Cleomenes, iv. 523-526, 533, 536-549.

ARATUS, son of the preceding, Aratus, v. 434, and after to 440.

ARAXES, river of Armenia, Lucullus, iii. 278; Pompey, iv. 104, 106; Antony, v. 216, 218.

ARBACES, a Mede, Artaxerxes, v. 454.

ARBELA, Camillus, i. 305; Pompey, iv. 108; Alexander, iv. 223.

ARCADIA and ARCADIANS, Numa, i. 161 (the Arcadian months); Coriolanus, ii. 61; Pelopidas, ii. 225, 246, and after; Philopœmen, ii. 412; Agesilaus, iv. 22, 32, 47, 48; Cleomenes, iv. 523, and after; Demosthenes, v. 31; Aratus, v. 389, 420.

ARCESILAUS, philosopher, Philopœmen, ii. 395; Aratus, v. 389.

ARCESILAUS, a Spartan, Agis, iv. 515.

ARCHEDEMUS, an Ætolian, Æm. Paulus, ii. 196; Flamininus, ii. 455.

ARCHEDEMUS, friend of Archytas, Dion, v. 276.

ARCHELAUS, general of Antigonus Gonatas, Aratus, v. 407, 408.

ARCHELAUS, king of Cappadocia, Antony, v. 227.

ARCHELAUS of Delos, Sylla, iii. 185.

ARCHELAUS, general of Mithridates, Marius, iii. 94; Sylla, iii. 168, 174-178, 180-188; Comparison, iii. 211; Lucullus, iii. 253, 255, 258.

ARCHELAUS, an Egyptian general, son of the preceding, Antony, v. 168.

ARCHELAUS, a writer, Cimon, iii. 219.

ARCHELAUS, a poet, Cimon, iii. 217.

ARCHELAUS, king of Sparta, Lycurgus, i. 94.

ARCHELAUS, in Phocis; Sylla, iii. 178.

INDEX 545

ARCHEPTOLIS, son of Themistocles, Themistocles, i. 283.
ARCHESTRATUS, an Athenian, Alcibiades, ii. 22; Lysander, iii. 135.
ARCHESTRATUS, an Athenian, Phocion, iv. 406.
ARCHESTRATUS, a dramatic poet, Aristides, ii. 308, 309.
ARCHIAS, an Athenian, Pelopidas, ii. 232.
ARCHIAS, a Theban, Pelopidas, ii. 225-228, 229-232; Agesilaus, iv. 34.
ARCHIAS, a Thurian, Demosthenes, v. 33, 34.
ARCHIBIADES, an Athenian, Phocion, iv. 378.
ARCHIBIUS, Antony, v. 252.
ARCHIDAMIA, grandmother of Agis, Pyrrhus, iii. 40; Agis, iv. 499, 517, 518. Perhaps not both the same.
ARCHIDAMIDAS, a Spartan, Lycurgus, i. 117.
ARCHIDAMUS II., king of Sparta, son of Zeuxidamus, father of Agesilaus, Lycurgus, i. 129; Pericles, i. 348, 379; Cimon, iii. 236; Crassus, iii. 353; Agesilaus, iv. 3, 5; Cleomenes, iv. 551.
ARCHIDAMUS III., king of Sparta, son of Agesilaus, Camillus, i. 306; Agesilaus, iv. 36, 37, 48, 50; Agis, iv. 498.
ARCHIDAMUS IV., king of Sparta, son of Eudamidas, Agis, iv. 498; Demetrius, v. 141.
ARCHIDAMUS V., king of Sparta, son of Eudamidas, brother of Agis, Cleomenes, iv. 520, 525; Comparison, iv. 623.
ARCHILOCHUS, the poet, Theseus, i. 5; Numa, i. 139; Pericles, i. 339; Marius, iii. 78; Phocion, iv. 374; Cato the Younger, iv. 420; Demetrius, v. 141; Galba, v. 506.
ARCHIMEDES, Marcellus, ii. 278-283, 285.

ARCHIPPE, wife of Themistocles, Themistocles, i. 283.
ARCHIPPUS, a comic poet, Alcibiades, ii. 4.
ARCHITELES, an Athenian, Themistocles, i. 253.
ARCHONIDES, a Sicilian, Dion, v. 302.
ARCHYTAS, Pythagorean philosopher, Marcellus, ii. 278; Dion, v. 276, 278.
ARCISSUS, a Spartan, Pelopidas, ii. 234.
ARDEA and ARDEATIANS, in Latium, Camillus, i. 302, 311-313.
ARDETTUS, in Athens, Theseus, i. 30.
AREIUS, or ARIUS, a philosopher, Antony, v. 246, 247.
AREOPAGUS, Solon, i. 195, 200, 211; Themistocles, i. 257; Pericles, i. 347, 350; Cimon, iii. 229, 234; Phocion, iv. 384; Demosthenes, v. 17, 29; Cicero, v. 64.
ARETÆUS, son of Dion, Dion, v. 291.
ARETE, wife of Dion, daughter of Dionysius, Timoleon, ii. 161; Dion, v. 264, 279, 291, 310, 317.
ARETHUSA, in Syria, Antony, v. 202.
AREUS I., king of Sparta, Pyrrhus, iii. 39, 40, 44, 47.
AREUS II., king of Sparta, Agis, iv. 499.
ARGAS, a poet, also a nickname of Demosthenes, Demosthenes, v. 5.
ARGILEONIS, mother of Brasidas, Lycurgus, i. 123.
ARGINUSÆ, islands off the coast of Æolis, Pericles, i. 391; Lysander, iii. 120.
ARGIUS, Galba's freedman, Galba, v. 507.
ARGOS and the ARGIVES, Lycurgus, i. 97 (the Argive kings); Alcibiades, ii. 15, 21; Pelopidas, ii. 245; Pyrrhus, iii. 44, and after; Lysander, iii. 113 (their shaving their hair); Nicias, iii. 321-322;

Agesilaus, iv. 25, 30, 45; Cleomenes, iv. 538, and after; Demetrius, v. 127; Aratus, v. 388, and after.
The ARGYRASPIDS, or Silver-Shields, Eumenes, iii. 457, and after.
ARIADNE, daughter of Minos, Theseus, i. 17-20, 23, 31; Comparison, i. 83, 85.
ARIÆUS, friend of Cyrus the Younger, Artaxerxes, v. 451.
ARIAMENES, admiral of Xerxes, Themistocles, i. 262.
ARIAMNES, an Arab, Crassus, iii. 377.
ARIARATHES II., king of Cappadocia, Eumenes, iii. 444, 445.
ARIARATHES, son of Mithridates, Sylla, iii. 168; Pompey, iv. 110.
ARIARATHES, Pompey, iv. 116.
ARIASPES, son of Artaxerxes II., Artaxerxes, v. 474, 475.
ARIMANIUS, the Persian god, Themistocles, i. 278.
ARIMINUM, in Umbria, Marcellus, ii. 265; Pompey, iv. 142; Cæsar, iv. 324, 325; Cato the Younger, iv. 471.
ARIMNESTUS, a Platæan, Aristides, ii. 324, 325.
ARIMNESTUS, a Spartan, Aristides, ii. 334.
ARIOBARZANES, king of Cappadocia, Sylla, iii. 157, 185, 187; Cicero, v. 99; Demetrius, v. 105.
ARIOMANDES, a Persian, Cimon, iii. 231.
ARIOVISTUS, a German chief, Cæsar, iv. 308-309.
ARIPHRON, son of Xanthippus, guardian of Alcibiades, Alcibiades, ii. 3, 8.
ARISTÆNUS, ARISTÆUS, or ARISTÆNETUS, a citizen of Megalopolis, Philopœmen, ii. 410, 416.
ARISTAGORAS, a Cyzicenian, Lucullus, iii. 256.
ARISTANDER of Telmessus, Alexander, iv. 179, 196, 213, 214, 224, 227, 249, 253.
ARISTEAS of Argos, Pyrrhus, iii. 44, 46.
ARISTEAS of Proconnesus, Romulus, i. 78.
ARISTIDES, son of Lysimachus, Life, ii. 308; Comparison of Aristides and Cato, ii. 388; Themistocles, i. 247, 250, 258, 261, 264, 265, 268, 269; Pericles, i. 345; Comparison of Alcibiades and Coriolanus, ii. 113, 116; Pelopidas, ii. 224; Cimon, iii. 220, 229; Nicias, iii. 324; Comparison, iii. 398; Phocion, iv. 370, 374; Demosthenes, v. 16.
ARISTIDES, a Locrian, Timoleon, ii. 126.
ARISTIDES, author of the Milesiaca, Crassus, iii. 394.
ARISTIDES, son of Xenophilus, Aristides, ii. 309.
ARISTION, tyrant of Athens, Numa, i. 148; Sylla, iii. 169, 171, 186; Lucullus, iii. 268.
ARISTIPPUS of Argos, Pyrrhus, iii. 44; Aratus, v. 411-415.
ARISTIPPUS of Cyrene, philosopher, Dion, v. 277, 278.
ARISTOBULUS, Alexander's historian, Alexander, iv. 196, 200, 202, 208, 243, 282; Demosthenes, v. 27.
ARISTOBULUS, king of Judæa, Pompey, iv. 112, 120; Antony, v. 167.
ARISTOCLITUS, father of Lysander, iii. 114.
ARISTOCRATES, an Athenian, Demosthenes, v. 15, 17.
ARISTOCRATES, son of Hipparchus, a Spartan writer; Lycurgus, i. 93, 132; Philopœmen, ii. 414.
ARISTOCRATES, a rhetorician, Antony, v. 236.
ARISTOCRITUS, Alexander, iv. 190.
ARISTODEMUS of Miletus, Demetrius, v. 110, 118.
ARISTODEMUS, tyrant of Megalopo-

INDEX

lis, Philopœmen, ii. 395; Agis, iv. 499.

ARISTODEMUS, the Heraclid, founder of the royal houses of Sparta, Lycurgus, i. 88; Agesilaus, iv. 28.

ARISTODICUS of Tanagra, Pericles, i. 352.

ARISTOGITON, companion of Harmodius, Aristides, ii. 346.

ARISTOGITON, an Athenian sycophant, Phocion, iv. 378-380; Demosthenes, v. 17.

ARISTOMACHE, wife of Dionysius the Elder, sister of Dion, Timoleon, ii. 161; Dion, v. 262, 264, 265, 272, 310, 317.

ARISTOMACHUS, Achæan general, Cleomenes, iv. 524.

ARISTOMACHUS, tyrant of the Argives, Aratus, v. 410, 420, 421, 430.

ARISTOMACHUS, a Sicyonian, Aratus, v. 389.

ARISTOMENES, the Messenian, Romulus, i. 74; Agis, iv. 519.

ARISTON of Ceos, a philosopher, Themistocles, i. 247; Aristides, ii. 311.

ARISTON of Chios, a philosopher, Cato the Elder, ii. 373; Demosthenes, v. 11, 34.

ARISTON, a Corinthian pilot, Nicias, iii. 337, 344.

ARISTON, Captain of the Pæonians, Alexander, iv. 234.

ARISTON, friend of Pisistratus, Solon, i. 210.

ARISTONICUS, admiral of Mithridates, Lucullus, iii. 258.

ARISTONICUS of Marathon, Demosthenes, v. 32.

ARISTONICUS of Pergamus, a son of Eumenes II.; Flamininus, ii. 452; Ti. Gracchus, iv. 592.

ARISTONUS, a musician, Lysander, iii. 134.

ARISTOPHANES, the comic poet, Themistocles, i. 268; Pericles, i. 375 (the verses), Alcibiades, ii. 4, 22; Cimon, iii. 221; Nicias, iii. 309 (the verse), 313, 318; Demetrius, v. 113; Antony, v. 237.

ARISTOPHANES, a Macedonian, Alexander, iv. 251.

ARISTOPHON, archon at Athens, Demosthenes, v. 27.

ARISTOPHON, an Athenian, Phocion, iv. 374.

ARISTOPHON, a painter, Alcibiades, ii. 23.

ARISTOTELES, an Argive, Cleomenes, iv. 543; Aratus, v. 430.

ARISTOTELES, a logician, Aratus, v. 388.

ARISTOTLE, Theseus, i. 3, 14, 26; Lycurgus, i. 87, 95, 96, 106, 126, 127, 131; Solon, i. 186, 203, 213; Themistocles, i. 257; Camillus, i. 310; Pericles, i. 341, 350, 352, 374, 376; Comparison of Alcibiades and Coriolanus, ii. 114; Pelopidas, ii. 223, 240; Aristides, ii. 345; Comparison, ii. 390; Lysander, iii. 114; Sylla, iii. 189; Cimon, iii. 227; Nicias, iii. 308; Crassus, iii. 354; Alexander, iv. 186-188, 202, 253, 256, 258, 281, 284; Cleomenes, iv. 529; Cicero, v. 63; Dion, v. 280.

ARISTOXENUS, a musician, Lycurgus, i. 132; Timoleon, ii. 137; Aristides, ii. 345; Alexander, iv. 182.

ARISTRATUS, tyrant of Sicyon, Aratus, v. 397, 398.

ARISTUS of Ascalon, Academic philosopher, Brutus, v. 320.

ARMENIA and ARMENIANS, Sylla, iii. 157; Cimon, iii. 216; Lucullus, iii. 261, 266, and after; Crassus, iii. 374, and after; Pompey, iv. 98, 104, and after; Cæsar, iv. 343; Antony, v. 199, 202, and after.

ARMILUSTRIUM, on the Aventine Mount, Romulus, i. 71.

INDEX

ARNACES, a Persian, Themistocles, i. 264.
ARPATES, a Persian, Artaxerxes, v. 475.
ARPINUM, town in Latium, Marius, iii. 54; Cicero, v. 46.
ARRHENIDÆS, an Athenian, Demosthenes, v. 29.
ARRHIDÆUS, son of Philip, and himself called PHILIP, Alexander, iv. 190, 284; Compare Eumenes, iii. 456, and Phocion, iv. 404.
QUINTUS ARRIUS, a senator, Cicero, v. 54.
ARRUNTIUS (Lucius), in command at Actium, Antony, v. 233.
ARSACES, king of the Parthians, Sylla, iii. 157; Crassus, iii. 373, 387; Pompey, iv. 165; Comparison of Demetrius and Antony, v. 255.
ARSACIDÆ, Crassus, iii. 395.
ARSAMES, son of Artaxerxes II., Artaxerxes, v. 474.
ARSANIAS, river of Armenia, Lucullus, iii. 285.
ARSIAN GROVE, Poplicola, i. 222.
ARSICAS, Artaxerxes, v. 441, 442.
ARSIS, river of Italy, Pompey, iv. 66.
ARTABANUS, a Persian, Themistocles, i. 276, 277.
ARTABAZES. See ARTAVASDES.
ARTABAZUS, father of Barsine, Eumenes, iii. 442; Alexander, iv. 208.
ARTABAZUS, a Persian, Aristides, ii. 335.
ARTAGERSES, leader of the Cadusians, Artaxerxes, v. 450, 451, 454, 456.
ARTASYRAS, a Persian, Artaxerxes, v. 452, 455.
ARTAVASDES, king of Armenia, the same as ARTABAZES, Crassus, iii. 375, 377; Antony, v. 203, 204, 217; Comparison, v. 258.
ARTAYCTES, a Persian, Themistocles, i. 261.

ARTAXAS, king of Armenia, Lucullus, iii. 285.
ARTAXATA, town of Armenia, Lucullus, iii. 285.
ARTAXERXES I., Longimanus, Alcibiades, ii. 55; Artaxerxes, v. 441.
ARTAXERXES II., Mnemon, Life, v. 441; Pelopidas, ii. 253.
ARTEMIDORUS of Cnidos, Cæsar, iv. 359.
ARTEMIDORUS, a Greek, Lucullus, iii. 262.
ARTEMISIA, queen of Caria, Themistocles, i. 263.
ARTEMISIUM, promontory in Eubœa, Themistocles, i. 252, 254, 255; Alcibiades, ii. 3.
ARTEMIUS of Colophon, Alexander, iv. 251.
ARTEMON, an engineer, Pericles, i. 376.
ARTHMIADAS, a Spartan, Lycurgus, i. 94.
ARTHMIUS of Zelea, Themistocles, i. 252.
MARCUS ARTORIUS, friend of Augustus, Brutus, v. 366.
ARUNS, son of Porsenna, Poplicola, i. 233, 234.
ARUNS, a Tuscan, Camillus, i. 301, 302.
ARUNS, son of Tarquin, Poplicola, i. 222.
ARUVENI, Cæsar, iv. 316.
ARVERNI. See ARUVENI.
ARYBAS, king of Epirus, Pyrrhus, iii. 1.
ARYMBAS, brother of Olympias, Alexander, iv. 179.
ASBOLOMENI, Cimon, iii. 215.
ASCALIS, son of Iptha, king of Mauretania, Sertorius, iii. 415.
ASCALON, in Syria, Lucullus, iii. 299; Cicero, v. 40; Brutus, v. 320.
ASCANIUS, son of Æneas, Romulus, i. 42.

INDEX 549

ASCLEPIADES, a grammarian, Solon, i. 177.
ASCLEPIADES, son of Hipparchus, Phocion, iv. 392.
ASCULUM of Apulia, Pyrrhus, iii. 31.
ASCULUM of Picenum, Pompey, iv. 62.
ASEA, or ALSÆA, Cleomenes, iv. 527.
ASIA, frequent; the Asiatic orators, Cicero, v. 41; the Asiatic style of speaking, Antony, v. 166.
ASIA, daughter of Themistocles, Themistocles, i. 284.
ASIATICUS, a freedman, Galba, v. 497.
ASINARUS, river of Sicily, and ASINARIAN feast, Nicias, iii. 346, 347.
ASINIUS POLLIO, Cæsar, iv. 325, 339, 346; Pompey, iv. 159; Cato the Younger, iv. 472; Antony, v. 173.
ASOPIA, a name of Salamis, Solon, i. 184.
ASOPUS, a river in Bœotia, Aristides, ii. 323, 328; Lucullus, iii. 273.
ASPASIA, Pericles, i. 371, 373, 381-384.
ASPASIA, or MILTO, of Phocæa, Pericles, i. 373; Artaxerxes, v. 470, 471, 472.
ASPENDUS, in Pamphylia, Alcibiades, ii. 40.
ASPETUS, a name for Achilles, Pyrrhus, iii. 1.
ASPHALIUS, a name of Neptune, Theseus, i. 40.
ASPIS, citadel of Argos, Pyrrhus, iii. 47, 48; Cleomenes, iv. 540, 544.
ASSUS, a stream, and the ASSIA, near Chæronea, Sylla, iii. 177, 178.
ASSYRIA and ASSYRIANS, Lucullus, iii. 277; Crassus, iii. 379.

ASTERIA, a woman of Salamis, Cimon, iii. 219.
ASTEROPUS, a Spartan ephor, Cleomenes, iv. 531.
ASTURA, in Latium, Cicero, v. 90.
ASTYANAX, Brutus, v. 343.
ASTYOCHUS, a Spartan, Alcibiades, ii. 37, 38.
ASTYPALÆA, an island, Romulus, i. 78.
ASTYPHILUS of Posidonia, or Pæstum, Cimon, iii. 240.
ASYLUM, Romulus, i. 67; ASYLÆUS, a god, Romulus, i. 51.
ATEIUS, tribune of the people, Crassus, iii. 371.
MARCUS ATEIUS, or TEIUS, Sylla, iii. 172.
ATELLIUS, Brutus, v. 363.
ATHAMANIA and ATHAMANES, Flamininus, ii. 443; Pompey, iv. 150.
ATHANIS, an historian, Timoleon, ii. 149, 167.
ATHENÆUM, a pass in Arcadia, Cleomenes, iv. 523.
ATHENODORUS, an actor, Alexander, iv. 220.
ATHENODORUS, surnamed Cordylio, a Stoic philosopher, Cato the Younger, iv. 423, 429.
ATHENODORUS of Imbros, Phocion, iv. 388.
ATHENODORUS, son of Sandon, a writer, Poplicola, i. 232.
ATHENOPHANES, an Athenian, Alexander, iv. 230.
ATHENS and ATHENIANS, frequent.
ATHESIS, the river Adige, Marius, iii. 79, 80.
ATHOS, Mount, Alexander, iv. 279.
ATILIUS. See ATTILIUS.
ATLANTIC ISLANDS, Sertorius, iii. 414.
ATLANTIC SEA, Timoleon, ii. 145; Sertorius, iii. 414, 436; Cæsar, iv. 314.
ATLANTIS, Plato's fable, Solon, i. 205, 212.

ATOSSA, daughter of Artaxerxes II., Artaxerxes, v. 466, 469, 471, 474.
ATREUS, Cimon, iii. 223; Cicero, v. 42.
ATROPATENE and ATROPATENIANS (Satrapenians), Lucullus, iii. 286; Antony, v. 203.
ATTALIA, in Pamphylia, Pompey, iv. 164.
ATTALUS, uncle of Cleopatra, wife of Philip, Alexander, iv. 189, 190.
ATTALUS, Alexander, iv. 258.
ATTALUS I., king of Pergamus, Flamininus, ii. 430; Antony, v. 227.
ATTALUS III., Philometor, Camillus, i. 306; Ti. Gracchus, iv. 538; Demetrius, v. 121.
ATTES, or ATTIS, Numa, i. 138; Sertorius, iii. 405.
ATTIA, mother of Augustus, Cicero, v. 88; Antony, v. 195.
ATTICA, frequent, see particularly Theseus, i. 1-41.
ATTICUS, Cicero's friend, Cicero, v. 88; Brutus, v. 351.
JULIUS ATTICUS, Galba, v. 504.
ATILIA, wife of Cato the Younger, iv. 420, 422, 439.
ATTILII, a probable correction for Hostilii, Comparison of Cato and Aristides, ii. 388.
MARCUS ATTILIUS (more correctly CAIUS), Numa, i. 163.
ATTILIUS VERGILIO, Galba, v. 504.
ATTIS, Numa, i. 138; Sertorius, iii. 405.
ATTIUS, see TULLUS and VARUS, below.
AUFIDIUS, lieutenant of Sertorius, Sertorius, iii. 438, 440.
AUFIDUS, river of Apulia, Fabius, i. 414.
AUGUSTUS, Numa, i. 162, 163. See CÆSAR.
AULIS, in Bœotia, Pelopidas, ii. 243; Lysander, iii. 146; Agesilaus, iv. 9.

AURELIA, mother of Cæsar, Cæsar, iv. 296-298; Cicero, v. 68.
CAIUS AURELIUS (in the text ONATIUS), Crassus, iii. 366; Pompey, iv. 87.
QUINTUS AURELIUS, Sylla, iii. 199.
AUTOCLIDES, a writer, Nicias, iii. 342.
AUTOLEON, king of the Pæonians, Pyrrhus, iii. 11.
AUTOLYCUS, an athlete, Lysander, iii. 131.
AUTOLYCUS, founder of Sinope, Lucullus, iii. 273.
AUXIMUM, a town of Picenum, Pompey, iv. 65.
AVENTINE MOUNT, Romulus, i. 57, 67, 71; Numa, i. 157; C. Gracchus, iv. 612.
AXIOCHUS of Miletus, father of Aspasia, Pericles, i. 371.
AXIUS, Cicero, v. 65.
AXIUS, river of Macedonia, Demetrius, v. 150.

B

BABYCA, a bridge near Sparta, Lycurgus, i. 95; Pelopidas, ii. 239.
BABYLON, BABYLONIA, BABYLONIANS, Lucullus, iii. 277; Crassus, iii. 373; Comparison, iii. 403; Eumenes, iii. 443; Alexander, iv. 229, 230, 260, 275, 279; Demetrius, v. 108; Antony, v. 213; Artaxerxes, v. 447, 462.
BACCHIADÆ of Corinth, Lysander, iii. 113.
BACCHIDES, Lucullus, iii. 265, 266.
BACCHYLIDES, a poet, Numa, i. 140.
BACTRA, BACTRIA, and the BACTRIANS, in Asia, Crassus, iii. 370; Comparison, iii. 403; Antony, v. 203; Bactrian horse, Alexander, iv. 225.
MARCUS BÆBIUS, consul, Numa, i. 167.

INDEX

BÆTICA, a part of Spain, Sertorius, iii. 419.
BÆTIS, the Guadalquivir, in Spain, Cato the Elder, ii. 361; Sertorius, iii. 414, 419.
BAGOAS, a Persian, Alexander, iv. 236.
BAGOAS, favorite of Alexander, Alexander, iv. 273.
BAÆ, in Campania, Marius, iii. 93.
BALBUS, an officer under Sylla, Sylla, iii. 195.
BALBUS, Cæsar's friend, Cæsar, iv. 354.
POSTUMIUS BALBUS, probably ALBUS, Poplicola, i. 237.
BALINUS, or CEBALINUS, a Macedonian, Alexander, iv. 247.
BALISSUS, river in Mesopotamia, Crassus, iii. 380.
BALTE, a nymph, mother of Epimenides, Solon, i. 188.
BAMBYCE, or HIERAPOLIS, Antony, v. 202.
BANDIUS. See BANTIUS.
BANTIA, a town in Apulia, Marcellus, ii. 299.
BANTIUS of Nola, Marcellus, ii. 273, 274.
BARBIUS, a *tesserarius*, Galba, v. 501.
BARCA, a friend of Cato, Cato the Younger, iv. 455.
BARCA, in Hannibal's army, Fabius, i. 416.
HAMILCAR BARCA, Hannibal's father, Cato the Elder, ii. 358.
BARDYÆI, slaves, Marius, iii. 106.
BARDYLLIS, king of Illyria, Pyrrhus, iii. 11.
BARGYLIANS, a people of Caria, Flamininus, ii. 438.
BARSINE, daughter of Artabazus, wife of Alexander, Eumenes, iii. 442; Alexander, iv. 208.
BARSINE, another sister, wife of Eumenes, Eumenes, iii. 442.
LUCIUS BASILLUS, Sylla, iii. 166.

BASTARNÆ, or BASTERNÆ, a Celtic tribe, Æm. Paulus, ii. 179, 181.
BATACES, a priest of Cybele, Marius, iii. 72.
BATALUS, a flute-player, nickname of Demosthenes, Demosthenes, v. 5.
BATAVIANS, a German tribe, Otho, v. 522.
BATHYCLES, Solon, i. 181.
LENTULUS BATIATES, Crassus, iii. 360, 362.
BATON of Sinope, a writer, Agis, iv. 511.
BATTI, kings of Cyrene, Coriolanus, ii. 72.
BEDRIACUM, near Cremona, town and field of battle, Otho, v. 518, 520, 523.
BELÆUS of Minturnæ, Marius, iii. 101.
BELBINA, town of Arcadia, Cleomenes, iv. 524.
BELGÆ, a Gallic tribe, Pompey, iv. 128; Cæsar, iv. 310.
BELITARAS, a Persian in the service of Parysatis, Artaxerxes, v. 461.
BELLEROPHON, Coriolanus, ii. 101.
BELLINUS, a prætor, Pompey, iv. 90.
The Temple of BELUS, Alexander, iv. 203.
BELURIS the secretary, a Persian, Artaxerxes, v. 465.
BENEVENTUM, a town of Italy, Pyrrhus, iii. 36.
BERENICE of Chios, wife of Mithridates, Lucullus, iii. 266.
BERENICE, wife of Ptolemy, Pyrrhus, iii. 5, 7.
BERENICIS, town of Epirus, Pyrrhus, iii. 7.
BERŒA, town of Macedonia, Pyrrhus, iii. 13; Pompey, iv. 146; Demetrius, v. 153.
BERYTUS, town of Phœnicia, Antony, v. 218.

BESSUS, a Persian, Alexander, iv. 241.
BESTIA, a Roman general, Marius, iii. 61.
BESTIA, a tribune, Cicero, v. 62.
BIAS of Priene, Solon, i. 181.
CALPURNIUS BIBULUS, Pompey, iv. 123, 124, 134; Cæsar, iv. 301, 302; Cato the Younger, iv. 440, 448, 466, 474; Antony, v. 169.
BIBULUS, step-son of Brutus, Brutus, v. 331, 344.
PUBLICIUS BIBULUS, a tribune, Marcellus, ii. 297.
BION (perhaps of Soli), a writer, Theseus, i. 27.
BIRCENNA, daughter of Bardyllis and wife of Pyrrhus, Pyrrhus, iii. 11.
BISALTÆ, a people of Thrace, Pericles, i. 354.
BISANTHE, a town in Thrace, Alcibiades, ii. 53.
BITHYNIA and BITHYNIANS, Numa, i. 138; Alcibiades, ii. 55; Flamininus, ii. 449, 450; Sylla, iii. 168, 185; Comparison, iii. 212; Lucullus, iii. 251, and after; Sertorius, iii. 435; Cæsar, iv. 287; Brutus, v. 339, 349.
BITHYS, general of Demetrius II., Aratus, v. 419.
BITON of Argos, Solon, i. 206.
BLOSSIUS of Cuma, philosopher, Ti. Gracchus, iv. 575, 588, 592.
BOCCHORIS, king of Egypt, Demetrius, v. 132.
BOCCHUS, king of Mauretania, Marius, iii. 62, 91; Sylla, iii. 154-158.
BOCCHUS, king of Mauretania, Antony, v. 227.
BŒI, a Gallic tribe, in the original of the verses, Romulus, i. 63.
BŒORIX, king of the Cimbri, Marius, iii. 82.
BŒOTIA and BŒOTIANS, frequent. See particularly Pelopidas, ii. 220-261; some passages in Themistocles, Pericles, and Alcibiades; Aristides, ii. 321, and after; Lysander, iii. 146, and after; Sylla, iii. 168, 174, and after; Cimon, iii. 213; Agesilaus, iv. 10, 24, and after; Phocion, iv. 393, 394; Demetrius, v. 146; Aratus, v. 400, 436; Bœotian months, Camillus, i. 305; Pelopidas, ii. 245; Aristides, ii. 335.
BOLA, a town of Latium, and BOLANI, Coriolanus, ii. 94.
BOLLA, or BOVILLÆ, another Latin town. Ibid.
BONONIA, Bologna, in Cisalpine Gaul, Cicero, v. 90.
BORYSTHENIS, or Olbia, on the Black Sea, Cleomenes, iv. 521.
BOSPORUS, the kingdom of, Sylla, iii. 168; Lucullus, iii. 274; Comparison, iii. 305; Cimmerian Bosporus, Theseus, i. 29.
BOTTLÆANS, Theseus, i. 14.
BRACHYLLES, a Theban, Flamininus, ii. 429.
BRASIDAS, Spartan general, Lycurgus, i. 123, 124, 130; Lysander, iii. 113, 134; Nicias, iii. 319.
BRAURON, in Attica, Solon, i. 186.
BRENNUS, king of the Gauls, Camillus, i. 302, 303, 309, 310, 318, 319.
BRIAREUS, the giant, Marcellus, ii. 281.
BRIGES, army servants, Brutus v. 370.
BRITAIN and BRITONS, Comparison of Nicias and Crassus, iii. 402; Pompey, iv. 128; Cæsar, iv. 304-314; Cato the Younger, iv. 470, but some read, *Germans*.
BRITOMARTUS, or VIRIDOMARUS, king of the Gæsatæ, Romulus, i. 61; Marcellus, ii. 267-270.
BRIXILLUM, a town of Cisalpine Gaul, Otho, v. 515, 519, 528.
BRUNDUSIUM, or BRUNDISIUM, Æm. Paulus, ii. 212; Cato the Elder,

INDEX 553

ii. 367; Sylla, iii. 190; Crassus, iii. 371; Pompey, iv. 94, 145-146; Cæsar, iv. 328, 330-332; Cato the Younger, iv. 428; Cicero, v. 73, 81, 84; Antony, v. 172, 199, 228.

BRUTI (Bruti and Cumæi), Cæsar, iv. 355.

BRUTTII and BRUTTIUM, Fabius, i. 422, 424; Timoleon, ii. 139, 143, 158; Crassus, iii. 358; Cato the Younger, iv. 471.

BRUTTIUS SURA, lieutenant of Sentius, Sylla, iii. 168, 169.

LUCIUS JUNIUS BRUTUS, Poplicola, i. 215-221, 224; Cæsar, iv. 355; Brutus, v. 318, 319, 328.

BRUTUS, TITUS, and TIBERIUS, sons of Lucius, Poplicola, i. 216-221.

BRUTUS, first tribune of the people, Coriolanus, ii. 66, 74.

BRUTUS, consul, B. C. 138, Ti. Gracchus, iv. 592.

BRUTUS, prætor in the time of Marius, Sylla, iii. 165.

BRUTUS, father of the following, Pompey, iv. 65, 78, 147.

MARCUS BRUTUS, Life, v. 318; Comparison with Dion, v. 381; Pompey, iv. 78, 147, 170; Cæsar, iv. 340, 347, 350, 355-365; Cato the Younger, iv. 453, 494; Cicero, v. 85, 86, 89, 91; Comparison, v. 99; Antony, v. 175, 178, 184, 185, 236; Comparison, v. 256; Dion, v. 259, 261.

DECIMUS BRUTUS ALBINUS, Cæsar, iv. 358, 360; Antony, v. 175; Brutus, v. 331, 339, 349.

BRUTUS, a steward, Brutus, v. 319.

BRUTUS, name of a book, Brutus, v. 320, 331.

BUBULCI, Poplicola, i. 226.

BUCEPHALAS, or BUCEPHALUS, Alexander, iv. 185, 200, 226, 242, 266.

BUCEPHALIA, a town, Alexander, iv. 266.

BUSIRIS, an Egyptian deity, Theseus, i. 10.

BUTAS, freedman of Cato, Cato the Younger, iv. 491.

BUTAS, a poet, Romulus, i. 69.

FABIUS BUTEO, Fabius, i. 407.

BUTES, a Persian, Cimon, iii. 222.

BUTHROTUM, seaport of Epirus, Brutus, v. 347.

BYLLIS, town of Illyria, Brutus, v. 347.

BYZANTIUM and BYZANTINES, Pericles, i. 365; Alcibiades, ii. 46, 47; Aristides, ii. 340; Cimon, iii. 221, 222, 226; Nicias, iii. 340; Alexander, iv. 188; Phocion, iv. 343; Cato the Younger, iv. 451, 453; Demosthenes, v. 10, 19; Cicero, v. 64, 76.

C

CABIRA, a town in Asia, Lucullus, iii. 261, 262, 265; Comparison, iii. 305.

CABIRI, Marcellus, ii. 302.

CADIZ or GADES, Sertorius, iii. 414.

CADMEA, citadel of Thebes, Theseus, i. 32; Pelopidas, ii. 225, 226, 234, 236; Agesilaus, iv. 33-36; Alexander, iv. 193; Phocion, iv. 397.

CADMEA, sister of Neoptolemus, Pyrrhus, iii. 6.

CADMUS, son of Agenor, Sylla, iii. 178.

CADUSIANS, a people of Asia, Artaxerxes, v. 449, 467, 468.

CÆCI, Roman surname, Coriolanus, ii. 72.

CÆCIAS, the name of a wind, Sertorius, iii. 426.

CÆCILIA, mother of Lucullus, Lucullus, iii. 243.

CÆCILIA, wife of Sylla, Sylla, iii. 161. See METELLA.

CÆCILIUS, a Sicilian, Cicero, v. 46.

CÆCILIUS, the rhetorician, Demosthenes, v. 3.

CÆCINA, commanding for Vitellius,

Otho, v. 514, 518, 520, 521, 523, 529.
MARCUS CÆDICIUS, Camillus, i. 300, 301.
CÆLIUS, or CÆCILIUS, the orator (M. Cælius Rufus), Cicero, v. 78.
CÆNINENSES, Romulus, i. 60, 61; Marcellus, ii. 270.
CÆNUM, a town in Pontus, Pompey, iv. 109.
CÆPIO (Q. Servilius), Camillus, i. 306; Marius, iii. 71, 74; Lucullus, iii. 280; Sertorius, iii. 407.
SERVILIUS CÆPIO, Pompey, iv. 124; Cæsar, iv. 301.
CÆPIO (Q. Servilius), brother of Cato the Younger, Cato the Younger, iv. 413, 415, 417, 421, 424.
CÆSAR (C. Julius Cæsar), Life, iv. 286; Romulus, i. 62, 68; Numa, i. 162; Marius, iii. 57; Lucullus, iii. 300; Crassus, iii. 354, 359, 367-371, 373-382; Comparison, iii. 399-402; Pompey, iv. 70, 79, 91, 121-129, 131-133, 137-159, 162-166, 170; Comparison, iv. 171-173; Alexander, iv. 178; Cato the Younger, iv. 437-441, 442, 447-451, 453, 457, 461, 464, 468-472, 473, 475, 478-480, 482-488, 490, 493, 494; Cicero, v. 58-64, 66, 68-72, 78-84, 86, 87, 88, 89; Antony, v. 169-180, 197, 221, 226, 228, 239, 247; Brutus, v. 318-343, 348, 351, 356, 358, 371; Comparison, v. 381-385; Otho, v. 514, 519.
LUCIUS CÆSAR, uncle of Antony, Cicero, v. 90; Antony, v. 182, 183.
LUCIUS CÆSAR, Cato the Younger, iv. 487.
CÆSAR (Sextus Julius), Sylla, iii. 156.
CÆSAR (C. Julius Cæsar Octavianus, called Augustus), Numa, i. 163; Poplicola, i. 232; Pericles, i. 337; Marcellus, ii. 302; Alexander, iv. 275; Cæsar, iv. 362; Cato the Younger, iv. 493; Cicero, v. 87-91, 93; Comparison, v. 97, 99; Antony, v. 179-186, 191, 195-197, 199, 200, 218-226, 227-236, 239-253; Brutus, v. 342, 343, 348-352, 355, 356, 358, 361, 362, 365-367, 372, 373, 375, 379; Comparison, v. 384, 385; Galba, v. 478.
CÆSAR, as a title of the Emperors, frequent in Galba and Otho; also Comparison of Pericles and Fabius, i. 434.
CAIUS CÆSAR, meaning Caligula, Antony, v. 253; Galba, v. 485, 487, 488.
CÆSARION, son of Cæsar and Cleopatra, Cæsar, iv. 343; Antony, v. 221, 247.
CAIETA (in the text CAPITÆ), town in Latium, Cicero, v. 91.
CALAICI, tribe in Spain, Cæsar, iv. 299.
CALANUS, an Indian philosopher, Alexander, iv. 188, 271, 275.
CALAURIA (a doubtful name), in Sicily, Timoleon, ii. 159.
CALAURIA, or CALAUREA, island on coast of Argolis, Pompey, iv. 89; Phocion, iv. 400; Demosthenes, v. 33, 35.
CALENUS (Q. Fufius Calenus), lieutenant of Cæsar, Cæsar, iv. 336; Brutus, v. 327.
CALLÆSCHRUS, an Athenian, Alcibiades, ii. 49.
CALLIADES, Athenian general, Nicias, iii. 315.
CALLIAS the Torchbearer, Aristides, ii. 315, 316, 343; Comparison of Aristides and Cato, ii. 393; Pericles, i. 372; Cimon, iii. 233.
CALLIAS the Rich, Pericles, i. 372; Alcibiades, ii. 12; Cimon, iii. 219.
CALLIAS of Syracuse, Demosthenes, v. 6.
CALLIBIUS, a Spartan, Lysander, iii. 131.

CALLICLES, son of Arrhenides, Demosthenes, v. 29.
CALLICLES, a money-lender, Phocion, iv. 376.
CALLICRATES, an Athenian Architect, Pericles, i. 358.
CALLICRATES, a Spartan, Aristides, ii. 332.
CALLICRATES, a Spartan, Agesilaus, iv. 51.
CALLICRATES, a Syracusan, Nicias, iii. 333.
CALLICRATIDAS, a Spartan, Lycurgus, i. 130; Pelopidas, ii. 221; Lysander, iii. 118, 120; Artaxerxes, v. 464.
CALLIDROMON, mountain of Thessaly, Cato the Elder, ii. 365.
CALLIMACHUS, Comparison of Cato and Aristides, ii. 354.
CALLIMACHUS, an engineer, Lucullus, iii. 267, 287.
CALLIMACHUS, the poet, Antony, v. 238.
CALLIMEDON the Crab, Phocion, iv. 357, 406, 409; Demosthenes, v. 31.
CALLINICUS, a surname, Coriolanus, ii. 71; Marius, iii. 52.
CALLIPHON, an Athenian, Sylla, iii. 173.
CALLIPPIDES, a tragedian, Alcibiades, ii. 47; Agesilaus, iv. 31.
CALLIPPUS, an Athenian, tyrant, of Syracuse, Timoleon, ii. 132; Comparison, ii. 217; Nicias, iii. 329; Dion, v. 274, 287, 313-317.
CALLISTHENES, Athenian orator, Demosthenes, v. 26.
CALLISTHENES, freedman of Lucullus, Lucullus, iii. 300.
CALLISTHENES, an Olynthian philosopher and historian, Camillus, i. 306; Pelopidas, ii. 238; Aristides, ii. 345; Sylla, iii. 204; Cimon, iii. 231, 232; Agesilaus, iv. 49; Alexander, iv. 217, 227, 228, 253-259.
CALLISTRATUS, an Athenian orator, Demosthenes, v. 15.

CALLISTRATUS, attendant of Mithridates, Lucullus, iii. 265.
CALLISTUS, freedman of Caligula, Galba, v. 485.
CALPURNIA, daughter of Piso, wife of Cæsar, Pompey, iv. 124; Cæsar, iv. 301, 357, 358; Antony, v. 178.
CALPURNII, Numa, i. 165.
CALPURNIUS BIBULUS. See BIBULUS.
CALPURNIUS LANARIUS, Sertorius, iii. 413.
CALPURNIUS PISO. See PISO.
CALPUS, son of Numa, Numa, i. 165.
CALVINUS' DOMITIUS, Pompey, iv. 71; Cæsar, iv. 337, 338.
CALVISIUS, follower of Cæsar, Antony, v. 225.
CALVISIUS SABINUS, Galba, v. 487.
CALVISIUS. See DOMITIUS.
CALYDON, CALYDONIA, (Calydonian Boar), Theseus, i. 32; Aratus, v. 400.
CAMARINEANS, Dion, v. 286.
CAMBYSES, Alexander, iv. 216.
CAMERINUM, in Umbria, Marius, iii. 86.
CAMERIUM, in Latium, Romulus, i. 73.
MARCUS FURIUS CAMILLUS, Life, i. 285; Romulus, i. 80; Numa, i. 148; Fabius, i. 397; Galba, v. 508.
LUCIUS CAMILLUS, son of Camillus, Camillus, i. 397.
CAMILLUS, a boy in Jupiter's temple, Numa, i. 143.
CAMIRUS, in Rhodes, Demetrius, v. 124.
CAMPANIA, Fabius Maximus, i. 402; Comparison, i. 431; Marcellus, ii. 1; Sylla, iii. 191; Crassus, iii. 379; Cato the Younger, iv. 450; Cicero, v. 43, 66; Campanian soldiers, Dion, v. 286.
CAMULATUS, a soldier, Brutus, v. 374.

CAMURIUS, a soldier, Galba, v. 505.
CANETHUS, father of Sciron, Theseus, i. 27.
CANIDIUS, lieutenant of Antony, Antony, v. 199, 209, 222, 229, 231, 234, 235, 239.
CANIDIUS (more correctly Canius), tribune of the people, Pompey, iv. 127.
CANIDIUS (perhaps Caninius), Cato the Younger, iv. 451-454; Brutus, v.
CANINIUS REVILIUS, i. e. REBILUS, Cæsar, iv. 350.
CANNÆ, Fabius, i. 407, 414; Æm. Paulus, ii. 170; Marcellus, ii. 271, 273, 276, 293.
CAIUS CANNICIUS, lieutenant of Crassus, Crassus, iii. 364.
CANOBUS, or CANOPUS, Solon, i. 204; Cleomenes, iv. 560; Antony, v. 194; Comparison, v. 257; Canobic mouth of the Nile, Alexander, iv. 215.
CANTHARUS, part of the harbor at Athens, Phocion, iv. 400.
CANULEIA, Vestal Virgin, Numa, i. 148.
CANUS, a musician, Galba, v. 492.
CANUSIUM, town of Apulia, Marcellus, ii. 271, 272.
CANUTIUS, an actor, Brutus, v. 342.
CAPANEUS, the hero, Pelopidas, ii. 223.
CAPENATES, the people of Capena, Camillus, i. 287, 290, 302.
CAPHIS, a Phocian, Sylla, iii. 170, 174.
CAPHISIAS of Sicyon, a friend of Aratus, Aratus, v. 391, 392.
CAPHISIAS, a musician, Pyrrhus, iii 10.
CAPHYÆ, town of Arcadia, Cleomenes, iv. 524; Aratus, v. 433.
CAPITÆ, i. e. CAIETA, Cicero, v. 91.
FONTEIUS CAPITO, Antony, v. 201.
FONTEIUS CAPITO, Galba, v. 491.

CAPITOLINUS, ædile with Marcellus, Marcellus, ii. 263.
QUINTIUS CAPITOLINUS, dictator, Camillus, i. 328.
MARCUS MANLIUS CAPITOLINUS, Camillus, i. 316, 327-328.
CAPPADOCIA and CAPPADOCIANS, Marius, iii. 90; Sylla, iii. 157, 165, 168, 185; Lucullus, iii. 250, 270, 277, 291; Sertorius, iii. 436; Eumenes, iii. 443, and throughout; Pompey, iv. 98, 120; Alexander, iv. 202; Cæsar, iv. 343; Cato the Younger, iv. 493; Cicero, v. 77; Comparison, v. 98, 99; Demetrius, v. 106; Antony, v. 227.
CAPRARII, Poplicola, i. 226.
NONÆ CAPROTINÆ, Romulus, i. 80; Numa, i. 134; Camillus, i. 324.
CAPUA, Fabius, i. 417; Comparison, i. 432; Sylla, iii. 192; Crassus, iii. 360, 361; C. Gracchus, iv. 603.
CARANUS, Alexander, iv. 178.
CARBO, consul, B. C. 85, Marius, iii. 71; Sylla, iii. 184, 193-195; Sertorius, iii. 411, 412, 433; Pompey, iv. 64-66, 69, 70; Brutus, v. 351.
CARDIA and CARDIANS, Sertorius, iii. 406; Eumenes, iii. 441, 444.
CARIA and CARIANS, Theseus, i. 9; Themistocles (his mother a Carian), i. 244; Aristides, ii. 334; Agesilaus, iv. 13, 14; Alexander, iv. 190, 209; Demetrius, v. 155; Aratus, v. 397; Artaxerxes, v. 450, 456.
THE CARINÆ, in Rome, Antony, v. 196.
CARINNA, or CARINNAS, of Carbo's party, Pompey, iv. 65.
CARMANIA, province of Persia, Alexander, iv. 272.
CARMENTA, a nymph, Romulus, i. 68.
CARMENTAL GATE, Camillus, i. 314.
CARNEADES, Academic philosopher, Cato the Elder, ii. 380, 381; Lucullus, iii. 299; Cicero, v. 40.

CARNUTES, or CARNUTINI, Gallic tribe, Cæsar, iv. 316.
CARRHÆ, town of Mesopotamia, Crassus, iii. 385, 388-390.
CARTHAGE and the CARTHAGINIANS. See the lives of Fabius (i. 395), Timoleon (ii. 118), Marcellus (ii. 262), Cato the Elder, the last two pages (ii. 385, 386), parts of Pyrrhus (iii. 31 to 35), Caius Gracchus (iv. 605 to 609), and Dion (v. 264, 265, 272, 284, 311). Also, Camillus, i. 306 (their unlucky days); Pericles, i. 368; Alcibiades, ii. 24; Flamininus, ii. 422; Marius, iii. 102; Lucullus, iii. 287 (the Armenian Carthage); Nicias, iii. 325; Cæsar, iv. 350; Ti. Gracchus, iv. 569; Comparison, 622.
NEW CARTHAGE, in Spain, Sertorius, iii. 413.
SPURIUS CARVILIUS, Comparison of Romulus and Theseus, i. 86; Comparison of Lycurgus and Numa, i. 174.
CARYATIDES, Artaxerxes, v. 459.
CARYSTUS, town in Eubœa, Brutus, v. 345.
PUBLIUS CASCA, the conspirator, Cæsar, iv. 360; Brutus, v. 334, 337, 371.
CASILINUM, in Campania, Fabius, i. 402.
CASINUM, in Latium, Fabius, i. 402.
CASPIAN SEA, Lucullus, iii. 277; Pompey, iv. 104-108; Alexander, iv. 242; Cæsar, iv. 351; Comparison of Antony and Demetrius, v. 255.
CASSANDER, son of Antipater, king of Macedon; Pyrrhus, iii. 3, 7; Eumenes, iii. 455; Alexander, iv. 281; Phocion, iv. 403, 404; Demosthenes, v. 15, 36; Demetrius, v. 109, 110, 119, 125, 137, 141, 144.

CASSANDRA, daughter of Priam, Agis, iv. 505.
CASSANDREA, town in Macedonia, Demetrius, v. 154.
CASSIUS, friend of Brutus, Crassus, iii. 375, 376, 379-380, 387-390; Pompey, iv. 79; Cæsar, iv. 350, 356, 359, 363, 364; Cicero, v. 85; Antony, v. 176-178, 184, 188; Comparison, v. 256; Brutus, v. 319, 324, 325, and after; Comparison, v. 381.
QUINTUS CASSIUS, tribune of the people, Antony, v. 171.
CASSIUS SABACO, Marius, iii. 56.
CASSIUS SCÆVA, Cæsar, iv. 304.
CASSIUS (C. Cassius Varus), Crassus, iii. 362.
CASTULO, in Spain, Sertorius, iii. 408.
CASTUS, lieutenant of Crassus, Crassus, iii. 364.
CATANA, Alcibiades, ii. 28; Timoleon, ii. 134, 142, 158, 161; Marcellus, ii. 302; Nicias, iii. 330-331; Dion, v. 317.
CATAONIA, Demetrius, v. 158.
LUCIUS CATILINE, the conspirator, Sylla, iii. 199; Lucullus, iii. 295; Crassus, iii. 367; Cæsar, iv. 293, 294; Cato the Younger, iv. 437, 441; Cicero, v. 49-57, 60, 62, 69; Comparison, v. 98; Antony, v. 166; Brutus, v. 323.
CATO, great-grandfather of the Censor, Cato the Elder, ii. 347.
MARCUS CATO, father of the Censor, Cato the Elder, ii. 347.
MARCUS CATO, the Censor, or CATO THE ELDER, Cato Major, Life, ii. 347; Comparison with Aristides, ii. 388; Coriolanus, ii. 66; Æm. Paulus, ii. 174, 194; Pelopidas, ii. 220; Flamininus, ii. 447, 448; Cato the Younger, iv. 413.
MARCUS CATO, son of the Censor, Æm. Paulus, ii. 194; compare

Cato the Elder, ii. 387, where his son is also mentioned.
CATO SALONIUS, or SALONIANUS, younger son of the Censor, Cato the Elder, ii. 383, 386, 387.
MARCUS, son of CATO SALONIUS, Cato the Elder, ii. 387, but the consul was his brother Lucius.
CATO THE YOUNGER, Life, iv. 413; Cato the Elder, ii. 387; Lucullus, iii. 294-297; Crassus, iii. 359, 369, 370; Comparison, iii. 399, 401, 402; Pompey, iv. 112, 119, 122-125, 134-138, 142, 143, 148, 151, 164; Cæsar, iv. 289, 294, 295, 300-303, 312, 313, 320, 334, 347, 355; Phocion, iv. 369-371; Cicero, v. 60, 62, 76, 79-82; Comparison, v. 96; Antony, v. 170; Brutus, v. 319-325, 330, 331, 352, 356, 364, 375; Otho, v. 522.
MARCUS CATO, son of Cato the Younger, Brutus, v. 375; Compare Cato the Younger, iv. 486-493.
CATOS, Crassus, iii. 368.
CATULI, Crassus, iii. 368; Cicero, v. 38.
LUTATIUS CATULUS, consul, B. C. 102, Marius, iii. 69, 79-85, 108; Sylla, iii. 156.
LUTATIUS CATULUS, consul, B. C. 78, Poplicola, i. 229; Sylla, iii. 202; Crassus, iii. 367; Pompey, iv. 78, 80, 92, 98, 101; Cæsar, iv. 292, 294; Cato the Younger, iv. 429, 430; Cicero, v. 60, 70; Galba, v. 478.
MOUNT CAUCASUS, Lucullus, iii. 261; Pompey, iv. 106, 108; Cæsar, iv. 351; Demetrius, v. 108; Antony, v. 199; Comparison, v. 255.
CAULONIA, town of Bruttium, Fabius, i. 423; Dion, v. 285.
CAUNUS, town of Caria, and CAUNIANS, Nicias, iii. 349; Demetrius, v. 159; Artaxerxes, v. 452, 453, 454.

CEBALINUS, or BALINUS, a Macedonian, Alexander, iv. 247.
CECROPS, Comparison of Theseus and Romulus, i. 85.
CELÆNÆ, town in Phrygia, Eumenes, iii. 451; Demetrius, v. 108.
CELER, Romulus, i. 52.
QUINTUS METELLUS CELER, Romulus, i. 53; Coriolanus, ii. 72.
QUINTUS METELLUS CELER, son of the preceding, Cicero, v. 54, 69.
CLODIUS CELSUS, Galba, v. 489.
MARIUS CELSUS, Galba, v. 503, 506; Otho, v. 509, 515, 517, 519, 522, 523.
CELTIBERIANS, Spanish tribe, M. Cato, ii. 361; Marius, iii. 54; Sertorius, iii. 408.
CELTS, and the CELTIC nation, Romulus, i. 63; Camillus, i. 300; Marius, iii. 63; Sertorius (a Celtic dress), iii. 407; Pompey, iv. 65. (But the Greek words Celt and Celtic are often used where the translation gives Gaul and Gallic.)
CELTORII, Gallic tribe, Camillus, i. 300.
CELTO-SCYTHIANS, Marius, iii. 64.
CENCHREÆ, town of Argolis, Pelopidas, ii. 246.
CENCHREÆ, port of Corinth, Cato the Younger, iv. 455; Demetrius, v. 125; Aratus, v. 408, 413, 430.
CENINENSES or CÆNINENSES, Romulus, i. 60, 61; Marcellus, ii. 270.
MARCIUS CENSORINUS, Coriolanus, ii. 59.
CENSORINUS, Sylla, iii. 158.
LUCIUS CENSORINUS, Antony, v. 186.
CENSORINUS, Crassus, iii. 383, 385.
CENTAURS, Theseus, i. 32, 33; Comparison, i. 82; Agis, iv. 495.
CEOS, island in the Ægean Sea, The-

INDEX 559

mistocles, i. 247; Timoleon, ii. 163; Aristides, ii. 311; Nicias, iii. 309; Demosthenes, v. 1.

CEPHALON, friend of Aratus, Aratus, v. 438.

CEPHALUS, a Corinthian, Timoleon, ii. 150.

CEPHISODORUS, a Theban, Pelopidas, ii. 233.

CEPHISODOTUS, an Athenian, Phocion, iv. 388.

CEPHISUS, river of Attica, Theseus, i. 10; Agesilaus, iv. 45.

CEPHISUS, river of Bœotia, Sylla, iii. 177, 178, 183; Alexander, iv. 189; Demosthenes, v. 21.

CERAMICUS, a part of Athens, Sylla, iii. 172, 173; Cimon, iii. 220; Phocion, iv. 407; Demetrius, v. 113, 114.

CERAUNIAN MOUNTAINS, Phocion, iv. 401.

CERAUNUS, a surname, Pyrrhus, iii. 31.

CERBERUS, Theseus, i. 34; Nicias, iii. 308.

CERCINA, island on the coast of Africa, Marius, iii. 103; Dion, v. 284.

CERCYON, an Arcadian, Theseus, i. 10, 31.

CEREATE, CEREATUM, or CIRRHEATÆ (in the text corruptly CIRRHÆATON), a village in Latium, Marius, iii. 54.

CERESSUS, a town of Bœotia, Camillus, i. 305.

CERMALUS, or CERMANUS, or GERMANUS, Romulus, i. 44.

CETHEGUS, companion of Catiline, Cæsar, iv. 294; Cato the Younger, iv. 437; Cicero, v. 54, 56, 57, 61, 62, 71.

CORNELIUS CETHEGUS, consul, B. C. 204, Marcellus, ii. 266.

PUBLIUS CORNELIUS [CETHEGUS], consul, B. C. 181, Numa, i. 167.

CETHEGUS, friend of Marius, Marius iii. 102; Lucullus, iii. 250-251.

CHABRIAS, an Athenian, Camillus, i. 306; Agesilaus, iv. 53, 57; Phocion, iv. 372-374; Demosthenes, v. 17.

CHÆRON, founder of Chæronea, Sylla, iii. 178.

CHÆRON of Megalopolis, Alexander, iv. 180.

CHÆRONDAS, archon, Demosthenes, v. 27.

CHÆRONEA, in Bœotia, and CHÆRONEANS, Theseus, i. 30; Camillus, i. 306; Pelopidas, ii. 240; Lysander, iii. 149; Sylla, iii. 168, 177-179, 184-186; Cimon, iii. 213-215; Lucullus, iii. 247, 258; Agesilaus, iv. 25; Alexander, iv. 189, 194; Phocion, iv. 385; Demosthenes, v. 21, 24, 27; Aratus, v. 400.

CHALASTRA, a town of Macedonia, Alexander, iv. 247, 248.

CHALCEDON, town of Bithynia, Alcibiades, ii. 43, 45; Lucullus, iii. 253, 254.

CHALCIDIANS, in Thrace, Lycurgus, i. 130; Nicias, iii. 315; Demosthenes, v. 10.

CHALCIS and CHALCIDIANS, in Eubœa, Theseus, i. 30; Pericles, i. 370; Philopœmen, ii. 415; Flamininus, ii. 435, 438, 444; Sylla, iii. 181, 182; Demetrius, v. 152.

CHALCODON, a hero, king of the Abantes, Theseus, i. 29, 38.

CHALCUS, DIONYSIUS so called, a poet, Nicias, iii. 313. Also a nickname (the Brazen), in Demosthenes, v. 13.

CHALDÆANS, Marius, iii. 105; Sylla, iii. 158, 204; Lucullus, iii. 260, 267; Alexander, iv. 280; Galba, v. 500.

CHAONIANS, a people of Epirus, Pyrrhus, iii. 26, 41.

CHARACITANIANS, a Spanish tribe, Sertorius, iii. 425, 426.
CHARES, an Athenian, Pelopidas, ii. 222; Phocion, iv. 371, 374, 382; Comparison of Demosthenes and Cicero, v. 97; Aratus, v. 400.
CHARES of Mitylene, a writer, Alexander, iv. 206, 213, 243, 257, 258, 276; Phocion, iv. 387.
CHARES, river in Argolis, Aratus, v. 412.
CHARICLES, an Athenian, Nicias, iii. 312.
CHARICLES, son-in-law of Phocion, Phocion, iv. 391, 392, 406, 409.
CHARICLO, wife of Sciron, Theseus, i. 10.
CHARIDEMUS, the general, Sertorius, iii. 405.
CHARIDEMUS, the orator, Phocion, iv. 384, 385; Demosthenes, v. 26.
CHARILAUS, king of Sparta, Lycurgus, i. 90, 94, 116; called also CHARILLUS, Cleomenes, iv. 532; Comparison of Agis and Cleomenes, with Gracchi, iv. 623.
CHARIMENES, an Argive diviner, Aratus, v. 410.
CHARINUS, an Athenian, Pericles, i. 380.
CHARMION, Antony, v. 226, 251.
CHARMUS, an Athenian, Solon, i. 178.
CHARON of Lampsacus, a writer, Themistocles, i. 276.
CHARON, a Theban, Pelopidas, ii. 228-232, 234, 246, 247.
CHARONITÆ, a nickname, Antony, v. 179.
CHAROPS, an Epirot, Flamininus, ii. 426.
CHARYBDIS, Dion, v. 277.
CHELIDONIAN ISLANDS, Cimon, iii. 230, 232.
CHERSONESUS, in Thrace, and CHERSONESIANS, Pericles, i. 354, 366, 367; Lysander, iii. 118, 122, 123; Cimon, iii. 223; Lucullus, iii. 248,
273; Eumenes, iii. 382; Comparison, iii. 467; Phocion, iv. 382; Demetrius, v. 136.
THE SYRIAN CHERSONESUS, Demetrius, v. 161-163.
CHILEUS, an Arcadian, Themistocles, i. 251.
CHILO, slave of Cato, Cato the Elder, ii. 376.
CHILONIS, daughter of Leonidas, Agis, iv. 513-514.
CHILONIS, daughter of Leotychidas, Pyrrhus, iii. 39, 41, 42.
CHIOS and CHIANS, in the Ægean Sea, Theseus, i. 19; Themistocles, i. 283; Alcibiades, ii. 15, 34, 52; Aristides, ii. 340; Cimon, iii. 225, 231; Lucullus, iii. 247, 266; Phocion, iv. 372; Brutus, v. 355.
CHIRON, the Centaur, Pericles, i. 342.
CHLIDON, a Theban, Pelopidas, ii. 229.
CHŒRILUS, a poet, Lysander, iii. 134.
CHOLARGUS, Attic township, Pericles, i. 340, 357; Nicias, iii. 305.
CHRYSA, Theseus, i. 29.
CHRYSANTES, a Persian, Comparison of Pelopidas and Marcellus, ii. 305.
CHRYSERMAS, an Egyptian, Cleomenes, iv. 559, 561.
CHRYSIPPUS, Stoic philosopher, Aratus, v. 386.
CHRYSIS, Demetrius, v. 126.
CHRYSOGONUS, freedman of Sylla, Cicero, v. 39.
CHRYSOGONUS, a flute-player, Alcibiades, ii. 47.
MARCUS TULLIUS CICERO, Life, v. 37; Comparison with Demosthenes, v. 95; Æm. Paulus, ii. 180; Cato the Elder, ii. 372; Flamininus, ii. 448; Lucullus, iii. 295, 298-300; Crassus, iii. 354, 367; Pompey, iv. 118, 122, 125, 126, 141, 145, 147; Cæsar, iv. 288,

INDEX

290, 293, 294, 303, 323, 347, 349-353; Phocion, iv. 369; C. Gracchus, iv. 595; Demosthenes, v. 3; Antony, v. 166, 170, 173, 180-183, 185; Comparison, v. 258; Brutus, v. 330, 339, 342-344, 347-350.

CICERO, son of the orator, Cicero, v. 89, 94; Brutus, v. 344, 347.

QUINTUS CICERO, brother of the orator, Cicero, v. 59, 75, 90, 93; Cæsar, iv. 315.

CILICIA and CILICIANS, Themistocles, i. 282; Lysander, iii. 122; Cimon, iii. 240; Lucullus, iii. 250, 251, 270, 273, 274, 277, 288; Crassus, iii. 363, and Sertorius, iii. 413, 415 (pirates); Eumenes, iii. 445-447; Pompey, iv. 88, and after (pirates), 120, 163; Alexander, iv. 201, and after; Cæsar, iv. 287; Cicero, v. 77, 79; Comparison, v. 98; Demetrius, v. 136, 137, 157, 159; Antony, v. 188, 189, 201, 221, 227; Brutus, v. 322.

CILLES, general of Ptolemy Lagus, Demetrius, v. 107.

TILLIUS CIMBER, Cæsar, iv. 360; Brutus, v. 336, 339.

CIMBRIANS, Camillus, i. 306; Marius, iii. 63-65, 69, 79, 82, 83, 108; Lucullus, iii. 280, 295; Sertorius, iii. 407; Cæsar, iv. 292, 307, 308, 317; Otho, v. 525.

CIMMERIANS, Marius, iii. 63, 64; Cimmerian Bosphorus, Theseus, i. 29.

CIMON, son of Miltiades, Life, iii. 213; Comparison with Lucullus, iii. 302; Theseus, i. 39; Themistocles, i. 249, 269, 273, 282; Pericles, i. 343, 346, 349-353, 377, 378; Comparison, i. 431, 433; Alcibiades, ii. 26, 31; Pelopidas, ii. 224; Aristides, ii. 323, 339, 340-344; Cato the Elder, ii. 354; Flamininus, ii. 437; Demosthenes, v. 16.

CIMON, called COALEMUS, father of Miltiades, Cimon, iii. 217.

CINEAS, an Athenian, Phocion, iv. 381.

CINEAS, minister of Pyrrhus, Pyrrhus, iii. 18-21, 25, 27-29, 32.

CINGONIUS VARRO, Galba, v. 490.

LUCIUS CINNA, consul, B. C. 87, Marius, iii. 103-105, 108; Sylla, iii. 167, 171, 184; Crassus, iii. 355, 356; Sertorius, iii. 409-411; Pompey, iv. 61-63; Cæsar, iv. 286; Cicero, v. 56; Brutus, v. 351.

CINNA, a poet, friend of Cæsar, iv. 363; Brutus, v. 340, 341.

CINNA, the conspirator, Cæsar, iv. 363; Brutus, v. 338.

CINNA, perhaps brother of the above, Brutus, v. 345.

CIRCE, the goddess, Romulus, i. 42.

CIRCEII or CIRCEUM, Coriolanus, ii. 94; Marius, iii. 96; Cæsar, iv. 351; Cicero, v. 91.

The CIRCUS MAXIMUS at Rome, Romulus, i. 46, 57, 67; Flamininus, ii. 422.

CIRRHA, town of Phocis, and CIRRHÆANS, Lycurgus, i. 132; Numa, i. 139; Solon, i. 186.

CIRRHÆATON (Cereatæ), near Arpinum, Marius, iii. 54.

CISSUS, a Macedonian, Alexander, iv. 238.

CISSUSA, fountain in Bœotia, Lysander, iii. 148.

MOUNT CITHÆRON, Aristides, ii. 324, 325, 327, 333; Lysander, iii. 147; Demosthenes, v. 26.

CITIUM, town of Cyprus, and CITIEANS, Cimon, iii. 241, 242; Alexander, iv. 226; Cleomenes, iv. 521.

CIUS, town of Bithynia, Phocion, iv. 388.

CLARIUS, river of Cyprus, Solon, i. 205.

CLAROS, in Ionia, Pompey, iv. 89.

CLASTIDIUM, in Cisalpine Gaul, Marcellus, ii. 267.

CLAUDIA, wife of Ti. Gracchus, iv. 569.
CLAUDII, Poplicola, i. 236; Coriolanus, ii. 72.
APPIUS CLAUDIUS. See APPIUS.
CLAUDIUS CÆSAR, emperor, Antony, v. 254; Galba, v. 487, 498.
CLAUSUS. See APPIUS.
CLAZOMENÆ, town of Ionia, Alcibiades, ii. 41; Nicias, iii. 327.
CLEÆNETUS, an Athenian, Demetrius, v. 126.
CLEANDER of Mantinea, Philopœmen, ii. 395.
CLEANDRIDES, a Spartan, Pericles, i. 370; Nicias, iii. 348.
CLEANTHES, a physician, Cato the Younger, iv. 491.
CLEANTHES, Stoic philosopher, Alcibiades, ii. 10.
CLEARCHUS, a Macedonian, Demosthenes, v. 20.
CLEARCHUS, a Spartan, Artaxerxes, v. 446, 448-449, 454, 459, 460.
CLEOCRITUS, a Corinthian, Aristides, ii. 320, 336.
CLEODÆUS, son of Hyllus, Pyrrhus, iii. 1.
CLEOMANTIS, a Spartan, Alexander, iv. 249.
CLEOMBROTUS I., king of Sparta, son of Pausanias, Pelopidas, ii. 234, 242, 244; Comparison of Lysander and Sylla, iii. 210; Agesilaus, iv. 35, 37, 41, 42; Agis, iv. 499, 512-515, 519.
CLEOMBROTUS II., king of Sparta, son-in-law of Leonidas, Agis, iv. 508, 509.
CLEOMEDES of Astypalæa, Romulus, i. 79.
CLEOMEDON, an Athenian, Demetrius, v. 126.
CLEOMENES, an Athenian, Lysander, iii. 130.
CLEOMENES, a Spartan, Solon, i. 186.

CLEOMENES II., king of Sparta, son of Cleombrotus, Agis, iv. 499.
CLEOMENES III., king of Sparta, son of Leonidas, Life, iv. 520; Comparison, iv. 619; Philopœmen, ii. 399; Agis, iv. 497; Aratus, v. 421-430, 432.
CLEON, of Athens, Pericles, i. 385, 388; Nicias, iii. 309, 310, 313, 316-319; Comparison, iii. 399-401; Ti. Gracchus, iv. 567; Demetrius, v. 113.
CLEON of Halicarnassus, writer, Lysander, iii. 143; Agesilaus, iv. 29.
CLEON, tyrant of Sicyon, Aratus, v. 387.
CLEONÆ, town of Argolis, and CLEONÆANS, Timoleon, ii. 122; Cimon, iii. 238; Phocion, iv. 400; Cleomenes, iv. 541; Demosthenes, v. 32; Aratus, v. 413, 414.
CLEONICE, a woman of Byzantium, Cimon, iii. 221, 222.
CLEONIDES, general of Ptolemy Lagus, Demetrius, v. 117.
CLEONYMUS, son of Cleomenes II., Pyrrhus, iii. 39-41; Agis, iv. 499; Demetrius, v. 146.
CLEONYMUS, a Spartan, son of Sphodrias, Agesilaus, iv. 36, 37, 42.
CLEOPATER, an Achæan officer, Aratus, v. 426.
CLEOPATRA, wife of Philip of Macedon, Alexander, iv. 189, 192, 214, 274.
CLEOPATRA, sister of Alexander the Great, Eumenes, iii. 444, 451.
CLEOPATRA, daughter of Mithridates, wife of Tigranes, Lucullus, iii. 272.
CLEOPATRA, queen of Egypt, Cæsar, iv. 341, 343; Antony, v. 175, 188, and after; Comparison, v. 255, 257.
CLEOPATRA, daughter of Antony

INDEX 563

and Cleopatra, Antony, v. 201, 252.
CLEOPHANES, an Athenian, Phocion, iv. 381.
CLEOPHANTUS, son of Themistocles, Themistocles, i. 283.
CLEOPTOLEMUS of Chalcis, Flamininus, ii. 444.
CLEORA, wife of Agesilaus, Agesilaus, iv. 28.
CLEPSYDRA, spring at Athens, Antony, v. 198.
CLIDEMUS, an historian, Theseus, i. 17, 29; Themistocles, i. 257; Aristides, ii. 335.
CLIMAX, mountain in Lycia, Alexander, iv. 202.
CLINIAS, Solon, i. 193.
CLINIAS, father of Alcibiades, Alcibiades, ii. 3, 15, 31.
CLINIAS, father of Aratus, Aratus, v. 387, 393.
CLISTHENES, Pericles, i. 340; Aristides, ii. 310; Cimon, iii. 235.
CLITARCHUS, an historian, Themistocles, i. 276; Alexander, iv. 243.
CLITOMACHUS, an Academic philosopher, Cicero, v. 39, 40.
CLITORIUM and CLITORIANS, Lycurgus, i. 89; Cimon, iii. 235.
CLITUS THE BLACK, a Macedonian, Alexander, iv. 195, 199, 249-253.
CLITUS, a Macedonian, Phocion, iv. 407, 408.
CLITUS, servant of Brutus, Brutus, v. 378.
CLODIA, wife of Lucullus, sister of P. Clodius, Lucullus, iii. 294.
CLODIA, called Quadrantaria, another sister, Cicero, v. 69.
CLODIA, daughter of P. Clodius and Fulvia, Antony, v. 183.
PUBLIUS CLODIUS, the tribune, Lucullus, iii. 289; Pompey, iv. 122, 126, 127; Cæsar, iv. 295-298, 303; Cato the Younger, iv. 434, 447, 449-451, 457, 464; Cicero, v. 68-72, 74-76; Antony, v. 166, 175; Brutus, v. 340.
CLODIUS, a commander during the servile war, Crassus, iii. 361.
CLODIUS, Antony, v. 181.
CLODIUS, a deserter, Brutus, v. 373.
CLODIUS CELSUS of Antioch, Galba, v. 489.
CLODIUS MACER, Galba, v. 481, 489, 491.
CLODIUS, an historian, Numa, i. 133.
CLŒLIA, Poplicola, i. 233.
CLŒLIA, wife of Sylla, Sylla, iii. 161.
CLŒLIAN, or CLUILIAN DITCHES, Fossæ Cluiliæ, Coriolanus, ii. 96.
CLŒLIUS, more correctly Cælius (C. Cælius Caldus), Pompey, iv. 65.
CLODONES, Alexander, iv. 180.
CLUNIA, a town in Spain, Galba, v. 482.
CLUSIUM, town of Etruria, and CLUSINIANS, Numa, i. 152; Poplicola, i. 230; Camillus, i. 301, 302, 303.
CLUVIUS RUFUS, governor in Spain, Otho, v. 511.
CLYMENE, Theseus, i. 37.
CNACION, river of Sparta, Lycurgus, i. 95; Pelopidas, ii. 239.
CNIDOS, in Caria, and CNIDIANS, Alcibiades, ii. 40; Cimon, iii. 230; Lucullus, iii. 247; Agesilaus, iv. 25; Cæsar, iv. 341; Artaxerxes, v. 463.
COALEMUS, surname of Cimon's father, Cimon, iii. 218.
COCCEIUS, more correctly SALVIUS, COCCEIANUS, Otho's nephew, Otho, v. 526.
HORATIUS COCLES, Poplicola, i. 231, 232.
CODRUS, Solon, i. 177.
CŒLIUS. See above, CLŒLIUS.
CŒLIUS, lieutenant of Antony, Antony, v. 231.

COENUS, a Macedonian, Alexander, iv. 265.
COLCHIS, Theseus, i. 32; Lucullus, iii. 261; Pompey, iv. 98, 104, 107, 120.
COLIAS, promontory of Attica, Solon, i. 184.
TARQUINIUS COLLATINUS, Poplicola, i. 215-221.
COLLINE GATE, at Rome, Numa, i. 149; Camillus, i. 310; Sylla, iii. 195.
COLLYTUS, part of Athens, Demosthenes, v. 13.
COLONIS, village in Messenia, Philopœmen, ii. 417.
COLOPHON and COLOPHONIANS, Timoleon, ii. 164; Lysander, iii. 134; Lucullus, iii. 247.
COMIAS, archon at Athens, Solon, i. 213.
COMINIUS, consul, Coriolanus, ii. 66, 71.
PONTIUS COMINIUS, Camillus, i. 313, 314, 315.
COMMAGENE, Pompey, iv. 120; Antony, v. 198, 227.
COMUM, the modern Como, called, when Cæsar planted his colony there, NEW COMUM, Cæsar, iv. 321.
CONNIDAS, tutor of Theseus, Theseus, i. 4.
CONON, the Athenian general, son of Timotheus, Alcibiades, ii. 55; Lysander, iii. 124, 125; Sylla, iii. 159; Agesilaus, iv. 25, 33; Artaxerxes, v. 463, 464.
CONOPION, an Athenian, Phocion, iv. 410.
CONSA, or COSSA, in Etruria, Flamininus, ii. 423.
CONSIDIUS, Cæsar, iv. 302.
PUBLIUS CONSTANS, perhaps COTTA, Cicero, v. 66.
CONSUS, a Roman God, Romulus, i. 57.
COPILLUS, general of the Tectosages, Sylla, iii. 155.

COPONIUS, lieutenant of Crassus, Crassus, iii. 388.
CORA, daughter of Aidoneus, Theseus, i. 34.
CORACESIUM, town in Spain, Pompey, iv. 95.
CORCYNA, nurse of Ariadne, Theseus, i. 20.
CORCYRA, the modern Corfu, Themistocles, i. 272; Pericles, i. 378, 379; Timoleon, ii. 128; Æm. Paulus, ii. 212; Pyrrhus, iii. 12-13; Cato the Younger, iv. 456; Demosthenes, v. 19.
CORDUBA, Cordova, in Spain, Cæsar, iv. 306.
CORDYLIO, ATHENODORUS so called, Cato the Younger, iv. 423, 428.
CORFINIUM, in Italy, Cæsar, iv. 327.
CORFINIUS, or CORNIFICIUS, Cæsar, iv. 336, 344.
CORINTH and CORINTHIANS, see many passages in the lives of Timoleon, ii. 118; Cleomenes, iv. 520, and Aratus, v. 386; and for general history, the following:—Pericles, i. 378; Alcibiades, ii. 19, 26; Cato the Elder, ii. 364; Philopœmen (its destruction), ii. 420; compare iv. 350; Lysander, iii. 139; Cimon, iii. 238; Nicias, iii. 315, 321, 334, 337, 344; Agesilaus, iv. 22, 24, 30, 31, 32; Cæsar (the new colony), iv. 350; Agis, iv. 511; Demosthenes, v. 19; Demetrius, v. 117, 127, 152, 161, 163; Dion, v. 259, 312. The meeting of the seven wise men, Solon, i. 180; Corinth, Chalcis, and Demetrius, Flamininus, ii. 435; Nero at Corinth, the same, ii. 440; Diogenes at Corinth, Alexander, iv. 195; the Isthmus, Cæsar, iv. 351; Simonides's line, Dion, v. 259.
CAIUS MARCIUS CORIOLANUS, Life, ii. 59; Comparison, ii. 112.

INDEX 565

CORIOLI, in Latium, Coriolanus, ii. 66, 67, 71.

CORNELIA, daughter of Scipio, mother of the Gracchi, Ti. Gracchus, iv. 566, 569, 575; C. Gracchus, iv. 599, 609, 617.

CORNELIA, wife of Marius, iii. 93.

CORNELIA, daughter of Cinna, wife of Cæsar, Cæsar, iv. 286, 291.

CORNELIA, daughter of Metellus Scipio, wife of Pompey, Pompey, iv. 135, 136, 150, 162, 163, 165, 167-170.

CORNELII, Marius, iii. 52; the three Cornelii, Cicero, v. 56. For others of the name, see CETHEGUS, COSSUS, DOLABELLA, LACO, LENTULUS, MERULA, SCIPIO, SYLLA.

CAIUS CORNELIUS, an augur at Padua, Cæsar, iv. 340.

CORNELIUS NEPOS, an historian, Marcellus, ii. 302; Comparison of Marcellus and Pelopidas, ii. 304; Lucullus, iii. 300; Ti. Gracchus, iv. 592.

CORNELIUS, freedman of Sylla, Cæsar, iv. 287.

LUCIUS CORNIFICIUS, Brutus, v. 348.

CORNUTUS, Marius, iii. 107.

COROEBUS, an architect, Pericles, i. 357.

CORONEA, town in Bœotia, Pericles, i. 366; Alcibiades, ii. 3; Lysander, iii. 150; Agesilaus, iv. 22, 25.

CORRHABUS, or CORRHAGUS, son of Demetrius Poliorcetes, Demetrius, v. 164.

CORRHÆUS, CORRHABUS, or CORRHAGUS, father of Demetrius's mother, Stratonice, Demetrius, v. 103.

CORSICA, Pompey, iv. 93, 150.

MESSALA CORVINUS, Brutus, v. 363-367, 370, 371, 379.

VALERIUS CORVINUS, or CORVUS, consul six times, Marius, iii. 87.

CORYNETES, name of Periphetes, Theseus, i. 8; Comparison, i. 82.

COS, in the Egean Sea, Solon, i. 180; Alcibiades, ii. 40; Lucullus, iii. 247.

COSCONIUS, Cæsar, iv. 344.

COSIS, brother to the king of the Albanians, Pompey, iv. 107.

COSSA, in Etruria, Flamininus, ii. 423.

COSSÆANS, a mountain tribe in Persia, Alexander, iv. 279.

COSSINIUS, Crassus, iii. 361.

CORNELIUS COSSUS, Romulus, i. 61; Marcellus, ii. 270.

LICINIUS COSSUS, Camillus, i. 289.

COTTA, or CONSTANS, Cicero, v. 66.

COTTA, prætor in Spain, Sertorius, iii. 419.

COTTA, consul, 634 B. C., Marius, iii. 55.

LUCIUS COTTA, Cicero, v. 67.

MARCUS COTTA, Lucullus, iii. 249, 251-253.

COTTA, lieutenant of Cæsar, Cæsar, iv. 315.

COTYLO, a nickname of Varius, Antony, v. 182.

COTYS, king of Paphlagonia, Agesilaus, iv. 16.

CRANIUM, or CRANEUM, at Corinth, Alexander, iv. 195.

CRANON, Camillus, i. 306; Phocion, iv. 395; Demosthenes, v. 32; Demetrius, v. 111.

CAIUS CRASSIANUS, a centurion, Pompey, iv. 157; C. CRASSINIUS, Cæsar, iv. 338.

CRASSUS, Fabius, i. 428.

PUBLIUS LICINIUS [CRASSUS], Æm. Paulus, ii. 178.

PUBLIUS CRASSUS, father-in-law of Caius Gracchus, and Pontifex Maximus, T. Gracchus, iv. 576, 592, and under the name of LICINIUS, C. Gracchus, iv. 614.

CRASSUS, son of the preceding, brother of Caius Gracchus's wife, C. Gracchus, iv. 613.

MARCUS CRASSUS, Life, iii. 351;

Comparison with Nicias, iii. 398; Sylla, iii. 194-196; Lucullus, iii. 293, 300; Nicias, iii. 307; Pompey, iv. 84-87, 101, 118, 122, 130-132, 135, 165; Cæsar, iv. 298-301, 312, 319; Cicero, v. 46, 47, 53, 65, 71, 75; Antony, v. 198, 202, 214; Brutus, v. 369.

PUBLIUS CRASSUS, son of the above, Crassus, iii. 367, 380, 383-386; Pompey, iv. 135, 162; Cicero, v. 75, 77.

CRASSUS, Cato the Younger, iv. 491.

CRASSUS (M. Licinius Crassus Frugi Magnus), father of Piso adopted by Galba, Galba, v. 499.

CRATERUS, Alexander's general, Eumenes, iii. 446-448, 454; Alexander, iv. 237-239, 245-247, 258; Phocion, iv. 388, 395, 396; Demosthenes, v. 32; Demetrius, v. 116.

CRATERUS, brother of king Antigonus Gonatas, an historical writer, Aristides, ii. 344; Cimon, iii. 233.

CRATES, a philosopher, Demetrius, v. 155.

CRATESICLEA, mother of Cleomenes, Cleomenes, iv. 526, 545, 562, 563.

CRATESIPOLIS, wife of Alexander, the son of Polysperchon, Demetrius, v. 110.

CRATINUS, comic poet, Solon, i. 203; Pericles, i. 341, 358, 372; Cimon, iii. 227.

CRATIPPUS, Peripatetic philosopher, Pompey, iv. 163; Cicero, v. 64; Brutus, v. 344.

CRAUGIS, father of Philopœmen, Philopœmen, ii. 395.

CREMONA, town of North Italy, Otho, v. 517, 518.

CREON, king of Thebes, Pelopidas, ii. 243; Alexander, iv. 230; Demosthenes, v. 34.

CREOPHYLUS, Homer's friend, the correct reading in Lycurgus, i. 92.

CRETE and the CRETANS, Theseus, i. 13, and after to 24, 40; Lycurgus, i. 92, 102, 132; Solon, i. 187 (Epimenides); Æmilius Paulus, ii. 196, 199, 208 (Cretan targets); Marcellus, ii. 286; Philopœmen, ii. 402, 409, 410; Pyrrhus, iii. 40, 43, 44, 45, 47; Lysander, iii. 137 (Cretan against Cretan), 148 (the Cretan Storax); Lucullus, iii. 245; Eumenes, iii. 465 (Nearchus the Cretan); Agesilaus, iv. 49; Pompey, iv. 96; Cleomenes, iv. 526, 544 (Cretan soldiers); C. Gracchus, iv. 613 (Cretan archers); Dion, v. 312; Brutus, v. 339; Artaxerxes, v. 463; Aratus, v. 414, 434, 436; Cretan sea, v. 436.

CRIMESUS, river of Sicily, Timoleon, ii. 152, 153, 155.

CRISPINUS (T. Quintius), colleague of Marcellus, Marcellus, ii. 300.

CRISPINUS (Rufus), first husband of Poppæa, Galba, v. 495.

CRISPINUS, killed by the Prætorians, Otho, v. 511.

CRITIAS, an Athenian, son of Callæschrus, Lycurgus, i. 100; Alcibiades, ii. 49; Cimon, iii. 227, 237.

CRITO, an Athenian, Aristides, ii. 310.

CRITOLAIDAS, a Spartan, Solon, i. 186.

CRITOLAUS, Peripatetic philosopher, Pericles, i. 347.

CROBYLUS, the nickname of Hegesippus, an orator, Demosthenes, v. 19.

CROBYLUS, a Corinthian, Alexander, iv. 208.

CRŒSUS, king of Lydia, Solon, i. 181, 205-208; Comparison, i. 239.

CROMMYON, in the district of Corinth, Theseus, i. 9.

CROTON, in South Italy, Romulus,

INDEX 567

i. 78; Alexander, iv. 229; Cicero, v. 57.

CRUSTUMERIUM, a Sabine town, Romulus, i. 62.

CTESIAS, physician of Cnidos, an historian, Artaxerxes, v. 441, 446, 449-454, 459, 460, 461, 463.

CTESIBIUS, Demosthenes, v. 6.

CTESIUM, port of Scyros, Cimon, iii. 224.

CTESIPHON, an Athenian, Demosthenes, v. 27.

CTESIPPUS, an Athenian, son of Chabrias, Phocion, iv. 373; Demosthenes, v. 17.

TERENTIUS CULEO, or CULLEO, tribune of the people, Flamininus, ii. 446.

CULLEO, a friend of Pompey, Pompey, iv. 126.

CUMA, in Campania, Ti. Gracchus, iv. 575, 588, 592.

CUMA, in Æolia. See CYME.

CUMÆANS, Cæsar, iv. 355.

CUNAXA, in Babylonia, Artaxerxes, v. 448.

CURES, city of the Sabines, Numa, i. 136; Compare Romulus, i. 66, 67, 80.

CURII, Comparison of Aristides and Cato, ii. 388.

CURIO, lieutenant of Sylla, Sylla, iii. 173; Cæsar, iv. 294; Cato the Younger, iv. 428; Antony, v. 166.

CURIO, son of the former, tribune of the people, Pompey, iv. 140, 141; Cæsar, iv. 321, 322; Cato the Younger, iv. 465; Antony, v. 166, 169.

MANIUS CURIUS (Dentatus), Cato the Elder, ii. 349, 358; Comparison, ii. 392; Pyrrhus, iii. 36.

MARCUS CURTIUS, Romulus, i. 64.

CURTAIN LAKE, Romulus, i. 64; Galba, v. 505.

CYANEAN ISLANDS, Cimon, iii. 232.

CYBERNESIA, Athenian feast, Theseus, i. 16.

CYBISTHUS, son of Thales, Solon, i. 182.

CYCHREUS, of Salamis, Theseus, i. 10; Solon, i. 185.

CYCLADES, islands in the Ægean Sea, Sylla, iii. 168; Demetrius, v. 135.

CYCNUS, the hero, Theseus, i. 10.

CYDNUS, river of Cilicia, Alexander, iv. 203; Antony, v. 189.

CYLLARABIS, or CYLARABIS, at Argos, Pyrrhus, iii. 47; Cleomenes, iv. 539, 550.

CYLON, an Athenian, Solon, i. 186-189.

CYME, town of Æolia, Themistocles, i. 274.

CYNÆGYRUS, brother of Æschylus, Comparison of Cato and Aristides, ii. 389.

CYNISCA, sister of Agesilaus, Agesilaus, iv. 29.

CYNOSARGES, Themistocles, i. 244.

CYNOSCEPHALÆ, Theseus, i. 31; Pelopidas, ii. 256; Flamininus, ii. 432.

CYNOSSEMA in Salamis, the Dog's Grave, Themistocles, i. 258; Cato the Elder, ii. 355.

CYPRUS and CYPRIANS, Theseus, i. 19; Solon, i. 205; Themistocles, i. 282; Pericles, i. 353 (Cimon's death), 374; Flamininus, ii. 437 (Cimon's battles); Lysander, iii. 125; Cimon, iii. 231, 240, 241; Lucullus, iii. 246, 300 (Cato's mission); Pompey, iv. 125, (the same) 165, 169; Dion, v. 280; Alexander, iv. 211, 219; Cæsar, iv. 312 (Cato's mission); Cato the Younger, iv. 451, and after, to 464; Cicero, v. 76 (Cato's mission); Demetrius, v. 106, 116-120, 123 (Cyprian cuirasses), 139, 141; Antony, v. 201, 221; Brutus, v. 321; Artaxerxes, v. 463.

CYPSELUS, tyrant of Corinth, Aratus, v. 389.

CYRENE and CYRENEANS, in Africa, Philopœmen, ii. 395; Lucullus, iii. 245; Cato the Younger, iv. 476; Cleomenes, iv. 554, 559; Demetrius, v. 116, 164; Antony, v. 228; Dion, v. 277.
CYRNUS, or CYRUS, river of Asia, Pompey, iv. 106, 107.
CYRRHESTICA, district of Syria, Demetrius, v. 159; Antony, v. 198.
CYRUS, founder of the Persian monarchy, Solon, i. 207; Alexander, iv. 223, 275; Antony, v. 171; Artaxerxes, v. 441, 442.
CYRUS THE YOUNGER, son of Darius Nothus, Pericles, i. 373; Alcibiades, ii. 52; Lysander, iii. 116, 117, 119-122, 134; Comparison, iii. 210; Artaxerxes, v. 441, 443, 445-453, 454-458, 459, 462, 469, 470.
CYTHERA, island on the coast of Laconia, Nicias, iii. 315; Comparison, iii. 401; Agesilaus, iv. 45; Cleomenes, iv. 554.
CYTHERIS (a name of Volumnia), Antony, v. 174.
CYZICUS and CYZICENIANS, Alcibiades, ii. 34, 41, 42; Lucullus, iii. 254-258, 288; Dion, v. 278; Brutus, v. 349.

D

DÆDALUS, Theseus, i. 18.
DAIMACHUS, an historian, Comparison of Solon and Poplicola, i. 242; Lysander, iii. 126.
DALMATIA, Otho, v. 513.
DAMAGORAS, a Rhodian, Lucullus, iii. 248.
DAMASCUS, in Syria, Alexander, iv. 206, 208, 211, 246.
DAMASTES, Theseus, i. 10.
DAMASTES, an historian, Camillus, i. 306.
DAMIPPUS, a Spartan, Marcellus, ii. 283, 284.

DAMOCHARES, a Spartan, Agis, iv. 515-517.
DAMOCLES, or DEMOCLES, Demetrius, v. 126.
DAMOCLIDAS, a Theban, Pelopidas, ii. 228, 232.
DAMOCRATES, a Platæan hero, Aristides, ii. 324.
DAMOCRATES, a Spartan, Cleomenes, iv. 524.
DAMON, a Macedonian, Alexander, iv. 208.
DAMON, a musician, Pericles, i. 341, 342; Aristides, ii. 310; Nicias, iii. 314.
DAMON, surnamed PERIPOLTAS, Cimon, iii. 213-215.
DAMONIDES of Œa, Pericles, i. 350.
DAMOPHANTUS of Elis, Philopœmen, ii. 403.
DAMOTELES, a Spartan, Cleomenes, iv. 552.
DAMYRIAS, river of Sicily, Timoleon, ii. 159.
DANAUS, founder of Argos, Pyrrhus, iii. 48.
DANDAMIS, an Indian, Alexander, iv. 188, 271.
DANDARIANS, a tribe of Pontus, Lucullus, iii. 263.
DANUBE, Æm. Paulus, ii. 179; Cato the Elder, ii. 363 (where the text has Istria); Alexander, iv. 192, 231.
DAOCHUS, a Thessalian, Demosthenes, v. 20.
DAPHNE, daughter of Amyclas, Agis, iv. 505.
DAPHNE (Antioch on Daphne). See ANTIOCH.
DARDANIANS, an Illyrian tribe, Æm. Paulus, ii. 178.
DARDANUS, founder of Troy, Camillus, i. 308.
DARDANUS, Brutus's shield-bearer, Brutus, v. 378.
DARDANUS, in the Troad, Sylla, iii. 187.

INDEX 569

DARIUS I., son of Hystaspes, king of Persia, Themistocles, i. 248; Aristides, ii. 314.

DARIUS II., Nothus, son of Artaxerxes I., Artaxerxes, v. 441, 442.

DARIUS III., Codomannus, Camillus, i. 306; Agesilaus, iv. 22; Alexander, iv. 198, 200, 203, 204, 209, 214, 220-227, 232, 233, 236, 239-241, 246, 259, 276; Phocion, iv. 387.

DARIUS, son of Artaxerxes II., Artaxerxes, v. 469-474.

THE LAKE DASCYLITIS, in Bithynia, Lucullus, iii. 256.

DASSARETIS, district of Illyria, Flamininus, ii. 426.

DATIS, the Persian general, Aristides, ii. 314.

DECELEA, in Attica, Alcibiades, ii. 32, 50; Lysander, iii. 122; Cimon, iii. 223.

THE DECHAS, at Sparta, Agis, iv. 517.

DECIMUS. See BRUTUS.

DEIANIRA, Pericles, i. 372.

DEIDAMIA, wife of Pirithous, Theseus, i. 33.

DEIDAMIA, sister of Pyrrhus, Pyrrhus, iii. 2, 4, 9; Demetrius, v. 127, 135, 137, 164.

DEIMACHUS, a Thessalian, Lucullus, iii. 273.

DEIONEUS, son of Eurytus, Theseus, i. 9.

DEIOTARUS, king of Galatia, Crassus, iii. 372; Pompey, iv. 161; Cato the Younger, iv. 425, 428; Antony, v. 229.

DELIUM, in Bœotia, Alcibiades, ii. 11; Lysander, iii. 150; Sylla, iii. 185; Nicias, iii. 315.

DELLIUS, an officer and historical writer, Antony, v. 188, 189, 226.

DELOS, island of the Ægean Sea, Theseus, i. 21; Pericles, i. 354; Aristides, ii. 342; Sylla, iii. 185; Nicias, iii. 311.

DELOS, a mountain of Bœotia, Pelopidas, ii. 237.

DELPHI and DELPHIANS, Theseus, i. 3, 5, 14, 16, 25, 28; Romulus, i. 79; Lycurgus, i. 93, 95, 128; Numa, i. 148; Solon, i. 180, 184, 186, 203; Camillus, i. 289, 294; Pericles, i. 369; Fabius, i. 418; Timoleon, ii. 128, 158; Æm. Paulus, ii. 202, 212; Marcellus, ii. 271; Aristides, ii. 323, 337; Philopœmen, ii. 396, 407; Flamininus, ii. 439; Lysander, iii. 113, 134, 145, 149; Sylla, iii. 169, 196; Cimon, iii. 238; Nicias, iii. 326; Agesilaus, iv. 28; Alexander, iv. 180, 195, 237, 281; Phocion, iv. 375; Agis, iv. 508; Cicero, v. 42; Demetrius, v. 113, 115, 148; Aratus, v. 438.

DELPHINIUM, temple of Apollo, Theseus, i. 11, 16.

DEMADES, Athenian orator, Solon, i. 194; Phocion, iv. 366, 384, 390, 392, 396, 402, 403; Cleomenes, iv. 550; Demosthenes, v. 9-13, 15, 27, 32, 35; Galba, v. 477.

DEMÆNETUS, a Syracusan, Timoleon, ii. 165.

DEMARATUS or DAMARATUS, a Corinthian, father of Tarquinius Priscus, Romulus, i. 62; Poplicola, i. 228.

DEMARATUS, a Corinthian, friend of Philip and Alexander, Agesilaus, iv. 21; Alexander, iv. 190, 233, 259.

DEMARATUS, of Rhodes, Phocion, iv. 388.

DEMARATUS, or DAMARATUS, deposed king of Sparta, Lycurgus, i. 116; Themistocles, i. 279; Artaxerxes, v. 442.

DEMARETUS, a Corinthian, Timoleon, ii. 146, 150, 154.

DEMARISTE, mother of Timoleon, Timoleon, ii. 122.

INDEX

DEMEAS, son of Demades, Phocion, iv. 402.

THE DEMETRIAD, an Attic tribe, Demetrius, v. 112.

DEMETRIAS, the new name of Sicyon, Demetrius, v. 129.

DEMETRIAS, a fortified town of Thessaly, Flamininus, ii. 435; Demetrius, v. 164; Brutus, v. 345.

DEMETRIUS I., POLIORCETES, son of Antigonus, Life, v. 101; Comparison with Antony, v. 255; Æm. Paulus, ii. 176; Pyrrhus, iii. 5, 8, 9, 12, 16, 37, 50; Eumenes, iii. 465; Demosthenes, v. 16.

DEMETRIUS, king of Cyrene, son of Demetrius Poliorcetes, Demetrius, v. 164.

DEMETRIUS, surnamed the Thin, another son of Poliorcetes, v. 164.

DEMETRIUS II., son of Antigonus Gonatas, Æm. Paulus, ii. 176; Aratus, v. 401, 419.

DEMETRIUS, son of Philip III. of Macedon, Æm. Paulus, ii. 177; Flamininus, ii. 434.

DEMETRIUS, an attendant of Cassius, Brutus, v. 370.

DEMETRIUS of Magnesia, a writer, Demosthenes, v. 17, 31, 32.

DEMETRIUS, a Peripatetic philosopher, Cato the Younger, iv. 487, 490.

DEMETRIUS, a Syracusan crier, Timoleon, ii. 169.

DEMETRIUS the Phalerian, Theseus, i. 22; Lycurgus, i. 120; Solon, i. 201; Aristides, ii. 309, 310, 316, 345; Phocion, iv. 409; Demosthenes, v. 11-13, 16, 32; Demetrius, v. 108, 109, 112.

DEMETRIUS, freedman of Pompey, Pompey, iv. 60, 112, 113; Cato the Younger, iv. 426.

DEMETRIUS of Pharos, Aratus, v. 436.

DEMETRIUS, surnamed Phidon, Alexander, iv. 257.

DEMO, Demetrius, v. 126, 131.

DEMOCLES, or DAMOCLES, an Athenian, Demetrius, v. 126.

DEMOCLIDES, or DROMOCLIDES, an Athenian, Demetrius, v. 115.

DEMOCHARES of Leuconoë, an Athenian, Demosthenes, v. 34; Demetrius, v. 127.

DEMOCHARES of Soli, Demetrius, v. 131.

DEMOCRATES, an Athenian, Alcibiades, ii. 6.

DEMOCRITUS, philosopher, Timoleon, ii. 119.

DEMOLEON, a Thessalian, Lucullus, iii. 273.

DEMON, an Athenian, Demosthenes, v. 26, 31.

DEMON, an historian, Theseus, i. 17, 24.

DEMONAX, Lucullus, iii. 255.

DEMOPHANES, Academic philosopher, Philopœmen, ii. 395.

DEMOPHILUS, an Athenian, Phocion, iv. 411.

DEMOPHON, son of Theseus, Theseus, i. 31, 37; Solon, i. 205.

DEMOPOLIS, son of Themistocles, Themistocles, i. 284.

DEMOSTHENES, father of the orator, Demosthenes, v. 4, 22.

DEMOSTHENES, the orator, Life, v. 1; Comparison with Cicero, v. 95; Alcibiades, ii. 14; Cato the Elder, ii. 350, 352; Pyrrhus, iii. 18; Alexander, iv. 192; Phocion, iv. 372, 374, 377, 384, 385, 396, 398, 400; Cicero, v. 42, 63.

DEMOSTHENES, an Athenian general, Alcibiades, ii. 1; Nicias, iii. 315-317, 337-340, 346, 348.

DEMOSTRATUS, an Athenian orator, Alcibiades, ii. 25; Nicias, iii. 326.

DEMOSTRATUS (probably ERASISTRATUS), son of Phæax, Agesilaus, iv. 22.

INDEX 571

DENSUS SEMPRONIUS, a faithful centurion, Galba, v. 505.
DERCETÆUS, Antony, v. 245.
DERCYLLIDAS, a Spartan general, Lycurgus, i. 108; Artaxerxes, v. 462.
DERCYLLUS, Phocion, iv. 404.
DEUCALION, son of Minos, Theseus, i. 18.
DEUCALION, son of Prometheus, Pyrrhus, iii. 1.
DEXITHEA, daughter of Phorbas, Romulus, i. 42.
DEXIUS, or DEXOUS, Pyrrhus, iii. 24.
DIADEMATUS, a name of one of the Metelli, Coriolanus, ii. 72.
DIAGORAS, victor at the Olympic games, Pelopidas, ii. 259.
DIAMPERES, gate of Argos, Pyrrhus, iii. 46.
DICÆARCHIA, DICÆARCHEA, near Naples, the same as PUTEOLI, Sylla, iii. 204.
DICÆARCHUS, a writer, Theseus, i. 21, 36; Agesilaus, iv. 28.
DICOMES, king of the Getæ, Antony, v. 229.
DIDIUS, Sertorius, iii. 407.
DIDIUS, Cæsar, iv. 349.
DIDYMA, near Miletus, Pompey, iv. 89.
DIDYMUS, a grammarian, Solon, i. 177.
DIEUTYCHIDAS, or DIEUCHIDAS, Lycurgus, i. 89.
DINARCHUS, of Corinth, Timoleon, ii. 146, 150; Phocion, iv. 406; Demosthenes, v. 36.
DINDYMENE, Themistocles, i. 281.
DINIAS, who killed Abantidas, Aratus, v. 388.
DINIAS, an historian, Aratus, v. 414.
DINOCRATES of Messene, Philopœmen, ii. 417-419; Flamininus, ii. 446.
DINOMACHE, mother of Alcibiades, Alcibiades, ii. 1.

DINON, an historian, Themistocles, i. 276; Alexander, iv. 231; Artaxerxes, v. 441, 446, 450, 454, 461, 464.
DIOCLES of Megara, Theseus, i. 10.
DIOCLES of Peparethus, Romulus, i. 43.
DIOCLES, one of four Syrians, Aratus, v. 402-404.
DIOCLES, son of Themistocles, Themistocles, i. 283.
DIOCLIDES, Alcibiades, ii. 28.
DIODORUS the geographer, Theseus, i. 40; Themistocles, i. 284; Cimon, iii. 235.
DIODORUS, son of Sophax, Sertorius, iii. 416.
DIOGENES, step-son of Archelaus, Sylla, iii. 184.
DIOGENES, general of Demetrius II., governor of the Piræus, Aratus, v. 419.
DIOGENES of Sinope, philosopher, Lycurgus, i. 131; Fabius, i. 408; Timoleon, ii. 138; Alexander, iv. 195, 271.
DIOGENES, Stoic philosopher, Cato the Elder, ii. 379.
DIOGITON, a Theban, Pelopidas, ii. 259.
DIOMEDES, an Athenian, Alcibiades, ii. 15.
DIOMEDE, Cleopatra's servant, Antony, v. 244.
DIOMEDE, the hero, Romulus, i. 42.
DIUM, town in Macedonia, Demetrius, v. 142.
DION of Syracuse, brother-in-law of Dionysius the Elder, Life, v. 259; Comparison with Brutus, v. 381; Timoleon, ii. 119, 135, 147, 161; Comparison, ii. 218; Aristides, ii. 309; Nicias, iii. 329, 341.
DIONASSA, mother of Lycurgus, Lycurgus, i. 88.
DIONYSIUS of Colophon, a painter, Timoleon, ii. 164.

DIONYSIUS, a Corinthian, Timoleon, ii. 150.
DIONYSIUS of Halicarnassus, an historian, Romulus, i. 62; Comparison of Alcibiades and Coriolanus, ii. 113; Pyrrhus, iii. 24, 30.
DIONYSIUS of Magnesia, an orator, Cicero, v. 41.
DIONYSIUS of Messene, Alexander, iv. 280.
DIONYSIUS THE ELDER, tyrant of Syracuse, Solon, i. 198; Timoleon, ii. 126, 137; Pelopidas, ii. 255, 258; Cato the Elder, ii. 383; Lysander, iii. 115; Agesilaus, iv. 48; Dion, v. 261-267, 269, 270, 312; Galba, v. 477.
DIONYSIUS THE YOUNGER, tyrant of Syracuse, Timoleon, ii. 119-121, 127, 129, 132, 134, 135, 138, 139, 161, 169; Comparison, ii. 217, 218; Nicias, iii. 341; Dion, v. 264, 267, 269-282, 285, and following; Comparison, v. 382-384.
DIONYSIUS, one of four Syrians, Aratus, v. 405.
DIONYSIUS CHALCUS, a poet, Nicias, iv. 329.
DIONYSODORUS of Trœzen, Aratus, v. 386.
DIOPHANES, general of the Achæans, Philopœmen, ii. 413; Flamininus, ii. 445; Comparison, ii. 456.
DIOPHANES of Mitylene, the rhetorician, Ti. Gracchus, iv. 575, 591.
DIOPHANTUS of Amphitrope, an Athenian, Aristides, ii. 344.
DIOPITHES, an Athenian, Pericles, i. 382.
DIOPITHES, an Athenian, Phocion, iv. 374; Comparison of Cicero and Demosthenes, v. 97.
DIOPITHES, a Spartan, Lysander, iii. 140; Agesilaus, iv. 6.
DIOSCORIDES, a writer, Lycurgus, i. 102; Agesilaus, iv. 50.

The DIOSCURI, Castor and Pollux, Theseus, i. 36.
DIPHILIDES, or PHILIDES, a horse-breeder, Themistocles, i. 249.
DIPHILUS, an Athenian, Demetrius, v. 155.
DIPHILUS, a comic poet, Nicias, iii. 307.
DIPHRIDAS, a Spartan, Agesilaus, iv. 24.
The DIPYLON, or DOUBLE GATE, at Athens, Pericles, i. 380; Sylla, iii. 173.
DIRADES, Attic township, Alcibiades, ii. 36.
DIRCE, a fountain at Thebes, Demetrius, v. 155.
DOCIMUS, a Macedonian, Eumenes, iii. 451.
DODONA, the oracle, Themistocles, i. 277; Pyrrhus, iii. 1; Lysander, iii. 114; Phocion, iv. 399.
The DOG'S GRAVE. See CYNOSSEMA just above.
The DOG'S HEADS. See CYNOSCEPHALÆ in the Index.
DOLABELLA, friend of Sylla, Sylla, iii. 193, 194; Cæsar, iv. 289.
DOLABELLA, friend of Cæsar, Cicero's son-in-law, Cæsar, iv. 344, 356; Cicero, v. 86; Antony, v. 173-176; Brutus, v. 320, 326, 345.
CORNELIUS DOLABELLA, son of the preceding, Antony, v. 250.
DOLABELLA, Galba, v. 499; Otho, v. 514.
DOLOPIANS, Theseus, i. 38 (in Scyros), Flamininus, ii. 443; Cimon, iii. 224.
DOMITIAN, the emperor, Numa, i. 162; Poplicola, i. 230; Æm. Paulus, ii. 199.
DOMITIUS (Ahenobarbus, of the party of Marius), Pompey, iv. 69, 71-73.
LUCIUS DOMITIUS AHENOBARBUS, Cato the Younger's brother-in-law, Crassus, iii. 369, 370; Com-

INDEX

parison, iii. 399; Pompey, iv. 130, 151, 152, 154; Comparison, iv. 175; Cæsar, iv. 327, 336, 337; Cato the Younger, iv. 458; Cicero, v. 80.

DOMITIUS AHENOBARBUS (Cnæus, son of Lucius the preceding), Antony, v. 207, 222, 229.

DOMITIUS AHENOBARBUS (Lucius, son of Cnæus the preceding), married to Antonia, Antony, v. 253.

[DOMITIUS] AHENOBARBUS (Cnæus, son of Lucius the preceding), married to the younger Agrippina, Antony, v. 253.

LUCIUS DOMITIUS (Nero Germanicus, the emperor Nero, son of Cnæus the preceding), Antony, v. 253. See NERO.

LUCIUS DOMITIUS, or CALVISIUS DOMITIUS (perhaps DOMITIUS CALVINUS), Sertorius, iii. 419.

DOMITIUS CALVINUS (Cnæus), Pompey, iv. 134, 154 (where the text is Lucius Domitius); Cæsar, iv. 337, 343.

DORIANS, Lycurgus, i. 102 (a Doric word); Pericles, i. 365 (Dorians in Asia Minor); Lysander, iii. 118 (the Dorian character), 143; Agesilaus, iv. 44; Agis, iv. 518; Cleomenes, iv. 481 (the Doric measure and rule of life); Aratus, v. 387 (Doric aristocracy), 394.

DORIS, the mother country of the Dorians, Themistocles, i. 255.

DORIS, wife of Dionysius the Elder, Dion, v. 262, 264.

DORYLAUS, general of Mithridates, Sylla, iii. 182; Lucullus, iii. 264.

DOSON, surname of Antigonus, Coriolanus, ii. 72. See ANTIGONUS.

DRACO, Solon, i. 194, 195, 196, 203.

DRACONTIDES, an Athenian, Pericles, i. 383.

DROMICHÆTES of Thrace (king of the Getæ), Demetrius, v. 147, 163.

DROMOCLIDES of Sphettus, Demetrius, v. 115, 140.

LIVIUS DRUSUS, Ti. Gracchus, iv. 567; C. Gracchus, iv. 603-607.

LIVIUS DRUSUS, uncle of Cato the Younger (son of the preceding); Cato the Younger, iv. 413, 415.

DRUSUS, son of Livia (brother of the emperor Tiberius), Antony, v. 254.

DURIS of Samos, an historian, Pericles, i. 376, 377; Alcibiades, ii. 47; Lysander, iii. 134; Eumenes, iii. 441; Agesilaus, iv. 5; Alexander, iv. 196, 243; Phocion, iv. 371, 387; Demosthenes, v. 21, 26.

DYME, or DYMÆ, in Achæa, Pompey, iv. 96; Cleomenes, iv. 536; Aratus, v. 396, 433.

DYRRACCHIUM, or DYRRHACHIUM, town of Illyria, Sylla, iii. 190; Pompey, iv. 145, 162; Cæsar, iv. 304, 328; Cato the Younger, iv. 472-475; Cicero, v. 73, 81; Brutus, v. 346.

E

EBRO, or IBERUS, the river in Spain, Sertorius, iii. 424.

ECBATANA, Pelopidas, ii. 253; Agesilaus, iv. 21; Alexander, iv. 278; Demosthenes, v. 16; Artaxerxes, v. 471.

ECDELUS of Megalopolis, Aratus, v. 389, 392.

ECDEMUS of Megalopolis, Philopœmen, ii. 395.

ECHECRATES, Pelopidas, ii. 237.

ECHECRATIDES, a sophist, Phocion, iv. 388.

ECHEDEMUS and ECHEDEMIA, Theseus, i. 36.

ECNOMUM, in Sicily, Dion, v. 285.

ECPHANES, a Spartan, Agis, iv. 501.

ECPREPES, a Spartan ephor, Agis, iv. 507.
EDESSA in Macedonia, Pyrrhus, iii. 12, 16; Demetrius, v. 151.
EDONIAN WOMEN, Alexander, iv. 180.
The EGEAN SEA, Cimon, iii. 224.
EGERIA, the goddess, Numa, i. 138, 153, 158.
EGNATIUS, lieutenant of Crassus, Crassus, iii. 388.
EGYPT and EGYPTIANS. For history, see Themistocles, i. 282; Pericles, i. 368, 390; Pyrrhus, iii. 5; Cimon, iii. 240; Lucullus, iii. 245, 246; Comparison, iii. 305; Crassus, iii. 367; Eumenes, iii. 450; Agesilaus, iv. 51-56; Pompey, iv. 127, 165-170; Comparison, 176, 177; Alexander, iv. 214-220; Cæsar, 339, 341-343; Cato the Younger, iv. 452, 460, 476; Cleomenes, iv. 545, 555, and after; Demetrius, v. 119, 164; Antony, v. 167, 188, and after, to the end; Brutus, v. 324, 349, 356; Artaxerxes, v. 465, 467; Aratus, v. 389, 397, 399, 432; Galba, v. 478, 489; Otho, v. 525. Also Romulus, i. 55 (the month Chœac); Lycurgus, (his visit to Egypt) i. 92; Numa, i. 138 (an Egyptian dogma); 156 (the Egyptian wheels); Solon, i. 179 (Plato's visit), 204 (Solon's visit); Nicias, iii. 318 (its productiveness of good and of ill); Demetrius, v. 131 (the story of Bocchoris); Antony, v. 191 (the Egyptian dialect).
EION, town in Thrace, Cimon, iii. 222-224.
ELÆA in Mysia, Lucullus, iii. 249; Phocion, iv. 388.
ELÆA, a spring of water in Bœotia, Pelopidas, ii. 237.
ELÆUS in the Chersonese, Lysander, iii. 122.

ELATEA, in Phocis, Sylla, iii. 175; Phocion, iv. 406; Demosthenes, v. 20.
ELATUS, a Spartan ephor, Lycurgus, i. 97.
ELEA, or VELIA, in Lucania, Brutus, v. 343. See VELIA.
ELECTRA, Agamemnon's daughter, Lysander, iii. 130.
ELEPHENOR, son of Chalcodon, Theseus, i. 39.
ELEUS, son of Cimon, Pericles, i. 378; Cimon, iii. 235.
ELEUSIS, Theseus, i. 10, 32, 33; Themistocles, i. 263; Pericles, i. 357; Alcibiades, ii. 32, 50; Pelopidas, ii. 236; Aristides, ii. 324; Agesilaus, iv. 36; Phocion, iv. 392, 399, 411; Demetrius, v. 139.
ELEUTHERÆ, in Attica, Theseus, i. 32.
ELICIUM, or ILICIUM, Numa, i. 158.
ELIMLÆ, or ELIMIA, in Macedonia, Æm. Paulus, ii. 178.
ELIS and ELEANS, Lycurgus, i. 116, 131, 132; Alcibiades, ii. 20; Pelopidas, ii. 245; Philopœmen, ii. 403; Nicias, iii. 322; Cleomenes, iv. 523, 525, 536.
ELPINICE, sister of Cimon, Pericles, i. 352, 377; Cimon, iii. 217, 218, 234.
ELYMÆANS, a Median people, Pompey, iv. 108.
ELYSIAN FIELDS, Sertorius, iii. 415.
EMATHION, son of Tithonus, Romulus, i. 42.
EMPEDOCLES the philosopher, Demetrius, v. 106.
EMPYLUS, a rhetorician, Brutus, v. 320.
ENAROPHORUS, Theseus, i. 34.
ENDEIS, daughter of Sciron, Theseus, i. 10.
ENDYMION, Numa, i. 138.
ENGYIUM, town in Sicily, Marcellus, ii. 286, 288.

INDEX 575

ENNA, town of Sicily, Marcellus, ii. 286.
EPAMINONDAS the Theban, Lycurgus, i. 105; Fabius, i. 430; Coriolanus, ii. 63; Comparison, ii. 116; Timoleon, ii. 164; Pelopidas, ii. 223, and after; Marcellus, ii. 288; Comparison, ii. 303, 305; Aristides, ii. 308, 309; Cato the Elder, ii. 358; Comparison, ii. 392; Philopœmen, ii. 397, 410; Comparison of Sylla and Lysander, iii. 210; Agesilaus, iv. 28, 39-50; Phocion, iv. 370; Demosthenes, v. 22; Aratus, v. 403.
EPAPHRODITUS, freedman of Augustus, Antony, v. 246.
EPAPHRODITUS (FELIX), surname of Sylla, Sylla, iii. 201.
EPERATUS, an Achæan, Aratus, v. 433.
EPHESUS and EPHESIANS, Alcibiades, ii. 13, 15, 43, 52; Marcellus, ii. 288; Flamininus, ii. 451; Lysander, iii. 116-118, 120; Sylla, iii. 188; Lucullus, iii. 272, 276; Agesilaus, iv. 10, 13; Alexander, iv. 181; Cato the Younger, iv. 427; Demetrius, v. 135; Antony, v. 186, 222, 225.
EPHIALTES, an Athenian, Pericles, i. 347, 350, 352; Cimon, iii. 229, 232, 234, 237; Demosthenes, v. 16.
EPHIALTES, an Athenian orator, Demosthenes, v. 26.
EPHIALTES, a Macedonian, Alexander, iv. 238.
EPHORUS, an historian, Themistocles, i. 276; Camillus, i. 306; Pericles, i. 375, 376; Alcibiades, ii. 48; Timoleon, ii. 123; Pelopidas, ii. 238; Lysander, iii. 132, 138, 144, 151; Cimon, iii. 231; Dion, v. 296.
EPICHARMUS, comic poet, Numa, i. 146; Poplicola, i. 230.

EPICLES of Hermione, Themistocles, i. 250.
EPICRATES of Acharnæ, an Athenian, Themistocles, i. 273.
EPICRATES the baggage-carrier, Pelopidas, ii. 254.
EPICURUS, an Athenian, Phocion, iv. 411.
EPICURUS, the philosopher, and EPICUREANS, Pyrrhus, iii. 28; Comparison of Lucullus and Cimon, iii. 302; Cæsar, iv. 360; Demetrius, v. 140; Brutus, v. 330, 359, 362.
EPICYDES, an Athenian, Themistocles, i. 251.
EPICYDIDAS, a Spartan, Agesilaus, iv. 20.
EPIDAMNUS. See DYRRHACHIUM.
EPIDAURUS, town of Argolis, and EPIDAURIANS, Theseus, i. 8; Pericles, i. 387; Sylla, iii. 169; Pompey, iv. 89; Cleomenes, iv. 541, 543; Aratus, v. 409, 430.
EPIGETHES, Aratus, v. 417.
EPIGONUS, tyrant of Colophon, Lucullus, iii. 247.
EPILYCUS, an Athenian, Pericles, i. 388.
EPIMENIDES, the Phæstian, of Crete, Solon, i. 187, 188.
EPIPOLÆ, in Syracuse, Timoleon, ii. 146; Nicias, iii. 332, 338; Dion, v. 286, 289.
EPIRUS and EPIROTS. See, in general, the Life of Pyrrhus, vol. iii. 1-51; Theseus, i. 34; Themistocles, i. 273; Æmilius Paulus, ii. 204; Flamininus, ii. 425-428; Alexander, iv. 190, 274; Cæsar, iv. 330; Demetrius, v. 142, 148; Antony, v. 228; Aratus, v. 437.
EPITADEUS, a Spartan ephor, Agis, iv. 500.
EPITIMUS, the Pharsalian, Pericles, i. 389.
EPIXYES, satrap of Phyrgia, Themistocles, i. 280.

576 INDEX

EPIZEPHYRII, see LOCRI EPIZEPHYRII, Marcellus, ii. 299.
ERASISTRATUS, father of Phæax, Alcibiades, ii. 16.
ERASISTRATUS, or DEMOSTRATUS, son of Phæax, an Athenian, Agesilaus, iv. 22.
ERASISTRATUS, the physician of Seleucus, Demetrius, v. 144, 145.
ERATOSTHENES, the chronologer, historian, geographer, and philosopher, Lycurgus, i. 87; Themistocles, i. 277; Alexander, iv. 181, 223; Demosthenes, v. 10, 34.
ERECHTHEUS, king of Athens, Theseus, i. 3, 12, 18, 35; Comparison, i. 85.
ERESUS in Lesbos, Solon, i. 213.
ERETRIA, town in Eubœa, Themistocles, i. 259, 277; Phocion, iv. 380, 381.
ERGADES, an Attic tribe, Solon, i. 201.
ERGINUS, one of four Syrians, Aratus, v. 403-407, 418.
ERGOTELES, Themistocles, i. 274.
ERIANTHUS, a Theban, Lysander, iii. 130.
ERICIUS, an officer under Sylla, Sylla, iii. 177, 179.
ERIGYIUS, a friend of Alexander in his youth, Alexander, iv. 191.
ERINEUS (a doubtful reading), Theseus, i. 10.
EROS, attendant of Antony, Antony, v. 243, 244.
ERYX, in Sicily, Pyrrhus, iii. 32; Marius, iii. 101.
The ESQUILINE HILL, Sylla, iii. 166.
ETEOCLES, a Spartan, Lysander, iii. 135.
ETHIOPIA and ETHIOPIANS, Cimon, iii. 216; Antony, v. 191, 228; Brutus, v. 374.
ETRURIA and ETRURIANS, or ETRUSCANS, TYRRHENIA and TYRRHENIANS (these are the Greek words always), TUSCANY and TUSCANS, Romulus, i. 41, 42, 53, 61, 74; Poplicola, i. 222, 223, 227, 231-234 (the war with Porsenna); Camillus, i. 286, 287, 291 (the war with Veii), 298, 301 (the original Tuscan territory), 305, 323, 325, 326, 330; Pericles, i. 368; Fabius, i. 396, 398, 428; Æmilius Paulus, ii. 174 (the Tuscan sea); Marcellus, ii. 270, 298, 300; Marius, iii. 63, 103; Sylla, iii. 162 (an Etruscan doctrine); Pompey, iv. 93 (the Tyrrhenian sea), 94; Ti. Gracchus, iv. 575; Cicero, v. 49, 52, 53; Antony, v. 228 (the Tuscan sea).
ETYMOCLES, a Spartan, Agesilaus, iv. 37.
EUBŒA, the island, and the EUBŒANS, Theseus, i. 5, 38; Solon, i. 190; Themistocles, i. 253; Pericles, i. 347, 365, 369, 370; Comparison, —; Flamininus, ii. 436; Sylla, iii. 168, 186; Phocion, iv. 380; Demosthenes, v. 19; Aratus, v. 397.
EUBULUS, an Athenian, Phocion, iv. 374.
EUCHIDAS of Platæa, Aristides, ii. 337.
EUCLIA, daughter of Hercules, Aristides, ii. 337.
EUCLIDAS, a Spartan, brother of Cleomenes, Philopœmen, ii. 400; Cleomenes, iv. 533, 552, 553; Comparison, iv. 623.
EUCLIDAS, a Spartan, Artaxerxes, v. 444.
EUCLIDES, archon at Athens 403 B. C., Aristides, ii. 309.
EUCLIDES or EURYCLIDAS, in power at Athens, Aratus, v. 427.
EUCLIDES, a Corinthian, Timoleon, ii. 134.
EUCTUS, a Macedonian, Æm. Paulus, ii. 196.

EUDÆMON, a surname, Coriolanus, ii. 72.
EUDÆUS, or EULÆUS, a Macedonian, Æm. Paulus, ii. 196.
EUDAMIDAS I., son of Archidamus, III., king of Sparta, Agis, iv. 498.
EUDAMIDAS II., son of Archidamus IV., king of Sparta, Agis, iv. 498.
EUDAMIDAS, a Spartan, Agis, iv. 498.
EUDAMUS, captain of the Elephants, Eumenes, iii. 462.
EUDEMUS of Cyprus, Dion, v. 280.
EUDEMUS of Pergamus, Ti. Gracchus, iv. 583.
EUDOXUS, a mathematician, Marcellus, ii. 278.
EUERGETES, or EVERGETES, a surname, Coriolanus, ii. 71.
EUIUS, or EVIUS, a flute player, Eumenes, iii. 442.
EUMELUS, Æm. Paulus, ii. 186.
EUMENES of Cardia, Life, iii. 441; Comparison with Sertorius, iii. 467; Sertorius, iii. 406; Antony, v. 227.
EUMENES II., king of Pergamus, Cato the Elder, ii. 358; Flamininus, ii. 452.
EUMOLPUS and the EUMOLPIDÆ, Alcibiades, ii. 32, 49, 50; Sylla, iii. 172.
EUNEOS, an Athenian, Theseus, i. 28.
EUNOMUS the Thriasian, an Athenian, Demosthenes, v. 7.
EUNOMUS, king of Sparta, Lycurgus, i. 88.
EUNUS, a slave, Sylla, iii. 204.
EUPHEMIDES, an Athenian, Themistocles, i. 251.
EUPHORION, father of Solon, Solon, i. 177.
EUPHRANOR, a machine maker, Aratus, v. 390.
EUPHRANTIDES the prophet, Themistocles, i. 261; Aristides, ii. 320.
EUPHRATES, the river, Sylla, iii. 157; Lucullus, iii. 270, 274, 292; Crassus, iii. 372; Pompey, iv. 102, 104, 105, 165; Alexander, iv. 220, 223, 273, 280; Demetrius, v. 108; Antony, v. 194, 227.
EUPHRONIUS, Antony's son's tutor, Antony, v. 240.
EUPOLEMUS, son of Hicetes, Timoleon, ii. 160.
EUPOLIA, daughter of Agesilaus, Agesilaus, iv. 28.ᵃ
EUPOLIA, wife of Archidamus, Agesilaus, iv. 3.
EUPOLIS, a comic poet, Pericles, i. 341, 372; Alcibiades, ii. 16; Cimon, iii. 235; Nicias, iii. 312.
EURIPIDES the tragic poet, Theseus, i. 3, 13, 32; Lycurgus, i. 131; Comparison, i. 173; Solon, i. 200; Fabius, i. 417; Alcibiades, ii. 4, 15; Pelopidas, ii. 223, 252; Marcellus, ii. 289; Comparison, ii. 306; Pyrrhus, iii. 18; Lysander, iii. 130; Sylla, iii. 156; Cimon, iii. 218; Nicias, iii. 314, 320, 332, 349; Crassus, iii. (the verses), 395, 396; Comparison, iii. 403; Alexander, iv. 191, 251, 256; Cato the Younger, iv. 472; Demosthenes, v. 8; Demetrius, v. 116, 155; Comparison, v. 257; Brutus, v. 377.
EUROPE, Themistocles, i. 264; Camillus, i. 300; Pericles, i. 365; Aristides, ii. 321; Pyrrhus, iii. 15; Pompey, iv. 121; Alexander, iv. 190; Brutus, v. 358.
EUROTAS, river of Sparta, Lycurgus, i. 104, 110, 112; Pelopidas, ii. 239, 245, 253; Comparison, ii. 305; Agesilaus, iv. 28, 45, 48, 49.
EURYBIADES, a Spartan, Themistocles, i. 252, 258, 265; Aristides, ii. 319.

EURYCLES, a Spartan, Antony, v. 234.
EURYCLES, a Syracusan, Nicias, iii. 347.
EURYCLIDAS, a Spartan, Cleomenes, iv. 528.
EURYDICE, wife of Demetrius Poliorcetes, Demetrius, v. 116, 164.
EURYDICE, sister of Phila, Demetrius, v. 155.
EURYLOCHUS of Ægæ, Alexander, iv. 238.
EURYMEDON, an Athenian officer, Nicias, iii. 336, 343.
EURYMEDON, river of Pamphylia, Flamininus, ii. 437; Cimon, iii. 231.
EURYPON, king of Sparta, and EURYPONTIDÆ, Lycurgus, i. 88, 89; Lysander, iii. 143, 151; Comparison of Agesilaus and Pompey, iv. 172; Agis, iv. 498.
EURYPTOLEMUS, kinsman of Pericles, Pericles, i. 346, probably the same as EURYPTOLEMUS, son of Megacles, Cimon's wife's father; Cimon, iii. 219, 235.
EURYPTOLEMUS, cousin of Alcibiades, Alcibiades, ii. 48.
EURYSACES, son of Ajax, Solon, i. 186; Alcibiades, ii. 3.
EURYTUS, king of Œchalia, Theseus, i. 9.
EUTERPE, mother of Themistocles, Themistocles, i. 244.
EUTHIPPUS, an Athenian of Anaphlystus, Cimon, iii. 239.
EUTHYDEMUS, an Athenian officer, Nicias, iii. 336.
EUTHYMUS, a Leucadian, Timoleon, ii. 158.
EUTHYMUS, an officer under Hicetes, Timoleon, ii. 160.
EUTHYNUS of Thespiæ, Agesilaus, iv. 49.
EUTYCHUS, or FORTUNATE, the ass-driver's name, Antony, v. 231.
EUXINE SEA, Theseus, i. 27; Marius, iii. 94, 109; Lucullus, iii. 248; Pompey, iv. 102; also Pericles, i. 367; Alexander, iv. 241.
EVAGORAS, king of Cyprus, Lysander, iii. 125.
EVALCUS, a Spartan, Pyrrhus, iii. 45.
EVANDER, the Arcadian, Romulus, i. 55, 69.
EVANDER, a Cretan, Æm. Paulus, ii. 196.
THE HILL OF EVANDER, near Messene, Philopœmen, ii. 417.
EVANGELUS, servant of Pericles, Pericles, i. 364.
EVANGELUS, a writer on Tactics, Philopœmen, ii. 398.
EVANTHES of Samos, Solon, i. 186.
EVERGETES, or EUERGETES, a surname, Coriolanus, ii. 71.
EVIUS, or EUIUS, a flute player, Eumenes, iii. 442.
EXATHRES, brother of Darius, Alexander, iv. 241.
EXECESTIDES, father of Solon, Solon, i. 177.

F

FABIA, sister of Cicero's wife Terentia, Cato the Younger, iv. 434.
FABII, Camillus, i. 302-305; Fabius, i. 395; Cæsar, iv. 303.
FABIUS, son of Hercules, Fabius, i. 395.
FABIUS, high priest, Camillus, i. 309.
QUINTUS FABIUS AMBUSTUS, Numa, i. 152; Camillus, i. 289, 303.
FABIUS PICTOR, historian, Romulus, i. 43, 50, 56; Fabius, i. 418.
FABIUS RULLUS MAXIMUS, Fabius, i. 395; Pompey, iv. 75.
FABIUS BUTEO, dictator, Fabius, i. 407.
FABIUS MAXIMUS VERRUCOSUS, Life, i. 395; Comparison with Pericles,

i. 430; Pericles, i. 340; Æm. Paulus, ii. 173; Marcellus, ii. 272, 289, 293, 295; Cato the Elder, ii. 349, 352; Comparison of Pompey and Agesilaus, iv. 176.

FABIUS MAXIMUS, son of the preceding, Fabius, i. 426; Compare Æm. Paulus, ii. 173; he is the father, by adoption, of the following.

FABIUS MAXIMUS, son of Æm. Paulus, Æm. Paulus, ii. 173, 186, 211.

FABIUS (Maximus Allobrogicus), C. Gracchus, iv. 601.

FABIUS (Adrianus), lieutenant of Lucullus, Lucullus, iii. 290.

[FABIUS] MAXIMUS, consul B. C. 45, Cæsar, iv. 350.

FABIUS VALENS, lieutenant of Galba, commanding for Vitellius, Galba, v. 486, 491, 499; Otho, v. 514, 516, 518, 521, 523.

FABIUS FABULUS, or FABULLUS, murderer of Galba, Galba, v. 506.

FABRICII, Comparison of Aristides and Cato, ii. 388.

CAIUS FABRICIUS, the Roman consul, Comparison of Aristides and Cato, ii. 392; Pyrrhus, iii. 25, 27, 28, 29; Galba, v. 508.

FALERII and FALERIANS, Camillus, i. 296-298; Fabius, i. 397.

FALERNIAN WINE, Antony, v. 226.

FALISCANS, people of the district of Falerii, Camillus, i. 287, 290, 295, 296, 298, 302; C. Gracchus, iv. 598.

FANNIA, Marius, iii. 99, 100.

FANNIUS, an historian, Ti. Gracchus, iv. 569.

CAIUS FANNIUS, C. Gracchus, iv. 603, 606, 607.

FAUNUS, Romulus, i. 70; Numa, i. 157; Cæsar, iv. 296.

FAUSTA, daughter of Sylla, Sylla, iii. 201.

FAUSTULUS, servant of Amulius, Romulus, i. 44-46, 49.

FAUSTUS, son of Sylla, Sylla, iii. 201; Pompey, iv. 116, 124; Comparison, iv. 171; Cæsar, iv. 301; Cicero, v. 68; Brutus, v. 327.

MARCUS FAVONIUS, friend of Cato, Pompey, iv. 143, 151, 161; Comparison, iv. 175; Cæsar, iv. 312, 326, 334; Cato the Younger, iv. 449, 465, 466; Brutus, v. 330, 356, 357.

FENESTELLA, an historian, Sylla, iii. 194; Crassus, iii. 356.

FERENTINE GROVE or GATE, Romulus, i. 73.

FIDENÆ and FIDENATES, Romulus, i. 62, 72, 73; Poplicola, i. 237, 238; Camillus, i. 302.

FIDENTIA, town of Cisalpine Gaul, Sylla, iii. 192.

FIMBRIA, commanding in Asia, Flamininus, ii. 452; Sylla, iii. 171, 187, 188; Lucullus, iii. 247, 248, 251, 289, 290; Sertorius, iii. 435.

FIRMANI (of Firmum in Picenum), Cato the Elder, ii. 365, 366.

HORDEONIUS FLACCUS, lieutenant of Galba, Galba, v. 486, 494, 498, 499.

VALERIUS FLACCUS, consul 195 B. C., Cato the Elder, ii. 350, 361, 371.

VALERIUS FLACCUS, consul with Marius, afterwards killed by Fimbria, Marius, iii. 87; Sylla, iii. 171, 182, 187; Lucullus, iii. 252, 289.

FLACCUS (Horace the Poet), Lucullus, iii. 295.

FLAVIUS FLACCUS, Ti. Gracchus, iv. 588 (probably FULVIUS).

LUCIUS FLAMININUS, Cato the Elder, ii. 371; Flamininus, ii. 425, 447, 448.

TITUS QUINTIUS FLAMININUS, Life, ii. 422; Comparison with Philopœmen, ii. 454; Æm. Paulus, ii. 177; Cato the Elder, ii. 364, 371,

374; Comparison, ii. 389; Philopœmen, ii. 396, 410-414, 416, 421; Sylla, iii. 170.

CAIUS FLAMINIUS, consul, Fabius, i. 397, 398; Marcellus, ii. 265, 267.

THE FLAMINIAN CIRCUS, Marcellus, ii. 297; Lucullus, iii. 293.

FLAVIUS, tribune of the people, Cæsar, iv. 355.

FLAVIUS SABINUS, brother of Vespasian, Otho, v. 514.

FLAVIUS, commanding Brutus's engineers, Brutus, v. 377.

FLAVIUS, tribune of the soldiers, Marcellus, ii. 296.

FLAVIUS GALLUS, lieutenant of Antony, Antony, v. 209, 210.

FLORA, Pompey, iv. 59, 60, 131.

MESTRIUS FLORUS, a consular, friend of Plutarch, Otho, v. 524.

FONTEIUS CAPITO, Antony, v. 201.

FONTEIUS, killed in Germany, Galba, v. 491.

FREGELLÆ and FREGELLANS, in Latium, Marcellus, ii. 301; Comparison, ii. 306; C. Gracchus, iv. 597.

FRENTANI, a Samnite people, Pyrrhus, iii. 23.

FUFIDIUS, or AFIDIUS, Sylla, iii. 198; Sertorius, iii. 419.

FULCINIA, mother of Marius, Marius, iii. 54.

FULVIA, a noble lady, Cicero, v. 54.

FULVIA, wife of Antony, Antony, v. 175, 183, 191, 192, 194, 196, 200, 220, 223, 239, 247, 253.

THE FULVIAN COURT, or BASILICA, Cæsar, iv. 321.

QUINTUS FULVIUS, consul and dictator, Comparison of Fabius and Pericles, i. 432 (where the text has Furius); Marcellus, ii. 294, 295.

CNÆUS FULVIUS, proconsul, Marcellus, ii. 293.

FULVIUS (Marcus Fulvius Flaccus, consul 125 B.C.), Ti. Gracchus, iv. 579, (not quite certainly the same) 588, (Flavius Flaccus) 593; C. Gracchus, iv. 605, 607, 609-616 (where his son is mentioned).

FULVIUS, tribune of the people, Flamininus, ii. 423.

FURII, Camillus, i. 286.

FURIUS. See CAMILLUS.

LUCIUS FURIUS, colleague with Camillus, Camillus, i. 329, 330.

FURIUS, consul with Flaminius, Marcellus, ii. 265.

FURIUS, an officer in the servile war, Crassus, iii. 361.

FURNIUS, Antony, v. 225.

G

GABENI, in Persia, Eumenes, iii. 460.

GABII, town of Latium, Romulus, i. 46; Camillus, i. 319.

AULUS GABINIUS, Pompey, iv. 91, 94, 124; Cato the Younger, iv. 450; Cicero, v. 70, 72; Antony, v. 166, 167, 172.

GABINIUS, an officer under Sylla, Sylla, iii. 177, 179.

GADES, or CADIZ, Sertorius, iii. 414.

GÆSATÆ, Gallic tribe, Marcellus, ii. 264, 267, 268, 269.

GÆSYLUS, a Spartan, Dion, v. 309.

GAIUS, foster-brother of Mithridates, Pompey, iv. 116.

GALATE, or ACRURIUM, a mountain of Phocis, Phocion, iv. 406.

GALATIA, province of Asia Minor, Marius, iii. 90; Lucullus, iii. 260, 292; Crassus, iii. 372; Pompey, iv. 98, 100, 105; Cato the Younger, iv. 425; Antony, v. 227.

SERVIUS GALBA, serving under Æmilius Paulus (afterwards consul), Æm. Paulus, ii. 205, 207; Cato the Elder, ii. 368; Comparison, ii. 389.

INDEX 581

GALBA, lieutenant of Sylla, Sylla, iii. 179.
CAIUS SULPICIUS [GALBA], prætor, Cicero, v. 57.
GALBA, an officer under Cæsar, Cæsar, iv. 406.
SULPICIUS GALBA (grandfather of the emperor), cited as an historian, Romulus, i. 63.
SULPICIUS GALBA, the emperor, Life, v. 476; Otho, v. 509, 515, 516.
GALEPSUS, town of Macedonia, Æm. Paulus, ii. 197.
ANNIUS GALLUS, general of Otho, Otho, v. 515, 517, 518, 523.
GALLUS, friend of Augustus Cæsar, Antony, v. 246.
FLAVIUS GALLUS, lieutenant of Antony, Antony, v. 209, 210, 515.
GANDARITANS, an Indian people, Alexander, iv. 266.
THE GANGES, Alexander, iv. 266, 267.
GARGETTUS in Attica, Theseus, i. 12, 38.
GAUGAMELA, where the battle of Arbela was fought, town of Assyria, Alexander, iv. 224.
GAUL and the GAULS. The capture of Rome by the Gauls, Camillus, i. 300-320, 328, 332-335; and compare Romulus, i. 63, 70, 80; Numa, i. 133, 152; Fabius, i. 417. The war before the second Punic war, Marcellus, ii. 264-270, and the Comparison, 303; and compare Romulus, i. 61; Fabius, i. 397. The war with the Cimbri in Gaul, Marius, iii. 68-78; and compare Sertorius, iii. 407. Cæsar's campaigns, Cæsar, iv. 303 and after; and compare Crassus, iii. 368, 371, and the Comparison, 402; Pompey, iv. 124, 125, 128, 130, 142, 147, 150, 152; Cato the Younger, iv. 450, 464, 468, 470; Cicero, v. 71; Antony, v. 169. The Gauls in Greece, Pyrrhus, iii. 31, 38, 41, 45, 46, 47; and compare Cimon, iii. 213; Comparison of Agis and Cleomenes and the Gracchi, iv. 621. Gauls near the Danube, Æm. Paulus, ii. 179, 183; Gallic horse, Lucullus, iii. 280; Crassus, iii. 372, 384, 385; Antony, v. 203, 208, 209, and compare Pompey, iv. 66. In the Servile War, Crassus, iii. 360, 362. The revolt of Gaul, Galba, v. 480-482, 486, 487, 494, 498; Otho, v. 516, 518. Also Solon, i. 179; Æm. Paulus, ii. 174; Caius Gracchus, iv. 612; Pompey, iv. 67; Cicero, v. 49, 50, 57; Antony, v. 182, 228; Ravenna in Gaul, Marius, iii. 53; Transalpine Gaul, Marius, iii. 65; Pompey, iv. 124; Cæsar, iv. 302; Cisalpine Gaul, or Gaul on the Po, Lucullus, iii. 249; Crassus, iii. 362; Sertorius, iii. 408; Pompey, iv. 78, 125; Cæsar, iv. 302, 309, 310, 317, 323, 324; Cicero, v. 49; Brutus, v. 325, 339; Comparison, v. 384, 385; Gallia Narbonensis, Sertorius, iii. 419. The Gallic dress, Otho, v. 516.
GAZA, town of Syria, Alexander, iv. 213; Demetrius, v. 107.
GEDROSIA, province of Persia, Alexander, iv. 272, 273.
GEGANIA, a vestal, Numa, i. 148.
GEGANIA, mother-in-law of Thalæa, Comparison of Lycurgus and Numa, i. 174.
GELA, town of Sicily, and GELOANS, Timoleon, ii. 163; Cimon, iii. 225; Dion, v. 285.
GELÆ, Scythian tribe, Pompey, iv. 108.
GELANOR, king of the Argives, Pyrrhus, iii. 48.
GELEONTES, or GEDEONTES, Attic tribe, Solon, i. 201.

INDEX

GELLIANUS, sent by Nymphidius into Spain, Galba, v. 486, 488.
LUCIUS GELLIUS, consul, Crassus, iii. 362; Pompey, iv. 86; Cato the Younger, iv. 421; Cicero, v. 66.
MARCUS GELLIUS, senator, Cicero, v. 68.
GELO, an Epirot, Pyrrhus, iii. 6, 7.
GELO, or GELON, tyrant of Syracuse, Coriolanus, ii. 77; Timoleon, ii. 150; Dion, v. 264.
GEMINIUS, companion of Antony, Antony, v. 225, 226.
GEMINIUS, companion of Pompey, Pompey, iv. 60, 79.
GEMINIUS of Terracina, Marius, iii. 96, 99.
GENTHIUS, king of Illyria, Æm. Paulus, ii. 179, 180.
GENUCIUS, tribune of the people, C. Gracchus, iv. 598.
GERADAS, a Spartan, Lycurgus, i. 110.
GERÆSTUS, promontory of Eubœa, Agesilaus, iv. 9.
GERANDAS, a Spartan, Pelopidas, ii. 247.
GERANEA, mountain of Corinth, Cleomenes, iv. 542; Aratus, v. 416.
GERGITHUS, town in the Troad, Phocion, iv. 388.
GERMANICUS, son of Drusus, Antony, v. 253.
GERMANICUS, surname of Nero, Antony, v. 253; of Vitellius, Galba, v. 499.
GERMANUS. See CERMALUS.
GERMANY and the GERMANS, Æm. Paulus, ii. 199 (the revolt of Antonius against Domitian); Marius, iii. 63; Crassus, iii. 362; Comparison with Nicias, 402; Pompey, iv. 152; Cæsar, iv. 308, 309, 312-314, 351; Cato the Younger, iv. 470 (where the text has Britons) Galba, v. 479, 481, 488, 491, 494, 498-499; Otho, v. 520, 522, 529.
GETÆ, Scythian tribe, Antony, v. 229.
GIGIS, maid of Parysatis, Artaxerxes, v. 461, 462.
GISCO, a Carthaginian commander, Timoleon, ii. 158, 162.
GISCO, with Hannibal at Cannæ, Fabius, i. 414.
MANIUS ACILIUS [GLABRIO], consul B. C. 191, Cato the Elder, ii. 363, 366, 367; Philopœmen, ii. 416, 421; Flamininus, ii. 443, 444; Sylla, iii. 170.
MANIUS GLABRIO, Sylla, iii. 200; Pompey, iv. 98, and compare 68.
GLAUCIA, tribune with Saturninus, Marius, iii. 86; Comparison of Sylla and Lysander, iii. 207.
GLAUCIAS, king of Illyria, Pyrrhus, iii. 3, 4.
GLAUCIPPUS, Athenian orator, Phocion, iv. 370.
GLAUCUS, a physician, Alexander, iv. 278; Antony, v. 226.
GLAUCUS, in the Trojan war, Dion, v. 259.
GLAUCUS, son of Polymedes, an Athenian, Phocion, iv. 381.
GLAUCUS PONTIUS (subject of a poem by Cicero), Cicero, v. 39.
GLYCON, an Athenian, Pericles, i. 382.
GNATHÆNION, an Argive sempstress, Æm. Paulus, ii. 178; Aratus, v. 440.
GNOSSUS, in Crete, Theseus, i. 18.
GOBRYAS, a Persian, Cimon, iii. 231.
GOMPHI, town of Thessaly, Cæsar, iv. 335.
GONATAS. See ANTIGONUS.
GONGYLUS, a Corinthian, Nicias, iii. 334, 335.
GORDIUM, town in Phrygia, Alexander, iv. 202.
GORDIUS, a Cappadocian, Sylla, iii. 157.

INDEX 583

GORDYÆAN MOUNTAINS, Alexander, iv. 224.
GORDYENE and GORDYENIANS, district of Armenia, Lucullus, iii. 270, 277, 283, 290; Pompey, iv. 108.
GORGIAS, an officer under Eumenes, Eumenes, iii. 449.
GORGIAS the Leontine, Cimon, iii. 227.
GORGIAS, a rhetorician, contemporary with Cicero, Cicero, v. 64.
GORGIDAS, a Theban, Pelopidas, ii. 233, 234, 239-241.
GORGO, wife of Leonidas, Lycurgus, i. 107.
GORGOLEON, a Spartan, Pelopidas, ii. 238.
GORGUS of Ceos, Timoleon, ii. 163.
GORTYNIANS, in Crete, Philopœmen, ii. 409, 410; Pyrrhus, iii. 40.
GRACINUS, companion of Sertorius, Sertorius, iii. 438.
GRACCHI, Ti. Gracchus, iv. 569, 575; C. Gracchus, iv. 599, 617; Comparison with Agis and Cleomenes, iv. 619.
TI. SEMPRONIUS GRACCHUS, father of the Gracchi, Marcellus, ii. 266; Cato the Elder, ii. 363; Ti. Gracchus, iv. 565, 566, 568, 588.
TIBERIUS GRACCHUS, Life, iv. 565; Comparison, iv. 619; Agis, iv. 497; C. Gracchus, iv. 594, and following.
CAIUS GRACCHUS, Life, iv. 594; Comparison, iv. 619; Agis, iv. 497; Ti. Gracchus, iv. 565, and following.
GRANICUS, river of Mysia, Camillus, i. 306; Lucullus, iii. 258; Alexander, iv. 198.
GRANIUS, stepson of Marius, iii. 95, 97, 101.
GRANIUS, a magistrate, Sylla, iii. 205.
GRANIUS PETRO, a quæstor under Cæsar, Cæsar, iv. 305.

GRYPUS, a surname, Coriolanus, ii. 71; Marius, iii. 52.
GURAS, brother of Tigranes, Lucullus, iii. 287.
GYARTA, or GYAR, district belonging to Syracuse, Dion, v. 297.
GYLIPPUS, a Spartan, Lycurgus, i. 130; Pericles, i. 370; Alcibiades, ii. 32; Comparison Æm. Paulus and Timoleon, ii. 218; Lysander, iii. 131; Nicias, iii. 333-335, 338, 344, 346-347; Dion, v. 309.
GYLIPPUS, a Spartan, Cleomenes, iv. 520.
GYLON, grandfather of Demosthenes, v. 4.
GYMNOSOPHISTS, Lycurgus, i. 93; Alexander, iv. 269.
GYRISŒNIANS (perhaps Oretanians) in Spain, Sertorius, iii. 408.
GYTHIUM, harbor of Laconia, Philopœmen, ii. 411; Cleomenes, iv. 553.

H

HÆMON, rivulet of Bœotia, Theseus, i. 30; Demosthenes, v. 21.
HÆMUS, mountain in Thrace, Alexander, iv. 180.
HAGNON, a Teian, Alexander, iv. 208, 236, 257.
HAGNON, an Athenian, Pericles, i. 383, perhaps the same as the father of Theramenes; Lysander, iii. 129; Nicias, iii. 309.
HAGNONIDES, or AGNONIDES, Phocion, iv. 401, 406-408, 411.
HAGNOTHEMIS, Alexander, iv. 284.
HAGNUS, Attic township, Theseus, i. 12.
HALÆ, burial-place of Timon, Antony, v. 238.
HALÆÆ, town of Bœotia, Sylla, iii. 190.
HALIARTUS, city of Bœotia, Lysander, iii. 147-150; Comparison of Lysander and Sylla, iii. 210.

584 INDEX

HALICARNASSUS, in Caria, Themistocles, i. 244; Alexander, iv. 200; Demetrius, v. 108.

HALIMUS, Attic township, Cimon, iii. 217.

HALONESUS, island on the coast of Thrace, Demosthenes, v. 11.

HALYCUS, or LYCUS, river in Sicily, Timoleon, ii. 162.

HAMILCAR, a Carthaginian commander, Timoleon, ii. 151.

HAMILCAR, surnamed BARCA, Fabius, i. 416; Cato the Elder, ii. 358.

HANNIBAL, Romulus, i. 71; Pericles, i. 340; Fabius, i. 396 and after; Æm. Paulus, ii. 176; Pelopidas, ii. 222; Marcellus, ii. 263, 271 and after, 293 and after; Comparison, ii. 304, 305; Cato the Elder, ii. 348, 363; Comparison, ii. 394; Flamininus, ii. 423, 425, 434, 435, 441, 449-452; Pyrrhus, iii. 10; Lucullus, iii. 285, 287; Sertorius, iii. 406, 434; Agesilaus, iv. 22; Ti. Gracchus, iv. 565; Otho, v. 525.

HANNO, Timoleon, ii. 143.

HARPALUS, Æm. Paulus, ii. 186; Alexander, iv. 188, 191, 231, 238; Phocion, iv. 390-392; Demosthenes, v. 28, 29; Comparison, v. 98.

HASDRUBAL, a Carthaginian commander, Timoleon, ii. 151.

HASDRUBAL, brother of Hannibal, Flamininus, ii. 425.

HEBREWS, Antony, v. 191.

HECALE, HECALENE, HECALESIA, Theseus, i. 12, 13.

HECATÆUS, tyrant of the Cardians, Eumenes, iii. 444.

HECATÆUS the Sophist (of Miletus), Lycurgus, i. 116.

HECATÆUS of Eretria (perhaps of Abdera), a writer, Alexander, iv. 243.

HECATOMBÆUM in Achæa, Cleomenes, iv. 536; Aratus, v. 424.

HECATOMPEDON, a name for the Parthenon, Cato the Elder, ii. 354.

HECATOMPEDON, in Syracuse, Dion, v. 304.

HECTOR, Theseus, i. 37; Pompey, iv. 97; Brutus, v. 343, 344; Aratus, v. 389.

HECUBA, Comparison of Theseus and Romulus, i. 86; Pelopidas, ii. 252.

HEDYLIUM, mountain in Phocis, Sylla, iii. 177, 178.

HEGEMON, an Athenian, Phocion, iv. 407, 409.

HEGESIAS, of Magnesia, a writer, Alexander, iv. 181.

HEGESIPYLE, daughter of Olorus, mother of Cimon, Cimon, iii. 217.

HEGESTRATUS, archon at Athens, Solon, i. 213.

HELEN, Theseus, i. 31, 33-35, 37; Comparison, i. 85; Solon, i. 180; Antony, v. 170; Galba, v. 495.

HELENUS, son of Pyrrhus, Pyrrhus, iii. 11, 48, 51.

HELICON, an armorer, Alexander, iv. 206.

HELICON, a Cyzicenian, Dion, v. 278.

HELICON, mountain in Bœotia, Lysander, iii. 150; Agesilaus, iv. 27.

HELICUS, perhaps HELISSON, in Arcadia, Cleomenes, iv. 546.

HELIOPOLIS in Egypt, Solon, i. 204.

HELIUS, Nero's favorite, Galba, v. 493.

HELLANICUS, of Mitylene, a historian, Theseus, i. 15, 27-29, 33; Alcibiades, ii. 29.

HELLANICUS, a Sicilian, Dion, v. 302.

HELLESPONT, Themistocles, i. 264; Pericles, i. 365; Alcibiades, ii.

INDEX

39, 40, 43, 44; Aristides, ii. 321; Lysander, iii. 122, 136, 142; Sylla, iii. 186; Lucullus, iii. 258; Agesilaus, iv. 12, 23; Alexander, iv. 197, 198; Phocion, iv. 382, 383.

HELVETIANS, Cæsar, iv. 307.

HELVIA, mother of Cicero, Cicero, v. 37.

HELVIDIUS PRISCUS, Galba, v. 507.

HENIOCHA, daughter of Pittheus, Theseus, i. 27.

HEPHÆSTION, friend of Alexander the Great, Pelopidas, ii. 258; Eumenes, iii. 442, 443; Alexander, iv. 219, 235, 238, 245, 248, 257, 278, 279, 282.

MOUNT HEPHÆUS, Sylla, iii. 191, perhaps TIFATA.

HEPTACHALCUM at Athens, Sylla, iii. 172.

HERACLEA in Bithynia, Cimon, iii. 222; Lucullus, iii. 259.

HERACLEA in Italy, Pyrrhus, iii. 22.

HERACLEA in Thessaly, Flamininus, ii. 443; Demetrius, v. 125.

HERACLEA, Lysander, iii. 134.

HERACLIDES of Cuma, a writer, Artaxerxes, v. 466.

HERACLIDES, of Pontus, philosopher, Solon, i. 177, 200, 211, 213; Themistocles, i. 276; Camillus, i. 310; Pericles, i. 376, 388; Alexander, iv. 214.

HERACLIDES, a Syracusan, Nicias, iii. 342.

HERACLIDES, a Syracusan, Dion, v. 270, 292, 293, 297, 298, 304, 306, 308, 309, 312, 313, 315.

HERACLITUS, the philosopher of Ephesus, Romulus, i. 79; Camillus, i. 305; Coriolanus, ii. 109.

HERÆA, town of Arcadia, Lysander, iii. 140; Cleomenes, iv. 527.

HERÆUM, promontory near Corinth, Agesilaus, iv. 31, 32; Cleomenes, iv. 542.

HERCULES the hero, frequent. See, in particular, the Life of Theseus. The Pillars of Hercules, Timoleon, ii. 145; Nicias, iii. 325; Pompey, iv. 91; Alexander, iv. 273; Antony, v. 168; Aratus, v. 399.

HERCULES, son of Alexander and Barsine, Eumenes, iii. 442.

HERCYNIAN FOREST, Marius, iii. 64.

HEREAS of Megara, historian, Theseus, i. 19, 36; Solon, i. 186.

HERENNIUS, lieutenant of Sertorius, Pompey, iv. 81.

CAIUS HERENNIUS and the family of the HERENNII, Marius, iii. 56.

HERENNIUS, a centurion, who killed Cicero, Cicero, v. 92, 93.

HERIPPIDAS, a Spartan, Pelopidas, ii. 234; Agesilaus, iv. 16.

HERMÆUS, a priest, Lucullus, iii. 264.

HERMAGORAS, a rhetorician, Pompey, iv. 117.

THE HERMÆUM (perhaps HERMUS), Phocion, iv. 392.

HERMINIUS, Poplicola, i. 231.

HERMIONE, daughter of Menelaus and Helen, Comparison of Solon and Lycurgus, i. 173.

HERMIONE, town of Argolis, and HERMIONIANS, Themistocles, i. 250; Pompey, iv. 89; Alexander, iv. 231; Cleomenes, iv. 541; Aratus, v. 420.

HERMIPPUS, philosopher and historian, Lycurgus, i. 94, 121; Solon, i. 178, 182, 186; Alexander, iv. 256; Demosthenes, v. 13, 32, 34.

HERMIPPUS, a comic poet, Pericles, i. 382, 385.

HERMOCRATES, son of Hermon, a Syracusan, Nicias, iii. 308, 331, 344, 348; Dion, v. 261.

HERMOLAUS, a Macedonian, Alexander, iv. 258.

HERMON, an Athenian, Alcibiades, ii. 38.

586　INDEX

HERMON, a Syracusan, Nicias, iii. 308.
HERMOTIMUS of Phocæa, Pericles, i. 373.
HERMUS, an Athenian, Theseus, i. 28.
HERMUS in Attica (according to a correction), Theseus, i. 10; Phocion, iv. 391.
HERO, niece of Aristotle, Alexander, iv. 258.
HEROD, king of Judæa, Antony, v. 227, 239, 240.
HERODES, friend of Cicero, Cicero, v. 64.
HERODORUS of Pontus, a writer, Theseus, i. 27, 31, 33; Romulus, i. 52.
HERODOTUS, a Bithynian, Numa, i. 138.
HERODOTUS of Halicarnassus, the historian, Themistocles, i. 253, 265, 269; Aristides, ii. 329, 335; Comparison, ii. 389.
HEROPHYTUS of Samos, Cimon, iii. 226.
HEROSTRATUS, Brutus, v. 344.
HERSILIA, wife of Romulus, Romulus, i. 58, 64, 66; Comparison, i. 85.
HESIOD, Theseus, i. 3, 14, 19; Numa, i. 139; Solon, i. 179; Camillus, i. 305; Comparison of Aristides and Cato, ii. 391; Galba, v. 492.
HESYCHIA (Quietness) priestess at Clazomenæ, Nicias, iii. 327.
HEXAPYLA, gate of Syracuse, Marcellus, ii. 284.
HICETES, tyrant of the Leontines, Timoleon, ii. 121, 127-135 and after to 161.
HICETES, a Syracusan, Dion, v. 317.
HIDRIEUS, or IDRIEUS, prince of Caria, Agesilaus, iv. 19.
HIEMPSAL, king of Numidia, Marius, iii. 102; Pompey, iv. 73.

HIERÆ (more correctly IETÆ), Timoleon, ii. 158.
HIERAPOLIS, town of Syria, Crassus, iii. 373; Antony, v. 202.
HIERO, Nicias, iii. 313.
HIERO, tyrant of Syracuse, Themistocles, i. 274; Marcellus, ii. 271, 278, 279.
HIERONYMUS of Cardia, an historian, Pyrrhus, iii. 24, 30, 41; Eumenes, iii. 456; Demetrius, v. 146.
HIERONYMUS of Carrhæ, Crassus, iii. 385.
HIERONYMUS of Rhodes, writer, Aristides, ii. 345; Agesilaus, iv. 20.
HIERONYMUS, tyrant of Syracuse, Marcellus, ii. 276.
HIMERA, town of Sicily, and HIMERÆANS, Timoleon, ii. 150; Pompey, iv. 70, 71.
HIMERÆUS, brother of Demetrius the Phalerian, Demosthenes, v. 32.
HIPPARCHUS, father of Asclepiades, Phocion, iv. 392.
HIPPARCHUS the Cholargian, Nicias, iii. 324.
HIPPARCHUS, Antony's freedman, Antony, v. 234, 241.
HIPPARCHUS, a Spartan, Lycurgus, i. 92, 132.
HIPPARETE, wife of Alcibiades, Alcibiades, ii. 12.
HIPPARINUS, father of Dion, Dion, v. 261.
HIPPARINUS, a son of Dion, Dion, v. 291.
HIPPIAS, an Epirot, Pyrrhus, iii. 2.
HIPPIAS the comedian, Antony, v. 174.
HIPPIAS the Sophist, of Elis, Lycurgus, i. 120; Numa, i. 134.
HIPPITAS, a Spartan, Cleomenes, iv. 561.
HIPPO, tyrant of Messina, Timoleon, ii. 162, 167.

HIPPO, a Syracusan, Dion, v. 297.
HIPPOCLUS, father of Pelopidas, Pelopidas, ii. 222.
HIPPOCOÖN, Theseus, i. 34.
HIPPOCRATES, an Athenian commander, Nicias, iii. 315.
HIPPOCRATES, the mathematician, Solon, i. 190.
HIPPOCRATES, the physician, Cato the Elder, ii. 381.
HIPPOCRATES, father of Pisistratus, Solon, i. 210.
HIPPOCRATES, a Spartan, Alcibiades, ii. 44.
HIPPOCRATES, commander in Syracuse, Marcellus, ii. 277, 278, 283.
HIPPODAMIA, wife of Pelops, Theseus, i. 7.
HIPPOLYTA, the Amazon, Theseus, i. 30.
HIPPOLYTUS, son of Theseus, Theseus, i. 3, 31; Numa, i. 139.
HIPPOMACHUS, the wrestling master, Dion, v. 260.
HIPPOMEDON, a Spartan, Agis, iv. 501, 512.
HIPPONICUS, one of Solon's friends, Solon, i. 193.
HIPPONICUS, father of Callias, Pericles, i. 372; Alcibiades, ii. 12.
HIPPONIUM, HIPPO, or VIBO, in Lucania, Cicero, v. 73.
HIPPOSTHENIDAS, a Theban, Pelopidas, ii. 228.
HIRTIUS, consul with Pansa, Æm. Paulus, ii. 214; Cicero, v. 86, 89; Antony, v. 180.
HISTIÆA and HISTIÆANS, in Eubœa, Themistocles, i. 254; Pericles, i. 371.
HOMER, Theseus, i. 5, 14, 19, 26, 37; Lycurgus, i. 88, 92; Solon, i. 185, 204, 210; Fabius, i. 419; Alcibiades, ii. 11; Coriolanus, ii. 99; Timoleon, ii. 164; Æm. Paulus, ii. 202, 210; Pelopidas, ii. 221, 239; Marcellus, ii. 262; Comparison of Cato and Aristides, ii. 391; Philopœmen, ii. 395, 398, 405; Pyrrhus, iii. 33; Marius, iii. 64; Cimon, iii. 223; Sertorius, iii. 406; Agesilaus, iv. 8; Alexander, iv. 214, 215; Phocion, iv. 385; Cleomenes, iv. 529, 530; Ti. Gracchus, iv. 593; Demetrius, v. 150; Antony, v. 188; Brutus, v. 343, 344, 357; Galba, v. 495. Quotations without the name, Theseus, i. 2; Coriolanus, ii. 87; Timoleon, ii. 118; Cato the Elder, ii. 389; Pyrrhus, iii. 16, 43; Nicias, iii. 313, 314; Pompey, iv. 133; Alexander, iv. 218, 256; Cleomenes, iv. 558; Demosthenes, v. 14; Dion, v. 277; Brutus, v. 345.
HOMOLOICHUS of Chæronea, Sylla, iii. 178-182.
ANTONIUS HONORATUS, Galba, v. 489.
HOPLIAS, river of Bœotia, Lysander, iii. 150.
HOPLITÆ, Attic tribe, Solon, i. 201.
HOPLITES, river near Haliartus, Lysander, iii. 149, 150, 180.
HORACE the poet, under the name of FLACCUS, Lucullus, iii. 295.
MARCUS HORATIUS, consul, Poplicola, i. 227-229.
HORATIUS COCLES, Poplicola, i. 231.
HORCOMOSIUM, at Athens, Theseus, i. 30.
HORDEONIUS FLACCUS, commanding in Germany, Galba, v. 486, 494, 498, 499.
HORTENSIUS, lieutenant of Sylla, Sylla, iii. 174, 179.
QUINTUS HORTENSIUS, the orator, Sylla, iii. 203; Lucullus, iii. 224; Cato the Younger, iv. 440, 441, 472; Cicero, v. 45, 76.
HORTENSIUS, son of the orator, Cæsar, iv. 324; Antony, v. 185; Brutus, v. 345, 349.
HOSTILIUS, grandfather of Tullus the king, Romulus, i. 58, 64.

TULLUS HOSTILIUS, king of the Romans, Romulus, i. 64; Numa, i. 166, 168; Coriolanus, ii. 59.
HOSTILIUS, Æm. Paulus, ii. 178.
LUCIUS HOSTIUS, Romulus, i. 71.
HYACINTHIA, a Spartan festival, Aristides, ii. 323.
HYACINTHUS, son of Amyclas, Numa, i. 139.
HYBLA, a fortress of Sicily, Nicias, iii. 330.
HYBREAS, an orator, Antony, v. 187.
HYCCARA, a town of Sicily, Alcibiades, ii. 58; Nicias, iii. 330.
HYDASPES, a river of India, Alexander, iv. 263, 264, 266.
HYDRUM (perhaps a false reading for Cyprus), Cimon, iii. 232.
HYLLUS, son of Hercules, Pyrrhus, iii. 1.
HYMENÆUS, Romulus, i. 58.
HYPATES, a Theban, Pelopidas, ii. 232, 233.
HYPERBATAS, Achæan prætor, Cleomenes, iv. 536.
HYPERBOLUS, an Athenian, Alcibiades, ii. 16, 17; Aristides, ii. 318; Nicias, iii. 323, 324; Comparison, iii. 399.
HYPERBOREANS, Camillus, i. 310.
HYPERIDES, an Athenian orator, Phocion, iv. 370, 374, 378, 385, 393, 396, 398, 400; Demosthenes, v. 14, 16, 32.
HYPSÆUS, Pompey, iv. 137; Cato the Younger, iv. 466.
HYPSECHIDAS, a Spartan, Solon, i. 186.
HYPSICRATIA, Pompey, iv. 103.
HYPSION, a Platæan hero, Aristides, ii. 324.
HYRCANIA, in Asia, Lucullus, iii. 292; Crassus, iii. 377; Comparison, iii. 403; Pompey, iv. 107, 108, 111; Alexander, iv. 241, 244 (the Caspian or Hyrcanian sea), Cæsar, iv. 351.

HYRODES, king of Parthia, Crassus, iii. 374, 377, 378, 394-396; Antony, v. 197, 202.
HYSLÆ, town of Bœotia, Aristides, ii. 324.

I

IACCHUS (BACCHUS), Themistocles, i. 261; Alcibiades, ii. 50; Phocion, iv. 399; the Iaccheum, Aristides, ii. 346.
IALYSUS, founder of Ialysus in Rhodes, Demetrius, v. 124. The town is also mentioned in the Greek as the native country of Timocreon, Themistocles, i. 255.
IAPYGIA, part of Italy, Theseus, i. 14; Pyrrhus, iii. 20; Dion, v. 283, 295.
IARBAS, king of Numidia, Pompey, iv. 73.
IBER, IBERUS, or EBRO, river of Spain, Sertorius, iii. 424.
IBERIANS, people of Asia, Lucullus, iii. 277, 286; Pompey, iv. 106, 109, 120; Antony, v. 199.
IBYCUS the poet, Comparison of Lycurgus and Numa, i. 172.
ICELUS MARCIANUS, a freedman, Galba's favorite, Galba, v. 482, 483, 497.
ICHNÆ, town in Mesopotamia, Crassus, iii. 385.
ICTINUS, the architect, Pericles, i. 357.
IDA, mountain in Phrygia, Numa, i. 157; Eumenes, iii. 450.
IDÆUS, or ADÆUS, secretary to Agesilaus, Agesilaus, iv. 19.
IDAS, brother of Lynceus, Theseus, i. 33.
IDOMENEUS, an historian, Pericles, i. 352, 388; Aristides, ii. 310, 313, 323; Phocion, iv. 370; Demosthenes, v. 17, 26.
IDRIEUS, or HIDRIEUS, prince of Caria, Agesilaus, iv. 19.

IETÆ (in the text HIERÆ), town in Sicily, Timoleon, ii. 158.
IGNATIUS, or EGNATIUS, lieutenant of Crassus, Crassus, iii. 388.
ILIA, daughter of Numitor, Romulus, i. 44, 49.
ILIA, wife of Sylla, Sylla, iii. 161.
ILICIUM, or ELICIUM at Rome, Numa, i. 158.
ILIUM and ILIANS, Lucullus, iii. 256, 258. See TROY and TROJANS.
ILLYRIA and ILLYRIANS, Æm. Paulus, ii. 179, 183, 206; Philopœmen, ii. 400; Pyrrhus, iii. 3, 11, 50 (an Illyrian sword); Pompey, iv. 124, 142; Alexander, iv. 181, 190; Cæsar, iv. 302, 323; Cato the Younger, iv. 450; Cleomenes, iv. 532, 551, 552; Comparison, iv. 621; Demetrius, v. 164; Antony, v. 222, 228; Illyric soldiers, Aratus, v. 423; Illyrian legion, Galba, v. 503.
IMBROS, island in the Ægean Sea, Phocion, iv. 388.
INDIA and the INDIANS, Alexander, iv. 195, 245, 259, 262-272, 275; compare Eumenes, iii. 441; other historical passages are Demetrius, v. 108, 138. See, also, Lycurgus, i. 93; Æm. Paulus, ii. 182; Crassus, iii. 370; Comparison, iii. 401, 402; Pompey, iv. 156; Antony, v. 203, 247; Indian kings, Comparison of Dion and Brutus, v. 383.
INO, daughter of Cadmus, Camillus, i. 290.
INORA or SINORA, castle of Mithridates, Pompey, iv. 103.
MARCUS INSTEIUS, lieutenant of Antony, Antony, v. 231.
INSUBRES, a tribe of Gauls, Marcellus, ii. 264, 265, 267.
IOLAUS, son of Antipater, Alexander, iv. 281, 283.
IOLAUS, companion of Hercules, Pelopidas, ii. 240.

IOLCUS in Thessaly, Demetrius, v. 164.
ION of Chios, poet and historian, Theseus, i. 19; Pericles, i. 343, 377; Comparison of Alcibiades and Coriolanus, ii. 113; Cimon, iii. 220, 225, 238; Demosthenes, v. 3.
ION, son of Xuthus, Solon, i. 201.
IONIA and IONIANS, Themistocles, i. 255; Pericles, i. 365, 377; Alcibiades, ii. 34, 35 and after; Aristides, ii. 344; Lysander, iii. 142; Cimon, iii. 230, 234; Demosthenes, v. 28; Antony, v. 194; Brutus, v. 355; Ionia and Peloponnesus, Theseus, i. 26. Salamis Ionian, Solon, i. 186; Ionian women, Themistocles, i. 275; Pericles, i. 371; Alcibiades, ii. 52; Lucullus, iii. 265; Crassus, iii. 395; Phocion, iv. 389; Artaxerxes, v. 470, 472. Ionian sumptuosity, Lycurgus, i. 92.
THE IONIAN SEA, Æm. Paulus, ii. 212; Pyrrhus, iii. 20 (in the Greek); Sylla, iii. 182; Cæsar, iv. 330; Antony, v. 172, 195, 228.
IOPE, daughter of Iphicles, Theseus, i. 92.
IOPHON, son of Pisistratus, Cato the Elder, ii. 383.
IOS, island in the Ægean Sea, Sertorius, iii. 406.
IOXUS and the IOXIDS, descended from Theseus, Theseus, i. 9.
IPHICLES, Theseus, i. 31.
IPHICRATES, the Athenian general, Pelopidas, ii. 221; Agesilaus, iv. 32; Artaxerxes, v. 467; Galba, v. 476.
IPHITUS, son of Eurytus, Theseus, i. 7; Lycurgus, i. 87, 121.
IPSUS, field of the battle, a town of Phrygia, Pyrrhus, iii. 5; Demetrius, v. 138.

IPHTHA, Sertorius, iii. 415.
IRAS, Cleopatra's maid, Antony, v. 226, 251.
ISÆUS the orator, Demosthenes, v. 6.
ISAURICUS (P. SERVILIUS), Cæsar, iv. 293; and (?) Sylla, iii. 194; Pompey, iv. 76.
SERVILIUS ISAURICUS, son of the preceding, Cæsar, iv. 329.
ISIAS, a Corinthian captain, Timoleon, ii. 146.
ISIDAS or ISADAS, the son of Phœbidas, Agesilaus, iv. 50.
ISIDORUS, admiral of Mithridates, Lucullus, iii. 258.
ISIS, the Egyptian goddess, Antony, v. 221, 241.
ISMENIAS, a Theban, Pelopidas, ii. 225.
ISMENIAS the Theban (son of the preceding?), Pelopidas, ii. 249, 252; Artaxerxes, v. 465.
ISMENIAS the flute-player, Pericles, i. 338; Demetrius, v. 102.
ISMENUS, river of Bœotia, Demetrius, v. 155.
ISOCRATES the orator, Alcibiades, ii. 16; Cato the Elder, ii. 381; Demosthenes, v. 6; Comparison, v. 97.
ISODICE, wife of Cimon, Cimon, iii. 219, 235.
ISOMANTUS, river of Bœotia, Lysander, iii. 150.
ISSORION, strong place in Sparta, Agesilaus, iv. 46.
ISSUS, field of the battle, a town in Cilicia, Alexander, iv. 211, 226.
ISTHMUS OF CORINTH, Theseus, i. 8, 27; Themistocles, i. 255, 258, 259, 264, 270; Pompey, iv. 89; Alexander, iv. 195; Cæsar, iv. 351; Cleomenes, iv. 541; Demetrius, v. 128, 136, 146; Aratus, v. 401, 430. The Isthmian games, Theseus, i. 27; Solon, i. 202;
Timoleon, ii. 152; Flamininus, ii. 435, 440; Agesilaus, iv. 30.
ISTER or ISTRUS, an historian, Theseus, i. 37; Alexander, iv. 243.
ITALIA, daughter of Themistocles, Themistocles, i. 283.
ITALUS, father of Roma, Romulus, i. 42.
ITALY and ITALIANS, Theseus, i. 14; Romulus, i. 42, 43, and elsewhere frequent. Italians, as distinct from the Romans, Æm. Paulus, ii. 186; Pyrrhus, iii. 26; Marius, iii. 75, 92, 93; Comparison of Lysander and Sylla, iii. 211; Compare Caius Gracchus, iv. 600, 606, but the original word here, and in Coriolanus, ii. 61, is that applied to the Italian Greeks. For Italian Greeks, see Æm. Paulus, ii. 198; Pyrrhus, iii. 17; Nicias, iii. 334; Alexander, iv. 229. Italian words, Romulus, i. 59. An Italian feeling, Æm. Paulus, ii. 192.
ITHAGENES of Samos, Pericles, i. 374.
ITHOME and THE ITHOMATAS, citadel of Messene, Pelopidas, ii. 246; Cimon, iii. 238; Aratus, v. 436.
ITONIAN, epithet of Minerva, Pyrrhus, iii. 38; Agesilaus, iv. 27.
IULIS, town in the island of Ceos, Demosthenes, v. 1.
IXION, Agis, iv. 495.

J

JANICULUM, Numa, i. 166; Marius, iii. 104.
JASON the hero, Theseus, i. 18, 32; Cimon, iii. 216.
JASON, tyrant of Pheræ, Pelopidas, ii. 251.
JASON of Tralles, an actor, Crassus, iii. 395.

INDEX 591

JUBA (I.), king of Numidia, Pompey, iv. 165; Cæsar, iv. 345, 346, 348.

JUBA (II.), (son of the preceding), king of Numidia, and an historian, Romulus, i. 58, 59, 63; Numa, i. 143, 154; Comparison of Pelopidas and Marcellus, ii. 304; Sylla, iii. 177; Sertorius, iii. 416; Cæsar, iv. 348; Antony, v. 253.

JUBIUS (probably L. Vibullius Rufus), Pompey, iv. 148.

JUDÆA and the JEWS, Pompey, iv. 112, 120; Cicero, v. 45; Antony, v. 167, 201, 227, 239; Galba, v. 489; Otho, v. 513, 525.

JUGURTHA, king of Numidia, Marius, iii. 58, 62, 91; Sylla, iii. 155, 158; C. Gracchus, iv. 616.

JULIA, mother of Antony, Antony, v. 166.

JULIA, wife of Marius, aunt of Cæsar, Marius, iii. 57; Cæsar, iv. 260, 290.

JULIA, wife of Pompey, daughter of Cæsar, Pompey, iv. 123, 126, 156; Cæsar, iv. 301, 314, 348; Cato the Younger, iv. 448.

JULIA, daughter of Augustus, Antony, v. 253.

JULIUS, Censor, Camillus, i. 299.

JULIUS PROCULUS, Romulus, i. 77; Numa, i. 134.

JULIUS SALINATOR, Sertorius, iii. 413.

JULIUS ATTICUS, Galba, v. 504.

JUNIA, sister of Brutus, wife of Cassius, Brutus, v. 325.

MARCUS JUNIUS, dictator, Fabius, i. 407.

JUNIUS, governor of Asia, Cæsar, iv. 288.

JUNIUS BRUTUS. See BRUTUS.

JUNIUS SILANUS, Cato the Younger, iv. 436, 438; Cicero, v. 53, 57-60.

JUNIUS or JULIUS VINDEX, commanding in Gaul, Galba, v. 479-482, 486, 494, 498, 508.

L

LABEO, friend of Brutus, Brutus, v. 330, 377.

LABIENUS, officer of Cæsar in Gaul, Pompey, iv. 147, 152; Cæsar, iv. 307, 327; Cato the Younger, iv. 476; Cicero, v. 81.

LABIENUS, commanding among the Parthians (son of the preceding), Antony, v. 191, 194, 197.

LACEDÆMONIUS, son of Cimon, Pericles, i. 378; Cimon, iii. 235.

LACEDÆMON and LACEDÆMONIANS, Theseus, i. 35, 37; Romulus, i. 60; Lycurgus, i. 87, throughout, and elsewhere continually. For Lacedæmonian habits see, besides Lycurgus, the lives of Lysander, iii. 114; Agesilaus, iv. 3; Agis, iv. 495; and Cleomenes, iv. 520. Lacedæmonian women, Lycurgus, i. 107; Alcibiades, ii. 3; Pyrrhus, iii. 40; Agis, iv. 502; Cleomenes, iv. 564. See, also, LACONIA.

LACETANI, people of Spain, Cato the Elder, ii. 362.

LACHARES, tyrant of Athens, Demetrius, v. 138, 139.

LACHARES, a Spartan, Antony, v. 234.

LACHARTUS, a Corinthian, Cimon, iii. 238.

LACIA and the LACIADÆ, an Attic township, Alcibiades, ii. 31; Cimon, iii. 217, 227.

LACINIUM, promontory of Bruttium, Pompey, iv. 89.

CORNELIUS LACO, favorite of Galba, Galba, v. 488, 503, 506, 508.

LACONIA, Lycurgus, i. 98 and after; Pelopidas, ii. 245, 246; Philopœmen, ii. 414; Pyrrhus, iii. 40; Nicias, iii. 315; Agesilaus, iv. 33, 41, 44, 45; Cleomenes, iv. 524, 532, 540, 543, 546, 550, 556; Demetrius, v. 141; Aratus, v. 420. See, also, Agis, iv. 504.

LACRATIDAS, an Athenian, Pericles, i. 388.

LACRATIDAS, a Spartan ephor, Lysander, iii. 151.

LACRITUS, the orator, Demosthenes, v. 32.

CAIUS LÆLIUS, the friend of Scipio, surnamed Sapiens, Cato the Younger, iv. 420; Ti. Gracchus, iv. 574.

LÆLIUS, contemporary with Cicero, Comparison of Demosthenes and Cicero, v. 99.

LÆLIUS, Antony, v. 181.

POPILIUS LÆNAS, a senator, Brutus, v. 334, 335, 336.

LAERTES, father of Ulysses, Cicero, v. 83.

LÆVINUS (P. Valerius), Pyrrhus, iii. 21, 24, 25, 27.

LAIS of Corinth, Alcibiades, ii. 57; Nicias, iii. 330.

LAIUS, father of Œdipus, Pelopidas, ii. 241.

LAMACHUS, an Athenian general, Pericles, i. 368; Alcibiades, ii. 25, 28, 31; Nicias, iii. 325, 328, 329, 333.

LAMACHUS the Myrinæan, a speaker, Demosthenes, v. 10.

LAMIA, Demetrius, v. 121, 126, 129, 130, 131, 132; Comparison, v. 256.

LAMIA, town of Thessaly, Pyrrhus, iii. 1; Eumenes, iii. 444; Phocion, iv. 393, 397; Demosthenes, v. 31; Demetrius, v. 111.

LAMPIDO, wife of Archidamus, Agesilaus, iv. 3.

LAMPON, an Athenian diviner, Pericles, i. 344.

LAMPONIUS, the Lucanian general, Sylla, iii. 194; Comparison, iii. 211.

LAMPRIAS, grandfather of Plutarch, Antony, v. 191.

LAMPSACUS, in Mysia, Themistocles, i. 280; Alcibiades, ii. 54; Lysander, iii. 122, 125.

LAMPTRA or LAMPRA, Attic township, Aristides, ii. 326; Phocion, iv. 405.

CALPURNIUS LANARIUS, Sertorius, iii. 413.

LANASSA, daughter of Agathocles, Pyrrhus, iii. 11-13.

LANASSA, daughter of Cleodæus, Pyrrhus, iii. 1.

LANGOBRITÆ, people of Spain, Sertorius, iii. 421.

LANGON, in Elis, Cleomenes, iv. 536.

LAODICE, daughter of Priam, Theseus, i. 37; Cimon, iii. 218.

LAODICÆA, in Syria, Antony, v. 240.

LAOMEDON, an Athenian, Cimon, iii. 225.

LAOMEDON of Orchomenus, Demosthenes, v. 7.

LAOMEDON, king of Troy, Nicias, iii. 308; Sertorius, iii. 405.

LAPHYSTIUS, a Syracusan, Timoleon, ii. 165.

LAPITHÆ, people of Thessaly, Theseus, i. 31, 33.

ACCA LARENTIA, and another LARENTIA, Romulus, i. 45.

LARISSA, in Thessaly, Pelopidas, ii. 248; Sylla, iii. 186; Agesilaus, iv. 24; Pompey, iv. 160; Demetrius, v. 134, 143; Brutus, v. 323.

LARISSA, in Syria, Antony, v. 202.

LARISSUS, river of Elis, Philopœmen, ii. 403.

TITUS LARTIUS, Coriolanus, ii. 67, 70.

LARYMNA, town of Bœotia, Sylla, iii. 190.

LATHYRUS, a surname, Coriolanus, ii. 72.

LATINS, Romulus, i. 42, 45, 46, 50, 72, 80, 81; Numa, i. 143, (early connection of Greek and Latin) 149; Poplicola, i. 222, 235; Camillus, i. 323, 326, 289, 336 and (the Latin feast or holidays); Coriolanus, ii. 61, 94, 97; Æm. Paulus, ii. 198; Marcellus, ii. 270; Flamininus, ii. 433; (Greek words in Latin) Pyrrhus, iii. 33; C. Gracchus, iv. 603, 604; Cicero, v. 37. In some other places, also, *Latin* for *the Latin language* is used in the translation, where the original has *the Roman language* or another phrase.

TITUS LATINUS or LATINIUS, Coriolanus, ii. 89, 90.

LATINUS, son of Telemachus, Romulus, i. 42.

LATTAMYAS, a Thessalian, Camillus, i. 305.

LAURENTUM, town of Latium, Romulus, i. 71, 72.

LAURIUM, in Attica, Themistocles, i. 248; Nicias, iii. 312.

LAURON, town of Spain, Sertorius, iii. 427, 428; Pompey, iv. 81.

LAVERNA at Rome, Sylla, iii. 160.

LAVICI, town of Latium, Coriolanus, ii. 94.

LAVINIA, daughter of Latinus, Romulus, i. 42.

LAVINIUM, town of Latium, Romulus, i. 71; Coriolanus, ii. 95.

LEBADEA, town of Bœotia, Lysander, iii. 147; Sylla, iii. 177.

LECANIUS, Galba, v. 505.

LECHÆUM, port of Corinth, Cleomenes, iv. 542; Aratus, v. 408.

LECTUM, promontory of the Troad, Lucullus, iii. 248.

LEGES, Scythian tribe, Pompey, iv. 108.

LEMNOS, island in the Ægean Sea, Pericles, i. 373; Aristides, ii. 346; Lucullus, iii. 258.

LENTULI, Pompey, iv. 161 (Spinther and Crus.)

CORNELIUS LENTULUS at Cannæ, Fabius, i. 416.

CORNELIUS LENTULUS (Clodianus), censor with Gellius, and also consul with him, Crassus, iii. 362; Pompey, iv. 86.

CORNELIUS LENTULUS SURA, accomplice of Catiline, Cæsar, iv. 294; Cicero, v. 55, 56, 57, 60-63, 71; Antony, v. 166.

LENTULUS SPINTHER (consul B. C. 57), with Pompey at Pharsalia, Pompey, iv. 127, 152; Cæsar, iv. 335; Cicero, v. 75, 80.

LENTULUS SPINTHER (son of the preceding), Cæsar, iv. 362.

LUCIUS LENTULUS (Crus, consul B. C. 49), Pompey, iv. 141, 142, 169; Cæsar, iv. 321, 323, 326; Antony, v. 170.

CORNELIUS LENTULUS, lieutenant of Flamininus, Flamininus, ii. 438.

LENTULUS, same as Dolabella, Cicero's son-in-law, a Lentulus by adoption, Cicero, v. 85.

LENTULUS BATIATES at Capua, Crassus, iii. 360.

VALERIUS LEO, Cæsar's host at Milan, Cæsar, iv. 306.

LEOBOTES of Agraule, son of Alcmæon, Themistocles, i. 271.

LEOCHARES, a sculptor, Alexander, iv. 237.

LEOCRATES, an Athenian, Pericles, i. 363; Comparison, i. 431; Aristides, ii. 336.

LEON of Byzantium, Nicias, iii. 340; Phocion, iv. 382.

LEON, father of Antalcidas, Artaxerxes, v. 464.

LEONIDAS, Alexander's tutor, Alexander, iv. 184, 209.

LEONIDAS (I.), king of Sparta, Lycurgus, i. 91, 107, 116; Themistocles, i. 254; Pelopidas, ii. 243; Agis, iv. 511; Cleomenes, iv. 522; Artaxerxes, v. 464.

LEONIDAS (II.), king of Sparta,

INDEX

Agesilaus, iv. 57; Agis, iv. 498-500, 503, 506, 509, 512-516, 518, 519; Cleomenes, iv. 520, 522, 523.

LEONNATUS, one of Alexander's officers, Eumenes, iii. 444, 445; Alexander, iv. 207, 236; Phocion, iv. 395.

LEONNATUS, a Macedonian, Pyrrhus, iii. 23.

LEONTIDAS, a Theban, Pelopidas, ii. 225, 226, 232, 233; Agesilaus, iv. 35.

LEONTINI, LEONTIUM, and the LEONTINES, in Sicily, Timoleon, ii. 140, 150, 160; Marcellus, ii. 276; Pyrrhus, iii. 31; Nicias, iii. 325, 329, 330; Dion, v. 286, 300-301.

LEONTIS, Attic tribe, Themistocles, i. 244; Aristides, ii. 315.

LEOS, an Athenian, Theseus, i. 12.

LEOSTHENES, an Athenian, Timoleon, ii. 126; Pyrrhus, iii. 1; Phocion, iv. 372, 392, 393, 394, 397; Demosthenes, v. 31; Comparison, v. 97.

LEOTYCHIDES (dialectically LEUTYCHIDAS), king of Sparta, Lycurgus, i. 105; Themistocles, i. 270; Comparison of Lucullus and Cimon, iii. 305.

LEOTYCHIDES, son of Agis II., Alcibiades, ii. 34; Lysander, iii. 139, 140; Agesilaus, iv. 5, 6; Comparison, iv. 171, 172.

LEOTYCHIDES, a Spartan, Pyrrhus, iii. 39.

LEPIDA, wife of Metellus Scipio, Cato the Younger, iv. 420.

MARCUS ÆMILIUS LEPIDUS, first senator, Æm. Paulus, ii. 215.

MARCUS LEPIDUS (consul, B. C. 78); Sylla, iii. 202, 205; Pompey, iv. 77-79, 101; Comparison, iv. 171.

MARCUS LEPIDUS the triumvir, Cæsar, iv. 357, 361; Cicero, v. 90; Antony, v. 171, 174, 178, 181-184, 195, 222; Brutus, v. 339, 349.

LEPTINES, brother of Dionysius the Elder, Timoleon, ii. 138; Dion, v. 268, 270.

LEPTINES, who killed Callippus, Dion, v. 317, perhaps the same as

LEPTINES, tyrant of Apollonia, Timoleon, ii. 150.

LERNA, in Argolis, Pyrrhus, iii. 27; Cleomenes, iv. 536; Aratus, v. 424.

LESBOS and LESBIANS, island of the Ægean Sea, Pericles, i. 365; Alcibiades, ii. 15, 34; Aristides, ii. 340; Nicias, iii. 314; Pompey, iv. 150.

LEUCARIA, LUCARIA, or LUCANIA, wife of Italus, Romulus, i. 42.

LEUCAS and LEUCADIANS, island on the coast of Acarnania, Themistocles, i. 272; Timoleon, ii. 128, 137; Pompey, iv. 89; Demosthenes, v. 19; Dion, v. 280.

LEUCASPIDES, or White-Shields, Cleomenes, iv. 546.

LEUCON, Platæan hero, Aristides, ii. 324.

LEUCONOE, Attic township, Demetrius, v. 127.

LEUCOTHEA, Camillus, i. 290.

LEUCTRA, field of battle, a town of Bœotia, Lycurgus, i. 131; Camillus, i. 305; Coriolanus, ii. 63; Pelopidas, ii. 242, 243, 253; Comparison, ii. 303, 305; Lysander, iii. 134; Comparison, iii. 210; Agesilaus, iv. 22, 41, 57; Comparison, iv. 172, 174; Agis, iv. 519; Artaxerxes, v. 464.

LEUCTRIDÆ or LEUCTRIDES, daughters of Scedasus, Pelopidas, ii. 242.

LEUCTRON, town of Arcadia, Pelopidas, ii. 243; Cleomenes, iv. 526.

LEUCUS, river of Macedonia, Æm. Paulus, ii. 194.

LIBETHRA in Macedonia, Alexander, iv. 196.

INDEX 595

LIBITINA, the Roman goddess, Numa, i. 151.

LIBO, one of Pompey's commanders by sea, Antony, v. 172.

LIBYA, frequent, as also AFRICA, by which the Greek word Libya has been frequently translated. See portions of the lives of Marius, Sylla, iii. 154; Sertorius, iii. 416; Pompey, Cæsar, Cato the Younger, and Antony. The Libyan piper, Lucullus, iii. 256. Libyssan earth, Flamininus, ii. 450. Proconsulate of Galba, Galba, v. 479.

LIBYS, a Spartan, Agis, iv. 501.

LIBYSSA, village of Bithynia, Flamininus, ii. 450.

LICHAS, a Spartan, Cimon, iii. 228.

LICINIA, wife of C. Gracchus, Ti. Gracchus, iv. 592; C. Gracchus, iv. 613, 616.

LICINIA, a vestal, Crassus, iii. 251.

PUBLIUS LICINIUS, commanding in Macedonia, Æm. Paulus, ii. 178.

LICINIUS, servant of Ti. Gracchus, Ti. Gracchus, iv. 568.

LICINIUS, friend of C. Gracchus, C. Gracchus, iv. 614.? Publius Crassus.

LICINIUS MACER, impeached by Cicero, Cicero, v. 47.

LICINIUS PHILONICUS, Æm. Paulus, ii. 214.

LICYMNIUS, his tomb at Argos, Pyrrhus, iii. 50.

CAIUS LIGARIUS, friend of Brutus, Brutus, v. 329.

QUINTUS LIGARIUS, defended by Cicero, Cicero, v. 82.

LIGURIANS or LIGUSTINES, in Northern Italy, Fabius, i. 396; Æm. Paulus, ii. 174, 190, 206, 216; Marius, iii. 69, 75.

LILYBÆUM, promontory of Sicily, Timoleon, ii. 151.

LIMNÆUS, a Macedonian, Alexander, iv. 268.

LIMNUS of Chalastra, a Macedonian, Alexander, iv. 247, 248.

LINDUS, town of Rhodes, Marcellus, ii. 302.

LINGONES, tribe of Gauls, Cæsar, iv. 317.

LIPAREANS, Camillus, i. 295.

LIRIS, river of Campania, Marius, iii. 98.

LISSUS, town of Dalmatia, Antony, v. 172.

LIVIA, wife of Augustus, Antony, v. 249, 253; Galba, v. 479, 489.

MARCUS LIVIUS, commanding in Tarentum, Fabius, i. 425.

LIVIUS DRUSUS. See two of the name under DRUSUS.

LIVIUS POSTUMIUS, a commander of the Latins, Romulus, i. 80.

LIVY the historian, Camillus, i. 292; Marcellus, ii. 274, 293, 302; Comparison, ii. 304; Cato the Elder, ii. 372; Flamininus, ii. 447, 450; Sylla, iii. 161; Lucullus, iii. 281, 286; Cæsar, iv. 340, 358.

LOCRI EPIZEPHYRII, town in Italy, Marcellus, ii. 299.

LOCRI and LOCRIANS, in Greece, Pericles, i. 365; Pelopidas, ii. 237, 238; Aristides, ii. 337; Flamininus, ii. 436; Dion, v. 261; Aratus, v. 400.

MARCUS LOLLIUS, a quæstor, Cato the Younger, iv. 430.

LOTHRONUS, Greek name of the Vulturnus, Fabius, i. 402.

LUCANIA and LUCANIANS, in Italy, Fabius, i. 421; Timoleon, ii. 162; Marcellus, ii. 294; Pyrrhus, iii. 21, 36; Sylla, iii. 195; Crassus, iii. 363, 365; Cato the Younger, iv. 434; Cicero, v. 73; Brutus, v. 343.

LUCCA, town of Etruria, Crassus, iii. 368; Pompey, iv. 129; Cæsar, iv. 311.

LUCERES, Roman tribe, Romulus, i. 67.
LUCILIUS, tribune of the people, Pompey, iv. 134.
LUCILIUS, friend of Brutus, Antony, v. 236; Brutus, v. 375, 376.
SEXTUS LUCINUS or LICINIUS, Marius, iii. 108.
LUCRETIA, wife of Numa, Numa, i. 165.
LUCRETIA, wife of Collatinus, Poplicola, i. 215, 227.
LUCRETIUS, father of Lucretia, Poplicola, i. 227.
TITUS LUCRETIUS, consul, Poplicola, i. 230, 237.
LUCIUS LUCRETIUS, Camillus, i. 321.
LUCRETIUS OFELLA, Sylla, iii. 196, 200; Comparison, iii. 208.
LUCIUS LUCULLUS, Life, iii. 243; Comparison, iii. 303; Camillus, i. 306; Cato the Elder, ii. 383; Flamininus, ii. 452; Marius, iii. 93; Sylla, iii. 160, 169, 192; Cimon, iii. 214-216; Crassus, iii. 364, 370, 374, 386; Comparison, iii. 401, 402; Pompey, iv. 61, 83, 98, 104, 105, 110, 111, 121, 125; Comparison, iv. 176; Cato the Younger, iv. 424, 434, 439, 445, 447, 448, 473; Cicero, v. 69, 72.
MARCUS LUCULLUS, brother of Lucullus, Sylla, iii. 192; Lucullus, iii. 244, 293, 301; Cæsar, iv. 289, 297.
THE TWO LUCULLI, Cæsar, iv. 303.
LUCUMO, an Etruscan, Camillus, i. 301.
LUPERCI and LUPERCALIA, Romulus, i. 69; Numa, i. 162; Cæsar, iv. 354; Antony, v. 176.
LUSITANIA and LUSITANIANS, Sertorius, iii. 416-417, 437; Comparison, iii. 439; Cæsar, iv. 299; Ti. Gracchus, iv. 592; Galba, v. 496, 498.

CAIUS LUSIUS, nephew of Marius, Marius, iii. 67, 68.
LUTATIUS CATULUS. See CATULUS.
LYCÆUM, mountain of Arcadia, Cleomenes, iv. 525; Aratus, v. 421.
LYCAONIA, in Asia Minor, Lucullus, iii. 274; Eumenes, iii. 453; Pompey, iv. 98; Antony, v. 227.
LYCEUM, gymnasium at Athens, Theseus, i. 30; Sylla, iii. 169; Phocion, iv. 411.
LYCIA, in Asia Minor, and LYCIANS, Alexander, iv. 201, 232; Brutus, v. 352-355.
LYCOMEDÆ or LYCOMIDÆ, an Attic family, Themistocles, i. 245.
LYCOMEDES, an Athenian, Themistocles, i. 263.
LYCOMEDES, king of Scyros, Theseus, i. 38; Cimon, iii. 224.
LYCON of Scarphia, an actor, Alexander, iv. 220.
LYCON, a Syracusan, Dion, v. 316.
LYCOPHRON, a Corinthian, Nicias, iii. 315.
LYCOPHRON of Pheræ, son of Jason, Pelopidas, ii. 260; Galba, v. 477, if he is the Pheræan.
LYCORTAS, father of Polybius the historian, Philopœmen, ii. 420.
LYCURGUS, an Athenian, Solon, i. 208.
LYCURGUS the Athenian orator, Flamininus, ii. 439; Comparison of Nicias and Crassus, iii. 398; Phocion, iv. 374, 378, 385; Demosthenes, v. 26.
LYCURGUS the lawgiver, Life, i. 87; Comparison, i. 169; Theseus, i. 1; Numa, i. 139; Solon, i. 193, 200; Alcibiades, ii. 34; Aristides, ii. 310; Comparison, ii. 390; Philopœmen, ii. 414; Agesilaus, iv. 38, 48; Phocion, iv. 390; Agis, iv. 500, 501, 504, 505, 516; Cleome-

nes, iv. 530, 531, 534, 538, 541; Comparison, iv. 621, 623.
LYCUS, a river of Phrygia, Demetrius, v. 156.
LYCUS, a river of Pontus, Lucullus, iii. 261.
LYDIA and LYDIANS in Asia Minor, Theseus, i. 7; Romulus, i. 42; Themistocles, i. 281; Aristides, ii. 332, 334; Lysander, iii. 116, 119; Cimon, iii. 226; Nicias, iii. 307 (Lydian cars); Eumenes, iii. 451; Agesilaus, iv. 14; Demetrius, v. 155; Antony, v. 194; Artaxerxes, v. 442.
LYDIADAS or LYDIADES of Megalopolis, Cleomenes, iv. 526; Aratus, v. 415, 416, 420-422.
LYGDAMIS, a leader of the Cimmerians, Marius, iii. 64.
LYNCEUS, brother of Idas, Theseus, i. 33.
LYNCEUS of Samos, a writer, Demetrius, v. 130.
LYNCUS, on the Macedonian border, Flamininus, ii. 426.
LYRA, the constellation, Cæsar, iv. 353.
LYSANDER of Alopece, Themistocles, i. 283.
LYSANDER, the Spartan general, Life, iii. 113; Comparison, iii. 207; Lycurgus, i. 129; Alcibiades, ii. 53-58; Flamininus, ii. 437; Nicias, iii. 348; Agesilaus, iv. 4-6, 9-12, 29; Comparison, iv. 171, 172; Agis, iv. 511.
LYSANDER, son of Lybis, a Spartan, Agis, iv. 501-505, 507, 508, 511, 516.
LYSANDRIDAS of Megalopolis, Cleomenes, iv. 547.
LYSANORIDAS, a Spartan, Pelopidas, ii. 234.
LYSIAS, the Athenian orator, Cato the Elder, ii. 356.
LYSICLES the sheep-dealer, Pericles, i. 372.

LYSIDICE, daughter of Pelops, Theseus, i. 7.
LYSIMACHUS the Acarnanian, Alexander's pedagogue, Alexander, iv. 184, 212.
LYSIMACHUS, father of Aristides, Themistocles, i. 247, 260; Aristides, ii. 308, 309, 343.
LYSIMACHUS, son of Aristides, Aristides, ii. 346.
LYSIMACHUS, grandson of Aristides, Aristides, ii. 346.
LYSIMACHUS, general of Alexander, and king of Thrace, Pyrrhus, iii. 8, 13-18, 42; Alexander, iv. 243, 257; Demetrius, v. 115, 119, 122, 129, 131, 136, 141, 147, 153-156, 158, 162, 163; Comparison, v. 257.
LYSIPPUS, general of the Achæans, Philopœmen, ii. 409.
LYSIPPUS the sculptor, Alexander, iv. 182, 200, 237.

M

MACARIA, daughter of Hercules, Pelopidas, ii. 243.
MACEDON and MACEDONIANS. See, in general, the lives of Æmilius Paulus, Flamininus, Pyrrhus, Eumenes, Alexander, Phocion, Cleomenes, Demosthenes, Demetrius, and Aratus, and the Comparisons. Also, Theseus, i. 5; Camillus, i. 306; Timoleon, ii. 138; Pelopidas, ii. 248; Aristides, ii. 329; Cato the Elder, ii. 363, 369; Philopœmen, ii. 401, 403, 408, 412; Sylla, iii. 168, 170, 174, 186, 187, 190; Cimon, iii. 215, 234; Agesilaus, iv. 22, 23; Pompey, iv. 106, 147; Cæsar, iv. 289, 333; Cato the Younger, iv. 422; Cicero, v. 50, 70, 90; Antony, v. 172, 184, 185, 221, 229, 234; Brutus, v. 322, 344, 345, 349, 350; Galba, v. 476, 477; Macedonian

months, Alexander, iv. 161, 198, 283. The Macedonian dialect, Eumenes, iii. 459, 460; Alexander, iv. 251; Antony, v. 191. The Macedonian hat or cap, Antony, v. 221. Compare Eumenes, iii. 448; Demetrius, v. 149.

MACEDONICUS, surname, see METELLUS, Marius, iii. 52.

LUCINIUS MACER, impeached by Cicero, Cicero, v. 47.

CLODIUS MACER, Galba, v. 481, 488, 491.

MACHANIDAS, tyrant of Lacedæmon, Philopœmen, ii. 405-408.

MACHARES, son of Mithridates, Lucullus, iii. 274.

MACHATAS, an Epirot, Flamininus, ii. 426.

MACRÆ or ACRÆ, in Sicily, Dion, v. 286.

MACRINUS, a surname, Marius, iii. 52.

MACRON. See CLODIUS MACER.

MÆCENAS, friend of Augustus, Comparison of Demosthenes and Cicero, v. 97; Antony, v. 199.

MÆCIUS or MARCIUS, a hill in Latium, Camillus, i. 323, 325.

MÆDI and MÆDICA in Thrace, Æm. Paulus, ii. 181; Sylla, iii. 186; Alexander, iv. 189.

SPURIUS MÆLIUS, killed by Ahala, Brutus, v. 319.

THE LAKE MÆOTIS, Marius, iii. 64; Sylla, iii. 168; Lucullus, iii. 263; Pompey, iv. 107; Alexander, iv. 241; Antony, v. 223.

MAGÆUS, a Persian, Alcibiades, ii. 57.

MAGAS, brother of Ptolemy Philopator, Cleomenes, iv. 557.

MAGNESIA, a town of Caria, Themistocles, i. 280-284.

MAGNESIA and MAGNESIANS in Thessaly, Pelopidas, ii. 255, 259; Flamininus, ii. 436, 438, 443.

MAGNUS, Pompey's surname, Sertorius, iii. 427; Pompey, iv. 75. Plutarch (except in a passage like p. 141) uses the original Latin word, which in the English is translated into The Great.

MAGO, a Carthaginian, Timoleon, ii. 141-148.

MAIA, mother of Mercury, Numa, i. 162.

MALACA, Malaga in Spain, Crassus, iii. 356.

MALCHUS, king of Arabia, Antony, v. 227.

MALCITAS or MALCITUS, a Theban, Pelopidas, ii. 259.

MALEA, promontory of Laconia, Sylla, iii. 168; Agis, iv. 503; Aratus, v. 396.

MALIAN GULF, Pericles, i. 365.

MALLIANS, an Indian people, Alexander, iv. 268, 273.

MAMERCI, Numa, i. 165.

MAMERCUS, tyrant of Catana, Timoleon, ii. 134, 158, 159, 161, 162, 167.

MAMERCUS, son of Numa, Numa, i. 146, 165.

MAMERCUS, son of Pythagoras, Numa, i. 146; Æm. Paulus, ii. 170.

MAMERTINES of Messena in Sicily, Pyrrhus, iii. 33, 35; Pompey, iv. 69.

MAMURIUS, Numa, i. 153, 154.

CAIUS MANCINUS, consul (137 B. C.), Ti. Gracchus, iv. 570, 572.

MANDONIUM. See MANDURIA.

MANDROCLIDAS, a Spartan, Pyrrhus, iii. 40.

MANDROCLIDAS, son of Ecphanes, Agis, iv. 501, 505, 508.

MANDURIA or MANDONIUM, a town of Italy, Agis, iv. 498.

MANILIUS, friend of Pompey, tribune, Pompey, iv. 98; Cicero, v. 47, 48.

MANILIUS, disgraced by Cato, Cato the Elder, ii. 372.

INDEX 599

MANIUS? i. e. AQUILIUS, Lucullus, iii. 249. In Plutarch's text, Marius.

MANLIUS, properly MANIUS, Manius Curius, a tribune, Flamininus, ii. 423.

MANLIUS, defeated by the Cimbri (consul 105 B. C.), Marius, iii. 74.

MANLIUS, Cicero, v. 52, 54.

LUCIUS MANLIUS, a soldier, Cato the Elder, ii. 365.

LUCIUS MANLIUS in Spain (? MANILIUS), Sertorius, iii. 419.

MARCUS MANLIUS CAPITOLINUS, Camillus, i. 316, 327, 328.

MANLIUS TORQUATUS, Fabius, i. 407.

TITUS MANLIUS, consul with Marcus (Caius) Atilius (235 B. C.), Numa, i. 163.

[MANLIUS] TORQUATUS, lieutenant of Sylla, Sylla, iii. 195.

MANLIUS, officer under Sertorius, Sertorius, iii. 437, 438.

MANLIUS of consular rank, Ti. Gracchus, iv. 579.

MANTINEA, a town of Arcadia, and MANTINEANS, Numa, i. 153; Alcibiades, ii. 20, 27; Comparison, ii. 113; Pelopidas, ii. 224; Philopœmen, ii. 395, 406; Nicias, iii. 322; Agesilaus, iv. 44, 48-50; Cleomenes, iv. 525, 527, 535, 546; Demetrius, v. 127, 141; Aratus, v. 410, 421, 424, 430-432.

MARATHON in Attica, Theseus, i. 12, 32, 36, 39; Themistocles, i. 247; Camillus, i. 305; Aristides, ii. 314-316, 330; Comparison, ii. 389, 393; Flamininus, ii. 437; Cimon, iii. 220; Demosthenes, v. 32; Aratus, v. 400.

MARATHUS, who gave name to Marathon, Theseus, i. 36.

MARCELLINUS, Crassus, iii. 369; Pompey, iv. 129.

MARCELLUS, a Roman surname, Marius, iii. 52.

MARCUS CLAUDIUS MARCELLUS, father of Marcellus, Marcellus, ii. 262.

MARCUS CLAUDIUS MARCELLUS, in the second Punic war, Life, ii. 262; Comparison, ii. 303; Romulus, i. 61; Fabius, i. 419, 423, 424; Flamininus, ii. 423, 446.

MARCUS MARCELLUS, son of the general, Marcellus, ii. 263, 301; Flamininus, ii. 446.

MARCUS MARCELLUS (consul 51 B. C.), Cæsar, iv. 321 (?); Cato the Younger, iv. 432; Cicero, v. 53.

MARCELLUS (Caius, consul 50 B. C. with Paulus), Pompey, iv. 140, 141; Cæsar, iv. 321; Antony, v. 169.

MARCELLUS (also Caius, consul 49 B. C. with Lentulus Crus, cousin of the preceding), Cæsar, iv. 321.

CAIUS MARCELLUS, first husband of Octavia, the sister of Augustus, Marcellus, ii. 302; Cicero, v. 87; Antony, v. 195, 253.

MARCELLUS, son of the preceding, adopted by Augustus, Marcellus, ii. 302; Antony, v. 253.

CLAUDIUS MARCELLUS, lieutenant of Marius, Marius, iii. 76, 77.

MARCIA, wife of Cato the Younger, Cato the Younger, iv. 439, 441, 455, 456, 471, 472.

MARCIANUS, new name given to Icelus, Galba, v. 483.

MARCII, Coriolanus, ii. 59.

MARCIUS, kinsman of Numa, Numa, i. 140, 141, 166.

MARCIUS, son-in-law of Numa, father of Ancus Marcius, Numa, i. 166.

ANCUS MARCIUS the king, Numa, i. 147, 166; Coriolanus, ii. 59.

CAIUS MARCIUS. See CORIOLANUS.

CAIUS MARCIUS, consul with Scipio

600 INDEX

Nasico (162 B.C.), Marcellus, ii. 266.
PUBLIUS and QUINTUS MARCIUS, Coriolanus, ii. 59.
MARCIUS CENSORINUS, ibid.
MARCIUS PHILIPPUS, censor, Æm. Paulus, ii. 215.
MARCIUS REX, brother-in-law to Clodius, Cicero, v. 69.
MARCIUS in Catiline's conspiracy, Cicero, v. 54.
MARCIUS in Pompey's camp, Cicero, v. 80.
MARDIANS, a people of Asia, Lucullus, iii. 286; Antony, v. 207, 214-216.
MARDION, Cleopatra's attendant, Antony, v. 226.
MARDONIUS the Persian, Themistocles, i. 249, 265; Aristides, ii. 316, 321, 322, 326, 327; Agis, iv. 498.
MARICA, her grove near Minturnæ, Marius, iii. 101.
MARII, Pompey, iv. 67.
CAIUS MARIUS, Life, iii. 52; Flamininus, ii. 452; Sylla, iii. 154, 158, 161-167, 171, 193, 197; Comparison, iii. 211; Lucullus, iii. 248, 295; Crassus, iii. 353, 354; Sertorius, iii. 407, 409-411; Pompey, iv. 71; Comparison, iv. 176; Cæsar, iv. 286, 287, 290, 292, 303, 308; Antony, v. 165; Brutus, v. 351; Otho, v. 519; Marius's mules, Marius, iii. 67.
MARIUS THE YOUNGER, son of the preceding, Marius, iii. 95, 102, 103; Sylla, iii. 193-195, 200; Sertorius, iii. 411, 412; Pompey, iv. 74; Cæsar, iv. 286, 287.
MARCUS MARIUS, killed by Catiline, Sylla, iii. 200.
MARCUS MARIUS or VARIUS, lieutenant of Sertorius, Lucullus, iii. 254, 259; Sertorius, iii. 436.
MARIUS CELSUS, commanding for Otho, Galba, v. 503, 506; Otho, v. 509, 515, 516-519, 522, 523.
MARGIANIAN steel, Crassus, iii. 381.
MARGITES, Demosthenes, v. 26.
MARPHADATES, a Cappadocian prince, Cato the Younger, iv. 493.
MARRUCINI, a people of Italy, Æm. Paulus, ii. 192.
MARSEILLES, MASSALIA, or MASSILIA, in Gaul, Solon, i. 179; Marius, iii. 78; Cæsar, iv. 304.
MARSI or MARSIANS, in Italy, and THE MARSIAN WAR, Fabius, i. 420; Lucullus, iii. 245; Crassus, iii. 357; Sertorius, iii. 408; Cicero, v. 39.
MARSIANS (uncertain), Sylla, iii. 155.
MARSYAS, an historian, Demosthenes, v. 20.
MARSYAS, under Dionysius the Elder, Dion, v. 268.
MARTHA, a Syrian woman, Marius, iii. 71.
MARTIALIUS or MARTIALIS, a tribune of the prætorian guard, Galba, v. 502.
MARTIANUS, a gladiator, Galba, v. 485.
MARULLUS, tribune of the people, Cæsar, iv. 355.
MASABATES, the king's eunuch, Artaxerxes, v. 458, 459.
MASISTIUS, a Persian, Aristides, ii. 327, 328.
MASINISSA, king of Numidia, Cato the Elder, ii. 385.
PAPIRIUS MASO, father-in-law of Æmilius Paulus, Æm. Paulus, ii. 173.
MASSILIA. See MARSEILLES.
MATUTA, MOTHER, the Roman goddess, Camillus, i. 290.
MAURISCUS or MAURICUS, a senator, Galba, v. 485.
MAURITANIA and MOORS in Africa,

INDEX

Marius, iii. 103; Sertorius, iii. 413, 415, 421, 440.

MAXIMUS, Roman surname, Pompey, iv. 75. See FABIUS.

MAZÆUS, a Persian, Alexander, iv. 225, 235.

MEDEA, Theseus, i. 11; Alexander, iv. 191, 230.

MEDIA and THE MEDES. See, in general, the lives of Themistocles, Aristides, Cimon, Lucullus, iii. 255, 261, and after, Alexander, Antony, v. 191, 198, and after, and Artaxerxes. Also, Theseus, i. 39; Numa, i. 148; Pericles, i. 371; Æm. Paulus, ii. 198; Sylla, iii. 172; Eumenes, iii. 462, 465; Agesilaus, iv. 33. The Median dress, Alexander, iv. 242; Antony, v. 221. Also Pompey, iv. 106, 108, 120; Demetrius, v. 156.

MEDIOLANUM or MILAN, Marcellus, ii. 269; Cæsar, iv. 306; Comparison of Dion and Brutus, v. 384.

MEDIUS, friend of Alexander and Antigonus, Alexander, iv. 282; Demetrius, v. 120.

MEGABACCHUS (perhaps Megabocchus), friend of Crassus, Crassus, iii. 383.

MEGABATES, a young Persian, Agesilaus, iv. 16, 17.

MEGABYZUS, a Persian, Alexander, iv. 239.

MEGACLES the archon, who killed Cylon, Solon, i. 186, 187.

MEGACLES, son of Alcmæon, opponent of Pisistratus, Solon, i. 208, 210.

MEGACLES, grandfather of Alcibiades, Alcibiades, ii. 1.

MEGACLES, father of Euryptolemus, Cimon, iii. 219, 235.

MEGACLES, friend of Pyrrhus, Pyrrhus, iii. 22, 24.

MEGACLES, brother of Dion, Dion, v. 287, 288.

MEGALEAS, or MEGALÆUS, a Macedonian, Aratus, v. 433.

MEGALOPHANES or DEMOPHANES, a Megalopolitan, Philopœmen, ii. 395.

MEGALOPOLIS, a town of Arcadia, and MEGALOPOLITANS, Pelopidas, ii. 243; Philopœmen, ii. 395, 399, 401, 409-420; Pyrrhus, iii. 39; Agis, iv. 498; Cleomenes, iv. 524, 526, 533, 546-550, 553, 562; Aratus, v. 389, 415, 421, 424.

MEGARA and MEGARIANS, historical notices, Theseus, i. 9, 10, 26, 30, 36; Solon, i. 183, 187; Comparison, i. 242; Themistocles, i. 261; Pericles, i. 369, 379, and after; Alcibiades, ii. 46; Aristides, ii. 327, 336; Philopœmen, ii. 408; Nicias, iii. 315; Cæsar, iv. 336; Phocion, iv. 383; Demosthenes, v. 19; Demetrius, v. 110, 135, 146; Brutus, v. 327. The Megarian territory is also mentioned, Pelopidas, ii. 234; Cimon, iii. 238; Agesilaus, iv. 39; Agis, iv. 510; Aratus, v. 416; Anecdotes, Lysander, iii. 139; Philopœmen, ii. 396; Phocion, iv. 411; Antony, v. 185; Dion, v. 275.

MEGARA, a town in Macedonia, Pyrrhus, iii. 2.

MEGARA, a town in Sicily, Marcellus, ii. 283, 286.

MEGELLUS of Elea or Velia, Timoleon, ii. 163.

MEGISTONUS, stepfather of Cleomenes, Cleomenes, iv. 527, 532, 541, 543; Aratus, v. 423, 427.

MELANIPPUS, a son of Theseus, Theseus, i. 9.

MELANOPUS, an Athenian, Demosthenes, v. 15.

MELANTAS or MELANTES, a Persian, Artaxerxes, v. 461.

MELANTHIUS, an Athenian, Phocion, iv. 389.

MELANTHIUS, a poet, Cimon, iii. 217, 218.
MELANTHUS, a painter of the school of Sicyon, Aratus, v. 397.
MELAS, a river of Bœotia, Pelopidas, ii. 237; Sylla, iii. 183.
MELEAGER the hero, Theseus, i. 32.
MELESIAS, father of Thucydides, Pericles, i. 348; Nicias, iii. 309.
MELESIPPIDAS, a Spartan, Agesilaus, iv. 3.
MELIBŒA, a town of Thessaly, Pelopidas, ii. 252.
MELICERTA, Theseus, i. 27.
MELISSUS of Samos, philosopher, Themistocles, i. 246; Pericles, i. 375.
MELITE or MELITA, a district in Athens, Solon, i. 186; Themistocles, i. 271; Phocion, iv. 388.
MELITEA, a town of Thessaly, Sylla, iii. 182.
MELLARIA, a town of Spain, Sertorius, iii. 419.
MELON, a Theban, Pelopidas, ii. 228, 232, 234, 246; Agesilaus, iv. 35.
MELOS and MELIANS, Alcibiades, ii. 23; Lysander, iii. 129; Comparison of Crassus and Nicias, iii. 401.
CAIUS MEMMIUS, accuser of Lucullus, Lucullus, iii. 293; Cato the Younger, iv. 419 (?), 445.
MEMMIUS, Pompey's sister's husband, Sertorius, iii. 431; Pompey, iv. 71.
MEMNON, general of Darius, Alexander, iv. 202, 208.
MEMPHIS in Egypt, Lucullus, iii. 246.
MENANDER, put to death by Alexander, Alexander, iv. 260.
MENANDER, friend of Antigonus, Eumenes, iii. 453.
MENANDER in the Syracusan expedition, Nicias, iii. 336.

MENANDER (perhaps the same), commanding at Ægos-potami, Alcibiades, ii. 54.
MENANDER, the comic poet, Alexander, iv. 201.
MENANDER, officer of Mithridates, Lucullus, iii. 264.
MENAS the pirate, Antony, v. 195, 196.
MENDE, a town in Macedonia, Comparison of Nicias and Crassus, iii. 403.
MENDES (THE MENDESIAN PROVINCE) in Egypt, Agesilaus, iv. 54, 55.
MENECLIDAS, an orator at Thebes, Pelopidas, ii. 246, 247.
MENECRATES, a writer, Theseus, i. 28.
MENECRATES, called Jupiter, a physician, Agesilaus, iv. 31.
MENECRATES under Sextus Pompeius, Antony, v. 195.
MENEDEMUS, attending on Lucullus, Lucullus, iii. 264.
MENELAUS in Sophocles, Demetrius, v. 154. PORT OF MENELAUS in Africa, Agesilaus, iv. 57.
MENELAUS, brother of Ptolemy Lagus, Demetrius, v. 117.
MENEMACHUS, officer of Mithridates, Lucullus, iii. 264.
MENENIUS AGRIPPA, Coriolanus, ii. 65.
MENESTHES, who went with Theseus to Crete, Theseus, i. 16.
MENESTHEUS, son of Peteus, who commanded the Athenians at Troy, Theseus, i. 35, 36, 39; Cimon, iii. 223.
MENESTHEUS, an Athenian commander (son of Iphicrates), Phocion, iv. 374.
MENINX, an island on the coast of Africa, Marius, iii. 101.
MENIPPUS, an Athenian, Pericles, i. 359.

INDEX

MENIPPUS of Caria, an orator, Cicero, v. 41.
MENITID or TEMENITID gates of Syracuse, Dion, v. 288.
MENŒCEUS, son of Creon, Pelopidas, ii. 243.
MENŒTIUS, father of Patroclus, Aristides, ii. 337.
MENON, father of Theano, Alcibiades, ii. 32.
MENON, a workman with Phidias, Pericles, i. 381, 382.
MENON the Thessalian, in the service of Cyrus the Younger, Artaxerxes, v. 460.
MENON the Thessalian, commanding in the Lamian war, Pyrrhus, iii. 1; Phocion, iv. 395.
MENTOR, in Alexander's service, Eumenes, iii. 442.
MENYLLUS, commanding the Macedonian garrison, Phocion, iv. 399, 400, 401, 403.
MERIONES, the Homeric hero, Marcellus, ii. 286.
MEROPE, daughter of Erechtheus, Theseus, i. 18.
CORNELIUS MERULA, consul with Octavius (87 B.C.), Marius, iii. 103, 109.
MESOPOTAMIA, Lucullus, iii. 278, 284; Crassus, iii. 372, 374, 375, 389; Pompey, iv. 120; Demetrius, v. 108; Antony, v. 191, 198.
MESSALA, father of Valeria, Sylla's wife, Sylla, iii. 203.
MESSALA, consul (53 B. C.), Pompey, iv. 134.
MESSALA CORVINUS, son of the preceding, Brutus, v. 345-367, 370, 371, 379.
MESSALÆ, Comparison of Poplicola, and Solon, i. 239.
MESSAPIANS, Pyrrhus, iii. 18, 20; Agis, iv. 498.
MESSENA or MESSANA, the modern Messina in Sicily, Alcibiades, ii. 31; Timoleon, ii. 144, 158, 162;

Pyrrhus, iii. 33; Pompey, iv. 69; Cato the Younger, iv. 472; Dion, v. 317.
MESSENIA, MESSENE, and THE MESSENIANS, in Peloponnesus, Romulus, i. 74 (story of Aristomenes); Lycurgus, i. 97, 127 (the revolt); Pelopidas, ii. 246, 253 (the restoration); Philopœmen, ii. 399, 408, 409, 417-420; Flamininus, ii. 446; Comparison, ii. 454-456; Cimon, iii. 237, 238 (the revolt); Agesilaus, iv. 49, 51 (the restoration); Comparison, iv. 173; Alexander, iv. 280 (a Messenian); Agis, iv. 519 (Aristomenes); Cleomenes, iv. 525, 531, 533, 547, 548, 558; Comparison, iv. 623; Demosthenes, v. 15 (a Messenian); Demetrius, v. 139; Aratus, v. 433-436. In Philopœmen, Flamininus, Cleomenes, Demetrius, and Aratus, the reference is generally to Messene, the new city.
MESTRIUS FLORUS, a consular, Otho, v. 524.
METAGENES of Xypete, an architect, Pericles, i. 357.
METAPONTUM, town of Lucania, Fabius, i. 420.
METELLA, wife of Sylla, Sylla, iii. 161, 162, 171, 184, 200, 202, 204; Pompey, iv. 68; Cato the Younger, iv. 416. She is CÆCILIA METELLA.
METELLI, Comparison of Lysander and Sylla, iii. 207; Cæsar, iv. 308. The house of Metellus, Cato the Younger, iv. 442.
QUINTUS METELLUS MACEDONICUS, Marius, iii. 52; Comparison of Nicias and Crassus, iii. 401; Ti. Gracchus, iv. 583.
METELLUS DIADEMATUS, Coriolanus, ii. 72.
CÆCILIUS METELLUS (called Dalmaticus), the chief priest, father

of Sylla's wife, Marius, iii. 54, 55; Sylla, iii. 161; Pompey, iv. 60.

CÆCILIUS METELLUS, surnamed NUMIDICUS (brother of Dalmaticus), Comparison of Alcibiades and Coriolanus, ii. 116; Marius, iii. 58-63, 86-90, 105; Lucullus, iii. 243; Cato the Younger, iv. 449.

METELLUS PIUS, son of Numidicus, Cato the Elder, ii. 383; Marius, iii. 105; Sylla, iii. 160, 194; Lucullus, iii. 251; Crassus, iii. 356; Comparison, iii. 401; Sertorius, iii. 406, 419-423, 425, 427-429, 432-433, 439; Pompey, iv. 67, 79, 101; Cæsar, iv. 293.

METELLUS, commanding in Crete (Creticus), Pompey, iv. 96, 97.

METELLUS, tribune of the people (son of the preceding), Pompey, iv. 144; Comparison, iv. 174; Cæsar, iv. 328.

QUINTUS METELLUS CELER, Romulus, i. 53; Coriolanus, ii. 72.

QUINTUS METELLUS CELER (son, by adoption, of the preceding), Cicero, v. 54, 69.

METELLUS NEPOS, tribune with Cato (brother, by blood, of the preceding), Cæsar, iv. 311; Cato the Younger, iv. 434, 435, 441-445; Cicero, v. 62, 66, 67.

METELLUS SCIPIO (son of Scipio Nasica, adopted by Metellus Pius), father of Cornelia, Pompey's wife, Pompey, iv. 135, 145, 150, 152, 154; Comparison, iv. 171, 176; Cæsar, iv. 323, 333, 335, 337, 345, 346, 348; Cato the Younger, iv. 420, 466, 476-478, 482; Cicero, v. 53; Brutus, v. 325; Galba, v. 508; Otho, v. 522.

CAIUS METELLUS, Sylla, iii. 198.

METHYDRIUM, in Arcadia, Cleomenes, iv. 524.

METILIUS, tribune, Fabius, i. 404-407.

METON the astronomer, Alcibiades, ii. 24; Nicias, iii. 327.

METON, a Tarentine, Pyrrhus, iii. 17.

METROBIUS the scrivener, Cimon, iii. 227.

METROBIUS the player, Sylla, iii. 154.

METRODORUS the dancing man, Antony, v. 186.

METRODORUS of Scepsis, counsellor of Mithridates, Lucullus, iii. 271.

MICION, powerful at Athens, Aratus, v. 427.

MICION, a Macedonian officer, Phocion, iv. 395.

MICIPSA, king of Numidia, C. Gracchus, iv. 596.

MIDAS, king of Phrygia, Poplicola, i. 230; Flamininus, ii. 450; Alexander, iv. 202; Cæsar, iv. 269.

MIDIAS, accused by Demosthenes, Alcibiades, ii. 14; Demosthenes, v. 14.

MIDIAS, an Athenian exile, Sylla, iii. 173.

MIEZA, town of Macedonia, Alexander, iv. 187.

MILETUS and MILESIANS, Solon, i. 180, 181, 188; Pericles, i. 371, 373, 376; Lysander, iii. 119, 121; Alexander, iv. 200; Cæsar, iv. 288; Demetrius, v. 155. Milesian purple, Alcibiades, ii. 33. Milesian women, Lucullus, iii. 266; Crassus, iii. 395. The Milesiaca or Milesian stories, Crassus, iii. 394, 395.

MILAN. See MEDIOLANUM.

ANNIUS MILO, Cicero's friend, Cato the Younger, iv. 466; Cicero, v. 75, 76, 77.

MILO, a Macedonian officer, Æm. Paulus, ii. 187.

MILTAS the Thessalian, a prophet, Dion, v. 280, 282.

MILTIADES, Theseus, i. 7; Themistocles, i. 247, 248; Aristides, ii.

INDEX

314, 330, 345; Comparison, ii. 389; Cimon, iii. 217, 219, 223; Demetrius, v. 116.

MILTO, called ASPASIA by Cyrus the Younger, Pericles, i. 373; compare Artaxerxes, v. 470-472.

MIMALLONES, Alexander, iv. 180.

MINDARUS, a Spartan admiral, Alcibiades, ii. 40, 42, 43.

MINOA, on the coast of Megara, Nicias, iii. 315; Comparison, iii. 401.

MINOA, a town in Sicily, Dion, v. 284.

MINOS, king of Crete, Theseus, i. 13-20; Numa, i. 139; Cato the Elder, ii. 381; compare Demetrius, v. 150.

MINOTAUR, Theseus, i. 13-15, 17.

MINTURNÆ, a town on the Liris, Marius, iii. 97, 99, 100.

CAIUS MINUCIUS, a private man, Poplicola, i. 216.

MINUCIUS, dictator, Marcellus, ii. 267.

LUCIUS MINUCIUS (more correctly MARCUS), master of the horse, Fabius, i. 399, 401, 405-412; Comparison, i. 432, 433.

MARCUS MINUCIUS, one of the two first quæstors, Poplicola, i. 226.

MINUCIUS THERMUS, tribune of the people with Cato, Cato the Younger, iv. 443.

MISENUM, promontory and town of Campania, Marius, iii. 93; C. Gracchus, iv. 617; Antony, v. 196.

MITHRAS, the Persian deity, Pompey, iv. 90; Alexander, iv. 222; Artaxerxes, v. 444.

MITHRIDATES, son of Ariobarzanes, founder of the kingdom of Pontus, Demetrius, v. 105, 106.

MITHRIDATES, king of Pontus, Flamininus, ii. 452; Marius, iii. 91, 93, 94, 103, 108-110; Sylla, iii. 161, 162, 164, 167, 168, 171, 174, 182, 184-188, 192; Comparison, iii. 211, 212; Lucullus, iii. 245-267, 271, 272, 274, 277, 278, 282, 284, 286, 289, 291; Comparison, iii. 305; Crassus, iii. 370; Sertorius, iii. 409, 435-436; Pompey, iv. 83, 88, 98, 101-111, 114-116, 120; Cæsar, iv. 343; also Numa, i. 148.

MITHRIDATES, king of Commagene, Antony, v. 227.

MITHRIDATES, cousin to Monæses, Antony, v. 213, 215.

MITHRIDATES, a Persian, Artaxerxes, v. 451, 455-458.

MITHRIDATES of Pontus, Galba, v. 489, 490.

MITHROBARZANES, general of Tigranes, Lucullus, iii. 276.

MITHROPAUSTES, cousin of Xerxes, Themistocles, i. 279.

MITYLENE, a town in Lesbos, Solon, i. 190; Lucullus, iii. 248; Pompey, iv. 116, 161, 163; Ti. Gracchus, iv. 575.

MNASITHEUS, a companion of Aratus, Aratus, v. 392.

MNEMON, a surname, Marius, iii. 52; compare Artaxerxes, v. 441.

MNESICLES, architect of the Propylæa, Pericles, i. 358.

MNESIPHILUS of Phrearrhi, a philosopher, Themistocles, i. 246.

MNESIPTOLEMA, daughter of Themistocles, Themistocles, i. 280, 281, 283.

MNESTRA, Cimon, iii. 219.

MŒROCLES, an orator, Demosthenes, v. 16, 26.

MŒSIA and MŒSIANS, Otho, v. 513, 518, 525.

MOLON (see APOLLONIUS), Cæsar, iv. 288; Cicero, v. 41.

MOLUS or MORIUS, a river of Bœotia, Sylla, iii. 178, 181.

MOLOSSIANS, a people of Epirus, Theseus, i. 34, 37; Themistocles,

606 INDEX

i. 273; Pyrrhus, iii. 1, 2, 4, 6, 13, 26, 38, 45, 46; Demetrius, v. 127.
MOLOSSUS, an Athenian commander, Phocion, iv. 382.
MOLPADIA, an Amazon, Theseus, i. 30.
MONÆSES, a Parthian exile, Antony, v. 202, 213.
MONIME of Miletus, Lucullus, iii. 260; Pompey, iv. 110.
MORIUS. See MOLUS.
MOSCHIAN MOUNTAINS, Pompey, iv. 106.
MOTHONE, beyond Malea, Aratus, v. 396.
MUCIA, wife of Pompey, Pompey, iv. 117.
MUCIANUS, governor of Syria, Otho, v. 513.
THE MUCII (Mucius Scævola, the augur), Cicero, v. 39.
MUCIUS SCÆVOLA, Poplicola, i. 232.
MUCIUS SCÆVOLA, the lawyer, Sylla, iii. 204; Ti. Gracchus, iv. 576.
MUCIUS, father-in-law of the Younger Marius, Marius, iii. 95.
MUCIUS, tribune with Ti. Gracchus, Ti. Gracchus, iv. 582, 588.
CAIUS MUMMIUS, under Sylla, Sylla, iii. 166.
LUCIUS MUMMIUS ACHAICUS, who took Corinth, Philopœmen, ii. 421; Marius, iii. 52; Lucullus, iii. 267; Comparison of Nicias and Crassus, iii. 401.
MUMMIUS, lieutenant of Crassus, Crassus, iii. 362.
MUNATIUS PLANCUS (Titus), Pompey, iv. 136; Cato the Younger, iv. 467; Cicero, v. 64.
MUNATIUS PLANCUS (Lucius, his brother), Antony, v. 182, 224; Brutus, v. 338.
MUNATIUS (Rufus), friend of Cato the Younger, Cato the Younger, iv. 422, 439, 443, 446, 453, 455, 471.

MUNDA, field of battle, a town in Spain, Cæsar, iv. 348.
MUNYCHIA, port of Athens, Solon, i. 188; Sylla, iii. 174; Phocion, iv. 398, 402, 403; Demosthenes, v. 32; Demetrius, v. 109, 111, 140; Aratus, v. 419.
MUNYCHUS, son of Demophon, Theseus, i. 37.
MURCUS, Galba, v. 503.
MURENA, lieutenant of Sylla, Sylla, iii. 178, 181.
LUCIUS LICINIUS MURENA, Lucullus, iii. 261, 268, 270, 278; Cato the Younger, iv. 436, 437, 444; Cicero, v. 53, 76; Comparison, v. 96.
MUSEUM, hill in Athens, Theseus, i. 29; Demetrius, v. 140.
MUSEUM at Chæronea, Sylla, iii. 179.
MUSÆUS the poet, Marius, iii. 97.
MUTINA, now MODENA, Pompey, iv. 78; Antony, v. 180.
MYCALE, where the battle was, Camillus, i. 305; Pericles, i. 340; Æm. Paulus, ii. 198.
MYCENÆ, city of Argolis, Sertorius, iii. 416; Aratus, v. 414.
MYGDONIA, district of Mesopotamia, Lucullus, iii. 287.
MYLÆ, a town of Sicily, Timoleon, ii. 167.
MYLASA in Caria, Phocion, iv. 388.
MYNDUS in Caria, Marius, iii. 72.
MYRINE in Mysia, Demosthenes, v. 10.
MYRON of Phlya, Solon, i. 187.
MYRON or MYRO, an officer of Mithridates, Lucullus, iii. 264.
MYRONIDES, an Athenian general, Pericles, i. 363, 372; Comparison, i. 431; Aristides, ii. 323, 336.
MYRSILUS, a writer, Aratus, v. 389.
MYRTILUS, Pyrrhus's cup-bearer, Pyrrhus, iii. 6.

INDEX

MYRTO, granddaughter of Aristides, Aristides, ii. 345.
MYRTO, sister of Patroclus, Aristides, ii. 337.
MYSIANS, in Asia Minor, Theseus, i. 5.
MYUS, a town of Caria, Themistocles, i. 280.

N

NABATÆAN or NABATHÆAN ARABS, Pompey, iv. 152; Demetrius, v. 108; Antony, v. 201.
NABIS, tyrant of Lacedæmon, Philopœmen, ii. 409-413, 418; Flamininus, ii. 440; Comparison, ii. 456.
NAPLES, NEAPOLIS, NEAPOLITANS, Marcellus, ii. 272; Lucullus, iii. 296; Comparison, iii. 303; Pompey, iv. 138; Cicero, v. 46; Brutus, v. 342.
NARBO, town in Gaul, and GALLIA NARBONENSIS, Sertorius, iii. 419; Galba, v. 487.
NARNIA, in Umbria, Flamininus, ii. 423.
NARTHACIUM or MOUNT NARTHACIUS, in Thessaly, Agesilaus, iv. 24.
PUBLIUS SCIPIO NASICA, consul with Marcius (162 B. C.), Æm. Paulus, ii. 185-190, 194, 200; Marcellus, ii. 266; Cato the Elder, ii. 385.
PUBLIUS NASICA, pontifex maximus, Ti. Gracchus, iv. 582, 589, 592, 593.
NAUCRATES, a Lycian, Brutus, v. 352.
NAUPACTUS, on the Gulf of Corinth, Flamininus, ii. 443.
NAUPLIA, town of Argolis, Pyrrhus, iii. 46.
NAUSICRATES the rhetorician, Cimon, iii. 242.

NAUSITHOÜS of Salamis, Theseus, i. 16.
NAXOS, island in Ægean Sea, Theseus, i. 19, 20; Themistocles, i. 274; Camillus, i. 306; Pericles, i. 354; Nicias, iii. 311; Phocion, iv. 373.
NAXOS, town of Sicily, Nicias, iii. 331.
NEALCES, a painter, Aratus, v. 398.
NEANDER, an Epirot, Pyrrhus, iii. 2.
NEANTHES, an historical writer, Themistocles, i. 244.
NEAPOLIS, a quarter in Syracuse, Marcellus, ii. 284.
NEAPOLIS, near Agrigentum, Dion, v. 308.
NEARCHUS, Alexander's admiral, of Crete, Eumenes, iii. 442, 465; Alexander, iv. 191, 272, 273, 279-253.
NEARCHUS, a Pythagorean, Cato the Elder, ii. 350.
NECTANABIS, an Egyptian king, Agesilaus, iv. 53-56.
NELEUS of Scepsis, Sylla, iii. 189.
NEMEA and NEMEAN GAMES, Pericles, i. 367; Timoleon, ii. 152; Philopœmen, ii. 407; Flamininus, ii. 438; Cleomenes, iv. 540; Aratus, v. 391, 412, 413; NEMEA, as a woman, personified, Alcibiades, ii. 23.
NEOCHORUS of Haliartus, who killed Lysander, Lysander, iii. 150.
NEOCLES, father of Themistocles, Themistocles, i. 244; Aristides, ii. 310.
NEOCLES, son of Themistocles, Themistocles, i. 283.
NEO the Bœotian, with Perseus, Æm. Paulus, ii. 196. More correctly NEON.
NEON the Corinthian, Timoleon, ii. 142.
NEOPTOLEMUS, son of Achilles,

Pyrrhus, iii. 1; Alexander, iv. 179.
NEOPTOLEMUS (I., king of the Molossians), Pyrrhus, iii. 2.
NEOPTOLEMUS (II., grandson of the preceding), Pyrrhus, iii. 4-6.
NEOPTOLEMUS, captain of Alexander's guard, Eumenes, iii. 441, 446-449.
NEOPTOLEMUS, general of Mithridates, Marius, iii. 94; Lucullus, iii. 248.
CORNELIUS NEPOS, the historian, Marcellus, ii. 302; Comparison, ii. 304; Lucullus, iii. 300; Ti. Gracchus, iv. 592.
METELLUS NEPOS, Cæsar, iv. 311; Cato the Younger, iv. 434, 435, 442, 445; Cicero, v. 62, 66, 67.
NERO, LUCIUS DOMITIUS GERMANICUS, the emperor, Flamininus, ii. 440; Antony, v. 253; Galba, v. 477 and after, throughout; Otho, v. 509, 514, 528.
NERO, assumed as a surname by Otho, Otho, v. 511.
NERVII, tribe of Gauls, Cæsar, iv. 310.
NESTOR in Homer, Pelopidas, ii. 239; Cato the Elder, ii. 368; Brutus, v. 357.
NEW COMUM (NEOCOMUM), Cæsar, iv. 321.
NICÆA, wife of Alexander, in possession of Acrocorinthus, Aratus, v. 401.
NICÆA, town of Bithynia, Theseus, i. 28.
NICAGORAS the Messenian, Cleomenes, iv. 558.
NICAGORAS of Trœzen, Themistocles, i. 257.
NICANOR, friend of Antigonus, Eumenes, iii. 463.
NICANOR, sent by Cassander to Munychia, Phocion, iv. 403-406.
NICARCHUS, great grandfather of Plutarch, Antony, v. 235.

NICATOR. See SELEUCUS.
NICERATUS, father of Nicias, Alcibiades, ii. 16; Nicias, iii. 309.
NICERATUS of Heraclea, a poet, Lysander, iii. 134.
NICIAS, Life, iii. 307; Comparison, iii. 398; Alcibiades, ii. 1, 16-20, 24, 25, 28, 31; Pelopidas, ii. 224; Aristides, ii. 318; Flamininus, ii. 437.
NICIAS, steward of Ptolemy, Cato the Younger, iv. 456.
NICIAS, citizen of Engyium, Marcellus, ii. 287, 288.
NICIAS, a friend of Agesilaus, Agesilaus, iv. 20.
NICOCLES, the friend of Phocion, Phocion, iv. 386, 409.
NICOCLES, tyrant of Sicyon, Philopœmen, ii. 395; Aratus, v. 389, 391, 394.
NICOCREON, king of Salamis in Cyprus, Alexander, iv. 220.
NICODEMUS the Messenian, Demosthenes, v. 15.
NICODEMUS, a blind cripple, Pelopidas, ii. 223.
NICOGENES, the richest man in Æolia, Themistocles, i. 275.
NICOLAUS the philosopher, Brutus, v. 379, 380.
NICOMACHE, daughter of Themistocles, Themistocles, i. 283.
NICOMACHUS, a Greek of Carrhæ, Crassus, iii. 385.
NICOMACHUS, a youth, Alexander, iv. 247.
NICOMACHUS, a painter, Timoleon, ii. 164.
NICOMEDES, married to Sybaris, Themistocles, i. 283.
NICOMEDES, king of Bithynia, Sylla, iii. 185, 187; Cæsar, iv. 287.
NICOMEDIA, town of Bithynia, Lucullus, iii. 259.
NICON, an elephant, Pyrrhus, iii. 49.

NICON, a servant of Craterus, Alexander, iv. 239.
NICON, conqueror, Eutychus's ass, Antony, v. 231.
NICONIDES of Thessaly, an engineer, Lucullus, iii. 256.
NICOPOLIS, a rich lady, Sylla, iii. 154.
NICOPOLIS, near Actium, Antony, v. 228.
NICOSTRATA, the proper name of CARMENTA, Romulus, i. 68.
NIGER, friend of Antony, Antony, v. 219.
NIGER, a surname, Coriolanus, ii. 72.
PUBLIUS NIGIDIUS, a philosophical friend of Cicero, Cicero, v. 59.
NILE, Solon, i. 204; Sylla, iii. 183; Alexander, iv. 215.
NIPHATES, mountain in Armenia, Alexander, iv. 224.
NISÆA, port of Megara, Solon, i. 185, 187; Nicias, iii. 315; Phocion, iv. 383.
NISÆAN horse, Pyrrhus, iii. 13.
NISIBIS, town of Mesopotamia, Lucullus, iii. 287, 293; Comparison, iii. 305.
NOLA, town of Campania, Marcellus, ii. 272, 273, 274, 275; Sylla, iii. 164, 165.
NONACRIS, town of Arcadia, Alexander, iv. 284.
NONIUS, killed by Saturninus, Marius, iii. 87.
NONIUS, nephew of Sylla, Sylla, iii. 167.
NONIUS, with Pompey, Cicero, v. 80.
NORA, town of Cappadocia, Eumenes, iii. 453-456.
NORBANUS, acting with Carbo, consul (83 B.C.), Sylla, iii. 191; Sertorius, iii. 411.
NORBANUS, commanding under Antony, Brutus, v. 361.

NORICI, of the north-east Alps, Marius, iii. 69.
NUMA POMPILIUS, Life, i. 133; Comparison, i. 169; Theseus, i. 1; Romulus, i. 64, 68, 70; Camillus, i. 303, 308, 321; Coriolanus, ii. 59, 90, 111; Æm. Paulus, ii. 170; Marcellus, ii. 271; Cæsar, iv. 352; Phocion, iv. 370.
NUMANTIA and NUMANTINES, in Spain, Æm. Paulus, ii. 195; Marius, iii. 54, 67; Lucullus, iii. 295; Ti. Gracchus, iv. 570-573, 582, 593; C. Gracchus, iv. 612; Comparison, iv. 622.
NUMERIUS, a friend of Marius, Marius, iii. 95.
NUMERIUS, a friend of Pompey (perhaps Numerius Magius), Pompey, iv. 146.
NUMIDIANS, in the Carthaginian service, Fabius, i. 410, 428; Timoleon, ii. 156; Marcellus, ii. 276, 302; Comparison, ii. 306. Numidian kings, Cato the Elder, ii. 385; Marius, iii. 91, 102; Sylla, iii. 154; Cæsar, iv. 345, 348 (king Juba); C. Gracchus, iv. 616. NUMIDIA, Pompey, iv. 73. A Numidian horseman, Otho, v. 521.
NUMIDICUS. See METELLUS.
NUMISTRO, town of Lucania, Marcellus, ii. 294.
NUMITOR, king of Alba, Romulus, i. 44, 50, 75.
NURSIA, in the country of the Sabines, Sertorius, iii. 406.
NYMPHÆUM, near Apollonia, Sylla, iii. 190.
NYMPHIDIA, mother of the following, Galba, v. 485, 489.
NYMPHIDIUS SABINUS, prætorian præfect, Galba, v. 478, 483, 485, 487-490, 500, 508.
NYPSIUS the Neapolitan, commander of the garrison in Ortygia, Dion, v. 300, 303, 306.

NYSA, Alexander, iv. 262.
NYSÆUS, ruling in Syracuse (Dionysius the Younger's half brother), Timoleon, ii. 120.
NYSSA, sister of Mithridates, Lucullus, iii. 265.

O

OARSES, Artaxerxes, v. 441.
OCHUS, son of Artaxerxes II., Alexander, iv. 274; Artaxerxes, v. 469, 472-477. He is ARTAXERXES III.
OCTAVIA, sister of Augustus, Poplicola, i. 232; Marcellus, ii. 302; Antony, v. 195, 197, 199, 200, 218, 225, 240, 249, 252, 253.
OCTAVIAN (OCTAVIANUS), Augustus Cæsar, Antony, v. 175. See CÆSAR.
OCTAVIUS, i. e. OCTAVIANUS, Brutus, v. 352. See the note.
OCTAVIUS, father of Augustus, Cicero, v. 88.
CAIUS OCTAVIUS, a pretendent conspirator, Cæsar, iv. 362.
CNÆUS OCTAVIUS, who took Perseus, Æm. Paulus, ii. 199, 200.
OCTAVIUS, consul with Cinna (87 B. C.), Marius, iii. 103, 104, 105, 109; Sylla, iii. 171; Sertorius, iii. 409.
OCTAVIUS, governor of Cilicia, Lucullus, iii. 250.
LUCIUS OCTAVIUS, lieutenant of Pompey, in Crete, Pompey, iv. 97.
MARCUS OCTAVIUS, tribune of the people, Ti. Gracchus, iv. 577-582, 584; C. Gracchus, iv. 599.
MARCUS OCTAVIUS, at Actium with Antony, Antony, v. 231.
MARCUS OCTAVIUS, in Africa with Cato, Cato the Younger, iv. 486.
OCTAVIUS, lieutenant of Crassus, Crassus, iii. 387, 390-393.

OCTAVIUS, of African descent, Cicero, v. 66.
ŒA, Attic township, Pericles, i. 350.
ŒCHALIA in Eubœa, Theseus, i. 9.
ŒDIPUS, in Sophocles, Demetrius, v. 156. Œdipus's well, Sylla, iii. 182.
ŒNANTHES, an Egyptian, Cleomenes, iv. 557.
ŒNARUS, priest of Bacchus, Theseus, i. 19.
ŒNEIS, Cimon's tribe, Cimon, iii. 238.
ŒNIADÆ, people of Acarnania, Pericles, i. 367; Alexander, iv. 249.
ŒNOPION, son of Theseus and Ariadne, Theseus, i. 19.
ŒNUS, river of Sparta, Lycurgus, i. 95.
ŒTÆANS, Pericles, i. 365.
LUCRETIUS OFELLA, Sylla, iii. 196, 200; Comparison, iii. 208.
OLBIANS, in Mauritania, Sertorius, iii. 416.
OLBIUS, servant of Nicogenes, Themistocles, i. 275.
OLIGYRTUS, a fortress in Arcadia, Cleomenes, iv. 550.
OLIZON, opposite Artemisium, Themistocles, i. 254.
OLOCRUM (MOUNT OLOCRUS), in Macedonia, Æm. Paulus, ii. 193.
OLORUS, king of Thrace, Cimon, iii. 217.
OLORUS, father of Thucydides, ibid.
OLTHACUS, chief of the Dandarians, Lucullus, iii. 263.
OLYMPIA and THE OLYMPIC GAMES, Theseus, i. 27; Lycurgus, i. 87, 116, 120 (usage for Spartan conquerors); Numa, i. 133 (visit of Pythagoras), 145; Solon, i. 201 (usage for Athenian conquerors); compare ii. 345; Themistocles, i. 250, 265, 274

INDEX 611

(Hiero's tent); Alcibiades, ii. 15; compare v. 1; Æm. Paulus, ii. 202 (Phidias's Jove); Pelopidas, ii. 259; Aristides, ii. 325, 345; Cato the Elder, ii. 354 (Cimon's horses); Sylla, iii. 169; Agesilaus, iv. 19, 29 (Cynisca); Alexander, iv. 181 (Philip's victory); Cato the Younger, iv. 465; Agis, iv. 508 (the oracle); Demosthenes, v. 1, 10; Demetrius, v. 113; Otho, v. 515. The Olympic truce, Lycurgus, i. 87, 121. Lists of victors, Numa, i. 134.

OLYMPIAS, wife of Philip of Macedon, Eumenes, iii. 456, 457; Alexander, iv. 179, 180, 181, 184, 189, 192, 214, 235, 274, 283, 285; Demetrius, v. 123.

OLYMPIC GAMES. See OLYMPIA.

OLYMPIODORUS, serving with Aristides, Aristides, ii. 327.

OLYMPUS, mountain in Thessaly, Æm. Paulus, ii. 183, 184, 186.

OLYMPUS, in Cilicia or Lycia, Pompey, iv. 89.

OLYMPUS, Cleopatra's physician, Antony, v. 248.

The OLYNTHIANS, of Olynthus in Macedonia, Demosthenes, v. 10, and compare Alexander, iv. 255.

OMISES, a Persian, Artaxerxes, v. 444.

OMPHALE, queen of Lydia, Theseus, i. 7; Pericles, i. 372; Comparison of Antony and Demetrius, v. 257.

ONEA, mountains in Megaris, Cleomenes, iv. 542.

ONESICRITUS, Alexander's historian, Alexander, iv. 188, 196, 243, 264, 266, 271, 272.

ONOMARCHUS, with Antigonus, Eumenes, iii. 465.

ONOMARCHUS, the Phocian, Timoleon, ii. 158.

ONOMASTUS, Otho's freedman, Galba, v. 501.

OPHELTAS, a king of the Bœotians, Cimon, iii. 213.

OPHELTAS, ruler of Cyrene, Demetrius, v. 116.

LUCIUS OPIMIUS, consul 121 B. C., C. Gracchus, iv. 607, 609-611, 613, 616.

OPLACUS, a Frentanian, Pyrrhus, iii. 23.

CAIUS OPPIUS, Cæsar's friend, Pompey, iv. 70; Cæsar, iv. 307.

OPUNTIANS (Locrians), Flamininus, ii. 428.

ORCHALIDES, hill in Bœotia, Lysander, iii. 150.

ORCHOMENUS, town in Arcadia, Cleomenes, iv. 524, 527, 546, 550; Aratus, v. 423, 431.

ORCHOMENUS and ORCHOMENIANS, in Bœotia, Pelopidas, ii. 237-238; Comparison, ii. 303; Lysander, iii. 147; Sylla, iii. 183-185, 190; Cimon, iii. 215; Lucullus, iii. 247, 258; Agesilaus, iv. 26.

ORCYNII, in Cappadocia, Eumenes, iii. 452.

ORESTEUM, town in Arcadia, Aristides, ii. 323.

ORESTES (L. Aurelius), the consul (B. C. 126), C. Gracchus, iv. 595, 596.

OREUS, town in Eubœa, Æm. Paulus, ii. 178.

OREXARTES, river of Scythia, Alexander, iv. 243.

ORFIDIUS, in command of a legion, Otho, v. 522.

ORICUS or ORICUM, seaport of Epirus, Æm. Paulus, ii. 204; Pompey, iv. 148; Cæsar, iv. 330.

ORITES, Indian people, Alexander, iv. 272.

ORNEUS, son of Erechtheus, Theseus, i. 35.

ORNIS, near Corinth, Aratus, v. 404.

ORNYTUS, Theseus, i. 9.

OROANDES of Crete, a shipmaster, Æm. Paulus, ii. 199.
OROBAZUS, Parthian ambassador, Sylla, iii. 157, 158.
OROMAZES or OROMASDES, the Persian divinity, Alexander, iv. 221; Artaxerxes, v. 474.
ORONTES, a Persian, Artaxerxes, v. 471; Aratus, v. 389 (? the same).
OROPUS and OROPIANS, in Attica, Cato the Elder, ii. 379; Demosthenes, v. 5.
ORPHEUS, Comparison of Lucullus and Cimon, iii. 302; Alexander, iv. 196.
ORSODATES, Alexander, iv. 260.
ORTHAGORAS, a diviner, Timoleon, ii. 123.
ORTHOPAGUS, a height near Chæronea, Sylla, iii. 178.
ORYSSUS of Crete, Pyrrhus, iii. 45.
OSCA, a city in Spain, Sertorius, iii. 422, 437.
OSTANES, younger son of Darius Nothus, Artaxerxes, v. 441, 445, 465.
OSTIA, seaport of Rome, Marius, iii. 95; Cæsar, iv. 352; Otho, v. 511.
OTACILIUS, brother of Marcellus, Marcellus, ii. 263.
OTRYÆ, in Phrygia, Lucullus, iii. 254.
MARCUS OTHO (Salvius), the emperor, Life, v. 509; Galba, v. 496-497, 499-502, 503, 506, 507.
MARCUS OTHO (Roscius, author of the Roscian law), Cicero, v. 51.
OVICULA, Fabius's surname, Fabius, i. 395.
OXATHRES, younger son of Darius Nothus, Artaxerxes, v. 441, 445.
OXUS, river in Asia, Alexander, iv. 260.
OXYARTES, a Persian, Alexander, iv. 261, 274.
OXYDRACÆ, Alexander, iv. 259.

P

PACCUS or PACCIUS, servant of Cato the Elder, Cato the Elder, ii. 362.
PACHES, the Athenian general, Aristides, ii. 345; Nicias, iii. 314.
PACHYNUS, cape in Sicily, Dion, v. 283.
CAIUS PACCIANUS, dressed up for Crassus, Crassus, iii. 394.
PACCIANUS, lieutenant of Sylla, Sertorius, iii. 415.
VIBIUS PACIANUS, friend of Crassus, Crassus, iii. 355, 356.
PACORUS, son of Hyrodes, Crassus, iii. 395, 397; Antony, v. 198.
PADUA or PATAVIUM, Cæsar, iv. 340.
PÆANIA, Demosthenes's township, Demosthenes, v. 31.
PÆDARETUS, a Spartan, Lycurgus, i. 123.
PÆON the Amathusian, a writer, Theseus, i. 19.
PÆONIANS, on the border of Thrace and Macedon, Æm. Paulus, ii. 190; Pyrrhus, iii. 11; Pompey, iv. 115 (Pannonia); Alexander, iv. 234.
PÆSTUM or POSIDONIA, the Greek colony in Lucania, Cimon, iii. 240.
PAGASÆ, port of Thessaly, Themistocles, i. 268.
PALATINE HILL or PALATIUM, at Rome, Romulus, i. 41, 65, 67, 70; Poplicola, i. 234 (Clœlia's statue); Camillus, i. 322 (Romulus's staff); Sertorius, iii. 436; C. Gracchus, iv. 607 (his house); Cicero, v. 46 (his house), 55, 60; Galba, v. 477, 479, 501-504; (Palatine Apollo) 501.
PALESTINE, Lucullus, iii. 261; Pompey, iv. 120.
PALLANTIUM, town of Arcadia,

INDEX

Cleomenes, iv. 524; Aratus, v. 421.
PALLAS, brother of Ægeus, and PALLANTIDÆ, Theseus, i. 4, 12.
PALLENE, Attic township, Theseus, i. 12.
PAMMENES, a Theban, Pelopidas, ii. 239, 249.
PAMPHILUS the painter, of the school of Sicyon, Aratus, v. 397.
PAMPHYLIA, in Asia Minor, Cimon, iii. 230; Pompey, iv. 164; Alexander, iv. 201; Brutus, v. 321.
PANACTUM, a fort in Attica, Alcibiades, ii. 18; Nicias, iii. 321; Demetrius, v. 125.
PANÆTIUS the philosopher, Aristides, ii. 309, 346; Cimon, iii. 219; Demosthenes, v. 15.
PANÆTIUS, in a Tenian galley, Themistocles, i. 260.
PANDION, king of Athens, Theseus, i. 12.
PANDOSIA, town of Italy, Pyrrhus, iii. 22.
PANNONIA and PANNONIANS, Otho, v. 513, 518; compare Pompey, iv. 115.
PANOPE or PANOPEUS, a town in Phocis, and PANOPEANS, Lysander, iii. 149; Sylla, iii. 176.
PANOPEUS, father of Ægle, Theseus, i. 31.
PANSA, consul with Hirtius, Æm. Paulus, ii. 214; Cicero, v. 86, 89; Antony, v. 180.
PANTALEON, the Ætolian, Aratus, v. 418.
PANTAUCHUS, Demetrius's general, Pyrrhus, iii. 9; Demetrius, v. 148.
PANTEUS, a Spartan, Cleomenes, iv. 546, 562, 563.
PANTHOIDES, married to Italia, Themistocles, i. 283.
PANTHOIDES, a Spartan, Pelopidas, ii. 236.

PAPHLAGONIA, in Asia Minor, Sylla, iii. 185, 186; Lucullus, iii. 288; Eumenes, iii. 443, 448; Agesilaus, iv. 16; Pompey, iv. 120; Alexander, iv. 202; Antony, v. 227.
PAPHOS, town in Cyprus, Cato the Younger, iv. 452.
PAPIRIA, wife of Æm. Paulus, Æm. Paulus, ii. 173.
MARCUS PAPIRIUS, Camillus, i. 311.
PAPPUS, an historian, Demosthenes, v. 34.
PARÆTONIUM, west of Alexandria, Antony, v. 236.
PARALUS, son of Pericles, Pericles, i. 372.
PARAPOTAMIANS, in Phocis, Sylla, iii. 177.
PARAUÆA, on the border of Macedonia, Pyrrhus, iii. 7.
PARIS, son of Priam, Theseus, i. 37; Comparison, i. 86; Comparison of Sylla and Lysander, iii. 211; Alexander, iv. 198 (Paris's harp); Comparison of Antony and Demetrius, v. 257; Galba, v. 495.
PARISCAS, attending on Cyrus, Artaxerxes, v. 452.
PARMA, town of Italy, Marius, iii. 85.
PARMENIDES the philosopher, Pericles, i. 342.
PARMENIO, Alexander's general, Alexander, iv. 181, 191, 198, 204, 208, 220, 224-226, 228, 236, 246, 247, 248, 249.
PARNASSUS, mountain in Phocis, Sylla, iii. 175.
PARRHASIUS the painter, Theseus, i. 5.
The PARTHENON at Athens, Pericles, i. 357; Demetrius, v. 125, 130; Comparison, v. 257, and, under the name of the Hecatompedon, Cato the Elder, ii. 354.

614 INDEX

PARTHIA and THE PARTHIANS. See, especially, the lives of Crassus, iii. 352, and from 370 to the end, with the Comparison; and Antony, v. 169, 188; and from 191 to 222 and the Comparison; also Sylla, iii. 157 (an embassy); Lucullus, iii. 261, 270, 284, 292, 293 (their relations to Tigranes); Nicias, iii. 307; Eumenes, iii. 465; Pompey, iv. 105, 108, 111 (his own dealings), 112, 130, 132, 135 (Crassus's disaster), 138, 156, 162, 164, 165; Alexander, iv. 242; Cæsar, iv. 319 (Crassus's death), 351, 353 (his designs); Cicero, v. 77; Demetrius, v. 122 (habit of their kings); Brutus, v. 325, 342, 343, 345, 369; Comparison, v. 384. The Parthian language, Antony, v. 191, 213.

PARYSATIS, wife of Darius Nothus, Artaxerxes, v. 441, 444, 446, 456-461, 466.

PASACAS, Cyrus's horse, Artaxerxes, v. 449.

PASARGADÆ, ancient city in Persia, Artaxerxes, v. 442.

PASEAS, tyrant of Sicyon, Aratus, v. 387, 389.

PASICRATES, king of Soli in Cyprus, Alexander, iv. 219.

PASIPHAE, wife of Minos, Theseus, i. 17.

PASIPHAE, her oracle, Agis, iv. 505; Cleomenes, iv. 527.

PASIPHON, a writer, Nicias, iii. 312.

PASITIGRIS, the Tigris river, Eumenes, iii. 459.

PASSARO, in the Molossian country, Pyrrhus, iii. 6.

PATÆCUS, who boasted he had Æsop's soul, Solon, i. 182.

PATAREANS, Brutus, v. 320, 354.

PATAVIUM or PADUA, Cæsar, iv. 340.

PATRÆ, town of Achaia, Alcibiades, ii. 21; Cato the Elder, ii. 364; Aratus, v. 433.

PATROBIUS, favorite of Nero, Galba, v. 493, 507.

PATROCLES, counsellor of Seleucus, Demetrius, v. 157.

PATROCLUS the hero, Theseus, i. 37; Aristides, ii. 337; Alexander, iv. 256; and compare p. 197.

PATRON, companion of Evander, Romulus, i. 55.

PATRONIS, village of Phocis, Sylla, iii. 175.

SUETONIUS PAULINUS, Roman general, Otho, v. 515, 517-518, 520, 522.

LUCIUS ÆMILIUS PAULUS, father of Æmilius Paulus, killed at Cannæ, Fabius, i. 413, 416; Æm. Paulus, ii. 170; Marcellus, ii. 273.

ÆMILIUS PAULUS (also Lucius), Life, ii. 170; Comparison, ii. 217; Timoleon, ii. 119; Cato the Elder, ii. 369, 377, 382; Sylla, iii. 170; Aratus, v. 440; Galba, v. 476.

PAULUS, consul with Marcellus (50 B. C.), brother of Lepidus, Pompey, iv. 139; Cæsar, iv. 321; Cicero, v. 90; Antony, v. 182; THE BASILICA PAULI, Cæsar, iv. 321; Galba, v. 504.

PAUSANIAS, assassin of Philip, Alexander, iv. 191; Demosthenes, v. 24.

PAUSANIAS the physician, Alexander, iv. 238.

PAUSANIAS, an officer of Seleucus, Demetrius, v. 161.

PAUSANIAS, son of Cleombrotus, regent of Sparta, Lycurgus, i. 117; Themistocles, i. 271, 272; Aristides, ii. 323, 327, 329, 333, 336, 339, 340; Comparison, ii. 389; Cimon, iii. 221; Comparison, iii. 305; Agis, iv. 498.

PAUSANIAS, son of Plistoanax, king

of Sparta, Lysander, iii. 128, 138, 147-149; Agis, iv. 498.

PEDA or PEDUM, town of Latium, Coriolanus, ii. 94.

PEDALIUM, near Sinope, Lucullus, iii. 273.

PEGÆ, the Fountains, port of Megara, Pericles, i. 367; Aratus, v. 428, 429.

PELAGON, an Eubœan, Themistocles, i. 253.

PELASGUS, Pyrrhus, iii. 1.

PELASGIANS, Romulus, i. 41.

PELEUS, Theseus, i. 10; Alexander, iv. 184.

PELIAS, father of Acastus, Sylla, iii. 204.

PELIGNIANS, people of Italy, Æm. Paulus, ii. 192.

PELLA, town of Macedonia, Æm. Paulus, ii. 196; Eumenes, iii. 444; Alexander, iv. 275; Demetrius, v. 151, 152.

LUCIUS PELLA, disgraced by Brutus, Brutus, v. 358.

PELLENE, town of Achæa, and PELLENIANS, Cleomenes, iv. 539; Aratus, v. 416, 425, 440.

PELLENE, in Laconia, Agis, iv. 503.

PELOPIDAS, Life, ii. 220; Comparison with Marcellus, ii. 303; Timoleon, ii. 164; Aristides, ii. 309; Agesilaus, iv. 35; Aratus, v. 400; Artaxerxes, v. 465.

PELOPONNESUS and THE PELOPONNESIANS, Theseus, i. 3, 7, 8, 26, and elsewhere frequent.

THE PELOPONNESIAN WAR, Lycurgus, i. 126 (Thucydides's history); Pericles, i. 378; Coriolanus, ii. 76; Aristides, ii. 309; Lysander, iii. 115, 150; Cleomenes, iv. 551; Antony, v. 237.

PELOPS, son of Tantalus, Theseus, i. 3, 7. PELOPIDÆ, Marius, iii. 52.

PELOPS the Byzantine, Cicero, v. 64.

PELUSIUM, town in Egypt, Pompey, iv. 165; Antony, v. 167, 241; Brutus, v. 355.

PENELOPE, wife of Ulysses, Demetrius, v. 129.

PENEUS, river of Thessaly, Flamininus, ii. 425.

PENTAPYLA, in Syracuse, Dion, v. 288.

PENTELICAN MARBLE, Poplicola, i. 229.

PENTELEUM, town of Arcadia, Cleomenes, iv. 539; Aratus, v. 425.

PENTHEUS, king of Thebes, Crassus, iii. 396.

PEPARETHUS, island in the Ægean Sea, Romulus, i. 43, 50.

PERDICCAS, king of Macedon, Comparison of Crassus and Nicias, iii. 400.

PERDICCAS, Alexander's general, Eumenes, iii. 441, 444-446, 450; Alexander, iv. 197, 238, 284; Demosthenes, v. 36.

PERGAMIA, in Crete, Lycurgus i. 132. (The district of Pergamus.)

PERGAMUS, in Mysia, Sylla, iii. 167, 168, 186; Lucullus, iii. 247; Cæsar, iv. 288; Cato the Younger, iv. 423; Antony, v. 225 (the library); Brutus, v. 320 (the Pergamenians).

PERIANDER, tyrant of Corinth, Solon, i. 180, 187; Aratus, v. 389.

PERIBŒA, mother of Ajax, Theseus, i. 31.

PERICLES, Life, i. 337; Comparison, i. 431; Lycurgus, i. 111; Themistocles, i. 246, 257; Alcibiades, ii. 3, 6, 10, 11, 18, 24; Pelopidas, ii. 224; Aristides, ii. 310, 341, 344, 345; Cato the Elder, ii. 358; Cimon, iii. 232, 234, 235, 239; Nicias, iii. 309, 310, 315, 320, 341; Comparison, iii. 398; Pompey, iv. 146; Phocion, iv. 374; Demosthenes, v. 7, 10, 16, 22; Cicero, v. 82.

PERICLIDAS, a Spartan envoy, Cimon, iii. 237.
PERIGUNE, daughter of Sinnis, Theseus, i. 8.
PERINTHUS, town of Thrace, and PERINTHIANS. Alexander, iv. 276; Phocion, iv. 382; Demosthenes, v. 19.
PERIPATETICS, Sylla, iii. 189; Cato the Younger, iv. 487, 489; Cicero, v. 64; Brutus, v. 344.
PERIPHEMUS, a hero of Salamis, Solon, i. 185.
PERIPHETES, called CORYNETES, Theseus, i. 8.
PERIPHORETUS, name given to Artemon, Pericles, i. 376.
PERIPOLTAS the prophet, Cimon, iii. 213.
PERIPOLTAS, surname of Damon, ibid.
PERITAS, Alexander's dog, Alexander, iv. 266.
PERITHŒDÆ, an Attic township, Alcibiades, ii. 16; Nicias, iii. 323.
PERPENNA VENTO, Sertorius, iii. 423, 424, 436-440; Pompey, iv. 69, 81, 83, 84.
PERRHÆBIA, part of Thessaly, and PERRHÆBIANS, Æm. Paulus, ii. 185; Flamininus, ii. 436.
PERSÆUS, a philosopher, commanding in Corinth, Aratus, v. 402, 408.
PERSEUS the hero, Cimon, iii. 216.
PERSEUS, king of Macedon, Æm. Paulus, ii. 176, 177, 180-183, 187, 192, 196-209, 213; Comparison, ii. 217; Cato the Elder, ii. 369, 377; Demetrius, v. 164; Aratus, v. 440.
PERSIA or PERSIS, meaning Persia proper, Eumenes, iii. 459; Alexander, iv. 232; Artaxerxes, v. 447. THE PERSIANS, see, in general, the lives of Themistocles, Aristides, Cimon, Agesilaus, Alexander, Artaxerxes, and the Comparisons. Also, Solon, i. 207; Camillus, i. 305; Pericles, i. 371-373; Alcibiades, ii. 33, 35; Æm. Paulus, ii. 182; Pelopidas, ii. 253; Cato the Elder, ii. 365; Flamininus, ii. 431; Lysander, iii. 116, 140; Comparison of Nicias and Crassus, iii. 401; Pompey, iv. 103, 106; Demosthenes, v. 23; Antony, v. 202; Brutus, v. 354; Persian women, Eumenes, iii. 442; Alexander, iv. 208; Demetrius, v. 136; Persian language, Themistocles, i. 279. Persian fashions, Eumenes, iii. 447; the dress, Alexander, iv. 223, 242, 251; the money, Agesilaus, iv. 23; Artaxerxes, v. 443. Compare MEDIA and THE MEDES.
PESSINUS, town of Galatia, Marius, iii. 72; Cato the Younger, iv. 428.
PETELIA, town of Bruttium, Marcellus, ii. 299. Mountains of Petelia, Crassus, iii. 364.
PETELINE GROVE at Rome, Camillus, i. 328.
PETEUS, son of Orneus, Theseus, i. 35.
PETICIUS, a shipmaster, Pompey, iv. 160, 161.
PETILIUS the prætor, Numa, i. 167.
THE PETILII, tribunes of the people, two brothers, Cato the Elder, ii. 367.
PETINUS, favorite of Nero, Galba, v. 493.
PETRA, town in Arabia, Pompey, iv. 114, 115; Antony, v. 236.
PETRA, town in Thessaly, Æm. Paulus, ii. 185.
PETROCHUS, above Chæronea, Sylla, iii. 179.
GRANIUS PETRO, quæstor, Cæsar, iv. 305.
PETRONIUS, lieutenant of Crassus, Crassus, iii. 392, 398.

INDEX

PETRONIUS TURPILIANUS, Galba, v. 490, 491, 493.
PEUCESTES, officer of Alexander, Eumenes, iii. 458, 459, 461, 463; Alexander, iv. 238, 239, 268, 269.
PHÆA, the Crommyonian sow, Theseus, i. 9.
PHÆAX of Salamis, Theseus, i. 16.
PHÆAX, an Athenian statesman, Alcibiades, ii. 16, 17; Nicias, iii. 325; Agesilaus, iv. 22 (?).
PHÆDIMUS, Eumenes, iii. 462.
PHÆDO, archon at Athens, Theseus, i. 39.
PHÆDRA, wife of Theseus, Theseus, i. 31.
PHÆNARETE, wife of Samon, Pyrrhus, iii. 7.
PHÆSTUS, in Crete, Solon, i. 187.
PHAETHON, first king of the Molossians, Pyrrhus, iii. 1.
PHALERUM, port of Athens, Theseus, i. 21; Themistocles, i. 259; Aristides, ii. 308, 345; Demetrius, v. 109, 110 (the Phalerian, i. e. Demetrius the Phalerian; see his name).
PHALINUS, a Zacynthian, Artaxerxes, v. 454.
PHANIAS the Lesbian, a philosopher and historian, Solon, i. 189; Themistocles, i. 244, 253, 262, 277, 280.
PHANIPPUS or PHÆNIPPUS, archon in the year of Marathon, Aristides, ii. 316.
PHANODEMUS, historian, Themistocles, i. 261; Cimon, iii. 231, 241.
PHARAX the Spartan, Timoleon, ii. 132; Comparison, ii. 218; Dion, v. 308.
PHARMACUSA, island near Miletus, Cæsar, iv. 287.
PHARNABAZUS, a Persian satrap, Alcibiades, ii. 34, 41, 45, 55, 58; Lysander, iii. 135, 137, 142; Agesilaus, iv. 12, 16-19, 25, 33; Artaxerxes, v. 463, 464, 467, 471.

PHARNABAZUS, son of Artabazus, Eumenes, iii. 448.
PHARNACES, son of Mithridates, Pompey, iv. 116; Cæsar, iv. 343.
PHARNACIA or PHERNACIA, town in Pontus, Lucullus, iii. 265.
PHARNAPATES, general of the Parthians, Antony, v. 197.
PHAROS, island in the Adriatic Sea (?), Aratus, v. 436.
PHAROS, in the port of Alexandria, Alexander, iv. 215; Cæsar, iv. 343; Antony, v. 194, 237.
PHARSALUS, PHARSALIA, and PHARSALIANS, Pericles, i. 389; Pelopidas, ii. 250, 256; Agesilaus, iv. 24; Pompey, iv. 152, 156; Comparison, iv. 175; Cæsar, iv. 335, 345, 355; Cato the Younger, iv. 475, 477; Cicero, v. 81, 82; Antony, v. 173, 228; Brutus, v. 323; Otho, v. 523.
PHARYGÆ, a small village of Phocis, Phocion, iv. 406.
PHASELIS, town of Lycia, Cimon, iii. 230; Alexander, iv. 202.
PHASIS, river of Pontus, Lucullus, iii. 288; Comparison, iii. 305; Pompey, iv. 107.
PHAYLLUS of Crotona, the wrestler, Alexander, iv. 229.
PHEGÆA, Attic township, Alcibiades, ii. 31.
PHENEUS, town of Arcadia, Cleomenes, iv. 539; Aratus, v. 425.
PHERÆ, town of Achæa, Cleomenes, iv. 536.
PHERÆ, town of Thessaly, and PHERÆANS, Pelopidas, ii. 248-250, 255, 261; Galba, v. 477.
PHEREBŒA, wife of Theseus, Theseus, i. 31.
PHERECLES, at Dodona, Lysander, iii. 144.
PHERECLUS, son of Amarsyas, Theseus, i. 16.
PHERECYDES, an historical writer, Theseus, i. 17, 27.

PHERECYDES the philosopher, Pelopidas, ii. 243; Sylla, iii. 204; Agis, iv. 506.

PHERENDATES, commander at the Eurymedon, Cimon, iii. 231.

PHERENICUS, a Theban exile, Pelopidas, ii. 225, 228.

PHERISTUS of Elea or Velia, Timoleon, ii. 163.

PHERNACIA, more correctly PHARNACIA, in Pontus, Lucullus, iii. 265.

PHIDIAS the sculptor, Pericles, i. 339, 357, 359, 381-383; Æm. Paulus, ii. 202.

PHIDON, Demetrius so named, Alexander, iv. 257.

PHILA, daughter of Antipater, wife of Demetrius, Demetrius, v. 116, 123, 131, 136, 137, 144, 154, 155, 164; Comparison, v. 255.

PHILADELPHUS, a surname, Coriolanus, ii. 71.

PHILADELPHUS, king of Paphlagonia, Antony, v. 227.

PHILAIDÆ, the township of Pisistratus, named from PHILÆUS, son of Ajax, Solon, i. 186.

PHILAGRUS, tutor of Metellus Nepos, Cicero, v. 67.

PHILARGYRUS, freedman of Cato the Younger, Cato the Younger, iv. 455.

PHILARUS, river of Bœotia, Lysander, iii. 150.

PHILETAS, a poet, Pericles, i. 339.

PHILIDES or DIPHILIDES, a breeder of horses, Themistocles, i. 249.

PHILINNA, mother of Philip Arrhidæus, Alexander, iv. 284.

PHILIPPI, town of Macedonia, and THE CAMPI PHILIPPI, field of battle, Sylla, iii. 187; Cæsar, iv. 364, 365; Cato the Younger, iv. 494; Antony, v. 236; Brutus, v. 345, 349, 359, 361, 379.

PHILIPPIDES, the comic poet, Demetrius, v. 114, 115.

PHILIP (II.), king of Macedon, father of Alexander. See the lives of Alexander, iv. 179-186, 188-192, 194, 200, 217, 218, 248, 256, 276, 284; Phocion, iv. 380, 382, 386, 400; Demosthenes, v. 10, 11, 14, 16, 18-20, 22-24; Comparison, v. 98. Some additional particulars are given in Pericles, i. 338; Timoleon, ii. 138; Pelopidas, ii. 240, 248; Eumenes, iii. 441; Demetrius, v. 123, 150. He is mentioned also in Camillus, i. 306; Æm. Paulus, ii. 182, 206; Sertorius, iii. 406; Eumenes, iii. 462, 464; Demetrius, v. 112, 128; Comparison, v. 257; Aratus, v. 397, 408.

PHILIP (III.) ARRHIDÆUS, son of Philip II. by Philinna, Eumenes, iii. 457; compare Alexander, iv. 190, 283, 284; Phocion, iv. 404-407.

PHILIP (IV.), son of Cassander, Demetrius, v. 141.

PHILIP (V.), son of Demetrius II., Æm. Paulus, ii. 176-178; Cato the Elder, ii. 363, 371; Philopœmen, ii. 403, 408, 410, 412; Flamininus, ii. 424-436, 438, 443; Comparison, ii. 454, 455; Demetrius, v. 105; Aratus, v. 401, 432-437, 440.

PHILIP THE ACARNANIAN, Alexander's physician, Alexander, iv. 204.

PHILIP, brother of Demetrius, Demetrius, v. 102, 126.

PHILIP of Chalcis, a writer, Alexander, iv. 243.

PHILIP, first husband of Berenice, Pyrrhus, iii. 5.

PHILIP, freedman of Pompey, Pompey, iv. 167-169.

PHILIP of Theangela, a writer, Alexander, iv. 243.

PHILIP, a Theban, Pelopidas, ii. 225, 227, 232.

INDEX

PHILIP, left in India, Alexander, iv. 266, supposed by some to be the father of Antigonus; compare Demetrius, v. 105.

MARCIUS PHILIPPUS, censor, Æm. Paulus, ii. 215.

LUCIUS PHILIPPUS, attached to Pompey, Pompey, iv. 59, 80.

PHILIPPUS, father of Marcia, and stepfather of Augustus, consul (56 B. C.), Cato the Younger, iv. 439, 441, 456; Cicero, v. 87.

PHILISTUS, the Syracusan historian, Timoleon, ii. 138; Pelopidas, ii. 258; Nicias, iii. 307, 308, 335, 348; Alexander, iv. 188; Dion, v. 269-272, 277, 283, 295, 297.

PHILLIDAS, a Theban, Pelopidas, ii. 227, 230-232.

PHILO'S ARSENAL, Sylla, iii. 174.

PHILO, philosopher of the New Academy, Lucullus, iii. 299; Cicero, v. 39, 40.

PHILO the Theban, a writer, Alexander, iv. 243.

PHILOBŒOTUS, in the plain of Elatea, Sylla, iii. 175.

PHILOCHORUS, an Attic historian, Theseus, i. 14, 16, 17, 27, 32, 38; Nicias, iii. 342.

PHILOCLES, a writer, Solon, i. 177.

PHILOCLES, an Athenian general, Lysander, iii. 123, 127; Comparison, iii. 211.

PHILOCRATES, an Athenian orator, Demosthenes, v. 18.

PHILOCRATES, servant of C. Gracchus, C. Gracchus, iv. 614.

PHILOCTETES the hero, Solon, i. 198; Themistocles, i. 254.

PHILOCYPRUS, king in Cyprus, Solon, i. 205.

PHILOLOGUS (correctly PHILOGONUS), freedman of Q. Cicero, Cicero, v. 93.

PHILOMBROTUS, archon at Athens, Solon, i. 190.

PHILOMEDES (or PHILOMELUS), of Lampra, Phocion, iv. 405.

PHILOMELUS the Phocian, Timoleon, ii. 158.

ATTALUS PHILOMETOR, Camillus, i. 306; Ti. Gracchus, iv. 583; Demetrius, v. 121.

PHILON. See PHILO.

PHILONICUS the Thessalian, Alexander, iv. 184.

LICINIUS PHILONICUS, Æm. Paulus, ii. 214.

PHILOPŒMEN, Life, ii. 395; Comparison with Flamininus, ii. 454; Flamininus, ii. 440, 445; Cleomenes, iv. 548; Aratus v. 408.

PHILOSTEPHANUS, a writer, Lycurgus, i. 120.

PHILOSTRATUS, a philosopher, Cato the Younger, iv. 477; Antony, v. 247.

PHILOTAS of Amphissa, a physician, friend of Plutarch's grandfather, Antony, v. 191, 192.

PHILOTAS, son of Parmenio, Alexander, iv. 191, 193, 223, 236, 246-249.

PHILOTIS or TUTULA, Romulus, i. 81; Camillus, i. 323, 324.

PHILOXENUS, officer of Alexander, Alexander, iv. 208.

PHILOXENUS, a Macedonian, Pelopidas, ii. 249.

PHILOXENUS, a dithyrambic poet, Alexander, iv. 188.

PHILOXENUS (correctly POLYXENUS), brother-in-law of Dionysius I., Dion, v. 279.

PHLIUS and PHLIASIANS, in Peloponnesus, Pericles, i. 342; Agesilaus, iv. 35; Cleomenes, iv. 541, 550; Aratus, v. 420-425.

PHLOGIDAS, a Spartan, Lysander, iii. 132.

PHLOGIUS, companion of Hercules, Lucullus, iii. 273.

PHLYA, an Attic township, Solon, i. 187; Themistocles, i. 245, also

(?) 263, Apollo the laurel-crowned a Phlya is another reading.

PHOCÆA and PHOCÆANS, in Ionia, Pericles, i. 373; Lysander, iii. 117; Artaxerxes, v. 470.

PHOCION, Life, iv. 366; Timoleon, ii. 126; Alexander, iv. 235; Agis, iv. 496; Demosthenes, v. 12, 16; Aratus, v. 403.

PHOCIS and PHOCIANS, in Northern Greece, Themistocles, i. 255; Pericles, i. 365, 369; Flamininus, ii. 436; Lysander, iii. 130, 146, 147, 149; Sylla, iii. 170, 175; Agesilaus, iv. 25, 41; Alexander, iv. 193; Phocion, iv. 407; Demosthenes, v. 14, 20; Aratus, v. 436.

PHOCUS, friend of Solon, Solon, i. 190.

PHOCUS, son of Phocion, Phocion, iv. 389, 402, 409, 411.

PHŒBIDAS, a Spartan, Pelopidas, ii. 225, 226, 236; Agesilaus, iv. 34, 50; Comparison, iv. 172.

PHŒBIS, a *mothax*, Cleomenes, iv. 528.

PHŒNICIA and PHŒNICIANS, Pericles, i. 374, 377; Alcibiades, ii. 36, 39; Timoleon, ii. 129, 131, 162; Æm. Paulus, ii. 182; Pyrrhus, iii. 32; Lysander, iii. 122; Sylla, iii. 178 (a Phœnician word); Cimon, iii. 231, 232, 240; Lucullus, iii. 270; Agesilaus, iv. 53; Pompey, iv. 101, 105, 120; Alexander, iv. 201, 211, 219; Antony, v. 194, 201, 221, 230.

PHŒNIX, Achilles's tutor, Philopœmen, ii. 395; Alexander, iv. 184, 212.

PHŒNIX of Tenedos, Eumenes, iii. 448.

PHŒNIX, a Theban, Alexander, iv. 193.

PHŒNIX, a spring in Bœotia, Pelopidas, ii. 237.

PHORBAS, Romulus, i. 42; Numa, i. 139.

PHORMION, an Athenian general, Alcibiades, ii. 3.

PHORMION, an Athenian, Demosthenes, v. 17; Comparison, v. 98.

PHRAATA, town in Media, Antony, v. 203, 205, 217.

PHRAATES, king of Parthia, Pompey, iv. 105; compare Lucullus, iii. 284.

PHRAATES, son of Hyrodes (grandson of the preceding), king of Parthia, Crassus, iii. 397; Antony, v. 202, 204, 206, 207, 218.

PHRASICLES, nephew of Themistocles, Themistocles, i. 283.

PHREARRHI, Attic township, Themistocles, i. 244, 250.

PHRIXUS the Spartan, Agesilaus, iv. 47.

PHRYGIA and PHRYGIANS, Numa, i. 138 (the fable of Attis); Themistocles, i. 280; Alcibiades, ii. 55; Flamininus, ii. 449 (defeat of Antiochus); Cimon, iii. 226; Lucullus, iii. 253, 254; Eumenes, iii. 444, 451; Agesilaus, iv. 13-16; Pompey, iv. 98; Alexander, iv. 202 (Gordium); Cæsar, iv. 296 (the Bona Dea); Phocion, iv. 401 (countryman searching for Antigonus); Demetrius, v. 106, 156.

PHRYNICHUS, an Athenian general, Alcibiades, ii. 36, 37.

PHRYNICHUS, the comic poet, Alcibiades, ii. 29; Nicias, iii. 313.

PHRYNICHUS, the tragic poet, Themistocles, i. 250.

PHRYNIS the musician, Agis, iv. 507.

PHTHIA, wife of Admetus, Themistocles, i. 273.

PHTHIA, mother of Pyrrhus, Pyrrhus, iii. 1, 2.

PHTHIOTIS, Pericles, i. 365; Pelopidas, ii. 255, 260; Flamininus, ii. 436.

PHYLACIA, Aratus, v. 419.

PHYLACION, mistress of Stratocles, Demetrius, v. 113.

PHYLARCHUS the historian, Themistocles, i. 284; Camillus, i. 306; Pyrrhus, iii. 41; Agis, iv. 505; Cleomenes, iv. 525, 552, 554; Demosthenes, v. 31; Aratus, v. 424.

PHYLE, fortress in Attica, Lysander, iii. 138, 147; Demetrius, v. 125.

PHYLLIUS, a Spartan, Pyrrhus, iii. 42.

PHYSCON, a surname, Coriolanus, ii. 71.

PHYTALIDÆ, an Attic house, Theseus, i. 10, 24.

PICENUM and PICENTINES, in Italy, Marcellus, ii. 265; Crassus, iii. 362; Pompey, iv. 64.

PICINÆ or PICTÆ, i. e. AD PICTAS, Sylla, iii. 165.

FABIUS PICTOR, the historian, Romulus, i. 43, 50, 56; Fabius, i. 418.

PICUS, a demigod, Numa, i. 157.

PIERION, a poet, Alexander, iv. 250.

PIGRES, Eumenes, iii. 448.

PINARII, Numa, i. 165. PINARIUS, Comparison of Lycurgus and Numa, i. 174.

PINARUS, river of Cilicia, Alexander, iv. 205.

PINDAR, Theseus, i. 31; Romulus, i. 79; Lycurgus, i. 119; Numa, i. 139; Themistocles, i. 253; Marcellus, ii. 288, 300; Marius, iii. 88; Nicias, iii. 307; Alexander, iv. 193; Demetrius, v. 150; Aratus, v. 386.

PINDARUS, freedman of Cassius, Antony, v. 184; Brutus, v. 369.

PINUS, son of Numa, ancestor of the Pinarii, Numa, i. 165.

PIRÆUS, port of Athens, Themistocles, i. 257, 267 (its construction), 284; Pericles, i. 348 (Ægina its eyesore); Alcibiades, ii. 39; Pelopidas, ii. 235; Lysander, iii. 129, 131 (its destruction); Sylla, iii. 169, 174 (its siege and capture), 189; Comparison, iii. 211; Nicias, iii. 349; Agesilaus, iv. 35; Phocion, iv. 404, 405; Demosthenes, v. 1 (the eyesore), 7, 31; Demetrius, v. 109 (his entrance), 140, 152 (in the text, at Athens), Brutus, v. 350; Aratus, v. 418-420. The Piraic gate at Athens, Theseus, i. 29; Sylla, iii. 173.

PIRITHOUS the hero, Theseus, i. 19, 32-35, 38.

PISA, town of Elis, Pericles, i. 339.

PISANDER, an Athenian, Alcibiades, ii. 38.

PISANDER, a Platæan hero, Aristides, ii. 324.

PISANDER the Spartan admiral, Agesilaus, iv. 16, 25.

PISAURUM, town of Umbria, Antony, v. 226.

PISIDIANS, Themistocles, i. 280; Alexander, iv. 202.

PISIS the Thespian, Demetrius, v. 146.

PISISTRATUS, tyrant of Athens, Theseus, i. 19; Solon, i. 177, 178, 184, 186, 208-212; Comparison of Solon and Poplicola, i. 241; Pericles, i. 340, 345; Cato the Elder, ii. 383.

PISO, called CAIUS, really LUCIUS, an historian, Numa, i. 166; Marius, iii. 110.

PISO, consul (67 B.C.), (opposed to both Pompey and Cæsar), Pompey, iv. 94; Cæsar, iv. 293; Cicero, v. 57.

PISO, consul (61 B.C.), an adherent of Pompey, Pompey, iv. 118; Cato the Younger, iv. 446.

CALPURNIUS PISO, father-in-law of Cæsar, consul (58 B.C.), Pompey, iv. 124; Cæsar, iv. 301, 329; Cato the Younger, iv. 450; Cicero, v. 70, 72. (The name Calpurnius is common to all the Pisos.)

Piso, Cicero's son-in-law, Cicero, v. 72, 85.

Piso, adopted by Galba, Galba, v. 499, 500, 503, 506, 507.

PISSUTHNES, a Persian, Pericles, i. 373.

PITANE, town of Mysia, Lucullus, iii. 247.

PITTACUS, tyrant of Mitylene, Solon, i. 190.

PITTHEUS, father of Æthra, Theseus, i. 3-7, 18, 25, 27, 37.

PITYUSSA, island on the coast of Spain, Sertorius, iii. 413.

PIXODORUS, more correctly PIXODARUS, prince of Caria, Alexander, iv. 190.

PLACENTIA, town in North Italy, Otho, v. 515, 516.

MUNATIUS PLANCUS (Titus), Pompey, iv. 136; Cato the Younger, iv. 467, 468; Cicero, v. 64.

MUNATIUS PLANCUS (Lucius, his brother), Antony, v. 182, 224; Brutus, v. 338.

PLATÆA and PLATÆANS, Themistocles, i. 265; Camillus, i. 305; Æm. Paulus, ii. 198; Pelopidas, ii. 236, 247; Aristides, ii. 310, 316, 323; and after to 340; Comparison, ii. 389, 393; Flamininus, ii. 437; Lysander, iii. 147, 149; Comparison, iii. 210; Cimon, iii. 232; Alexander, iv. 193, 228; Agis, iv. 498.

PLATO, the comic poet, Themistocles, i. 284; Pericles, i. 342; Alcibiades, ii. 17; Nicias, iii. 324; Antony, v. 237.

PLATO, the philosopher, Comparison of Romulus and Theseus, i. 82; Lycurgus, i. 90, 96, 107, 110, 126, 127, 131; Numa, i. 144, 150,

164; Solon, i. 179, 205, 212; Themistocles, i. 248, 283; Pericles, i. 347, 362, 372; Alcibiades, ii. 1, 8; Coriolanus, ii. 77; Comparison, ii. 115; Timoleon, ii. 126; Pelopidas, ii. 240; Marcellus, ii. 278; Aristides, ii. 309, 343; Cato the Elder, ii. 350, 356; Philopœmen, ii. 411; Marius, iii. 53, 111; Lysander, iii. 115, 134; Lucullus, iii. 318; Comparison, iii. 302, 304; Nicias, iii. 308, 341; Phocion, iv. 369, 371; Cato the Younger, iv. 489; Comparison, iv. 620; Demosthenes, v. 6; Cicero, v. 39, 63; Comparison, v. 98; Demetrius, v. 103, 138; Antony, v. 193, 201; Dion, v. 259, 262, 263, 267-271, 273-280, 311-313; Brutus v. 320; Comparison, v. 383, 384; Galba, v. 476.

PLEMMYRIUM, promontory of Sicily, Nicias, iii. 336.

The PLESIANACTIUM or POECILE at Athens, Cimon, iii. 218.

PLISTARCHUS, brother of Cassander, Demetrius, v. 137.

PLISTINUS, brother of Faustulus, Romulus, i. 52.

PLISTOANAX, king of Sparta, Lycurgus, i. 117; Pericles, i. 369; Agis, iv. 498.

PLOTINUS or PLOTIUS, Crassus, iii. 351.

PLUTARCH, tyrant of Eretria, Phocion, iv. 380, 381.

THE Po, Romulus, i. 63; Marcellus, ii. 267; Marius, iii. 81; Crassus, iii. 362; Pompey, iv. 79; Cæsar, iv. 309, 311, 316; Brutus, v. 339; Otho, v. 515, 520.

POLEMON, commanding with Eumenes, Eumenes, iii. 451.

POLEMON the geographer, Aratus, v. 398.

POLEMON, king of Pontus, Antony, v. 204, 227.

INDEX 623

POLIARCHUS or POLYARCHUS, of Ægina, Themistocles, i. 267.
POLLICHUS, a Syracusan, Nicias, iii. 342.
ASINIUS POLLIO, the friend of Cæsar, Pompey, iv. 159; Cæsar, iv. 325, 339, 346; Cato the Younger, iv. 472; Antony, v. 173.
POLLIO, prætorian prefect (? PLOTIUS), Otho, v. 528.
POLLIS the Spartan, Dion, v. 263.
POLUS of Ægina, the actor, Demosthenes, v. 32.
POLYÆNUS, Philopœmen, ii. 407.
POLYALCES, a Spartan ambassador, Pericles, i. 380.
POLYBIUS the historian, Æm. Paulus, ii. 186, 187, 191; Pelopidas, ii. 238; Comparison, ii. 304; Cato the Elder, ii. 359, 361; Philopœmen, ii. 414, 420, 421; Cleomenes, iv. 549, 552; Ti. Gracchus, iv. 569; Brutus, v. 322; Aratus, v. 424.
POLYCLETUS the sculptor, Pericles, i. 339.
POLYCLETUS or POLYCLITUS, an historian, Alexander, iv. 243.
POLYCLETUS, a favorite of Nero, Galba, v. 493.
POLYCRATES, tyrant of Samos, Pericles, i. 375; Lysander, iii. 121.
POLYCRATES of Sicyon, friend of Plutarch, Aratus, v. 386.
POLYCRATES, son of the preceding, Aratus, v. 387.
POLYCRATIDAS, a Spartan, Lycurgus, i. 123.
POLYCRITE, granddaughter of Aristides, Aristides, ii. 345.
POLYCRITUS of Mende, a physician, Artaxerxes, v. 463.
POLYDECTES, king of Sparta, Lycurgus, i. 88, 89.
POLYDORUS, king of Sparta, Lycurgus, i. 96, 98.
POLYEUCTUS, son of Themistocles, Themistocles, i. 283.

POLYEUCTUS the Sphettian, Phocion, iv. 371, 377; Demosthenes, v. 11, 16, 26.
POLYGNOTUS the painter, Cimon, iii. 218.
POLYGNOTUS'S TOWER, Aratus, v. 391.
POLYIDUS, Platæan hero, Aristides, ii. 324.
POLYMACHUS of Pella, a Macedonian, Alexander, iv. 275.
POLYMEDES, Phocion, iv. 381.
POLYPHRON, uncle of Alexander of Pheræ, Pelopidas, ii. 252.
POLYSPERCHON, one of those who killed Callippus, Dion, v. 317.
POLYSPERCHON, Alexander's general, Pyrrhus, iii. 10; Eumenes, iii. 455, 457; Phocion, iv. 403-407; Demetrius, v. 110.
POLYSTRATUS, present at the death of Darius, Alexander, iv. 241.
POLYTION, companion of Alcibiades, Alcibiades, ii. 26, 31.
POLYXENUS, married to the sister of Dionysius the Elder, Dion, v. 279.
POLYZELUS'S HOUSE, Nicias, iii. 346.
POLYZELUS the Rhodian, a writer, Solon, i. 193.
POMAXATHRES, a Parthian, Crassus, iii. 393, 396.
POMENTIUM (Suessa Pometia), town of Latium, Cæsar, iv. 351.
POMPÆDIUS SILO, Cato the Younger, iv. 415.
POMPEIA, wife of Cæsar, Cæsar, iv. 291, 295-298; Cicero, v. 68, 69.
POMPEII, town of Campania, Cicero, v. 46.
THE POMPEII, Marius, iii. 52.
AULUS POMPEIUS, a tribune, Marius, iii. 72, 73.
[POMPEIUS] STRABO, father of Pompey, Pompey, iv. 58, 59, 62.
POMPEY THE GREAT (Cn. Pompeius Magnus), Life, iv. 58; Comparison with Agesilaus, iv. 171. See,

also, the contemporary lives, Sylla, iii. 194, 200, 202, 205; Comparison, iii. 208; Lucullus, iii. 244, 249, 251, 289-300; Comparison, iii. 305; Crassus, iii. 354, 357-359, 364-371, 377; Comparison, iii. 399-402; Sertorius, iii. 406, 419, 423, 427-433, 439, 440; Comparison, iii. 468; Cæsar, iv. 291, 298-303, 310, 312, 314, 316, 319-323, 326-329, 332-341, 344, 348-350, 355, 359, 361, 363; Cato the Younger, iv. 416, 423, 426, 427, 433, 435, 445-447, 450, 452, 457-461, 464-476, 478, 482; Cicero, v. 46-48, 50, 52, 56, 62, 67, 71-72, 74-77, 78-81, 83, 84; Comparison, v. 97; Antony, v. 169-173, 174, 183, 228; Brutus, v. 321-324, 327, 329, 333, 336, 345, 351, 355, 363; Comparison, v. 382, 383. The day of his death is given in Camillus, i. 306, and his name occurs in Numa, i. 162; Alexander, iv. 178; and Otho, v. 519.

CNÆUS POMPEIUS, son of Pompey, Pompey, iv. 145; Cato the Younger, iv. 475, 481; Cicero, v. 81; Antony, v. 189.

SEXTUS POMPEIUS, younger son of Pompey, Cato the Younger, iv. 476; Antony, v. 195, 196, 200, 221.

SEXTUS POMPEIUS, nephew of Pompey, Cato the Younger, iv. 416.

QUINTUS POMPEIUS, consul with Sylla (88 B.C.), Sylla, iii. 161, 164.

POMPEIUS, opponent of Gracchus, Ti. Gracchus, iv. 583.

POMPILIA, daughter of Numa, Numa, i. 165.

POMPILIUS. See NUMA.

POMPO, son of Numa, ancestor of the Pomponii, Numa, i. 165.

POMPONIA, wife of Quintus Cicero, Cicero, v. 93.

POMPONIUS, father of Numa, Numa, i. 136. THE POMPONII, Numa, i. 165.

POMPONIUS, prætor in the year of the battle of Thrasymene, Fabius, i. 398.

POMPONIUS, friend of C. Gracchus, C. Gracchus, iv. 614.

POMPONIUS, taken by Mithridates, Lucullus, iii. 261.

PONTIUS, Sylla, iii. 192.

PONTIUS COMINIUS, who climbed the capitol, Camillus, i. 313, 314.

PONTUS, Lycurgus, i. 104; Aristides, ii. 344; Marius, iii. 64, 91; Lysander, iii. 144; Sylla, iii. 168, 185, 188; Lucullus, iii. 253 and after, as far as 291; Sertorius, iii. 434; Eumenes, iii. 444; Pompey, iv. 101, 106, 107, 115, 120; Cæsar, iv. 344, 348, 351; Cato the Younger, iv. 447; Cicero, v. 49; Demetrius, v. 105; Antony, v. 227; Galba, v. 489. The Pontic trumpeter, Lucullus, iii. 256. Salt fish of Pontus, Antony, v. 194. See, also, THE EUXINE. Pontus signifies, sometimes the sea, more generally its Asiatic shore and the adjoining country.

POPILIUS, concerned in killing Cicero, Cicero, v. 92.

POPILIUS, opponent of the Gracchi, C. Gracchus, iv. 599.

POPILIUS LÆNAS, a senator, Brutus, v. 334-336.

CAIUS POPILIUS, Cæsar, iv. 290.

PUBLIUS VALERIUS POPLICOLA or PUBLICOLA, Life, i. 214; Comparison with Solon, i. 239; Romulus, i. 62; Coriolanus, ii. 102.

POPPÆA, wife of Crispinus, Otho, and Nero, Galba, v. 495, 496; (name given to Sporus), 485.

PORCIA, sister of Cato the Younger, Cato the Younger, iv. 413, 458.

PORCIA, daughter of Cato the

Younger, wife of Brutus, Cato the Younger, iv. 440, 494; Brutus, v. 320, 331, 332, 335, 343, 344, 379, 380.

THE PORCII, Poplicola, i. 226. THE PORCIAN BASILICA, Cato the Elder, ii. 374; Cato the Younger, iv. 418.

PORCIUS, i. e. Cato's son, Cato the Younger, iv. 493. See CATO.

LARS PORSENNA, king of Clusium, Poplicola, i. 230-234; Comparison, i. 242, 243.

PORUS, Indian king, Alexander, iv. 263-266.

POSIDONIA or PÆSTUM, Cimon, iii. 240.

POSIDONIUS, historian of Perseus, Æm. Paulus, ii. 191, 192, 194.

POSIDONIUS of Rhodes, philosopher and historian, Fabius, i. 419; Marcellus, ii. 262, 272, 288, 302; Marius, iii. 52, 110; Pompey, iv. 117; Cicero, v. 41; Brutus, v. 319.

POSTUMA or POSTHUMA, daughter of Sylla, Sylla, iii. 205.

POSTUMIUS BALBUS (Albus), Poplicola, i. 237.

POSTUMIUS TUBERTUS, Poplicola, i. 234.

POSTUMIUS TUBERTUS, dictator, Camillus, i. 286.

SPURIUS POSTUMIUS, Ti. Gracchus, iv. 575.

POSTUMIUS, a soothsayer, Sylla, iii. 165.

POSTUMIUS. See LIVIUS and ALBINUS.

POSTUMUS, a surname, Coriolanus, ii. 72.

POSTUMUS, in the Greek OPSIGONUS, i. e. Mucius Scævola, Poplicola, i. 232.

POTAMON of Lesbos, an historian, Alexander, iv. 266.

POTAMUS, Attic township, Aristides, ii. 346.

POTHINUS the eunuch, Pompey, iv. 166, 170; Cæsar, iv. 341, 342; Antony, v. 226.

POTIDÆA, town of Macedonia, Pericles, i. 379; Alcibiades, ii. 11; Alexander, iv. 181.

VALERIUS POTITUS, envoy to Delphi, Camillus, i. 289.

PRÆCIA, Lucullus, iii. 251.

PRÆNESTE and PRÆNESTINES, in Latium, Camillus, i. 329; Marius, iii. 112; Sylla, iii. 194, 196, 199.

PRÆSIANS, an Indian people, Alexander, iv. 266, 267.

PRANICHUS, a poet, Alexander, iv. 250.

PRAXAGORAS, a Neapolitan, Pompey, iv. 138.

PRAXIERGIDÆ, an Attic priestly family, Alcibiades, ii. 50.

PRIAM, king of Troy, Agis, iv. 505.

PRIENE, town of Ionia, Solon, i. 181; Pericles, i. 373; Antony, v. 223.

PRISCUS, a surname, Cato the Elder, ii. 347.

HELVIDIUS PRISCUS, Galba, v. 507.

PROCLES or PATROCLES, king of Sparta, Lycurgus, i. 88.

PROCONNESUS, on the Propontis, Romulus, i. 78; Alcibiades, ii. 41.

PROCRUSTES, name of Damastes, Theseus, i. 10; Comparison, i. 82.

PROCULEIUS, friend of Augustus, Antony, v. 245, 246.

PROCULUS, a surname, Coriolanus, ii. 72.

JULIUS PROCULUS, Romulus, i. 77; Numa, i. 134, 140.

PROCULUS, Otho's general and prætorian prefect, Otho, v. 518, 520, 522. See, also, 528, note.

PROLYTA, daughter of Agesilaus, Agesilaus, iv. 28.

PROMACHUS, a Macedonian, Alexander, iv. 276.

PROMATHION, an historian of Italy, Romulus, i. 43.
PROMETHEUS, in Æschylus, Pompey, iv. 58.
PROPHANTUS, a Sicyonian, Aratus, v. 388.
PROPONTIS, Lucullus, iii. 251.
PROTAGORAS the sophist, Pericles, i. 389; Nicias, iii. 341.
PROTEAS, Alexander, iv. 235.
PROTHOUS, a Lacedæmonian, Agesilaus, iv. 41.
PROTHYTES, a Theban, Alexander, iv. 193.
PROTIS or PROTUS, founder of Marseilles, Solon, i. 179.
PROTOGENES the painter, Demetrius, v. 124.
PROTUS the pilot, Dion, v. 283.
PROXENUS, a Macedonian, Alexander, iv. 260.
PRUSIAS, king of Bithynia, Flamininus, ii. 449, 459, 462.
PRYTANIS, king of Sparta, Lycurgus, i. 88.
PSAMMON, an Egyptian philosopher, Alexander, iv. 218.
PSENOPHIS of Hierapolis, Solon, i. 204.
PSILTUCIS, island of the Indian Sea, Alexander, iv. 272.
PSYCHE, wife of Marphadates, Cato the Younger, iv. 494.
PSYLLI, people of Libya, Cato the Younger, iv. 476.
PSYTTALEA, islet near Salamis, Aristides, ii. 320.
PTŒODORUS the Megarian, Dion, v. 275.
PTOLEMAIS, daughter of Ptolemy Lagus, married to Demetrius, Demetrius, v. 137, 155, 164.
PTOLEMY (I.) SOTER, son of Lagus, Alexander's general, king of Egypt, Pyrrhus, iii. 5, 7, 8, 13; Eumenes, iii. 442, 446; Alexander, iv. 191, 233, 243; Demetrius, v. 106-109, 116, 117, 120, 122-125; Comparison, v. 256, 257; also Coriolanus, ii. 72.
PTOLEMY (II.) PHILADELPHUS, king of Egypt, Philopœmen, ii. 403; Aratus, v. 389, 396, 399, 427; also Coriolanus, ii. 72.
PTOLEMY (III.) EUERGETES (I.), king of Egypt, Philopœmen, ii. 403; Agis, iv. 502; Cleomenes, iv. 542, 545, 554-557; Aratus, v. 409, 427; also Coriolanus, ii. 72.
PTOLEMY (IV.) PHILOPATOR, king of Egypt, Cleomenes, iv. 557-560, 562; Demetrius, v. 152.
PTOLEMY (V.) EPIPHANES, king of Egypt, Philopœmen, ii. 409.
PTOLEMY (VII.) PHYSCON (or EUERGETES II.), king of Egypt, Ti. Gracchus, iv. 566; also Coriolanus, ii. 71.
PTOLEMY (VIII.) LATHYRUS, king of Egypt, Coriolanus, ii. 72.
PTOLEMY (XI.) AULETES, king of Egypt, Lucullus, iii. 246; Pompey, iv. 127; Cato the Younger, iv. 451, 452; Antony, v. 167.
PTOLEMY (XII.), son of the preceding, brother of Cleopatra, king of Egypt, Pompey, iv. 165, 168, 170; compare Cæsar, iv. 341, 344.
PTOLEMY, king of Cyprus, son of Ptolemy Lathyrus, brother of Auletes, Cato the Younger, iv. 453; Brutus, v. 321.
PTOLEMY, prefect of Alexandria, Cleomenes, iv. 561.
PTOLEMY, nephew of Antigonus, Eumenes, iii. 454.
PTOLEMY, son of Antony and Cleopatra, Antony, v. 221.
PTOLEMY, son of Chrysermas, Cleomenes, iv. 560, 561.
PTOLEMY CERAUNUS, king of Macedon, Pyrrhus, iii. 31.
PTOLEMY, king of Macedon, Pelopidas, ii. 249.

INDEX

PTOLEMY, attendant of Mithridates, Lucullus, iii. 265.
PTOLEMY, son of Pyrrhus, Pyrrhus, iii. 7, 11, 41, 42, 45.
PTOLEMY (or PTOLEMÆUS, which is the full Greek form of the name), Galba, v. 500.
PTOUM, mountain in Bœotia, Pelopidas, ii. 237.
PUBLICIUS BIBULUS, Marcellus, ii. 297.
PUBLICOLA. See POPLICOLA.
PUBLICOLA, lieutenant of Antony at Actium, Antony, v. 231, 232.
PYDNA, town of Macedonia, field of battle, Themistocles, i. 274; Æm. Paulus, ii. 187, 191, 196, 197.
PYLADES the musician, Philopœmen, ii. 408.
PYLIUS, an Athenian, Theseus, i. 37.
PYLOS, harbor of Messenia, Alcibiades, ii. 18; Coriolanus, ii. 76; Nicias, iii. 316, 301, 322; Comparison, iii. 400.
PYRAMIA in Thyreatis, Pyrrhus, iii. 48.
THE PYRENEES, Camillus, i. 300; Sertorius, iii. 413, 423, 427.
PYRILAMPES, an Athenian, Pericles, i. 359.
PYRRHA, wife of Deucalion, Pyrrhus, iii. 1.
PYRRHUS, surname of Neoptolemus, Pyrrhus, iii. 1.
PYRRHUS, king of Epirus, Life, iii. 1; Cato the Elder, ii. 349; Flamininus, ii. 428, 451; Sertorius, iii. 434; Cleomenes, iv. 540; Demetrius, v. 127, 136, 142, 147, 148, 151-155; Otho, v. 525.
PUTEOLI, or DICÆARCHEA, Sylla, iii. 204.
PYTHAGORAS the philosopher, Numa, i. 133, 144-146, 150, 155, 167; Pythagorean sect, Dion, v. 269, 276. Also Æm. Paulus, ii.

170; Cato the Elder, ii. 350; Alexander, iv. 271.
PYTHAGORAS the soothsayer, Alexander, iv. 280.
PYTHEAS, an Athenian speaker, Phocion, iv. 390; Demosthenes, v. 9, 22, 31; Comparison, v. 95.
PYTHOCLES, condemned with Phocion, Phocion, iv. 409.
PYTHOCLES, descended from Aratus, Aratus, v. 387.
PYTHOCLIDES, a musician, Pericles, i. 341.
PYTHODORUS, Themistocles, i. 274.
PYTHODORUS the torch-bearer, Demetrius, v. 129.
PYTHOLAUS, one of Thebe's three brothers, Pelopidas, ii. 260.
PYTHO, i. e. DELPHI, Lycurgus, i. 96. THE PYTHIAN GAMES, Solon, i. 186; Pelopidas, ii. 259; Lysander, iii. 134; Demetrius, v. 148; Otho, v. 515. The Pythoness, Aratus, v. 438.
PYTHON the dragon, Pelopidas, ii. 238.
PYTHON, a musician, Pyrrhus, iii. 10.
PYTHON, officer of Alexander, Alexander, iv. 283.
PYTHON the Byzantine, Demosthenes, v. 10.
PYTHONICE, Harpalus's mistress, Phocion, iv. 391.
PYTHOPOLIS, town of Bithynia, Theseus, i. 28.

Q

QUADRANTARIA, Clodia's nickname, Cicero, v. 70.
QUINDA, the treasure-town in Cilicia, Eumenes, iii. 457; Demetrius, v. 137.
QUINTIO, Cato's freedman, Cato the Elder, ii. 379.
QUINTIUS CAPITOLINUS, dictator, Camillus, i. 327.

Lucius Quintius, tribune and prætor, Lucullus, iii. 250, 288.
Titus Quintius Flamininus. See Flamininus.
Quintius, one of Crassus's officers, Crassus, iii. 364.
Quirinal Hill, Romulus, i. 80; Numa, i. 154.
Quirinus, Romulus, i. 78, 80; Numa, i. 135; Camillus, i. 309; Marcellus, ii. 271.
Quirites, inhabitants of Cures, Romulus, i. 67, 80; Numa, i. 136.

R

Ramnenses, the first of the three Roman tribes, Romulus, i. 67.
Ratumena, gate of Rome, Poplicola, i. 228.
Ravenna in Gaul, visited by Plutarch, Marius, iii. 53.
The Regia at Rome, Romulus, i. 65, 80; Numa, i. 154.
Remonium or Remonia, on The Aventine, Romulus, i. 51, 53.
Remus, brother of Romulus, Romulus, i. 42, 46-52, 69; Comparison, i. 82, 85.
Caninius Revilius, consul for a day, Cæsar, iv. 350.
Marcius Rex, husband of Tertia, Cicero, v. 69.
Rex, a surname of the Mamerci or Mamercii (Marcii), Numa, i. 165.
Rhadamanthus the judge, Theseus, i. 15; Lysander, iii. 148.
Rhamnus, freedman of Antony, Antony, v. 215.
Rhamnus, a town of Attica, Phocion, iv. 395; Demetrius, v. 139.
Rhea, daughter of Numitor, Romulus, i. 44.
Rhea, mother of Sertorius, Sertorius, iii. 407.
Rhegium, a Greek town in Bruttium, and Rhegians, Fabius, i. 423; Alcibiades, ii. 28; Timoleon, ii. 129-131, 143; Crassus, iii. 363; Dion, v. 285, 317.
Rhenea, island near Delos, Nicias, iii. 311.
The Rhine, Cæsar, iv. 309, 312, 313; Otho, v. 522.
Rhodes and Rhodians, Themistocles, i. 270; Pericles, i. 365; Marius, iii. 89; Lucullus, iii. 246; Pompey, iv. 117; Alexander, iv. 226; Cæsar, iv. 288; Phocion, v. 388; Cato the Younger, iv. 473; Demosthenes, v. 28; Cicero, v. 41, 78, 80; Demetrius, v. 122-125; Brutus, v. 321, 352, 355.
Rhodogune, daughter of Artaxerxes, Artaxerxes, v. 471.
Rhodon, tutor of Cæsarion, Antony, v. 247.
Rhœsaces, a Persian at Athens, Cimon, iii. 229.
Rhœsaces, a Persian at the Granicus, Alexander, iv. 199.
Rhœteum, a village of Arcadia, Cleomenes, iv. 546.
The Rhone, Solon, i. 179; Sertorius, iii. 407; Cæsar, iv. 306.
Rhosus, a town in Syria, Demetrius, v. 137.
Rhus, at Megara, Theseus, i. 30.
Rhymitalces the Thracian, Romulus, i. 62.
Rhyndacus, river in Bithynia, Lucullus, iii. 257.
Rignarium or Remonium, Romulus, i. 51.
Riphæan Mountains, Camillus, i. 300.
Roma, a Trojan woman, Romulus, i. 41; Roma, wife of Latinus, and Roma, daughter of Italus, Romulus, i. 42.
Romanus, son of Ulysses, Romulus, i. 42.
Rome and Romans, frequent. See, also, under Latin. In all the

following passages the original has "the *Roman* language, &c.," Æm. Paulus, ii. 213; Lucullus, iii. 243, 244; Crassus, iii. 388, 389; Pompey, iv. 167; Cæsar, iv. 339, 344, 360; Demosthenes, v. 2; Cicero, v. 42, 83; Brutus, v. 320, 336. Grecian and Roman learning, Sertorius, iii. 422. Roman months, Romulus, i. 54, 68; Numa, i. 160-163; Cæsar, iv. 329, 352.

ROMULUS, Life, i. 41; Comparison of Theseus and Romulus, i. 82; Theseus, i. 1, 2; Numa, i. 134, 135, 137, 158, 160, 161; Poplicola, i. 220; Camillus, i. 321-324; Marcellus, ii. 270; Pompey, iv. 92; Phocion, iv. 369.

ROMUS, king of the Latins, and ROMUS, son of Emathion, Romulus, i. 42.

ROSCIUS, two brothers of the name, Crassus, iii. 392.

ROSCIUS, defended by Cicero, Cicero, v. 39.

ROSCIUS the comedian, Sylla, iii. 203; Cicero, v. 42.

ROSCIUS, opponent of Pompey, Pompey, iv. 92.

ROXANA, wife of Alexander, Pyrrhus, iii. 4; Alexander, iv. 245, 284.

ROXANA, sister of Mithridates, Lucullus, iii. 265.

ROXANES, a Persian, Themistocles, i. 278.

RUBICON, river of Italy, Pompey, iv. 142; Cæsar, iv. 309, 325.

MARCUS RUBRIUS, with Cato at Utica, Cato the Younger, iv. 483.

RUBRIUS, tribune of the people, C. Gracchus, iv. 605.

RUBRIUS, prætor in Macedonia, Cato the Younger, iv. 422.

RUFINUS, Sylla's ancestor, Sylla, iii. 152.

CLUVIUS RUFUS, governor of Spain, Otho, v. 511.

LUCIUS RUFUS, Ti. Gracchus, iv. 590.

VIRGINIUS RUFUS, commanding in Germany, Galba, v. 481, 494, 498; Otho, v. 509, 529.

FABIUS RULLUS MAXIMUS, Fabius, i. 395; Pompey, iv. 75.

RUMILIA, and the fig-tree RUMINALIS, Romulus, i. 44.

RUTILIUS the historian, Marius, iii. 62, 87; Pompey, iv. 110.

S

CASSIUS SABACO, friend of Marius, Marius, iii. 56.

SABBAS, an Indian king, Alexander, iv. 269, 270.

SABINES, people of Italy, Romulus, i. 57, 68, 80; Comparison, i. 82; Numa, i. 134, 137, 140, 142, 160; Poplicola, i. 214, 234-237; Coriolanus, ii. 64, 102; Cato the Elder, ii. 347; Sertorius, iii. 406; Pompey, iv. 63; Cæsar, iv. 287.

SABINUS, friend of Cicero, Cicero, v. 64.

CALVISIUS SABINUS, in Caligula's time, Galba, v. 487.

FLAVIUS SABINUS, Vespasian's brother, Otho, v. 514.

NYMPHIDIUS SABINUS, prætorian prefect, Galba, v. 478, 483, 485, 487-490, 500, 508.

SACCULIO, a buffoon, Brutus, v. 371.

SADALAS, king of Thrace, Antony, v. 227.

SAGRA, a river of Italy and field of battle, Æm. Paulus, ii. 198.

SAGUNTUM, a town of Spain, Sertorius, iii. 431.

SAIS, a town of Egypt, Solon, i. 212.

SALAMIS, island on the coast of Attica, Theseus, i. 10, 16; Solon,

i. 184-187, 213; Comparison, i. 242; Themistocles, i. 256, 264; Camillus, i. 306; Pelopidas, ii. 243; Aristides, ii. 319, 320, 322, 330; Cato the Elder, ii. 354; Comparison, ii. 389; Flamininus, ii. 437; Lysander, iii. 122, 130; Cimon, iii. 219, 220, 232; Alexander, iv. 229; Phocion, iv. 405; Demetrius, v. 117; Aratus, v. 409, 419. The SALAMINIAN galley, Pericles, i. 347; Alcibiades, ii. 30.

SALAMIS, town in Cyprus, Alexander, iv. 219; Demetrius, v. 117.

SALII, Roman priests, Numa, i. 151, 153, 154.

JULIUS SALINATOR, Sertorius, iii. 413.

SALINÆ (in Campania?), Crassus, iii. 361.

SALIUS, probably SALVIUS, commander of the Pelignians, Æm. Paulus, ii. 192.

SALIUS, a dancing-master, Numa, i. 153.

SALLUST the historian, Comparison of Lysander and Sylla, iii. 209; Lucullus, iii. 257, 288.

SCIPIO SALLUTIO, Cæsar, iv. 345.

SALONIUS, a clerk, Cato the Elder, ii. 382.

CATO SALONIUS or SALONIANUS, son of Cato the Elder, Cato the Elder, ii. 383, 387.

SALVENIUS, soldier of Sylla, Sylla, iii. 178.

SALVIUS, a centurion, one of Pompey's murderers, Pompey, iv. 167, 168.

SAMNITES, a people of Italy, Marcellus, ii. 293; Cato the Elder, ii. 349; Pyrrhus, iii. 18, 24, 27-29, 31, 34, 36; Sylla, iii. 194, 195; Ti. Gracchus, iv. 572.

SAMON, an Epirot, Pyrrhus, iii. 7.

SAMOS and SAMIANS, island of Ionia, Themistocles, i. 246; Pericles, i. 349, 371, 373-378; Comparison, i. 432; Alcibiades, ii. 36, 39, 53; Pelopidas, ii. 222; Aristides, ii. 340, 342; Lysander, iii. 117-119, 121, 129, 134; Cimon, iii. 226; Lucullus, iii. 247; Alexander, iv. 218; Antony, v. 223; Brutus, v. 320.

SAMOSATA, a town of Commagene, Antony, v. 198.

SAMOTHRACE, island on the coast of Thrace, Numa, i. 153; Camillus, i. 308; Æm. Paulus, ii. 197, 199; Marcellus, ii. 302; Lucullus, iii. 259; Pompey, iv. 89; Alexander, iv. 179.

SANDAUCE, sister of Xerxes, Themistocles, i. 261; Aristides, ii. 320.

SANDON, father of Athenodorus, Poplicola, i. 232.

SAPHA, in Mesopotamia, Lucullus, iii. 272.

SAPPHO the poetess, Demetrius, v. 145.

SARDINIA, the island, Cato the Elder, ii. 355; Pompey, iv. 79, 93, 128, 150; Cæsar, iv. 311; C. Gracchus, iv. 595; Comparison, iv. 622; Antony, v. 196.

SARDIS, capital of Lydia, and SARDIANS, Romulus, i. 74 (Sardians for sale); Solon, i. 207; Themistocles, i. 279, 281; Alcibiades, ii. 41; Aristides, ii. 314; Lysander, iii. 116, 119, 122; Eumenes, iii. 451; Agesilaus, iv. 14, 16; Pompey, iv. 110; Alexander, iv. 200; Phocion, iv. 388; Demosthenes, v. 23; Demetrius, v. 156; Brutus, v. 356, 358.

SARMENTUS, Cæsar's little page, Antony, v. 226.

SARPEDON, tutor of Cato the Younger, Cato the Younger, iv. 414, 416.

SATIBARZANES, eunuch of Artaxerxes, Artaxerxes, v. 453.

INDEX 631

SATIPHERNES, a Persian, Artaxerxes, v. 451.
SATRICUM, a town of Latium, Camillus, i. 330.
PUBLIUS SATUREIUS, tribune of the people, Ti. Gracchus, iv. 590.
LUCIUS SATURNINUS, Marius, iii. 68, 86-89, 94.
SATURNINI, Comparison of Lysander and Sylla, iii. 207.
SATYRUS, a Corinthian diviner, Timoleon, ii. 123.
SATYRUS the actor, Demosthenes, v. 8.
CASSIUS SCÆVA, soldier of Cæsar, Cæsar, iv. 304.
MUCIUS SCÆVOLA, Poplicola, i. 232.
MUCIUS SCÆVOLA the lawyer, Sylla, iii. 204; Ti. Gracchus, iv. 576.
SCAMBONIDÆ, Attic township, Alcibiades, ii. 31.
SCANDEA, in the island of Cythera, Comparison of Crassus and Nicias, iii. 403.
SCAPTE HYLE, in Thrace, Cimon, iii. 217.
SCARPHIA or SCARPHEA, in Locris, Alexander, iv. 220.
SCAURI, Cicero, v. 38.
SCAURUS, former husband of Metella, Sylla's wife, Sylla, iii. 200; Pompey, iv. 68.
SCEDASUS of Leuctra, Pelopidas, ii. 242.
SCELLIUS, companion of Antony's flight, Antony, v. 233.
SCEPSIS, town in Mysia, Sylla, iii. 189; Lucullus, iii. 271.
SCIATHUS, island in the Ægean Sea, Themistocles, i. 252.
SCILLUSTIS, island in the Indian Sea, Alexander, iv. 272.
SCIONÆANS, of Scione in Macedonia, Lysander, iii. 129.
CORNELIUS SCIPIO, master of the horse to Camillus, Camillus, i. 289.

CNÆUS CORNELIUS [SCIPIO], Marcellus, ii. 267-269.
CORNELIUS SCIPIO AFRICANUS (the Elder), Fabius, i. 427-429; Comparison, i. 432; Æm. Paulus, ii. 173, 186; Comparison, ii. 304; Cato the Elder, ii. 352, 362, 363, 367, 369, 383; Comparison, ii. 389, 394; Flamininus, ii. 425, 447, 451; Pyrrhus, iii. 10; Marius, iii. 52, 65; Lucullus, iii. 257 (?); Crassus, iii. 386 (?); Pompey, iv. 75; Ti. Gracchus, iv. 565, 569, 575, 588; C. Gracchus, iv. 617; Galba, v. 508.
SCIPIO AFRICANUS (the Younger), son of Æmilius Paulus (Æmilianus), Romulus, i. 76; Æm. Paulus, ii. 173; Cato the Elder, ii. 359, 369; Marius, iii. 54, 67; Lucullus, iii. 295; Cato the Younger, iv. 420; Ti. Gracchus, iv. 566, 569, 572, 574, 582, 593; C. Gracchus, iv. 605.
LUCIUS SCIPIO (Asiaticus), brother of the elder Africanus, Cato the Elder, ii. 368, 372, 373; Flamininus, ii. 453; Lucullus, iii. 257; Crassus, iii. 386.
SCIPIO (Asiaticus), consul (83 B. C.), Sylla, iii. 193; Sertorius, iii. 411; Pompey, iv. 66.
PUBLIUS SCIPIO NASICA, son-in-law of the elder Africanus, Æm. Paulus, ii. 185, 190, 194, 200; Marcellus, ii. 266; Cato the Elder, ii. 385.
PUBLIUS [SCIPIO] NASICA, Ti. Gracchus, iv. 582, 590, 592, 593.
SCIPIO SALLUTIO, Cæsar, iv. 345.
METELLUS SCIPIO, father-in-law of Pompey (see METELLUS), Pompey, iv. 135, 145, 150, 152, 154; Comparison, iv. 171, 176; Cæsar, iv. 323, 333, 335, 337, 345, 346, 348; Cato the Younger, iv. 420, 466, 476-479, 482; Cicero, v.

53; Brutus, v. 325; Galba, v. 508 (?); Otho, v. 522.

SCIPIOS, Sertorius, iii. 405; Pompey, iv. 67; Cæsar, iv. 303, 345.

SCIRADIUM, promontory of Salamis, Solon, i. 185.

SCIRAPHIDAS, a Spartan, Lysander, iii. 132.

SCIRON, Theseus, i. 9, 10, 27, 36; Comparison, i. 82.

SCIRUS of Salamis, Theseus, i. 16.

SCOPAS the Thessalian, Cato the Elder, ii. 373. THE SCOPADS, Cimon, iii. 228.

SCOTUSSA, town of Thessaly, Theseus, i. 31; Æm. Paulus, ii. 177; Pelopidas, ii. 252; Flamininus, ii. 430; Pompey, iv. 153; Cæsar, iv. 337.

SCRIBONIA, mother of Piso, Galba, v. 499.

SCROFA, quæstor with Crassus, Crassus, iii. 364.

SCYLLA and CHARYBDIS, Dion, v. 277.

SCYROS, island of the Ægean Sea, Theseus, i. 38; Cimon, iii. 224.

SCYTHES, a slave of Pompey, Pompey, iv. 167.

SCYTHES, a Spartan, Agesilaus, iv. 24.

SCYTHIA and SCYTHIANS, Theseus, i. 1 (Scythian ice); Marius, iii. 64 (origin of the Cimbri); Sylla, iii. 175 (Scythian coats); Crassus, iii. 377, 381, 382; Pompey, iv. 115, 120 (Scythian women), 155, 156; Alexander, iv. 243; Cæsar, iv. 351; Demetrius, v. 121 (habits in drinking).

SECUNDUS the rhetorician, Otho's secretary, Otho, v. 519.

SELEUCIA or SELEUCEA, on the Tigris, Lucullus, iii. 272; Crassus, iii. 373, 374, 376, 378, 394.

SELEUCIA or SELEUCEA, in Syria or in Cilicia, Pompey, iv. 165.

SELEUCUS (I.) NICATOR, general of Alexander and king of Syria, Æm. Paulus, ii. 209 (?); Cato the Elder, ii. 363; Lucullus, iii. 261; Alexander, iv. 239, 267, 283; Demetrius, v. 108, 119, 128, 134, 136-138, 144, 145, 152, 157-163.

SELEUCUS (II.) CALLINICUS, Agis, iv. 499, 502, 508.

SELEUCUS, steward of Cleopatra, Antony, v. 241, 249.

SELINUS, a town of Sicily, Lycurgus, i. 117.

SELLASIA, town of Laconia and field of battle, Philopœmen, ii. 400; Agis, iv. 503; Cleomenes, iv. 546, 552, 555; Aratus, v. 432.

SELYMBRIA, a town of Thrace, Alcibiades, ii. 44, 45.

SEMPRONIUS DENSUS, a faithful centurion, Galba, v. 505.

SENECA the philosopher, Galba, v. 496.

SOSIUS SENECIO, Plutarch's friend, see SOSIUS.

SENONES, a tribe of Gauls, Camillus, i. 300.

SENTIUS, governor of Macedon, Sylla, iii. 168.

SEPTEMPAGIUM, Romulus, i. 74.

SEPTIMIUS, a tribune, one of Pompey's murderers, Pompey, iv. 166-168.

SEPTIMIUS, Galba, v. 490.

SEPTIMULEIUS, C. Gracchus, iv. 615.

SEQUANI, a tribe of Gauls, Marius, iii. 81; Cæsar, iv. 309, 317.

SERAPION, a youth, Alexander, iv. 235.

SERAPIS, Alexander, iv. 280, 283.

SERBONIAN MARSH, Antony, v. 167.

SERGIUS, an actor, Antony, v. 174.

SERIPHUS, island in the Ægean, Themistocles, i. 266.

SERRANUS, in Plutarch's text SORANUS, Cato the Younger, iv. 420.

QUINTUS SERTORIUS, Life, iii. 405; Comparison with Eumenes, iii. 467; Marius, iii. 52, 108; Lucul-

INDEX

lus, iii. 250, 251, 254, 259; Crassus, iii. 365; Pompey, iv. 75, 79-85.
SERVILIA, sister of Cato the Younger, mother of Marcus Brutus, Cato the Younger, iv. 413, 436, 439; Brutus, v. 319, 323, 379.
SERVILIA, another sister of Cato the Younger, wife of Lucullus, Lucullus, iii. 294; Cato the Younger, iv. 439, 445, 473.
SERVILII, Cæsar, iv. 355.
SERVILIUS AHALA, Brutus, v. 319.
SERVILIUS the augur, Lucullus, iii. 243.
[SERVILIUS] CÆPIO, Cato's half brother, Cato the Younger, iv. 413, 415, 421, 424. See, also, 428.
[SERVILIUS] ISAURICUS, Cæsar, iv. 293; and probably Sylla, iii. 194; Pompey, iv. 76.
SERVILIUS ISAURICUS, son of the preceding, Cæsar, iv. 329.
MARCUS SERVILIUS, of consular dignity, Æm. Paulus, ii. 206.
SERVILIUS, prætor, Sylla, iii. 165.
SERVILIUS, lieutenant of Pompey, Pompey, iv. 107.
SERVILIUS, instead of SERVIUS, is in one or two places attached to the name of Galba. See GALBA.
SERVIUS [TULLIUS], king of the Romans, Numa, i. 148.
SERVIUS (or SERVEIUS), Sylla, iii. 167.
SESSORIUM, near Rome, Galba, v. 507.
SESTIUS, Brutus, v. 322.
SESTOS, town of Thrace, Alcibiades, ii. 54; Lysander, iii. 122, 124, 129; Cimon, iii. 226.
SETIA, town of Latium, Cæsar, iv. 351.
SEUTHAS, a servant of Aratus, Aratus, v. 390.
SEXTILIUS'S WATERS (Aquæ Sextiæ), in Gaul, Marius, iii. 73.

SEXTILIUS, governor of Africa, Marius, iii. 102.
SEXTILIUS, lieutenant of Lucullus, Lucullus, iii. 276, 277.
SEXTILIUS, a prætor, seized by the pirates, Pompey, iv. 90.
LUCIUS SEXTIUS, first plebeian consul, Camillus, i. 336.
PUBLIUS SEXTIUS, defended by Cicero, Cicero, v. 66.
SEXTIUS SYLLA, the Carthaginian, Romulus, i. 59.
TIDIUS SEXTIUS, Pompey, iv. 147.
SIBYLS and SIBYLLINE BOOKS, Theseus, i. 25; Poplicola, i. 235; Fabius, i. 399; Marcellus, ii. 265; Marius, iii. 105; Demosthenes, v. 21; Cicero, v. 56.
SIBYRTIUS, governor of Arachosia, Eumenes, iii. 466.
SIBYRTIUS's wrestling ground, Alcibiades, ii. 6.
SICILY and SICILIANS. See, in general, for history, the lives of Timoleon, Marcellus, Nicias, Dion, and the Comparisons; also, Alcibiades, ii. 24-28, 32, 48, 58; Pyrrhus, iii. 19, 31-37; Pompey, iv. 69, 71, 84, 93, 128, 143, 150; Cæsar, iv. 345; Cato the Younger, iv. 472, 473, 477; Cicero, v. 38, 43-46, 73; Comparison, v. 98, 99; Antony, v. 195, 196, 200, 221. For other notices, Theseus, i. 18 (Dædalus's visit); Lycurgus, i. 130; Themistocles, i. 273 (his visit); Camillus, i. 306 (a date); Pericles, i. 368, 370; Fabius, i. 423, 428; Pelopidas, ii. 255; Cato the Elder, ii. 352; Marius, iii. 101; Lysander, iii. 115, 131; Sylla, iii. 204 (Eunus the slave); Cimon, iii. 225 (Æschylus there); Crassus, iii. 363, 386; Agesilaus, iv. 5, 48; Demetrius, v. 128. Native Sicilians or Sicels, Nicias, iii. 331. Sicilian manufactures, Lysander, iii. 115; Al-

exander, iv. 226. Sicilian lard, Nicias, iii. 307.

SICINIUS, a public speaker, Crassus, iii. 360.

SICINNIUS VELLUTUS, tribune of the people, Coriolanus, ii. 66, 74, 82.

SICINNUS, a Persian captive, Themistocles, i. 259, 260.

SICYON and SICYONIANS, in Peloponnesus, Numa, i. 139 (Hippolytus); Pericles, i. 367; Cato, ii. 379; Philopœmen, ii. 395; Cleomenes, iv. 538, 539-543; Demetrius, v. 117, 127; Antony, v. 194 (Fulvia's death); and Aratus throughout. The Sicyonian school of painting, Aratus, v. 397 and after.

SIDON, seaport of Syria, Demetrius, v. 137; Antony, v. 218.

SIGLIURIA, Poplicola, i. 230.

SIGNIA, a town of Latium, Sylla, iii. 193.

SILANIO, a statuary, Theseus, i. 5.

JUNIUS SILANUS, husband of Servilia, Cato's sister and Brutus's mother, Cato the Younger, iv. 436-438; Cicero, v. 53, 57-60.

MARCUS SILANUS, driven away by Cleopatra, Antony, v. 226.

SILENUS, a youth of Pontus, Lysander, iii. 145.

PUBLIUS SILICIUS, proscribed, Brutus, v. 348.

SILLACES, a Parthian, Crassus, iii. 377, 395.

POMPÆDIUS SILO, an Italian deputy, Cato the Younger, iv. 415.

PUBLIUS SILO, an Italian, Marius, iii. 92.

SILVIA, daughter of Numitor, Romulus, i. 44.

SILVIUM, a town of Apulia, Sylla, iii. 192.

SIMÆTHA, at Megara, Pericles, i. 381.

SIMMIAS, accuser of Pericles, Pericles, i. 388.

SIMMIAS, companion of Philopœmen, Philopœmen, ii. 407.

SIMONIDES of Ceos, the poet, Theseus, i. 9, 16; Lycurgus, i. 88; Themistocles, i. 245, 250, 263; Timoleon, ii. 165; Agesilaus, iv. 3; Dion, v. 259; Aratus, v. 431, 432.

SIMYLUS the poet, Romulus, i. 63.

SINNACA, town of Babylonia, Crassus, iii. 390, 391.

SINNIS, a robber, Theseus, i. 8, 27, 31; Comparison, i. 82.

SINOPE, daughter of Asopus, Lucullus, iii. 273.

SINOPE and SINOPIANS, a town of Pontus, Pericles, i. 368; Lucullus, iii. 273; Comparison, iii. 305; Pompey, iv. 116.

SINORA, SINORIA, or INORA, a town of Pontus, Pompey, iv. 103.

SINUESSA, town of Italy, Marcellus, ii. 297; Otho, v. 510.

SIPPIUS, an effeminate man, Cato the Younger, iv. 417.

SIRIS, a river of Lucania, Pyrrhus, iii. 22.

SISENNA, an historian, Lucullus, iii. 244.

SISIMITHRES, a cowardly Persian, Alexander, iv. 261.

SISMATIAS, a place in Sparta, Cimon, iii. 237.

SMYRNA, a town of Ionia, Sertorius, iii. 406; Brutus, v. 350, 352.

SOCHARES of Decelea, perhaps the same as SOPHANES, Cimon, iii. 223.

SOCRATES the philosopher, Lycurgus, i. 131; Pericles, i. 357, 371; Alcibiades, ii. 3, 6-11, 24; Aristides, ii. 308, 310, 343; Cato the Elder, ii. 356, 376, 381; Marius, iii. 111; Lysander, iii. 115; Nicias, iii. 327, 341; Alexander, iv. 271; Phocion, iv. 412.

INDEX

SOLI, a town of Cilicia, Demetrius, v. 122, 131.
SOLI, a town of Cyprus, Solon, i. 205; Alexander, iv. 220.
SOLON, the Athenian lawgiver, Life, i. 177; Comparison with Publicola, i. 239; Poplicola, i. 214; Themistocles, i. 246; Phocion, iv. 374; Cleomenes, iv. 540; Antony, v. 201.
SOLON of Platæa, Phocion, iv. 406.
SOLONIUM, Marius, iii. 95.
SOLOON, or SOLUS, a young man of Athens and a river of Bithynia named after him, Theseus, i. 28.
SONCHIS the Saite, Solon, i. 204.
SOPHANES, Comparison of Aristides and Cato, ii. 389. See SOCHARES.
SOPHAX, son of Hercules, Sertorius, iii. 416.
SOPHENE and SOPHENIANS, district of Armenia, Lucullus, iii. 275, 283; Pompey, iv. 105.
SOPHOCLES the poet, Numa, i. 139; Comparison, i. 173; Solon, i. 177; Pericles, i. 349; Timoleon, ii. 164; Cimon, iii. 225; Nicias, iii. 329; Pompey, iv. 168; Alexander, iv. 186, 188; Phocion, iv. 366; Agis, iv. 495; Demosthenes, v. 8; Demetrius, v. 154, 156; Antony, v. 186; Artaxerxes, v. 472.
SOPHROSYNE, daughter of Dionysius the Elder, Dion, v. 264.
SORANUS, probably SERRANUS, Cato the Younger, iv. 420.
SOREX the mime, Sylla, iii. 203.
SORNATIUS, lieutenant of Lucullus, Lucullus, iii. 264, 274, 284, 290.
SOSIBIUS, favorite of Ptolemy Philopator, Cleomenes, iv. 557-559.
SOSIBIUS, a writer, Lycurgus, i. 122.
SOSICLES the Pedian, at the battle of Salamis, Themistocles, i. 262.
SOSIGENES, friend of Demetrius, Demetrius, v. 160.

SOSIS, a Syracusan speaker, Dion, v. 294-295.
SOSISTRATUS, a Syracusan, Pyrrhus, iii. 34.
SOSIUS SENECIO, friend of Plutarch, Theseus, i. 1; Demosthenes, v. 1, 36; Dion, v. 259.
SOSO, sister of Abantidas of Sicyon, Aratus, v. 388.
SOSSIUS, lieutenant of Antony, Antony, v. 199.
SOTER, a surname, Coriolanus, ii. 71.
SOTION, a writer, Alexander, iv. 266.
SOUS, king of Sparta, Lycurgus, i. 88, 89.
SPAIN and SPANIARDS (IBERIA and IBERIANS), Lycurgus, i. 93 (his supposed voyage thither); Fabius, i. 404, 427, 428 (Scipio); Timoleon, ii. 156; Æm. Paulus, ii. 172, 175 (their mixture with Ligurians), 216; Marcellus, ii. 276; Comparison, ii. 306; Cato the Elder, ii. 355, 361, 362; Comparison, ii. 393; Flamininus, ii. 425; Marius, iii. 52, 57, 67; Lucullus, iii. 250, 254, 289; Crassus, iii. 355, 359, 364, 365, 370; Sertorius and the Comparison throughout; Pompey, iv. 75, 78-84 (campaign against Sertorius), 96, 111, 130, 145-148, 150; Cæsar, iv. 291 (quæstor there), 299 (proprætor there), 311, 321, 329 (defeat of Afranius); 334, 348 (battle of Munda); Cato the Younger, iv. 447, 460, 481; Ti. Gracchus, iv. 570; C. Gracchus, iv. 601; Cicero, v. 79; Antony, v. 171, 175, 203, 228; Galba, v. 479, 481, 482, 486, 488, 498; Otho, v. 511.
SPANUS, a Lusitanian, Sertorius, iii. 417.
SPARAMIZES, a eunuch of Parysatis, Artaxerxes, v. 456, 457.

SPARTA, Theseus, i. 34; Lycurgus, i. 87, and frequent throughout the Lives. See, also, LACEDÆMON and LACONIA.

SPARTACUS, the leader in the servile war, Crassus, iii. 360-365; Comparison, iii. 400; Pompey, iv. 101; Cato the Younger, iv. 421.

SPARTON, Bœotian commander at the first battle of Coronea, Agesilaus, iv. 27.

SPARTON, a Rhodian, Phocion, iv. 388.

SPENDON, a poet of Sparta, Lycurgus, i. 127.

SPERCHIUS, river of Thessaly, Theseus, i. 37.

SPEUSIPPUS the philosopher, Dion, v. 275, 280, 296.

SPHACTERIA, island on the coast of Messenia, Alcibiades, ii. 19; Nicias, iii. 316.

SPHÆRUS the Borysthenite, a philosopher, Lycurgus, i. 95; Cleomenes, iv. 521, 533.

SPHETTUS, an Attic township, Theseus, i. 12; Demetrius, v. 115.

SPHINES, the proper name of Calanus the Indian philosopher, Alexander, iv. 271.

SPHODRIAS, a Spartan, Pelopidas, ii. 235; Agesilaus, iv. 35-37, 42; Comparison, iv. 172.

NYMPHS called SPHRAGITIDES, Aristides, ii. 324, 335.

SPICLUS, SPICULUS, or SPICILLUS, the gladiator, Galba, v. 485.

LENTULUS SPINTHER, consul (57 B.C.), Pompey, iv. 127, 152; Cæsar, iv. 335; Cicero, v. 75, 80.

LENTULUS SPINTHER, his son, Cæsar, iv. 362.

SPITHRIDATES, a Persian, Lysander, iii. 142; Agesilaus, iv. 12, 16.

SPORUS, Galba, v. 485.

SPURINA, commanding for Otho, Otho, v. 515-517.

STAGIRA or STAGIRUS, town of Macedonia, Alexander, iv. 186.

STAPHYLUS, son of Theseus, Theseus, i. 19, 20.

STASICRATES, an architect, Alexander, iv. 279.

STATIANUS, lieutenant of Antony, Antony, v. 203, 204.

STATILIUS, an Epicurean, Brutus, v. 330.

STATIRA, wife of Artaxerxes II., Artaxerxes, v. 445, 446, 459-461.

STATIRA, wife of Darius, Alexander, iv. 221, 222.

STATIRA, daughter of Darius, married to Alexander, Alexander, iv. 276, 284.

STATIRA, sister of Mithridates, Lucullus, iii. 265, 266.

STATYLLIUS (or STATILIUS), Cato the Younger, iv. 487, 488, 494; Brutus, v. 377, 378.

STEPHANUS, Demosthenes, v. 17.

STEPHANUS, a boy, Alexander, iv. 230.

STERTINIUS, probable correction of TITILLIUS, lieutenant of Flamininus, Flamininus, ii. 438.

STESILAUS of Ceos, Themistocles, i. 247; Aristides, ii. 311.

STESIMBROTUS of Thasos, a writer, Themistocles, i. 246, 249, 273; Pericles, i. 349, 359, 374, 389; Cimon, iii. 218, 234, 235.

STHENIS of Himera, Pompey, iv. 70, 71.

STHENIS the statuary, Lucullus, iii. 273.

STILBIDES, a diviner, Nicias, iii. 342.

STILPO, the philosopher at Megara, Demetrius, v. 111.

STIRIA, Attic township, Alcibiades, ii. 39.

STIRIS, a town of Phocis, Cimon, iii. 215.

STOIC Philosophers, Cato the Elder, ii. 379; Lucullus, iii. 296; Cato the Younger, iv. 417, 423,

487. Doctrines, Cato the Younger, iv. 436, 489; Cleomenes, iv. 522; Cicero, v. 41, 65; Comparison, v. 96.
LICINIUS STOLO, tribune of the people, Camillus, i. 331, 332.
STRABO, philosopher and historian, Sylla, iii. 189; Lucullus, iii. 281; Cæsar, iv. 357.
STRABO, father of Pompey, Pompey, iv. 58, 62.
STRATO, a rhetorician, Brutus, v. 379.
STRATOCLES, an Athenian demagogue, Demetrius, v. 113, 114, 127, 129, 130.
STRATONICE, the daughter of Corrhæus or Corrhagus, wife of Antigonus, Demetrius, v. 103.
STRATONICE, daughter of Demetrius, married to Seleucus and to Antiochus, Demetrius, v. 136, 137, 144, 146, 161-164.
STRATONICE, one of the wives of Mithridates, Pompey, iv. 108, 109.
STRATONICUS, Lycurgus, i. 130.
STRŒBUS, servant of Callisthenes, Alexander, iv. 256.
STRYMON, river of Thrace, Cimon, iii. 222, 223.
STYMPHÆA or TYMPHÆA, on the borders of Macedon and Epirus, Pyrrhus, iii. 8.
SUCRO, river in Spain, Sertorius, iii. 429; Pompey, iv. 81.
SUETONIUS PAULINUS, commanding for Otho, Otho, v. 515, 517-518, 520, 522.
SUEVI or SUEVIANS, a German people, Pompey, iv. 128; Cæsar, iv. 313.
SUGAMBRI, a German people, Cæsar, iv. 313.
SUILLII, a Roman name, Poplicola, i. 226.
SULPICIUS, consular tribune, Camillus, i. 318.

QUINTUS SULPICIUS, pontifex maximus, Marcellus, ii. 266.
SULPICIUS, commanding in Macedonia, Flamininus, ii. 424.
SULPICIUS, tribune of the people, Marius, iii. 93-95; Sylla, iii. 163-166.
SULPICIUS, interrex and consul (51 B. C.), Pompey, iv. 135; Cato the Younger, iv. 468.
SULPICIUS GALBA. See GALBA.
SUNIUM, promontory of Attica, Aratus, v. 419.
SUPERBUS. See TARQUINIUS.
LENTULUS SURA, accomplice of Catiline, Cæsar, iv. 294; Cicero, v. 55-57, 60-62, 71; Antony, v. 166.
BRUTTIUS SURA, Sylla, iii. 168, 169.
SURENA, commander of the Parthians, Crassus, iii. 377, 380, 389-397.
SUSA, town of Persia, Pelopidas, ii. 253; Comparison of Crassus and Nicias, iii. 403; Agesilaus, iv. 21; Alexander, iv. 203, 231, 232, 276; Demosthenes v. 16; Artaxerxes v. 447.
SUSAMITHRES, uncle of Pharnabazus, Alcibiades, ii. 57.
SUTRIUM, town of Etruria, Camillus, i. 323, 326, 327.
SYBARIS and SYBARITES, Greek town in Italy, Pericles, i. 354; Pelopidas, ii. 220; Crassus, iii. 395.
SYBARIS, daughter of Themistocles, Themistocles, i. 283.
LUCIUS CORNELIUS SYLLA, Life, iii. 152; Comparison with Lysander, iii. 207. See, also, the contemporary and nearly contemporary lives. Marius, iii. 62, 82, 83, 92, 93, 94, 108, 109, 112; Lucullus, iii. 243-245, 247-252, 267, 269, 273, 293, 301; Crassus, iii. 352, 357-358; Comparison, iii. 398; Sertorius, iii. 406, 409, 411, 412, 415, 427, 428, 433, 434-437; Pompey,

638 INDEX

iv. 64-71, 74-78, 85, 99, 116, 124; Comparison, iv. 171; Cæsar, iv. 286-288, 290, 291, 301, 303, 329; Cato the Younger, iv. 416, 431, 433; Cicero, v. 39, 40, 48, 50-52, 55, 68. Also, Poplicola, i. 229; Flamininus, ii. 452; Antony, v. 165; Brutus, v. 327; Otho, v. 519.

SEXTIUS SYLLA the Carthaginian, Romulus, i. 59.

SYMBOLUM, near Philippi, Brutus, v. 361.

SYNALUS, a Carthaginian, Dion, v. 284, 285, 289.

SYRACUSE and SYRACUSANS. See, in general, the lives of Timoleon and Dion, Marcellus, ii. 276-293; Nicias, iii. 308, 327 to the end, and the Comparisons; also, Alcibiades, ii. 24-32; Pyrrhus, iii. 11, 31, 34; Coriolanus, ii. 77; Agesilaus, iv. 39; Cato the Younger, iv. 472.

SYRIA and SYRIANS, Æm. Paulus, ii. 176; Flamininus, ii. 446; compare, also, Philopœmen, ii. 415; where *Syrians* occurs in the original; these passages refer to the war of Antiochus with the Romans;—Lucullus, iii. 261 (Tigranes), 269, 273 (the Cappadocian Syrians); Crassus, iii. 370, 373, 390; Pompey, iv. 105, 111, 112, 120, 130, 145; Alexander, iv. 205, 213; Cæsar, iv. 343; Cato the Younger, iv. 426, 460; Cicero, v. 50, 65, 67, 70, 77, 86; Demetrius, v. 106, 107, 117, 136, 138 (the Syrian sea), 158; Antony, v. 167, 169, 191, 194, 198, 201, 221, 222, 241, 250; Brutus, v. 349, 350; Aratus, v. 397, 402 (four Syrian brothers), 408, 418; Galba, v. 489; Otho, v. 513, 525. Cœle-Syria, Antony, v. 201, 221. A Syrian woman, Marius, iii. 71. Syriac, Antony, v. 213. The Syrian Chersonese, Demetrius, v. 161.

SYRMUS, king of the Triballians, Alexander, iv. 192.

GREAT SYRTIS, Dion, v. 284.

SYRUS, son of Apollo and Sinope, Lucullus, iii. 273.

T

TACHOS, king of Egypt, Agesilaus, iv. 51-54.

TACITA, one of the Muses, Numa, i. 145.

TÆNARUS, promontory of Laconia, Pompey, iv. 89; Phocion, iv. 401; Cleomenes, iv. 545, 563; Antony, v. 234.

TAGUS, the river, Sertorius, iii. 425.

TALASIUS and TALASIO, Romulus, i. 55; Pompey, iv. 63.

TALAURA, town of Cappadocia, Lucullus, iii. 266.

TAMYNÆ, town of Eubœa, Phocion, iv. 380.

TANAGRA, town of Bœotia, Pericles, i. 351; Pelopidas, ii. 236; Cimon, iii. 238, 239.

TANAIS, the river Don, Alexander, iv. 243.

TANUSIUS, an historian, Cæsar, iv. 313.

TAPHOSIRIS, town of Egypt, Comparison of Antony and Demetrius, v. 257.

TARCHETIUS, king of the Albans, Romulus, i. 42, 43.

TARCONDEMUS, king of Cilicia, Antony, v. 227.

TARENTUM, Greek town in Italy, Fabius, i. 422-425; Comparison, i. 432; Marcellus, ii. 289, 295; Cato, ii. 349, 367; Philopœmen, ii. 406 (Tarentine soldiers in Peloponnesus); Flamininus, ii. 423; Pyrrhus, iii. 16, 18, 19, 20, 25-32, 34, 36; Sylla, iii. 191; Alexander, iv. 208 (a Tarentine);

Cleomenes, iv. 526 (Tarentine soldiers); C. Gracchus, iv. 603; Cicero, v. 81; Antony, v. 199, 228.

TARPEIA, daughter of Tarpeius, Romulus, i. 62, 63.

TARPEIA, a vestal, Numa, i. 148.

TARPEIUS, a Roman captain, Romulus, i. 62.

TARPEIAN HILL, Romulus, i. 64; Numa, i. 143; Marius, iii. 109.

TARQUINIA, a vestal, Poplicola, i. 222.

TARQUINIUS, son of Damaratus, the Elder, Romulus, i. 62, 63; Poplicola, i. 228.

TARQUINIUS SUPERBUS, Comparison of Lycurgus and Numa, i. 174; Poplicola, i. 213-234; Coriolanus, ii. 61; Ti. Gracchus, iv. 585.

TARQUINIUS COLLATINUS, Poplicola, i. 215-221.

THE TARQUINS, Poplicola, i. 217; Comparison, i. 242; Æm. Paulus, ii. 198; Brutus, v. 318.

TARRACINA or TERRACINA, town of Latium, Marius, iii. 96, 99; Cæsar, iv. 351.

TARRUTIUS, friend of Varro, Romulus, i. 54, 55.

TARRUTIUS, Romulus, i. 46.

TARSUS, town of Cilicia, Marius, iii. 111; Ti. Gracchus, iv. 575; Demetrius, v. 157.

TATIA, daughter of Tatius, Numa, i. 137, 165.

TATIENSES, the second Roman tribe, Romulus, i. 67.

TATIUS, king of the Sabines, Romulus, i. 62, 63, 67, 71-73; Numa, i. 135, 137, 140, 142.

TAUREAS, an Athenian, Alcibiades, ii. 23.

TAURION, officer of Philip III. of Macedon, Aratus, v. 438.

TAUROMENIUM, town of Sicily, Timoleon, ii. 131, 133.

TAURUS, mountains of Asia, Æm.

Paulus, ii. 176; Lucullus, iii. 275, 276, 278, 285; Comparison, iii. 305; Pompey, iv. 95; Demetrius, v. 157.

TAURUS, a Cretan, Theseus, i. 14, 17.

TAURUS, lieutenant of Octavianus, Antony, v. 231.

TAXILES, king of the Indians, Alexander, iv. 262, 271.

TAXILES, general of Mithridates, Sylla, iii. 162, 181; Lucullus, iii. 277-278.

TAYGETUS, mountain of Laconia, Lycurgus, i. 110; Pelopidas, ii. 253; Cimon, iii. 236; Agis, iv. 503.

TECHNON, a servant of Aratus, Aratus, v. 390, 392, 404.

TECTOSAGES, a tribe of Gauls, Sylla, iii. 155.

TEGEA, town of Arcadia, and TEGEATANS, Theseus, i. 34; Aristides, ii. 325, 329, 335; Lysander, iii. 150; Agesilaus, iv. 49; Agis, iv. 498, 509, 512; Cleomenes, iv. 524, 536, 544, 546, 549.

TEGYRÆ, town of Bœotia, Pelopidas, ii. 237, 238, 241; Comparison, ii. 303, 304; Agesilaus, iv. 39.

TELAMON, son of Æacus, Theseus, i. 10.

TELAMON, town of Etruria, Marius, iii. 103.

TELECLIDES the comic poet, Pericles, i. 341, 362; Nicias, iii. 312.

TELECLIDES, a Corinthian, Timoleon, ii. 127.

TELEMACHUS, a Corinthian captain, Timoleon, ii. 134.

TELEMACHUS, son of Ulysses, Romulus, i. 42.

TELEPHUS, son of Hercules, Romulus, i. 42.

TELES, a coward, Pericles, i. 385.

TELESIDES, a Sicilian, Dion, v. 301.

TELESINUS the Samnite, Sylla, iii. 194; Comparison, iii. 211.

640 INDEX

TELESIPPA, Alexander, iv. 238.
TELESTES, a dithyrambic poet, Alexander, iv. 188.
TELEUTIAS, half brother of Agesilaus, Agesilaus, iv. 30.
TELLUS, Solon, i. 206; Comparison, i. 239.
TELMESSUS, town of Lycia, Alexander, iv. 179.
TEMENITID or MENITID, gate of Syracuse, Dion, v. 288.
TEMPE, pass of Thessaly, Themistocles, i. 252; Flamininus, ii. 425; Pompey, iv. 160.
TENEDOS, island on the coast of Troas, Lucullus, iii. 248; Eumenes, iii. 448.
TENOS, island in the Ægean Sea, Themistocles, i. 260.
TENTERITÆ, a German nation, Cæsar, iv. 312.
TEOS and TEIANS, town of Ionia, Romulus, i. 54; Sylla, iii. 189; Alexander, iv. 236.
TERATIUS, Romulus, i. 43.
TERENTIA, wife of Cicero, Cato the Younger, iv. 434; Cicero, v. 46, 59, 69, 71, 84.
TERENTIUS CULLEO or CULEO, tribune of the people, Flamininus, ii. 446.
[TERENTIUS] CULLEO, friend of Pompey, Pompey, iv. 126.
LUCIUS TERENTIUS, in the tent with Pompey, Pompey, iv. 61.
TERENTIUS, Galba, v. 505.
TERENTIUS VARRO, defeated at Cannæ, Fabius, i. 412-416.
TERENTIUS VARRO the author, Romulus, i. 54, 61; Cæsar, iv. 329.
TERIBAZUS, a Persian, Artaxerxes, v. 445, 447, 450, 467, 471-473, 475.
TERMERUS, a robber, Theseus, i. 10.
TERMINUS, Numa, i. 158.
TERPANDER, the poet and musician, Lycurgus, i. 118, 127; Agis, iv. 506.

TERTIA, daughter of Æm. Paulus, Æm. Paulus, ii. 180; Cato the Elder, ii. 377.
TERTIA, sister of Clodius, Cicero, v. 69.
TETHYS, Romulus, i. 43.
TETRAPOLIS, in Attica, Theseus, i. 12.
TEUCER, an Athenian informer, Alcibiades, ii. 29.
TEUTAMUS, commander of the Argyraspids, Eumenes, iii. 457, 462, 463.
TEUTONES, a German people, Marius, iii. 63, 69, 73, 76, 81; Sertorius, iii. 407; Cæsar, iv. 307.
THAIS, mistress of Ptolemy, Alexander, iv. 233.
THALÆA, wife of Pinarius, Comparison of Numa and Lycurgus, i. 174.
THALAMÆ, town of Laconia, Agis, iv. 505.
THALES, a Cretan, Lycurgus, i. 91; Agis, iv. 506.
THALES of Miletus, the wise man, Solon, i. 179, 182, 188.
THALLUS, an Athenian, Phocion, iv. 381.
THAPSACUS, town of Mesopotamia, Alexander, iv. 273.
THAPSUS, town of Africa, field of battle, Cæsar, iv. 346; Cato the Younger, iv. 479.
THAPSUS, town of Sicily, Nicias, iii. 332.
THARGELIA, an Ionian woman, Pericles, i. 371.
THARRHYPAS, king of Epirus, Pyrrhus, iii. 1.
THASOS and THASIANS, island in the Ægean Sea, Cimon, iii. 233; Cato the Younger, iv. 424 (Thasian marble); Demetrius, v. 121 (Thasian wine); Brutus, v. 361, 369.
THEAGENES, a Theban, Alexander, iv. 194.

THEANGELA, town of Caria, Alexander, iv. 243.
THEANO, daughter of Menon, Athenian priestess, Alcibiades, ii. 32.
THEARIDAS of Megalopolis, Cleomenes, iv. 548.
THEARIDES, brother of Dionysius the Elder, Dion, v. 264.
THEBE, daughter of Jason, wife of Alexander of Pheræ, Pelopidas, ii. 251, 255, 260.
THEBES and THEBANS, of Bœotia, Theseus, i. 32 (his expedition thither); Lycurgus, i. 105, 127, 131; Solon, i. 180; Themistocles, i. 269; Camillus, i. 306 (date of its destruction by Alexander); Fabius, i. 430 (funeral of Epaminondas); Alcibiades, ii. 6 (flute playing); Pelopidas and the Comparison throughout; Aristides, ii. 330, 334; Flamininus, ii. 429 (his entrance); Lysander, iii. 130, 146-148 (his death); Sylla, iii. 182; Agesilaus, iv. 10 (where the translation has Bœotians), and generally, 23-50, and the Comparison; Alexander, iv. 193-194; Phocion, iv. 385, 396; Demosthenes, v. 10, 19, 21, 26; Demetrius, v. 110, 147, 148, 155; Dion, v. 275; Artaxerxes, v. 465.
The Thebans' sacred band, Pelopidas, ii. 239-242; Alexander, iv. 189.
THEMISCYRA, a town of Pontus, Lucullus, iii. 260.
THEMISTOCLES, Life, i. 245; Theseus, i. 7; Pericles, i. 345; Alcibiades, ii. 55; Comparison, ii. 113; Pelopidas, ii. 224, 243; Aristides, ii. 311, 313-315, 317, 320, 321, 339, 342-344; Cato the Elder, ii. 357, 358; Comparison, ii. 389, 394; Flamininus, ii. 450; Lysander, iii. 130; Cimon, iii. 220, 223, 225, 229, 236, 241; Comparison,

iii. 305; Comparison of Crassus and Nicias, iii. 401; Pompey, iv. 146; Comparison, iv. 175; Phocion, iv. 370; Comparison of Cicero and Demosthenes, v. 99; Antony, v. 202.
THEMISTOCLES, an Athenian, friend of Plutarch, Themistocles, i. 284.
THEOCRITUS the augur, Pelopidas, ii. 244.
THEODECTES of Phaselis, the philosopher, Alexander, iv. 202.
THEODORUS the atheist, Phocion, iv. 411.
THEODORUS the high-priest, Alcibiades, ii. 49.
THEODORUS, tutor of Antyllus, Antony, v. 247.
THEODORUS of Phegæa, companion of Alcibiades, Alcibiades, ii. 26, 31.
THEODORUS, a Tarentine, Alexander, iv. 208.
THEODOTES, uncle of Heraclides, Dion, v. 270, 304, 306, 307.
THEODOTUS of Chios, a rhetorician in Egypt, Pompey, iv. 166, 170; Cæsar, iv. 341; Brutus, v. 355.
THEODOTUS the prophet, Pyrrhus, iii. 8.
THEOGITON the Megarian, Aristides, ii. 336.
THEOMNESTUS the Academic philosopher, Brutus, v. 344.
THEOPHANES the Lesbian, Pompey, iv. 110, 116, 127, 165, 167; Cicero, v. 80.
THEOPHILUS, Antony's steward, Antony, v. 234.
THEOPHILUS, an armorer, Alexander, iv. 226.
THEOPHRASTUS, a Macedonian officer in Corinth, Aratus, v. 408.
THEOPHRASTUS the philosopher, Lycurgus, i. 100; Solon, i. 180, 212, Themistocles, i. 274; Pericles, i. 370, 388, 391; Aristides, ii. 342;

Lysander, iii. 127, 135; Sylla, iii. 189; Nicias, iii. 320, 324; Sertorius, iii. 421; Agesilaus, iv. 5, 53; Cato the Younger, iv. 454; Agis, iv. 496; Demosthenes, v. 11, 19; Cicero, v. 63.

THEOPOMPUS the historian, Themistocles, i. 267, 274, 281; Alcibiades, ii. 48; Timoleon, ii. 123; Lysander, iii, 132, 151; Agesilaus, iv. 15, 45, 47; Demosthenes, v. 4, 15, 16, 20, 23, 29; Dion, v. 283.

THEOPOMPUS of Cnidos, author of a collection of fables, Cæsar, iv. 341.

THEOPOMPUS the comic poet, Lysander, iii. 128.

THEOPOMPUS, king of Sparta, Lycurgus, i. 96, 97, 117, 130; Agis, iv. 519.

THEOPOMPUS, a Spartan officer, Pelopidas, ii. 238.

THEOPOMPUS, a Theban, Pelopidas, ii. 228.

THEORIS the priestess, Demosthenes, v. 17.

THEORUS, Alcibiades, ii. 4.

THERAMENES, son of Hagnon, Alcibiades, ii. 3, 46; Lysander, iii. 129; Nicias, iii. 309; Cicero, v. 82.

THERICLEAN cups, Æm. Paulus, ii. 209; the epithet also occurs in the Greek, Philopœmen, ii. 405.

THERMODON, rivulet of Bœotia, afterwards called HÆMON, Theseus, i. 30; Demosthenes, v. 21.

THERMODON, a river of Pontus, Lucullus, iii. 260; Pompey, iv. 108.

THERMODON, a hero, Demosthenes, v. 21.

THERMOPYLÆ, the pass, Themistocles, i. 254; Cato the Elder, ii. 364; Comparison, ii. 389; Flamininus, ii. 428, 437, 443; Agesilaus, iv. 25; Alexander, iv. 192; Demetrius, v. 125, 147.

MINUCIUS THERMUS, Cato the Younger, iv. 443.

THERSIPPUS, Solon, i. 211.

THERYCION, a Spartan, Cleomenes, iv. 527, 528, 554, 555.

THESEUS, Life, i. 1; Comparison with Romulus, i. 82; Solon, i. 205; Sylla, iii. 172; Cimon, iii. 224.

THESPÆ, town of Bœotia, Pelopidas, ii. 235, 236; Lysander, iii. 149; Agesilaus, iv. 35; Demetrius, v. 147.

THESPIS, the tragic poet, Solon, i. 209.

THESPROTIANS, people of Epirus, Pyrrhus, iii. 1.

THESSALONICA, wife of Cassander, Pyrrhus, iii. 7; Demetrius, v. 142.

THESSALONICA, town of Macedonia, Cato the Younger, iv. 424; Brutus, v. 371.

THESSALUS, son of Cimon, Pericles, i. 378; Alcibiades, ii. 26, 31; Cimon, iii. 235.

THESSALUS, son of Pisistratus, Cato the Elder, ii. 383.

THESSALUS, an actor, Alexander, iv. 190, 191.

THESSALY and THESSALIANS, Theseus, i. 30, 37; Romulus, i. 42; Themistocles, i. 252, 269; Camillus, i. 305 (date of their defeat by the Bœotians); Pericles, i. 365; Alcibiades, ii. 33; Æm. Paulus, ii. 176, 178; Pelopidas, ii. 248-251, 255-259; Aristides, ii. 319, 321; Flamininus, ii. 428-439 (battle of Cynoscephalæ); Pyrrhus, iii. 1 (Menon), 9, 15, 18 (Cineas), 24; Sylla, iii. 168 (dominion of Mithridates), 174, 182, 185, 190; Cimon, iii. 213 (Bœotian migration), 224, 234; Lucullus, iii. 256 (Niconides the

INDEX 643

engineer), 273 (Autolycus the hero); Agesilaus, iv. 24; Pompey, iv. 150; (Pharsalia) Comparison, iv. 175; Alexander, iv. 184 (Bucephalas), 193, 211 (Thessalians at Issus), 226 (at Arbela), 239; Cæsar, iv. 333, 335, 341 (campaign of Pharsalia); Phocion, iv. 395 (Menon); Demosthenes, v. 20 (Daochus); Demetrius, v. 130; Dion, v. 280 (Miltas); Brutus, v. 345; Galba, v. 477.

THESTE, the name of the sister of Dionysius the Younger, Dion, v. 279.

THETIDIUM or THETIDEUM, in Thessaly, Pelopidas, ii. 256.

THIMBRON, a Spartan officer, Artaxerxes, v. 462.

THOAS, an Athenian, Theseus, i. 28.

THŒNON, a Syracusan, Pyrrhus, iii. 34.

THONIS, an Egyptian woman, Demetrius, v. 132.

THORANIUS, lieutenant of Metellus, Sertorius, iii. 419.

THORAX of Larissa, Demetrius, v. 134.

THORAX, a Spartan officer, Lysander, iii. 122, 136.

THRACE and THRACIANS, Theseus, i. 14 (Bottiæans); Romulus, i. 62 (Rhymitalces); Themistocles, i. 244 (his mother, born in Thrace); Pericles, i. 354, 365, 367; Alcibiades, ii. 33, 45, 53, 55; Æm. Paulus, ii. 186, 187, 190 (Thracian soldiers); Cato the Elder, ii. 363; Flamininus, ii. 438; Pyrrhus, iii. 13; Lysander, iii. 131, 137; Sylla, iii. 168 (dominion of Mithridates), 174; Cimon, iii. 217 (his Thracian blood), 222, 233; Lucullus, iii. 280 (Thracian horse); Nicias, iii. 315; Crassus, iii. 360, 362 (the servile war), 364; Agesilaus, iv. 23; Alexander, iv. 180 (bacchantes), 194, 279 (Athos); Phocion, iv. 400; Cato the Younger, iv. 424 (his brother's death); Demosthenes, v. 33, 34; Demetrius, v. 147, 152, 163 (Dromichætes); Antony, v. 227, 229.

THRACIAN VILLAGE, near Cyzicus, Lucullus, iii. 255.

THRASEA (Pætus, the Stoic), his life of Cato, Cato the Younger, iv. 439, 454.

THRASON, Alcibiades, ii. 53.

THRASYBULUS, son of Thrason, Alcibiades, ii. 53.

THRASYBULUS of Stiria, who expelled the Thirty Tyrants, Alcibiades, ii. 3, 39; Pelopidas, ii. 227, 234; Lysander, iii. 147, 149; Aratus, v. 400.

THRASYDÆUS, envoy of Philip of Macedon, Demosthenes, v. 20.

THRASYLLUS, an Athenian, Alcibiades, ii. 43.

THE LAKE THRASYMENE, field of battle, Fabius, i. 398.

THRIASIAN GATE, at Athens, Pericles, i. 380.

THRIASIAN PLAIN, in Attica, Themistocles, i. 263; Pelopidas, ii. 228; Agesilaus, iv. 36; Aratus, v. 418.

THUCYDIDES, son of Melesias, Pericles, i. 344, 348, 353, 360-363; Comparison, i. 433; Nicias, iii. 309, 324; Demosthenes, v. 16.

THUCYDIDES, son of Olorus, the historian, Lycurgus, i. 125; Themistocles, i. 274, 276; Pericles, i. 349, 362, 376, 378, 384; Fabius, i. 396; Alcibiades, ii. 10, 15, 16, 28; Comparison, ii. 113; Aristides, ii. 341; Cato the Elder, ii. 350; Cimon, iii. 217; Nicias, iii. 307, 308, 312, 335, 337, 348; Agesilaus, iv. 48; Demosthenes, v. 6.

THURII, town of Italy, Pericles, i. 354; Alcibiades, ii. 31, 32; Timoleon, ii. 139, 143; Nicias, iii. 314; Demosthenes, v. 32.

THURIUM, a height above Chæronea, Sylla, iii. 178-182.

THURO, mother of Chæron, Sylla, iii. 178.

THYATIRA, town of Lydia, Sylla, iii. 188.

THYESTES, Cicero, v. 42.

THYMŒTADÆ, Attic township, Theseus, i. 18.

THYREA, town, and THYREATIS, district of Argolis, Nicias, iii. 316; Pyrrhus, iii. 48.

THYRSUS, freedman of Augustus, Antony, v. 241.

TIBARENIANS, people of Pontus, Lucullus, iii. 260, 261, 267.

TIBER, the river, Romulus, i. 41; Camillus, i. 304; Fabius, i. 395; Æm. Paulus, ii. 205; Cæsar, iv. 351; Otho, v. 514. The Tiberine island, Otho, ibid.; and compare Poplicola, i. 221.

TIBERIUS the emperor, and the DOMUS TIBERIANA, Galba, v. 502.

TIDIUS SEXTIUS, Pompey, iv. 147.

TIGELLINUS, Nero's favorite and prætorian prefect, Galba, v. 478, 483, 488, 493, 500, 508; Otho, v. 510.

TIGRANES (II.), king of Armenia, Camillus, i. 306; Sylla, iii. 182; Lucullus, iii. 255, 261, 266, 269-293; Comparison, iii. 305; Crassus, iii. 370, 386; Pompey, iv. 96, 98, 104, 105, 108, 120, 152; Comparison, iv. 174.

TIGRANES (III.), king of Armenia, Pompey, iv. 104, 105, 120, 125.

TIGRANOCERTA, town of Armenia, Lucullus, iii. 276-278, 293; Comparison, iii. 305.

TIGRIS, river of Asia, Lucullus, iii. 272, 275; Comparison, iii. 305.

TIGURINI, Helvetian tribe, Cæsar, iv. 307.

TILLIUS CIMBER, Cæsar, iv. 360; Brutus, v. 336, 339.

TILPHOSSIUM, mountain of Bœotia, Sylla, iii. 182.

TIMÆA, wife of Agis, Alcibiades, ii. 34; Lysander, iii. 140; Agesilaus, iv. 5.

TIMÆUS, friend of Andocides, Alcibiades, ii. 30.

TIMÆUS, the Sicilian historian, Lycurgus, i. 88, 132; Timoleon, ii. 123, 131, 164; Comparison, ii. 218; Nicias, iii. 307, 335, 348; Dion, v. 264, 272, 291, 296.

TIMAGENES, an historian, Pompey, iv. 127; Antony, v. 240.

TIMAGORAS, Athenian envoy to Persia, Pelopidas, ii. 254; Artaxerxes, v. 465.

TIMANDRA, Alcibiades, ii. 57, 58.

TIMANTHES (not the famous Timanthes), a painter, Aratus, v. 418.

TIMANTHES, friend of Aratus (perhaps the same), Aratus, v. 396, 397.

TIMESILEUS, tyrant of Sinope, Pericles, i. 368.

TIMESITHEUS, general of the Lipareans, Camillus, i. 295.

TIMOCLEA, sister of Theagenes, a woman of Thebes, Alexander, iv. 193.

TIMOCLIDES, magistrate of Sicyon, Aratus, v. 387.

TIMOCRATES, Demosthenes, v. 17.

TIMOCRATES the Rhodian, sent with money into Greece, Artaxerxes, v. 463.

TIMOCRATES, married to Dion's wife, Dion, v. 279, 285-287.

TIMOCREON of Rhodes, the poet, Themistocles, i. 269, 270.

TIMODEMUS, father of Timoleon, Timoleon, ii. 121, 169.

INDEX 645

TIMOLAUS, a Spartan, Philopœmen, ii. 413.
TIMOLEON, Life, ii. 118; Comparison with Æm. Paulus, ii. 217; Camillus, i. 306; Dion, v. 317.
TIMOLEONTEUM, at Syracuse, Timoleon, ii. 169.
TIMON the misanthrope, Alcibiades, ii. 23; Antony, v. 237, 238.
TIMON the Phliasian, a writer, Numa, i. 145; Pericles, i. 342; Dion, v. 275.
TIMONASSA of Argos, wife of Pisistratus, Cato the Elder, ii. 383.
TIMONIDES the Leucadian, Dion's friend, Dion, v. 280, 291, 296.
TIMOPHANES, brother of Timoleon, Timoleon, ii. 122-124.
TIMOTHEUS, son of Conon, Athenian general Timoleon, ii. 164; Pelopidas, ii. 222; Sylla, iii. 159; Demosthenes, v. 17.
TIMOTHEUS, a Macedonian soldier, Alexander, iv. 208.
TIMOTHEUS, the poet and musician, Philopœmen, ii. 408; Agesilaus, iv. 20; Agis, iv. 507; Demetrius, v. 150.
TIMOXENUS, general of the Achæans, Cleomenes, iv. 543; Aratus, v. 423, 433.
TINGA, wife of Antæus, Sertorius, iii. 416.
TINGIS, town of Mauritania, Sertorius, iii. 415.
TINNIUS of Minturnæ, Marius, iii. 99.
TIREUS, eunuch of Darius, Alexander, iv. 221, 222.
TIRIBAZUS, a Persian, Agesilaus, iv. 33.
TIRO, freedman of Cicero, Cicero, v. 84, 93.
TISAMENUS the Elean, a prophet, Aristides, ii. 323.
TISANDER, an Athenian, Pericles, i. 388.
TISAPHERNES, a Persian satrap, Alcibiades, ii. 33-38, 40; Comparison, ii. 114; Lysander, iii. 116; Agesilaus, iv. 13-15; Artaxerxes, v. 443, 444, 446, 459, 463, 465.
TISIAS, an Athenian, Alcibiades, ii. 16.
TISIPHONUS, one of Thebe's three brothers, Pelopidas, ii. 260.
TITHORA, town of Phocis, Sylla, iii. 175.
TITHRAUSTES, a Persian, Cimon, iii. 231.
TITHRAUSTES, a Persian, Agesilaus, iv. 15.
TITIANUS, brother of Otho, Otho, v. 517, 523.
TITILLIUS, probably STERTINIUS, Flamininus, ii. 438.
TITINIUS, friend of Cassius, Brutus, v. 368.
TITIUS the quæstor, and TITIUS the consular, Antony, v. 209, 224.
QUINTUS TITIUS, a Roman merchant in Greece, Sylla, iii. 177.
TITUS, a native of Croton, Cicero, v. 57.
TITURIUS, officer of Cæsar in Gaul, Cæsar, iv. 315.
TITYUS, Pelopidas, ii. 238.
TOLERIA, town of Latium, Coriolanus, ii. 94.
TOLMÆUS, Pericles, i. 366.
TOLMIDES, an Athenian general, Pericles, i. 363, 366; Comparison, i. 431, 433; Agesilaus, iv. 27.
TOLUMNIUS, king of the Etruscans, Romulus, i. 61; Marcellus, ii. 270.
TORQUATUS, a name, Marius, iii. 52.
TORQUATUS, under Sylla, Sylla, iii. 195.
MANLIUS TORQUATUS, Fabius, i. 407.
TORYNE, town in Epirus, Antony, v. 228.
TRACHIS, town of Thessaly, Theseus, i. 33.
TRAGIA, island near Samos, Pericles, i. 374.

TRAGISCUS, a Cretan, Aratus, v. 414.
TRALLES, town of Lydia, Crassus, iii. 395; Cæsar, iv. 340.
TRALLIANS, a Thracian people, Agesilaus, iv. 23.
TRAPEZUS. See TREBIZOND.
TREBATIUS, one of Cæsar's friends, Cicero, v. 79.
TREBELLIUS, tribune with Dolabella, Antony, v. 173.
TREBIA, river of north Italy, field of battle, Fabius, i. 396, 398.
TREBIZOND (TRAPEZUS), town of Pontus, Eumenes, iii. 444.
CAIUS TREBONIUS, conspirator with Brutus, Pompey, iv. 130; Cato the Younger, iv. 460; Antony, v. 177; Brutus, v. 336, 339.
TREBONIUS, Marius, iii. 68.
TREBONIUS, in Africa, Galba, v. 491.
TRIARIUS, lieutenant of Lucullus, Lucullus, iii. 290; Pompey, iv. 111.
TRIBALLIANS, a Thracian people, Alexander, iv. 192.
TRIOPIAN HEADLAND, in Caria, Cimon, iii. 230.
TRIPYLUS, Aratus, v. 427.
TRITÆA and TRITÆANS, in Achæa, Cleomenes, iv. 538; Aratus, v. 396.
TRITYMALLUS, Cleomenes, iv. 542.
TROAS, mother of Æacides, Pyrrhus, iii. 1.
TROAS, daughter of Æacides, Pyrrhus, iii. 2.
TRŒZEN, town of Argolis and TRŒZENIANS, Theseus, i. 3, 6, 18, 31, 37, 40; Comparison, i. 85; Themistocles, i. 256; Cleomenes, iv. 541; Demosthenes, v. 30; Aratus, v. 386, 409.
TROGLODYTES, people of Ethiopia, Antony, v. 191.
TROPHONIUS, Aristides, ii. 334; Sylla, iii. 177.

TROY and TROJANS, Theseus, i. 37, 39; Romulus, i. 41, 42; Comparison, i. 86; Solon, i. 180; Camillus, i. 306 (date of the taking of Troy), 308 (the Palladium); Cimon, iii. 218, 223 (verses); Lucullus, iii. 256 (Ilium), 258 (Ilians); Nicias, iii. 308; Sertorius, iii. 405; Alexander, iv. 197; Antony, v. 170; Dion, v. 259 (Simonides's verse). THE TROAD, Sylla, iii. 187; Lucullus, iii. 238, 258. The game called Troy, Cato the Younger, iv. 416.
ÆLIUS TUBERO, son-in-law of Æm. Paulus, Æm. Paulus, ii. 174, 201, 203.
TUBERO the Stoic (son of the preceding), Lucullus, iii. 295.
POSTUMIUS TUBERTUS, Poplicola, i. 234.
POSTUMIUS TUBERTUS, Camillus, i. 286.
TUDER or TUDERTIA, town in Umbria, Marius, iii. 72; Crassus, iii. 357.
TUDITANUS, an historian, Flamininus, ii. 442.
TULLIA, daughter of Cicero, Cicero, v. 85.
TULLIUS, Cicero, v. 37. See CICERO.
TULLUS ATTIUS, leader of the Volscians, Cicero, v. 37. Called TULLUS AUFIDIUS in Coriolanus, ii. 86, and after.
TULLUS, a consular, Pompey, iv. 143.
TULLUS, friend of Cicero, Cicero, v. 69.
TULLUS HOSTILIUS, the king, Romulus, i. 64; Numa, i. 166, 168; Coriolanus, ii. 59.
PETRONIUS TURPILIANUS, Galba, v. 490, 491.
TURPILLIUS, friend and officer of Metellus, Marius, iii. 59.
TUSCANS and TUSCANY. See ETRURIA and ETRUSCANS.

INDEX

TUSCULUM and TUSCULANS, a town of Latium, Camillus, i. 330; Cato the Elder, ii. 347; Lucullus, iii. 296, 301; Pompey, iv. 151; Cæsar, iv. 334; Cicero, v. 83, 90.

TUTTIA, town in Spain, Sertorius, iii. 428, but the reading is uncertain.

TUTULA or TUTOLA, a maid, Romulus, i. 81; Camillus, i. 323, 324.

TYCHA, part of Syracuse, Marcellus, ii. 284.

TYCHON, a name given to a spear, Pelopidas, ii. 252.

TYDEUS, an Athenian officer, Alcibiades, ii. 54; Lysander, iii. 124.

TYMPHÆA or STYMPHÆA, border district of Macedon and Epirus, Pyrrhus, iii. 8.

TYNDARUS, Theseus, i. 34, and THE TYNDARIDS, Flamininus, ii. 440.

TYNNONDAS, tyrant of Eubœa, Solon, i. 190.

TYPHON, Antony, v. 167.

TYRANNION, a grammarian, Sylla, iii. 189; Lucullus, iii. 268.

TYRE, town of Phœnicia, Alexander, iv. 212, 213; Demetrius, v. 137.

TYRRHENIA and TYRRHENIANS. See ETRURIA and ETRUSCANS.

TYRTÆUS the poet, Lycurgus, i. 96; Cleomenes, iv. 522.

U

ULIADES of Samos, Aristides, ii. 340.

ULYSSES, Romulus, i. 42; Solon, i. 210; Alcibiades, ii. 29; Coriolanus, ii. 87; Marcellus, ii. 286; Cato the Elder, ii. 359; Lysander, iii. 137; Agesilaus, iv. 8.

UMBRIANS, Crassus, iii. 357.

USIPETES or USIPES, people of Germany, Cæsar, iv. 312.

UTICA, Marius, iii. 60; Pompey, iv. 71, 74; Cæsar, iv. 347; Cato the Younger, iv. 478-488, 493.

V

VACCÆANS, people of Spain, Sertorius, iii. 432.

VAGA or VACCA, town of Numidia, Marius, iii. 59.

VAGISES, Parthian ambassador, Crassus, iii. 374.

VALENTIA, town of Spain, Pompey, iv. 81.

VALERIA, sister of Poplicola, Coriolanus, ii. 102, 103.

VALERIA, daughter of Poplicola, Poplicola, i. 233, 234.

VALERIA, daughter of Messala, married to Sylla, Sylla, iii. 203, 205.

THE VALERII, Comparison of Solon and Poplicola, i. 239.

VALERIUS ANTIAS, an historian, Romulus, i. 58; Numa, i. 167; Flamininus, ii. 447.

VALERIUS CORVINUS (i. e. CORVUS), six times consul, Marius, iii. 87.

VALERIUS FLACCUS, consul and censor, Cato the Elder, ii. 350, 351, 361, 371.

VALERIUS FLACCUS, consul with Marius, Marius, iii. 87; Sylla, iii. 171, 182, 187; Lucullus, iii. 252, 289.

VALERIUS LEO, at Milan, Cæsar, iv. 306.

MARCUS VALERIUS MAXIMUS, brother of Poplicola, Poplicola, i. 218, 219, 229; Coriolanus, ii. 64; Pompey, iv. 75.

VALERIUS MAXIMUS, an historian, Marcellus, ii. 302; Brutus, v. 379.

[VALERIUS] MESSALA CORVINUS. See MESSALA.

VALERIUS POPLICOLA. See POPLICOLA.

VALERIUS POTITUS, Camillus, i. 289.

648 INDEX

QUINTUS VALERIUS, put to death by Pompey, Pompey, iv. 70.

VALERIUS, VOLESUS, or VELESUS, founder of the Valerian house, Numa, i. 140; Poplicola, i. 214.

FABIUS VALENS, commanding for Vitellius, Galba, v. 486, 491, 499; Otho, v. 514, 516, 518, 521, 523.

VARGUNTINUS, probably VARGUNTEIUS, lieutenant of Crassus, Crassus, iii. 388.

PUBLIUS VARINUS the prætor, in the servile war, Crassus, iii. 361.

VARIUS, called COTYLON, Antony, v. 182.

TERENTIUS VARRO, consul, defeated at Cannæ, Fabius, i. 412-416.

TERENTIUS VARRO, the writer, Romulus, i. 54, 61; Cæsar, iv. 329.

CINGONIUS VARRO, Galba, v. 490.

ALFENUS VARUS, commanding the Batavians at Bedriacum, Otho, v. 499.

ATTIUS VARUS, governor of Africa, Cato the Younger, iv. 476, 477.

VATINIUS, Pompey, iv. 130; Cato the Younger, iv. 459; Cicero, v. 47, 66; Brutus, v. 346.

VEII, town of Etruria, and VEIENTES, VEIENTINES, or VEIENTANI, Romulus, i. 73, 75; Poplicola, i. 227; Camillus, i. 286, 288-291, 294, 302, 305, 313, 320.

VELABRUM, at Rome, Romulus, i. 46.

VELESUS or VOLESUS, Numa, i. 140; compare Poplicola, i. 214.

VELIA, part of the Palatine Hill at Rome, Poplicola, i. 224, 238.

VELIA or ELEA, town in Lucania, Timoleon, ii. 163; Æm. Paulus, ii. 215; Brutus, v. 343. Zeno the Eleatic, Pericles, i. 342.

VELITRÆ and THE VELITRANI, town in Latium, Camillus, i. 335; Coriolanus, ii. 73, 74.

SCINNIUS VELLUTUS, tribune of the people, Coriolanus, ii. 66, 74, 81, 82.

VENTIDIUS, two brothers of that name, Pompey, iv. 65.

VENTIDIUS, lieutenant of Antony, Antony, v. 197-198.

PERPENNA VENTO, Sertorius, iii. 423, 424, 436-440; Pompey, iv. 69, 81, 83, 84.

VENUSIA, town of Apulia, Fabius, i. 415; Marcellus, ii. 299.

VERANIA, wife of Pisol, Galba, v. 507.

VERCELLÆ, town of Cisalpine Gaul, Marius, iii. 82.

VERENIA or VERANIA, one of the first vestals, Numa, i. 148.

VERGENTORIX or VERCINGETORIX, king of the Gauls, Cæsar, iv. 316, 319.

VERGILIA, wife of Coriolanus, Coriolanus, ii. 102-104.

ATILLIUS VERGILIO, Galba, v. 504.

CAIUS VERGILIUS, prætor of Sicily, Cicero, v. 73.

VERRES, prætor of Sicily, Cicero, v. 45, 46.

VERRUCOSUS, name given to Fabius, Fabius, i. 395.

VESPASIAN the emperor, Poplicola, i. 229; Otho, v. 514, 515.

SPURIUS VETTIUS, *interrex*, Numa, i. 142.

VETTIUS, defended by C. Gracchus, C. Gracchus, iv. 594.

VETTIUS, Lucullus, iii. 300.

CAIUS VETURIUS, sentenced to death, C. Gracchus, iv. 598.

PUBLIUS VETURIUS, one of the first quæstors, Poplicola, i. 226.

VETURIUS MAMURIUS, Numa, i. 154, 155.

VETURIUS, an *optio*, Galba, v. 501.

VETUS, prætor in Spain, Cæsar, iv. 291.

VIBIUS PACIANUS, friend of Crassus, Crassus, iii. 355, 356.

INDEX 649

VIBIUS, a Sicilian (VIBO SICA), Cicero, v. 73.
VIBO, a town of Lucania, Cicero, v. 73.
VICA POTA, Poplicola, i. 225.
CAIUS VILLIUS, cruelly put to death, Ti. Gracchus, iv. 591.
PUBLIUS VILLIUS, commanding in Macedonia, Flamininus, ii. 425, 438.
VINDICIUS, a slave, Poplicola, i. 218, 220.
VINDIUS or VEDIUS, Pompey, iv. 64.
JUNIUS, i. e. JULIUS, VINDEX, commanding in Gaul, Galba, v. 479-482, 494, 498, 508.
VIRIDOMARUS or BRITOMARTUS, king of the Gauls, Romulus, i. 61; Marcellus, ii. 267-270.
TITUS VINIUS, Galba's favorite, Galba, v. 480, and after throughout.
THE VIPSANIAN PORTICO, Galba, v. 503.
VIRGINIUS, tribune of the people, Sylla, iii. 167.
VIRGINIUS RUFUS, commanding in Germany, Galba, v. 481, 494, 498; Otho, v. 509, 529.
VITELLII, Poplicola, i. 217.
VITELLIUS, the emperor, Poplicola, i. 229; Galba, v. 495, 498, 499, 506; Otho, v. 513, and after throughout.
LUCIUS VITELLIUS, brother of the emperor, Otho, v. 422.
VOCONIUS, lieutenant of Lucullus, Lucullus, iii. 259.
VOCONIUS, father of three daughters, Cicero, v. 68.
VOLSCI or VOLSCIANS, people of Italy, Camillus, i. 286, 302, 323, 325, 326, 329; Coriolanus, ii. 66-70, 72, 73, 86-88, 91, and after; Comparison, ii. 113-115; Cicero, v. 37.

VOLUMNIA, mother of Coriolanus, Coriolanus, ii. 63, 102, 105.
PUBLIUS VOLUMNIUS, a philosopher, friend of Brutus, Brutus, v. 373, 377, 378.
VOLUMNIUS, a player, Brutus, v. 371.
VOPISCUS, a Roman surname, Coriolanus, ii. 72.
VULTURNUS or LOTHRONUS, river of Campania, Fabius, i. 402.

X

XANTHIPPIDES, archon at Athens, Aristides, ii. 316.
XANTHIPPUS, father of Pericles, Themistocles, i. 257, 270; Pericles, i. 340; Alcibiades, ii. 3; Aristides, ii. 323; Cato the Elder, ii. 354.
XANTHIPPUS, son of Pericles, Pericles, i. 372, 388, 389.
XANTHUS and XANTHIANS, town of Lycia, Alexander, iv. 201; Brutus, v. 321, 353, 354.
XENAGORAS, son of Eumelus, Æm. Paulus, ii. 186.
XENARCHUS, a writer, Nicias, iii. 308.
XENARES, a Spartan, Cleomenes, iv. 523.
XENOCLES of Adramyttium, an orator, Cicero, v. 41.
XENOCLES of Cholargus, an architect, Pericles, i. 357.
XENOCLES, an exile of Sicyon, Aratus, v. 390.
XENOCLES, a Spartan, Agesilaus, iv. 24.
XENOCRATES, the Academic philosopher, Flamininus, ii. 439; Marius, iii. 53; Comparison of Cimon and Lucullus, iii. 302; Alexander, iv. 188; Phocion, iv. 371, 397, 398, 401.
XENODOCHUS the Cardian, Alexander, iv. 251.

XENOPHANTUS the musician, Demetrius, v. 163.
XENOPHILUS, Aristides, ii. 309.
XENOPHILUS, a captain of robbers, Aratus, v. 390.
XENOPHON, commanding in Chalcidice, Nicias, iii. 315.
XENOPHON the writer, Lycurgus, i. 88; Alcibiades, ii. 48; Marcellus, ii. 288; Comparison, ii. 305; Lysander, iii. 131; Agesilaus, iv. 13, 25, 29, 42, 49; Comparison, iv. 173; Antony, v. 212; Artaxerxes, v. 443, 448, 450, 454.
XERXES, Themistocles, i. 248, 254, 255, 260-265, 268, 276; Aristides, ii. 319-321; Comparison, ii. 393; Sylla, iii. 175; Agesilaus, iv. 23; Alexander, iv. 232; Artaxerxes, v. 441, 442. Xerxes in a gown, Lucullus, iii. 296.
XUTHUS the flute-player, Antony, v. 186.
XYPETE, Attic township, Pericles, i. 357.

Z

ZACYNTHUS, the island of Zante, Flamininus, ii. 445; Nicias, iii. 341; Dion, v. 281, 316; Artaxerxes, v. 454.
ZALEUCUS, lawgiver of Locri, Numa, i. 139.
ZARBIENUS, king of Gordyene, Lucullus, iii. 270, 283.
ZARETRA, town of Euboea, Phocion, iv. 381.
ZELA, town of Pontus, field of battle, Cæsar, iv. 344.
ZELEA, town in the Troad, Themistocles, i. 251.
ZENO of Citium, the Stoic philosopher, Lycurgus, i. 131; Phocion, iv. 371; Cleomenes, iv. 522; Aratus, v. 408.
ZENO, a Cretan, Artaxerxes, v. 463.
ZENO, the Eleatic philosopher, Pericles, i. 342, 343.
ZENODOTIA, town in Mesopotamia, Crassus, iii. 372.
ZENODOTUS of Trœzen, Romulus, i. 58.
ZEUGMA, on the Euphrates, Crassus, iii. 375, 388.
ZEUXIDAMUS, father of Archidamus II., Cimon, iii. 236; Agesilaus, iv. 1.
ZEUXIS the painter, Pericles, i. 357.
ZOILUS, a smith, Demetrius, v. 123.
ZOPYRUS, tutor of Alcibiades, Lycurgus, i. 111; Alcibiades, ii. 3.
ZOPYRUS, a Macedonian, Pyrrhus, iii. 50.
ZOROASTER, Numa, i. 139.
ZÓSIME, wife of Tigranes, Pompey, iv. 120.

www.ingramcontent.com/pod-product-compliance
Lightning Source LLC
Chambersburg PA
CBHW020628230426

43665CB00008B/86